# The Wiley Blackwell Companion to Cultural Geography

# Wiley Blackwell Companions to Geography

*Wiley Blackwell Companions to Geography* is a blue-chip, comprehensive series covering each major subdiscipline of human geography in detail. Edited and contributed by the disciplines' leading authorities each book provides the most up to date and authoritative syntheses available in its field. The overviews provided in each *Companion* will be an indispensable introduction to the field for students of all levels, while the cutting-edge, critical direction will engage students, teachers, and practitioners alike.

# The Wiley Blackwell Companion to Cultural Geography

*Edited by*

Nuala C. Johnson, Richard H. Schein, and Jamie Winders

**WILEY** Blackwell

This paperback edition first published 2016
© 2013 John Wiley & Sons, Ltd

Edition history: John Wiley & Sons Ltd (hardback, 2013)

*Registered Office*
John Wiley & Sons Ltd, The Atrium, Southern Gate, Chichester, West Sussex, PO19 8SQ, UK

*Editorial Offices*
350 Main Street, Malden, MA 02148-5020, USA
9600 Garsington Road, Oxford, OX4 2DQ, UK
The Atrium, Southern Gate, Chichester, West Sussex, PO19 8SQ, UK

For details of our global editorial offices, for customer services, and for information about how to apply for permission to reuse the copyright material in this book please see our website at www.wiley.com/wiley-blackwell.

The right of Nuala C. Johnson, Richard H. Schein, and Jamie Winders to be identified as the authors of the editorial material in this work has been asserted in accordance with the UK Copyright, Designs and Patents Act 1988.

*Library of Congress Cataloging-in-Publication Data*

The Wiley Blackwell companion to cultural geography / edited by Nuala C. Johnson, Richard H. Schein, and Jamie Winders.
    pages cm. – (Blackwell companions to geography)
  Includes index.
  ISBN 978-0-470-65559-7 (hardback) ISBN 978-1-119-25071-5 (paperback)
  1. Human geography.  I. Johnson, Nuala Christina, 1962–
  GF41.W534 2013
  304.2—dc23
                                                            2012038979

A catalogue record for this book is available from the British Library.

Cover image: La Grande Arche du Palais (de la Grande Arche de la Défense au Port du Palais) from the series "Le Triomphe de Belle-Île-en-Mer," 1964–1994 (collage and photo), by Gerard Fromanger / Private Collection / Giraudon / The Bridgeman Art Library

Set in 9/12.5pt Sabon by SPi Global, Pondicherry, India
Printed in Singapore by C.O.S. Printers Pte Ltd

1  2016

# Contents

# Notes on Contributors

**John Agnew** is Distinguished Professor of Geography and Italian at UCLA (University of California, Los Angeles) where he teaches political geography and the urban geography of Europe. He is the author or co-author of the following recent books: *Place and Politics in Modern Italy* (2002); *Hegemony: The New Shape of Global Power* (2005); *Berlusconi's Italy: Mapping Contemporary Italian Politics* (2008); and *Globalization and Sovereignty* (2009).

**Derek H. Alderman** is Professor and Head of the Department of Geography at the University of Tennessee. His research interests include the politics of public memory and heritage tourism in the American South, particularly the commemoration of the civil rights movement and the slave experience. He is the co-author (with Owen Dwyer) of *Civil Rights Memorials and the Geography of Memory* (2008).

**Ben Anderson** is a Reader in human geography at Durham University. His current research focuses on the politics of affect and emotion, with particular reference to spaces of war and security in the early twenty-first century. His most recent work has focused on how states govern in and through emergencies.

**Andrew Boulton** is a PhD candidate in the Department of Geography, University of Kentucky. His research focuses on the intersections of cultural landscapes and emerging locative media.

**Tim Bunnell** is Associate Professor in the Department of Geography at the National University of Singapore, where he also holds a joint appointment in the Asia Research Institute. He moved to Singapore after completing doctoral work at the University of Nottingham on the politics of urban landscape change in Malaysia and is the author of *Malaysia, Modernity and the Multimedia Super Corridor: A Critical Geography of Intelligent Landscapes* (2004).

**Paul Cloke** is Professor of Human Geography at the University of Exeter, with research interests in social and cultural geographies of rurality, nature–society relations, ethics and care, and landscapes of spirituality. He is co-author of the following recent books: *Globalizing Responsibility* (2011); *A Companion to Social Geography* (2011); *Swept Up Lives?*

*Re-envisioning the Homeless City* (2010); *International Perspectives on Rural Homelessness* (2006); and *Faith-based organisations and exclusion in European cities* (2012).

**Ian Cook** and Peter Jackson, Allison Hayes-Conroy, Sebastian Abrahamsson, Rebecca Sandover, Mimi Sheller, Heike Henderson, Lucius Hallett, Shoko Imai, Damian Maye, and Ann Hill, are a collection of faculty, post-docs, and students who came together to write their chapter online in 2010–2012. They all study food from different perspectives, and not all as cultural geographers. More information about their work can be found at foodculturalgeographies.wordpress.com.

**Meghan Cope** is Professor of Geography at the University of Vermont. A specialist in urban social geography, she examines how urban spaces and landscapes are produced and how different groups, especially youth and children, use, redefine, and make sense of those spaces. Cope also focuses on combining qualitative research with geographic information systems (GIS).

**Jeremy W. Crampton** is Associate Professor of Geography at the University of Kentucky. His research on mapping and the state has covered the role of geographers during World Wars I and II, and how geographical knowledges are produced through mapping technologies. He is currently working on the geographies of the US intelligence community and its use of social-geographic analysis. His most recent book is *Mapping: A Critical Introduction to Cartography and GIS* (Wiley-Blackwell, 2010).

**Declan Cullen** is a doctoral candidate in geography at Syracuse University. His research uses postcolonial theory to examine Newfoundland, Canada, in the 1930s and its place in wider transatlantic flows and political-economic transitions. He has also examined the relationship between race, nation, and the diaspora in early twentieth-century Ireland, through a postcolonial lens.

**David Delaney** is the author of *Race, Place and the Law* (1998), *Law and Nature* (2003), *Territory: A Short Introduction* (2005, Blackwell), and *The Spatial, the Legal and the Pragmatics of World-Making: Nomospheric Investigations* (2011) as well as numerous articles on the theme of legal geography. He is also the co-editor (with Nick Blomley and Richard T. Ford) of the *Legal Geographies Reader* (2001, Blackwell). He teaches in the Department of Law, Jurisprudence, and Social Thought at Amherst College.

**Caitlin DeSilvey** is Senior Lecturer in the Environment and Sustainability Institute at the University of Exeter. Her research explores landscape, material culture, memory, heritage management, and the intersection between geography and contemporary arts practice. Current projects include a connective ethnography of copper-mining regions, a study of anticipatory history, and a collaborative documentary project on mending and repair practices.

**Deborah Dixon** is Professor of Geography at the University of Glasgow. Her work is driven by an interest in the ideas, concepts, ethics, and politics of poststructuralist and feminist theories, grounded in case study analysis of monstrous, media, and marginal geographies, topics which overlap time and again in often unexpected ways.

**Mona Domosh** is the Joan P. and Edward J. Foley, Jr. 1933 Professor of Geography at Dartmouth College. Her research focuses on the cultural and economic practices involved in the making of an American commercial empire in the first half of the twentieth century.

**Robyn Dowling** is an urban cultural geographer at Macquarie University in Sydney. Her research focuses on daily practices of urban life, especially vis-à-vis homes and neighborhoods. Her current research examines the institutions and processes through which carbon is governed and the ways individual identities are imagined in these processes.

**Patricia Ehrkamp** is Associate Professor of Geography at the University of Kentucky. She studies the politics of immigrant incorporation and the changing geographies of citizenship in the context of migrant transnationalism. She has published widely on her research in Germany and the US South in journals such as *Transactions of the Institute of British Geographers*, *Urban Geography*, *Environment and Planning A*, *Journal of Ethnic and Migration Studies*, and *Gender, Place and Culture*.

**Berrak Çavlan Erengezgin** is a doctoral student in the Department of Geography at the University of British Columbia, Vancouver, Canada. Her research interests include the Kurdish women's movement in Turkey, decolonization movements, feminisms in the Middle East, state violence, race, gender and memory, and reflexive/collaborative feminist ethnographies.

**Elizabeth A. Gagen** is a lecturer in geography at the University of Hull. Her research examines discourses of mental and physical health and their role in shaping bodies and identities. Her work has focused on the US playground movement and military recreation during World War I and emotional health in UK education policy.

**Chris Gibson** is Professor in Human Geography at the University of Wollongong, Australia. His books include *Sound Tracks* (2003); *Music and Tourism* (2005); and *Creativity in Peripheral Places* (2012).

**Joshua F.J. Inwood** is Assistant Professor in the Africana Studies Program and the Department of Geography at the University of Tennessee. His research interests focus on processes of racialization, landscape studies, and contested notions of identity as well as justice studies. His current research explores the United States' first ever truth and reconciliation commission.

**Tariq Jazeel** teaches human geography at the University of Sheffield in the UK. His research is situated at the intersections of postcolonial theory, South Asian studies, and critical geography, and he has published on the politics of Sri Lankan "nature" and National Parks, Sri Lanka's tropical modern architecture, literary geographies, and on various diasporic and "multicultural" formations.

**Nuala C. Johnson** is a Reader in Geography at Queen's University Belfast, UK. An historical geographer with research interests that include the relationships between identity politics, memory and representation, as well as the role of aesthetics in the making of scientific spaces. Dr. Johnson is the author of *Nature Displaced, Nature Displayed: Order and Beauty in Botanical Gardens* (2011); *Ireland, the Great War and the Geography of Remembrance* (2003); and she is editor of *Culture and Society* (2008).

**John Paul Jones III** is Professor in the School of Geography and Development and Dean of the College of Social and Behavioral Sciences at the University of Arizona. He has also taught at the University of Kentucky, where he was co-founder and co-director of that institution's Committee on Social Theory.

**Audrey Kobayashi** is a Professor of Geography at Queen's University (Canada). She has published widely on social justice issues including anti-racism, immigration, employment equity, and critical disability studies. Her edited collections include *The Companion to Gender Studies* (with David Theo Goldberg and Philomena Essed; Wiley-Blackwell, 2009) and *Geographies of Peace and Armed Conflict* (2012).

**David N. Livingstone** is Professor of Geography and Intellectual History at Queen's University Belfast. His recent books include *Putting Science in its Place* (2003); and *Adam's Ancestors: Race, Religion and the Politics of Human Origins* (2008).

**Hayden Lorimer** teaches at the University of Glasgow where he is a Reader in Human Geography. His research and writing cut across lots of corresponding subjects, materiality being just one of them. Others are landscape, memory, place, fieldwork, biography, and the life of the senses.

**Jamie Lorimer** is University Lecturer in the School of Geography and the Environment at the University of Oxford. His research develops new approaches to animal and environmental geographies that do not need to make recourse to modern understandings of nature – as a pure, stable set of objects governed solely by science and markets.

**Niall Majury** lectures in economic geography at Queen's University Belfast. He undertook his postgraduate training in Canada, earning degrees from the University of British Columbia and University of Toronto. His research focuses on the construction and governance of markets, in particular financial markets.

**Linda McDowell** is Professor of Human Geography at the University of Oxford. Her research examines connections between new forms of work and the transformation of gender relations. Her book, *Working Bodies* (2009), examines interactive service employment and workplace identities. Her most recent book, *Working Lives* (2013), is about women migrants in the postwar UK labor market.

**Tom Mels** is an Associate Professor of Human Geography at Gotland University, Sweden, and associate editor of *Landscape Research*. His research is broadly concerned with the intersections of capitalist modernity and the politics of landscape and nature.

**Don Mitchell** is a Distinguished Professor of Geography at Syracuse University. His research focuses on the role of labor and capital in producing landscapes, struggles over and in public space, and Marxist theories of space and culture.

**John Morrissey** lectures on political and cultural geography at National University of Ireland, Galway, where he is Programme Director of the MA in Environment, Society and Development. His current research is focused on contemporary US geopolitics in the Middle East and its array of military, economic and biopolitical securitization practices. He is the author of *Negotiating Colonialism* (2003); and co-author of *Key Concepts in Historical Geography* (2013).

**Catherine Nash** is Professor of Human Geography at Queen Mary, University of London. Her research interests are in geographies of identity, belonging and relatedness, and she is currently exploring these themes in accounts of human genetic diversity and popular historical practices.

**Natalie Oswin** is Assistant Professor of Geography at McGill University. Her publications include articles on South Africa's post-apartheid gay and lesbian movement, the cultural politics of heteronormativity in Singapore, and conceptual pieces on queer geographies.

**Anssi Paasi** is Professor of Geography at the University of Oulu and currently an Academy Professor (2008–2012) at the Academy of Finland. He has published widely on the sociocultural construction of political boundaries and spatial identities, as well as on new regional geography and region/territory building.

**Bronwyn Parry** is Professor of Social Science, Health and Medicine at King's College London. A geographer by training she has longstanding interests in investigating the way human–environment relations are being recast by technological, economic, and regulatory change. She has published widely on the rise and operation of the life sciences industry, informationalism, the commodification of life forms, posthumanism, bioethics, and systems for knowing, disciplining, and governing nature and is author of *Trading the Genome: Investigating the Commodification of Bioinformation* (2004); and *Mind over Matter: Memory, Forgetting, Brain Donation and the Search for Cures for Dementia* (2011).

**Emma R. Power** is a lecturer in geography and urban studies at the University of Western Sydney. Her research examines urban natures, everyday practices of sustainability and homemaking, and human–animal relations. Current research projects are examining the place of dogs in Australian cities.

**Geraldine Pratt** is Professor of Geography at the University of British Columbia. She is author of *Working Feminism* (2004) and *Families Apart: Migrant Mothers and the Conflicts of Labor and Love* (2012); co-author of *Gender, Work and Space* (1995); and co-editor of *The Global and the Intimate: Feminism in Our Time* (2012). She also co-wrote *Nanay, a Testimonial Play*.

**Patricia L. Price** is Professor of Geography at Florida International University in Miami, Florida. She researches a variety of topics including critical race theory, the comparative Latinization of US cities, popular religiosity in the US–Mexico borderlands, and ethics in geographic research with human subjects.

**Paul Robbins** holds a PhD from Clark University and is Director of the Nelson Institute for Environmental Studies at the University of Wisconsin-Madison. His research centers on the relationships between individuals (homeowners, hunters, and foresters), environmental actors (lawns, elk, and mosquitoes), and the institutions that connect them.

**James Ryan** is Associate Professor of Historical and Cultural Geography at the University of Exeter. His research interests contribute to geographies of colonialism and postcolonialism, visual culture and geography, and the history of geographical knowledge and science.

**Richard H. Schein** is Professor of Geography at the University of Kentucky, where he also is a member of the Committee on Social Theory and the American Studies Faculty. He is a cultural and historical geographer interested in the place of land and landscape in the processes of everyday life. His work often is focused on the racialized US south, and especially in urban settings. He is the editor of *Landscape and Race in United States* (2006).

**Rachel Silvey** is Associate Professor of Geography at the University of Toronto. Her research examines the gendered dimensions of migration and economic change in Indonesia, as well as the role of religion in the gender politics of migration more broadly. She has published in the fields of feminist theory, critical development studies, and transnationalism.

**Matthew Sparke** is Professor of Geography and International Studies and Director of the Global Health Minor at the University of Washington. He is the author of *In the Space of*

*Theory: Postfoundational Geographies of the Nation-State* (2005); and *Introducing Globalization: Ties, Tensions and Uneven Integration* (2013).

**Krithika Srinivasan** has recently completed a PhD from the Department of Geography, King's College London. Her research uses Michel Foucault's work on biopower to critically examine concepts and practices of wildlife conservation and animal welfare. Her academic interests encompass the arenas of environment-development, animal and more-than-human geographies, and Foucauldian theory.

**Elizabeth R. Straughan** is currently working as an AHRC/NSF funded postdoctoral research fellow on a project exploring art–science collaborations at the University of Glasgow. Her research considers the body through an attendance to the skin as well as the material and metaphorical dynamics of touch, to unravel the volatile nature of the body enhanced and manipulated by technology.

**Mary E. Thomas** is Associate Professor of Geography and Women's, Gender, and Sexuality Studies at Ohio State University. Her book, *Multicultural Girlhood: Racism, Sexuality, and the Conflicted Spaces of American Education*, came out in 2011. She is currently doing research at a juvenile detention facility with teenage girls.

**Robert M. Wilson** is Associate Professor of Geography at Syracuse University. He is the author of *Seeking Refuge: Birds and Landscapes of the Pacific Flyway* (2010). His more recent work examines the historical geography of Japanese American incarceration during World War II and the geographies of the climate movement.

**Jamie Winders** is Professor in Geography at the Maxwell School of Citizenship and Public Affairs, Syracuse University, USA. An urban social geographer with a focus on social theory and qualitative methods, she has published widely in geography and related fields on international migration, racial politics, urban governance, postcolonial theory, pedagogy, and historical geography.

**Matthew Zook** is Associate Professor in the Department of Geography at the University of Kentucky with interests in technological change and sociospatial organization in the economy and society. A selection of his work about locative media, the geoweb, and online mapping can be found at his research blog floatingsheep.org.

Chapter 1

# Introduction

*Nuala C. Johnson, Richard H. Schein, and Jamie Winders*

It is hard to find a key word or topic in cultural geography these days that does not enjoy an interdisciplinary constituency. That is a good thing. The contemporary fascination with the "cultural" has generated an enormous body of work on which cultural geographers draw and to which they contribute. Cultural geography as a subdiscipline brings to the conversations a long tradition, most notably attention to space and place, to the spatiality of everyday life at multiple and fluid scales, to landscapes as the re-suturing of human and physical worlds, and to the politics and epistemological implications of these engagements. In the past decade, these traditional foci have remained intact, even as some have garnered renewed enthusiasm (such as nature–society questions), others have undergone increased conceptual scrutiny (such as the "cultural landscape" concept), and many have engaged new conceptual or theoretical possibilities (such as increased interest in affect and emotion or consideration of the "posthuman"). All of these developments are present in this volume, and this introductory chapter signposts some of these traditional, new, and renewed areas of interest in cultural geography and the ways these topics have shifted in the last decade. This chapter is not, however, meant as a comprehensive introduction to the subdiscipline of cultural geography. Instead, it is an invitation to examine the field's ever-changing contours through the ensuing essays.

Cultural geography has been a foundational building block of human geography since the discipline formally was established in the nineteenth century. Documenting spatial patterns in human interaction with, responses to, and transformations of the natural landscape, raising questions about how landscape itself was shaped by and shaped social dynamics, and problematizing the ideas of culture, landscape, and nature have been cultural geography's contributions to the ways that human geographers have thought about the world around them, past and present. Today, the line between human geography as a discipline and cultural

*The Wiley Blackwell Companion to Cultural Geography*, First Edition.
Edited by Nuala C. Johnson, Richard H. Schein, and Jamie Winders.
© 2013 John Wiley & Sons, Ltd. Published 2016 by John Wiley & Sons, Ltd.

geography as a subdiscipline is blurred to the point that cultural geography *is* human geography in some corners of our field. Recent intellectual and scholarly developments within geography have drawn cultural geographers closer to the fold and to deeper engagements with colleagues and ideas once thought beyond cultural geography's purview – political, economic, historical, or environmental geography, for example. These connections have been strengthened through cultural geography's embrace of and relevance to the so-called cultural and spatial turns across the human sciences as well as its engagement with social theory and concepts of interest to a broad range of scholars within and beyond the discipline. In short, cultural geographers today study nearly every aspect of human geography and do so in ways that simultaneously reinforce the subdiscipline's place in geography and question the logic and locations of its boundaries.

Cultural geography is itself deeply geographic in terms of what places and spaces cultural geographers study and how cultural-geographic scholarship is conducted across institutional and national contexts. Although cultural geography developed historically and intellectually in relation to other areas of human geography, such as cultural ecology and social geography, it also has developed in relation to its practical and institutional contexts. Cultural geography means different things in different places *and* is enacted in different ways, especially between its North American and British variants (see, for example, Audrey Kobayashi's discussion of this phenomenon in relation to geographic treatments of race in Chapter 9). *Where* cultural geography is performed, and where cultural-geographic research is produced, then, shapes what cultural-geographic scholarship looks like as much as does the widening array of spaces and places that cultural geographers now study. In all these ways, cultural geography, as a body of work, is as unruly as ever in its wanderings into other subdisciplines and disciplines, is as spatial as ever in the different strands of theories and writings that coexist as cultural geography in different places, and is as foundational as ever to the field of human geography in its interrogation of the relationship between the spatial and the social, landscape and cultural processes, past and present.

The chapters commissioned for this new companion to cultural geography take up the difficult task of sorting through the unruliness, spatiality, and continuing centrality of contemporary cultural geography. The chapters are written by scholars who self-identify as cultural geographers and by geographers who write about cultural themes from the perspective of other subdisciplines. Thus, this companion reflects on the field of cultural geography from within and from without. While this approach might problematize the notion of a coherent subdiscipline, it also makes a claim about the continuity and relevance of cultural geography as a way of looking at the world, from the past to the future. That claim is especially salient today. Scholarly and intellectual inquiry focused on the social, political, cultural, and economic worlds must respond to changes in the intellectual worlds of theory, the academic worlds of changing scholarly subjects, and, ultimately, the worlds of everyday social practice.

In the midst of these multiple, sometimes competing, foci, there is also a critical argument to be made for the normative qualities of any intellectual activity that might claim, even demand, that scholars go beyond "response" to the world around them to contribute to the shaping of that world in which they operate and upon which they gaze. This argument, of course, sat at the center of critical human geography as it emerged in the late 1990s. With a dual focus on critically interrogating the categories, lenses, and frameworks through which geographers examined the social world *and* on working to envision a more just and equitable version of that social world, critical human geography began from the presumption that geographers can, and should, do more than report on the world and, instead, should be part of interventions that improve it. Cultural geography played a key role in the development of critical human geography. Its connection to questions of emancipatory visions, interventions, and social justice is evident here in chapters covering such issues as the Occupy movement, the global financial crisis, the politics of food, and the continuing centrality of race and racism within the neoliberal rhetoric of a post-racial world. In the process, and in multiple ways, these chapters call for a politics of *relevance* in contemporary cultural geography and for engaging not only academic theoretical debates but also the everyday world around us.

To maintain that relevance, scholarly inquiry must remain vigilant of itself: always looking backward and looking forward, always remaining cognizant of the aims, intents, and consequences of a defined field, past and present, no matter how difficult the task of locating "the center" of that field. So it is with cultural geography. In responding to the ever-changing nature of the field of cultural geography and the world in which it practices, we introduce this *new* companion to cultural geography as a contribution to the ongoing conversation around this particular subdiscipline of human geography. It is emphatically a new volume, even as it follows almost ten years on the heels of the first companion (Duncan, Johnson, and Schein 2004). Some of the authors in this volume are the same; many are different. All of the essays are original and were commissioned specifically for this volume, with the intent of continuing to look forward and of looking at cultural geography from more than its center. As any review of the field makes clear, cultural geography has meant many things in many contexts; and that vibrancy must continue if it is to survive in the contemporary world of interdisciplinary study and challenges to intellectual orthodoxy, even those that fostered the subdiscipline in the first place.

Defining cultural geography, indeed any discipline or subdiscipline, is tricky; and different, imbricated categorical criteria often are employed. For cultural geography, these criteria might include attention to tradition or genealogies (which themselves have a geography, see Tolia-Kelly 2010); to personalities or hagiographies of specific cultural geographers; to theoretical and conceptual paradigms and debates over their utility and appropriateness across time and space; to thematic focus on some aspect of the world; to disciplinary key words and ideas; to calls for particular research agendas. Each of these categories is represented in this volume's essays; and together, they comprise a broad introduction to cultural geography, albeit an introduction located in the Anglophone world and largely stemming from British and US traditions.

Those more generally interested in the definitional breadth of cultural geography *per se* also might look at other sources. This volume's predecessor, for instance, presented three chapters which, at the time, proclaimed the *fin-de-siècle* revival of cultural geography as a field and attempted to trace traditions and a set of genealogies reflecting the differential nature of cultural geography across (part of) the Anglophone world (Schein 2004; Scott 2004; Barnett 2004). The fact that there were *three* chapters dedicated to "Introducing Cultural Geographies" explicitly recognized that disciplinary genealogies can be notoriously teleological and tend to present neat historical progressions that elide difference – including geographical difference – conflict, tension, and those who "lost" in the process. Designed to be read in stereo, one of those chapters told the perhaps "standard" genealogy of cultural geography from a US-based perspective (Schein 2004). This cultural geography, particularly in the United States, is sometimes referred to as *traditional* cultural geography. It generally is traced to the fifty-plus-year corpus of work produced by Carl Sauer, most famously associated with the geography department at the University of California, Berkeley, and ultimately known in shorthand as "the Berkeley School."

Sauer himself was heavily influenced by German geography and American anthropological ideas of culture. His work drew on extensive fieldwork in the Americas; and as is the case with any active scholar, his approach to geography changed over the years, making any attempt to accurately characterize a fundamental or essential "Sauerian" position problematic. Nevertheless, there came to be something identified *as* a Sauerian, or Berkeley School, approach to cultural geography that seemed to take on a life of its own across the discipline. By the 1980s, that approach was under attack on primarily ontological and epistemological grounds that were part of human geography's general critique of positivism at the time. In that critique, the two immediate targets of a so-called Sauerian cultural geography were, theoretically, the concept of culture and, substantively, the focus upon cultural landscapes. The challenge to both pillars of a "Sauerian" cultural geography came from British and US academics and, in its earliest manifestation, was perhaps most associated with the work of Denis Cosgrove, Jim Duncan, and Peter Jackson (e.g., Cosgrove 1984; Duncan 1980; Jackson 1989). These geographers were joined in short order, however, by other scholars, trained in cultural geography, who saw the opportunity to bring to the critique a continued interest in "cultural" geographies that took on board serious theoretical questions of social power, especially around questions of race, gender, class, nature, and the nature of fieldwork (e.g., Anderson 1995; Domosh 1991; Kobayashi 1989; Mitchell 1995; Nast 1994; Rose 1993). That challenge to *traditional* cultural geography by what became called the *New* cultural geography constituted a series of debates and battles over ownership of concepts, epistemologies, and subject matter. These struggles became known as a Civil War (although like most paradigm clashes, it was not always so civil) and helped to catalyze a round of disciplinary positioning in the 1990s that reinvigorated cultural geography as part of the larger discipline's critical turn (see, for instance, Price and Lewis 1993; Duncan 1993; Cosgrove 1993; Jackson 1993; Foote *et al.* 1994).

Meanwhile, Heidi Scott could write in the *second* of those introductory chapters in 2004 that "recent decades have witnessed the meteoric rise of 'culture' and its study to a position of prominence across the social sciences and humanities." Scott traced this "cultural turn" in British geography to Raymond Williams and the Birmingham Centre for Cultural Studies, thus marking a different genealogy of cultural geography from a different geographic starting point in Britain. While Scott acknowledged transatlantic links to American cultural geography through geographers like Jackson and Cosgrove, her genealogy took little note of traditional (American) cultural geography and demonstrated that (then) recent British cultural geography was more closely aligned with cultural studies, British sociology, and social geography (but see Peach 2002) – a subdiscipline that never had a strong counterpart in the US and, instead, was absorbed by urban and cultural geography (del Casino and Marston 2006). Britain's new cultural geography, from Scott's perspective, "embraced and was profoundly shaped by feminist scholarship, as well as by poststructuralist, postmodern, and postcolonial theory" (Scott 2004: 24). Its most recent, and perhaps most volatile and productive, set of debates focused around the non- or more-than-representational challenge to the genealogy established in that chapter.

Clive Barnett, in the *third* "introducing" chapter, took exception to (mostly British) geography's (claim to a) cultural turn *per se* and worried about intellectual fashion and theoretical fetishizing, especially the "othering" of Marxism, positivism, and realism. He also raised concerns about claims on the part of one (sub)discipline ("cultural geography") to stand for the whole of human geography, as well as what he perceived as the short shrift given to actually defining the culture of cultural geography and the workings of power and politics in the process.

What was meant then (*c.* 2002) to be a simple introductory chapter on cultural geography's genealogy metamorphosed into three chapters demonstrating differing claims to tradition, different kinds of intellectual impetuses, and different institutional geographies and debates over what cultural geography comprised. More positively, the need for three chapters demonstrated the (re)invigoration of cultural geography itself, whether old or new, Marxian, poststructuralist or positivist, or focused on landscape, individuals, societies, or natures. In the 2000s, conceptual and theoretical debate joined a pluralism of substantive foci as the breadth of cultural geography expanded.

This reinvigoration was captured in geographical journals as well. The founding of new international journals *Gender, Place and Culture* in 1994, *Ecumene* (now *Cultural Geographies*) in 1995, and *Social and Cultural Geography* in 2000 gave new outlets to cultural-geographic scholarship, where previously the only subdisciplinary journal had been the US-based *Journal of Cultural Geography*. The foment of cultural geography in the past ten years can also be traced in the periodic "progress reports" that are the staple of the journal *Progress in Human Geography*. The fact of cultural geography's joining the mainstream of Anglo-American human geography led to both a commonality of substantive topics in the subfields and to inevitable clashes over relevant and critical theoretical perspectives that are the hallmark of any vibrant intellectual pursuit. In a series of reports, Catherine Nash noted, for example, that cultural geographers' concern with meaning, belonging, place, and identity mandated an engagement with other realms of social inquiry; and she called forth the necessary ties between cultural geography and the study of the nation, especially the postcolonial condition and links with anti-racist geographies (Nash 2002, 2003). Subsequent reports broadened cultural geography's thematic or substantive engagement with human geography to take up intersections with geographies of home, migration, transnationalism, mobility, and diaspora (Blunt 2005, 2007). Other reports urged a reexamination of cultural geographies of race and racism and the body and a renewed engagement with the politics of visual culture itself (Tolia-Kelly 2010, 2012).

Meanwhile, theoretical challenges also were published. For example, Hayden Lorimer charged cultural geographers to move beyond their ostensible reliance upon the representational epistemology of cultural studies to engage the non- or more-than-representational aspects of everyday life (2005, 2007). This debate over representation has, in many ways, structured contemporary cultural geography for the last decade, splitting the subdiscipline into "representational" and "non-representational" camps in a manner that has yet to be fully articulated, yet which runs as a *leitmotif* though many chapters in this volume. The dichotomies presented in such debates, however, are never so simple; and the charges on all sides generally are made through metonymic arguments that single out individual works to represent the entirety of the corpus under attack. The positive outcome of these dialogues, though, has been the animation of cultural geography itself. They have also driven us to continually (re)evaluate the terms of our academic and scholarly inquiry, to seriously engage in cultural geographies of practice, and to meet the rest of the discipline – and scholars in other disciplines – on the common grounds of substantive scholarly inquiry. For the moment, then, we are left with a set of new concerns for the next generation of cultural geographers, concerns which are unavoidably caught up in the traditions and disciplines of our scholarly writing and journals but which also are captured in this volume as moments to look forward to.

## Volume Structure/Summary

The previous volume of this companion was a response to renewed intellectual vigor/rigor in the post-positivist and culturalist/critical turns that marked cultural geography at the *fin de siècle*. Through its chapters, it attempted to bring progress reports (and especially theory) to the subdiscipline and those at large. Since that volume, much has changed in cultural geography, especially around theory, which has been so incorporated into much of cultural geography, if not the discipline as a whole, that an explicit discussion of it no longer seems necessary. Instead, this volume more often represents important thinkers and writers in the field (and its subfields) who offer new directions, reflective essays, as well as overviews and entries into their respective literatures. The authors here were given a broad scope to address their topics with the aim of capturing the best of cultural-geographic thinking exemplifying a topic or an approach. Because cultural geography has been so thoroughly and explicitly "theorized," we revised the volume's format to include only a few "theoretical dispatches" to signpost (some) dominant theoretical or conceptual positions in the field.

We hope that these essays and dispatches, in addition to capturing or reflecting the state of cultural geography, also serve as interventions into its ongoing reinvention and reinvigoration. These essays prompt consideration on a number of themes that we offer as part of a new set of conversations about the direction that the discipline of geography, and the subdiscipline of cultural geography, might take in the next generation.

The volume opens with the theoretical dispatches. We do not proclaim these dispatches to be an exhaustive list. We offer them, instead, as some of the more important theoretical moments that underpin contemporary cultural geography and as reminders (following Eagleton 1983) that cultural geography, like any academic inquiry, is always and everywhere party to some theoretical framing, whether intentionally or consciously invoked. Given that premise, it follows that we should always be cognizant of the theoretical genealogies, assumptions, and implications of cultural-geographic scholarship. Chapters 2 through 7, thus, offer short introductions to the imbrications of cultural geography with: postcolonialism (Chapter 2 by Tariq Jazeel), poststructuralism (Chapter 3 by John Paul Jones III), feminism (Chapter 4 by Mary E. Thomas and Patricia Ehrkamp), materiality (Chapter 5 by Hayden Lorimer), affect (Chapter 6 by Deborah Dixon and Elizabeth R. Straughan), and historical materialism (Chapter 7 by Don Mitchell).

The rest of the book is divided into four thematic sections, somewhat heuristically determined and titled, in order: Foundations, Landscapes, Natures/Cultures, Circulations/Networks/Fixities. The first three of these sections capture cultural geography's traditional foci in their contemporary moments. The last presents new directions, engagements, and developments not always considered heretofore as central to cultural geography but which have been engaged by cultural geography in name and in spirit.

The Foundations section begins with Catherine Nash's essay (Chapter 8), which serves as an introduction to some of the creative ways in which cultural geographers are doing cultural geography that stretch and test the limits of established approaches to the practice and dissemination of research. It also works with an elastic sense of cultural geography that not only describes wider cultural geographies at large beyond the academy but also attends to the ways in which cultural themes and cultural approaches now span subdisciplinary areas and weaken rigid definitions of their boundaries. Audrey Kobayashi treats "race" in Chapter 9 as both a fundamental product of Western cultures and an analytical concept of central importance to cultural geography. Cultural geography for a long time either ignored race altogether or took for granted seemingly pre-given racial categories that emerged from Enlightenment thinking. Her focus on the social construction of race, the importance of tackling racism, and processes of racialization charts the intellectual history of "race" in geography across several national contexts and several hundred years.

Geraldine Pratt and Berrak Çavlan Erengezgin's chapter on gender (Chapter 10) traces three strands of thinking that have produced gender as a foundational/non-foundational category of analysis in cultural geography. As they show, gender is now seen as so infused, and destabilized, by other social and cultural relations as to be unthinkable on its own. Pratt and Erengezgin discuss three areas of contemporary interest and debate about gender: retheorizations of the relations between biology, the non-human, and social constructions of gender; the challenges of transgender studies for both re- and de-centering gender; and the unfinished business of provincializing Western theorizing about gender to make room for fuller, richer understandings of the world. Linda McDowell's chapter (Chapter 11) on social class offers a rich discussion of cultural geographies of class and class identities. Moving across both theoretical perspectives on class and the multi-scalar geographies of class politics themselves, McDowell highlights the complexities of class as it intersects with other systems of difference, especially gender and race/ethnicity, and the ongoing importance of class as a shaper of life chances and outlooks. In doing so, her chapter pays particular attention to the links between class, place, and culture, as well as to the relationships among theory, methods, and geographical analysis in thinking about class. As she shows, class is both economic and cultural in geographically and temporally contingent ways; and studies of class must treat it as such.

Natalie Oswin (Chapter 12) examines the place of sexuality, and geographies of sexualities, in cultural geography and the discipline at large. As she shows, sexuality has been "on the map" for geographers since the 1990s, when the "cultural turn" enabled a focus on issues of sexual difference and facilitated engagement with queer theory. Over the last decade or so, the literature on geographies of sexualities has been healthy, with a fairly strong interdisciplinary presence. Sexuality is still, nonetheless, largely cast as a peripheral disciplinary concern, even in cultural geography. Oswin's chapter surveys the recent geographies of sexualities literature, arguing that sexuality should be taken more seriously as a central critical geographical concern. In Chapter 13, Patricia L. Price takes on "Place" as one of cultural geography's "key words." Starting with the heuristic utility of seeing place as simultaneously concerned with location, material form, and meaning, she takes us beyond simple definitions to explore questions of identity and authenticity as bound to notions of place in ways that are often problematic. The humanistic approach to place taken in this chapter emphasizes the narrative qualities of place, bodies, and mobilities in experiencing as well as constructing place, and the emotional dimensions of place.

John Agnew (Chapter 14) addresses the enduring significance of nationalism to the exercise and expression of group identity in the modern world. By taking seriously the power of nationalism to influence both the ideas and practices of political life, he traces the territorial and cultural underpinnings of nationalist identity in the conduct of everyday life across a range of different contexts. Caitlin DeSilvey's chapter (Chapter 15) on objects narrates a series of events in the geobiography of a pair of granite bookends. Positioning the bookends as "potent objects" that illuminate multiple paths of inquiry and the fluidity between matter, material, and objects, her chapter explores the complexities of the cultural geography of material culture. The bookends' mobile history allows DeSilvey to explore geographical perspectives on the underlying dynamism of ostensibly inert matter, the labor required to maintain the durability of cultural artifacts, and the importance of material mediation in the performance of cultural memory and the construction of individual identity. In doing so, it offers both methodological and theoretical arguments for a critical approach to material culture.

The Landscapes section begins with Chapter 16, where Niall Majury argues that over the past decade scholarship within economic geography has drawn upon an increasingly pluralist, heterodox intellectual culture. The chapter explores the cultural politics of homeownership and mortgage finance in the United States, arguing that economic landscapes can fruitfully be thought of in terms of situated logics and imperatives that animate a variegated geography of "worth" permanently "under construction." Nuala C. Johnson (Chapter 17) explores how the politics of landscape overlaps and intersects with representational, material, and performative approaches to interpretation. Focusing on three arenas of everyday life – nation, map, nature – she investigates how the cultural geographies of landscape reflect and refract with deeply political questions that are anchored in debates about identities and power relations.

Derek H. Alderman and Joshua F.J. Inwood (Chapter 18) trace the significance of commemoration in the conjugation of historical and contemporary memory and its possibilities in developing social justice. Drawing largely from African American experiences in the southeastern United States, this chapter reviews the importance of landscape to remembering (and forgetting) the past and discusses the narrative and arena frameworks for interpreting memorials and heritage sites. Mona Domosh (Chapter 19) explores the differing meanings contained within the terms consumption and landscape and highlights some of the commonalities (both terms draw their contemporary meanings from the early modern period) and some of the overlaps (both terms touch on issues related to the economy and economic class) that may not be immediately apparent from their everyday usage. She draws on some of these similarities to focus on the ways in which landscape is consumed and the ways in which consumption produces landscape.

In Chapter 20, Tom Mels and Don Mitchell introduce us to two seemingly disparate landscape transformations – in Gotland, Sweden, and Ohio, United States – as a prelude to discussing the relationship between land, landscape, and social, economic, and environmental justice. They present cultural landscapes as the hard material of life, the very places where (and through which) injustice lives as they interrogate both liberal and radical notions of justice, the role of oppression and exploitation in considering justice, and, finally, the politics of landscape and the possibility of landscapes as sites of justice. In Chapter 21 Paul Cloke examines how rural landscapes have been differently understood in terms of history, cultural politics, performance, and assemblage. In using these categories as convenient pegs on which to hang different ways of stretching ideas about rural landscape, he suggests that these seemingly "distinct" approaches are not mutually exclusive but intersect and co-constitute in different ways.

David Delaney (Chapter 22) presents a "culturalist" conception of the legal landscape, particularly considered for its utility in cultural geography and with especial attention to interpreting cultural landscapes. He first discusses varying uses and conceptions of "culture" and "law" in cultural geography before exploring the idea of law and/as culture in combination, where the law is central to the socio-spatializations that concern cultural geographers. He concludes with examples drawn from the realm of aesthetic nuisance litigation and landscape practices. Elizabeth A. Gagen's chapter (Chapter 23) on aging asks readers to think beyond age-related categories, such as childhood and adulthood, and to approach aging itself as a relational process. Drawing on work in children's geographies and geographical gerontology, she argues for increased attention to intergenerationality, life course, and age-related transitions as key aspects of understanding cultural geographies of aging itself. Gagen's chapter examines the ways that assumptions about age are incorporated into the built environment and highlights some recent efforts to work against age-related segregation. To conclude, she reflects on the complexities of multigenerational living in both the global North and South and the economic imperatives and social choices bound up with the act of cohousing.

In Chapter 24, Meghan Cope reviews themes in the growing literature on children's geographies, paying particular attention to where children's geographies and cultural geography intersect and can inform each other. Organizing her chapter around the workings of power, landscape, and material culture in children's geographies, she examines the role of agency, identity, context, place, and discourse in thinking through how youth and children experience, transform, and produce space across sites and scales. Through a discussion of public and private, intimate and institutional spaces of childhood and adolescence, Cope's chapter lays out ways that cultural geography can contribute to the area of children's/youth geographies and that children's/youth geographies can draw on the insights of cultural geography. Tim Bunnell (Chapter 25) challenges cultural geography's traditional rural-centrism to realize what he calls our increasingly urbanized (and decreasingly Atlantic-centered) world. Drawing upon over a decade of work in Kuala Lumpur, he demonstrates the complementary approaches to the urban landscape that are iconographic and interpretive with those that move beyond representation toward questions of embodiment, experience, and affect. His rapprochement joins contemporary debates regarding cultural geography's theoretical, epistemological, and methodological direction.

In Chapter 26, Robyn Dowling and Emma R. Power examine domesticities – the processes and sites through which people create senses of belonging, safety, security, and comfort. As they show, domesticities are produced in myriad ways, in diverse sites, and across scales and are always already imbricated with relations of power. Through a discussion of feminist, material-culture, and postcolonial perspectives on domesticities, Dowling and Power argue that for cultural geographers, domesticities can illuminate connections between identities, imaginaries, and geographies. Their chapter reviews trends in the study of domesticities, from examinations of everyday practices of homemaking to the more-than-human nature of domesticities, to argue for the importance of bringing cultural geography home.

The Natures/Cultures section begins with Chapter 27, where Paul Robbins assesses the importance of metaphors as necessary cultural artifacts that stand for and help us to make sense of the relationship between humans and non-humans, especially as considered within environmental geography, cultural ecology, and political ecology. He traces a critical genealogy of geographical approaches to the nature–society nexus through themes such as determinism, functionalism, adaptation, networking, and mutuality, as a prelude to establishing a new vocabulary for our present epoch, the "Anthropocene." Bronwyn Parry (Chapter 28) traces the ethical, epistemological, and economic implications of historical and recent developments in biotechnology through case studies of agricultural biotechnology, posthuman enhancement, and synthetic biology. She delves into the question of why genetically modified organisms have been subject to such approbation before turning to investigate the implications of their profound capacity to rewrite human–animal–technology relations in unprecedented ways in the twenty-first century.

In Chapter 29 Jamie Lorimer and Krithika Srinivasan review the work in animal geographies over the last decade. They differentiate work concerned with what animals tell us about people from that concerned with the agencies and lived experiences of animals in their interactions with people and reflect on the consequences of each for the development of a more-than-human geography. The chapter on food (Chapter 30) offers an innovative approach to not only the topic of food but also the act of writing itself. Initially written as a collective blog by Ian Cook and ten other food scholars, it examines emerging cultural geographies of food. Taking inspiration from recent reflections on cultural geography's past and future, the chapter develops a series of arguments about the texture, creativity, and activism embedded in geographies of food. In doing so, the authors highlight what cultural geography can bring to geographic research on food, as well as how geographers can join ongoing activisms associated with the politics of food across space and scales.

Robert M. Wilson's chapter (Chapter 31) provides an insightful review of key themes in environmental history, especially from the perspective of North America, in the last two decades. His chapter addresses work on topics from the management of nature to environmental politics, from transnational and urban environmental histories to disease and animal geographies. Grounding his review in cultural geography's own engagement with nature–society relations, Wilson highlights both points of divergence between environmental history and cultural geography and areas of current and possible convergence, especially vis-à-vis recent trends in environmental history to write for a wider audience and to address themes like evolutionary history. David N. Livingstone's essay (Chapter 32) critically examines some contemporary scientific debates in relation to Darwinism in general and natural selection in particular. He focuses on how the cultural as much as the scientific informs the terms and boundaries around which these debates – or science wars – are prosecuted.

The final section on Circulations, Networks, and Fixities begins with Chapter 33, where Matthew Sparke develops an argument about the worldly cultural geography of activism in Occupy Wall Street. Drawing on a range of activists and scholars, Sparke shows how cultural geographers can learn from and contribute to the cultural work in which Occupy activists and their supporters are engaged as they reflect on the complex, multi-scalar geographies built into activist space. A local repossession of spaces in lower Manhattan and elsewhere draws attention to global dispossessions of various sorts, bringing into focus what Sparke describes as seven "problem spaces" associated with Occupy activism. In this way, Sparke suggests, the Occupy movement offers the opportunity not only to think critically about the geographies embedded in and produced through activism but also to bring the insight of cultural geography and efforts toward global justice together.

Rachel Silvey's chapter on migration (Chapter 34) examines the increasing centrality of migration studies to cultural geography as a field. Locating the migrant as a key figure in an era of globalization, Silvey offers three themes in which the insights from cultural geography, especially feminist cultural geography, illuminate the lived politics of migration and the changing link between place and culture associated with migration: concepts of control and dominance, especially the relationality of inequalities and workings of gender; migrant subjectivities, particularly vis-à-vis religion and the intimate labor of social reproduction; and geographies of im/migrant justices through sanctuary cities and remittance justice. To conclude, the chapter argues that acts of migration are bound up with cultural geographies from the home to the transnational and that migration politics *are* cultural politics that merit more attention from cultural geographers.

Jeremy W. Crampton's chapter (Chapter 35) on "Mappings" takes us through several cartographic revolutions, material and epistemological. He treats the emergence of modern mapping as part of the political turn in critical cartography and geographic information systems (GIS) and specifically engages maps through three themes rather than by a strict chronology: mapping as material form, mapping as knowledge(s), and mapping as practice and performance. He concludes by juxtaposing the surveillant capacity of new (and exciting) mapping and location technologies, often serving the interests of the state, with the possibilities for counter-mapping in an open-source world. In Chapter 36, Andrew Boulton and Matthew Zook articulate at the place of "locative digital technologies" – software, code, smartphones, online maps, georeferenced data sets – as actants in everyday life. Their exploration of these technologies in mediating the production of space, landscapes, and subjectivities addresses the "inner workings" and duplicity of code itself, before using examples to look at the imbrication of code with questions of visuality, positionality, and memory in our mundane engagements with the world around us.

Ben Anderson's chapter (Chapter 37) reflects on what difference attention to affect and emotion makes to cultural geography as a field. Through a discussion of recent work on both topics, he argues that incorporating affect and emotion promises a cultural geography sensitive to the dynamics of how life is lived and how a life takes place. Highlighting shifts away from culture as a signifying system, the chapter lays out key elements of a politics of affect and emotion, of ways of being political, that can enrich scholarship in cultural geography. To end, Anderson raises the question of whether the "turn" to affect and emotion heralds a "new" cultural geography attuned to life and living. In Chapter 38 Chris Gibson navigates a course through two prominent threads in tourism geographies. The first starts with neo-Marxist research critiquing tourism capitalism (very much the antecedent for later critical tourism geographies) and then discusses post-capitalist and relational approaches to understand the situatedness of tourism work, livelihoods, and performativities. The second thread considers the theme of spaces of encounter, embodiment, and ethics.

Anssi Paasi's chapter (Chapter 39) on borders and border-crossings examines the meanings of borders, arguing for their importance not only in political but also in cultural geography. Drawing on geographers who call for a relational approach to the production of space and identity, Paasi lays out the historical context for the emergence of border studies in geography and discusses two modalities – landscapes of social power and landscapes of social control – that both destabilize traditional approaches to borders and illustrate their contemporary operations and politics as more than "mere lines." As Paasi shows, borders no longer are "fixed" at the territorial edges of states; and a cultural-geographic approach to borders contributes to stronger understandings of topics from citizenship to memory, from daily life to nation-states. John Morrissey, in Chapter 40, reflects on the key themes and theoretical concerns of geographers working on imperialism today. The chapter begins by sketching the development of "postcolonialism" and outlines the various functions and legacies of imperial discourse, the critical challenge of theorizing resistance, and the enduring imperial modalities of power operative in our contemporary moment.

Chapter 41, by Declan Cullen, James Ryan, and Jamie Winders, examines the relationship between cultural geography and postcolonial studies itself. Through a discussion of the idea of postcolonial geographies, it lays out the different meanings associated with the term "postcolonial" and reflects on what a distinctly *postcolonial* cultural geography might entail. It identifies three broad themes within postcolonial geographies and shows how cultural geographers can both draw on and contribute to the wider field of postcolonial studies for each topic. The chapter concludes by calling for more attention to the geographic and historical specificities of how colonial power works, as well as to the very material and discursive manifestations of that power and resistances to it.

## References

Anderson, K. (1995) *Vancouver's Chinatown*. Toronto: McGill-Queen's University Press.

Barnett, C. (2004) A critique of the cultural turn. In J.S. Duncan, N.J. Johnson and R.H. Schein (eds.), *A Companion to Cultural Geography*. Oxford: Blackwell, pp. 38–48.

Blunt, A. (2005) Cultural geography: Cultural geographies of home. *Progress in Human Geography*, 29 (4), 505–515.

Blunt, A. (2007) Cultural geographies of migration: Mobility, transnationality and diaspora. *Progress in Human Geography*, 31 (5), 684–694.

Cosgrove, D. (1984) *Social Formation and Symbolic Landscape*. London: Croom Helm.

Cosgrove, D. (1993) On "The reinvention of cultural geography" by Price and Lewis, commentary. *Annals, Association of American Geographers*, 83 (3), 515–517.

Del Casino, V.A. and Marston, S.J. (2006) Social geography in the United States: Everywhere and nowhere. *Social and Cultural Geography*, 7 (6), 995–1009.

Domosh, M. (1991) Toward a feminist historiography of geography. *Transactions of the Institute of British Geographers*, 16 (1), 95–104.

Duncan, J.S. (1980) The superorganic in American cultural geography. *Annals: Association of American Geographers*, 70 (2), 181–198.

Duncan, J.S. (1993) On "The reinvention of cultural geography" by Price and Lewis, commentary. *Annals, Association of American Geographers*, 83 (3), 517–519.

Duncan, J.S., Johnson, N.J. and Schein, R.H. (eds.) (2004) *A Companion to Cultural Geography*. Oxford: Blackwell.

Eagleton, T. (1983) *Literary Theory*. Minneapolis: University of Minnesota Press.

Foote, K.E., Hugill, P.E., Mathewson, K. and Smith, J. (eds.) (1994) *Re-reading Cultural Geography*. Austin: University of Texas Press.

Jackson, P. (1989) *Maps of Meaning*. London: Unwin Hyman.

Jackson, P. (1993) On "The reinvention of cultural geography" by Price and Lewis, commentary. *Annals, Association of American Geographers*, 83 (3), 519–520.

Kobayashi, A. (1989) A critique of dialectical landscapes. In A. Kobayashi and S. McKenzie (eds.), *Remaking Human Geography*. London: Unwin Hyman, pp. 164–183.

Lorimer, H. (2005) Cultural geography: The busyness of being "more-than-representational." *Progress in Human Geography*, 29 (1), 83–94.

Lorimer, H. (2007) Cultural geography: Worldly shapes, differently arranged. *Progress in Human Geography*, 31 (1), 89–100.

Mitchell, D. (1995) There's no such thing as culture: Toward a reconceptualization of the idea of culture in cultural geography. *Transactions of the Institute of British Geographers* NS, 20, 102–116.

Nash, C. (2002) Cultural geography: Postcolonial cultural geographies. *Progress in Human Geography*, 26 (2), 219–230.

Nash, C. (2003) Cultural geography: Anti-racist geographies. *Progress in Human Geography*, 27 (5), 637–648.

Nast, H.J. (1994) Opening remarks on "women in the field." *Professional Geographer*, 46 (1), 54–66.

Peach, C. (2002) Social geography: New religions and ethnoburbs – contrasts with cultural geography. *Progress in Human Geography*, 26 (2), 252–260.

Price, M. and Lewis, M. (1993) The reinvention of cultural geography. *Annals, Association of American Geographers*, 83 (1), 1–17.

Rose, G. (1993) *Feminism and Geography*. Minneapolis: University of Minnesota Press.

Schein, R.H. (2004) Cultural traditions. In J.S. Duncan, N.J. Johnson and R.H. Schein (eds.), *A Companion to Cultural Geography*. Oxford: Blackwell, pp. 11–23.

Scott, H. (2004) Cultural turns. In J.S. Duncan, N.J. Johnson and R.H. Schein (eds.), *A Companion to Cultural Geography*. Oxford: Blackwell, pp. 24–37.

Tolia-Kelly, D.P. (2010) The geographies of cultural geography I: Identities, bodies and race. *Progress in Human Geography*, 34 (3), 358–367.

Tolia-Kelly, D.P. (2012) The geographies of cultural geography II: Visual culture. *Progress in Human Geography*, 36 (1), 135–142.

# Theoretical Dispatches

*The Wiley Blackwell Companion to Cultural Geography*, First Edition.
Edited by Nuala C. Johnson, Richard H. Schein, and Jamie Winders.
© 2013 John Wiley & Sons, Ltd. Published 2016 by John Wiley & Sons, Ltd.

# Chapter 2

# Postcolonialism

## Tariq Jazeel

With its origins in late 1970s literary studies, postcolonialism has made lasting interventions across the social sciences and humanities, not least within cultural geography. Postcolonialism's particular point of departure has always been colonialism or colonization, and it is strongly influenced by poststructural urges to show the constructedness of the "real" and to expose the often occluded power relations and effects of those constructions. It is, however, no simple celebration of the formal end of colonialism, as the hyphenated time period "the post-colonial" might imply (Sharp 2009: 3–5). Postcolonial scholarship has instead aimed at exposing colonialism's continued presence and exclusionary effects within the period we designate "after-the-colonial" (see McClintock 1992; Nash 2002: 220). In this dispatch I briefly outline three of postcolonialism's key politico-intellectual interventions; firstly, around power/knowledge and Orientalism; secondly, around interstitiality, hybridity, and identities; and thirdly, around subalternity and the politics of representation. All three of these postcolonial theoretical interventions have had a significant bearing on cultural geography (for surveys, see Sharp 2009; Nash 2002; Sidaway 2002).

## 1

In 1978, the literary critic Edward Said published his pathbreaking book *Orientalism*, a text that for many marks the beginning of postcolonial studies. *Orientalism* lucidly demonstrated how the very categories of East and West, or for Said the "Orient" and "Occident," were not and are not in any sense natural. By engaging a vast archive of work by eighteenth-, nineteenth-, and early twentieth-century European poets, artists, and scholars, Said showed how the "Orient" and "Occident" were in fact made by a litany of ways of talking about, painting, and writing on "the Orient." Drawing upon Michel Foucault's work, Said was

*The Wiley Blackwell Companion to Cultural Geography*, First Edition.
Edited by Nuala C. Johnson, Richard H. Schein, and Jamie Winders.
© 2013 John Wiley & Sons, Ltd. Published 2016 by John Wiley & Sons, Ltd.

interested in the discursive production of the West's commonplace knowledges and assumptions about the East. In doing so, *Orientalism*, and subsequently Said's *Culture and Imperialism* (1993), identified the discursive strategies of debasement, domination, and the power/knowledge relationships through which imperialism worked. For Said and a generation of postcolonial scholars to come, this persistent discursive articulation of a self/other binary was central to imperial domination and its continued afterlife.

Said's thesis is profoundly geographical (Blunt and McEwan 2002). As he put it, *Orientalism* was essentially concerned with "two geographical entities [that] support and to an extent reflect each other" (1991/1978: 5). Equally, *Orientalism* is a profoundly representational thesis, and given cultural geography's turn toward representation through the 1980s (see Gregory 1994), Said's work has proved a lasting inspiration for geographical scholarship exploring the unequal economies of representation and power/knowledge central to the perpetuation of colonial and imperial power geometries. For example, geographers have shown geography's own eighteenth- and nineteenth-century disciplinary claims as a preeminent science of exploration to be entirely complicit with British colonialism and imperialism (Livingstone 1992; Bell, Butlin, and Heffernan 1995; Driver 1992, 2001; Lambert 2009). Similarly, cultural-geographical scholarship has tackled the cartographic (Carter 1987; Edney 1997; Driver 2010), photographic (Lutz and Collins 1993; Ryan 1997), and literary (Gregory 1995; Phillips 2001) productions of colonial space and imperial selfhood, and more recently cultural geographers have made concerted attempts to displace pervasive distorted geographical imaginations of the Islamic world (see Gregory 2004; Attewell 2012; Phillips 2011).

## 2

From the early 1990s postcolonial theory focused more explicitly on the border zones of the binary differences that Said's work helped identify; on where cultures, spaces, and identities meet, overlap, and displace one another. It was the literary theorist Homi Bhabha's (1994) book *The Location of Culture* that focused a new generation of postcolonial scholars on the productively unstable cultural borders that colonialism instantiated. If borders are ideological and geographical markers of separation and exclusion, they are also spaces of emergence (see Perera 2009). As Bhabha suggested, it is in the colonially inscribed border zones between rigid and distinct cultural, ethnic, and geographical differences – what Bhabha termed the "interstices" (1994: 2) – where the overlapping and rewriting of cultural, ethnic, and geographical purity occurs.

Bhabha's work not only drew attention to the hybridities, creolizations, and syncretizations that resulted from colonial encounter, it also heightened a sense that notions of cultural purity and authenticity are themselves but myths (see also Young 2006; Griffiths 1994). In work that emerged from British cultural studies in particular, border dynamisms and cultural fluxes became something of a metaphor for the workings of postcolonial culture itself; for example, in Stuart Hall's (1996) assertion that ethnicities are always newly emergent, and Paul Gilroy's work on the "Black Atlantic" (1993) as a space of creative cultural production connecting Africa, North America, and the United Kingdom.

Not least because of the explicitly spatial language of borders and contact zones, geographers have taken much from these developments, particularly in explorations of the hybridity of postcolonial spaces and identities. For example, in work on the global colonial processes and architectural hyrbidities of both colonial and imperial cities (Jacobs 1996; King 2004;

Driver and Gilbert 1999), as well as on other syncretic modes of transnational cultural production tied to the diasporic experience, for instance British Asian dance music (Jazeel 2005),
or food and fashion (Jackson, Crang, and Dwyer 2004). Geographers have also usefully
explored the manifold hybridities, stretched belongings, and diasporic identities resulting
from colonial and post-independent migration (for example, Blunt 2005, 2007; Lahiri 2000,
2003; Jazeel 2006; Kofman and Raghuram 2005; Tolia-Kelly 2004). However, as Robert
Young has stressed, even the metaphor of "hybridity" carries its own risks. Just as it implies
a "making one of distinct things" (Young 2006: 158), its logic unwittingly reinstantiates an
unhelpful notion of antecedent cultural purity.

## 3

The concept of "representation" has a twofold connotation: first, as a form of textual presentation, and second, as a political mechanism for "speaking for." Postcolonialism has typically engaged the ways these two senses of representation slide over one another, particularly
in the context of discerning a politics of marginality and exclusion, or in other words, to
tackle questions like whose and which narratives are able to come into representation, and
who speaks for those typically occluded from histories still largely written by the powerful.

From the late 1970s, the Subaltern Studies Collective has pushed in a concerted way at
this postcolonial politics of representation, initially in the context of the colonial historiography of India, and subsequently in much broader terms. Inspired by the writings of the
Italian Marxist Antonio Gramsci, founding members of the Collective – Ranajit Guha, Shahid
Amin, David Arnold, Partha Chatterjee, David Hardiman, and Gyanendra Pandey – were
dissatisfied with extant historical interpretations of India's "Freedom Movement," which
tended to celebrate elite contributions to Indian nationalism whilst invisibilizing the contributions of "the people." Put simply, this was because historical records, and the colonial archive
more generally, were written by the powerful, not by illiterate peasant movements key to the
Indian national struggle. Theoretically, therefore, subalternity is created by the very elitism
of history writing. The Collective set about revising these histories in a series of writings (see
Guha 1982, 1983a, 1983b, 1984; Pandey 1991; Chatterjee 1993) that aimed to read archives
against their authorial grain, teasing out their multiple silences and erasures, and in those
silences reinserting subaltern agency into the narrative of Indian nationalism, making visible
"the contribution made by the people *on their own*" (Guha 2000: 2).

Geographers too have worked to bring subaltern spatialities and narratives into representation (see Featherstone 2005, 2007; Gidwani 2006; Sharp 2011), but perhaps more influential within the discipline have been Dipesh Chakrabarty's interventions into subaltern
studies. Chakrabarty (2000, 2002) effectively broadened the Collective's engagement with
the colonial archive to critically engage knowledge production more generally. He argued
that everyday intellectual habits of theorization are inescapably Eurocentric; in his words,
"'political modernity' . . . is impossible to *think* of anywhere in the world without invoking
certain categories and concepts, the genealogies of which go deep into the intellectual and
even theological traditions of Europe" (2000: 4). His book *Provincializing Europe* (2000)
was a concerted attempt to decenter the Euro-American intellectual tradition, revealing its
hegemony and thus clearing space for non-Western politico-intellectual thought. This critical
postcolonial maneuver has proved influential amongst geographers in, for example, urban
geographies committed to reading southern cities on their own terms rather than through
prevalent Euro-American urban theory (Robinson 2006; McFarlane 2010), engagements with

the Eurocentric spatiality of theory culture itself (Sparke 2005; Jazeel 2009), and in work advocating more responsible Euro-American research praxis on the global South (Jazeel and McFarlane 2010; Noxolo 2009). With its focus on the global South, much of this scholarship has constituted something of a bridge between cultural and development geography.

Despite the postcolonial intellectual's best efforts, however, there remain real questions around subalternity's ability to ever effectively come into representation. Does the making visible of the excluded (whether a person, figure of thought, theoretical tradition, or anything else) not always leave an even more excluded residue, and is "speaking for" the subaltern not an act of ventriloquism itself? As Gayatri Spivak famously put it, there is a political necessity to ask: "Can the subaltern speak?" (1988).

In closing, it is worth stressing that postcolonialism is a power-laden theoretico-intellectual field (see Jazeel 2011; Scott 2005). In this sense, if much of postcolonialism's political promise is its persistent effort to unsettle the contours of power, it seems contradictory to try to map or survey postcolonialism as a "body of theory" (Sidaway 2002: 11). Though I have written here about "postcolonial theory" as such, the implications of the word "theory" toward a universal, disinterested, and stable intellectual system might be a little misleading (see Spivak 1993: 3). Perhaps more useful is the challenge to think of postcolonialism instead as a *method* for thinking against the grain of colonial power's lingering and subjugating effects, or as Spivak (1993: 1–24) has put it, a "strategy" to achieve particular politico-intellectual goals.

## References

Attewell, W. (2012) Every Iraqi's nightmare: Blogging peace in occupied Baghdad. *Antipode*, 44 (3), 621–639.

Bell, M., Butlin, R.A., and Heffernan, M.J. (eds.) (1995) *Geography and Imperialism, 1820–1940*. Manchester: Manchester University Press.

Bhabha, H. (1994) *The Location of Culture*. London and New York: Routledge.

Blunt, A. (2005) *Domicile and Diaspora: Anglo-Indian Women and the Spatial Politics of Home*. Oxford: Blackwell.

Blunt, A. (2007) Cultural geographies of migration: Mobility, transnationality and diaspora. *Progress in Human Geography*, 31, 684–694.

Blunt, A. and McEwan, C. (2002) Introduction. In *Postcolonial Geographies*, ed. A. Blunt and C. McEwan. New York and London: Continuum, pp. 1–8.

Carter, P. (1987) *The Road to Botany Bay*. London and Boston: Faber and Faber.

Chakrabarty, D. (2000) *Provincializing Europe: Postcolonial Thought and Historical Difference*. Princeton: Princeton University Press.

Chakrabarty, D. (2002) *Habitations of Modernity: Essays in the Wake of Subaltern Studies*. Chicago: University of Chicago Press.

Chatterjee, P. (1993) *The National and its Fragments: Colonial and Postcolonial Histories*. Princeton: Princeton University Press.

Driver, F. (1992) Geography's empire: Histories of geographical knowledge. *Environment and Planning D: Society and Space*, 10, 23–40.

Driver, F. (2001) *Geography Militant: Cultures of Exploration and Empire*. Oxford: Blackwell.

Driver, F. (2010) In search of the imperial map: Walter Crane and image of empire. *History Workshop Journal*, 69, 146–157.

Driver, F. and Gilbert, D. (eds.) (1999) *Imperial Cities: Landscape, Display and Identity*. Manchester: Manchester University Press.

Edney, M. (1997) *Mapping an Empire: The Geographical Construction of British India, 1765–1843*. Chicago: University of Chicago Press.

Featherstone, D.J. (2005) Atlantic networks, antagonisms and the formation of subaltern political identities. *Social and Cultural Geography*, 6 (3), 387–404.

Featherstone, D.J. (2007) Skills for heterogeneous associations: The Whiteboys, collective experimentation and subaltern political ecologies. *Environment and Planning D: Society and Space*, 25 (2), 284–306.

Gidwani, V. (2006) What's left? Subaltern cosmopolitanism as politics. *Antipode*, 38 (1), 8–21.

Gilroy, P. (1993) *The Black Atlantic: Modernity and Double Consciousness*. London: Verso.

Gregory, D. (1994) *Geographical Imaginations*. Oxford: Blackwell.

Gregory, D. (1995) Between the book and the lamp: Imaginative geographies of Eygpt, 1849–50. *Transactions of the Institute of British Geographers*, 20, 29–57.

Gregory, D. (2004) *The Colonial Present*. Oxford: Blackwell.

Griffiths, G. (1994) The myth of authenticity: Representation, discourse and social practice. In *De-Scribing Empire: Post-Coloniality and Textuality*, ed. C. Tiffin and A. Lawson. London: Routledge, pp. 70–85.

Guha, R. (ed.) (1982) *Subaltern Studies I: Writings on South Asian History*. Delhi: Oxford University Press.

Guha, R. (ed.) (1983a) *Subaltern Studies II: Writings on South Asian History*. Delhi: Oxford University Press.

Guha, R. (1983b) *Elementary Aspects of Peasant Insurgency in Colonial India*. Delhi: Oxford University Press.

Guha, R. (ed.) (1984) *Subaltern Studies III: Writings on South Asian History*. Delhi: Oxford University Press.

Guha, R. (2000) On some aspects of the historiography of colonial India. In *Mapping Subaltern Studies and the Postcolonial*, ed. V. Chaturvedi. London and New York: Verso, pp. 1–7.

Hall, S. (1996) New ethnicities. In *Stuart Hall: Critical Dialogues in Cultural Studies*, ed. D. Morley and K.H. Chen. London and New York: Routledge, pp. 442–453.

Jackson, P., Crang, P., and Dwyer, C. (eds.) (2004) *Transnational Spaces*. London and New York: Routledge.

Jacobs, J. (1996) *Edge of Empire: Postcolonialism and the City*. London and New York: Routledge.

Jazeel, T. (2005) The world is sound: Geography, musicology and British-Asian soundscapes. *Area*, 37 (3), 233–241.

Jazeel, T. (2006) Postcolonial geographies of privilege: Diaspora space, the politics of personhood and the "Sri Lankan Women's Association in the UK." *Transactions of the Institute of British Geographers*, 31 (1), 19–33.

Jazeel, T. (2009) Governmentality. *Social Text*, 27 (3 100), 136–140.

Jazeel, T. (2011) The geography of theory: Knowledge, politics and the postcolonial present. In *Postcolonial Spaces: The Politics of Place in Contemporary Culture*, ed. A. Teverson and S. Upstone. Basingstoke: Palgrave Macmillan, pp. 164–184.

Jazeel, T. and McFarlane, C. (2010) The limits of responsibility: A postcolonial politics of academic knowledge production. *Transactions of the Institute of British Geographers*, 35 (1), 109–124.

King, A. (2004) *Spaces of Global Cultures: Architecture, Urbanism, Identity*. London and New York: Routledge.

Kofman, E. and Raghuram, P. (2005) Gender and skilled migrants: Into and beyond the workplace. *Geoforum*, 36, 149–154.

Lahiri, S. (2000) *Indians in Britain: Anglo-Indian Encounters, "Race" and Identity, 1880–1930*. London: Frank Cass.

Lahiri, S. (2003) Performing identity: Colonial migrants, passing and mimicry between the wars. *Cultural Geographies*, 10, 408–423.

Lambert, D. (2009) "Taken captive by the mystery of the Great River": Towards an historical geography of British geography and Atlantic slavery. *Journal of Historical Geography*, 35, 44–65.

Livingstone, D.N. (1992) *The Geographical Tradition: Episodes in the History of a Contested Enterprise*. Oxford: Blackwell.

Lutz, C. and Collins, J. (1993) *Reading National Geographic*. Chicago: University of Chicago Press.

McClintock, A. (1992) The angel of progess: Pitfalls of the term "postcolonialism." *Social Text*, 31/32, 84–98.

McFarlane, C. (2010) The comparative city: Knowledge, learning, urbanism. *International Journal of Urban and Regional Research*, 34 (4), 725–742.

Nash, C. (2002) Cultural geography: Postcolonial cultural geographies. *Progress in Human Geography*, 26 (2), 219–230.

Noxolo, P. (2009) My paper, my paper: Reflections on the embodied production of postcolonial geographical responsibility in academic writing. *Geoforum*, 40 (1), 55–65.

Pandey, G. (1991) In defence of the fragment: Writing about Hindu–Muslim riots in India today. *Economic and Political Weekly*, 26 (11–12), 559–572.

Perera, N. (2009) Rebuilding lives, undermining oppositions: Spaces of war and peace in the north. In *Spatialising Politics: Culture and Geography in Postcolonial Sri Lanka*, ed. C. Brun and T. Jazeel. London, Thousand Oaks, and New Delhi: Sage, pp. 168–193.

Phillips, R. (2001) Decolonising geographies of travel: Reading James/Jan Morris. *Social and Cultural Geography*, 2 (1), 5–24.

Phillips, R. (2011) Remembering Islamic empires: Speaking of imperialism and Islamophobia. *New Formations*, 70, 94–112.

Robinson, J. (2006) *Ordinary Cities: Between Modernity and Development*. London and New York: Routledge.

Ryan, J. (1997) *Picturing Empire: Photography and the Visualization of the British Empire*. London: Reaktion Books.

Said, E. (1991/1978) *Orientalism*. London: Penguin.

Said, E. (1993) *Culture and Imperialism*. London: Vintage.

Scott, D. (2005) The social construction of postcolonial studies. In *Postcolonial Studies and Beyond*, ed. A. Loomba, S. Kaul, M. Bunzl, A. Burton, and J. Esty. Durham, NC: Duke University Press, pp. 385–400.

Sharp, J. (2009) *Geographies of Postcolonialism: Spaces of Power and Representation*. London: Sage.

Sharp, J. (2011) Subaltern geopolitics: Introduction. *Geoforum*, 42, 271–273.

Sidaway, J. (2002) Postcolonial geographies: Survey–explore–review. In *Postcolonial Geographies: Writing Past Colonialism*, ed. A. Blunt and C. McEwan. New York and London: Continuum, pp. 11–28.

Sparke, M. (2005) *In the Space of Theory: Post-Foundational Geographies of the Nation-State*. Minneapolis: University of Minnesota Press.

Spivak, G.C. (1988) Can the subaltern speak? In *Marxism and the Interpretation of Culture*, ed. C. Nelson and L. Grossberg. London: Macmillan, pp. 271–313.

Spivak, G.C. (1993) *Outside in the Teaching Machine*. London and New York: Routledge.

Tolia-Kelly, D. (2004) Locating processes of identification: Studying the precipitates of re-memory through artefacts in the British Asian home. *Transactions, Institute of British Geographers*, 29, pp. 314–329.

Young, R. (2006) The cultural politics of hybridity. In *The Post-Colonial Studies Reader*, 2nd edition, ed. B. Ashcroft, G. Griffiths, and H. Tiffin. London and New York: Routledge, pp. 158–161.

# Chapter 3

# Poststructuralism

*John Paul Jones III*

Poststructuralism is a multi-faceted intellectual movement that emerged in the 1960s, largely out of French continental philosophy and literary criticism. Its arrival marked a departure from several strands of structuralist thought that dominated theoretical approaches to language, culture, economy, and psyche during the first half of the twentieth century. The keystone of structuralist thought is the view that structures are real, but underlying, well-ordered systems that govern the relations of the parts that comprise them, and that "events" – whether a linguistic convention, a cultural practice, an economic regularity, or a recurrent dream – are the surface manifestations of a structure's deeper operation. Social explanation under structuralism involves linking such events to the causal forces that underlie them, though these, just like events, are generally assumed to be historically and socially determined and hence mutable. Influential thinkers in structuralism include the linguist Ferdinand de Saussure, the anthropologist Claude Lévi-Strauss, the Marxist philosopher Louis Althusser, and the psychoanalyst Jacques Lacan.

Poststructuralists criticize the systematicity and perceived rigidity of structuralism; in the hands of some there is also an explicit rejection of its "depth ontology." Among the key thinkers who helped define the movement are Roland Barthes, Jean Baudrillard, Judith Butler, Gilles Deleuze, Jacques Derrida, Umberto Eco, Michel Foucault, Elizabeth Grosz, Félix Guattari, Stuart Hall, Julia Kristeva, Ernesto Laclau, Bruno Latour, Jean-François Lyotard, Chantal Mouffe, Edward Said, and Gayatri Chakravorty Spivak. Through their reworking of literary analysis, cultural studies, science studies, feminism, Marxism, and postcolonial and psychoanalytic theory, these and other theorists profoundly changed the social sciences, including most subfields of human geography, and especially cultural geography.

Geographers began to employ poststructuralist ideas in the 1980s (Cosgrove and Daniels 1987; Driver 1985; Harley 1989; Olsson 1980). At the time, however, it was difficult to

*The Wiley Blackwell Companion to Cultural Geography*, First Edition.
Edited by Nuala C. Johnson, Richard H. Schein, and Jamie Winders.
© 2013 John Wiley & Sons, Ltd. Published 2016 by John Wiley & Sons, Ltd.

disentangle its contributions from postmodernism, which was a more diffuse, but nonetheless related intellectual, cultural, artistic, and architectural movement. Postmodernism's epochal character – nominally disclosed as a break from modernity's facile allegiance to, on the one hand, social, political, and technological progress, and, on the other hand, scientific authority, objectivity, and rigor – led some to announce a sea change in thought: "we are all postmodern now," one saying went. And yet, as David Harvey (1990) and Fredric Jameson (1991) pointed out, postmodernism's disparate cultural logics – play, difference, flexibility, irony, performance – were all too readily turned into commodities. In a stinging rejection of postmodernism's fascination with surfaces, Harvey offered his own depth-ontology explanation, accounting for postmodernism's many forms through the drifting uncertainties brought about by time–space compression under post-Fordist capitalism. For Harvey, it was postmodern politics that were most troubling, as they were seen to offer little more than diversions in the name of difference. In reply, feminists like Rosalyn Deutsche (1991) and Doreen Massey (1991) countered that difference was central to thinking politics, well, differently. These squabbles aside, postmodernism might well have survived if not for the publication of physicist Alan Sokal's hoax on the purportedly postmodern editors and readers of *Social Text*, the journal which in 1996 published his paper announcing a "transformative hermeneutics of quantum gravity" – a pseudoscientific masterwork that tested the movement's standards of strong evaluation, and found them wanting.

Not that poststructuralism was off the hook in terms of strong evaluation – charges of relativism, subjectivism, and indeterminacy were also leveled against it (Wolin 1992). But there were, and there continue to be, a set of theoretic and analytic signposts (Natter and Jones 1993) that both constrain and make more attractive postmodernism's narrower and more precise cousin. This so much so today that one can find many cultural geographers who self-identify as poststructuralists, but few who accept the lapel button of postmodernism.

Among those signposts there is, first, a critical stance toward meaning and interpretation, a position summarized by the term "crisis of representation." At one level, the crisis refers to a radical approach toward the study of signs, the relational composites of signifiers (words, images) and signifieds (concepts, things) we use to generate understanding. Though Saussure's structural linguistics had long proposed that meaning was forged by differences among signs, rather than through a word's inherent qualities, Derrida's (1976, 1981) elaboration of *différance* suggests a more profound instability. *Différance*: (a) undermines the long-established hierarchy between writing (as a less authentic form of communication) and the spoken word (as a more reliable one – a consequence of the speech act's "logocentricism" of presence); (b) challenges non-relational approaches toward binaries, asserting not just differences between terms but the co-constitutive (and often violent) character of the hierarchies established by them (e.g., master/slave); and (c) proposes, in contrast to a structure maintained by differences, the endless deferral of meaning, part of the "incessant movement of recontextualisation" that sets the terms for his method of deconstruction (Derrida 1988: 136; Dixon and Jones 2005). The stakes here are far more than wordplay: they raise doubts about our representations of the world, suggesting that, in having only partial or context-determined access to reality, we might even be "socially constructing" (Hacking 1999) something that doesn't exist (Baudrillard 1994). In the midst of this referential abyss, cultural geographers found purpose studying the context-dependent gaps between worlds and the many texts purporting to capture them, whether these were mathematical/statistical models, legal and scientific reports, and maps, or travel writing, photographs, and cinema (see, for example, Aitken and Dixon 2006; Barnes 1996; Barnes and Duncan 1991; Dixon and Hapke 2003; Morin 1999; Pickles 2004; Willems-Braun 1997).

That these gaps were not simply contextual but also political should not surprise. After all, poststructuralism emerged at a time when questioning authority was popular, and many literary critics did just that when they dispensed with efforts to wrestle intentionality out of the minds of writers. In place of the dispatched author (Barthes 1967), feminist and Marxist critics came to fancy a more democratic and diverse strategy focused on readers who activate the polymorphous meanings in texts in ways never imagined by authors (some of whom, being quite literally dead, had long since ceded the adjudication of meaning to readers). Yet, as Stanley Fish (1980) argued, the determination of meaning is not a pure effect of subjectivity: we are all members of "interpretive communities"; furthermore, no one reads outside of the expectations of form and genre that, in Hayden White's (1987) view, predetermine content. For cultural geographers, these insights have proven as productive for spatial texts as they have for literary ones (e.g., DeLyser 1999). Implicitly they suggest that interpretive attention and even explanatory power shift from "authors" – the machinations of capital – to "operators" (de Certeau 1984), those who do their own readings as they walk the streets and transgress social and spatial boundaries (e.g., Brown 2000; Cresswell 1996; Domosh 1998; Secor 2004).

Second, poststructuralism issued a warning to those who would seek refuge from the above in the certainty of the self. Derrida's early challenge (1970) to Identity was part of a multi-pronged attack on the enduring and self-evident elements that organize structures, such as Reason and Truth. In them he discovered not only centers and peripheries, but also the in-between grounds of "freeplay" that testify to the contingent historicity of all centers. Viewing "Man" through this analytic is an enlightening exercise for those willing to historicize the "I" who nominates himself as a subject; as Laclau and Mouffe (1985) made clear, appeals to positive identity are nothing more than the policing (i.e., patrolling the "freeplay") of difference in the effort to stabilize the referential subject. The politics here are critical, for not only were all manner of Others necessarily made peripheral in the process of constructing identity, but the centers then made (say, male, white, European) were to forever bear the mark (the "trace") of the excluded. This dependent process, in which the identity of a subject is not founded on any owned certitude but rather on the negation of the traits of the excluded Other – the so-called "constitutive outside" – is what makes whiteness such a prime target of deconstruction (Dwyer and Jones 2000; Kobayashi and Peake 2000; Morrison 1992). But what, one might ask, about sex, male and female? Is there not some sort of foundation to identity rooted in the materiality of the body? Well, no. Drawing largely from Foucault, to whom I turn next, it was Butler's (1990) central insight that gender is not given corporeally but is maintained through performance: the iterative, citational repetitions of difference that continually reproduce the heteronormative field that makes possible the very interpretation of gender (see also Gregson and Rose 2000; Peake 2010).

Third and finally, there is a poststructuralist theory of power. One of Foucault's (1980) many important insights was to look small when looking for power – to the tiny plays of mind, matter, language, and practice that create effects, often imperceptibly and over long periods of time. This micro-power often operates as a self-regulating form of bio-power, a corporeal form of adherence to authority that ensures proper comportment. So while the state, for example, may have heavy machinery and secret forces capable of killing and torture, it may be its trappings of micro-power – the display of the flag, the awe-inspiring magnificence of a court of justice, the pompous formalism of its uniforms and ceremonies – that produce genuine allegiance. Such power is not the product of a structure, but of untold dispersals, including, through the work of "discourse," the linguistic regulation of the possible and the impossible, the sane and the mad, and the healthy and the diseased (Sharp, Routledge, Philo, and Paddison 2000). Foucault was especially concerned to elaborate this notion of power

within the work of institutions (the hospital and the prison most prominently), but his theories have been very influential, taken up by geographers in the widest of contexts (Crampton
and Elden 2007). As a result, to apply the label "critical" to a geographic subfield – as has
been done for cartography, geopolitics, health and medical geography, and development
studies, to name a few – often enough conjures Foucault-style (1972) questions, such as: Who
has the power to designate a norm as the limit to the sensible, appropriate, and the legal?
And how does that power work through language, rules, and practices? The traditional
objects of cultural geography – the built environment and landscapes – are taken as special
cases of such power (i.e., as space/power). Such "discourse materialized" (Schein 1997) both
divulges and conceals: think, for example, how a fence marking an owner's territory also
normalizes the wider system of private property that permits it.

I conclude with two remarks to situate poststructuralism in relation to some of the other
topics raised in this volume. Speaking substantively, I would note that while cultural geographers have tended to be more receptive to poststructuralism than geographers working in
other subfields of human geography, it has by no means been evenly adopted across cultural
geography's objects of analysis (e.g., class, race, gender, sexuality, disability; nation and postcolonialism; nature, landscape, and the built environment; popular media, consumption, and
tourism; politics, both mainstream and alternative; and food, animals, and biotechnology).
This unevenness is largely historical: to understand it one has to inquire about the purchase
other theories (e.g., historical materialism) had on these objects during and after poststructuralism's arrival. Keep in mind, moreover, that some objects of analysis – for example,
animals – owe their ascendency *as* worthy objects to poststructuralism's insights (in this case
to the destabilizing power of deconstruction on the human–animal binary; e.g., Delaney
2001). Finally, speaking theoretically, I should address one of the more repeated criticisms of
poststructuralism, namely, its apparent privileging of epistemology over ontology – or, in a
similar vein, of representation over materiality. An early rallying point for this critique was
Derrida's claim that "there is nothing outside the text," a provocative if misinterpreted
(Derrida 1988) fragment that lent weight to charges that poststructuralists had so thoroughly
textualized the world that they had lost touch with reality. This criticism, repeated in scores
of conference-hotel meeting rooms throughout the 1990s, has by now largely been exhausted,
replaced by an ontologically "flat," materialist poststructuralism inspired by Deleuze and
Guattari (1987; Bonta and Protevi 2004; Jones, Woodward, and Marston 2007; Massumi
2002). What seems plausible to conjecture in hindsight is that poststructuralism, for all its
contributions, at some point wandered into a cul-de-sac of representation that was difficult
to exit. Once there, research objects could be subjected to predictable questions about their
categorical framing and discursive positioning, but overlooked in that neighborhood might
have been some of their liveliness and force. The more recent turns to materiality and affect
– as discussed elsewhere in this volume – are welcomed in that regard.

## References

Aitken, S. and Dixon, D. (2006) Imagining geographies of film. *Erdkunde*, 60, 326–336.
Barnes, T. (1996) *Logics of Dislocation: Models, Methods, and Meanings of Economic Geography*. New
    York: Guilford Press.
Barnes, T. and Duncan, J. (eds.) (1991) *Writing Worlds: Discourse, Text, and Metaphors in the Repre-
    sentation of Landscape*. London: Routledge.

Barthes, R. (1967) The death of the author. In R. Barthes, *Image-Music-Text*, trans. S. Heath. New York: Noonday, pp. 142–148.

Baudrillard, J. (1994) *Simulacra and Simulation*, trans. S. Faria Glaser. Ann Arbor: University of Michigan Press.

Bonta, M. and Protevi, J. (2004) *Deleuze and Geophilosophy: A Guide and Glossary*. Edinburgh: Edinburgh University Press.

Brown, M. (2000) *Closet Space: Geographies of Metaphor from the Body to the Globe*. London: Routledge.

Butler, J. (1990) *Gender Trouble: Feminism and the Subversion of Identity*. London: Routledge.

Cosgrove, D. and Daniels, S. (eds.) (1987) *The Iconography of Landscape*. Cambridge: Cambridge University Press.

Crampton, J. and Elden, S. (eds.) (2007) *Space, Knowledge and Power: Foucault and Geography*. Aldershot: Ashgate.

Cresswell, T. (1996) *In Place/Out of Place: Geography, Ideology, and Transgression*. Minneapolis: University of Minnesota Press.

de Certeau, M. (1984) *The Practice of Everyday Life*, trans. S. Rendall. Berkeley: University of California Press.

Delaney, D. (2001) Making nature/marking humans: Law as a site of (cultural) production. *Annals of the Association of American Geographers*, 91, 487–503.

Deleuze, G. and Guattari, F. (1987) *A Thousand Plateaus: Capitalism and Schizophrenia*, trans. B. Massumi. Minneapolis: University of Minnesota Press.

DeLyser, D. (1999) Authenticity on the ground: Engaging the past in a California ghost town. *Annals of the Association of American Geographers*, 89, 602–632.

Derrida, J. (1970) Structure, sign and play in the discourses of the human sciences. In *The Structuralist Controversy*, ed. R. Macksey and E. Donato. Baltimore: Johns Hopkins University Press, pp. 247–265.

Derrida, J. (1976) *Of Grammatology*, trans. G. C. Spivak. Baltimore: Johns Hopkins University Press.

Derrida, J. (1981) *Positions*, trans. A. Bass. Chicago: University of Chicago Press.

Derrida, J. (1988) *Limited Inc.*, trans. S. Weber. Evanston: Northwestern University Press.

Deutsche, R. (1991) Boys town. *Environment and Planning D: Society and Space*, 9, 5–30.

Dixon, D.P. and Hapke, H.M. (2003) Cultivating discourse: The social construction of agricultural legislation. *Annals of the Association of American Geographers*, 93, 142–164.

Dixon, D.P. and Jones III, J.P. (1998) My dinner with Derrida, or spatial analysis and poststructuralism do lunch. *Environment and Planning A*, 30, 247–260.

Dixon, D.P. and Jones III, J.P. (2005) Derridean geographies. *Antipode*, 37, 242–245.

Doel, M. 2000. *Poststructuralist Geographies: The Diabolical Art of Spatial Science*. Edinburgh: University of Edinburgh Press.

Domosh, M. (1998) Those "gorgeous incongruities": Polite politics and public space on the streets of nineteenth-century New York City. *Annals of the Association of American Geographers*, 88, 209–226.

Driver, F. (1985) Power, space, and the body: A critical assessment of Foucault's *Discipline and Punish*. *Environment and Planning D: Society and Space*, 3, 425–446.

Dwyer, O. and Jones III, J.P. (2000) White socio-spatial epistemology. *Social and Cultural Geography*, 1, 209–222.

Fish, S. (1980) *Is There a Text in this Class? The Authority of Interpretive Communities*. Cambridge, MA: Harvard University Press.

Foucault, M. (1972) *The Archaeology of Knowledge*. London: Tavistock.

Foucault, M. (1980) *Power/Knowledge: Selected Interviews and Other Writings, 1972–77*, ed. C. Gordon. Brighton: Harvester Press.

Gregson, N. and Rose, G. (2000) Taking Butler elsewhere: Perfomativities, spatialities and subjectivities. *Environment and Planning D: Society and Space*, 18, 433–452.

Hacking, I. (1999) *The Social Construction of What?* Cambridge, MA: Harvard University Press.

Harley, B.J. (1989) Deconstructing the map. *Cartographica*, 26, 1–20.

Harvey, D. (1990) *The Condition of Postmodernity: An Enquiry into the Origins of Cultural Change*. Oxford: Blackwell.

Jameson, F. (1991) *Postmodernism, or, the Cultural Logic of Late Capitalism*. Durham, NC: Duke University Press.

Jones III, J.P., Woodward, K., and Marston, S.A. (2007) Situating flatness. *Transactions of the Institute of British Geographers*, 32, 264–276.

Kobayashi, A. and Peake, L. (2000) Racism out of place: Thoughts on whiteness and an antiracist geography in the new millennium. *Annals of the Association of American Geographers*, 90, 392–403.

Laclau, E. and Mouffe, C. (1985) *Hegemony and Socialist Strategy: Towards a Radical Democratic Politics*. London: Verso.

Lefebvre, H. (1991) *The Production of Space*, trans. D. Nicholson-Smith. Oxford: Blackwell.

Massey, D. (1991) Flexible sexism. *Environment and Planning D: Society and Space*, 9, 31–57.

Massumi, B. (2002) *Parables for the Virtual: Movement, Affect, Sensation*. Durham, NC: Duke University Press.

Morin, K. (1999) Peak practices: Englishwomen's "heroric" adventures in the nineteenth-century American West. *Annals of the Association of American Geographers*, 89, 489–514.

Morrison, T. (1992) *Playing in the Dark: Whiteness and the Literary Imagination*. Cambridge, MA: Harvard University Press.

Natter, W. and Jones III, J.P. (1993) Signposts toward a poststructuralist geography. In *Postmodern Contentions: Epochs, Politics, Space*, ed. J.P. Jones III, W. Natter, and T. Schatzki. New York: Guilford Press, pp. 165–204.

Natter, W. and Jones III, J.P. (1997) Identity, space and other uncertainties. In *Space and Social Theory: Interpreting Modernity and Postmodernity*, ed. G. Benko and U. Strohmayer. Oxford: Blackwell, pp. 141–161.

Olsson, G. (1980) *Birds in Egg – Egg in Birds*. London: Pion Press.

Peake, L. 2010. Gender, race, sexuality. In *The Sage Handbook of Social Geographies*, ed. S.J. Smith, R. Pain, S.A. Marston, and J.P. Jones III. London: Sage, pp. 55–77.

Pickles, J. (2004) *A History of Spaces: Cartographic Reason, Mapping and the Geo-coded World*. New York: Routledge.

Schein, R. (1997) The place of landscape: A conceptual framework for interpreting an American scene. *Annals of the Association of American Geographers*, 87, 660–680.

Secor, A. (2004) "There is an Istanbul that belongs to me": Citizenship, space, and identity in the city. *Annals of the Association of American Geographers*, 94, 352–368.

Sharp, J.P., Routledge, P., Philo, C., and Paddison, R. (2000) Entanglements of power: Geographies of domination/resistance. In *Entanglements of Power: Geographies of Domination/Resistance*, ed. J.P. Sharp, P. Routledge, C. Philo, and R. Paddison. London: Routledge, pp. 1–42.

Sokal, A. (1996) Transgressing the boundaries: Towards a transformative hermeneutics of quantum gravity. *Social Text*, 46/47, 217–252.

White, H. (1987) *The Content of the Form: Narrative Discourse and Historical Representation*. Baltimore: Johns Hopkins University Press.

Willems-Braun, B. (1997) Buried epistemologies: The politics of nature in (post)colonial British Columbia. *Annals of the Association of American Geographers*, 87, 3–31.

Wolin, R. (1992) *The Terms of Cultural Criticism: The Frankfurt School, Existentialism, Poststructuralism*. New York: Columbia University Press.

Chapter 4

# Feminist Theory

*Mary E. Thomas and Patricia Ehrkamp*

Feminist thought roams through many topics, philosophies, and cultures, but perhaps one connection between these is paramount: feminist thought has concerned itself with questions of power. Lively debate grapples with the question of just how patriarchy works, but also where knowledge about place, nature, culture, and people has been constructed, to whose benefit, and how best to challenge the biases embedded in the masculinist ways the world has come to be represented. "Feminist" thus insinuates a *confrontation* of patriarchal power and asks how differently ordered institutions, material and natural resource allocation, symbolic meanings, and cultural practices might lead to less disparity and suffering. Central to this politics is the idea that the division of life into hierarchical categories of social difference has greatly benefited those occupying the proffered universal subject-position at the expense of those who can never begin to approach its constructed ideals (Spivak 2010). As such, feminism has extended far from an examination of "women" to consider the dictates of compulsory heterosexuality, sexual difference, racism and ethnocentrism, norms of embodiment and ability, capitalism, colonialism, and masculinist orderings of space (see, for example, Blunt 2005; Colls 2012; Gökarıksel 2009; Oswin and Olund 2010; Tolia-Kelly 2010).

Indeed, evidencing gender, sexual, or racial injustice by describing its effects does precious little to offer radical departures from the discourses and resources of Western, white supremacist patriarchy. To be clear, in our view there is potential danger in normative accounts for social justice movements, as feminists have long suggested (e.g., Razack 2008). The quest for an end to domination has always been a politicized one and thus involves reimagining politics itself (Wright 2010). Consider, for example, that numerous assumptions about equality inherent in understandings of liberal democracy are themselves cultural values (Brown 2006). This is not to say that gender equity is not an important aspect of feminist-inspired cultural geographies, but that we need to be aware of and make assumptions and values about "rights"

*The Wiley Blackwell Companion to Cultural Geography*, First Edition.
Edited by Nuala C. Johnson, Richard H. Schein, and Jamie Winders.
© 2013 John Wiley & Sons, Ltd. Published 2016 by John Wiley & Sons, Ltd.

explicit, not inevitable or natural as liberalism might have it. This also entails not simply looking for resistance or struggles in the usual places and subjects (Butler 1993) and in forms that are recognizable to the Western, often masculinist gaze (Mohanty 1988).

Mahmood's (2005) study of the women's mosque movement in Cairo, Egypt, for example, finds notions of agency that are "illiberal," that is, they do not entail public demonstrations for women's rights or claims to equality rooted in liberal democracy. Instead, women articulate their claims to space, knowledge, and education through piety and their reading of Islamic texts. And while feminist scholarship has helped lay bare the practices of domination that continue to shape the (cultural) geographies of racism and racial violence in places like the United States and Canada, McKittrick (2006) also shows that the struggle to "respatialize" understandings about, in this case, black women's bodies can realize geography as "an alterable terrain" (p. xvii). She argues that making black women's geographies intelligible means revamping the ways geographers are trained to see in the first place through masculinist, supremacist eyes (see also Rose 1993). McKittrick writes: "What you cannot see, and cannot remember, is part of a broader geographic project that thrives on forgetting and displacing blackness" (2006: 33).

Clearly, there are areas of the discipline where feminist and anti-racist thought have been carelessly dismissed. However, it is difficult to discern aspects of cultural geography that have not been impacted by feminist thinking. Indeed, the cultural turn in geography occurred at the same time as the explosion of feminist approaches and critiques, and their histories are intimately linked. Whether delving into questions of representation, approaches to methodologies, or understandings of what exactly "culture" is, feminist thought has insisted that the very doing of intellectual work is an embodied, positioned, and power-laden practice (Rose 1993; Sangtin Writers and Nagar 2006; Thien 2005). Feminism deserves more than just a little credit for introducing the attention in cultural geography to social difference. Unfortunately, it is not difficult to point out how masculinist academic behavior placates the potentials of feminist political interventions and seeks to maneuver around the ways that feminism has altered cultural fields of study. Reductive attitudes to feminism stem from those who concentrate on only a narrow range of continental theory, thereby reproducing "expert" and truer-than-thou knowledge, not to mention white male privilege. Likewise, it is easy to ignore "what you cannot see" by only engaging with communities of like-minded and like-embodied thinkers and by reducing feminism to stereotypical critiques.

There is still, of course, much to anticipate in continuing the rich history of feminism's internal debates. While feminism is no longer (indeed, if it ever was) merely concerned with "women" or gender alone, it is too often reduced to a gendered approach in contemporary cultural geography (see Sharp 2011, on the history of gender in geography). Simply evidencing gender, while situated as a laudable goal in the expansion of geographic empirics, does little to theorize the complexity of the term or the work it does conceptually and politically. For feminisms to continue to exert a trenchant, critical force in cultural geographies, feminist theorizing must continue to push past the categories and assumptions that potentially restrain it.

## References

Blunt, A. (2005) *Domicile and Diaspora: Anglo-Indian Women and the Spatial Politics of Home*. Oxford: Blackwell.

Brown, W. (2006) *Regulating Aversion: Tolerance in the Age of Identity and Empire*. Princeton: Princeton University Press.

Butler, J. (1993) *Bodies That Matter: On the Discursive Limits of "Sex."* New York: Routledge.

Colls, R. (2012) Feminism, bodily difference and non-representational geographies. *Transactions of the Institute of British Geographers*. 37 (3), 430–445.

Gökarıksel, B. (2009) Beyond the officially sacred: Religion, secularism, and the body in the production of subjectivity. *Social and Cultural Geography*, 10 (6), 657–674.

Mahmood, S. (2005) *Politics of Piety: The Islamic Revival and the Feminist Subject*. Princeton: Princeton University Press.

McKittrick, K. (2006) *Demonic Grounds: Black Women and the Cartographies of Struggle*. Minneapolis: University of Minnesota Press.

Mohanty, C.T. (1988) Under Western eyes: Feminist scholarship and colonial discourses. *Feminist Review*, 30, 65–88.

Oswin, N. and Olund, E. (2010) Governing intimacy. *Environment and Planning D: Society and Space*, 28 (1), 60–67.

Razack, S. (2008) *Casting Out: The Eviction of Muslims from Western Law and Politics*. Toronto: University of Toronto Press.

Rose, G. (1993) *Feminism and Geography: The Limits of Geographical Knowledge*. Minneapolis: University of Minnesota Press.

Sangtin Writers and Nagar, R. (2006) *Playing with Fire: Feminist Thought and Activism through Seven Lives in India*. Minneapolis: University of Minnesota Press.

Sharp, J. (2011) Gender: Part II. In *A Companion to Human Geography*, ed. J. Agnew and J. Duncan. Oxford: Blackwell, pp. 501–511.

Spivak, G.C. (2010) Situating feminism. *Beatrice Bain Research Group Presents: Annual Keynote Talk*, University of California, Berkeley. http://www.youtube.com/watch?v=garPdV7U3fQ (accessed October 16, 2012).

Thien, D. (2005) After or beyond feeling? A consideration of affect and emotion in geography. *Area*, 37 (4), 450–454.

Tolia-Kelly, D.P. (2010) The geographies of cultural geography I: Identities, bodies and race. *Progress in Human Geography*, 34 (3), 358–367.

Wright, M. (2010) Geography and gender: Feminism and a feeling of justice. *Progress in Human Geography*, 34 (6), 818–827.

Chapter 5

# Materialities

*Hayden Lorimer*

As a key term in this *Companion*, the choice of "materialities" is one that immediately indicates things that are multiple. Where once the singular root, "materiality," might once have done the job, there is now, it seems, much more matter in need of our geographical attention. Just for a minute, select a single thing from this list – petrol, perfume, pigs, pineapples, pathogens – and then imagine the possible ways that it could be mapped into place and across the planet (cf. Ian Cook's excellent online resource: http://www.followthethings.com). The ways you now have in mind will be multiple and mobile, encompassing organic and artificial processes, to be positioned along a spectrum of scales running from the molecular to the mega-structural. But more than this, "materialities" is a term suggestive of emerging theories about how we should understand the very existence of stuff, and our diverse experiences of, or encounters with it. These ontological and metaphysical theories explore how material properties relate, change, and actively proliferate, sometimes signaling abundances of a more radical or volatile sort. This then is to invoke the term "materialities" as one concerned with complex spatial relations and with the quality or consistency of matter, and its elements, potentially in different states. However, among the broad community of human geography, a vocabulary of "materiality" also has been used as a determining measure of research with real-world application or significance, based upon a principled model of critical academic engagement. As a fullest expression of political and social commitment, the *materializing* of an abstract idea is its real, observable instantiation in a more just society. Both of these qualities of materiality – of spatial-physical composition and of politico-social relevance – have fused in recent debate about the spirit, purpose, and direction of contemporary cultural geography. What is at stake when the term "materialities" is employed is nothing less than the geographical authority to describe the nature of the lived world.

*The Wiley Blackwell Companion to Cultural Geography*, First Edition.
Edited by Nuala C. Johnson, Richard H. Schein, and Jamie Winders.
© 2013 John Wiley & Sons, Ltd. Published 2016 by John Wiley & Sons, Ltd.

Even the most capsular history of the relation between geography and materiality has to take root somewhere: the turn of the millennium offers as good a starting point as any. Back then clarion calls to *re*materialize this, that, or the next thing began to populate geographical journal issues and annual conference sessions. The prefatory "*re-*" was specifically reactive; in expression, it could be just a touch irascible, and had not yet seen its rhetorical impact reduced to that of a rather tired cliché. This "*re-*" implied that one theoretical twist too many had been taken in the sunlit uplands of geography's celebrated "cultural turn." It was directed at a novel form of geographical inquiry motivated by a deep engagement with social and cultural theory, and perceived to have become unhealthily fixated with an *im*material realm of image, text, process, and identity. The same "*re-*" also held out the promise of reclamation and rehabilitation, as if snapping fingers to break a spell of undisciplined, wandering thought. Efforts at rapprochement with cognate fields of geographical inquiry (the urban; the social) sought to wrestle back the political initiative for a re-routed form of research: materialist in foundation, empirically based, and primarily concerned with explaining structurally signifi- cant kinds of social difference and injustice (Jackson 2000; Lees 2002). The urge to re- materialize by "getting real" is ongoing, regularly exercised through vocal opposition to what is labeled – in academic vernacular – as "theory for theory's sake."

The perceived need to establish a firmer material footing for studies in cultural geography has opened a parallel debate about the very definitional terms for (and metaphysical attributes of) materiality, and, by a relational logic, its binary opposite, immateriality (Anderson and Wylie 2009). The case for a renewed emphasis on the social and experiential as it exists in a textured "'thingy,' bump-into-able" world of solidity and matter (Philo 2000: 33) has met with constructive critique, insisting that a language of "grounding" studies in the "concrete" actualities of the everyday creates an unhelpful limit point for cultural inquiries, being prem- ised on false distinctions between the organic/inorganic, inside/outside, architectural/environ- mental, biological/artificial. Instead, force, feeling, and form must be understood relationally, opening possibilities for alternative spatial formations. Only by more seriously and affirma- tively accommodating the affective, the habitual, the technological, the excessive, and the processural – or simply put, the more-than-representational (Lorimer 2005; cf. Thrift 2007) – is it possible to properly treat materials as ongoing phenomena activated in ordinary worlds of practice. The endless reinventions of the globalized city offer one test-bed for such experi- mental thinking about, variously: affective flows of feeling and mood (Latham and McCor- mack 2004); the pull exacted on experience by the psychic subconscious (Pile 2005); the digital choreographing and software programming embedded in ordinary experience (Kitchin and Dodge 2011); the wholesale redesign of technologies of security to safeguard city-systems (Graham 2011); the cultural commemoration and re-fabrication of urban neighborhoods (Till 2005; Cresswell 2012); the decommissioning of residential architectures (Jacobs, Cairns, and Strebel 2006); and the disassembly, demolition, and disposal of major transportation infra- structures (Gregson 2011). Such recombinant urban materialities are everywhere in operation, their fluctuating states dependent on different durations of movement and thresholds of consistency. Beyond the city limits, experimental explorations of uncertain materialities have turned to atmospheric conditions and elemental states (Martin 2011; McCormack 2010; Lorimer and Wylie 2010), the body-subject, sense, and matter (Wylie 2005); the shifting, inter-species ecologies of landscape (Lorimer 2010; Jones 2011), and site-specific approaches to entropic decomposition (DeSilvey 2007).

Already well established, this "material turn" in geographical thinking has been closely informed by strands of vitalist, phenomenological, and feminist philosophy (Gilles Deleuze and Félix Guattari, Brian Massumi, Alphonso Lingis, Manuel De Landa, and Elizabeth Grosz rank among the most cited), and is thickening satisfactorily through more direct kinds of interdisciplinary conversation with scholars in political science (Jane Bennett), social anthropology (Tim Ingold, Kathleen Stewart), archaeology (Christopher Tilley), performance studies (Mike Pearson), and strands of object-oriented philosophy, most notably speculative realism (Graham Harman). The focusing of attention on materialities has also reawakened – at the same time as reworking – a more obvious and older tradition of disciplinary alliance between human and physical geographers. Arguably, it is the versatility and elasticity of "materialities" as a conceptual resource that makes it suited to new anticipative geographies, aimed at rethinking society–environment relations in the near future (Clark 2010; Lane *et al.* 2011; Braun 2007; Shaw, Robbins, and Jones 2010; DeSilvey, Naylor, and Sackett 2011). Here, familiar measures of research relevance and social impact re-materialize, sometimes by creative configuration. What does yet remain largely unrealized is the real need for an inventively kaleidoscopic language, more faithful to, and intimate with, the materials themselves, and the social practices or cultural customs in which they play a part. Many more words for worlding "materialities" would be welcome: words that speak of the tactile and the toxic, of the companionable and the combustible, of friction and fluidity, of sensate and stable properties, of heady influence and heavy engineering. Too often, geographical writing about materialities slavishly rehashes the *ur*-lexicon coined by the canon of source-philosophers. Writing that springs from our more watchful observation of the situated geographies of material use and material circumstance would complement the sociocultural pluralism inherent to the concept.

## References

Anderson, B. and Wylie, J. (2009) On geography and materiality. *Environment and Planning A*, 41, 318–335.

Braun, B. (2007) Biopolitics and the molecularization of life. *Cultural Geographies*, 14, 6–28.

Clark, N. (2010) *Inhuman Nature: Sociable Life on a Dynamic Planet*. London: Sage.

Cook, I. *et al.* (2012) http://www.followthethings.com (accessed October 16, 2012).

Cresswell, T. (2012) Value, gleaning and the archive at Maxwell Street, Chicago. *Transactions of the Institute of British Geographers*, 37, 164–176.

DeSilvey, C. (2007) Salvage memory: Constellating material histories on a hardscrabble homestead. *Cultural Geographies*, 14, 401–424.

DeSilvey, C., Naylor, S., and Sackett, C. (eds.) (2011) *Anticipatory History*. Axminster: Uniform Books.

Graham, S. (2011) *Cities Under Siege: The New Military Urbanism*. London: Verso.

Gregson, N. (2011) Performativity, corporeality and the politics of ship disposal. *Journal of Cultural Economy*, 4, 137–156.

Jackson, P. (2000) Rematerializing social and cultural geography. *Social and Cultural Geography*, 1, 9–14.

Jacobs, J.M., Cairns, S., and Strebel, I. (2006) "A tall story . . . but, a fact just the same": The Red Road highrise as a black box. *Urban Studies*, 44, 609–629.

Jones, O. (2011) Lunar–solar rhythmpatterns: Towards the material cultures of tides. *Environmental and Planning A*, 43, 2285–2303.

Kitchin, R. and Dodge, M. (2011) *Code/Space: Software and Everyday Life*. Cambridge, MA: MIT Press.

Lane, S.N., Odoni, N., Landström, C., Whatmore, S.J., Ward, N., and Bradley, S. (2011) Doing flood risk science differently: An experiment in radical scientific method. *Transactions of the Institute of British Geographers*, 36, 15–36.

Latham, A. and McCormack, D.P. (2004) Moving cities: Rethinking the materialities of urban geographies. *Progress in Human Geography*, 28 (6), 701–724.

Lees, L. (2002) Rematerializing geography: The "new" urban geography. *Progress in Human Geography*, 26, 101–112.

Lorimer, H. (2005) Cultural geography: The busyness of being more-than-representational. *Progress in Human Geography*, 29, 83–94.

Lorimer, H. (2010) Forces of nature, forms of life: Calibrating ethology and phenomenology. In *Taking Place: Non-Representational Geographies*, ed. B. Anderson and P. Harrison. London: Ashgate, pp. 55–78.

Lorimer, H. and Wylie, J.W. (2010) LOOP (a geography). *Performance Research*, 15, 6–13.

Martin, C. (2011) Fog-bound: Aerial space and the elemental entanglements of body-with-world. *Environment and Planning D: Society and Space*, 29, 454–468.

McCormack, D.P. (2010) Remotely sensing affective afterlives: The spectral geographies of material remains. *Annals of the Association of American Geographers*, 100, 640–654.

Philo, C. (2000) More words, more worlds: Reflections on the cultural turn and human geography. In *Cultural Turns/Geographical Turns: Perspectives on Cultural Geography*, ed. I. Cook, D. Crouch, S. Naylor, and J. Ryan. Harlow: Prentice Hall, pp. 26–53.

Pile, S. (2005) *Real Cities: Modernity, Space and the Phantasmagorias of City Life*. London: Sage.

Shaw, I., Robbins, P., and Jones, J.P. (2010) A bug's life and the spatial ontologies of mosquito management. *Annals of the Association of American Geographers*, 100, 373–392.

Thrift, N. (2007) *Non-Representational Theory: Space, Politics, Affect*. London: Routledge.

Till, K. (2005) *The New Berlin: Memory, Politics, Place*. Minneapolis: University of Minnesota Press.

Wylie, J.W. (2005) A single day's walking: Narrating self and landscape on the South West Coast Path. *Transactions of the Institute of British Geographers*, 30, 234–247.

Chapter 6

# Affect

*Deborah Dixon and Elizabeth R. Straughan*

As with all manner of key concepts, affect has been used to underpin a wealth of geographic analysis and writing whilst eluding precision, in terms of a circumscribed definition, and specificity, in terms of what it appropriately illuminates. What is more, this geographic engagement itself rubs up against other disciplinary explorations and deployments of affect, each of which has a particular intellectual lineage (see Thrift 2004). Nevertheless, within geography an understanding of affect as unfolding from a modern-day appraisal by Gilles Deleuze (amongst others) of seventeenth-century philosopher Baruch Spinoza's ideas has tended to predominate, such that it has become bound up with other, equally unsettled, concepts such as materialism, embodiment, performance, and aesthetics, as well as poststructural theories more broadly. Of interest to geographers is how affect, in concert with these concepts, can help to reanimate the disciplinary imagination with regard to such long-standing concerns as site, topology, and territory.

Affect, as the non-cognized, non-symbolic, sensuous, rhythmic interplay between person and environment that allows for the emergence of a "sense of place," appears in Buttimer's (1976) essay on the "lifeworld." It is with the development of "non-representational theory" in the late 1990s, however, that affect is placed under sustained examination as a means of "livening," it was argued, a geographic discipline overly preoccupied with the interpretation of meaning and the key role of the intellect in such a process (Thrift and Dewsbury 2000). Subsuming the more specifically corporeal notions of percept (that is, a mental impression of something perceived) and sensation (that which is felt physiologically), affect became a reference for various forces that, with varying speeds and intensities, constitute (as opposed to direct or emanate from) the composing and recomposing of bodies.

Such bodies, following Deleuze's appraisal of Spinoza's immanent ontology, are by no means synonymous with the individuated, corporeal form of an organism. Rather, bodies are

*The Wiley Blackwell Companion to Cultural Geography*, First Edition.
Edited by Nuala C. Johnson, Richard H. Schein, and Jamie Winders.
© 2013 John Wiley & Sons, Ltd. Published 2016 by John Wiley & Sons, Ltd.

an assemblage of materials that are rendered distinct from each other by virtue of their capacity to do particular things (Ruddick 2010). Difference, here, ensues from what a particular
body can do rather than by virtue of, for example, taxonomies based on appearance, reproductive function, or DNA. As numerous geographers have pointed out, we can thus talk of
bodies as composed of individuals acting in concert with inhuman elements, non-human
animals, and technologies, that undertake certain practices such as fishing (Bear and Eden
2011), sitting comfortably on a chair (Bissell 2008), or living in a building (Kraftl 2008). The
emotional registers mobilized by these performances are thus part and parcel of affect, rather
than innate passions belonging to the corporeal. We can also talk of a multitude of bodies
extending in and through that which we consider to be "our" corporeal form – including,
for example, the viral infection that extends from animal reservoir to human host to fomite
(infectious surface) and so on – such that instead of a body's interior, surface, and exterior
we can think instead of windows, portals, and passages.

Importantly, however, such a "posthumanism" is tempered. That is, whilst affect undercuts
the notion of agency as a uniquely human capacity (Woodward 2010), and promotes an
ethics of cooperation that extends beyond the social (Anderson and Harrison 2010), both
Spinoza and Deleuze emphasize the fact that the reflective capacity for and of thought (albeit
enabled by an embodied way of knowing, and prompted by a reassembling of materialities
anew) provides for a crucial human/non-human distinction. Indeed, it is this distinction that
has prompted some geographers to unpack those capacities deemed to be the prerequisite of
human beings, such as the creative act and its pure potentiality (Thrift 2004), suffering
(Lorimer 2010), and vulnerability (Harrison 2008).

In explicitly methodological terms, an emphasis upon affect requires the abandoning of
pre-given categories, such as class, gender, and so on, that project rather than discover difference. Instead, Dewsbury asks that we work with a microscopic intensity to become sensitive to the researcher as, to use Grosz's (1994) terminology, a "volatile body," whose
experiences in place emerge "through the sensation of spacing that is material and immaterial,
human and animal, organic and inorganic" (2009: 326). Such experiences allow insight into
how bodies – extending in and through the corporeality of the researcher, affecting and affective of each other – are constituted from materials that, as Bennett puts it, do not flow so
much as they "collide, congeal, morph, evolve, and disintegrate" (2010: xi).

Such a methodology also requires the abandoning of pre-given spatial analytics, such as
scale, that purport to capture a fundamental order to the world. In arguing for a "flat ontology," for example, Marston, Jones, and Woodward point instead to an analytic based on sites,
insofar as these draw out the play of affect in the material composition and recomposition
of bodies, a play that sometimes leads to "the creation of new, unique events and entities,
but more often to relatively redundant orders and practices" (2005: 422). In similar vein,
Allen (2011) has eschewed a lexicon based on absolute location and distance; instead, materialities are stretched, reworked, and appropriated, such that proximity, presence, and absence
become "topological twists" in a scrumpled-up geography of affect. And, for Dixon, Hawkins,
and Straughan (forthcoming), an acknowledgment of the intensification of affect within
mating rituals, wherein certain material movements and transformations become fraught with
desire, prompts a reconsideration of territory as the product of innate aggression; instead,
territory becomes a form of art tied to expression.

Indeed, space as a geographic analytic has itself been recast in light of the play of affect.
Whilst diverse critical frameworks have eschewed a simple Euclidean (or topographic) rendering of space as the mere backdrop to events, an emphasis upon affect draws attention to the

as yet undisclosed heterogeneity and multiplicity of space. Here, to point to sites, topologies, and territories as they appear before us is not to circumscribe them as the innate qualities of bodies, but is rather to acknowledge their mutability, as well as our own openness, as researchers, to being surprised by such mutability, such that we can develop, hopefully, new ways of thinking.

## References

Allen, J. (2011) Topological twists: Power's shifting geographies. *Dialogues in Human Geography*, 1 (3), 283–298.

Anderson, B. and Harrison, P. (eds.) (2010) *Taking-Place: Non-Representational Theories and Geography*. Farnham: Ashgate.

Bear, C. and Eden, S. (2011) Thinking like a fish? Engaging with non-human difference through recreational angling. *Environment and Planning D: Society and Space*, 29 (2), 336–352.

Bennett, J. (2010) *Vibrant Matter: A Political Ecology of Things*. Durham, NC: Duke University Press.

Bissell, D. (2008) Comfortable bodies: Sedentary affects. *Environment and Planning A*, 40, 1697–1712.

Buttimer, A. (1976) Grasping the dynamism of the lifeworld. *Annals of the Association of American Geographers*, 66 (2), 277–292.

Dewsbury, J.-D. (2009) Performative, non-representational, and affect-based research: Seven injunctions. In *The Sage Handbook of Qualitative Research in Human Geography*, ed. D. Delyser *et al*. London: Sage, pp. 321–334.

Dixon, D.P., Hawkins, H., and Straughan, E.R. (forthcoming) Of human birds and living rocks: Remaking aesthetics for post-human worlds. Dialogues in Human Geography.

Grosz, E. (1994) *Volatile Bodies: Toward a Corporeal Feminism*. Bloomington: Indiana University Press.

Harrison, P. (2008) Corporeal remains: Vulnerability, proximity, and living on after the end of the world. *Environment and Planning A*, 40, 423–445.

Kraftl, P. (2008) Architecture/affect/inhabitation: Geographies of being-in buildings. *Annals of the Association of American Geographers*, 998 (1), 213–231.

Lorimer, J. (2010) Ladies and gentlemen, behold the enemy. *Environment and Planning D: Society and Space*, 28, 40–42.

Marston, S., Jones, J.P., and Woodward, K. (2005) Human geography without scale. *Transactions of the Institute of British Geographers*, 30 (4), 416–432.

Ruddick, S. (2010) The politics of affect: Spinoza in the work of Negri and Deleuze. *Theory, Culture and Society*, 27 (4), 21–45.

Thrift, N. (2004) Intensities of feeling: Towards a spatial politics of affect. *Geografiska Annaler*, 86 B.1, 57–78.

Thrift, N. and Dewsbury, J.-D. (2000) Dead geographies – and how to make them live again. *Environment and Planning D: Society and Space*, 18 (4), 411–432.

Woodward, K. (2010) Events, spontaneity and abrupt conditions. In *Taking-Place: Non-Representational Theories and Geography*, ed. B. Anderson and P. Harrison. Farnham: Ashgate, pp. 321–340.

Chapter 7

# Historical Materialism

## *Don Mitchell*

Almost three decades ago David Harvey (2001/1984) argued that all geography must be historical-materialist. He was right, but we have yet to realize the implications. If geography must be historical-materialist then *there can be no "cultural geography" as such.*[1]

By far the more important of the two words – "historical materialism" – is the first one. Without it any theory of materialism[2] becomes a pure, untenable, total, and totalizing theory of immanence.[3] It is as if the world just is and as if there is nothing outside of experience (such a theory of immanence is clearly at the root of, if unacknowledged by, the so-called new materialists in cultural geography like Wylie 2005; Bissell 2010). It turns "culture," and "cultural experience," into a mere "realm," an "affect,"[4] rather than a constitutive part of the social totality.

As E.P. Thompson (1978: 70) wrote: "Historical materialism offers to study social process in its totality; that is, it offers to do this when it appears, not as another 'sectoral' history [such as economic or labor history] . . . but as a total history of society, in which all other histories are convened." Historical-materialist geography must find ways of "convening" the history and practice of social, material life; to ignore the former – history – is to ignore the very constitution of the world we live in.

To convene history and practice, we must begin from the premise that the world is produced, not immanent. Then, we must seek to understand the unfolding *history* of this production (which is a natural history and a social history, as well as their ineluctable dialectical entwining: Smith 2008/1984). History in this sense is *internal* to materiality and to ignore it is thus to ignore precisely the ingredients of geography; it is to fall back on a fully idealist (to say nothing of solipsistic) view of the world. Or as Denis Cosgrove (1983: 1) long ago argued: "Both Marxism [historical materialism] and cultural geography commence at the same ontological point. In strict opposition to any form of determinism of linear causal

*The Wiley Blackwell Companion to Cultural Geography*, First Edition.
Edited by Nuala C. Johnson, Richard H. Schein, and Jamie Winders.
© 2013 John Wiley & Sons, Ltd. Published 2016 by John Wiley & Sons, Ltd.

explanation they insist on characterizing the relationship between humans and nature as historical. That men and women make their history and themselves is the first premise of historical materialism." The second premise is that they make the world out of an already produced world. This is not a world that suddenly rears up in order to be experienced (as most "new materialists" seem to think), but a world that has always already been historically constructed, over the long haul of natural history and the shorter haul of social struggle.

This already constructed world sets humanity problems that must be solved, and re-solved again. As people – perhaps divided into the bearers of capital and the bearers of labor-power, into men and women, into "Americans" and "Zimbabweans," into landlords and peasants, into the broad and mythical "middle classes" – confront the world as historically given, they must confront the problem of how they are to produce and reproduce their very existence as well as their consciousness under historically given social conditions, or they must figure out how to change existence itself. In a world where capitalism has become hegemonic (that is, in the world we actually live in, rather than the utopian world various "post-capitalist" theorists like to pretend we live in: e.g., Gibson-Graham 2006), the problems to be solved involve, at base, "the fundamental processes of capital accumulation that generate social change" (Harvey 2001/1992: 121) and that shape everything from the basics of reproduction (what to eat and how, where to live and how) to the most ethereal and seemingly rarified forms of cultural provision (art songs, string theory in physics). If we don't like any of these – the relations of accumulation and the injustices to which it gives rise, the annual *New York Times Magazine* article on string theory and its discontents – then we have to change history and geography itself: we have to change the historically, geographically *structured* world.

This can be a lot of work. For these problems *are* the social totality, and they are and can never be simply "cultural." "Culture," in this historical sense, is epiphenomenal.[5] It is epiphenomenal to the struggle to produce existence (which is not to say that it is not, at the same time, a critical ingredient of this struggle; of course it is), and thus cannot be studied in and of itself. Rather, culture must always be seen as something to be explained, and what needs to be explained is its historical as well as its geographical existence and ongoing redevelopment. That's the true importance of understanding that geography must always be historical-materialist. It asks us to see the world "not as we would like it to be but as it really is, the material manifestation of human hopes and fears" – and labor! – "mediated by powerful and conflicting processes of social reproduction" (Harvey 2001/1984: 116). And then, especially, it asks us to *explain* it.

### Notes

1  Nor can there be geography as such: Eliot Hurst (1985).
2  Materialism: "The doctrine that nothing exists except matter and its movements and modifications. Also, the doctrine that consciousness and will are wholly due to the operation of material agencies" (*Shorter Oxford English Dictionary*).
3  Immanent: "1. Indwelling, inherent (in); (of God) permanently pervading the universe; 2. Of an action: that is performed entirely within the mind of the subject, and produces no external effect" (*Shorter Oxford English Dictionary*).
4  Affect: "1. Mental or physical disposition or constitution; 2. An emotion, mood" (*Shorter Oxford English Dictionary*).
5  Epiphenomenon: "A concomitant or by-product of something" (*Shorter Oxford English Dictionary*).

## References

Bissell, D. (2010) Vibrating materialities: Mobility–body–technology relations. *Area*, 42, 479–486.

Cosgrove, D. (1983) Towards a radical cultural geography. *Antipode*, 15, 1–11.

Eliot Hurst, M. (1985) Geography has neither existence nor future. In *The Future of Geography*, ed. R.J. Johnston. London: Methuen, pp. 59–91.

Gibson-Graham, J.K. (2006) *The End of Capitalism (As We Knew It): A Feminist Critique of Political Economy* (with a new introduction). Minneapolis: University of Minnesota Press.

Harvey, D. (2001/1984) On the history and present condition of geography: An historical materialist manifesto. In *Spaces of Capital: Towards a Critical Geography*. New York: Routledge, pp. 108–120.

Harvey, D. (2001/1992) Capitalism: The factory of fragmentation. In *Spaces of Capital: Towards a Critical Geography*. New York: Routledge, p. 121.

Smith, N. (2008/1984) *Uneven Development: Nature, Capital, and the Production of Space*, 3rd edition. Athens, GA: University of Georgia Press.

Thompson, E.P. (1978) The poverty of theory: An orrery of errors. In *The Poverty of Theory and Other Essays*. New York: Monthly Review Press, pp. 1–210.

Wylie, J. (2005) A single day's walking: Narrating self and landscape on the South West Coast Path. *Transactions of the Institute of British Geographers*, 30, 37–51.

# Foundations

*The Wiley Blackwell Companion to Cultural Geography*, First Edition.
Edited by Nuala C. Johnson, Richard H. Schein, and Jamie Winders.
© 2013 John Wiley & Sons, Ltd. Published 2016 by John Wiley & Sons, Ltd.

Chapter 8

# Cultural Geography in Practice

*Catherine Nash*

## Introduction

In 2000 the journal *Cultural Geographies* established a new section entitled *Cultural Geographies in Practice*. It was set up to provide a place to feature the range of ways in which cultural geography is practiced. At one level this refers to the research practices of this subdisciplinary area. But the section was not conceived as a forum for academic cultural geography alone. "Cultural geographies" in the title of *Cultural Geographies in Practice* stands both for an academic pursuit and a wider range of ideas, practices, and concerns that span the academy and wider public culture. This reflects a sense of geography as more-than-academic, as an engagement with the world that is formally organized as a branch of academic knowledge but which also describes a broader set of practices, knowledges, and imaginations (Bonnett 2008). It was inspired by other efforts to consider popular or public forms of knowledge and the academic reflections upon them such as the *History Workshop Journal*'s section *Histories at Large*. This move to provide a place to feature the interesting and innovative work of "non-geographers" also pursuing the key themes of cultural geography through their cultural practices sought to challenge a conventional model of academic expertise by recognizing the significance of these public cultural geographies. It also was set up to feature the work of those crossing the boundaries between these categories through adopting modes of working that are academic, creative and involve collaborative relationships. This sort of creative cultural geography is not confined to this section of the journal. Lots of interesting work occurs on the ground and is documented in other ways. But it is one sign of a vibrant and lively strand of cultural geography in practice.

The title of this chapter also echoes that of a guide to research methods in cultural geography. In *Cultural Geography in Practice* (Blunt *et al*. 2003) the contributors bring together key

*The Wiley Blackwell Companion to Cultural Geography*, First Edition.
Edited by Nuala C. Johnson, Richard H. Schein, and Jamie Winders.
© 2013 John Wiley & Sons, Ltd. Published 2016 by John Wiley & Sons, Ltd.

themes that are the focus of interest in cultural geography and examples of how those themes can be addressed though specific sources and approaches, to show how cultural geography can be done. Reflecting the efflorescence of cultural geography in the previous decade and remedying the lack of practical guidance on how to undertake cultural geography, the book demonstrates the ways in which a range of methodologies (from textual interpretation to ethnography) and sources (including archives, the Internet, exhibitions, newspapers, visual images of many kinds, buildings, and sound) can be used to explore specific issues and themes by unpicking the process of producing research in cultural geography. This chapter has a related but distinctive aim. It is not to provide a condensed account of a range of methodologies in cultural geography, but an introduction to some of the creative ways in which cultural geographers are doing cultural geography that stretch and test the limits of established approaches to the practice and dissemination of research. It also works with an elastic sense of cultural geography that not only describes wider cultural geographies at large beyond the academy, but also attends to the ways in which cultural themes and cultural approaches now span subdisciplinary areas and weaken rigid definitions of their boundaries. In considering the creative practices of geographers under the heading of Cultural Geography in Practice I am, like Phil Crang in his recent reflections of this subject, including work by geographers (and others) who would not necessarily describe their work in this way (Crang 2010).

The founding of *Cultural Geographies in Practice* also coincided with one prominent and provocative criticism of cultural geography. In one of a series of influential reflections on the emphasis on representation and interpretation in cultural geography, Nigel Thrift criticized what he saw as its methodological narrowness and conservatism. He encouraged a turn to new methods which attempt to "co-produce the world" and reimagine the world including performance arts and theater, dance and music therapy, performative writing and creative storytelling (Thrift 2000: 3). The work of academic cultural geographers experimenting with new approaches that foreground the performative, practiced, and embodied dimensions of investigation and expand the creative practice and presentation of academic research has preceded or emerged through similar concerns or has been prompted through different directions and developments including interests in participatory collaboration and innovative forms of public engagement. Here I want to give a sense of the sets of overlapping orientations and sensibilities that underpin new experimental or creative strategies. A series of specific cases from a rich, diverse, and expanding range of possible examples will be used to represent and reflect on creative methodologies, unconventional ways of conveying research, disciplinary boundary crossing, and collaborative practice in cultural geography.

## Cultural Practice as Cultural Geography

The striking expansion of cultural geography over the last twenty years from its roots in studies of polite and vernacular material and visual culture has partly been about the expanded range of cultural practices and forms that have been addressed by cultural geographers. A wide range of cultural practices have been explored in terms of the ways they co-constitute places, spaces, landscapes, natures, identities, and social relations: routine but culturally significant practices such as cooking, shopping, sorting domestic stuff out; leisure practices such as gardening, rambling, cycling, making and listening to music (see Crouch 1999). In some cases their geographical dimensions are obvious. In other cases, particular cultural practices are explored as implicitly but inescapably bound up with wider social, economic, and political geographies. But this expansion has not simply meant the repeated application of an analytical framework concerned with the production and politics of meaning through culture onto new or hitherto overlooked cultural practices. Instead, cultural practices are being addressed in ways that both continue or rework long-standing interests in embodiment in phenomenological and social terms, for example, and in ways that depart from previous models of research through participatory approaches by directly engaging in the practice under consideration as a methodological, reflective, and interpretive strategy – a sort of hands-on cultural geography in practice – and are framed as new developments and through particular theoretical frameworks. Moreover, a focus on cultural geography in practice encompasses not only academic considerations of cultural practices in themselves but also the cultural practice of academic geography – the creativity of the ways in which cultural geography is both done and disseminated. A sense of these intertwining strands can be conveyed through a focus on the cultural geography of one cultural practice – walking – before considering further the ideas that inform and are expressed through creative cultural geographies of many different kinds.

Walking is a practice that has an established place in geography's disciplinary tradition of fieldwork. It is also the focus of a growing body of work by geographers and others, especially social anthropologists, considering walking as a lived and embodied practice and addressing its cultural meanings and social and spatial embeddedness (Lorimer 2010; Middleton 2011). In contrast to the sometimes universalizing claims about its meaning and value, especially in relation to spiritual, psychic, and physical health in popular accounts, these new pedestrian studies address all sorts of contexts of walking and a range of embodied walking practices and the specific meanings attached to walking in particular ways in particular places. David Matless (1998), for example, has traced the ways in which walking as one of a range of outdoor leisure pursuits in the interwar period in England was entangled with discourses of healthy citizenship, national prosperity, and tensions over class-based claims about countryside conduct and property rights.

Walking is not only the subject of cultural research in geography in this rich historical and cultural interpretive tradition but has also recently been revitalized as a research practice in its own right. Over the last decade geographers have been exploring direct and participatory forms of engagement as a way of understanding in a more embodied and direct way, a range of cultural-geographic practices and concerns. This includes dance as well as walking (see McCormack 2004, 2008; Revill 2004). A study of the lived meanings and experience of hill walking in Scotland, for example, was undertaken through a mobile participatory approach, researching walking while walking with others, as a sort of ethnography of walking (Lorimer 2010). Talking together while walking has also been proposed as a methodology through which understandings, reflections, emotions, and beliefs are collectively elucidated by research subjects and the researcher (Anderson 2004). In contrast, walking has been explored as a solitary undertaking in the work of John Wylie (2002, 2005) as a means to pursue his "post-phenomenological" consideration of landscape, subjectivity, corporality, and affect. In line with a broadly non-representational approach (Anderson and Harrison 2010), the emphasis is less on the meaning of landscape than on the way in which people make sense of the world through embodied and affective experience and in relation to the active effects of other people, objects, texts, and technologies. Other geographers combine the narrative form of an account of a walk in ways which attend both to its embodied practice and to the way the landscape can be read in terms of the interweaving of personal experience and affect and local, national, and global political geographies. This is the focus of James Sidaway's account of a single evening's walk on part of the coastal path that runs through the city of Plymouth that tells a multi-layered story of "how geopolitics affects us" and of how "the repercussions of militarism, war and death are folded into the textures of an everyday urban landscape" (Sidaway 2009: 1091).

Just as Wylie's work on rural landscapes emerges through and in relation to a long tradition of scholarly and social interest in the meaning and practice of being in "nature" Sidaway's urban walk can be situated within the fertile field of activist, artistic, and academic engagements with the questions of urban space through practices centered on walking (Phillips 2005; Pinder 2005). This includes the tradition of marches as forms of popular protest and a range of artistic interventions that use walking creatively to point to or explore the changing nature and experience of cities being reshaped by waves of capital and redevelopment. Artistic walking interventions are being undertaken through collaborative participation by cultural geographers (Fenton 2005). The redeveloping area of King's Cross in London, for example, has been the focus of a "treasure hunt" designed by a collaborative team, including geographer Steve Pile, to be undertaken as a suggestive exploration of the area's past and possible future (Battista et al. 2005).

These participatory and artistic-activist approaches are also linked to efforts to convey cultural geographies of walking in more creative ways. John Wylie (2006) has worked within the journal paper format with photographs and texts arranged to convey the rhythm of his walking and reflections on landscape and subjectivity around a section of the north Devon coast. Others have approached walking from the perspective of artists interested in exploring the nature of geographical practice, especially field walking. This is one strand of the considerable amount of work by visual artists on geographical knowledges, approaches, and themes that reflects the "spatial turn" in arts practice as well as cultural critical theory over the last two decades. Australian artist Perdita Phillips has worked with geographers, and as an artist in residence in the spaces of academic geography, and explored the relationship between the role of the artist and the natural scientist by adopting the techniques of field walking. A series of her art works explores the specificity of this spatial and embodied practice and ideas of sustained depth of relation to place or more ephemeral and transient encounters (Phillips 2004). For other creative geographers the walk is not only undertaken as a research method that can be communicated through the use of creative approaches via words and visual images, but a walk can be the research "output" that is actively reenacted and remade each time it is undertaken. This is the basis of Toby Butler's innovative work in constructing sound walks which are composed of a series of spoken extracts of oral history testimony and other sounds that are organized along a set route. He has used this to create powerful and poignant resonances between accounts of experience and their associated sites along the River Thames in his Memoryscape project (Butler 2006). Knowledge is thus not simply gathered and conveyed but co-created by the walker in the practice of undertaking the audio walk.

These different but overlapping approaches to walking reflect several key themes of creative cultural geographies: an emphasis on practice, performance, process and embodiment, participation and collaboration, on creative styles of engagement and forms of representation. The next section outlines the wider field of these developments through the theme of creative public geographies.

## Creative Public Geographies

In July 2009 Ian Cook and Kathryn Yussoff organized an event on behalf of the Social and Cultural Geography Research Group of the Royal Geographical Society (with the Institute of British Geographers) at the University of Exeter entitled "Creative Public Geographies." The seminar was one of a program of events entitled "Engaging Geography" devoted to exploring the relationship between academic geography and wider society. The "creative public geography" seminar was set out to

> examine how, in recent years, an increasing number of geographers and artists, poets, filmmakers, and other creative professionals etc. have worked collaboratively, broadening the remit of research and its outputs beyond the traditional texts and spaces of university education. In addition, geographers, artists, filmmakers, etc. are often one in the same person, and artists, filmmakers, etc. seem more and more interested in drawing upon geographical themes and vocabularies in their work.

It sought to

> explore the collaborative potentials, working practices, forms and spaces of engagement, and publics generated through recent academic/creative work on, for example, climate change, GM foods, animal geographies, ethical/sustainable consumption and postcolonial curating through a variety of project work underpinned by academic/creative collaborations. (Engaging Geography n.d.)

The event thus responded to the lively interest of creative practitioners in geographical subjects and approaches and to the ways in which geographers are becoming involved in creative practice (sometimes through collaborative working relationships) and producing cultural geographies in a range of forms including exhibitions, drama, films, radio programs, art projects, and audio walks. The Engaging Geography website features over one hundred examples of creative public geographies and thus provides the beginnings of an archive of geographical engagement that would otherwise be lost as a source of inspiration now and historical record in the future (Merriman 2010; see also Fuller and Askins 2010).

The current flourishing and increased visibility of creative public geographies of this kind extends a significant and well-established strand of work by cultural geographers such as Stephen Daniels, who have curated exhibitions of historical and contemporary art in regional and national museums and galleries. Other geographers have used the exhibition format within research projects to display objects, texts, and visual images that open up their research to potentially wide audiences and exploit the engaging potential of this creative mode of public engagement. They include Lowri Jones and Felix Driver inviting a subtly postcolonial reconsideration of British exploration through the archival materials of the Royal Geographical Society (2009), David Gilbert's exhibition on "Swinging London" at the Victoria and Albert Museum (2006), and Divya Tolia-Kelly's exhibition and education pack, "An Archaeology of 'Race'," challenging the idea of pure Britishness through a focus on Roman Britain and Hadrian's Wall (2009). Other geographers have worked with the expressive potential of words and photography but within the format of academic papers (DeSilvey 2007), or used new digital technologies to create websites that invite viewers to engage actively with themes of urban change (Pryke 2002), environmental memory (Cameron 1997), or urban experience (Rose, Basdas, and Degen 2009) by following different (structured or unstructured) pathways though a range of texts, images, and sounds. Cultural geographers are thus well placed to respond to increasing government concerns that state funding for research should make a clearly demonstrable contribution to wider society. "Impact," as it is being described, is a new measure of the value of academic research and has become a key criterion for research funding in the UK. Yet the development of creative public geography is underpinned by approaches to the value of research that resist narrowly economic or quantitative measures of impact and have a more challenging vision of a public cultural geography than the transfer of "useful" knowledge from the academy to the "public" (Pain, Kesby, and Askins 2010).

The increasingly creative practice of geographers has also been significantly shaped by social geography's tradition of participatory, activist, and action research that has challenged the hierarchical model of the academic expert and passive research subjects by redistributing authority in the research relationship through collaborative participation and involvement. This includes the use of the arts – performance, video, theater, photography – in innovative participatory research (Pain 2004). Film, for example, not only represents a cultural form – films – to be analyzed by cultural geographers, however valuable this remains, but is also a practice – filmmaking – that has been actively explored by geographers sometimes as a means of conveying research in ways that better match its subjects or approaches (Evans and Jones 2008; Gandy 2009) but also as a participatory practice. Hester Parr has used collaborative filmmaking with people with severe and enduring mental health problems as part of her commitment to using diverse approaches to access and include their voices and affectual worlds in geographical research. The filmmaking process was a way to explore the value of creative practice for mental health and the mutual benefit of the redistribution of expertise and authority in research through practical creative collaboration (Parr 2007). While this film was both a collaborative research practice and a representation of her wider work on the arts and mental health, for Parr the process is valued as much as the product for "it is through the creative processes such as this, and the unscripted negotiating of meaning through the *doing* of film, that the significance of arts work for this group comes alive and becomes more accessible" (Parr 2007: 131).

This strong sense of the value of creative and collaborative engagement similarly informs the work of geographers Caleb Johnston and Geraldine Pratt. In 2009 they wrote and produced a site-specific play, *Nanay* (Mother), in collaboration with the Philippine Women Centre of British Columbia. The play, which was staged in Vancouver and later Berlin, took conventional research materials in the form of transcripts from interviews with Filipino migrant domestic workers and children and from Canadian employers and nanny agents from Geraldine Pratt's work on the feminist geographies of childcare, and created an intimate, small-scale, and temporary performance installation "with the objective of bringing academic research to a wider public in an immediate, engaging way" (Johnston and Pratt 2010: 123). The play was an effort to build up public interest in and knowledge about the important social issue of the experience of Filipino migrant workers and their treatment by employers and authorities through the temporary migrant worker scheme. It was crafted to prompt the Canadian audience to reflect on their own complicity and the wider underlying issues of labor inequalities and immigrant experience, but also to create possibilities of new solidarities and alliances across different subject positions and opportunities for change. As the authors write in reflection:

> The play forced a sensual exchange, involving much more than words, often evoking an emotional, visceral response. We understand *Nanay* to be an attempt to create – and not just describe – emotional geographies of public significance. Of course, a theatrical event is fleeting – and extremely expensive to reproduce. Our challenge remains one of assessing whether and how its intensities travel beyond the event. (Johnston and Pratt 2010: 133)

This is one striking example of the work that does not "just describe" preexisting geographies but instigates and collaboratively engages in creative practice to produce in this case "emotional geographies of public significance."

The sense of meaning, understanding, or knowledge being co-produced in this collaboration is a key idea of what has recently been described as "organic public geographies" that go beyond the traditional idea of public engagement whereby academic research is presented in accessible formats to the wider public (Fuller 2008; Fuller and Askins 2010; Ward 2006). Inspired by the elaboration of these ideas in relation to sociology, organic public geography is underpinned by a more radical reimagining of the relationship between the academy and the public. Instead of relying on a model of academic expertise and a relatively uninformed, unthinking, and passive audience, the emphasis is on the value of non-academic knowledge and experience, and the possibility of working with people in forms of democratic and non-hierarchical collaboration and to engage in the collective co-production of knowledge. Academic authority is decentered, academic control over the process is redistributed, and the outcomes of working in this way are uncertain.

The varied work of cultural geographers engaging in creative practices does not necessarily neatly align with this idea of organic public geographies. Forms of collaboration and degrees of academic control vary. Yet the turn to creative practice is part of the wider overlapping interest in creativity as a form of collective engagement, the value of creative practice as a process, and the expressive and critical potential of creative forms as the products of research in cultural geography. Collaborations between geographers and creative practitioners of different kinds are one notable dimension of these creative public geographies. The final section of this chapter turns to the question of collaboration to consider how ideas of authority, expertise, and established ways of working are foregrounded and sometimes shifted in collaborative practice.

## Boundary Crossings: Geography, Art, and Collaboration

Collaborations between geographers and creative practitioners are not limited to those between geographers and visual artists. But art–geography collaborations are among the most well-established and have been subject to considerable reflection. The coming together of artists and geographers has partly arisen through a now deeply rooted interest in the place of art outside the confines of the art gallery that underpins the practice of funding artists through residencies in a range of institutional settings. With the rise of funding for science–art collaborations, spaces of scientific knowledge production, including more recently university geography departments, have become sites of creativity and collaboration (Foster and Lorimer 2007). As artists have become increasingly interested in the language of spatial theory and geographical practices (especially environmental field and laboratory work), cultural geographers in turn have been increasingly interested not only in the discipline's own visual traditions but also in the embodied making of art and the expressive potential of the visual arts.

These explorations of geographical and artistic connections and possible points of connection sometimes cohere around interests in cartography. One recent example was the "Crossing Boundaries" symposium in 2010, a collaborative venture between the Royal Geographical Society (with the Institute of British Geographers) and the Institute of International Visual Arts that aimed to "blur the boundaries between the art and science of mapping." The associated exhibition "Whose Map Is It? New Mapping by Artists" featured new work contributing to the now well-established tradition of visual artists working with and reworking the form and authority of conventional maps. These are occasions for the realization of shared interests, but artists and geographers can also find themselves misunderstood or misrepresented in the process. Despite the interests of conceptual artists in the theoretical vocabulary of cultural geography, academic geography can also be figured as the domain of positivist scientific knowledge production to be critically undermined by visual artists. The categories of "artist" and "academic geographer" are not simply dissolved in collaborative practice but can be put in tension, defended, reified, as well as crossed and reconsidered.

It was this question of the nature and meaning of these categories and the implications of collaboration across them that was subject to a short but intense period of investigation in the project *Visualising Geography*. This was itself a collaboration I co-ordinated between Felix Driver and myself as academic geographers, the artist Kathy Prendergast, and art curator Ingrid Swenson that instigated a series of collaborative relationships between artists and academics in the Department of Geography, Royal Holloway, University of London in 2002. These pairings were not the first or only collaborations between artists and geographers. In the UK context they have been a feature of the work of Divya Tolia-Kelly; artist Derek Hampson has worked with geographer Gary Priestnall to explore subjective versions of place, and with four geographers and a surveyor from the University of Nottingham to address the changing geographies of the town of Margate in Kent; and artist Catrin Webster and geographer Peter Merriman have explored their shared interests in landscape and mobility (Merriman and Webster 2009). Health geographer Edward Kinman and ceramic artist John Williams, based at Longwood University in Virginia, have similarly collaborated on a creative cartographic project (Kinman and Williams 2007; see also Dwyer and Davies 2010). As one contribution to this developing area, the *Visualising Geography* project fostered a variety of collaborative relationships and tried to create opportunities for some explicit discussion and documentation of the diverse dynamics and difficulties as well as the mutual benefits and insights of geography–art collaboration.

*Visualising Geography* was at once a tentative and ambitiously experimental attempt to consider the relationships between intellectual, empirical, and creative practices in geography and the visual arts. Though, as we realized, the project's title might imply that the role of the artists was simply to "illustrate" the work of geographers, our aim was to explore distinctions and possible crossovers between the categories of artist and academic, to consider the similarities and differences between ideas of individual autonomy and achievement in both domains, and the ways the value of art–academic collaborations are conceived of from both sides. As we recounted in the catalogue of the work-in-progress exhibition *Landing*, one of the project's insights was the inadequacy of distinguishing between art and academic geography on the basis of the intellectual and research-based work of geographers and the creative and practice-based work of artists. This was clear from the degree to which much contemporary art is underpinned by, or is constituted as, a form of empirical research. In our workshop discussions the categories of artist and academic "began to shift, realign, dissolve and sometimes re-crystalise as people talked about what they did and how and why. A description of ethnographic research at one point was redefined as art by artists. In other instances academics interested in more imaginative or inventive research methods encountered artists committed to rigorous empirical research" (Driver *et al.* 2002: 8). Collaborations varied in their dynamics, depth, and character. Some took the form of thoughtful conversations and rewarding exchanges; others stalled or faltered, "marked by senses of diffidence, insecurity, defensiveness, resistance or assumptions of authority" (Driver *et al.* 2002: 9).

Very few resulted in the actual co-production of the art itself. Collaboration is not an easy process. It involves a delicate negotiation of boundaries of expertise and authority. It may be easier to relinquish a degree of academic authority than to achieve acceptance as a creative practitioner. This is not surprising given how the easy adoption of the role of artist by an academic geographer could be seen to overlook or undermine the distinctive skills and training that make "art" a special form of cultural practice.

These issues were addressed in much more depth in Holly McLaren's doctoral research, which extended recent geographical engagement with artistic practice concerned with the making rather than interpretation of art, and sought to explore how "site-specific" art can capture the "fleeting, sensuous, unspoken geographies that constitute the 'lived complexities' of place" (McLaren 2007: 4). Through her role commissioning three pieces of new art focused on the Welsh border around the town of Oswestry, and organizing a scattered-site exhibition and crafting an exhibition catalogue (McLaren 2007), the project was a practical and sustained reflection on the nature of collaboration and the position of "curator" as well as "geographer." Each of the three resulting art works involved different configurations of the relationship between artists and geographer and different negotiations of their boundaries and conventions of autonomy and authority. Possibilities of direct creative collaboration in which the geographer is directly engaged in the creative process rather than in a facilitating or supportive role, or supplying ideas or research materials, remain relatively rare and depend on the contingent dynamics of the particular relationship. The relative openness of cultural geography to experimental ventures means that art–geography collaborations have been welcomed. But understandable and justified arguments that artistic achievement is hard earned rather than easy, and based upon the particular training, expertise, and skill of artists as well as talent, may mean that it might be more possible for an artist to become an artist-geographer than it is for a geographer to become a geographer-artist. The possibilities will of course vary in different contexts and for different individuals. The work of Trevor Paglan (2006), Helen Scalway (2006), and Perdita Phillips (2004), who as artists have forged innovative positions inhabiting both domains, points to the semi-permeable borders between academic geography and creative practice.

## Conclusion

This is a necessarily selective and partial account of recent strands of cultural geography and it reflects the geography of my own encounters with these developments. But what I hope comes through is the energetic and energizing spirit of creative, practice-led, and public cultural geographies. There is much inspiration to be found in these examples but also a sense of the challenges and difficulties of this work. While these innovations in the practice of cultural geography deserve recognition, this is not meant to be a simply celebratory account, nor one that simply lauds novelty for novelty's sake. There is a danger that the content of research is subordinated to a concern with form and aesthetics or overlooked in a focus on new technical possibilities. Nor is this chapter an argument that conventional formats and methods are being or should be superseded by new approaches. Most cultural geography as practiced within geography continues to reach its audiences via books, journals, and conference papers. And these forms of dissemination should not simply be seen as dull, limited, and conventional in contrast to new creative or technologically mediated forms and practices. In many respects these formats work very well, and can be worked with in ways that harness the expressive potential of writing and speaking to produce evocative, compelling, and convincing narrative accounts of their subjects within the constraints of traditional formats. There are moves to consider the possibilities of creative writing (Brace and Johns-Putra 2010) and to enliven conventional printed formats through "geo/graphic" approaches (Barnes 2011). Developments in electronic publishing offer new possibilities for linking journal papers to other material in a range of media, or of alternative forms of dissemination in their own right. But it is not the novelty of the form itself that determines the value of the work.

This question of value is, however, complicated by the economies of academic knowledge production. In the context of the increasing marketization of higher education, the value of scholarship is often conceived in monetary terms. This is most immediately obvious in the UK's competitive research assessment system whereby funding is awarded to departments on the basis of judgments about the academic significance of a department's published research. While non-standard outputs of innovative research practices are not explicitly excluded (and indeed are important in practice-based subjects such as architecture), the general conservatism of social research cultures, including geography, means that assessed work is effectively limited to journals, books, and book chapters. This means that the efforts of those engaged in creative, public, and participatory cultural geographies are not formally recognized and that the often demanding and time-consuming nature of this work has to be paralleled by the production of standard research papers in order to fulfill personal and institutional pressures to be productive in the conventional sense. This is an issue about public geographies of all kinds, including creative public geographies.

However, this continued primacy of books and papers in academic knowledge production is also being complicated by new requirements that government research funding to universities be linked to the proven wider public usefulness or "impact" of academic research. It is thus the case that more and more academics, cultural geographers included, will be involved in "impact activities" that seek to widen the audiences for their work through creative forms such as exhibitions. While the cultural geography in practice that I have highlighted here provides some significant precedents to learn from, it is also entangled in contested versions of relevance. In the context of measuring "impact," audience figures for a community engagement event, for example, may be deemed more significant than the much more subtle and hard-to-quantify significance of academic contributions to knowledge and understanding in the widest sense, or the value of collaborative creative research as a process in itself. These tensions and challenges within the wider institutional context of knowledge production or the social relations of collaboration do not undermine the creative cultural geographies that I have featured here but have come to the fore as this work has expanded and become more visible. More reflections on them will follow these moves to rework old forms and methods, engage in creative practices, develop participatory and collaborative approaches, and pursue creative public geographies, which mark the vitality of contemporary cultural geography.

## References

Anderson, B. and Harrison, P. (eds.) (2010) *Taking Place: Non-Representational Geographies*. Farnham: Ashgate.

Anderson, J. (2004) Talking whilst walking: A geographical archaeology of knowledge. *Area*, 36 (3), 254–261.

Barnes, A. (2011) *Realising the Geo/Graphic Landscape of the Everyday: A Practice-Led Investigation into an Interdisciplinary Geo/Graphic Design Process*. Unpublished PhD thesis, University of the Arts London.

Battista, K., LaBelle, B., Penner, B., Rendell, J., and Pile, S. (2005) Exploring "An Area of Outstanding Unnatural Beauty": A treasure hunt around King's Cross, London. *Cultural Geographies*, 12 (4), 429–462.

Blunt, A., Gruffudd, P., May, J., and Ogborn, P. (eds.) (2003) *Cultural Geography in Practice*. London: Hodder Arnold.

Bonnett, A. (2008) *What is Geography?* London: Sage.

Brace, C. and Johns-Putra, A. (2010) Recovering inspiration in the spaces of creative writing. *Transactions of the Institute of British Geographers*, 35, 399–413.

Butler, T. (2006) A walk of art: The potential of the sound walk as practice in cultural geography. *Social and Cultural Geography*, 7 (6), 889–908.

Cameron, L. (1997) *Openings: A Meditation on History, Method and Sumas Lake*. Montreal and Kingston: McGill University Press.

Crang, P. (2010) Cultural geography: After a fashion. *Cultural Geographies*, 17 (2), 191–201.

Crouch, D. (ed.) (1999) *Leisure Practices and Geographical Knowledge*. London: Routledge.

DeSilvey, C. (2007) Salvage memory: Constellating material histories on a hardscrabble homestead. *Cultural Geographies*, 14 (3), 401–424.

Driver, F., Nash, C., Prendergast, C., and Swenson, I. (2002) *Landing: Eight Collaborative Projects between Artists and Geographers*. Egham: Royal Holloway, University of London.

Dwyer, C. and Davies, G. (2010) Qualitative methods III: Animating archives, artful interventions and online environments. *Progress in Human Geography*, 34 (1), 88–97.

Engaging Geography (n.d.) Creative Public Geographies page of the Engaging Geography website, http://engaginggeography.wordpress.com/2-seminars/creative-public-geographies/ (accessed October 17, 2012).

Evans, J. and Jones, P. (2008) Towards Lefebvrian socio-nature? A film about rhythm, nature and science. *Geography Compass*, 2 (3), 659–670.

Fenton, J. (2005) Space, chance, time: Walking backwards through the hours on the left and right banks of Paris. *Cultural Geographies*, 12 (4), 412–428.

Foster, K. and Lorimer, H. (2007) Some reflections on art-geography as collaboration. *Cultural Geographies*, 14 (3), 425–432.

Fuller, D. (2008) Public geographies: Taking stock. *Progress in Human Geography*, 32 (6), 834–844.

Fuller, D. and Askins, K. (2010) Public geographies II: Being organic. *Progress in Human Geography*, 34 (5), 654–667.

Gandy, M. (2009) Liquid city: Reflections on making a film. *Cultural Geographies*, 16 (3), 403–498.

Johnston, C. and Pratt, G. (2010) *Nanay* (Mother): A testimonial play. *Cultural Geographies*, 17 (1), 123–133.

Kinman, E.L. and Williams, J.R. (2007) Domain: Collaborating with clay and cartography. *Cultural Geographies*, 14 (3), 433–444.

Lorimer, H. (2010) Walking: New forms and spaces for studies of pedestrianism. In *Geographies of Mobilities: Practices, Spaces and Subjects*, ed. T. Cresswell and P. Merriman. London: Ashgate, pp. 19–34.

Matless, D.S. (1998) *Landscape and Englishness*. London: Reaktion Books.

McCormack, D.P. (2004) Drawing out the lines of the event. *Cultural Geographies*, 11 (2), 211–220.

McCormack, D.P. (2008) Geographies for moving bodies: Thinking, dancing, spaces. *Geography Compass*, 2 (6), 1822–1836.

McLaren, H. (2007) *Bordering: An Art–Geography Collaboration*. London: Queen Mary, University of London.

Merriman, P. (2010) Creating an archive of geographical engagement. *Area*, 2 (3), 387–390.

Merriman, P. and Webster, C. (2009) Travel projects: Landscape, art, movement. *Cultural Geographies*, 16 (4), 525–535.

Middleton, J. (2011) Walking in the city: The geographies of everyday pedestrian practices. *Geography Compass*, 5 (2), 90–105.

Paglan, T. (2006) Late September at an undisclosed location in the Nevada desert. *Cultural Geographies*, 13 (2), 293–300.

Pain, R. (2004) Social geography: Participatory research. *Progress in Human Geography*, 28 (5), 652–663.

Pain, R., Kesby, M., and Askins, K. (2010) Geographies of impact: Power, participation and potential. *Area*, 43 (2), 183–188.

Parr, H. (2007) Collaborative film-making as process, method and text in mental health research. *Cultural Geographies*, 14 (1), 114–138.

Phillips, A. (2005) Walking and looking. *Cultural Geographies*, 12 (4), 507–513.

Phillips, P. (2004) Doing art and doing cultural geography: The fieldwork/field walking project. *Australian Geographer*, 35 (2), 151–159.

Pinder, D. (2005) Arts of urban exploration. *Cultural Geographies*, 12 (4), 383–411.

Pryke, M. (2002) The white noise of capitalism: Audio and visual montage and sensing economic change. *Cultural Geographies*, 9 (4), 427–477.

Revill, G. (2004) Performing French folk music: Dance, authenticity and non-representational theory. *Cultural Geographies*, 11 (2), 119–209.

Rose, G., Basdas, B., and Degen, M. (2009) Using websites to disseminate research on urban spatialities. *Geography Compass*, 3 (6), 2098–2108.

Scalway, H. (2006) A patois of pattern: Pattern, memory and the cosmopolitan city. *Cultural Geographies*, 13 (3), 451–457.

Sidaway, J.D. (2009) Shadows on the path: Negotiating geopolitics on an urban section of Britain's South West Coastal Path. *Environment and Planning D: Society and Space*, 27 (6), 1091–1116.

Thrift, N. (2000) Dead or alive. In *Cultural Turns/Geographical Turns: Perspectives on Cultural Geography*, ed. I. Cook, D. Crouch, S. Naylor, and J.R. Ryan. Harlow: Prentice Hall, pp. 1–6.

Ward, K. (2006) Geography and public policy: Towards public geographies. *Progress in Human Geography*, 30, 495–503.

Wylie, J. (2002) An essay on ascending Glastonbury Tor. *Geoforum*, 33 (4), 441–454.

Wylie, J. (2005) A single day's walking: Narrating self and landscape on the South West Coast Path. *Transactions of the Institute of British Geographers*, 30 (2), 234–247.

Wylie, J. (2006) Smoothlands: Fragments/landscapes/fragments. *Cultural Geographies*, 13 (3), 458–465.

# Chapter 9

# Critical "Race" Approaches

*Audrey Kobayashi*

Arguably, the most unpleasant, and deeply troubling, product of the struggle for culture is race. I approach the concept of "race" in two ways. First, it is a way of life, a fundamental product of Western cultures, deeply embedded in the European colonial past, lived out in the present as a taken-for-granted reality. Second, it is an analytical concept that has conditioned both academic and everyday ways of interpreting the world around us. For cultural geographers, it is important that race was part of our earliest scholarly efforts, rooted in the geographical lore that accompanied the first European voyages of exploration that brought knowledge, riches, and power to the imperial/colonial dynasties. It developed as a fully fledged theoretical system by Enlightenment thinkers whose treatises on such far-fetched theories as environmental determinism fit so neatly with the purposes of expanding European powers and with the by then highly developed sense of European cultural superiority and civilization.

Theories of cultural geographers of the twentieth century by and large eschewed environmental determinism in favor of understanding cultural phenomona. Consider the founding legacy of the Berkeley School in establishing cultural geography, with its emphasis on the creative transformation of human landscapes, on the cohesive nature of human communities, and on the many fascinating ways in which cultural practices and artifacts differentiate one part of the world from another (see especially the collection by Wagner and Mikesell 1962). Indeed, when I was a student during the 1970s, one of the things I found most exciting about my geography courses was the prospect of learning all the fascinating things I could about people in different parts of the world – and about what made them different from one another. But the cultural geographies during most of the twentieth century tended to ignore race – leaving it to the anthropologists – rather than addressing racism. They maintained an implicit belief in the fundamental differences that race makes, and failed to apply a critical

*The Wiley Blackwell Companion to Cultural Geography*, First Edition.
Edited by Nuala C. Johnson, Richard H. Schein, and Jamie Winders.
© 2013 John Wiley & Sons, Ltd. Published 2016 by John Wiley & Sons, Ltd.

understanding to the human fallout of racialization: inequality; poverty; degradation; denial of human rights and dignity; erasure or exotification of the very cultures that we study with such enthusiasm. If cultural geographers are not directly culpable in the creation of inequality, they have certainly been complicit in erasure and exotification.

More recently, although the tendency to study the world as an intriguing mosaic of difference remains very strong, critical cultural geographers have placed a new emphasis on what makes human beings different from one another, replacing what many would view as a naïve fascination with the exotic with a critical recognition that the exotic is a social production, both of the scholar and of the historical context in which the scholar works. Don Mitchell (2000) refers to "culture wars" as a more appropriate way of designating the struggles over identity, power, and territory that he sees as inherent in the development of human culture. Such an approach requires that we treat race as a historical product of colonialism and its associated processes that have resulted in a mapping of human value upon the earth according to the geographical distribution of phenotypical characteristics.

In this short essay, I am concerned with the latter definition of race. I wish to show that geographies have geography; that our ideas are produced in context, and in turn contribute to the production of that context, as we express ourselves as members of cultural systems, and as our intellectual ideas and our actions as scholars influence the world around us. I wish both to chart some of the intellectual history of geographical ideas about race, and to speculate on how the course of our history might be altered by critical assessment of our role in the process of racialization. The chapter begins with a review of the concept of "race" as it is understood in contemporary anti-racist geography, then moves to a brief analysis of how the production of anti-racist geography has developed in three contemporary Western and Northern contexts.

## The Geographical Concept of Race

Recent cultural geography has seen a proliferation of studies of race embedded in a larger discourse on social construction. Although the concept of social construction is perhaps the intellectual hallmark of the paradigmatic shift that underlies all poststructuralist thinking, nowhere has the concept more salience than in understanding the construction of race or the process of racialization.

What does the term "social construction" mean? It suggests that the attributes that are historically associated with the human body – the qualities that are said to constitute gender or race in particular – are socially constructed, or invented, rather than biologically determined. For example, traits associated with femininity, such as passivity, dependence, or emotionality, or traits associated with race, such as low intelligence or "uncivilized" behavior, result from the ascription of such qualities to specific groups, not to some necessary or intrinsic aspect of their physical makeup. Similarly, opposite traits that are usually viewed positively, such as strength, rationality, or the capacity for "civilized" behavior, are ascribed historically to white males. It is through the *practice* of racism or sexism, therefore, that people are given attributes based on skin color or sex and belief in those attributes is reinforced.

A theory of social construction also implies that *all* aspects of human being are socially constructed. There are not some areas that are socially constructed and others that are not – or that the "invention" of some traits is somehow just made up and therefore invalid, insignificant, arbitrary, or "not real" – but, rather, social construction constitutes the entire human experience. This point runs counter to any interpretation – for example, that of realism – that would suggest that some things are *only* socially constructed, as though there is some realm of human existence that is more basic, more true. In other words, a social construction-ist approach begins with social construction; it does not add it on to a "natural" base. Indeed, in a social constructionist interpretation, the term "natural" has no meaning, if that meaning concerns something that is prior to, determinate of, or independent of human discourse. Moreover, there is no need to resort to idealist interpretations that divide the world into that which is material and non-material, since the world may be interpreted as material existence with geohistorical meaning. Again, no part of the material world is without meaning. A social constructionist position is therefore simultaneously contingent, meaning that it is subject to change according to social context, and materialist, meaning that no social construction – including thought itself – occurs as anything except a material act.

A socially constructed world – filled with socially constructed human bodies – does not become less meaningful for having been invented. It is on the contrary *full* of meaning, replete with the tremendous range of discursive and imaginative actions that constitute human life. There is no meaningless human life, no meaningless human act or gesture; nor is there any meaning that is not social. The term "social" in this sense refers to all that is shared in being human, to common meaning based on shared history, filled with power and ideology, and systematically produced within social, cultural systems that are themselves socially con-structed. Because social systems are systematically produced, however, it is also possible for some social constructions to be more meaningful, and more powerful, than others, to be more historically significant or more materially durable upon the landscape. Both concepts of race and gender or sex are examples of extremely powerful constructions.

The socially constructed is also profoundly normative, as notions of good and bad, beautiful and ugly, civilized and uncivilized, strong and weak, are built into notions of the power, and the place, of human bodies within a social context. The strength of a social construction to regulate, or structure, human life depends very strongly upon its status as a normatizing concept, and therefore upon the ways in which human beings have invested it with power. The social constructions that are most powerful are those that display two main features: they are so deeply normatized that they seem to those who invoke or practice them to be natural ("well, *naturally*, black people have a tendency towards . . ."); and they are systematically embroiled within a wide spectrum of social life, including the family, the workplace, educational systems, expressions of national identity, and a range of cultural practices.

Recognition of the profound impossibility of accounting for any bodily trait as purely "biological" has occurred largely through the collision of theoretical perspectives on the construction of sex, gender, and race. Second-wave feminist theory underwent a series of disruptive shock waves when challenged to reexamine what had become a somewhat com-placent view that gender is built upon biological sex. These waves became a major force when non-white feminists, arguing along the same lines, claimed that biological assumptions of difference and sameness underlay a pervasive whiteness within the feminist movement (for a review, see Lovell 2000/1996). This recognition strengthened the understanding that we need to speak of feminisms and anti-racisms – and as a corollary of sexisms and racisms – because all are socially constructed and reflect specific historical circumstances. Nonetheless, the struggle to overcome whiteness in the feminist movement continues, as it does among those who would overcome racism. Theoretical understanding notwithstanding, both movements, and the relationship between them, have shown how hard it is to overcome our own normatized thinking, much less to marshal the social forces of change, fraught as these are with the results of historical constructions.

Building upon the historicity of the social construction of "race," it has become customary to refer to the process of "racialization" as what Miles (following upon Fanon 1966; Banton 1977; and Guillaumin 1980) defines as "a representational process whereby social significance is used to refer to certain biological (usually phenotypical) human features, on the basis of which those people possessing those characteristics are designated as a distinct collectivity" (1989: 74). The concept of racialization implies that races are constructed through historical processes, that they emerge in specific historical contexts without which they would have no meaning. By shifting from the *idea* of race to its social production, we are also able to analyze racism – the belief in the concept of race as a marker of human difference, as well as actions taken based on such a belief, whether implicit or explicit – as dynamic, discursive, and complex.

For the geographer, it is axiomatic to claim that all human processes *take place* in context. They occur within historically produced landscapes; they have spatial extent and distribution. It makes as much sense, therefore, to speak of *spatialization* as it does of racialization. Indeed, the two occur simultaneously. Racialization, therefore, is always a historical geography. In the context of Western society, notwithstanding its considerable prehistory, most writers place the construction of races within the so-called Enlightenment period of the latter half of the eighteenth century, simultaneous with the age of imperialism, the spread of systems of capitalism, and the burgeoning and spread of modern scientific discourse.[1] During that period was established much of the geography of the world: the building of nation-states based on ideas of inherent superiority and inferiority, the mapping of the world into "civilized" and "uncivilized" sections, the establishment of trade, production, and other economic factors that would profoundly influence human outcomes for centuries to come. During that period also the discipline of geography came into its own, as both a product and a producer of imperial, colonial systems. While cartographers mapped the world as a grid of political power, early human geographers speculated on whether climate was the dominant factor explaining the putative superiority of the white European man over the black African. In so doing, they legitimized and fed the notion of race that would by the end of the nineteenth century become a thoroughly naturalized and normatized part of modern Western life. In retrospect, they were entirely complicit in strengthening a racialized – and racist – society, while establishing the map as a significant statement not simply of location, but of moral values. As Livingstone's detailed account of the development of geography in the nineteenth century shows, the "interlacing of geographical knowledge and imperial drives" (1992: 219) in the expansion of imperial power represented not only an economic and political bid for power, but also an attempt to establish moral authority. The result was a racialized landscape that reflected the dominant values of the time and conditioned the values of the future.

Racialization, then, has a historical geography, in which we can understand the production of power, territory, and inequality in a systematic way, as systems through which the thread of race runs deeply, justifying the actions of the white North against the black and brown South and East, as well as the production and justification of racial inequality in the creation of modern multicultural societies. The most important lesson of racialization, perhaps, is understanding not only that these large-scale historical processes have produced specific results, but also that such processes occur through the imposition of the human imagination upon specific landscapes (Said 1978). The human imagination is the collective – and usually also contested – discourse through which the normative, the taken-for-granted, and the implicit is worked out, acted upon, coded and decoded, as it is integrated into every aspect of living. I turn now to a brief discussion of the ways in which cultural geographies of race have been thus produced, through the geographical imaginations of three social, cultural contexts.

## Anti-Racist Geography in Context

It would be difficult, indeed hypocritical, to avoid the fact that the discipline of geography is dominated by Northern, Western, white scholars whose lives and careers have been constructed out of the very colonial systems that produced them. If the most important precept of critical thinking is continually to cast back our ideas upon themselves, examining not only their logical consistency but also the motives through which they are produced, then our ideas about "race" are supremely susceptible to critical analysis. Part of that analysis, especially for the geographer, consists in recognizing that if racialization has a geography, so too does our attempt to understand it.

My purpose in this discussion, however, is not only to show that intellectual endeavors have a context. It is also to say something about the discourse of "race" itself. One of the most important features of contemporary anti-racist theory is the recognition that racisms are so highly variable and adaptable. This adaptability is based in what Foucault (see especially Foucault 1985) defines as a series of historical (and geographical) discourses mapping the "technologies of power" through which times and places gain their specific characteristics. As Laura Stoler (1995: 72) suggests, "race is a discourse of vacillations. It operates at different levels and moves not only between different political projects but seizes upon *different* elements of earlier discourses reworked for new political ends." This observation rests on the assumption not only that racism – and by extension attempts to overcome racism – gains its power in specific contexts, but also that it is not "independently derived" (Stoler 1995: 72) but implicated in a series of overlapping and intersecting discourses that drive political and cultural goals. It is not unreasonable to expect, therefore, that a critical anti-racist geography should be concerned with its own technologies of power and influence.

## British Geographies of Racialized Discourse

The very idea, "British," is historically synonymous with racial superiority, and many geographers have documented the fundamental ways in which British society is built upon a racialized discourse rooted in colonial expansion (e.g., Jacobs 1996; Clayton 2003; King 2003). We need only look to British imperial, social, scientific, and broadly intellectual history to see the forms of racialized discourse that have resulted both in the uneven development of colonialism and in the construction of the racialized "other" as inferior, uncivilized, and even inhuman. As Paul Gilroy (1987) put it, "There Ain't No Black in the Union Jack."

During the 1980s and 1990s, British academics produced a series of powerful critiques of British colonialism. These works provided international leadership in understanding the fundamental relationship between "race" and class, colonialism, and the downfall of empire marked by racial tensions as Britons came to terms with social change during the 1970s. The editors of *The Empire Strikes Back* (CCCS 1982) depicted a national crisis in which the contradictions established during years of colonial domination were being worked out upon the postcolonial British landscape (Solomos *et al.* 1982).[2]

The crisis to which they refer began in Britain as a result of post-World War II labor migration from former British colonies. This is not to say that British racialization began in the postwar period, especially if we consider the relative lack of non-white bodies in the British landscape prior to that time as itself a racialized expression of exclusion and of the notion of "British" as an exclusively white race. Nonetheless, it was during the early 1950s that Britain underwent a transition from racialization at a distance, becoming the multicultural society that it is today through the movement of thousands of former colonial inhabitants to British cities, especially to London and the Midlands. Geographers such as Ceri Peach responded to the transformation of the British landscape with well-established methodologies to study changes in residential patterns (Peach 1975; Peach, Robinson, and Smith 1981) that drew much from the rich dialogue between geographers and urban sociologists, in both Britain and the United States, but particularly those of the Chicago School. The students of the next generation writing in the late 1980s, including such scholars as Anderson (1987, 1988), Jackson (1987, 1988), Keith (1987, 1988, 1989), and Smith (1989a, 1989b), built upon this perspective by applying the lessons of the new cultural studies approach, which Bonnett and Nayak (2003) have described as "representations of race and place."

Bonnett and Nayak describe more recent work, again occurring primarily but not exclusively in a British context, as moving generally from the study of representations to deeper critical cultural understanding of the symbolic meaning of such representations, that encompass "new theories of cultural identity: beyond 'race'" (Bonnett and Nayak 2003: 306–307). Strongly influenced by postcolonial theorists, such work begins with Jackson's (1995) *Maps of Meaning* and extends to Ruth Frankenberg's (1993) account of the meaning of landscape racialization in childhood, Heidi Nast's (2000) psychoanalytical account of the construction of family in racialized Chicago, Peter Jackson's work on the racialization of shopping patterns (1998) or labor relations (1992), Anderson's (2002) call to examine the nature of racialized discourse, and Kobayashi and Peake's (2000) discussion of whiteness as a basis for both local and national identity in the framing of the events at Littleton, Colorado. All of these studies share an emphasis on both the geographical and historical nature of racialized landscapes, and the very important perspective that we cannot understand the construction of race as non-white without at least as much attention to the ways in which whiteness itself is constructed and performed as a dominant map for modern life. Bonnett (1993, 1997, 2000a, 2000b) draws out the theoretical implications of focusing on whiteness as a geographical and historicized social product.

What stands out about most of the works cited above is that they occur at a methodological distance from the "sites of struggle" in which racialized discourse occurs. Although a few of the works cited involve the collection of interview material, and all of them depend upon detailed archival research, none involves the immediate engagement of members of racialized communities, nor a political – much less activist – commitment to the places involved. The politics of difference and cultural identity are, therefore, constituted as analytical categories that – notwithstanding their obviously political roots – need to form the basis for scholarship:

> We have argued in this chapter that it is only by understanding such normative terms as "white" and "western" – the ones against which others are defined as exotic – that wider systems of racial privilege can be brought into view. By making it clear that categories such as whiteness are also the products of racialization, that they too have a history and a geography and, hence, are

changeable, we can help transform the critique of race and ethnicity from a "subfield" into an essential theme running throughout a rigorous geographical education. (Bonnett and Nayak 2003: 309)

In a recent review, Bonnett (2008) reiterates the relevance of ongoing whiteness studies, not only because whiteness remains dominant, but also because it is subject to change, especially in a context of "deracinating neoliberalism" (p. 193). As Jackson (2008) has pointed out, the course of anti-racist British geography since the 1980s shows two major trajectories: first, greater attention to public policy issues, including the impact of increased levels of immigration and increased government security in a post-9/11 world; second, greater attention to the lives of racialized people, especially through qualitative methods that allow their voices to be heard. Examples from Dwyer and Bressey's (2008) collection show increasing complexity, intersectionality, and attention to cultural nuance in documenting their everyday geographies. They also raise new questions about understanding race through anti-foundational theories that transcend social construction, a topic to which I return after additional discussion of the American context.

## The American Context

If British culture can be defined historically as racism at a distance, American society has by contrast been built upon the notion of a landscape shared, albeit unevenly and unequally, by white and non-white. Both the institution of slavery and the practice of ridding the land of aboriginal cultures are fundamental to what defines "America," and between the two account for most of the bloodshed that has occurred on American soil (Foote 1997). The refinements associated with whiteness that are a trademark of British culture developed a much more blunted popular appeal as a result. It is perhaps not insignificant that whereas British anti-racist scholarship has been characterized as somewhat aloof and theory-driven, American scholarship has been on the whole more empirical, as well as more fraught and engaged with social struggle.

The roots of anti-racist scholarship in the American context arose not through the direct application of social theory but through a very raucous discourse over the moral obligations of geographers as citizens that began with an Association of American Geographers (AAG) meeting in Ann Arbor, Michigan, in 1971, and led to the establishment of the journal *Antipode*. American anti-racist scholarship has emerged from not only the deep social division of the legacy of slavery but the post-World War II social responses that include reactions to the Cold War, the civil rights movement in the context of the peace movement of the 1960s, and geographers' early attempts to combat racism on the ground through such pedagogic experiments as Bunge's "Detroit Expedition" (Bunge 1971; Kobayashi 2003). For many American scholars, colonialism has meant not the construction of the other from a distance that spans all the pink on the globe, but colonialism represented by "the ghetto as neo-colony" (Blaut 1974). Others, while eschewing the rhetoric of radicalism as well as that of postcolonial theory, set their sights more immediately upon the lived conditions of African Americans, and upon a policy–as well as research–driven agenda for eradicating the results of a historical geography based on slavery (Rose 1970, 1972, 1978; Tyner 2004, 2005, 2006). Many have applied an anti-racist theoretical perspective to engage in direct political action to intervene with and on behalf of racialized people (Kobayashi 1994, 2001; Pulido 1996, 2000, 2002; Gilmore 1998–1999, 2002; Peake and Kobayashi 2002; Schein 2002; Wilson

2000a, 2000b, 2002; Woods 2002). These works discuss blood and guts, racialized killing, environmental degradation, the abuse of women and children, the burning of neighborhoods, and cultural genocide. They ask for an accounting not only of the cultural construction of whiteness, but also of the power of whiteness to exclude in ways that are often violent (Dwyer and Jones 2000) or that invoke the potential violence of the state (Delaney 2002). The focus shifts in such works from the actions of the dominant majority to define and represent racialized subjects to the actual experiences of those subjects in everyday landscapes, with a reflexive agenda for the role of the geographer in his or her subjects' lives. In addition, the majority of the geographical scholars working in an American context are themselves members of racialized minority groups (see also Frazier and Tettey-Fio 2006).

These two broadly based approaches to the study of racism in geography, one dominated by British scholars and focused on postcolonial theories of cultural representation, the other dominated by American scholars and focused on on-the-ground struggles that often involve participant activism on the part of the researcher, as well as coming to terms with the violence and human degradation that racism brings, are not meant as a clear-cut categorization of the two contexts. Indeed, there has been over the years a great deal of interaction between the two contexts, whether in the pages of *Antipode*, at both general and specialized academic conferences, and in joint publications. Indeed, there is some overlap among the scholars whom I have named above; a number of them work in both broadly described fields and in a number of empirical sites. Not all can be categorized according to nationality. Nor would I want to forget the contributions that have come from other parts of the world, notably southern Africa and the Caribbean. There are in addition a number of Canadians on the list – in addition to myself – whose work represents its own context, including that of recognizing the Aboriginal presence in Canada, but which often occurs in collaboration with both American and British colleagues. By all means, therefore, I wish to avoid lapsing into a new form of naïve cultural reductionism.

In both countries, of course, the complexity of racialization cross-cuts the landscape of racism in various ways. The two contexts are not unique, both because they have much cultural history in common, and because there is a wealth of collaboration among many countries. My distinction is therefore partly a heuristic one. It illustrates, however, the important fact that the discernibly different manifestations of race in the two national contexts need to be linked to the distinctive ways in which geographers have approached the study of racialization. The point is that the two countries illustrate the profound historical effects of such forces as colonialism, slavery, and state policy, to the extent that these processes can become dominant, if by no means monolithic, forces in the development of racialized cultural conditions. The extent to which geographical scholarship reflects that dominance is an expression both of our reaction to a distinctive cultural milieu and of the extent to which our own work is normatized and reflects common experiences and conditioning discourses. I believe that the dominant historical fact in Britain of racism at a distance through the process of global colonialism (brought home most definitively in the postwar era), set against the historical fact of slavery in the United States, with its legacy of deeply racialized and divided American cities, and a particular history of social activism among American geographers, point to some significant contextual differences that deserve serious further consideration. At least one major difference between the two contexts is that the British scene remains dominated by white geographers (hence an understandable focus on the significance of whiteness in geographical scholarship), while the American scene is much more diverse, but owes much to both the scholarship and the dedication to social change of African American and other minority group geographers. At the very least, my analysis points to a need to understand studies of racialization as themselves racialized.

## New Directions in Anti-Racist Geography: Reontologizing the Subject?

A number of geographers have gone beyond social constructionism to consider race in a "more than human" context. For Kay Anderson (2011), this project involves decentering the human body, partly as a corrective to the imperial, especially Victorian, construction of the indigenous body as inferior to the centered and superior European body, in both social and scientific racialism. Drawing from Latour (2005, 2008) she maintains that notwithstanding the political need to maintain an emphasis on social constructions of race within a "wholly racialized world" (Anderson 2011: 443, quoting Delaney 2002: 6), it is also necessary both to go beyond human exceptionalism and to transcend semiotic approaches to racialized discourse. She wants to take account of both the material and the conceptual.

Anderson's suggestions have two aspects, which should not be confused. First, she makes a distinction between the material and the conceptual, which must be interpreted cautiously, so as not to confuse the task of understanding the sociohistorical process of construction with what is constructed. Anderson maintains the constructivist position that race is a geo-historical product of human discourse, not something either prior to or beyond human action. It is worthwhile to remind ourselves that discourses, while *always* material, materialize in different ways. Indeed, it is their contingency that makes them subject to political interventions. The thought process itself is of course a material process; it is oxymoronic to depict thought as having a non-material existence. But nor do concepts materialize fully formed as a product of any individual thinker. Concepts are always relational, always geohistorically situated. Some concepts materialize with more power, have a greater spatial extent, and engage more people. Race is one of the most powerful of social constructions because it has been invested with so much power and spatial extent. The difference between the *concept* of race and its materiality is not an ontological difference therefore, but a question of identifying its myriad, intersecting geohistorical trajectories, its sticking power to paraphrase Jackson (2008: 30), and its shiftiness in different times and places. We do not need to re-ontologize race as a pre-given or biologically determined category in order to recognize the power involved in social construction. Its interpretation requires a historical materialism that is not at odds with a social constructionist approach.

Anderson's second objective is to decenter and destabilize Eurocentric assumptions of racial superiority, and to adopt a "broader ecological concern with the multiplicity of rela-tionships in which human beings are embedded" (2011: 448). To do so allows a relational understanding of the intersecting discourses of which race is a part, while at the same time providing an opportunity for different parts of the discipline of geography to share their concerns. Anderson's charge requires, however, that we consider the specific material forms of racialization, and that we engage the process at a more than intellectual level, a point to which I return later.

Saldanha (2006, 2011) departs from Anderson to claim that social constructionist approaches are idealist and unsuited to the challenging conversation between critical geog-raphy and biology. Surely, Saldanha is setting up a straw person when he contends that poststructuralist accounts of race have been limited to the ideational accounts in which race is not real, in the sense of being accessible to a search for scientific truth. It is a very perilous act to separate truth from ideology, or the material from the discursive, as Saldanha wants to do. Many geographers and others who address the social construction of race hold the process to be very real; indeed, to represent one of the most powerful realities of human existence. An analogy would be to assert that a building constructed by human beings is somehow less "real" than a "natural" rock formation. As biologists Lewontin, Rose, and Kamin (1982) pointed out years ago, to ontologize race independently of social construction is to adopt a form of essentialism in which the "real" is distinguished from, and possibly privileged over, that which is "only" socially constructed. Folly.

A key linkage in deciphering this controversy is that between the poststructural and the representational. While it is certainly possible to allow representations of reality to obscure reality (Saldanha 2011: 454), like opposing mirrors in which the body can only be cast back and forth without ever reaching the body itself, it is not necessary to separate the two. A constructionist approach would describe human action as a constant *material* process of respresentation/discourse, an engagement not only between identified bodies and ideas, but also between all bodies and all things (including bodies-as-things). A material attention to social construction, which describes nearly all such work in geography, is certainly not anti-realist. But nor is it a capitulation of discursive significance to an external world that is not part of the project of giving it meaning. To address these challenges, I turn to another European intellectual context, France, where anti-racist geographies have played a lesser role, although poststructuralism has played an extremely important role in influencing anti-racist geographies in the English-speaking context.

## Poststructuralist Anti-Racism: The French Context

Counter to claims set out in many geographical "more than human" discussions of race and poststructuralism, the roots of anti-racism in continental, especially French, thought are thoroughly material. To develop this point, we need to turn to the work of those scholars in post-World War II France who *actually* wrote about race. Preeminent among them was Jean-Paul Sartre, whose *Anti-Semite and Jew* and *Black Orpheus*[3] inspired Frantz Fanon's *Black Skin, White Masks* as well as Albert Memmi's *The Coloniser and Colonised* (1966).[4] Sartre's comment that "It is the anti-Semite that makes the Jew" set in train the dialectic that was the basis for both Memmi's and Fanon's depiction of the relationship between colonizer and colonized, racist and racialized, but also the basis for his spatial dialectic – "spatializing–spatialized" – which depicts the human relationship as always material and situated (Boyle and Kobayashi 2011; Kobayashi and Boyle forthcoming).

Intellectual anti-racist activists in Paris in the 1950s and 1960s included members of the negritude poetic movement (Senghor, Césaire, Lumumba, Damas), all of whom were directly involved in anti-racist, anti-colonial struggles (and influenced the American civil rights movement), and a range of anti-colonialist activists, including Sartre, Fanon, Jeanson, and others, for whom theorizing about the existence and construction of race was always situated, both historically and through direct political action. Indeed, Deleuze writes that it was Sartre's spatial dialectic of situation that made the emergence of poststructuralism even possible (van de Weil 2008).[5] Nowhere is the spatial dialectic of situation more clear than in a 1962 letter written by Sartre and published with the signatures of 136 French leftist intellectuals, coining the term "New Racism" ("le nouveau racisme") to describe a situation in which the racism of the metropole toward the distant colonial other is re-placed in a postcolonial context in the *banlieues* of Paris as a consequence of the racism of the French toward the new migrants who arrived in France after the dismantling of colonial regimes (Arthur 2008: 82–83). The work of these political French "poststructuralists" is not only the inspiration for much of the anti-racist writing by scholars such as Homi Bhabha, Paul Gilroy, Collette Guillaumin, and Robert Miles (all of whom influenced British anti-racist geography in the 1980s), but also a *geographical* inspiration for understanding the dialectic of racializing–racialized as fundamentally spatial, situated, placed.[6]

So it is not only problematic politically, but also inaccurate theoretically to describe poststructuralist accounts of race and racism as limited to a limited definition of representation. If, as I have suggested, there is a stronger tendency among British geographers to work through representational analysis at a greater distance from their subjects, and among North American geographers to engage directly with the violence of racism, without glossing over the significant range of theoretical approaches that both contexts encompass, that difference is as much about scholarly choices and specific contexts as it is about the theoretical limits of poststructuralism. A dialectical, historical-material account situates the practices of racism in relation to processes of colonialism, violence, and migration, and it identifies the specific spatial forms that accompany racist formations in different places historically, whether in the anti-colonial liberation movements of the 1960s, or the recent reinvention of racialized discourses that accompany neoliberalism (Goldberg 2009). It is about actual bodies, situated in relation to one another, and not only the things that bodies do to one another, but the systems of governance, dominance, and oppression that bodies – including the bodies of geographers – create.

## Political Anti-Racist Geographies for the Twenty-First Century

There is a cultural geography of anti-racist scholarship. It matters not only where but *who* does the work (as well, no doubt, as who speaks to whom, who reads whom), that there can be no disengagement of the political and the academic, and that in the end our discipline is thoroughly socially constructed, within a broader historico-intellectual context. My purpose here is to engage that process of construction, not only by pointing out discernible differences in intellectual contexts, but also by promoting dialogue between/among geographical cultures. For that project, too, is part of the political project of destabilizing the categories of race. In that political project we would abandon the tenets of social construction to our great detriment.

Is it possible, then, ever to achieve a "post-race" world as long as social constructions based on essentialist racial ideas continue to exist? Probably not. Post-race theories are social constructions like any other, but they depend not on fixed and bounded bodies and identities but on contingent realities that we can only *imagine* as possible (Gilroy 2000). The geographical imagination, however, needs not only to project a possible future, but also to understand how imaginations of the past have brought us to the present, how race has been inscribed on bodies, in boundaries and landscapes, and how that racialized legacy continues to work its way into every material thing. As Nayak (2006: 23) implores:

> In recognizing the interconnections between essentialist, constructionist and post-race ideas I would contend that race and ethnic scholars can benefit from listening to and becoming conversant in contemporary post-race dialogues, whether they chose to subscribe to these positions or not. Primarily there are also at least some compelling reasons to envisage new spaces and forms of cultural identification that cross the colour line and can engender "other ways of being." Secondly, by opening up the category of race to epistemological and ontological scrutiny we can

yet appreciate that race comes "with no guarantees." This anti-foundationalist approach is particularly helpful for recognizing race as a practice with no solid basis outside the discursive, material, structural and embodied configurations through which it is repetitively enacted, performed and, tenuously, secured.

Race remains on the global agenda, written as broadly and as forcefully as ever, although its landscapes continue to change. As Puar (2007) suggests, international geopolitics bring renewed intersections in new technologies of governance. Cities remain layers of racialized dispossession (Shaw 2007) challenged to redefine themselves in "perilous times" (Boggs and Kurashige 2011: 1). The shadow of neoliberalism is worldwide, bringing not only reinforcement of racialized difference through diverse processes such as commodification, surveillance, governmentality, and global interactions of values (Goldberg 2009), but also "post-racial" thinking that would undermine and deny race as though it *were just a figment of someone's imagination*. There is ironic danger in a convergence between a left that would abandon race as the imagined product of racists and a right that would abandon it as the imagined product of anti-racists. Meanwhile, as Tolia-Kelly (2010) reminds us, it is on the bodies of the racialized that the legacy of social constructions is all too real.

## Notes

1  For accounts of the history of racialization see Malik (1996) or West (2002). While many writers see antecedents to racial thinking in certain Greek and Roman writings, the modern concept arises in the writings of eighteenth-century thinkers, whose power to normatize the concept was considerable (Livingstone 1992). I have confined my discussion here to racism in the Western context, recognizing both that similar forms of creating difference exist in other contexts, and that there has been considerable historical overlap in various parts of the world, especially through the agency of colonialism. At the same time, however, I do not wish to reduce racialization to a single universal process.

2  I could also point to work done in France during the same era, especially that of Guillaumin (1980) or Fanon (1966), building upon the philosophies of Jean-Paul Sartre and Hannah Arendt. But while these works are of tremendous importance in geographical theories today, they did not play such a significant role in the production of geographical works in France at the time, and my purpose is to discuss the context of anti-racist geography.

3  Written in 1948 as an introduction to the *Anthologie de la Nouvelle Poésie nègre et malgache.*

4  Sartre reviewed *The Coloniser and Colonised* in 1957, and wrote the introduction to the 1966 publication, whose title draws on the Sartrean dialectic (Boyle and Kobayashi 2011; Kobayashi and Boyle forthcoming).

5  van de Wiel (2008: n.p.) cites Deleuze from the original French in Colombel (2005: 39).

6  For a full discussion see Kobayashi and Boyle (forthcoming).

## References

Anderson, K. (1987) Chinatown as an idea: The power of place and institutional practice in the making of a racial category. *Annals of the Association of American Geographers*, 77, 580–598.

Anderson, K. (1988) Cultural hegemony and the race-definition process in Chinatown, Vancouver: 1880–1980. *Environment and Planning D: Society and Space*, 6, 127–149.

Anderson, K. (2002) The racialization of difference: Enlarging the story field. *Professional Geographer*, 54 (1), 25–30.

Anderson, K. (2011) Race – Part I. In *The Wiley-Blackwell Companion to Human Geography*, ed. J. Agnew and J.S. Duncan. Oxford: Wiley-Blackwell, pp. 440–452.

Arthur, P. (2008) The persistence of colonialism: Sartre, the left, and identity in postcolonial France, 1970–1974. In *Race after Sartre: Antiracism, Africana Existentialism, Postcolonialism*, ed. J. Judaken. Albany: SUNY Press, pp. 77–98.

Banton, M. (1977) *The Idea of Race*. London: Tavistock.

Blaut, J.M. (1974) The ghetto as an internal neo-colony. *Antipode*, 6 (1), 37–41.

Boggs, G.L. and Kurashige, S. (2011) *The Next American Revolution: Sustainable Activism for the Twenty-First Century*. Berkeley, Los Angeles, and London: University of California Press.

Bonnett, A. (1993) Forever "white"? Challenges and alternatives to a "racial" monolith. *New Community*, 20 (1), 173–180.

Bonnett, A. (1997) Geography, "race" and whiteness: Invisible traditions and current challenges. *Area*, 29 (3), 193–199.

Bonnett, A. (2000a) *White Identities: Historical and International Perspectives*. Harlow: Pearson.

Bonnett, A. (2000b) *Anti-Racism*. London and New York: Routledge.

Bonnett, A. (2008) Whiteness and the West. In *New Geographies of Race and Racism*, ed. C. Dwyer and C. Bressey. Aldershot: Ashgate, pp. 17–28.

Bonnett, A. and Nayak, A. (2003) Cultural geographies of racialization – the territory of race. In *Handbook of Cultural Geography*, ed. K. Anderson, M. Domosh, S. Pile, and N. Thrift. London: Sage, pp. 300–312.

Boyle, M. and Kobayashi, A. (2011) Metropolitan anxieties: A critical appraisal of Sartre's theory of colonialism. *Transactions of the IBG* NS, 63, 408–424.

Bunge, Jr., W. (1971) Fitzgerald: The Geography of an American Revolution. Cambridge: Cambridge University Press.

Centre for Contemporary Cultural Studies (CCCS) (eds.) (1982) *The Empire Strikes Back: Race and Racism in '70s Britain*. London, Auckland, Sydney, Melbourne, and Johannesburg: Hutchinson and the Centre for Contemporary Cultural Studies.

Clayton, D. (2003) Critical imperial and colonial geographies. In *Handbook of Cultural Geography*, ed. K. Anderson, M. Domosh, S. Pile, and N. Thrift. London: Sage, pp. 354–368.

Colombel, J. (2005) Deleuze–Sartre: pistes. In *Deleuze épars: approches et portraits*, ed. André Bernold and Richard Pinhas. Paris: Hermann Editeurs, pp. 39–47.

Delaney, D. (2002) The space that race makes. *Professional Geographer*, 54 (1), 6–14.

Dwyer, C. and Bressey, C. (eds.) (2008) *New Geographies of Race and Racism*. Aldershot: Ashgate.

Dwyer, J.O. and Jones III, J.P. (2000) White socio-spatial epistemology. *Social and Cultural Geography*, 1 (2), 209–222.

Fanon, F. (1966) *The Wretched of the Earth*. Harmondsworth: Penguin.

Foote, K.E. (1997) *Shadowed Ground: America's Landscapes of Violence and Tragedy*. Austin: University of Texas Press.

Foucault, M. (1985) *History of Sexuality*. New York: Vintage Books.

Frankenberg, R. (1993) Growing up white: Feminism, racism and the social geography of childhood. *Feminist Review*, 45, 51–84.

Frazier, J.W. and Tettey-Fio, E.L. (eds.) (2006) *Race, Ethnicity, and Place in a Changing America*. Binghamton, NY: Global Academic Publishing and Harpur College, Binghamton University.

Gilmore, R. (1998–1999) Globalisation and US prison growth: From military Keynesianism to post-Keynesian militarism. *Race and Class*, 40 (2–3), 177–188.

Gilmore, R.W. (2002) Fatal couplings of power and difference: Notes on racism and geography. *Professional Geographer*, 54 (1), 15–24.

Gilroy, P. (1987) *There Ain't No Black in the Union Jack*. London: Routledge.

Gilroy, P. (2000) *Against Race: Imagining Political Culture Beyond the Color Line*. Cambridge, MA: Harvard University Press.

Goldberg, D.T. (2009) *The Threat of Race: Reflections on Racial Neoliberalism*. Oxford: Blackwell.

Guillaumin, C. (1980) The idea of race and its elevation to autonomous scientific and legal status. In UNESCO *Sociological Theories: Race and Colonialism*. Paris: UNESCO.

Jackson, P.J. (ed.) (1987) *Race and Racism: Essays in Social Geography*. London: Allen and Unwin.

Jackson, P.J. (1988) Street life: The politics of carnival. *Environment and Planning D: Society and Space*, 6, 231–237.

Jackson, P.J. (1992) The racialization of labour in post-war Bradford. *Journal of Historical Geography*, 18 (2), 190–209.

Jackson, P.J. (1995) *Maps of Meaning: An Introduction to Cultural Geography*. London: Routledge.

Jackson, P.J. (1998) Constructions of "whiteness" in the geographical imagination. *Area*, 30 (2), 99–106.

Jackson, P.J. (2008) Afterword: New geographies of race and racism. In *New Geographies of Race and Racism*, ed. C. Dwyer and C. Bressey. Aldershot: Ashgate, pp. 297–304.

Jacobs, J. (1996) *Edge of Empire: Postcolonialism and the City*. London: Routledge.

Keith, M. (1987) "Something happened": The problems of explaining the 1980 and 1981 riots in British cities. In *Race and Racism: Essays in Social Geography*, ed. P. Jackson. London: Allen and Unwin, pp. 275–303.

Keith, M. (1988) Racial conflict and the "no-go areas" of London. In *Qualitative Methods in Human Geography*, ed. J. Eyles and D.M. Smith. Cambridge: Polity, pp. 39–48.

Keith, M. (1989) Riots as "social problem" in British cities. In *Social Problems and the City*, ed. D.T. Hiebert and D.M. Smith. Oxford: Oxford University Press, pp. 289–306.

King, A.D. (2003) Cultures and spaces of postcolonial knowledges. In *Handbook of Cultural Geography*, ed. K. Anderson, M. Domosh, S. Pile, and N. Thrift. London: Sage, pp. 381–397.

Kobayashi, A. (1994) Coloring the field: Gender, "race," and the politics of fieldwork. *Professional Geographer*, 45 (1), 73–80.

Kobayashi, A. (2001) Negotiating the personal and the political in critical qualitative research. In *Qualitative Methodologies for Geographers*, ed. M. Limb and C. Dwyer. New York: Arnold and Oxford University Press, pp. 55–72.

Kobayashi, A. (2003) The construction of geographical knowledge – racialization, spatialization. In *Handbook of Cultural Geography*, ed. K. Anderson, M. Domosh, S. Pile, and N. Thrift. London: Sage, pp. 544–556.

Kobayashi, A. and Boyle, M. (forthcoming) The colonizer and the colonized: Sartre and Fanon. In *Marxism and Anti-Racism: Conversations*, ed. A. Bakan and E. Dua.

Kobayashi, A. and Peake, L. (2000) Racism out of place: Thoughts on whiteness and an antiracist geography in the new millennium. *Annals of the Association of American Geographers*, 90 (2), 392–403.

Latour, B. (2005) *Reassembling the Social*. Oxford: Oxford University Press.

Latour, B. (2008) Will non-humans be saved? An argument in ecotheology. *Journal of the Royal Anthropological Association*, 15, 459–475.

Lewontin, R., Rose, S., and Kamin, L. (1982) Bourgeois ideology and the origins of biological determinism. *Race and Class*, 24, 1–16.

Livingstone, D.N. (1992) *The Geographical Tradition*. Oxford: Blackwell.

Lovell, T. (2000/1996) Feminisms of the second wave. In *The Blackwell Companion to Social Theory*, ed. B.S. Turner. Oxford: Blackwell, pp. 299–324.

Malik, K. (1996) *The Meaning of Race: Race, History and Culture in Western Society*. Houndmills: Macmillan.

Miles, R. (1989) *Racism*. London and New York: Routledge.

Mitchell, D. (2000) *Cultural Geography: A Critical Introduction*. Oxford: Blackwell.

Nast, H. (2000) Mapping the "unconscious": Racism and the Oedipal family. *Annals of the Association of American Geographers*, 90 (2), 215–255.

Nayak, A. (2006) After race: Ethnography, race and post-race theory. *Ethnic and Racial Studies*, 29 (3), 411–430.

Peach, C. (ed.) (1975) *Urban Social Segregation*. London: Longman.

Peach, C., Robinson, V., and Smith, S. (eds.) (1981) *Ethnic Segregation in Cities*. London: Croom Helm.

Peake, L. and Kobayashi, A. (2002) Policies and practices for an anti-racist geography at the millennium. *Professional Geographer*, 54 (1), 50–61.

Puar, J.K. (2007) *Terrorist Assemblages: Homonationalism in Queer Times*. Durham, NC: Duke University Press.

Pulido, L. (1996) *Environmentalism and Economic Justice*. Tucson: University of Arizona Press.

Pulido, L. (2000) Rethinking environmental racism: White privilege and urban development in southern California. *Annals of the Association of American Geographers*, 90 (1), 12–40.

Pulido, L. (2002) Reflections on a white discipline. *Professional Geographer*, 54 (1), 25–30.

Rose, H.M. (1970) The development of an urban subsystem: The case of the Negro ghetto. *Annals of the Association of American Geographers*, 60, 1–17.

Rose, H.M. (1972) The spatial development of black residential subsystems. *Economic Geography*, 48, 43–65.

Rose, H.M. (1978) The geography of despair. *Annals of the Association of American Geographers*, 68 (4), 453–464.

Said, E. (1978) *Orientalism*. New York: Vintage.

Saldanha, A. (2006) Re-ontologising race: The machinic geography of phenotype. *Environment and Planning D: Society and Space*, 24, 9–24.

Saldanha, A. (2011) Race – Part II. Part I. In *The Wiley-Blackwell Companion to Human Geography*, ed. J. Agnew and J.S. Duncan. Oxford: Wiley-Blackwell, pp. 453–464.

Sartre, J.-P. (1972) Le nouveau racisme. *Le Nouvel Observateur*, December, pp. 18–22.

Schein, R. (2002) Race, racism, and geography: Introduction. *Professional Geographer*, 54 (1), 1–5.

Shaw, W. (2007) *Cities of Whiteness*. Oxford: Blackwell.

Smith, S. (1989a) *The Politics of "Race" and Residence*. Cambridge: Polity.

Smith, S. (1989b) Race and racism. *Urban Geography*, 10, 593–606.

Solomos, J., Findlay, B., Jones, S., and Gilroy, P. (1982) The organic crisis of British capitalism and race: The experience of the seventies. In *The Empire Strikes Back: Race and Racism in '70s Britain*, ed. Centre for Contemporary Cultural Studies. London, Auckland, Sydney, Melbourne, and Johannesburg: Hutchinson and the Centre for Contemporary Cultural Studies, pp. 9–46.

Stoler, L. (1995) *Race and the Education of Desire: Foucault's History of Sexuality and the Colonial Order of Things*. Duke, NC: Duke University Press.

Tolia-Kelly, D. (2010) The geographies of cultural geography I: Identities, bodies and race. *Progress in Human Geography*, 34 (3), 358–367.

Tyner, J. (2004) Territoriality, social justice and gendered revolutions in the speeches of Malcolm X. *Transactions, Institute of British Geographers* NS, 29, 330–343.

Tyner, J. (2005) *The Geography of Malcolm X: Black Radicalism and the Remaking of American Space*. New York: Routledge.

Tyner, J. (2006) "Defend the ghetto": Space and the urban politics of the Black Panther Party. *Annals of the Association of American Geographers*, 96 (1), 105–118.

van de Weil, R. (2008) Deleuze and Sartre: From praxis to production. Unpublished paper presented at the First International Deleuze Studies Conference, Cardiff, UK, August 13. http://www.raymondvandewiel.org/deleuze-sartre.html (accessed November 7, 2012).

Wagner, P.L. and Mikesell, M.W. (eds.) (1962) *Readings in Cultural Geography*. Chicago and London: Chicago University Press.

West, C. (2002) A genealogy of modern racism. In *Race Critical Theories*, ed. P. Essed and D.T. Goldberg. Oxford: Blackwell, pp. 90–112.

Wilson, B.M. (2000a) *America's Johannesburg: Industrialization and Racial Transformation in Birmingham*. Totowa, NJ: Rowman and Littlefield.

Wilson, B.M. (2000b) *Race and Place in Birmingham: The Civil Rights and Neighborhood Movements*. Totowa, NJ: Rowman and Littlefield.

Wilson, B.M. (2002) Critically understanding race-connected practices: A reading of W.E.B. Du Bois and Richard Wright. *Professional Geographer*, 54 (1), 31–41.

Woods, C. (2002) Life after death. *Professional Geographer*, 54 (1), 62–66.

Chapter 10

# Gender

*Geraldine Pratt and Berrak Çavlan Erengezgin*

This beyond [sex and gender] is a strange place . . . where the "what" and the "we" of feminist scholarly work is so undecided or so disseminated that it can no longer bound such work, where the [foundational] identity . . . has dissolved yet oddly has not dissolved the field [of study] itself.

Brown (2003: 3)

Indeed, the study of gender is in a strange time and place; and it is at once obvious, wrong, and right to think of gender as foundational for cultural geography (and vice versa). It is obvious because almost nothing at any geographical scale or within any area of the discipline can be fully understood outside of a gender analysis. Gender as systems of meaning and regulation, identification, social roles, and kinship relations structures what counts as knowledge (Rose 1993) and is no less central to analyses of critical geopolitics, transnationalism, globalization, labor markets, and urban development than to analyses of the spaces of the family and home; generations of feminist geographical analyses have demonstrated this point (e.g., Hyndman 2007; Nagar *et al.* 2002; Gibson-Graham 1996). It is, nonetheless, simultaneously wrong to claim gender as foundational because so much theoretical, cultural, and political work over at least the last forty years has unmoored gender from its foundation in biological sex, such that gender (and sexuality) are now loosely defined as "heuristics that describe the social meanings by which we figure out who is masculine and who is feminine and what those gendered bodies do with one another and feel about one another in a realm we call sex" (Valentine 2004: 215). It is also right because disarticulating gender from biological sex renders gender as a fully cultural category, one that must be foundational to cultural geography.

In this chapter, we trace three strands of thinking that have produced this strangely foundational/non-foundational category of analysis, now recognized to be so infused and

*The Wiley Blackwell Companion to Cultural Geography*, First Edition.
Edited by Nuala C. Johnson, Richard H. Schein, and Jamie Winders.
© 2013 John Wiley & Sons, Ltd. Published 2016 by John Wiley & Sons, Ltd.

destabilized by other social and cultural relations as to be unthinkable on its own. We then turn to three areas of contemporary interest and debate about gender: retheorizations of the relations between biology, the non-human, and social constructions of gender; the challenges that transgender studies pose for both recentering and decentering gender; and the unfinished business of recognizing the limits of Western theorizing about gender so as to "provincialize" these knowledge claims and make room for fuller and richer understandings of the world. All three areas of debate push toward a more worldly practice of cultural geography and emerge from the impulse to imagine and create other worlds and other possible ways of living.

## Destabilizing Gender Binaries

Twenty years ago, Gillian Rose (1993) argued that human geography is fundamentally masculinist. She identified two traditions of masculinist geographical knowledge production which produce and relate to constructions of femininity in differing ways. She argued that masculinity and femininity function as a self-reinforcing binary constructed within a masculinist frame of reference that defines itself in opposition to what is conceived as feminine: the subjective, emotional, and embodied. Social-scientific masculine knowledge, she argued, represses femininity and is conceived as rational, neutral, universal, and exhaustive – the product of a detached, objective observer. Aesthetic masculinity, which she located in cultural (in particular, humanistic) geography, may include the emotional and non-rational but continues to operate within the dualism of masculine and feminine. It does so because it feminizes nature, landscapes, and place and posits its authority to know these places in universalizing ways. On the cover of the book in which she developed her critique of the masculinisms underpinning geographical knowledge is a photograph by the artist Barbara Kruger. Framing the image of a woman's face is the text: "We won't play nature to your culture." This is a refusal, not only to embody nature, but also to participate in the dualisms (i.e., nature/culture, feminine/masculine) that structure masculinist knowledges. Below, we trace three of the strands of thinking in which this refusal has taken shape.

### Gender as Performativity

Within Anglophone feminism one means of refusing to play nature to a masculinist culture has involved disarticulating sex and gender, tethering the former to biology and understanding both femininity and masculinity to be social constructions (Rubin 1975; for a recent reassessment of Rubin's influence, see Love 2011). The criticism of this conceptual tactic is longstanding, in the first instance because it does little to disrupt the dualism between nature and culture. This is because the social (gender) is presumed to act upon the passive surface of sex. As Judith Butler (1993: 4) asked, "Is sex to gender as feminine to masculine [as nature to culture]?" So too, within this binary, once sex is gendered, it tends to be absorbed by the more active term (gender) and disappears as a focus of inquiry (for an early discussion of this tendency within geography, see Nast 1998).

Butler (1990) sought to create some genuine trouble for gender and the binary between sex and gender by privileging a third term: normative heterosexuality. As she argued, neither sex nor gender has an ontological status; the sexed body, no less so than gender, is brought into being through regulatory regimes of heteronormativity. Heteronormativity dictates that to be fully human, individuals must be sexed as either male or female; and these norms literally bring such bodies into being. Those not "properly" sexed (for instance, those born with indeterminate sex characteristics who might be classified as intersexed, estimated to be 1 in 2,000 births; Rubin 2010) risk social abjection. Butler argued that gender is a regulated "doing" rather than a stable and primary identity or static role. It is an identity or truth effect that emerges, not from the interior "truth" of biological sex, but through repeated gender performances, each performance an instantiation or unstable repetition of the gender ideal or norm.

While not uncontested (Nelson 1999), the influence of this notion of gender performativity has been substantial in geography. Butler wrote of her theory of performativity as "a gendered corporealization of time" (1990: 141); geographers have developed the spatiality of her theory by arguing that, like gender identity, spaces and places "do not preexist their performances" and that specific spaces and geographies are part of the process through which gender per- formances come into being (Gregson and Rose 2000; see also Pratt 2004), likely differently in different places.

Butler drew heavily on Foucault's theory of sexuality to trouble gender. Other feminists have rerouted his theory through a more expansive geographical argument. In the first volume of *The History of Sexuality*, Foucault documented an extraordinary proliferation of dis- courses about sexuality within European societies from the seventeenth century on and argued that these discourses multiplied because sexuality became "an especially dense transfer point for relations of power . . . useful for the greatest number of maneuvers and capable of serving as a point of support, as a linchpin, for the most varied strategies" of power rela- tions (1978: 103). Ann Stoler has argued that the geography and timing of Foucault's argu- ment are wrong and that discourses of sexuality first emerged, not in Europe, but in its colonies amidst concerns about white degeneracy and miscegenation. Gendered prescriptions of motherhood for middle-class women, she suggests, were an exceedingly important "part of the scaffolding" (1995: 93) through which racialized discourses of sexuality and European bourgeois presumptions of cultural and moral superiority were constructed and maintained.

Other scholars have written about the centrality of patriarchal gender relations to the violent process of colonial domination in North America. Citing a diverse range of non- hierarchical genders and sexual practices among some First Nations peoples prior to coloni- zation, Andrea Smith, for example, argues that instilling a gender-binary system and patriarchal dominance was key to the process of achieving colonial control. Gender violence, she suggests, is "a primary tool of colonialism and white supremacy . . . It is through sexual violence that a colonizing group attempts to render a colonized people inherently rapable, their lands inherently invadable, and their resources inherently extractable" (2010: 61; see also Mor- gensen 2011).

And yet, given that sexuality (and associated gender relations) is a dense transfer point for relations of power, its effects can be complex and differentiated. In a rich ethnography of Filipina women migrating to work as entertainers in an isolated rural area of Japan, Lieba Faier (2009) tells of a shift in the social meanings attached to these women as they settle and marry local men. Filipina women, previously stigmatized as hostesses, come to be viewed locally as exemplary *ii oyomesan* (good bride and daughter-in-law) and key participants in the maintenance of traditional Japanese values of family and home. Their acceptance in rural Japanese society takes place within closely scripted patriarchal norms and practices. Respect and care for the elderly, dedication to preparing meals and tidying the house, giving priority to husband and children: these performances provide the grounds for Filipinas' social inclusion. Reproducing traditional gender relations, these Filipina women are also redefining what is required to be Japanese, displacing a biogenetic criterion for national belonging with one established through performance. While these women are still required to assimilate into a national-racial sameness, the traditional heteronormative gender performance is redefining the grounds for national identity by relocating national belonging in performance rather than biogenetics.

## Gender, Intersectionality and Interlocking Systems of Oppression

If a larger discussion of gender–race–colonial–national formations has emerged within Fou-cauldian-inspired scholarship, critical race feminism has provided another route toward the realization that the analysis of gender alone is insufficient. African American feminists such as bell hooks (1981, 1984, 1990) and Audre Lorde (1984) have been hugely influential as early strong critics of the second-wave feminist tendency to ignore the experiences of non-white women and to take those of white, middle-class women as the norm. An exclusive focus on gender creates an odd optics, simultaneously too narrow and too expansive. hooks (1990) exposed, for instance, the limitations of second-wave feminists' rendering of the home as a privatized, isolating site of gender oppression. "Throughout our history, African-Amer-icans have recognized the subversive value of homeplace" as a private space affording tem-porary respite from white aggression and functioning as a "crucial site" for organizing (p. 47). hooks, then, called on black feminists to reclaim for themselves this meaning and poten-tial of homeplace.

Even as second-wave women's organizations sought to make connections with racialized women, analyses based solely on gender can have the effect of shoring home and nation "as a space of whiteness," an argument made by Jenna Loyd (2009) in relation to Another Mother For Peace (AMP), a US-based anti-war women's organization active in the late 1960s and 1970s. In many ways, AMP was an expansive and progressive movement which grew from a narrow focus on protecting activists' (and other) sons from military enlistment into a larger consumer protest against the war profiteering of companies such as General Motors and Dow Chemical and the toxic living conditions that they created both in war zones and domesti-cally, in the United States. However, their vision of a healthy home, Loyd argues, assumed and naturalized a fundamentally white and suburban model of family life. So too the links that AMP attempted to forge between the health of children in the United States and within war zones (in the case of AMP, Vietnam) "can dangerously erase differences between war zone and homefront, thereby obscuring who is responsible for mass violence" (2009: 416) and the extent to which and processes (both geopolitical and national) through which some groups of women (and men) are made especially vulnerable to violence.

Recognizing that differently racialized, classed, sexed, abled (etc.) women and men live gender differently is one issue; but the point goes beyond specifying and pluralizing under-standings of gender. Gender, race, and class identifications and oppressions intersect and interlock; and spatial practices and imaginations are integral to the processes through which this interlocking occurs (Ruddick 1996). Attempting to explain why two white middle-class, 19-year-old male university students received only a conviction for manslaughter for the murder of an aboriginal woman, Pamela George, in Regina, Saskatchewan, in 1995, Sherene Razack (2000) notes that Pamela George was a woman, that she was an aboriginal woman, and that she was an aboriginal woman sex worker. More than this, she was an aboriginal woman who lived in a racialized space of prostitution "where violence is innate," while the young men lived in white, middle-class spaces "far removed from spaces of violence" (p. 126). As Razack (2000) argues, Pamela George "was of the space where murders happen; they [the young men] were not" (p. 126). These positionings naturalized and made relatively unremarkable the violence inflicted upon George and the innocence of the young men, such that manslaughter seemed more apt than a conviction of murder.

Along with this kind of alignment of stigmatized places and race, bodies themselves territorialize an accretion of meanings when they are marked by race, gender, sexuality, class, and disability as primitive, bestial, and sexed. To be unmarked by race, gender, sexuality, class, or disability is a privileged subject position. Black, female, pervert, poor are meanings that overcome, *and become*, the body. Such subjects *are* their materiality; they cannot transcend it (Mohanram 1999). (See also Wright 2006 for the spatialized production of racialized women factory workers and sex workers as waste.)

If an intersectional approach decenters gender, it is important to recognize that it simultaneously insists on its centrality. Critical of Native activists who defer gender issues until some later time when more critical issues of survival have been addressed, Andrea Smith writes: "the Native nationhood that becomes articulated under this strategy of futurity is one that supports heteropatriarchy, U.S. imperialism, antiblack racism, and capitalism" (2010: 47). While gender alone is not enough to sustain scholarship inspired by critical race theory and politics, an intersectional approach insists that it cannot be ignored. Gender discourses and practices are integral to processes of racialization; they flow through each other in diverse but often reinforcing ways that must be taken seriously in any consideration of the cultural geographies of gender.

## Masculinities

Familiar dichotomies within gender-binary systems are those of mind/body or rational/emotional, the first terms gendered as masculine and the latter feminine. In an odd twist, those rendered as rational and disembodied can appear as ungendered. Another approach to destabilizing the fixity of gender, then, has been to make masculinity visible in its plural forms, to trace connections to "feminine" qualities and to demonstrate how masculinity is constructed in relation to femininity.

In her study of investment banking in London, England, for instance, Linda McDowell (1997) demonstrated that the conduct of business is far from rational and disembodied; masculine performances are integral to it. She identified two very different masculinities at work: the sober, rational patriarch of corporate finance and the youthful virility of the "Big Swinging Dick" on the trading floor and in the dealing rooms. McDowell quotes the novelist Margaret Atwood's tongue-in-cheek description of the former:

> only the heads, the unsmiling heads, the talking heads, the decision making heads, and maybe a little glimpse, a coy flash of suit. How do we know there's a body under all that discreet pinstriped tailoring? We don't and maybe there isn't. (Atwood 1992: 80, quoted in McDowell 2010: 653)

Of the traders, McDowell notes, they are "only too embodied" as "the quintessence of masculine energy . . . shouting, sweating and screaming" (2010: 653) on the trading floors. She describes an exaggerated masculine culture of sexualized jokes, aggressive talk, and sexual harassment and the extent to which much of the socializing takes place in masculine spaces of golf clubs, hospitality suites of football clubs, and lap-dancing clubs. Reflecting on her book after the financial collapse of 2008, McDowell (2010) wondered whether she had underestimated the effects of this masculine culture, especially the propensity toward and "whole-hearted embrace" of adventurous risk-taking. Rather than an interesting "add-on" to the study of the economy, McDowell reveals masculinity (and cultural geography) to be fundamental to understanding how the economy works (and fails).

At the other end of the economy, McDowell (2003) has also examined the ways in which working-class, often racialized young men have become defined as redundant and as problems. Cowen and Siciliano (2011) ask us to consider how this so-called redundancy and the devaluation and criminalization of racialized working-class men are being profitably recycled through growing security industries. They describe a re-masculinization of the nation in the United States, Canada, and Britain through renewed cultures of military masculinity. They cite as evidence the recruitment strategies of the US Army, in particular the increasing tendency to target ex-cons, youth detention centers, and poor African American men, the latter creating a "warrior class" through the "poverty draft." The use of "moral waivers" to enlist recruits has expanded significantly in recent years. In 2005 almost one in five individuals admitted to the US Army was admitted under a waiver, including a growing number of gang members. As Cowen and Siciliano note, "graffiti from turf in Chicago and LA now marks military installations across Iraq" (2011: 1517).

Men's reactions to aggressive and violent forms of masculinity inform their perceptions of women's vulnerability at a variety of spatial scales, in ways that throw into relief the relational nature of gender and raise questions about who in fact inhabits cultures of femininity. Masculine protection of vulnerable women, for instance, has a long history within colonial and military ventures. A desire to save Afghan women has played a significant role in justifying US (and Canadian) military violence in Afghanistan (Fluri 2012). At a different scale, Kristen Day (2001) has complicated a long-standing "fact" within urban and social geography: that women are more fearful in and of public space. Drawing on interviews with male undergraduate students at the University of California, Irvine, one of the two safest cities in the United States, she found that young men had largely realistic and differentiated assessments of the geography of their own safety: they felt safe in Irvine but more vulnerable in spaces such as South Central Los Angeles. Women, they felt, were unsafe everywhere, including Irvine. Day identifies two versions of masculinity: "bad ass" and "chivalrous"; while different in significant respects, both were constructed through an understanding of women as fearful and in need of male protection. Day does not discount women's real material vulnerability in some public spaces; but she argues that different forms of masculinity co-construct, reinforce, and perpetuate feminine identities that are oppressive. Constructions of masculinity, in other words, are fundamentally dependent on particular constructions of femininity. Men are not the autonomous beings portrayed in hegemonic representations of masculinity.

## Current Debates

### Biology and Animality

Reflecting on her study of the masculinity of investment bankers in the City of London, Linda McDowell remarked on its enduring, even increasing, significance over a decade after it was first published: "[i]n the intervening years, my arguments there seemed to become even more apposite as increasing numbers of cases of sexual harassment, as well as a sexualized culture have continued to dominate" (2010: 652). She then, however, took her gender analysis in a direction that would have been unimaginable when she first wrote her book in the mid-1990s to consider the role of hormones and the biological basis for decision-making. Feminists have long been wary of the ways that hormonal arguments are deployed to exclude women, but McDowell offers an equal-opportunity approach to hormonal explanation by considering how men are also "prisoners" of their biology. She introduces empirical research by "neuro-economists" that indicates that a trader's morning testosterone level predicts his day's profitability. Testosterone increases "persistence, appetite for risk and fearlessness in the face of novelty" that can advantage the trader (Coates and Herbert 2008, quoted in McDowell 2010: 656), although prolonged heightened levels tend to lead to impulsivity and reduced profitability. Coates speculated that traders during the "dot-com" crisis were displaying "classic symptoms of mania" (p. 656) associated with high levels of testosterone and mused that a "bull market" may be more than metaphorical. As McDowell writes, "Coates suggested that traders behave uncannily like real bulls and other male animals. A rutting stag, he noted, enjoys a testosterone surge if he beats off a sexual rival" (2010: 656). Hormones and animals: McDowell introduces two strands of thinking pursued within new materialist approaches in cultural geography, though the latter more profoundly dissolve a dichotomy between nature and culture than a "prisoner of biology" approach suggests.

Some of the best writing on the new feminist materialism locates the feminist separation of gender from biology within its intellectual and historical context. Gayle Rubin's disarticulation of gender from biology (1975) and then gender from sexuality (1984), for instance, must be understood in relation to specific debates at the time: the former within debates between feminists and Marxists in the 1970s and the latter within the pornography wars raging among different camps of feminists in the 1980s (Wilson 2010; see also Rubin 2011). Careful critics of earlier generations of gender theorists note as well that theorists such as Foucault and Butler recognized the relevance of materiality and the body (Barad 2003) and that Butler offered a specific theory of how sex and the body are materialized, not a theory of the material world (Ahmed 2008).

Nonetheless, feminists writing within "new materialism" argue that anti-biologism has been a pervasive tendency within feminism; it "is often the ignition that starts the theoretical engine" (Wilson 2010: 196). There is a deep-rooted anxiety within feminism of explanations that posit biological determinism: of their tendency to simultaneously depoliticize and, for non-hegemonic groups, have deleterious social and political effects. Biology tends to be "both a dank, disreputable mode of explanation and a site of political vulnerability" (Wilson 2010: 195). Feminists writing in this vein of new materialism argue that feminists have tended to conceive of biology as the substrate (or "underbelly") on which social processes act and of gender as a vast and complex system of social meaning. Elizabeth Wilson argues that one effect of this approach is that "feminism got smart by refusing biology" (2010: 202).

The problems with a social-constructivist approach to gender, theorists such as Wilson argue, is that it reinstates the dualism between nature and culture, rendering matter as passive and leaving relatively unexamined the fundamental sociality of biology. Recognizing that Butler's theory of gender performativity is precisely about the ways in which the social brings matter into being as sexed and gendered, Karen Barad, nonetheless, is critical of the fact that Butler (and a Foucauldian analytic of power upon which she draws) forestalls "an understanding of precisely *how* discursive practices produce material bodies" (2003: 808). It misses, in other words, some of the agency of matter and obscures the fact that matter is also a "doing" or "congealing of agency." Further, Wilson underlines the notion that there is no mode of embodiment or sexual and gender identification that is not simultaneously cultural and biological. There is no biologically pure object: serotonin levels, for instance, are linked to diet and are, thus, always already thoroughly social. Biology and culture, then, are not autonomous systems; they are fundamentally inter- and internally related. To say that testosterone is implicated in the financial crisis, then, is not a purely biological argument. No less than the serotonin studied by Wilson, testosterone levels are in a non-trivial way likely socially produced. This point is extremely important for cultural geographers because it insists that culture is integral to realms of life traditionally seen as non-cultural, for instance, biology.

And what of traders and bulls? In line with "the new materiality," McDowell embodies the human as animal. Another strand of argumentation has examined how non-humans are "enrolled" in the construction of the gendered identities of humans and the "collusions" between animal and gender (and often implicitly racialized) ontologies (Collard 2012). In an early article within "animal geographies," Jody Emel (1995) traced the interrelationships between constructions of masculinity, racism, the domination of nature, and the abuse of animals through a detailed examination of the eradication of wolves in North America. The wholesale slaughter of wolves, she argued, was not solely about the protection of livestock because it persisted long after wolves ceased to be an economic threat. It was tied up instead with constructions of masculinity in diverse, intertwined, and contradictory ways. Hunting is a performance and instantiation of a kind of frontier masculinity; that it was practiced with such a vengeance on wolves, she argues, demands a deeper gender analysis. Masculinity requires killing within acceptable conventions, in this case norms of hunting; and wolves were seen to both violate and embody what is required in a proper hunt. Hunting in packs, wolves were conceived to be cowards deserving to be killed; admired for their intelligence, endurance, and social skills, they were also considered worthy adversaries.

Rosemary Collard (2012), too, examines how "predation" functions "in the material–semiotic configurations of cougars, humans, and performances of gender" (p. 3). Curious about the figure of "the cougar," a term used to signify older women "preying" on younger men, and the contemporary celebration of "Cougar Annie" within hipster Pacific Northwest culture in Canada and the United States, she interrogates how these two figures derive their power from predation and, hence, are "not as liberatory as proponents of these figures might hope" (p. 3).

## Transgender

Reflecting on a rapid societal change in gender norms in the United States in the late 1990s, Susan Stryker (1998: 145) noted that in the spring of 1997, Cheryl Chase characterized her goal of abolishing medically unnecessary cosmetic surgery on infants with ambiguous genitals as "radical"; by September of that year, even a mainstream news outlet like ABC's *Prime Time Live* was editorializing in favor of this position. In 2005, Judith Halberstam wrote that many young gays and lesbians "think of themselves as part of a 'post-gender' world and for them the idea of 'labeling' becomes a sign of an oppression they have happily cast off in order to move into a pluralistic world of infinite diversity" (p. 19). Transgender negotiates and mediates and is, thus, a key site for thinking about the relations between gender as identity and as biology, and as both fluid and fixed.

Fittingly, what is meant by transgender is itself in transit, taking somewhat different forms in relation to other terms and within different debates. Stryker writes of "a 'bumptious heteroglossia' of competing accounts of what properly constitutes transgenderism and who gets to talk in which ways for what purposes" (1998: 147). Kath Browne (2004) characterizes it as gender disidentification and the act of living between genders. Stryker writes that she uses transgender

> not to refer to one particular identity or way of being embodied but rather as an umbrella term for a wide variety of bodily effects that disrupt or denaturalize heteronormatively constructed linkages between an individual's anatomy at birth, a nonconsensually assigned gender category, psychical identifications with sexed body images and/or gendered subject positions, and the performance of specifically gendered social, sexual, or kinship functions. (1998: 149)

Transgender, transsexual, and queer, she states, "are hopelessly entangled"; and transgender is often used to disrupt a creeping gender binarism within the other categories and social groupings. As Halberstam puts it:

> Sometimes transgender and transsexual are synonymous . . . [and set] in opposition to queer, which is presented as maintaining the same relationship between gender identity and body morphology as is enforced within heteronormative culture. Sometimes, transgender and queer are synonyms whose disruptive refigurations of desires and bodies are set in opposition to (nonhomosexual) transsexuality's surgical and hormonal recapitulation of heteronormative embodiment – its tendency to straighten the alignment between body and identity. (1998: 291)

Broadly, then, transgender approaches refigure genders – in the plural – "as potentially porous and permeable spatial territories (arguably numbering more than two), each capable of supporting rich and rapidly proliferating categories of embodied difference" (Stryker, Currah, and Moore 2008: 12).

The spatialized language that Stryker, Currah, and Moore use in their introduction to the "Trans-" issue of *Women's Studies Quarterly* is largely metaphorical, but geography is central to transgender experiences and analyses. With an emphasis on diversity, trans-analyses tend to emphasize the particularity and instability of gender embodiment; context (or geography) is central to how gender is performed and experienced (Browne 2010; Doan 2010; Nash 2010). Under this approach, clichéd assumptions about the embrace of gender diversity in the city as opposed to strict gender norms in rural areas have been scrutinized to better understand both the nature and diversity of transgendered experiences in the latter and the policing of gender in urban gay ghettoes and lesbian spaces (Halberstam 2005; Crawford 2008). The extent to which sexual and gender dichotomies are produced and regulated through space and place has been another focus of attention, with the toilet or bathroom, for example, being a rigidly sexual dichotomized and sometimes dangerous place (Browne 2004). Browne (2004) terms the policing of gender transgression "genderism" and Petra Doan (2010) writes autobiographically of the violent policing of gender in such seemingly nongendered spaces as airports, public transit, elevators, and the university classroom.

It is worth underlining the importance of keeping an appreciation of gender diversity in close conversation with more traditional gender (and intersectional) analyses, previously described. In a discussion of the contentious "border wars" that have taken place between transgender butches and female-to-male transsexuals (FTMs) (the latter undergoing surgery and/or hormonal treatment), Halberstam considers the implicit gender binaries that lie at the heart of much of the disagreement (i.e., accusations that FTMs are "traitors" to the woman's movement or configuring butches as fearful or "not man enough" to face surgically produced transition). Halberstam also advises butches and FTMs to "think carefully" about the kinds of "men or masculine beings that we become and lay claim to: alternative masculinities . . . will fail to change existing gender hierarchies to the extent that they fail to be feminist, anti-racist, anti-elitist and queer" (1998: 306–307). The same undoubtedly is true for alternative femininities. As this work shows, the cultural and spatial politics of transgender are complex and increasingly central to understanding cultural geographies of gender.

## More Worldly Gender Analyses

There is nothing inherently progressive about a gender analysis. Nancy Fraser (2009), for instance, scrutinizes the argument that in the United States, second-wave feminism has been a cultural success but has largely failed institutionally. Gender inequity, sexual harassment, and domestic violence are now widely believed to be unacceptable; "yet this sea-change at the level of attitudes has by no means eliminated those practices" (2009: 98). To explain the disjuncture between ideals and practice, she traces an uncomfortable "elective affinity" between contemporary variants of neoliberalism and second-wave feminist gender analysis and strategy. "Disturbing as it may sound, I am suggesting that second-wave feminism [especially the tendency to link women's emancipation to waged labor, feminist critiques of the family wage, and skepticism toward the paternalistic state, which supported widespread "NGO-ization"] has unwittingly provided . . . key ingredient[s] of a new spirit of neoliberalism" (2009: 110). A withering away of "the family wage" and massive expansion of female employment in low-paid, flexible service-sector jobs are the bleak outcomes "of a feminist romance that [has had the unintended outcome of investing] flexible capitalism with a higher meaning and a moral point" (2009: 110). (See also Stratigaki 2004 on the co-optation of gender equality objectives in European Union policy.)

It is not only that the meaning of gender equality often has been co-opted, thinned, and distorted by capitalist and other policy priorities; organizations can also reproduce gender and other hierarchies of class and race even as they advocate gender equality. When in 2002 the Sangtin Writers, most of whom were grassroots workers for the same large government-sponsored non-governmental organization in the Sitapur District of India's Uttar Pradesh, embarked on a journey of narrating their individual and collective experiences, they wrote intimate stories of their marginalization by urban elites within their women's organization. "Sometimes all the talk of equality sounds like the hollow beating of distant drums" (2006: 117). Frustrated by the active silencing of their criticisms within their NGO and the extent to which their work in rural areas nurtured the upward mobility of more advantaged women, they wrote:

> When we know that the nature and form of gender differences cannot be comprehended in any context without connecting them with caste and class difference, then the inability to raise questions about classism in our own organizations gives our work the shape of an animal who uses one set of teeth to show and another one to chew! (2006: 116)

Decades of critiques of the limitations and unintended consequences of a feminism focused too exclusively on gender have led to a moment of open, unbounded inquiry into what gender can mean and the possibilities for more diverse strategies that might lead toward more broadly conceived social justice. One approach is to decolonize gender analysis and more fully explore the diversity of actually existing gender meanings. In his work on Filipino sea-farers, for instance, Kale Fajardo (2011) explains that sex/gender are not distinct in the Fili-pino language and that the language is gender inclusive and gender neutral; there are, for instance, no gendered pronouns ("he" or "she"). As he writes, "Social and interpersonal contexts and self and social identifications are more important than rigid anatomical under-standings or biological readings of 'the body'" (p. 154). Tomboy transgender masculinity, thus, reads very differently within Filipino culture than it does in Euro-American contexts; and there are "connections, fluidities, and nondualities among and between conventional Filipino masculinities/manhoods/lalaki-ness and alternative (tomboy) masculinities/man-hoods/lalaki-ness" that one does not expect in the latter (p. 157). Recognizing the existence of fe/male men within Filipino society, then, is one step toward decolonizing both Filipino/American and masculinity studies.

Taking a very different example, Turkish has a term equivalent to biological sex (*cinsiyet*) while "*toplumsal cinsiyet*" is an equivalent for gender. However, in the Turkish context, "*toplumsal cinsiyet*" refers more to the social structures, actors, mechanisms, norms, and hierarchies governing femininity and masculinity than to the subject's individual performance of gender. Thus, it is perhaps closer to Butler's concept of "heteronormativity" as a regulative regime. "Sex," on the other hand, is used in place of Butler's notion of "gender" as the per-formative category. (See also Kamal 2008 for the challenges of translating gender into Arabic and the political nature of translation.)

Rethinking gender in more worldly terms, thus, involves situating and making less uni-versal assumptions about kinship and gender relations, and aspirations for, means toward, and the language of gender equity. Sherif-Trask (2006), for instance, is critical of the way in which "the Middle-Eastern family" is typically homogenized, essentialized, and rendered static and eternal within academic writing (see also Hammami and Rieker 1988; Harker 2010). Similarly, non-Euro-American cultures are often portrayed as violently patriarchal. To counter these stereotypical representations, critics have insisted on the existence of differenti-ated, context-specific patriarchies. As Homi Bhabha argued many years ago,

> Put "patriarchy" in the dock by all means, but put it in a relevant context. . . . "Patriarchy" in India, for instance, intersects with poverty, caste, illiteracy; patriarchy in liberal America is shored up, among other things, by racism, the gun culture, desultory welfare provision . . . (1999: 81)

Patriarchal relations, in other words, operate unevenly across places or even within places and cultures; and patriarchal practices develop in relation to other social relations: for example, the caste system in India, gun culture in the United States. So too, Western feminists have needed to rethink how their own assumptions about rights and equality may have reinforced punitive policies directed to some categories of women, in the current period, toward Muslim women in particular (Scott 2007; Razack 2008). Feminists recognize as well the need to question implicit assumptions about a natural alignment of secularism, anti-religiosity, and gender equality and to rethink secularism as a political-theological concept (Butler 2008; Reilly 2011), along with the utility of discourses of individual rights and empowerment in particular contexts.

All of this work places geographical analysis at the center of gender analyses. The time of assuming that gender unifies women (and divides them from men) is long past. Cindi Katz has developed the metaphor of counter-topography as a way of imagining how the particularity of gender relations and gendered experiences in any one place can be in the first instance more fully appreciated. Beyond this, she imagines counter-topographies as providing the grounds for developing solidarities and alliances. Topography, she writes, is "the accurate and detailed description of any locality," the three-dimensionality of which is produced by a patient layering of contour lines, one on top of the other (2001: 1214). She imagines particular processes – say, domestic violence – as contour lines of constant elevation, connecting people and places. But such processes are always situated within and altered by the specifics of their fully three-dimensional place in relation to other "contour lines" that define the topography of that place. This is a geographical rendering of intersectionality, animated across places. Tracing counter-topographies involves the simultaneous labor of following contour lines across places and understanding how the same processes are embedded in particular places. We suggest that they might offer a starting point for more sustained conversations about gender relations in different places.

Or, they might start conversations about different structured oppressions, problems, or issues; this is what it means to unbound studies of gender. After the Sangtin Writers published their critique of their NGO, for instance, they resolved to build a people's movement without depending on donors' funds. While their first writing project had detailed the various forms of violence that they had experienced as women, unlike donor groups that often target women in isolation from their communities, they understood that "violence against women [cannot] be addressed in isolation from the violence generated against rural livelihoods by everyday sociopolitical and economic processes" (2012: 290). Their first campaign, involving two thousand women and sixty men, was to restore irrigation waters to a distributary channel that had been unusable for sixteen years.

This beyond sex and gender is indeed a strange place, one where gender is both dissolved (and reimagined, rearranged, subverted) and yet oddly not dissolved at all. In her speculations about this place, Wendy Brown resolves that this beyond sex and gender is not, ultimately, a place but a time: it is a "peculiar offering that only temporality makes" (2003: 3). The force of our argument is that space, place, and geography are central to an unbounded study of gender and that these cultural geographies are key to thinking about new engagements between biology, sex, and gender.

## References

Ahmed, S. (2008) Imaginary prohibitions: Some preliminary remarks on the founding gestures of the "new materialism." *European Journal of Women's Studies*, 15, 23–39.

Atwood, M. (1992) *Good Bones*. Bloomsbury: London.

Barad, K. (2003) Posthumanist performativity: Towards an understanding of how matter comes to matter. *Signs: Journal of Women in Culture and Society*, 28, 801–831.

Bhabha, H. (1999) Liberalism's sacred cow. In *Is Multiculturalism Bad For Women?*, ed. J. Cohen, M. Howard, and M.C. Nussbaum. Princeton: Princeton University Press, pp. 79–84.

Brown, W. (2003) Feminism unbound: Revolution, mourning and politics. *Parallax*, 9, 3–16.

Browne, K. (2004) Genderism and the bathroom problem: (Re)materializing sexed sites and (re)creating sexed bodies. *Gender, Place and Culture*, 11 (3), 331–346.

Browne, K. (2010) Introduction: Towards trans geographies. *Gender, Place and Culture*, 17 (5), 573–577.

Butler, J. (1990) *Gender Trouble: Feminism and the Subversion of Identity*. New York: Routledge.

Butler, J. (1993) *Bodies That Matter: On the Discursive Limits of "Sex."* New York: Routledge.

Butler, J. (2008) Sexual politics, torture, and secular time. *British Journal of Sociology*, 59 (1), 1–23.

Coates, J.M. and Herbert, J. (2008) Endogenous steroids and financial risk taking on a London trading floor. *Proceedings of the National Academy of Sciences of the United States of America*, 105 (16), 6167–6172.

Collard, R.-C. (2012) Cougar figures, gender, and the performances of predation. *Gender, Place and Culture: A Journal of Feminist Geography*, 19 (4), 518–540.

Cowen, D. and Siciliano, A. (2011) Surplus masculinities and security. *Antipode*, 43 (5), 1516–1541.

Crawford, L.C. (2008) Transgender without organs? Mobilizing a geo-affective theory of gender modification. *WSQ*, 36 (3/4), 127–143.

Day, K. (2001) Constructing masculinity and women's fear in public space in Irvine, California. *Gender, Place and Culture*, 8 (2), 109–127.

Doan, P. (2010) The tyranny of gendered spaces: Reflections from beyond the gender hierarchy. *Gender, Place and Culture*, 17 (5), 635–654.

Emel, J. (1995) Are you man enough, big and bad enough? Ecofeminism and wolf eradication in the USA. *Environment and Planning D: Society and Space*, 13, 707–734.

Faier, L. (2009) *Intimate Encounters: Filipino Women and the Remaking of Rural Japan*. Berkeley: University of California Press.

Fajardo, K.B. (2011) *Filipino Crosscurrents: Oceanographies of Seafaring, Masculinities, and Globalization*. Minneapolis: University of Minnesota Press.

Fluri, J. (2012) Capitalizing on bare life: Sovereignty, exception, and gender politics. *Antipode*, 44 (1), 31–50.

Foucault, M. (1978) *The History of Sexuality*, vol. 1, trans. R. Hurley. New York: Vintage.

Fraser, N. (2009) Feminism, capitalism and the cunning of history. *New Left Review*, 56, 97–117.

Gibson-Graham, J.K. (1996) *The End of Capitalism (As We Knew It): A Feminist Critique of Political Economy*. Oxford: Blackwell.

Gregson, N. and Rose, G. (2000) Taking Butler elsewhere: Performativities, spatialities and subjectivities. *Environment and Planning D: Society and Space*, 18, 433–452.

Halberstam, J. (1998) Transgender butch: Butch/FTM border wars and the masculine continuum. *GLQ*, 4 (2), 287–310.

Halberstam, J. (2005) *In a Queer Time and Place: Transgender Bodies, Subcultural Lives*. New York: New York University Press.

Hammami, R. and Rieker, M. (1988) Feminist Orientalism and Orientalist Marxism. *New Left Review*, 170, 93–106.

Harker, C. (2010) On (not) forgetting families: Family spaces and spacings in Birzeit, Palestine. *Environment and Planning A*, 42, 2624–2639.

hooks, b. (1981) *Ain't I a Woman? Black Women and Feminism*. Boston: South End Press.

hooks, b. (1984) *Feminist Theory: From Margin to Center*. Boston: South End Press.

hooks, b. (1990) *Yearning: Race, Gender and Cultural Politics*. Boston: South End Press.

Hyndman, J. (2007) Feminist geopolitics revisited: Body counts in Iraq. *Professional Geographer*, 59, 35–46.

Kamal, H. (2008) Translating women and gender: The experience of translating *The Encyclopedia of Women and Islamic Culture* into Arabic. *WSQ*, 36 (3/4), 254–268.

Katz, C. (2001) On the grounds of globalization: A topography for feminist political engagement. *Signs*, 26 (4), 1213–1234.

Lorde, A. (1984) *Sister Outsider: Essays and Speeches by Audre Lorde*. Trumansburg: Crossing.

Love, H. (ed.) (2011) Rethinking sex. *GLQ*, 17 (1).

Loyd, J. (2009) War is not healthy for children and other living things. *Environment and Planning D: Society and Space*, 27, 403–424.

McDowell, L. (1997) *Capital Culture: Gender at Work in the City*. Oxford: Blackwell.

McDowell, L. (2003) *Redundant Masculinities? Employment Change and White Working-Class Youth*. Oxford: Blackwell.

McDowell, L. (2010) Capital culture revisited: Sex, testosterone and the city. *International Journal of Urban and Regional Research*, 34 (3), 652–658.

Mohanram, R. (1999) *Black Body: Women, Colonialism and Space*. Minneapolis: University of Minnesota Press.

Morgensen, S. (2011) *Spaces Between Us: Queer Settler Colonialism and Indigenous Decolonization*. Minneapolis: University of Minnesota Press.

Nagar, R., Lawson, V., McDowell, L., and Hanson, S. (2002) Locating globalization: Feminist (re)readings of the subjects and spaces of globalization. *Economic Geography*, 78, 257–284.

Nash, C. (2010) Trans geographies, embodiment and experience. *Gender, Place and Culture*, 17 (5), 579–595.

Nast, H. (1998) Unsexy geographies. *Gender, Place and Culture*, 5, 191–206.

Nelson, L. (1999) Bodies (and spaces) do matter: The limits of performativity. *Gender, Place and Culture*, 6, 331–353.

Pratt, G. (2004) *Working Feminism*. Edinburgh: University of Edinburgh Press.

Razack, S. (2000) Gendered racial violence and spatialized justice: The murder of Pamela George. *Canadian Journal of Law and Society*, 15, 91–130.

Razack, S.H. (2008) *Casting Out: The Eviction of Muslims from Western Law and Politics*. Toronto: University of Toronto Press.

Reilly, N. (2011) Rethinking the interplay of feminism and secularism in the neo-secular age. *Feminist Review*, 97, 4–31.

Rose, G. (1993) *Feminism and Geography: The Limits of Geographical Knowledge*. Minneapolis: University of Minnesota Press.

Rubin, D. (2010) Intersex Before and After Gender. Unpublished PhD thesis. Women's Studies, Emory University.

Rubin, G.S. (1975) The traffic in women: Notes on the political economy of sex. In *Toward an Anthropology of Women*, ed. R. Reiter. New York: Monthly Review Press, pp. 157–210.

Rubin, G.S. (1984) Thinking sex: Notes for a radical theory of the politics of sexuality. In *Pleasure and Danger*, ed. C. Vance. London: Routledge and Kegan Paul.

Rubin, G.S. (2011) Blood under the bridge: Reflections on "thinking sex." *GLQ*, 17, 15–48.

Ruddick, S. (1996) Constructing difference in public spaces: Race, class, gender as interlocking systems. *Urban Geography*, 17, 132–151.

Sangtin Writers and Nagar, R. (2006) *Playing with Fire: Feminist Thought and Activism through Seven Lives in India*. Minneapolis: University of Minnesota Press.

Sangtin Writers (Reena, R. Nagar, R. Singh, Surbala) (2012) Solidarity, self-critique, and survival: Sangtin's struggle with fieldwork. In *The Global and the Intimate: Feminism in Our Time*, ed. G. Pratt and V. Rosner. New York: Columbia University Press.

Scott, J.W. (2007) *The Politics of the Veil*. Princeton: Princeton University Press.

Sherif-Trask, B. (2006) Families in the Islamic Middle-East. In *Families in Global and Multicultural Perspective*, ed. B. Ingoldsby and S. Smith, 2nd edition. London: Sage.

Smith, A. (2010) Queer theory and native studies: The heteronormativity of settler colonialism. *GLQ*, 16 (1/2), 41–68.

Stoler, A.L. (1995) *Race and the Education of Desire: Foucault's History of Sexuality and the Colonial Order of Things*. Durham, NC: Duke University Press.

Stratigaki, M. (2004) The cooptation of gender concepts in EU policies: The case of "Reconciliation of Work and Family." *Social Politics*, 11 (1), 30–56.

Stryker, S. (1998) The transgender issue: An introduction. *GLQ*, 4 (2), 145–158.

Stryker, S., Currah, P., and Moore, L.J. (2008) Introduction: Trans-, trans, or transgender? *WSQ*, 36 (3/4), 11–22.

Valentine, D. (2004) The categories themselves. *GLQ*, 10 (2), 215–220.

Wilson, E.A. (2010) Underbelly. *Differences*, 21, 194–208.

Wright, M. (2006) *Disposable Women and Other Myths of Global Capitalism*. New York: Routledge.

Chapter 11

# Social Class: Position, Place, Culture, and Meaning

*Linda McDowell*

It is widely believed that the British are obsessed with class.

(David Cannadine, 2000)

We are all middle class now.

(John Prescott, 1997)

## Introduction: Class Matters

A chapter such as this one inevitably is a compromise. It reflects personal as well as wider research interests and, as class analysis expands and deepens its focus, inevitably reflects a particular view of the field. As I shall illustrate, the ways in which class is theorized and measured are multiple and depend on the perspective and approach of the analyst. Some approaches are mutually exclusive; others are compatible. But, as Andrew Sayer (a geographer who now works in a sociology department) insists, "class is a contested concept, both in academe and everyday life, and how academic and lay actors understand class makes a difference to the moral significance they attach to it" (2005: 19). How we behave toward others reflects our views about the extent and legitimacy of class differences, as well as our histories, education, employment, and place in the world. For most people, however, class is position in the labor market – that of their family in childhood, their own as they become adults. This influences their social class and the ability to acquire goods, resources, and reputational attributes that endow social status. And "although both the contours and the content of this [labor market] structure have changed, differentiated and unequal rewards to relative positions within it have remained comparatively stable" (Crompton 2010: 22). Indeed, in post-industrial economies, those at the top of the class structure seem to have gained an even more disproportionate share of income, wealth, and associated power.

*The Wiley Blackwell Companion to Cultural Geography*, First Edition.
Edited by Nuala C. Johnson, Richard H. Schein, and Jamie Winders.
© 2013 John Wiley & Sons, Ltd. Published 2016 by John Wiley & Sons, Ltd.

Nevertheless, as Crompton also notes, "material rewards, esteem and capacities for self-expression are not shaped solely by the requirements of capitalist production" (p. 22), nor may class consciousness be read from this location. People may act against, as well as in, their own class interests; and as both Bourdieu (1984) and Sayer (2005) have noted, for the less powerful, resistance may be more painful than acceptance. Governments may introduce policies to ameliorate the harshest of class inequalities or to enhance them, as well as to encourage or suppress actions based on class solidarity. In a globalizing world, facing in the second decade of the new millennium an economic crisis that may yet surpass that of the 1930s in significance and depth, the importance of class, as a position and a set of practices and meanings, remains a key issue for cultural geographers to investigate, even as new forms of organization and politics, as exemplified by the Occupy[1] movement in 2011, based on a politics of recognition (Butler 1998; Fraser 1995, 2000; Young 1997), become important.

The significance of class is evident in its continuing centrality as an object of analysis in our discipline. There is a growing focus in labor geography on class and class politics (Herod 2003; Wills 2008); in economic geography, on labor-market changes (Castree *et al.* 2004), regional growth and decline, and, more recently, the implications of the financial crisis, recession, and current regimes of economic austerity for spatial and social divisions of labor (Kitson, Martin, and Tyler 2011). Feminist geographers, too, are interested in the effects of recessions, as well as the implications of the rise of service-based economies in the global North (McDowell 2009) and growing industrialization in the South (Wright 2006), as more people across the world enter the labor market and as women's lives are transformed. For many women entering the labor market for the first time, their participation confers on them a class identity separate from that of their father or husband (Chant 2010; Kessler Harris 2007).

As well as an economic location, class affects modes of living, structures of feeling, esteem, and self-worth and so is an object of concern for social and cultural geographers. Here, analysts have investigated associations between class and lifestyle: how social and cultural practices and the consumption of particular goods mark class differences (McRobbie 2004). More recently, there has been a coincidence of interest across the discipline, as social and cultural geographers have turned to the sphere of employment to explore the ways in which workplace cultures differently position embodied workers in the labor market. They have also explored the social effects of inequality and, drawing on a longer sociological tradition, mapped the ways in which identities and class meanings are changing as geographical mobility transforms the links between class and place (Dorling 2011). And, while spatial mobility increases, social or class mobility, at least in the West, seems to have come to a halt, raising new questions and anxieties about the chances of the next generation vis-à-vis those of their parents (Aldridge 2004; Finnegan 1998).

Despite this growing body of work, indeed perhaps because of it, class is a difficult word to define. It is one of those complex terms that are both contested and defined in particular ways within different theoretical traditions. The simplest definition, perhaps, is a Marxist one; but even within Marxist approaches, class is theorized as more than an objective position in the sphere of production, in part depending on the questions theorists want to answer. As Eric Ohlin Wright, a significant Marxist class analyst in the United States, noted, "a concept [i.e., of class] whose task is to help answer a question about broad historical variations in the social organisation of inequality is likely to be defined quite differently from a concept used to answer a relatively narrow question about the subjective identity of individuals in contemporary society" (2005: 180). In other theoretical traditions, such as studies drawing on a Weberian notion of social status, class is defined as an identity (although notice Wright's mention of subjective identity), a process, and performance constructed not only through forms of participation in class struggle and class politics, but also through habits and aspirations, consumption practices, daily behavior, manners, symbols, dress, language, and embodied performances in a wide range of spatial arenas including the home, the street, leisure arenas, and the workplace. Class affects access to goods, to social experiences, to life itself, as there are large class-based differences between people and places, even in the affluent West.

Social class also affects how people are treated, as it informs value judgments about ways of living and personal attitudes: Sayer's argument about morality above. People make judgments about others, in large part based on assumptions about their class position, as the long discourse of condescension of the working class by the middle class makes clear (Skeggs 2004; Jones 2011). Whether "rednecks" in the US or "chavs" in the UK, the working class are often constructed as too loud, too noisy, too careless of the future, "welfare dependents" or "feckless" in societies increasingly marked by a rhetoric of individualism rather than class solidarity (Savage 2000). These discourses are also reflected through gender and ethnic differences, as the stereotypical construction of, for example, the "ladette" in the UK (a loud, often drunken, phallic hedonist version of femininity; McRobbie 2009) or the African American "welfare queen," a hate figure of the US right wing, make clear. Increasingly, these social and cultural practices and moral evaluations are extended across distanciated spatial scales as internal migration within nation-states disrupts older patterns based on workplace-based solidarity and as transnational migration tears apart the relations between class and place. Both internal and external migration alters class position, identities, and solidarity as diasporic communities construct networks of interest and solidarity across spatially separated ethnic/national communities (Portes and Rumbaut 2001; Waldinger and Fitzgerald 2004; Waldinger and Soehl 2010; Winders 2009).

In this chapter I want to explore some of these different dimensions of class and classed identities through the explicit lens of place-based class communities. My aim, then, is to address two interconnected questions:

- What are the links between class, place, and culture?
- How have they changed over (recent) time?

I want to assess a claim that local class cultures have disappeared in the "post-Fordist" era (Amin 1992), drawing on UK examples in the main, but also explore the consequences of transnational migration for the associations between class and place. In doing so, I want to insist on the intersections of class, gender, and ethnicity in the construction of place-based identities, arguing that class is always inflected through other social divisions. I explore the links between class, place, and culture as both practices and meaning through the lens of different theoretical traditions. Although it is hard to avoid the implication of chronological development, this is not intended, at least not in assessing theoretical traditions, although it is, of course, a definitional consequence in discussions of occupational change.

As well as addressing these central geographical questions, I want also to think about the links between theory, methods, and geographical analysis. Thus, a set of subquestions is threaded through the chapter.

- How is class defined conceptually?
- How do these concepts of class influence methodological approaches?

• What has been the nature of empirical work on class and place by geographers (and others)?

## What Is Class?

One of the simplest, empirically based ways of defining social class is on the basis of occupation. In the UK, there is a tradition of research, typically associated with a group of sociologists in Oxford (see Goldthorpe and Lockwood 1963; Goldthorpe *et al.* 1969), that has been drawn on in analyses of the changing relationships between home, community, and occupation. This group of class analysts has undertaken a long-term study of the links between occupation and social mobility in the second half of the twentieth century in Great Britain as the structure of jobs changed. Their work relies on an official definition of class based on categories devised by the Registrar General which, although it is straightforward and has been refined over the course of the study, has a number of drawbacks, including a relatively undifferentiated classification of the occupations undertaken by women. Individuals without employment are also excluded, which also means that less is known about women's lives and their understanding of class before their entry into the labor market. Indeed, the studies of social mobility by the Oxford school entirely neglected women, focusing only on men's occupational moves over the lifetime and assuming that a woman's class position reflected either that of her father or that of her husband. This assumption led to a lively exchange between Goldthorpe (1983), one of the most significant of the Oxford school, and Stanworth (1984), a feminist sociologist who insisted that women may have independent class positions, an argument now generally accepted.

The neglect of women's lives in these sorts of studies is problematic, leading the historian Cannadine (2000) to regret the serious absence of women in many considerations of social class. As he notes, "It seems likely that women visualise the social world, and their place within it, in some ways that are different from men," resulting in "a serious gap in our knowledge" (2000: xi). This gap is apparent in the many twentieth-century studies of working-class communities in Britain and the US in which steelworkers, fishermen, miners, and factory workers were the foci (Beynon 1984; Dennis, Henriques, and Slaughter 1956; Lucas and Tepperman 2001; Samuel 1977), although some feminist scholarship documented the implications for women's domestic labor of men's hard, physical work (Luxton 1980; McDowell and Massey 1984). As the occupational structure changed in the post-Fordist era, from around 1973 (Harvey 1989), analysts typically focused on the effects of the decline of the industrial or manual working class. This work in part substantiates the claim at the head of this chapter by the UK Labour Party politician John Prescott that the British "are all middle class now." It also encouraged claims from more theoretically oriented scholars, such as the French Marxist Gorz (1982), to bid "farewell to the working class" as male manual occupations disappeared. As feminist writer Wilson (1992) pointed out, however, this claim ignores not only growing numbers of women workers in low-paid service occupations but also women industrial workers in the global South. In later sections, I return to these studies to assess the effect of occupational change on the spatial distribution of class-based communities, as well as the consequences of women's growing labor-market participation for class analysis.

The focus on occupations in this tradition, however, is not misplaced as it reflects the crucial significance of the sphere of production in class analysis. As Crompton (2010: 11) noted, "class and employment have been linked from the 'founding fathers' onwards." Marx argued in the mid-nineteenth century that in capitalism, the proletariat are dependent on the sale of their labor-power in the market, exploited by the owners of the means of production, the bourgeoisie, who both buy and control this labor. As the structure of capitalist societies became more complex, additional class locations were distinguished, including the lumpen-proletariat whose attachment to the labor market was irregular and insecure, and a managerial class, who, while not owners of the means of production themselves, controlled the workers in the interests of the bourgeoisie. In Marx's schema, class interests are antagonistic and may lead to class conflict.

An alternative definition of class position was outlined by Weber at the end of the nineteenth century. He, like Marx, identified the sale of labor as crucial to class position but took a different view about the attributes available for sale by workers, including, for example, the possession of a range of social attributes, such as an elite education or a particular accent, that had value in the market. Weber identified a broader range of class positions associated with differential rewards, and his concept of class is often termed social stratification in which both class and social status are significant. Unlike Marx, Weber did not believe that class interests inevitably led to class conflict based on communal solidarity but regarded the bases of social action as less predictable. Distinction in status between, for example, old and new money often divides the interests of the wealthy, as does the development of particular values and lifestyles. Weber argued that the wealthy develop mechanisms of exclusion based on social restrictions such as marriage patterns or residential location to maintain their status, whereas the poor and the propertyless develop solidaristic practices to challenge their exclusion, often based in spheres other than the workplace, such as the housing market. Both definitions of class have been influential in geographic scholarship. The key exponent of Marxist approaches has been Harvey, whose focus has been closer to Ohlin Wright's first question about large-scale social organization of inequality and exploitation. The work of the urban scholar Saunders (1986) is a good example of a Weberian approach, as is the long tradition in the 1980s of work on the significance of collective consumption (see for example Pinch 1985).

The definitions of class developed by Marx (and Weber to a degree), as well as more empirical studies using occupation as a proxy for class, are what might be termed objective definitions of class. Class here is not an idea or a belief, not a set of meanings, but instead is an economic location. Position in the sphere of production determines the interests of individuals or groups; and, theoretically at least, the development of class consciousness and practices such as trade union membership and voting patterns reflect class interests. Unlike class or gender, social class in these schemas is not a mutable category; it is an objective distinction not subject to change. In these perspectives, class is not mapped onto the body, for example, through sets of regulatory structures or social meanings, as Bourdieu (1984) would argue later, but, instead, is a definition fixed by location in the sphere of production and the access this position brings to goods and services.

As Weber recognized, however, individuals and groups are unpredictable, not always acting in their own class interests; so political identification and actions cannot be read off class position. In interesting empirical work, class analysts mapped phenomena such as "working-class Tories" – manual workers in the UK who voted with the ruling class. Working-class Republican supporters are perhaps the US equivalent, as would be the working-class Tea Party members who vote against healthcare reforms and other policies to support the poor and disenfranchised. The Oxford school discussed above argued that with growing affluence and rising living standards in the UK, working-class consciousness and solidaristic forms of politics declined as a newly privatized working class retreated to the home and a distinct working-class culture based on communal activities began to dissolve. This conclusion was based on research among car workers and their families in Luton (Goldthorpe *et al.* 1969); and, as the study showed, the new lifestyle demanded long hours and overtime, as well as continued support for trade unions, thus refuting arguments that the working class were becoming middle class in lifestyle and attitudes.

## Class and Community

Arguments about the new forms of privatized lifestyles developing in the 1960s were, in part, a response to an older tradition of studies of class and class practices undertaken in single-industry communities and emphasizing the particularity of place-based cultures. Most of these studies are nostalgic, regretful, and dominated by studies of working-class communities in which a single industry provided employment for a large proportion of men in a local labor market. They look back to an earlier era when a shared sense of place, shared values, and a shared community were significant factors in the construction of solidaristic communities.

Here are US geographers Michael Storper and Dick Walker (1989: 28) explaining the significance of the connections between occupation and locality:

> Local labour markets deserve special emphasis because of labour's relative day-by-day immobility which gives an irreducible role to place-bound homes and communities . . . It takes time and spatial propinquity for the central institutions of daily life – family, church, clubs, schools, sports teams, union locals, etc – to take shape . . . Once established, these outlive individual participants to benefit, and be sustained by, generations of workers. The result is a fabric of distinctive, lasting local communities and cultures woven into the landscape of labour.

This sense of place, of a deep-rootedness in the locality in which customs and local institutions are structured by the dominant form of work, has been a key feature of twentieth-century economic development in Western economies. However, it might also be argued that the sorts of local institutions that became most significant in industrial communities were those based on masculine interests and identities, as the shared camaraderie that develops among men when work is hard and dangerous is transferred into the social arena. Thus, industrial employment for men was associated with particular forms of communal association and political beliefs, such as working men's clubs, a culture of drinking, and left-wing politics organized in the public arena though clubs, marches, and (often) industrial protest, including strike action, which largely excluded women. It is now commonplace to argue that the decline of manufacturing destroyed these class-based localities, and perhaps a sense of masculine identity. The UK films *Brassed Off* and *The Full Monty* set in Yorkshire, where coal and steel were key industries until the 1980s, are popular representations of these claims (the US version of *The Full Monty* transferred the action to Buffalo, New York, also a declining steel town). Most of the studies of industrial employment ignored the ways in which women's work was also reflected in a particular sense of place and local politics. As Doreen Massey and I argued in a critique of this work about the connections between place, masculinity, and class politics (1984), women's lives, too, reflected local employment opportunities, directly for women working in the textile mills of Lancashire and indirectly for women faced with the heavy demands of domestic labor when their menfolk worked in heavy, dirty industries.

These areas were usually Labour strongholds, in which the population was bound together through a set of cultural practices that cultural critic Raymond Williams (1977) termed a "structure of feeling." When women's political actions are added to the analyses, however, class solidarity may be riven by gender conflicts. In the early twentieth century in the UK, for example, not all working-class men appreciated women's involvement in the suffrage movement. In later actions, including strikes by women workers of color, local communities were not necessarily supportive (Pearson, Anitha, and McDowell 2010; McDowell, Anitha, and Pearson 2012).

In the two decades since Storper and Walker's claim, there has been not only an accelerated decline in employment in primary and manufacturing industries but also a great expansion in the extent of globalization, a spatial disconnection between employment and ownership, the spread of new forms of work, especially in the service sector, and the rise of mobile workers. Nevertheless, it is still worth considering the importance of place, even in an era when the new knowledge economy is purportedly "living on air" (Leadbeater 2000). It is important to remember the situatedness of most work and workers (and of unemployment), especially in the years of austerity following the financial crisis in 2008. The "airiest" of industries – global finance – had place-specific effects, not only on the bankers in London, New York, and other global financial sectors who lost their jobs, but also on the households who lost their homes in the sub-prime mortgage scandal. As unemployment rises, most people are trapped in place; and, as Sennett (1998) suggested, as certainty in the workplace, associated with permanent lifetime employment (for men) for a single employer, disappears, working-class communities may turn inward, building networks in the locality, based on the exclusion of unwanted "others," perhaps people of different origins or skin colors. In the UK, this tendency has led to the representation of the white working class as a backward-looking, nostalgic *ethnic* formation (Haylett 2001). During the New Labour governments between 1997 and 2009, the construction of the working class as a cultural formation rather than economic location became increasingly significant. In part in response to working-class opposition to immigration in certain localities, the working class as a whole was differentiated by nationality and skin color and the white working class became defined as a cultural problem, "one marginalised ethnic minority among others" (Jones 2011: 103). Before exploring the construction of class as a cultural formation in more detail, I look at one more recent argument about the changing connections between occupation and class position, in which gender differences play a key part, drawing on work by Esping-Andersen (1993), not so far widely discussed by geographers.

## Post-Fordist Class Change: Two Gender-Specific Structures?

Although Goldthorpe, Lockwood, and others recognized that new forms of privatized living often demanded dual-household incomes, they failed to see the significance of the women's rising labor-market participation, admittedly a phenomenon that accelerated after the date when they completed the affluent worker studies. Esping-Andersen's (1993) study – primarily a statistical analysis of the link between class and occupations – casts light not only on the implications of women's employment but also on the effects on social mobility as service-sector employment increased in the post-Fordist era.

As more women enter the labor market in post-industrial societies, in service-sector occupations in the public and private sector, it becomes possible to allocate a class position to women in their own right. Esping-Andersen (1993) suggested that if the occupational distribution of women is compared to that of men, there seemed to be evidence for *two* emergent class structures in the contemporary capitalist West, differentiated by gender. He also suggested that the emergent patterns may restrict class mobility, as the shift toward a more polarized occupational structure results in stronger processes of class closure as opportunities for social mobility are reduced. Thus, a new class dualism is emerging with "at the top, a closed professional elite stratum and, at the bottom, a new servant class, a new post industrial proletariat" (p. 16) as middle-level, middle-income jobs, including industrial employment for men and middle-management jobs accessible through internal promotion seemed to be disappearing. As the US economist Barry Bluestone (1995) also argued, the US economy was "hollowing out."

At the bottom end, growing numbers of men are disqualified from low-wage, low-status jobs by their inappropriate (stereotypical) gender attributes. Desirable labor-market characteristics of docility, deference, and a neat embodied performance are mapped onto socially constructed attributes of femininity, excluding young working-class men from the fastest-growing (albeit poorly remunerated) jobs in Western capitalist economies (Bourgois 1995; McDowell 2003; Newman 1999). At the top end, class membership increasingly is also closed. Members are admitted on the basis of elite educational and professional qualifications. An important question, thus, is the extent to which women's improved rates of educational participation and attainment will be reflected in rising rates of social mobility among young women or in (many) women's entrapment in bottom-end jobs. There are claims, however, that access to the "best" jobs – in the professions, in politics, the arts and creative industries, and the City – is increasingly restricted to middle-class, well-educated children from affluent families, many if not all of them young men, who are able to draw on social contacts, often to provide unpaid internships, that lead to paid employment (Perlin 2011). Later, I introduce Bourdieu's concept of social capital, which is a way of explaining the significance of these personal networks.

Although scholars have debated the contours of a post-Fordist labor market (e.g., Esping-Andersen 1993), there is clear evidence for the feminization of the bottom end of the hierarchy (McDowell 2009). These jobs demand empathy, deference, and social skills of persuasion in the retail sector, bars and clubs, gyms, massage parlors, various therapeutic occupations, child and elder care, and so on. Such work is concerned with the reproduction of the population, in public workspaces rather than in the private spaces of the home. Evelyn Glenn (2001) has shown how in the US the labors of women of color have been transferred from the homes of largely middle- and upper-class families into the market; and I (McDowell 2009) have explored the same shift in the UK. This transformation also has wide geographical implications, as the sorts of "reproductive employment" here are distributed more evenly than the older manufacturing employment with its regional differentiation. This largely female employment deepens on the distribution of demand from a local population. Public-sector employment (that is, for the national or local state) is also a key sector for women. In the UK in 2010, 40 percent of all women workers, compared to 11 percent of men, worked for the state; and it, too, is more evenly spread across places than male-dominated manufacturing used to be.

The particular effects of this transformation to an increasingly female-dominated service economy will work out geographically in different ways in different localities, depending on both the history of particular places and their current patterns of economic growth. The old manufacturing areas in the UK were badly hit by deindustrialization from the 1980s (Alcock *et al.* 2003) and attempted to attract a range of new employments. However, many of them are now heavily dependent on public-sector work and, thus, vulnerable to the program of cuts instituted by a neoliberal coalition government anxious to reduce public spending. Whether this more even spread of a new female working class will make resistance easier to organize remains to be seen.

The shift in Great Britain and the US toward a "workfare" model of welfare provision, in which both men and women are expected to work for wages, supported by what are euphemistically termed work/life balance policies and new forms of childcare support, provides a clear example of the new assumptions about gendered responsibilities. Women are often hired by employers for what may be class reasons – on average, their labor is cheaper than that provided by men. But, as this low cost is also connected to their gender, an approach that looks at the specific connections between class and gender in different national and local labor markets is essential. Such an approach to class analysis might be termed, after Acker (2000), a "regimes of inequality" (p. 193) approach. It is clear that there remains a need to explore the implications of this new regime for understandings of class practices, for class politics (women are often hard to organize as they work in small, unorganized workplaces), and especially for representations of class identities. Films, novels, and other representations of women as "heroic" members of the working class may yet emerge from this shift in the nature of the workplace and the spatiality of class identities. The women strikers at Fords in the 1970s, for example, are now immortalized in the film *Made in Dagenham*; but so far, secretaries, nurses, primary-school teachers, and waitresses tend to be seen as individuals, whose focus is on their personal lives, rather than as representatives of new forms of class struggle.

The connections between "race," ethnicity, and skin color and social class also need integrating into class analyses as there are not only evident "ethnic penalties" that affect the occupational position of minority groups but also sets of moral judgments that are mapped onto nationality and skin color (Bauder 2006). However, arguing for complexity and a focus on the intersection of social divisions in explaining what seem like class inequalities is easier said than done (Valentine 2007). As Castree *et al.* (2004) noted, "the specific way that class and non-class differences articulate is complex" (p. 55). Similarly, Acker (2000) noted that while feminist scholars have expressed a commitment to studying gender, class, and race together, "it was easier to make the pledge than to carry it out in a thorough way" (p. 193). It does seem evident, however, that adding gender and ethnicity/race opens up a new set of questions about the links between occupational change and class composition, especially in the new "age of austerity" in a post-crisis world.

## Class Beliefs, Class Cultures, the Body, and the Home

I turn now to approaches to class analysis that have addressed questions about assumptions, ideologies, meaning, and practices. Class is not only an occupational position but also a set of meanings that is significant in the construction of self- and group-worth and in the ways social groups view each other and interact. Indeed, occupational positions are more than just slots in the labor market; they also confer meaning on the holders of the jobs. See, for example, the attribution of unworthiness to people who perform low-grade "dirty work" in public-sector services (Dyer, McDowell, and Batnitzky 2008) or the "natural" feminine skills assumed for women in female-dominated jobs such as nursing (Hanson and Pratt 1995). First, however, I want to shift to the very local scale of the body and the home: both locations once considered as private. In contemporary class analysis, however, the body and the home have come to have an increasing significance. To a large extent, this significance reflects the importance of Bourdieu's work, which has influenced geographical and sociological analyses of how class attributes are embodied, reflected in, and constructed through social practices including consumption. Space permits only a brief summary of his arguments. However, good summaries are available (Jenkins 2002; Adkins and Skeggs 2004).

Bourdieu's key concepts include field, capital, and habitus through which he combines a structural analysis of class position and a more fluid understanding that positions are negotiated through the use of knowledge and resources. The field consists of a structured set of positions within a particular domain – the labor market, for example – which are independent of the characteristics of those occupying each position (Bourdieu 1993: 72). However, people come to occupy a position though struggles in which they deploy knowledge, capitals, and dispositions, summed up as habitus, to assert their authority and reputation within a particular field. These struggles, what Bourdieu called playing the game, define fields which themselves are open to change. Power to act in a field, to play the game, is based on the use of a range of what Bourdieu named capitals: economic, cultural, linguistic, symbolic, and social, which are both the means and the ends of playing the game in the pursuit of distinction within a field. These capitals include money, influence, an elite education, social networks, and "taste," which constitute the embodied disposition of the habitus: the "habitual or typical condition, state or appearance, particularly of the body" (Jenkins 2002: 74). While Bourdieu has been criticized for his complex writing style and his theorization as reductive, static, and insensitive to spatial differences below the national level, his work has been extremely influential for geographers and sociologists, including in my own work on labor-market change and segmentation (McDowell 1997, 2009).

Bourdieu's insistence that social action and practices are always embodied and his emphasis on cultural meaning led to a coincidence between his work and more recent feminist scholarship on identity, the body, femininity, motherhood, and class condescension, even though Bourdieu himself was uninterested in gender differences until later in his life. McRobbie (2004), for example, has demonstrated that classed distinctions are reproduced though the bodies of women, while Skeggs (1997, 2004) has shown how class differences within the working class – the respectable and unruly distinction – are reproduced though the education system and working-class women's practices. In an interesting collection of essays (Adkins and Skeggs 2004), McRobbie, Skeggs, Lawler, and others document the ways in which class is written on the bodies, clothes, and homes of women, showing how middle-class notions of acceptable and legitimate embodiment and actions deny authority to working-class women. These theorists argue that class is more than practices and meanings but also works through visceral emotions, such as rage, pain, fear, anger, and resentment. Bauder (2006), too, has drawn on these ideas to explain discrimination against minorities in the Canadian labor market. However, attitudes, emotions, and behavior that are outside the domain of exchange and instrumentality are problematic in a Bourdieusian framework, an issue for feminist analysis as empathy, care for others, and self-sacrifice without expectation of financial reward typically are part of the social construction of femininity (Gilligan 1982).

Studies of class differences based on embodiment, cultural meaning, and visceral emotions raise interesting questions for inter-class interactions in a period in which working middle-class women increasingly rely on the labor of working-class women, not only to clean their homes but also to raise their children. Skeggs (2004) has argued that the middle class increasingly use strategies of spatial separation and exclusion, through, for example, gated communities, private schooling, and private transport, to distance themselves from various others, including the working class, who are constructed as too fat, too noisy, too aggressive, and too poorly spoken. Indeed, in Britain in the new millennium, "geographical referencing is one of the contemporary shorthand ways of speaking class" (Skeggs 2004: 15). This claim is reinforced by a large-scale UK-based statistical analysis based on geodemographics (Burrows and Gane 2006). In a comment to delight geographers, sociologists Savage and Burrows (2007: 7) suggest that "it turns out that knowledge of the *spatial* location of someone is increasingly an important proxy for all manner of sociological information; indeed to the extent that there is *no need* for other social measures" (emphasis added). As the measures are based on household variable, the possibility of individuals of different class positions sharing a home is neglected.

While location and the strategies adopted to produce class boundaries might successfully maintain spatial and social segregation in public space, it is the "private" sphere of the home where increasing class contact is emerging, raising interesting questions for the reproduction of class-specific cultural practices that have so far received insufficient attention from geographers (McDowell 2008). If the working class as a group are constructed as conservative, anti-modern, despised, and unrestrained in their propensity to place immediate pleasures above deferred gratification, then how is it that working-class women may be relied on to care for middle-class children? What are the consequences for daily/weekly interactions in the home, as personal face-to-face contacts between classes, especially women, are growing, as the "new servant class" (Green 2006) cleans, cooks, and cares for middle-class households? How is the contradiction to be resolved (indeed even raised) between seeing working-class women as poor mothers, inadequate providers of income and material benefits, unskilled and poorly educated, and yet, when they enter the relations of wage labor in low-paid work, caring for middle-class households, as women whose "natural" caring and interpersonal skills make them ideal? The trend toward increasing spatial separation of the classes and the cultural condescension of the middle class is, thus, challenged every day through the labor of working-class women who care for middle-class children in childcare centers, nurseries, after-school clubs, and in the homes of childminders and of parents, bringing classes into intimate contact through the bodily care for children and class difference into the home.

Sayer (2005), one of the most interesting class analysts writing at present, has taken seriously the need to bring emotions and morals into class analysis by addressing what he terms "lay normativity" or the ethics of everyday life. As he argues, "people experience class in relation to others partly via moral and immoral sentiments such as benevolence, respect, compassion, pride and envy, contempt and shame" (2005: 3). He rejects philosophical claims that see these sentiments as unreasonable, that is as counterposed to reason. They are, instead, "embodied evaluative judgements of matters influencing people's well-being and that of others" (p. 3). Here, he is close to the work of feminist scholars outlined above and, while explicitly acknowledging his debt to Bourdieu, argues that Bourdieu neglects the moral dimensions of lay understandings in his notion of habitus. Sayer is interested in moral or non-instrumental judgments or commitments that affect class practices, drawing on moral philosophers, including Adam Smith and Martha Nussbaum, in his argument that social actors are able to think beyond their own social position and self-interest, in moral justifications of their own and others' class position, privilege, or disadvantage. Sayer's analysis differs from other studies referred to in this section in that it is a theoretical rather empirical analysis. However, it is interesting that methodologically, most of the studies of class inspired by Bourdieu rely on detailed empirical and ethnographic work. This is what is required to tease out both the connections between different aspects of class positions, dispositions, and practices and the relationships between class and other social characteristics. Analysis of intersections remains complex, but it is an essential task for cultural geographers.

## Transnational Class Mobility

It may seem perverse, having made a claim about the value of small-scale studies, to end with a discussion of transnational class mobility. However, this is not necessarily a contradiction. Large-scale movements, such as migration across national borders, are open to investigation though detailed case studies of, for example, the position of migrants in the labor market in their destination location, as well as through quantitative analyses of flows. What has long been recognized by migration theorists is that movement typically is associated with downward social mobility, at least for the majority and at least for a temporary period (which may stretch into many years for minority communities) (Platt 2005; Stein 1979). In the explanation of why this downward mobility happens, recent studies have drawn on some of the frameworks outlined above (Glick-Schiller, Basch, and Blanc 1995; Levitt 2001). Class dispositions, assumptions, embodied social practices, and cultural meanings both reflect the customs and structures of the societies that are left behind and influence the position in which migrants find themselves in the host society (Batnitzky, McDowell, and Dyer 2008). Here, there is a need for more research that uncovers the ways in which misunderstandings and different moral attitudes and meaning affect the class positioning of new entrants to a society and a locality and which affect who is successful and who is unsuccessful in achieving class mobility in a new context. At a broader scale, new entrants to a labor market and society typically find themselves in the position of what Marx termed the lumpenproletariat, or what more recently the Italian Operaismo school (Hardt and Negri 2000) have termed the precariat, susceptible to the booms and busts of the economy as job opportunities open up or close. Large-scale statistical analyses have shown, for example, that foreign-born men, especially men of color, are often the most disadvantaged in post-Fordist labor markets, although it is important to recognize that economic migration also includes the highly skilled who in a globalized economy move between high-status positions in, for example, the finance sector or education with no loss of position.

Migration has also changed in nature: it is no longer a permanent move from the homeland (if indeed it ever was); so the connections between class, place, and culture are complicated by multiple movements, by continuing associations, and by new relations. For transnational communities, class identities are complicated by the connections maintained between different places, often through marriage links, which may challenge class identities or produce cross-class households. Class then is played out across diverse registers and spaces and is further complicated by its intersections with racialized/ethnicized and gendered identities. To understand the complex ways in which class identities are constructed, change, and are associated with forms of resistance may require research that moves between different sites, not only between the home and the workplace in the home and host society but also between the sometimes multiple disaporic communities of which they are members. This agenda is challenging for geographers interested in the ways in which movement and place affect and reflect changing class identities as it may necessitate time-consuming multi-sited fieldwork.

## Conclusions

As I argued at the start of this chapter, the content here reflects my own interests and expertise; so there is perhaps greater emphasis on the labor market and the workplace than readers of a handbook of cultural geography might have expected. However, this is not an apology as it is participation in the labor market, for almost all of us over most of our adult lives, that designates our social class position, our standard of living, and the types of goods and services we are able to purchase in the market. An accident of birth places us in a particular locality – for some for their entire life and for most for their childhood – although in an increasingly mobile world, a growing proportion of the world's population may die far from where they were born. Over the life span, class position may change with spatial mobility, as well as participation in the labor market. Furthermore, the ideas, social practices, attitudes, and assumptions mapped onto class and written onto the body may also change over time. As I have argued, in the post-industrial West, the large-scale transformation of the economy and the labor market have radically altered the nature of social class and patterns of class practices and politics, as well as the connections between class and place.

There are several key points that follow from this argument. First, at the risk of repeating the argument *ad nauseam*, class is both an economic and a cultural formation which takes different forms over space and time. While economic position and cultural practices cannot be read off each other, it is clear that, despite ambivalence and contradictions, there are evident and enduring associations between class position and class practices. How we understand the world, how we walk down the street, how we speak, how we interact with others, as well as our attitudes, homes, the books we buy, the newspapers we read, our political practices, life chances, and opportunities, are all related to our position in the class structure.

This leads to my second point: class position is intercut by, and intersects with, other dimension of social difference, most notably with gender and ethnicity. The long history of discrimination and racist practices in the West results in what Roediger (1999) termed "the wages of whiteness," as, within all social classes but especially within the working class, more advantaged positions were and still often are closed to people of color and in-migrants in societies where white-skinned people were the majority and/or the most powerful. As many geographers have documented, this discrimination in the labor market was and is paralleled by discrimination and exclusion in other social spheres, perhaps most visibly in the housing market. Gender is the second major axis of what Tilly (1998) termed that durable set of "categorical inequalities." As I have argued here, the shift to a service-dominated economy, as well as the industrialization of parts of the global South, have resulted in a growing feminization of the labor market and the increasing representation of women among the working class. Women are an awkward problem for class analysts. Their concentration in the labor market makes it difficult to measure and assess the significance of class differences (or perhaps reflects outdated forms of occupational classification). But many women also live with partners (and men, too, of course, but this was not seen as a classificatory problem), leading to a question about how to categorize what are known as cross-class households. If a female primary-school teacher lives with, say, a motor mechanic, what is the class position of their household, predictions about their consumption behavior, their voting practices, and expectations of their children's education: all arenas where class has been regarded as a key determinant of attitudes and behaviors? Unlike the social theorist Ulrich Beck, I do not accept that class and gender have become what he refers to as zombie categories in the current era, devoid of significance in an individualized world of reflexive modernity (Beck 1992, 1997); but I do insist that their significance and connections are changing in ways that demand more analysis in specific contexts.

Third, I have argued that the spatialities of class have changed in the post-Fordist period. The old connections between class-based solidarity and local place-based communities have largely disappeared in the UK and the US but are being reconstructed in different ways. Most individuals for long periods of their life engage in a daily set of practices within a tightly defined locality. Even global bankers have a home and a headquarters where they sleep and work for at least part of the year. As for the rest of us, we mainly shop, cook, care for our children locally, and, if in employment, work quite close to home, even if daily commutes are becoming longer. As Hanson and Pratt (1995) and others noted, it is women who have more spatially confined lives than men in general, even if they are in waged employment, although these differences have a class pattern too. I have also argued here that class relations within the household are changing for many as an older class-specific pattern of living-in servants is being resuscitated, as an ethnically distinctive, spatially mobile population provides care for the children of middle-class "working" women and increasingly for the growing older population. Thus, class relations are apparent in the most intimate of daily practices and the "private" spaces of the home.

The changing configuration of gender, class, ethnicity, and place (and I have ignored aging, sexual identification, and religion, which are all key characteristics whose intersection with class would repay attention) raises complex questions for geographical analysis, especially in a period of hardship, most notably for the working class, as programs of austerity are introduced across Europe and in North America and income differentials between the rich and the poor increase. Exploring the connections between class and spatial particularities at different geographical scales, between patterns of investment, flows of people, and new configurations of class, gender, and ethnicity demands not only theoretical sophistication but also careful attention to methodological strategies as cultural geographers continue to explore the lived meaning of class position.

## Note

1 In 2011, mainly young, anti-capitalist, anti-bankers protesters occupied key public spaces such as parks and squares in many Western cities, including London and New York.

## References

Acker, J. (2000) Revisiting class: Thinking from gender, race and organisations. *Social Politics*, Summer, 192–214.

Adkins, L. and Skeggs, B. (eds.) (2004) *Feminism after Bourdieu*. Oxford: Blackwell.

Alcock, P., Beatty, C., Fothergill, S., Macmillan R., and Yeandle, S. (2003) *Work to Welfare: How Men Become Detached from the Labour Market*. Cambridge: Cambridge University Press.

Aldridge, S. (2004) *Life Chances and Social Mobility: An Overview of the Evidence*. Prime Minister's Strategy Unit, London: The Cabinet Office.

Amin, A. (1992) *Post-Fordism: A Reader*. Oxford: Blackwell.

Batnitzky, A., McDowell, L., and Dyer, S. (2008) A middle class global mobility: The working lives of Indian men in a west London hotel. *Global Networks*, 8, 51–70.

Bauder, H. (2006) *Labour Movement: How Migration Regulates Labour Markets*. Oxford: Oxford University Press.

Beck, U. (1992) *Risk Society: Towards a New Modernity*. London: Sage.

Beck, U. (1997) *The Reinvention of Politics: Rethinking Modernity in the Global Social Order*. Cambridge: Polity.

Beynon, H. (1984) *Working for Ford*. London: Penguin.

Bluestone, B. (1995) *The Polarisation of American Society*. New York: Twentieth Century Fund Press.

Bourdieu, P. (1984) *Distinction: A Social Critique of the Judgement of Taste*. London: Routledge.

Bourdieu, P. (1993) *Sociology in Question*. London: Sage.

Bourgois, P. (1995) *In Search of Respect: Selling Crack in El Barrio*. Cambridge: Cambridge University Press.

Burrows, R. and Gane, N. (2006) Geodemographics: Software and class. *Sociology*, 40 (5), 793–812.

Butler, J. (1998) Marxism and the merely cultural. *New Left Review*, 227, 33–44.

Cannadine, D. (2000) *Class in Britain*. London: Penguin.

Castree, N., Coe, N., Ward, K., and Samers, M. (2004) *Spaces of Work: Global Capitalism and Geographies of Labour*. London: Sage.

Chant, S. (ed.) (2010) *The International Handbook of Gender and Poverty*. Cheltenham: Edward Elgar.

Crompton, R. (2010) Class and employment. *Work, Employment and Society*, 24 (1), 9–26.

Dennis, N., Henriques, S., and Slaughter, C. (1956) *Coal is Our Life*. London: Eyre and Spottiswood.

Dorling, D. (2011) *So You Think You Know about Britain?* London: Constable.

Dyer, S., McDowell, L., and Batnitzky, A. (2008) Emotional labour/body work: The caring labours of migrants in the UK's National Health Service. *Geoforum*, 39, 2030–2038.

Esping-Andersen, G. (ed.) (1993) *Changing Classes: Stratification and Mobility in Post-Industrial Societies*. London: Sage.

Finnegan, W. (1998) *Cold New World*. New York: Random House.

Fraser, N. (1995) From redistribution to recognition? Dilemmas of social justice in a post-socialist age. *New Left Review*, 212, 68–94.

Fraser, N. (2000) Rethinking recognition. *New Left Review*, 3, 107–120.

Gilligan, C. (1982) *In a Different Voice: Psychological Theory and Women's Development*. Cambridge, MA: Harvard University Press.

Glenn, E.N. (2001) From servitude to service work: Historical continuities in the racial division of paid reproductive labour. *Signs: A Journal of Women and Culture*, 18, 1–43.

Glick-Schiller, N., Basch, L., and Blanc, C.S. (1995) From immigrant to transmigrant: Theorising transnational migration. *Anthropological Quarterly*, 68 (1), 48–63.

Goldthorpe, J. (1983) Women and class analysis: In defence of the conventional view. *Sociology*, 17, 465–488.

Goldthorpe, J. and Lockwood, D. (1963) Affluence and the British class structure. *Sociological Review*, 11 (2), 133–163.

Goldthorpe, J., Lockwood, D., Bechofer, F., and Platt, J. (1969) *The Affluent Work in the Class Structure*. Cambridge: Cambridge University Press.

Gorz, A. (1982) *Farewell to the Working Class*. London: Pluto.

Green, F. (2006) *Demanding Work: The Paradox of Job Quality in the Affluent Economy*. Princeton: Princeton University Press.

Hanson, S. and Pratt, G. (1995) *Gender, Work and Space*. London: Routledge.

Hardt, M. and Negri, A. (2000) *Empire*. Cambridge, MA: Harvard University Press.

Harvey, D. (1989) *The Condition of Post-Modernity*. Oxford: Blackwell.

Haylett, C. (2001) Illegitimate subjects? Abject whites, neoliberal modernisation and middle class multiculturalism. *Environment and Planning D: Society and Space*, 19, 351–379.

Herod, A. (2003) Workers, space and labor geography. *International Labour and Working Class History*, 64, 112–138.

Jenkins, R. (2002) *Pierre Bourdieu*. London: Routledge.

Jones, O. (2011) *Chavs: The Demonization of the Working Class*. London: Verso.

Kessler Harris, A. (2007) *Gendering Labour History*. Urbana: University of Illinois Press.

Kitson, M., Martin, R., and Tyler, P. (2011) The geographies of austerity. *Cambridge Journal of Regions, Economy and Society*, 4 (3), 289–302.

Lawler, S. (2004) Rules of engagement: Habitus, power and resistance. In *Feminism after Bourdieu*, ed. L. Adkins and B. Skeggs. Oxford: Blackwell, pp. 110–128.

Leadbeater, C. (2000) *Living on Thin Air: The New Economy*. London: Penguin.

Levitt, P. (2001) Transnational migration: Taking stock and future directions. *Global Networks*, 1 (3), 1470–2266.

Lucas, R. and Tepperman, L. (2001) *Minetown, Milltown, Railtown: Life in Canadian Communities of Single Industry*. Oxford: Oxford University Press.

Luxton, M. (1980) *More Than a Labour of Love*. Toronto: Canadian Scholars Press.

McDowell, L. (1997) *Capital Culture: Gender at Work in the City*. Oxford: Blackwell.

McDowell, L. (2003) *Redundant Masculinities? Employment Change and White Working Class Youth*. Oxford: Blackwell.

McDowell, L. (2008) Thinking through work: Complex inequalities constructions of difference and transnational migrants. *Progress in Human Geography*, 28, 145–163.

McDowell, L. (2009) *Working Bodies: Interactive Service Employment and Workplace Identities*. Oxford: Wiley-Blackwell.

McDowell, L. and Massey, D. (1984) A woman's place. In *Geography Matters!*, ed. D. Massey and J. Allen. Cambridge: Cambridge University Press.

McDowell, L., Anitha, S., and Pearson, R. (2012) Striking similarities: Representing South Asian women's industrial action in Britain. *Gender, Place and Culture: A Journal of Feminist Geography*, 19 (2), 133–152.

McRobbie, A. (2004) Notes on "what not to wear" and post-feminist symbolic violence. In *Feminism after Bourdieu*, ed. L. Adkins and B. Skeggs. Oxford: Blackwell, pp. 99–109.

McRobbie, A. (2009) *The Aftermath of Feminism: Gender, Culture and Social Change*. London: Sage.

Newman, K. (1999) *There's No Shame in My Game: The Working Poor in the Inner City*. New York: Russell Sage Foundation.

Pearson, R., Anitha, S., and McDowell, L. (2010) Striking issues: From labour process to industrial dispute at Grunwick and Gate Gourmet. *Industrial Relations Journal*, 40, 408–428.

Perlin, R. (2011) *Intern Nation: How to Earn Nothing and Learn Little in the Brave New Economy*. London: Verso.

Pinch, S. (1985) *Cities and Services: The Geography of Collective Consumption*. London: Routledge and Kegan Paul.

Platt, L. (2005) *Social Mobility and Migration*. York: Joseph Rowntree Foundation.

Portes, A. and Rumbaut, G. (2001) *Legacies: The Story of the Immigrant Second Generation*. Berkeley: University of California Press.

Roediger, D. (1999) *The Wages of Whiteness: Race and the Making of the American Working Class, Revised Edition*. London: Verso.

Samuel, R. (ed.) (1977) *Miners, Quarrymen and Saltworkers*. London: Routledge and Kegan Paul.

Saunders, P. (1986) *Social Theory and the Urban Question*. London: Hutchinson.

Savage, M. (2000) *Class Analysis and Social Transformation*. Buckingham: Open University Press.

Savage, M. and Burrows, R. (2007) The coming crisis of empirical sociology. *Sociology*, 41, 885–899.

Sayer, A. (2005) *The Moral Significance of Class*. Cambridge: Cambridge University Press.

Sennett, R. (1998) *The Corrosion of Character: The Personal Consequences of Work in the New Capitalism*. New York: W.W. Norton.

Skeggs, B. (1997) *Formations of Class and Gender*. London: Routledge.

Skeggs, B. (2004) *Class, Self, Culture*. London: Routledge.

Stanworth, M. (1984) Women and class analysis: A reply to John Goldthorpe. *Sociology*, 18, 159–170.

Stein, B. (1979) Occupational adjustment of refugees: Vietnamese in the United States. *International Migration Review*, 13 (1), 25–45.

Storper, M. and Walker, R. (1989) *The Capitalist Imperative: Territory, Technology and Industrial Growth*. Oxford: Blackwell.

Tilly, C. (1998) *Durable Inequality*. Berkeley: University of California Press.

Valentine, G. (2007) Theorising and researching intersectionality: A challenge for feminist geography. *Professional Geographer*, 59, 10–21.

Waldinger, R. and Fitzgerald, D. (2004) Transnationalism in question. *American Journal of Sociology*, 109 (5), 1177–1195.

Waldinger, R. and Soehl, T. (2010) Making the connections: Latino immigrants and their cross-border ties. *Ethnic and Racial Studies*, 33 (9), 1489–1510.

Williams, R. (1977) *Marxism and Literature*. Oxford: Oxford University Press.

Wills, J. (2008) Making class politics possible: Organizing contract cleaners in London. *International Journal of Urban and Regional Research*, 32 (2), 305–324.

Wilson, E. (1992) *The Sphinx in the City*. London: Virago.

Winders, J. (2009) Placing Latino migration and migrant experiences in the U.S. South: The complexities of regional and local trends. In *Global Connections and Local Receptions: New Latino Immigration to the Southeastern U.S.*, ed. J. Shefner and F. Ansley. Knoxville: University of Tennessee Press, pp. 223–244.

Wright, E.O. (ed.) (2005) *Approaches to Class Analysis*. Cambridge: Cambridge University Press.

Wright, M. (2006) *Disposable Women and Other Myths of Global Capitalism*. London: Routledge.

Young, I.M. (1997) Unruly categories: A critique of Nancy Fraser's dual systems theory. *New Left Review*, 1 (222), 147–160.

## Chapter 12

# Geographies of Sexualities: The Cultural Turn and After

*Natalie Oswin*

"Sexuality is – at last – finding a voice as a legitimate and significant area for geographical research" (Bell and Valentine 1995a: 11). This statement, from Bell and Valentine's editorial introduction to the landmark volume *Mapping Desire: Geographies of Sexualities*, appeared in print in 1995. While the radical geography project put class and, to a lesser extent, race and gender onto the disciplinary agenda as early as the 1960s, very little work on sexuality was published in geography prior to the 1990s.[1] Some geographers suggest that this late arrival is due to "squeamishness" (Binnie 1997) and enduring homophobia and heterosexism (Brown and Knopp 2003) within the discipline. I begin with this timeline to situate the geographies of sexualities[2] literature as a product of the discipline's "cultural turn." As Bell has reflected,

> The mid-1990s were an exciting time, even – or maybe especially – in geography. The porosity of the discipline, its magpie-like ability to pick things from elsewhere and put them to (usually) productive use, was in full flow. The so-called cultural turn in geography and the so-called spatial turn in the social sciences had both made geography "sexy." (2007: 83)

Alongside new disciplinary engagements with feminist, critical-race, postcolonial, post-modern, psychoanalytic theories and more, "the cultural turn made room for a queer turn in geography" (Bell 2007: 83). The shift away from Sauerian "superorganic" notions of culture and toward a cultural studies-inspired approach to culture as constructed, contested, embodied, and political created affinities with the poststructuralist, anti-assimilationist ideas about sexuality emerging contemporaneously in the humanities under the label "queer theory." As such, while sexuality is finally "on the map" in geography and is now frequently given a place in proliferating disciplinary compendiums, handbooks, companions, and

*The Wiley Blackwell Companion to Cultural Geography*, First Edition.
Edited by Nuala C. Johnson, Richard H. Schein, and Jamie Winders.
© 2013 John Wiley & Sons, Ltd. Published 2016 by John Wiley & Sons, Ltd.

encyclopedias, geographical studies of sexuality have a particularly strong tie to the subdiscipline of cultural geography.

Existing surveys of the geographies of sexualities literature have well laid out the contours and contributions of this 1990s "queer turn" within the "cultural turn" (Binnie and Valentine 1999; Brown *et al.* 2007; Brown and Knopp 2003). Persuaded by poststructuralist queer theory's insight that sexual categories and identities (along with all categories and identities) are socially and linguistically performed rather than biologically determined, a handful of geographers began to explore the ways in which space matters to the performance of sexualities (Bell *et al.* 1994; Bell and Valentine 1995b; Binnie 1997). They concomitantly moved away from previous geographical approaches to sexuality that mapped sexual difference *in place* to interrogate how sexual norms come to *take and make place*; for "the straightness of our streets is an artefact, not a natural fact" (Bell and Valentine 1995a: 19). This project was overtly political. Rejecting the dominant casting of heterosexuality as "normal" and homosexuality as "abnormal," geographers engaging with queer theory set out to denaturalize and reconfigure dominant cultural logics surrounding sexual acts and identities, proprieties and improprieties. As a result, as Brown and Knopp note,

> Sexual identities are now most fruitfully seen as culturally and ideologically constructed subjectivities and significations that serve and resist dominant forms of power. Power, meanwhile, is seen as working through discourses and representations as much as through more conventional material practices. (2003: 313)

It is further worth noting that the intellectual conversation between queer theory and geography has by no means been unidirectional. Binnie and Valentine state:

> Work on geographies of sexualities has to date been characterized by an emphasis on both the material and the everyday – how sexualities are lived out in particular places and spaces. This is the major contribution that geographers can therefore offer other disciplines concerned with sexuality. (1999: 183)

Existing surveys in geography have also well laid out the shortcomings and limitations of the geographies of sexualities literature. Most significantly, its insights have not been widely taken up in the discipline as a whole. In Bell's appraisal,

> sexuality is now more or less routinely and more or less unproblematically part of cultural geography ... Urban geography has been home to research on, among other things, gay gentrification and gay urban politics ... Political geography has accommodated talk of queer politics and of the spaces of sexual citizenship, though this hasn't really reshaped the main agenda or curriculum of the subdiscipline. (2007: 85)

He further notes some scattered work in rural geography and historical geography but overall bemoans the fact that geography's "queer turn" has spread only to "those parts of geography most infected and affected by the cultural turn" (2007: 83). Brown and Knopp similarly argue that "the discipline's traditional corpus has been largely untouched by a queer sensibility" and that "work on sexuality and space in geography remains largely peripheral even within cultural geography" (2003: 318).[3] These statements, unfortunately, still ring true. The literature on geographies of sexualities is certainly robust. Indeed, Brown, Browne, and Lim, in the introduction to their important edited volume *Geographies of Sexualities*, rightfully characterize the literature as "an exciting and proliferating field of studies" that "has blossomed over the last decade or so" (2007: 1). Nonetheless, it still has limited reach within the discipline itself. The vast majority of work in this vein is published in a narrow band of geography journals – most notably, *Social and Cultural Geography*, *Gender, Place and Culture*, and, on a smaller scale, *Environment and Planning D: Society and Space*. Though geographers working on sexuality have situated their work in multiple subfields (social, cultural, urban, political, and, to a lesser extent, economic, population, rural, and historical geographies), it has yet to be a central geographical concern. Even while "gender, race, and class" has become something of a mantra for critical cultural geographers (at least), sexuality is all too frequently left out of the analysis.

In light of these two facts, the vibrancy of the field of geographies of sexualities and its peripheral position within the discipline, this chapter has two aims. First, it is intended to survey the geographies of sexualities literature, focusing on work published since 2000 in the spirit of this *new* companion to cultural geography. Second, it argues for broader consideration of sexuality as an area of geographical concern. The first aim is addressed in the next two sections that deal with work on homosexualities and heterosexualities, respectively. That these topics now deserve nearly equal billing is one of the most significant developments in the field. Throughout the 1990s, the literature's focus was almost exclusively on gay and lesbian geographies. Since then, however, as Hubbard notes, "straight geographies have gone queer too" (2007: 154). The final section addresses the problematic fact that sexuality, despite growing attention to it, is so rarely taken seriously by geographers in their analyses of sociocultural phenomena. The "cultural turn" certainly spurred an exciting array of geographical work on sexuality that has especially well examined the ways in which sexual identities are contextual, contingent performances. To sustain this "queer turn" and increase its impact within the discipline, however, geographers working across subdisciplines need to pay much more critical attention both to the performances of heterosexualities and homosexualities and to the cultural politics of heteronormativity itself.

## Spacing Sexual Difference: Gay, Lesbian, "Queer"

The literature on geographies of sexualities that took shape in the 1990s was an overt attempt to "queer" the discipline. In their introduction to *Mapping Desire*, Bell and Valentine (1995a) laid out this project, stating that "a whole body of work is emerging in geography that explores the performance of sexual identities and the way that they are inscribed on the body and the landscape" (p. 8). They attribute the flourishing of the geographies of sexualities literature to the development of a "greater recognition of the multiplicity of sexualities and the fluid and contextual nature of sexual identities" (p. 9). The volume's chapters, as the editors described them, "expose the many ways of 'being' and 'doing' sexuality" (p. 10) and "begin to reveal that th[e] heterosexing of space is a performative act naturalized through repetition – and destabilized by the mere presence of invisibilised sexualities" (p. 18). This approach to sexuality as performed, multiple, and contextual is clearly indebted to queer theory and its critique of sexual identity as fixed. It also explicitly embraces "queer" in the second sense of the term, as derived from its use within AIDS activist organizations in the US and UK in the early 1990s. In this usage, "queer" signifies an alternative sexual identity that embodies a radical, sex-positive, activist, and anti-assimilationist politics. Following this second definition, for Bell and Valentine, a queer identity and politics encompass "anyone who refuse[s] to play by the rules of heteropatriarchy" (p. 21).[4]

*Mapping Desire* has shaped subsequent geographic work in many ways. Most fundamentally, its deployment of "queer" as both a critical epistemological approach and a radical identity simultaneously introduced geographers to a novel and productive way to think about sexuality and space while validating "deviant," marginalized, or non-dominant sexual identities and practices as worthy topics of study. Indeed, before Hubbard's (2000) call for more attention to heterosexualities, the focus of the geographies of sexualities literature was placed squarely on non-heterosexual or "queer" lives. More precisely, gay and lesbian geographies were the main concern.[5] Binnie and Valentine, in a 1999 survey, grouped the literature into three main fields – urban geography, rural geography, and geographies of sexual citizenship – none of which moved far from the study of "queer" lives. Since that time, however, much has changed. I turn now to a brief overview of the topical emphases found within the literature since 2000, before discussing a significant reconfiguration of the queer theoretical underpinnings of this recent literature.

As in the literature Binnie and Valentine surveyed, urban gay and lesbian geographies are still the mainstay of the field. Studies of residential spaces, formerly a key topic, have surprisingly fallen away, although Andrew Gorman-Murray's work (2008) on gay and lesbian uses of home spaces in Australia may be changing this trend. Work on commercial spaces, though, remains strong. Catherine Nash (2005), for instance, examines the emergence of Toronto's "gay ghetto" in the 1970s as a product of the gay movement's shift from a "liberationist" to an "ethnic minority" approach. Julie Podmore (2006) has looked at Montreal's lesbian bar cultures since 1950 to demonstrate the shifting territorial practices of lesbian subcultures. Gilbert Caluya's (2008) ethnography of gay Asian male experiences of Sydney's "gay scene" considers gay space as segregated space, while Andrew Tucker (2009) and Gustav Visser (2003) examine the racialization of gay spaces with a focus on Cape Town's de Waterkant district. Bell and Binnie (2004) have critiqued the ways in which the "active state promotion of gay spaces in cities has brought them into the entrepreneurial, neo-liberal frame" (p. 1815; on this theme, see also Andersson 2011 and Rushbrook 2002).

Beyond the geographies of commercial spaces, much work has attended to gay and lesbian appropriations of urban public spaces. Kath Browne (2008) and Lynda Johnston (2005), for instance, have studied the claiming of queer space through Pride celebrations in the UK and Australia. Gordon Waitt (2006) has looked at the 2002 Sydney Gay Games, while Sallie Marston (2002) has analyzed the exclusion of gays and lesbians from the New York St. Patrick's Day parade. Along similar lines, Adrian Mulligan (2008) has examined the "St. Pat's for All" parade as a gay and lesbian "counter-public" that emerged in response to this exclusion. In the context of New Orleans, Kathleen O'Reilly and Michael Crutcher (2006) have considered the "parallel politics" of African American and gay Labor Day parades, while John Paul Catungal and Eugene McCann (2010) have looked at the moral and sexual geographies of Vancouver's Stanley Park. In contrast to this strong body of work on urban areas, work on rural geographies of gay and lesbian lives has faded somewhat, though important contributions have been made. Phillips, Watt, and Shuttleton's edited collection *De-centring Sexualities* (2000) is perhaps the most concerted effort to take the study of gay and lesbian geographies "beyond the metropolis." More recently, Waitt and Stapel (2011) and Waitt and Gorman-Murray (2011) take up the call to disrupt notions of the rural as backward sexual spaces through their studies of gay and lesbian lives in Townsville, Australia.

Work on sexual citizenship continues to bring gay and lesbian issues into the subdiscipline of political geography. The legal status of sexual minorities within various national contexts, for example, is a central theme within this genre. In the UK, Stychin (2006) has deconstructed the ideological underpinnings of civil partnership legislation, while Browne (2011) has scrutinized persistent inequalities along class lines that have followed from such legislation. Baird (2006) has analyzed the provision of gay and lesbian rights in Tasmania in relation to its government's neoliberal approach to globalization. In my own work on Singapore, I examine the maintenance of a colonial-era sodomy law (Oswin 2010b). In the context of public health politics in Seattle, Washington, Brown (2006) extends the concept of sexual citizenship through his attention to political obligation. Electoral geographies, particularly in the US, have been another key concern (see Brown, Knopp, and Morrill 2005; Webster, Chapman, and Leib 2010), as have the sexual politics of immigration (see Coleman 2008; Simmons 2008) and, to a lesser extent, the relationship between sexuality and the state in the context of transnationality and diaspora (Sandell 2010; Sugg 2003).

In addition, a focus on sexuality and space has expanded in piecemeal fashion into a range of other areas. Work now exists on gay and lesbian geographies of the closet (Brown 2000), sport (Muller 2007), emotion (Gruszczynska 2009; Wilkinson 2009), affect (Brown 2008a; Lim 2007), animals (Talburt and Matus 2012), mobilities (Gorman-Murray 2009), family (Valentine, Skelton, and Butler 2003), diverse economies (Brown 2007), health (Sothern 2007), religion (Vanderbeck *et al.* 2011), mapping (Brown and Knopp 2006), civil society (Andrucki and Elder 2007), globalization (Oswin 2007), and more. As this list makes clear, recent work on the geographies of sexualities picks up on many themes present in the 1990s literature while examining "queer" lives in relation to ever more areas of geographical concern.

Beyond certain topical similarities, an important theoretical reconfiguration is evident between work on geographies of sexualities in the 1990s and work on the topic in the 2000s. In short, the assertion made in much of the 1990s literature that queerness is radical has given way to more careful and ambivalent readings of sexual cultural politics. In study after study, geographers' examinations of gay/lesbian/"queer" spaces find that a straightforwardly subversive, resistant, and inclusive sexual politics is hard to find. For instance, Johnston (2005) argues that gay Pride Parades contain both possibilities and paradoxes. She suggests that these events can be emancipatory for some while reinscribing hegemonies along race, class, and gender lines for others. Waitt, in his study of Sydney's Gay Games, argues that

> despite the best intentions, the social diversity of every iteration of the Gay Games has been restricted. The implied invitation is always to "come out" and celebrate being part of a remarkably white, gay, metropolitan community that operates across cultural distinctions. (2006: 773)

In their study of Toronto women's bathhouse events, Nash and Bain found schisms along class and gender lines and argue that "while queer spaces are often presented as progressive, inclusive and tolerant, these same spaces may be exclusionary or limiting despite efforts at openness" (2007: 58). Finally, Doan, in a survey of transgender persons in various US cities, argues that "the rush to celebrate some urban areas as inclusive queer spaces is premature, particularly with respect to gender variant individuals" (2007: 70).[6]

By now, it is well recognized that while gay and lesbian claims to space may challenge heterosexual dominance, they are not necessarily radical in the fullest sense of the term. This realization has made many geographers (though certainly not all) back away from labeling non-heterosexual identities as inherently anti-assimilationist or "queer." More fundamentally, it has spurred on recognition that positing space as dominantly heterosexual, waiting to be disrupted through "queering," "reifies a heterosexual/homosexual split [and] effaces other kinds of identities – race, ethnicity, nationality, class, and gender" (Puar 2002: 935–936; see also Nast 2002). In other words, heterosexual space is not just heterosexual space. Likewise, "queer" space is not just "queer" space, since sexuality is not an autonomous dimension of human experience. Instead, it is part of a broader social/cultural/political field and, thus, sexual norms cannot be understood apart from hierarchies of race, class, gender, and nationality. I now turn to the geographies of heterosexualities literature and return to this point about the possibilities of a "queer" critique that does more than add sexuality in the concluding section.

## Interrogating the "Center": Heterosexualities

While the queer turn that *Mapping Desire* inaugurated led at first to the almost exclusive production of work on gay and lesbian geographies, it opened the door for the exploration of the geographies of heterosexuality. After all, a queer geographical approach is based on the notion that space is actively heterosexualized rather than naturally heterosexual. Thus, Hubbard (2000), in his influential essay "Desire/Disgust: Mapping the Moral Contours of Heterosexuality," challenged geographers to think about sexuality more expansively. He called for work that addressed "how heterosexual identities are spatially constructed and negotiated," noting that conceptualizing space as either "gay" or "straight" "ignore[s] the complex way in which heterosexual spaces are themselves variously sexualized or desexual-ized by different people at different times" (2000: 192). Recognizing heterosexuality as multiple rather than monolithic, he argued for greater understanding of the ways in which heterosexual practices and identities tend to be cast as either "moral" or "immoral," norma-tive or non-normative. Hubbard's call has been so well heeded that studies of contingent, contextual heterosexualities are now plentiful, even if the literature is still not so extensive as is that on homosexualities. This new body of scholarship, however, is fairly amorphous. Studies of the urban geographies of prostitution and red-light districts are most abundant in this scholarship, although engagement with health geographies is on the rise and various other topics are emergent.

A focus on prostitution, as Hubbard notes, helps to clarify "how heteronormativity is reproduced spatially through the exclusion and containment of commercial sex work away from "family spaces" (2008: 646). Work in this vein includes Hubbard's (2004) examination of "Zero Tolerance" policies in Paris and London that displace sex workers from the city centers, Adler Papayanis' (2000) look at the use of zoning regulations to regulate the sale of pornographic materials in New York, Sanders' (2004) consideration of the ways in which sex workers in Britain employ spatial strategies to manage occupational hazards, Pitman's (2002) analysis of media coverage of the disappearance of sex workers from inner-city Van-couver, and Wright's (2004) analysis of sex workers' protests in Mexico's Ciudad Juárez. There has also been significant work on historical geographies of prostitution. Howell (2009) and Legg (forthcoming), for example, excavate the regulation of sex work as a tool of British colonial power; and Olund (2009) examines social reformers' efforts to discourage white working-class women from entering "white slavery" in the Progressive-era United States.

Work on the health geographies of sexuality has also been strong. Faria (2008) has studied Ghanaian HIV/AIDS prevention efforts, critiquing the focus of public health campaigns on heterosexual sex beyond the marital/domestic sphere. Raimondo has examined media representations of Belle Glade, Florida, as the "AIDS capital of the world" and interrogated the "role of racialized constructions of space in producing the category of heterosexual transmission and in establishing its distinction from normative heterosexuality" (2005: 53). Brown and Knopp (2010) have considered the regulation of certain heterosexual bodies – specifically, young, working-class white women and working-class African American men – during a moral panic around venereal disease in World War II Seattle, while Del Casino (2007a) has argued for the importance of considering the geographies of drug use and sexual health.[7] Beyond these literatures on sex work and health, the geographies of heterosexualities have touched on the topics of migration (Elder 2003; Richardson, Poudel, and Laurie 2009; Walsh, Shen, and Willis 2008), mobility (Bieri and Gerodetti 2007), family (Cowen and Gilbert 2008; Nast 2000), youth (Thomas 2004), home (Oswin 2010a; Robinson, Hockey, and Meah 2004), religion (Phillips 2012), political mobilization (Rasmussen 2006), emotion (Morrison 2012), leisure spaces (Boyd 2010), and tourism (Malam 2008).

That this exciting range of work has come into existence over the last decade or so means that it is no longer necessary to bemoan the dearth of geographical scholarship on hetero-sexualities. We now have a much more developed sense of how space is produced as hetero-sexual and how heterosexualities are contextually performed. This new literature also makes many important conceptual, political, and empirical contributions. Fundamentally, it very well supports Hubbard's claim that "the sexualized identity of space is not simply the result of a struggle between dominant, rigid heterosexuality and alternative homosexual identities" (2000: 211). That a person may identify as "heterosexual" and engage only in sex acts considered heterosexual does not necessarily ensure that she/he will enjoy heteronormative privilege. Many "heterosexual" subjects are rendered non-normative by notions of familial propriety and respectable domesticity. Second, and closely related to the first contribution, this literature points out that the determination of the proper heterosexual subject is not just a sexuality thing. Heterosexual normativities and non-normativities are mutually constituted by race, class, and gender norms (at least). I conclude this chapter with some thoughts on the ways in which these insights, in combination with the reconfigured queer critique found in the homosexualities literature, point to the relevance of geographies of sexualities to broader disciplinary concerns.

## Envisioning Critical Geographies of Heteronormativity

As this chapter has shown, the literature on geographies of sexualities is now more vibrant than ever. With recent work, many previous shortcomings have been productively addressed. Studies of gay and lesbian lives have become more nuanced, the geographies of the lives of transgender persons have finally received attention, and there is now a wealth of work on heterosexualities. More and more topics have been critically examined, and engagements have been made with a number of geography's subdisciplines. Race is no longer ignored in discussions of sexualities,[8] and the literature now covers a greater range of geographical sites.[9] As Hubbard notes, "rather than circling endlessly around the same debates concerning 'gay ghettos' and the spatial expressions of homophobia, current interventions offer a wide purview of sexual geographies" (2008: 654). This literature, I suggest, has much to offer the wider discipline of geography. Though it is unlikely that its poststructuralist insights will be widely taken up in those still (or again) positivist areas of the discipline, it is time that critical geographers interested in cultural politics take closer notice of sexuality. Nearly a decade ago, Brown and Knopp made the following plea:

we would ask all cultural geographers to recognize the centrality of sexuality to all aspects of culture. Sexuality is an always present aspect of the human experience. As such, it is always implicit, if not explicit, in cultural constructs. We think it crucial, therefore, that cultural geographers be open to exploring this dimension of whatever their topical concerns may be. (2003: 319)

I want to advance this call here, by building briefly on the contributions of the recent literature that I have pulled out in this chapter.

There may well be some truth to Bell's assertion that the sexualities literature is peripheral within geography because "institutionalised homophobia and erotophobia at the heart of geography is still there, arguably as strong as ever" (2007: 86). The general lack of consideration of gays, lesbians, and trans persons in most geographical work certainly suggests a fundamental heterosexist bias. It is also troubling, however, that even where engagements are made with the geographies of sexualities project within the wider critical geography literature, this engagement often does not amount to more than a brief acknowledgment of the exclusion of non-heterosexuals. This approach is problematic, first, because gay, lesbian, and transgender issues should not be simply tacked on to disciplinary concerns. Further, it is problematic because the ways in which sexuality is central to a huge range of social and spatial processes are generally ignored in critical geographical analyses that tend to focus squarely on gender, race, and/or class dynamics. Simply put, there is a geographical failure to critique heteronormativity as a normalizing regime.

This failure can perhaps be traced, at least in part, to the dominant perception within the discipline that the literature on the geographies of sexualities focuses only on interrogating the heterosexual/non-heterosexual binary. As shown above, geographical engagements with queer theory have opened up the discipline (if only partially) to gay, lesbian, and transgender lives as valid objects of study and spurred many geographers to advance analyses that challenge heterosexist discrimination. Geographers have also shined the spotlight on heterosexual experiences as multiple and contingent. In short, the literature on the geographies of sexualities does indeed interrogate the heterosexual/non-heterosexual binary. It does so usefully and out of necessity since heteronormativity, as Brown, Browne, and Lim state, "allows heterosexuality to go unmarked and unremarked upon – to be thought of as normal – by making homosexuality [and other non-heterosexualities] operate as heterosexuality's binary opposite" (2007: 8). But heteronormativity has more far-reaching effects. It makes not just heterosexuality, but *particular forms of heterosexuality*, seem right. Therefore, to understand the geographies of sexualities, we must consider more than the ways in which this sexual binary gets policed. Much recent literature has recognized this fact. Both implicitly and explicitly, then, geographers must interrogate heteronormativity as the coincidence of sexual norms with race, class, and gender norms.

Sexual norms certainly exclude marginal sexual identities and practices. They work in various ways to stigmatize non-heterosexuals – i.e., gay, lesbian, transgender, bisexual – as well as heterosexuals – i.e., prostitutes, bigamists, and sadomasochists – deemed "perverse" or "dangerous." Beyond their effects on such overtly sexualized figures, sexual norms also, however, play an often subtle, but always central, role in wide-ranging and fundamental processes of social reproduction and the management of populations. Beyond the ways in which they set out sexual "deviants" from "proper" sexual citizens, sexual norms work in tandem with hierarchies of race, class, gender, and nationality to determine who fits into, for instance, notions of acceptable family forms and kinship structures, "quality" citizens and migrants, and healthy bodies. Thus, a queer approach, as I have argued elsewhere, "can be deployed to understand much more than the lives of 'queers' " (Oswin 2008: 90) and ought to be articulated in concert with the feminist, materialist, critical-race, and postcolonial theories that have gained more traction within the discipline. Critical geographers, especially since the cultural turn, are centrally concerned with the ways in which discourse and practices pertaining to culture and cultural groups render some lives privileged and others precarious in social space. Work in this vein will be unduly partial until the insights of the new literature on the geographies of sexualities gain broader reach and until critical geographers more fully interrogate the politics of heteronormativity.

## Notes

1 The beginnings of the geographies of sexualities literature are generally traced to scattered studies of gay residential and commercial spaces and the geographies of prostitution in the late 1970s and 1980s. For a discussion of this early work, see Brown, Browne, and Lim (2007).

2 Throughout the history of geographic work on sexuality, various terms have been used to describe the field, including "sexuality and space," "queer geographies," and "geographies of sexualities." I use "geographies of sexualities" in this chapter because it is the broadest descriptor of the literature. It alludes to the variety of sexual subjectivities and spatial experiences while capturing work informed by both "queer" and other conceptual approaches.

3 A more positive appraisal can be made of the reach of the geographies of sexualities literature beyond geography. Many non-geographers have been publishing work on sexuality in space in geography journals, especially over the last decade; and much explicitly queer geography work is well cited across multiple disciplines.

4 For an excellent, concise introduction to queer theory, see Jagose (1996).

5 David Bell (2004) has also written about the geographies of bisexuality, but this area has not been widely taken up.

6 See the special issue on "trans geographies" edited by Browne, Nash, and Hines (2010) for articles that address the failure of geographers to consider gender-variant lives.

7 Del Casino also provides a useful conceptual discussion of "the possibility to queer the subject of health and medical geographic inquiry by challenging the presumptive heteronormativities implicit in medical geography" (2007b: 39).

8 Thomas (2011) makes a necessary critique of the implicit whiteness of sexuality studies within geography.

9 This increase in geographical coverage is largely attributable to the new literature on heterosexualities. With some notable exceptions, work on gay, lesbian, and trans lives within geography is concentrated on a limited range of mostly Western sites. For critiques of uneven geographies of work on homosexualities, see Brown (2008b) and Oswin (2006).

## References

Andersson, J. (2011) Vauxhall's post-industrial pleasure gardens: "Death wish" and hedonism in 21st-century London. *Urban Studies*, 48, 85–100.

Andrucki, M. and Elder, G. (2007) Locating the state in queer space: GLBT non-profit organizations in Vermont, USA. *Social and Cultural Geography*, 8, 89–104.

Baird, B. (2006) Sexual citizenship in the "new Tasmania." *Political Geography*, 25, 964–987.

Bell, D. (2004) Bisexuality: A place on the margins. In *The Margins of the City*, ed. S. Whittle. Aldershot: Ashgate, pp. 129–141.

Bell, D. (2007) Fucking geography, again. In *Geographies of Sexualities: Theory, Practices and Politics*, ed. K. Browne, J. Lim, and G. Brown. Burlington: Ashgate, pp. 81–86.

Bell, D. and Binnie, J. (2004) Authenticating queer space: Citizenship, urbanism and governance. *Urban Studies*, 41, 1807–1820.

Bell, D. and Valentine, G. (1995a) Introduction: Orientations. In *Mapping Desire: Geographies of Sexualities*, ed. D. Bell and G. Valentine. London: Routledge, pp. 1–27.

Bell, D. and Valentine, G. (eds.) (1995b) *Mapping Desire: Geographies of Sexualities*. London: Routledge.

Bell, D., Binnie, J., Cream, J., and Valentine, G. (1994) All hyped up and no place to go. *Gender, Place and Culture*, 1, 31–47.

Bieri, S. and Gerodetti, N. (2007) "Falling women" – "saving angels": Spaces of contested mobility and the production of gender and sexualities within early twentieth-century train stations. *Social and Cultural Geography*, 8, 217–234.

Binnie, J. (1997) Coming out of geography: Towards a queer epistemology? *Environment and Planning D: Society and Space*, 15, 223–237.

Binnie, J. and Valentine, G. (1999) Geographies of sexualities: A review of progress. *Progress in Human Geography*, 23, 175–187.

Boyd, J. (2010) Producing Vancouver's (hetero)normative nightscape. *Gender, Place and Culture*, 17, 169–189.

Brown, G. (2007) Thinking beyond homonormativity: Performative explorations of diverse gay economies. *Environment and Planning A*, 41, 1496–1510.

Brown, G. (2008a) Ceramics, clothing and other bodies: Affective geographies of homoerotic cruising encounters. *Social and Cultural Geography*, 9, 915–932.

Brown, G. (2008b) Urban (homo)sexualities: Ordinary cities and ordinary sexualities. *Geography Compass*, 2, 1215–1231.

Brown, G., Browne, K., and Lim, J. (2007) Introduction, or why have a book on geographies of sexualities? In *Geographies of Sexualities: Theory, Practices and Politics*, ed. K. Browne, J. Lim, and G. Brown. Burlington: Ashgate, pp. 1–18.

Brown, M. (2000) *Closet Space: Geographies of Metaphor from the Body to the Globe*. New York: Routledge.

Brown, M. (2006) Sexual citizenship, political obligation and disease ecology in gay Seattle. *Political Geography*, 25, 874–898.

Brown, M. and Knopp, L. (2003) Queer cultural geographies – We're here! We're queer! We're over there, too! In *Handbook of Cultural Geography*, ed. K. Anderson, M. Domosh, N. Thrift, and S. Pile. London: Sage, pp. 313–324.

Brown, M. and Knopp, L. (2006) Places or polygons? Governmentality, scale, and the census in *The Gay and Lesbian Atlas*. *Population, Space and Place*, 12, 223–242.

Brown, M. and Knopp, L. (2010) Between anatamo- and bio-politics: Geographies of sexual health in wartime Seattle. *Political Geography*, 29, 392–403.

Brown, M., Knopp, L., and Morrill, R. (2005) The culture wars and urban electoral politics: Sexuality, race and class in Tacoma, Washington. *Political Geography*, 24, 267–291.

Browne, K. (2008) A party with politics? (Re)making LGBTQ Pride spaces in Dublin and Brighton. *Social and Cultural Geography*, 8, 63–87.

Browne, K. (2011) "By partner we mean . . .": Alternative geographies of "gay marriage." *Sexualities*, 14, 100–122.

Browne, K., Nash, C., and Hines, S. (eds.) (2010) Towards trans geographies. *Gender, Place and Culture*, 17.

Caluya, G. (2008) "The Rice Steamer": Race, desire and affect in Sydney's gay scene. *Australian Geographer*, 39, 283–292.

Catungal, J.P. and McCann, E. (2010) Governing sexuality and park space: Acts of regulation in Vancouver, BC. *Social and Cultural Geography*, 11, 75–94.

Coleman, M. (2008) US immigration law and its geographies of social control: Lessons from homosexual exclusion during the Cold War. *Environment and Planning D: Society and Space*, 26, 1096–1114.

Cowen, D. and Gilbert, E. (2008) Citizenship in the "homeland": Families at war. In *War, Citizenship, Territory*, ed. D. Cowen and E. Gilbert. New York: Routledge, pp. 261–280.

Del Casino, V. (2007a) Flaccid theory and the geographies of sexual health in the age of Viagra. *Health and Place*, 13, 904–911.

Del Casino, V. (2007b) Health/sexuality/geography. In *Geographies of Sexualities: Theory, Practices and Politics*, ed. K. Browne, J. Lim, and G. Brown. Burlington: Ashgate, pp. 39–52.

Doan, P. (2007) Queers in the American city: Transgendered perceptions of urban space. *Gender, Place and Culture*, 14, 57–74.

Elder, G. (2003) *Hostels, Sexuality and the Apartheid Legacy: Malevolent Geographies*. Athens: Ohio University Press.

Faria, C. (2008) Privileging prevention, gendering responsibility: An analysis of the Ghanaian campaign against HIV/AIDS. *Social and Cultural Geography*, 9, 41–73.

Gorman-Murray, A. (2008) Reconciling self: Gay men and lesbians using domestic materiality for identity management. *Social and Cultural Geography*, 9, 283–301.

Gorman-Murray, A. (2009) Intimate mobilities: Emotional embodiment and queer migration. *Social and Cultural Geography*, 10, 441–460.

Gruszczynska, A. (2009) "I was mad about it all, about the ban": Emotional spaces of solidarity in the Poznan March of Equality. *Emotion, Space and Society*, 2, 44–51.

Howell, P. (2009) *Geographies of Regulation: Policing Prostitution in Nineteenth-Century Britain and the Empire*. Cambridge: Cambridge University Press.

Hubbard, P. (2000) Desire/disgust: Mapping the moral contours of heterosexuality. *Progress in Human Geography*, 24, 191–217.

Hubbard, P. (2004) Cleansing the metropolis: Sex work and the politics of Zero Tolerance. *Urban Studies*, 41, 1687–1702.

Hubbard, P. (2007) Between transgression and complicity (Or: can the straight guy have a queer eye?) In *Geographies of Sexualities: Theory, Practices and Politics*, ed. K. Browne, J. Lim, and G. Brown. Burlington: Ashgate, pp. 151–156.

Hubbard, P. (2008) Here, there, everywhere: The ubiquitous geographies of heteronormativity. *Geography Compass*, 2, 640–658.

Jagose, A. (1996) *Queer Theory: An Introduction*. New York: New York University Press.

Johnston, L. (2005) *Queering Tourism: Paradoxical Performances of Gay Pride Parades*. New York: Routledge.

Legg, S. (forthcoming) Stimulation, segregation and scandal: Geographies of prostitution regulation in British India, between registration (1888) and suppression (1923). *Modern Asian Studies*. DOI: 10.1017/S0026749X11000503

Lim, J. (2007) Queer critique and the politics of affect. In *Geographies of Sexualities: Theory, Practices and Politics*, ed. K. Browne, J. Lim, and G. Brown. Burlington: Ashgate, pp. 53–68.

Malam, L. (2008) Bodies, beaches and bars: Negotiating heterosexual masculinity in southern Thailand's tourism industry. *Gender, Place and Culture*, 15, 581–594.

Marston, S. (2002) Making difference: Conflict over Irish identity in the New York City St. Patrick's Day parade. *Political Geography*, 21, 373–392.

Morrison, C.-A. (2012) Heterosexuality and home: Intimacies of space and spaces of touch. *Emotion, Space and Society*, 5 (1), 10–18.

Muller, T. (2007) "Lesbian community" in Women's National Basketball Association (WNBA) spaces. *Social and Cultural Geography*, 8, 9–28.

Mulligan, A. (2008) Countering exclusion: The "St Pat's for all" parade. *Social and Cultural Geography*, 15, 153–167.

Nash, C.J. (2005) Contesting identity: Politics of gays and lesbians in Toronto in the 1970s. *Gender, Place and Culture*, 12, 113–135.

Nash, C. and Bain, A. (2007) "Reclaiming raunch"? Spatializing queer identities at Toronto women's bathhouse events. *Social and Cultural Geography*, 8, 47–62.

Nast, H. (2000) Mapping the "unconscious": Racism and the Oedipal family. *Annals of the Association of American Geographers*, 90, 215–255.

Nast, H. (2002) Queer patriarchies, queer racisms, international. *Antipode*, 34, 874–909.

Olund, E. (2009) *Traffic in Souls*: The "new woman," whiteness and mobile self-possession. *Cultural Geographies*, 16, 485–504.

O'Reilly, K. and Crutcher, M. (2006) Parallel power: The spatial politics of New Orleans' Labor Day Parades. *Social and Cultural Geography*, 7, 245–265.

Oswin, N. (2006) Decentering queer globalization: Diffusion and the "global gay." *Environment and Planning D: Society and Space*, 24, 777–790.

Oswin, N. (2007) The end of queer (as we knew it): Globalization and the making of a gay-friendly South Africa. *Gender, Place and Culture*, 14, 93–110.

Oswin, N. (2008) Critical geographies and the uses of sexuality: Deconstructing queer space. *Progress in Human Geography*, 32, 89–103.

Oswin, N. (2010a) The modern model family at home in Singapore: A queer geography. *Transactions of the Institute of British Geographers*, 35 (2), 256–268.

Oswin, N. (2010b) Sexual tensions in modernizing Singapore: The postcolonial and the intimate. *Environment and Planning D: Society and Space*, 28, 128–141.

Papayanis, M.A. (2000) Sex and the revanchist city: Zoning out pornography in New York. *Environment and Planning D: Society and Space*, 18, 341–353.

Phillips, R. (2012) Interventions against forced marriage: Contesting hegemonic narratives and minority practices in Europe. *Gender, Place and Culture: A Journal of Feminist Geography*, 19 (1), 21–41.

Phillips, R., Watt, D., and Shuttleton, D. (eds.) (2000) *De-centring Sexualities: Politics and Representation Beyond the Metropolis*. New York: Routledge.

Pitman, B. (2002) Re-mediating the spaces of reality television: *America's Most Wanted* and the case of Vancouver's missing women. *Environment and Planning A*, 34, 167–184.

Podmore, J. (2006) Gone "underground"? Lesbian visibility and the consolidation of queer space in Montréal. *Social and Cultural Geography*, 7, 595–625.

Puar, J. (2002) A transnational feminist critique of queer tourism. *Antipode*, 34, 935–946.

Raimondo, M. (2005) "AIDS capital of the world": Representing race, sex and space in Belle Glade, Florida. *Gender, Place and Culture*, 12, 53–70.

Rasmussen, C.E. (2006) We're no metrosexuals: Identity, place and sexuality in the struggle over gay marriage. *Social and Cultural Geography*, 7, 807–825.

Richardson, D., Poudel, M., and Laurie, N. (2009) Sexual trafficking in Nepal: Constructing citizenship and livelihoods. *Gender, Place and Culture*, 16, 259–278.

Robinson, V., Hockey, J., and Meah, A. (2004) "What I used to do . . . on my mother's settee": Spatial and emotional aspects of heterosexuality in England. *Gender, Place and Culture*, 11, 417–435.

Rushbrook, D. (2002) Cities, queer space, and the cosmopolitan tourist. *GLQ*, 8, 183–206.

Sandell, J. (2010) Transnational ways of seeing: Sexual and national belonging in *Hedwig and the Angry Inch*. *Gender, Place and Culture*, 17, 231–247.

Sanders, T. (2004) The risks of street prostitution: Punters, police and protestors. *Urban Studies*, 41, 1703–1717.

Simmons, T. (2008) Sexuality and immigration: UK family reunion policy and the regulation of sexual citizens in the European Union. *Political Geography*, 27, 213–230.

Sothern, M. (2007) You could truly be yourself if you just weren't you: Sexuality, disabled body space, and the (neo)liberal politics of self-help. *Environment and Planning D: Society and Space*, 25, 144–159.

Stychin, C. (2006) "Las Vegas is not where we are": Queer readings of the Civil Partnership Act. *Political Geography*, 25, 899–920.

Sugg, K. (2003) Migratory sexualities, diasporic histories, and memory in queer Cuban-American cultural production. *Environment and Planning D: Society and Space*, 21, 461–477.

Talburt, S. and Matus, C. (2012) Orienting ourselves to the gay penguin. *Emotion, Space and Society*, 5 (1), 36–44.

Thomas, M.E. (2004) Pleasure and propriety: Teen girls and the practice of straight space. *Environment and Planning D: Society and Space*, 22, 773–789.

Thomas, M.E. (2011) Sexuality – Part II. In *The Wiley-Blackwell Companion to Human Geography*, ed. J. Agnew and J. Duncan. Oxford: Blackwell, pp. 475–485.

Tucker, A. (2009) *Queer Visibilities: Space, Identity and Interaction in Cape Town*. Oxford: Wiley-Blackwell.

Valentine, G., Skelton, T., and Butler, R. (2003) Coming out and outcomes: Negotiating lesbian and gay identities with, and in, the family. *Environment and Planning D: Society and Space*, 21, 479–499.

Vanderbeck, R., Andersson, J., Valentine, G., Sadgrove, J., and Ward, K. (2011) Sexuality, activism, and witness in the Anglican Communion: The 2008 Lambeth Conference of Anglican bishops. *Annals of the Association of American Geographers*, 101, 1–20.

Visser, G. (2003) Gay men, leisure space and South African cities: The case of Cape Town. *Geoforum*, 34, 123–137.

Waitt, G. (2006) Boundaries of desire: Becoming sexual through the spaces of Sydney's 2002 Gay Games. *Annals of the Association of American Geographers*, 96, 773–787.

Waitt, G. and Gorman-Murray, A. (2011) Journeys and returns: Home, life narratives and remapping sexuality in a regional city. *International Journal of Urban and Regional Research*, 35 (6), 1239–1255.

Waitt, G. and Stapel, C. (2011) "Fornicating on floats"? The cultural politics of the Sydney Mardi Gras Parade beyond the metropolis. *Leisure Studies*, 30, 197–216.

Walsh, K., Shen, H.-H., and Willis, K. (eds.) (2008) Heterosexuality and migration in Asia. *Gender, Place and Culture*, 15.

Webster, G., Chapman, T., and Leib, J. (2010) Sustaining the "societal and scriptural fence": Cultural, social, and political topographies of same-sex marriage in Alabama. *Professional Geographer*, 62, 211–229.

Wilkinson, E. (2009) The emotions least relevant to politics? Queering autonomous activism. *Emotion, Space and Society*, 2, 36–43.

Wright, M. (2004) From protests to politics: Sex work, women's worth, and Ciudad Juárez modernity. *Annals of the Association of American Geographers*, 94, 369–386.

## Chapter 13

# Place

*Patricia L. Price*

## Approaching Place

What could be simpler than place? The (stereo)typical "You are here" definition of the term indicates an unembellished punctuality that could hardly be more straightforward. Why then a whole chapter on place? By way of prelude and as Raymond Williams (1983) was fond of pointing out, there is quite possibly an inverse relationship between the apparent simplicity of a term (e.g., "nature," "culture") and its genealogical depth as well as complexity of current usage.

> "Place" (like space and time) also has an extraordinary range of metaphorical meanings. We talk about the place of art in social life, the place of men in society, our place in the cosmos, and we internalize such notions psychologically in terms of knowing our place or feeling we have a place in the affections or esteem of others. We express norms by putting people, events, and things in their "proper" place and seek to subvert norms by struggling to define a new place . . . from which the oppressed can freely speak. *Place has to be one of the most multilayered and multipurpose keywords in our language.* (Harvey 1996: 208, emphasis added)

Though Williams failed to include "place" among his keywords, place's seeming simplicity obscures a multiplicity of meaning.[1] Inspired by Williams' deft approach to unpacking the density of meanings held within keywords, this chapter excavates the wealth of meaning in "place." Given the centrality of place to cultural geography – indeed, to human geography as a discipline overall – there could hardly be a more central task for this volume.

I begin with a working understanding of the word "place." Without overly belaboring the definitional task, Gieryn's (2000) tripartite definition of place as location, material form,

*The Wiley Blackwell Companion to Cultural Geography*, First Edition.
Edited by Nuala C. Johnson, Richard H. Schein, and Jamie Winders.
© 2013 John Wiley & Sons, Ltd. Published 2016 by John Wiley & Sons, Ltd.

and meaningfulness seems reasonable, as does his insistence that all three aspects of place remain bundled together.

> They cannot be ranked into greater or lesser significance for social life, nor can one be reduced down to an expression of another. Place has a plenitude, a completeness, such that the phenomenon is analytically and substantively destroyed if the three become unraveled or one of them forgotten. (p. 466; see also Agnew 2004)

To inquire into place takes us as far as written records on human musings about the world around us go. As philosopher Edward Casey (1997) has discussed at some length, notions of nothingness based in the absence of place play a central role in most theories of creation. From what Casey terms "the sheer void" – not just emptiness, but "*no-place-at-all*: utter void" (p. 3, emphasis in original) – arose the differentiation that defines place as the scission between heaven and earth, and the differentiation amongst places, whether in the cosmogonies of the Judeo-Christian Bible, Hesiod's *Theogony*, or Navajo creation accounts. When, according for instance to the Book of Genesis, God created dry land and light from the formless darkness, it was place itself that emerged, with its connotations of order, hierarchy, boundaries, specificity, and anchoring. As Casey (1997: 5) asserts, "[c]osmogenesis is topogenesis – throughout and at every step."

Not only is place central to accounts of how the world as we know it came to be, place is also central to historical accounts of how we came to know our world and our place in it. Humans are innately curious about the world around us and about those who occupy territories near and far. Travel writings of explorers from ancient empires are replete with musings about the strange lands and their inhabitants. The Greek geographer Strabo, traveling the circum-Mediterranean world from Egypt to Ethiopia to Rome in the first century CE, invoked the "different good and bad attributes" of place as a key area of inquiry about the world around us (quoted in Relph 1976: 1). Hippocrates' typology of the four bodily humors – phlegmatic, sanguine, choleric, and melancholic – was based upon the relative location of different lands (northern, southern, eastern, and western, respectively) and their influence on human temperament and health. Bernal Díaz del Castillo's (1996) narrative of the conquest of the ancient Aztec empire in the early sixteenth century recounts the astonishment of the Spaniards upon touring Tenochtitlan (Mexico City).

> [S]ome of our soldiers even asked whether the things we saw were not a dream. It is not to be wondered at that I here write it down in this manner, for there is so much to think over that I do not know how to describe it, seeing things as we did that had never been heard of or seen before, not even dreamed about. (pp. 190–191)

In short, human beings are not simply social animals; we are too *spatial* animals, inasmuch as territory – knowing it, owning it, exploring it – matters a great deal.

## Space, Place, and Time

There is a notable tendency among scholars to typologize space, and to hold place as a type of space that has accrued meaning through symbolic investment and repetitive engagement.[2] Though often used interchangeably in everyday parlance, space and place are differentiated from each other in various ways that have implications for the connotations of both. Most simple is a geometric distinction, whereby "Spaces have areas and volumes. Places have space between them" (Cresswell 2004: 8). This definition indicates that space and place are inter-related terms: they need each other in order to exist. A second sort of attempt to distinguish space from place invokes a distinct ontology whereby spaces *are* and places *are produced*; in other words, places are social products. While the "mere existence" of space has been pro-ductively interrogated (Lefebvre 1991; Casey 1997; Massey 2005; Harvey 2006), this second distinction between space and place assigns an abstract, smooth, limitless quality to space, while place – "human in scale and dense with feeling" (Tuan and Strawn 2009: 38) – is associated with specificity, immediacy, stasis, and uniqueness. Space is cerebral, place is expe-riential. Space is thus made into place through human intervention:

> Space is product, the geographical equivalent of the commodity; place, on the other hand, is product *and* work, with the uniqueness of the work of art of the craft of the artisan. Space and place stand in opposition to one another, as the opposition of different kinds of labor (and dif-ferent stages in the production of space). (Dirlik 2001: 18, emphasis in original)

Or as Relph (1976: 29) notes, "[places] are sensed in a chiaroscuro of setting, landscape, ritual, routine, other people, personal experiences, care and concern for home, and in the context of other places." Thus place *qua* place, as opposed to particular places or certainly to space, is notoriously resistant to intellectualization.

Finally, and to add time to the dynamic, places can be approached as pauses of sorts in what would otherwise be an overwhelming, meaningless flow of space-time.

> [M]uch of what is traditionally discussed as "time" and "space" is to be understood ultimately in terms of place: time and space meet in place, through whose needle's eye they are densely threaded together and at once. (Casey 2001: 226)

Or, in the words of David Harvey (1996: 261), "The process of place formation is a process of carving out 'permanences' from the flow of processes creating spatio-temporality. But the 'permanences' – no matter how solid they may seem – are not eternal but always subject to time as 'perpetual perishing'." This continuous crumbling away of the seeming solidity of place is a question to which we will return in more detail later.

The distinction between the smoothness of space and the texture of place has in turn unfurled in multiple additional understandings of space and place, understandings which map onto the principal oppositional categories of modernity. Thus space is active while place is passive, space is cerebral whereas place is experiential, space is associated with male and place with female, space is the arena of capital and place that of labor, and so on. Typically, then, in this modern understanding space is privileged over place. The privileging of space over place is all the more evident when the space/place pairing is aligned with that of the scalar pairing of global/local (Dirlik 2001). In the discourse of globalization, the rapidity of mobility – bodily through travel, economically through trade and capital flows, and intellectu-ally through the movement of ideas – is afforded by the nature of global space, which is hardly ever thought of as punctuated by places; rather, "the global" approaches the feature-lessness of the idealized isotropic plane. The local, by contrast, is particularity and rootedness taken to the extreme.

Some have found the fluidity of the global exhilarating in its association with freedom, lack of recurring encounters, and the shedding of the accountabilities and obligations

associated with being emplaced. Loosening the bonds of place-based (place-bound?) solidarities, such as the village or the nation-state, can constitute an awakening of identity. On the
other hand, some view the emergence of the global with deep trepidation, due to at least two
related factors linked to place: (1) the perception of placelessness as a condition of globalization, and (2) the emergence of an inauthentic relationship between people and place. On the
former, Marc Augé (1995) has labeled those sites associated with global transience – airports,
train stations, hotels – *non-places* precisely to note the slipping away of place particularity
under globalization. Places become emptied out of meaning, indistinguishable and interchangeable, and the self moving through them becomes lost – a condition that Fredric
Jameson (1991) has likened to schizophrenia. As Harvey contends, capitalism reverses the
equation whereby space is transformed into place, unraveling place back to space. As such,
and under late capitalism in particular, place becomes more like space: abstract, smooth,
masculine, cerebral, unanchored. It is important to note that this sentiment predates the late
modern era, surfacing for instance in the work of J.B. Jackson (1970) decrying "other-directed
places" (see also Relph 1976).

Indeed, mid-twentieth-century philosophical work is permeated with concern over the
emergence of a profound sort of homelessness associated with modernity writ large, as well
as modern capitalist relationships, in part because modernity is seen to sunder the previously
authentic ties between people and place. In other words, economic, cultural, and/or political
filters come to mediate what is (usually tacitly) understood to be formerly unmediated and
basic relationships; in particular, the relationship between humans and nature, and the relationship of individual humans to one another. What Gaston Bachelard (1994) understands
quite romantically in terms of the childhood home, or Martin Heidegger (1971) in terms of
"dwelling," is prised open and a level of remove inserted that renders these primal relationships inauthentic. There is thus a profound sense of homelessness, of being adrift in the
world – of displacement – which is associated with late modernity. And, to return to Jameson's
notion of schizophrenia, this prising apart can also be seen to occur within the
individual, who becomes alienated even from her (authentic) self.

Given the term's central status in the discipline of geography, there is a wealth of scholarship on place. To adequately discuss all of this would require a book of its own, and not
surprisingly, such books exist (see for instance Tuan 1977; Adams, Hoelscher, and Till 2001b;
Cresswell 2004). The relationship between place and landscape, for instance, reveals how
the framing and representation of place in particular ways shapes how we value specific
places, how certain patterns of power relations become normalized, how those with less
privilege are erased from view, and underscores the centrality of the visual (Cosgrove 1998;
contributions to Low and Lawrence-Zúñiga 2003; Price 2004; Wylie 2007; contributions to
Malpas 2011). The relationship between place and nature is another voluminous area of
study, interrogating the limits of the human, the dynamic relationship between humans and
nature as well as the flexible boundary between these two notions, and the whole issue of
culture itself (Smith 1984; Jones and Cloke 2002; Castree 2005). In terms of what is seen as
the central and driving characteristics of space, as well, there are wide variations within
approaches by geographers. Those of a more Marxist-inspired bent centralize labor, capital,
and production of place in their scholarship, while those of a more humanistic strain will, as
humanists are wont to do regardless of disciplinary affiliation, focus on the redemptive power
of the human spirit in their work. That humanistic scholars have worked so closely with
place is unsurprising, as many have posited that place awareness, place attachment, and
place-making are central activities of the human condition. "To be human is to live in a world

that is filled with significant places: to be human is to have and to know *your* place" (Relph 1976: 1, emphasis in original; see also Buttimer 1993). Because of the author's own inclination toward a humanistic approach, the balance of this chapter will explore this in more detail with respect to place. This is more a matter of housekeeping than anything else, and is not intended to discount in the slightest the wide topical and political latitude as well as the contradictions amongst geographers in our understandings of place.

## Crafting Place

Geographers and others working from a more or less humanistic perspective centralize place as a lived and dynamic entity. Places are made through human interaction over time with a locale and its elements; in turn, identities both individual and collective are solidified through human relationships to place. "In our inhabitation of places there is a looping effect between our identification of places and our identities" (Sundstrom 2003: 90). Seen through the lens of the individual, place is subjective and very much in the eye of the beholder. Indeed, the uniqueness of place is such that no two people will have exactly the same experience of place. Seen as a collectively generated entity, place is frequently portrayed as a weaving together of diverse individual experiences, and as such having a textural dimensionality. "If space is rather a simultaneity of stories-so-far, then places are collections of those stories, articulations within the wider power-geometries of space" (Massey 2005: 130). Metaphoric allusions to arts of all sorts – weaving, painting, writing, dance, and theater chief amongst them – prevail in humanistic understandings of place as an actively crafted entity.

### Writing Place

That "text" nests within the term "texture" is no accident, for narrative plays an important role in the construction of place, just as places themselves play important roles in narratives. The human relationship to place is mediated symbolically, with our most important symbolic structure being language. As Relph (1976) notes, it is requisite that places be named, as opposed to spaces which are typically unnamed: place-naming is a way that "space is claimed for man [*sic*]" (p. 16). Beyond naming, there is an important relationship between narrative and place, for place-worlds are, fundamentally, story-worlds. Narrative is a primary approach to the carving out of the "permanences" invoked by Harvey to define the act of place-making. Narrative allows the flow of time-space to be arrested and shaped in ways that make deliberate sense of events' interlinkages to one another and to a broader trajectory of meaning, and that allows us to emplace ourselves in that flow of events in meaningful ways (Price 2010). In other words, narrative allows us to plot place. Thus "places not only feature in inhabitants' (and geographers') narratives, they are narratives in their own right" (Rodman 2003: 206).

Yet a tendency in place-narratives is to posit a romantic notion whereby places are timeless and unchanging, as are the pre-given identities seen to be rooted in those places. Perhaps the fiction of place and identity as permanent serves, religion-like, as a mental bulwark of sorts against the inexorabilities of time and space upon ourselves as ultimately impermanent, mortal, corruptible. "Since time and space are intangible and dauntingly infinite, we cling intellectually and emotionally to our experiences and memories of the material world that is so reassuringly solid" (Adams, Hoelscher, and Till 2001a: xiii). Yet the fictional permanence of places and identities as unchanging also serves to entrap people in the pre-given notions about the places they are associated with, and to allow for defensive senses of place which are intolerant of difference and change. Doreen Massey has long cautioned about the regressive sense of place, arguing instead for an "extroverted" notion of places, which, rather than having boundaries around them, are more like nodes in open and multi-scalar networks of connectivity. Most recently, Massey's (2005) concept of the "thrown-together-ness" of place explicitly works against the romantic notions of timeless places and pre-given identities rooted in places. Massey notes that places have no inherent coherence; rather, it is we who construct that notion, through our stories about places and ourselves in relation to places. She notes that this is the case even when we are talking about the geological makeup of places, using the example of Skiddaw, a "massive block of a mountain, over 3000 feet high, grey and stony; not pretty, but impressive; immovable, timeless" (p. 131) in England's Lake District where Massey was staying with her sister. Viewed in the long span of geological time, even the massive Skiddaw – seemingly so fixed and emblematic of this place and people's relationships to it over the centuries – was on the move. "*Immigrant rocks*: the rocks of Skiddaw are immigrant rocks, just passing through here, like my sister and me only rather more slowly, and changing all the while" (p. 137, emphasis in original).

Massey's approach to the impermanence of place through geological time might be termed a place-biography. Biographies spanning a mere human lifetime are another way that place is shaped through what Hayden Lorimer (2003) calls "small stories." In Lorimer's approach, place is constituted as a nexus of intersecting biographies. He used the historical traces offered by notebooks, photographs, journal entries, personal accounts, and letters to glimpse into how a month-long winter residential field course at Glenmore Lodge, located below Scotland's Cairngorm Mountains, brought together biographies that shaped places at a particular moment in time. In 1951, 14-year-old Margaret Jack was invited to attend a month-long winter residential field course for girls at Glenmore Lodge. Robin Murray, a PhD student in Aberdeen University's Geography Department, was the girls' field studies instructor. The intersecting biographical experiences of Margaret and Robin, argues Lorimer, are every bit as important in understanding the construction of place – the place of the geography department where Robin studied and worked, the Lodge, the Cairngorm Mountains, and of Scotland itself – as the grander historical narratives that often encourage us to overlook these "small stories." "As unlikely subjects, Margaret Jack and Robin Murray do more than simply put this story *in place*: their presence, captured in a variety of forms, propels its narrative" (Lorimer 2003: 202, emphasis in original). And in turn, biographies provide a way (through narrative) of participating in place as a part of one's own history. It is to the participatory dimension of place that we now turn.

## Place and Bodies in Motion

Humanistic understandings of place emphasize its sensory, experiential dimensions. It is through participating, over time, in a locale and with others who also inhabit that locale, that place emerges. This participation typically involves some sort of active engagement of the body. With respect to place, the body is important "as a physical and biological entity, as lived experience, and as a center of agency, a location for speaking and acting on the world" (Low 2009: 26). Phenomenology, a branch of philosophy that centralizes the role of intentional experience in generating knowledge of the world, has been employed by geographers who suggest that bodily engagement in the world around us creates an experiential lifeworld and, thereby, an operational definition of place rooted in experience (Relph 1976; Seamon 1979; Tuan 1991). A phenomenological approach to place might well be a strategy for recovering the unmediated and authentic relationship to nature, other, and self, and as such reactionary in its stance vis-à-vis modernity (but see Rose 2010); alternatively, it can be seen as a way of highlighting the role of the human body in our experience of the world. Edward Casey (2009) goes so far as to assert that places can *only* be experienced through bodies, while place itself is scaled to the human body:

> A place cannot be too enormous or it ceases to be a place (i.e., it becomes a "region" in the usual sense of this term as signifying a large stretch of space), nor can it be too tiny (then it becomes a mere "spot"): it is scaled to the lived body, I would insist. (Casey 2001: 229)

The most common form of human bodily engagement with place, and certainly the most commonly remarked upon in writings by British geographers, is walking (Edensor 2000; Gray 2003; Wylie 2002, 2005; Murphy 2011). Our upright bipedal motion, variously purposeful and pleasureful, shapes our experience of place, as well as shaping place itself.

> Walking has created paths, roads, trade routes, generated local and cross-continental senses of place, shaped cities, parks, generated maps, guidebooks, gear, and, further afield, a vast library of walking stories and poems, of pilgrimages, mountaineering expeditions, meanders, and summer picnics. (Solnit 2001: 4)

Put more directly by the artist Andy Goldsworthy (1990: 1), "Place is found by walking." Walking generates a particular way of meditatively, deeply experiencing place, leading to what Adams (2001) has termed a "peripatetic sense of place."

The peripatetic sense of place is, however, becoming progressively eroded in a world where humans are ever more moved and informed by technologies rather than the power of two feet. Adams' (2001: 187) lament that the disappearing "stroll as a source of pleasure and the foot as a means of serious transportation, which together were for a long time at the root of a strong and deep sense of place," can surely be seen as part and parcel of the general regret at the loss of place in modern times discussed earlier. The experience of place is thinned as the experience of walking becomes less necessary, and less possible with the concomitant loss of public places through which to walk.

Other forms of bodily movement, as well, are the subject of geographers' musings about place. Dance (Thrift 1997), aeromobility (Cwerner 2009), automobility (Featherstone 2005), and cycling (Spinney 2009) provide some examples. As with walking, these modalities of bodily engagement with place go beyond the functional to constitute creative activities through which place and self are literally mobilized. Remarking on setting up camp, for instance, John Wylie (2002) asserts that the overnight stay leads to a different, not just an enhanced, experience of place, as compared to a day trip:

> The erection of the tent (the building of a dwelling) does not "add" to the experience, does not give "depth and texture" to an otherwise "shallow" or fleeting vision, does not make one feel "more connected" with the environment than a camera-toting tourist. Driving the pegs into the ground, muddying one's shoes and knees, does not bring one "closer" to the landscape "itself," rather it is a *creative* act which opens up a *new* spatiality and a *new* temporality. (p. 449, emphasis in original)

The non-representational view of place as dynamic and sensual in turn touches on debates with respect to the fragility of place and its ever-crumbling and reassembling nature (e.g., Malpas 1999) versus the perdurability of place (e.g., Casey 2001); in short, to the permanence or perishability of place and of self (see also Lorimer 2005). In addition, to view movement as constitutive of both place and self tacitly counters notions of place as pause in the flow of space-time. Movement of the self through space, rather than arrest through representation, catalyzes place, as for instance an asphalt road becomes a place "remade each time I walk down it" (Low 2009: 30; see also Macpherson 2010). In this view, which touches on non-representational theories in geography, place is dynamic and in tension with the self, rather than a structured (through the framing of landscape, narrative, or biography) pause amidst flow onto which meaning is layered over time. Thus walking and biography are two very different ways of being in-place.

## The Intimacy of Place

Last but not least, there is an important emotional component to the relationship between self and place (Tuan 1991, Smith *et al.* 2009). Place is deeply felt in childhood, a time when the conventions encouraging socio-spatial distancing – respect, fear, suspicion, and restraint among them – do not have as strong a hold as they do on adults. "Children relate to people and objects with a directness and intimacy that are the envy of adults bruised by life" (Tuan 1991: 137). Yet place attachments deepen and strengthen as experience accumulates – indeed, the need for place is one of the most elemental of human needs. The formation of emotional, sentimental bonds between people and a place, and people with one another in place, is an important component of being human in the world. Place attachments play central roles in human biographies.

> Place attachments result from accumulated biographical experiences: we associate places with the fulfilling, terrifying, traumatic, triumphant, secret events that happened to us personally there. The longer people have lived in a place, the more rooted they feel, and the greater their attachment to it. (Gieryn 2000: 481)

The positioning inside versus outside of place is an important distinction with respect to identity, resting as heavily as it does on belonging and exclusion. Thus one of the most central emotional needs with respect to place is belonging; concomitantly, one of the most universally feared conditions is that of exclusion. This is surely evidenced in the fact that exile – the forceful removal of the self from place – is one of the most universally grieved plights.

> Place-making, by setting up boundaries, gives rise to the polarities of "in" and "out," "us" and "them." Being "in," an insider, is good; being "out," an outsider, is bad. And so it is a great misfortune to be exiled – as an outcast or only a little less so, to be a stranger or foreigner, raised in villages and towns beyond the pale. (Tuan and Strawn 2009: 30)

The removal from place, and even more so the removal of place, or even the prospect of an unknown place, can incite emotions of anxiety, dread, terror, and panic amongst humans, because it violates our elemental need for place predicated on experience, and leads to "the existential predicament of place-bereft individuals. That predicament is one of place-panic: depression or terror even at the idea, and still more in the experience, of an empty place"

(Casey 1997: 6). At best, exile accounts are replete with emotions of sadness, nostalgia, and longing.

Home, "the topography of our intimate being" (Bachelard 1994: xxxvi), is the site of our most intimate of relationships with place, as well as one of the first that we experience. Homes (places invested with meaning and experience) and houses (the physical structures within which most human homes reside) frame the family dynamics that are so central to shaping us as adults. They provide refuge from the outside world at times in life (infancy, illness, old age) when we are particularly fragile. They nurture us by providing a place for reproduction, regeneration, and respite. The houses of childhood are familiar territory, one to which we return in our memories as adults as we seek to stabilize our sense of self. "[B]y remembering 'houses' and 'rooms,' we learn to 'abide' within ourselves . . . the house images move in both directions: they are in us as much as we are in them" (Bachelard 1994: xxxvii).

Homemaking, as with place-making more generally, is closely connected to boundaries and processes of inclusion and exclusion.

> "[H]ome" is often understood as a place within which only certain people and things belong . . .
> For example, a house or a flat where a person lives is made into "home" partly through their ability to spatially exclude certain people. (Holloway and Hubbard 2001: 77)

In turn, one of the hallmarks of an established place is the ability to articulate and enforce its boundaries. Over time, the coherence and solidification of distinctive places sharpen the boundaries between that place and others: "Social and cultural cohesion within each place gains at the expense of its people's sympathy for outsiders and the outside" (Tuan and Strawn 2009: 30).

Love is not a tremendously common theme in the scholarship on place attachments and emotions. Yet "love of place" – topophilia – is a well-recognized hallmark of the positive human relationship to place. Yi-Fu Tuan, whose book *Topophilia* (1974) provides a lengthy consideration of the affective bond between people and place, asserts that those with the most intimate connections to place, namely, children and farmers, have the strongest experience of topophilia. Gaston Bachelard (1994), who also employs the term topophilia, takes a more romantic approach to the affective connections to place through what he terms "the poetics of the house."

## Rethinking Place

Without a doubt, the sort of unwavering, unconditional love of place expressed by Tuan and Bachelard is an idealized relationship, one that is quickly belied by the too often violent, tragic realities of the social relationships that occur in places. A more realistic treatment of love in relationship to place may be found in work that deals, for instance, with landscapes of memory, for such work is cognizant of the multiple emotions associated with love and place. In the case of the seaside memorial benches on Mullion Cove, for example, love works in tandem with other emotions: loss, melancholy, loneliness. Indeed, the openness presupposed by love invites fracture and distancing and loss, of the self from others, of the self from place, of the self from the self. "The constitutive fissure of the geographies of love thus becomes the ruination of any phenomenological sense of the 'world' " (Wylie 2009: 285). Emotions (and philosophical approaches) predicated on union of self and place instead reveal the impossibility of such a union, and of the self as precariously placed at best.

Thus questions about place, and the role of the self and the self's experiences, emotions, and movements as they relate to place, dredge up some of the most profound questions about human existence on earth. Can such a thing as a dis-emplaced self exist? Is there such a thing as place at all without the self? What is the nature of the human need for place – is it an innate component of the human soul, or a learned trait? Is an unmediated relationship to nature, others, and oneself possible? What does it mean to be in the world? How do we understand the balance between the permanence and the fragility of place, and of self?

Far from being a dead-end topic, place continues to encapsulate some of the deepest human desires and paradoxes.

## Notes

1   Place is, however, a particular focus in many of Williams' novels.
2   Though see Casey (1996), who argues that in fact place precedes space, with the latter being a modern derivation of the former.

## References

Adams, P.C. (2001) Peripatetic imagery and peripatetic sense of place. In *Textures of Place: Exploring Humanist Geographies*, ed. P.C. Adams, S. Hoelscher, and K.E. Till. Minneapolis: University of Minnesota Press, pp. 186–206.

Adams, P.C., Hoelscher, S., and Till, K.E. (2001a) Place in context: Rethinking humanist geographies. In *Textures of Place: Exploring Humanist Geographies*, ed. P.C. Adams, S. Hoelscher, and K.E. Till. Minneapolis: University of Minnesota Press, pp. xiii–xxxiii.

Adams, P.C., Hoelscher, S., and Till, K.E. (2001b) Place in context: Rethinking humanist geographies. In *Textures of Place: Exploring Humanist Geographies*, ed. P.C. Adams, S. Hoelscher, and K.E. Till. Minneapolis: University of Minnesota Press, pp. xiii–xxxiii.

Agnew, J. (2004) Space-place. In *Spaces of Geographical Thought*, ed. P. Cloke and R. Johnston. London: Sage, pp. 81–96.

Augé, M. (1995) *Non-Places: Introduction to an Anthropology of Supermodernity*. London: Verso.

Bachelard, G. (1994/1958) *The Poetics of Space*, trans. M. Jolas, foreword by J.R. Stilgoe. Boston: Beacon Press.

Buttimer, A. (1993) *Geography and the Human Spirit*. Baltimore: Johns Hopkins University Press.

Casey, E.S. (1996) How to get from space to place in a fairly short stretch of time: Phenomenological prolegomena. In *Senses of Place*, ed. S. Feld and K. Basso. Santa Fe: School of American Research Press, pp. 13–52.

Casey, E.S. (1997) *The Fate of Place: A Philosophical History*. Berkeley: University of California Press.

Casey, E.S. (2001) J.E. Malpas's *Place and Experience*: A philosophical topography. *Philosophy and Geography*, 4 (2), 225–230.

Casey, E.S. (2009) *Getting Back into Place, Second Edition: Toward a Renewed Understanding of the Place-World*. Bloomington: Indiana University Press.

Castree, N. (2005) *Nature*. New York: Routledge.

Cosgrove, D. (1998) *Social Formation and Symbolic Landscape*. Madison: University of Wisconsin Press.

Cresswell, T. (2004) *Place: A Short Introduction*. Oxford: Blackwell.

Cwerner, S. (2009) Introducing aeromobilities. In *Aeromobilities*, ed. S. Cwerner, S. Kesselring, and J. Urry. Abingdon: Routledge, pp. 1–22.

Díaz del Castillo, B. (1996/1956) *The Discovery and Conquest of Mexico: 1517–1521*, trans. and intro. A.P. Maudslay, new intro. by H. Thomas. Cambridge, MA: Da Capo Press.

Dirlik, A. (2001) Place-based imagination: Globalism and the politics of place. In *Places and Politics in an Age of Globalization*, ed. R. Prazniak and A. Dirlik. Lanham: Rowman and Littlefield, pp. 15–51.

Edensor, T. (2000) Walking in the British countryside: Reflexivity, embodied practices and ways to escape. *Body and Society*, 6 (3/4), 81–107.

Featherstone, M. (2005) Automobilities: An introduction. In *Automobilities*, ed. M. Featherstone, N. Thrift, and J. Urry. Thousand Oaks, CA: Sage, pp. 1–24.

Gieryn, T.F. (2000) A space for place in sociology. *Annual Review of Sociology*, 26, 463–496.

Goldsworthy, A. (1990) *A Collaboration with Nature*. New York: Abrams.

Gray, J. (2003) Open spaces and dwelling places: Being at home on the hill farms in the Scottish Borders. In *The Anthropology of Place and Space: Locating Culture*, ed. S.M. Low and D. Lawrence-Zúñiga. Oxford: Blackwell, pp. 224–244.

Harvey, D. (1996) *Justice, Nature and the Geography of Difference*. Oxford: Blackwell.

Harvey, D. (2006) *Spaces of Global Capitalism: A Theory of Uneven Geographical Development*. New York: Routledge.

Heidegger, M. (1971) *Poetry, Language, Thought*, trans. and intro. A. Hofstadter. New York: Harper and Row.

Holloway, L. and Hubbard, P. (2001) *People and Place: The Extraordinary Geographies of Everyday Life*. Harlow: Prentice Hall.

Jackson, J.B. (1970) Other-directed houses. In *Landscapes: Selected Writings of J.B. Jackson*, ed. E.H. Zube. Amherst: University of Massachusetts Press, pp. 55–72.

Jameson, F. (1991) *Postmodernism, or the Cultural Logic of Late Capitalism*. Durham, NC: Duke University Press.

Jones, O. and Cloke, P. (2002) Orchard. In *Tree Cultures: The Place of Trees and Trees in their Place*, ed. O. Jones and P. Cloke. Berg: Oxford, pp. 123–142.

Lefebvre, H. (1991/1974) *The Production of Space*, trans. D. Nicholson-Smith. Oxford: Blackwell.

Lorimer, H. (2003) Telling small stories: Spaces of knowledge and the practice of geography. *Transactions of the Institute of British Geographers*, 28 (2), 197–217.

Lorimer, H. (2005) Cultural geography: The busyness of being "more-than-representational." *Progress in Human Geography*, 29 (1), 83–94.

Low, S.M. (2009) Towards an anthropological theory of place and space. *Semiotica*, 175, 21–37.

Low, S.M. and Lawrence-Zúñiga, D. (eds.) (2003) *The Anthropology of Place and Space: Locating Culture*. Oxford: Blackwell.

Macpherson, H. (2010) Non-representational approaches to body–landscape relations. *Geographical Compass*, 4 (1), 1–13.

Malpas, J.E. (1999) *Place and Experience: A Philosophical Topography*. Cambridge: Cambridge University Press.

Malpas, J.E. (ed.) (2011) *The Place of Landscape: Concepts, Contexts, Studies*. Cambridge, MA: MIT Press.

Massey, D. (2005) *For Space*. London: Sage.

Murphy, J. (2011) Walking a public geography through Ireland and Scotland. *Geographical Journal*, 177 (4), 367–379.

Price, P.L. (2004) *Dry Place: Landscapes of Belonging and Exclusion*. Minneapolis: University of Minnesota Press.

Price, P.L. (2010) Cultural geography and the stories we tell ourselves. *Cultural Geographies*, 17 (2), 203–210.

Relph, E. (1976) *Place and Placelessness*. London: Pion.

Rodman, M. (2003) Empowering place: Multilocality and multivocality. In *The Anthropology of Place and Space: Locating Culture*, ed. S.M. Low and D. Lawrence-Zúñiga. Oxford: Blackwell, pp. 204–223.

Rose, M. (2010) Back to back: A response to "Landscape, absence, and the geographies of love." *Transactions of the Institute of British Geographers*, 35, 141–144.

Seamon, D. (1979) *A Geography of the Lifeworld*. New York: St. Martin's.

Smith, M., Davidson, J., Cameron, L., and Bondi, L. (2009) Geography and emotion – emerging constellations. In *Emotion, Place and Culture*, ed. M. Smith, J. Davidson, L. Cameron, and L. Bondi. Farnham: Ashgate, pp. 1–20.

Smith, N. (1984) *Uneven Development: Nature, Capital, and the Production of Space*. Oxford: Blackwell.

Solnit, R. (2001) *Wanderlust: A History of Walking*. New York: Penguin.

Spinney, J. (2009) Cycling the city: Movement, meaning and method. *Geography Compass*, 3 (2), 817–835.

Sundstrom, R.R. (2003) Race and place: Social space in the production of human kinds. *Philosophy and Geography*, 6 (1), 83–95.

Thrift, N. (1997) The still point: Expressive embodiment and dance. In *Geographies of Resistance*, ed. S. Pile and M. Keith. London: Routledge, pp. 124–151.

Tuan, Y.F. (1977) *Space and Place: The Perspective of Experience*. Minneapolis: University of Minnesota Press.

Tuan, Y.F. (1991) Language and the making of place: A narrative-descriptive approach. *Annals of the Association of American Geographers*, 81 (4), 684–696.

Tuan, Y.F. and Strawn, M.A. (2009) *Religion: From Place to Placelessness*. Chicago: Center for American Places at Columbia College Chicago.

Williams, R. (1983/1976) *Keywords: A Vocabulary of Culture and Society*, revised edition. London: Fontana.

Wylie, J. (2002) An essay on ascending Glastonbury Tor. *Geoforum*, 33 (4), 441–454.

Wylie, J. (2005) A single day's walking: Narrating self and landscape on the South West Coast Path. *Transactions of the Institute of British Geographers*, 30 (2), 234–247.

Wylie, J. (2007) *Landscape*. New York: Routledge.

Wylie, J. (2009) Landscape, absence and the geographies of love. *Transactions of the Institute of British Geographers*, 34 (3), 275–289.

# Chapter 14

# Nationalism

## John Agnew

March 17, 2011 marked the 150th anniversary of the formal Unification of Italy, although that task was not completed until Rome was conquered and the pope retreated to the Vatican some ten years later. There was not much celebration. While there were formal ceremonies and some commentators decried the lack of popular enthusiasm, many historians and political activists of various stripes either declared the Italian national project a failure for not having created a strong sense of nationhood (e.g., Ginsborg 2010; Gentile 2011) or saw the day as an opportunity to declare their indifference or their preference for local and regional identities over the putative national one (Biorcio 2010; *La Repubblica* 2011). This could be seen as exemplary of a more general crisis of the so-called nation-hyphen-state. Localisms and region-alisms, religious affiliations, supranational and international organizations, and the increasing difficulties of national-state governments in managing economic and cultural challenges would all seem to threaten the apparent monopoly that nation-states and the nationalist movements that often inspired them, as in the Italian case, have long had in defining popular political identities and interests (e.g., Antonsich 2009).

Yet, I think that this claim is overstated. Italy was never successfully unified in the sense typically given to "unified" as the achievement of a powerful national identity that over-whelmed or subordinated all others (Patriarca 2010). The originating movement of the Risorgimento in the mid-nineteenth century split into parts at the time of Unification, none of which thereafter engaged the political imagination of the mass of the population of the peninsula and islands that became its territory (Banti 2011). The experience of fascism can be seen as an effort at forced unification that finally failed to have that effect even if it did arguably make the trains run on time. Of course, during that period Italians seemed to be among the most nationalist of peoples. That this proved to be temporary should give us pause. What are the lessons here? There are two, I think, which provide the basis for thinking

*The Wiley Blackwell Companion to Cultural Geography*, First Edition.
Edited by Nuala C. Johnson, Richard H. Schein, and Jamie Winders.
© 2013 John Wiley & Sons, Ltd. Published 2016 by John Wiley & Sons, Ltd.

about nationalism in a cultural-geographical framework. Nationalism does not have a timeless popular appeal and it does not appeal equally everywhere.

Probably the best definition of nationalism I have been able to find comes from the historian Robert H. Wiebe (2002: 5), who wants to avoid demonizing nationalism (as is typical among many contemporary intellectuals) but nevertheless take it seriously as a powerful political sentiment and program in the modern world: "Nationalism is the desire among people who believe that they share a common ancestry and a common destiny to live under their own government on land sacred to their history." It is, therefore, the most territorial of political ideologies based on cultural beliefs about a shared space occupied by a kin-like, ethnic, or affinity group who face common dangers and bring to these a social bond forged through the trials and tribulations of a common history brought about by a common geography. The very space occupied by the group is seen as part and parcel of the group's identity in a way that is not the case with the major political ideologies with which nationalism has competed over the past two hundred years or so: liberalism and socialism. When economic transactions are powerfully contained by state boundaries, nationalism gains a material basis that the other ideologies lack and which makes them ever vulnerable to collapsing into a nationalist form. It is no coincidence, therefore, that much socialism has been of the "national" or "in-one-country" varieties and that liberalism is usually hedged by claims about individual rights, property claims, and trade relationships that are enforced and defended by national states. Nationalism has benefited immeasurably from its alliance with states but this has also led to its greatest excesses.

Writing about nationalism is fraught with intellectual and political dangers. On the one hand, there is a tendency to diminish nationalism because of the presumed intemperance it has generated in modern politics or the seemingly irrational challenge, particularly to intellectuals, it poses to preferred brands of liberalism or socialism. On the other hand, there is a tendency to celebrate it as a means for groups subordinated by others to "liberate" themselves or to see it as reflecting deep-seated or primordial attachments to group and territory that provide "roots" in an otherwise chaotic and disturbing world. The political theorist John Dunn (1979: 55) captures this duality to nationalism eloquently when he writes:

> Nationalism is the starkest political shame of the twentieth century, the deepest, most intractable and yet most unanticipated blot on the political history of the world since the year 1900. But it is also the very tissue of modern political sentiment, the most widespread, the most unthinking and the most immediate political disposition of all at least among the literate populations of the modern world.

From this viewpoint, ignoring nationalism is as dangerous as mindlessly celebrating it.

Defining it is one thing, but how is this explosive sentiment usually regarded? It is often thought of as a political ideology lauding a preference for and the superiority of one's nation and nationality in comparison to those of foreigners. One influential strand of thinking, associated above all with the early nineteenth-century philosopher Hegel and those following in his footsteps, views nationalism as an autonomous force or causal power that brings about the end of history with the emergence of the modern (national) state. Nationalism as the "spirit of the people" is a form of consciousness that will come to dominate all others. In fact, its history is intimately connected to the growth of popular sovereignty (the people should rule) in relation to state power and the challenge to state power from liberal and socialist ideologies (Yack 2001). But this history is also one in which nationalism has had to be *articulated* and *organized* as a form of political expression and has had to be *based* on popular support gained from populations with alternative political possibilities. In other words – and this is what a second strand of thinking emphasizes – nationalism is a practical politics and not an autonomous force. It is not just a popular sentiment but also a program of political action. In this light, nationalism's key claims are that (1) those who constitute a nation should have their own state; (2) the nation and the state should map onto one another by means of a common territory that is the historic "homeland" of the nation; and (3) a national identity (or sense of belonging) should win out over other possible political identities (Breuilly 1982; Conversi 1999; Yiftachel 2000).

The two strands of thinking – nationalism as an autonomous force in history and nationalism as practical politics – persist, even if the second is today somewhat ascendant. What is certain is that academic interest in nationalism has exploded since the 1980s after a long period, dating from the 1940s, when interest faded except among those focused on the independence movements in the colonies of Europe's declining empires. An undoubted revival of academic interest in nationalism since the 1980s after a long hiatus can be read as symptomatic of the revival of nationalism in the world at large following the end of the US–Soviet Cold War and the stability it imposed on the world's political map. But even this claim fails to engender consensus. Much of what is today often put down to "nationalism" is in fact either a revival of extreme religious beliefs (as in the usage of Islamic *jihad* by many groups such as al-Qaeda and Hamas) or an upsurge of local warlordism in the face of weak governments (as in Somalia and Afghanistan) rather than the expression of true national groups in search of or reviving states on their collective behalf (Wiebe 2002). Nevertheless, reports of nationalism's death or decline have proved premature before. Indeed, in contemporary Europe, Asia, and the United States, nationalism seems anything but a spent force (e.g., Comaroff and Stern, 1995; Roshwald 2006; Ó Tuathail 2009; Meer, Dwyer, and Modood 2010; Webster 2011). To a considerable extent it is fair to say that "Rulers in modern nation-states are no longer legitimized by the principles of dynastic succession, God's grace, or civilizational progress but that they are expected to care for their own, ethnically defined people" (Cederman, Wimmer, and Min 2010: 94). Perhaps seven specific aspects of nationalism define the main features of contemporary debate and dissent. In this chapter I take each of these in turn to illustrate the ways in which "nationalism" currently figures in cultural geography and closely allied fields.

## Taking Nationalism More Seriously

With nationalism, as opposed to socialism and liberalism, many of those who study or make proclamations about it tend to see the people who subscribe to it as cultural dopes. "They should know better" is the implicit subtext, but they have been fooled or misled into it by self-serving state elites inventing traditions or by their own atavistic attachments to place and linguistic/religious groups. The implication is, obviously, that identifying by social class or pursuing individual interests are rational approaches to self-identification. In this way frequently undeclared and normative commitments to class and individual self as better sources of identification than nationality lead to a dismissal of nationalism as a legitimate type of political ideology.

Three ways of seeming to engage with nationalism but essentially dismissing it have achieved dominance in contemporary Western social and cultural studies. These must be challenged in order to take nationalism seriously as a powerful type of politics in the contemporary world. The first, associated most closely with the widely cited book by Benedict Anderson, *Imagined Communities: Reflections on the Origins and Spread of Nationalism* (1983), is that nationalism appeals simply to an "imagined community" that is created and organized by the spread of books and reading in national vernacular languages. In fact, of course, "print capitalism," as Anderson terms it, is only one of a mass of technological and cultural innovations that have materially ordered the world into national-state spaces – from highways and railways radiating from capital cities, national currencies and economic regulation, and systems of weights and measures to school systems and educational credentials, national churches, government systems, and cultural production of books, films, and music. The appeal of nationalism rests initially and finally in the fact that in many parts of the world the political organization of territory into national states has created real, not simply imagined, *material* communities of interest and identity in which large numbers of residents see their fate tied to that of the national state or, if they do not have one of their own, obtaining one for themselves. The crucial alliance of putative nation (imagined as it certainly is) with state-organized territory, therefore, provides the breeding ground for nationalism (Mann 1992; Smith 1999; Wiebe 2000).

Second, nationalism is often discussed independently of its ideological competitors, as if its development were separate from that of socialism and liberalism. With remarkably few exceptions, the study of nationalism has become separated from the study of the other great "isms" that took root in late nineteenth-century Europe and spread with it into the rest of the world with European colonialism. Yet all three grew in the context of the disruption of local peasant societies by industrialization and urbanization, mass migration, and ideologies promising totalistic solutions to contemporary problems of exploitation (socialism), limited citizenship rights (liberalism), and increased economic and military competition (nationalism). Although they were often competitors, after 1914 they also became collaborators, with nationalism as the victor, as socialism and liberalism both came to define their goals in national-state terms. One important cause of nationalism's success was its ability to combine an appeal to fictive kinship often based on teaching a common vernacular language in elementary schools with a clear identification of an "enemy" against whom the nation was embattled for this or that reason (economic, social, religious, etc.). Neither socialism nor liberalism had this mobilizing power: they could appeal to specific interests but not to the lethal combination of identity and interests fused with territory that nationalism encouraged (Dunn 1979; Brustein 1996; Hechter 2000; Harmes 2011).

Finally, nationalism undoubtedly did develop in popular appeal alongside the growth of industrial capitalism and "modernization" in Europe in the late nineteenth and early twentieth centuries (Gellner 1983). It received a further boost during the process of decolonization in the years following World War II, both in former colonies as they embarked on "nation-building" and in the "home countries" as they adjusted to an unaccustomed smallness with the loss of their empires (Murray 1997). A good case can be made that in fact European colonialism provided a necessary circumstance for the development of nationalism in Europe in the first place, with regard to both competition between European states for overseas empires' stimulating national enmities and empire-building's encouraging a sense of national-civilizational (and racial) superiority on the part of European nationalities over the colonized natives within "their" empires (Said 1993; Agnew and Corbridge 1995). But, the conventional wisdom suggests, following the view that nationalism is "caused" by, not just correlated with, modernization or industrial capitalism, that (1) nations are always the product of nationalism and (2) in the face of economic globalization and massive international migration nationalism can be expected to go into decline (e.g., Hobsbawm 1992).

With respect to the first of these points, it is not difficult to show, at least in many European cases, that some kind of proto-nation preexisted the arrival of nationalism (see, e.g., Smith 2002). Though nationalism is a modern phenomenon, therefore, there is no need to presume that nations or nationalities are likewise. This is a fallacy present in much of the contemporary literature. The second point, if anything, is made more insistently but is equally wrong-headed. To Nigel Harris (1990: 284), for example, "migration subverts the artificial cultural homogeneity which states have instilled in their citizens. . . . The greater the movement of peoples, the more that culture will come to be fashioned by people from many other sources." If anything, however, migration has often underwritten nationalism rather than written its epitaph. For example, the rise of Irish nationalism in the mid-nineteenth century is closely connected to emigration to the United States and the radical Irish nationalism of Irish Americans. Likewise, Jewish nationalism or Zionism grew out of large-scale international migration and the search for a Jewish homeland to bring the diaspora together in a single territory. Increased movement, therefore, can stimulate identity with a lost homeland rather than wipe it out. More generally, actually existing nationalism is complexly related to religious, linguistic, and economic divisions all held in tension by a primary group commitment to occupation and domination of a common space or national territory. It is not and never has been simply a "functional" response to modernization, the rise of the state, or industrial capitalism. As a result, nationalism will not soon decline or disappear (Chatterjee 1986; Mortimer 1999; Peckham 2001; Wiebe 2002).

## Nationalism and Territory

To geographers the most outstanding feature of nationalism is its unvarying claim to a territorial homeland (Anderson 1988; Murphy 2002; Yiftachel 2000, 2002). This is the feature shared by all nationalisms regardless of how they came about or where they are. Many students of nationalism are confused about the relationship between nationalism and territory. Wiebe (2000: 54), for example, misses the point when he states that "nationalist loyalties are . . . geographically indeterminate. They move wherever people move; they do not bounce off boundary walls, as Anderson would have it." Here the fact that supporters of a nationalist movement may be widely scattered is used to deny that nationalism *always* involves claiming a physical national homeland or, in other words, that nationalism is inherently territorial in its central claim, as Wiebe (2002: 5) himself suggests elsewhere, to monopolize for their nation "land sacred to their history." The fusion of a piece of land with the symbolic and mythified history of the nation is what gives nationalism such symbolic power immediately related to the sites and circumstances of everyday life when compared to the often more abstract claims of liberalism and socialism. The Serb nationalist obsession with Kosovo as the "historic core" of Serbia and the competing claims of Zionists and Palestinian nationalists to the same patches of land are only two of the best known cases of this relentless focus by nationalists on "our" territory. Incompatible land claims are also what make so many nationalist conflicts intractable and violent. At the same time, it is the sacredness of the land that makes the possibility of redemption through violent "cleansing" or removal of the competing other not only feasible but mandatory (Thrift 2007).

Two questions as to the precise character of the relationship between nationalism and territory have exercised considerable recent interest. One asks: when did the nation-in-its-territory become a subject of veneration? The purpose here is to ascertain how the map-image of the national territory and sense of "territorial destiny" figure in the genesis of nationalism. The other asks: how did nationalism reconfigure understandings of "home" such that the local (and familiar) became part of a nationalist "homeland"? The focus here is on the local production of the nation.

Responses to the first question tend to place the origins in either late medieval/early modern Europe or in Europe in the eighteenth century. Writers in the former camp tend to emphasize the experience of England and France as exemplary (see, e.g., Reynolds 1984; Hastings 1997; Schulze 1994). For example, Scattergood (2001) emphasizes how England was increasingly imagined as a separate space by poets and playwrights over the course of the fifteenth and sixteenth centuries in essentially modern terms – trade, merchants, money, networks of exchange. Neocleous (2003) emphasizes the role of the map after 1600 – and the borders depicted therein – as the instrument for violently imposing national-state logic onto what was often a more complex sociocultural reality. In accounts accepting this sort of genealogy, state elites elsewhere are then alleged to have later imitated the founding nations in pursuit of nationalist "modernity" (Greenfeld 1992). Those in the second group look to the eighteenth century, again largely also to England (now usually rewritten as "Britain") and France, as the period when popular political association with national territory crystallized (e.g., Colley 1992; Bell 2001). If in the British case wars served as the most important ingredient in promoting a popular British nationalism, in France it was the nationalist project that developed through the Revolution of 1789, notwithstanding the universalistic elements often seen in that moment of political upheaval. Yet, until the end of the century, "the sense of a British nation was not geographically tied to Britain itself" according to Stephen Conway (2001: 893), since it had a strong transatlantic element and was resisted by many in England who feared the rise of a culturally mixed "Britishness" (e.g., Ragussis 2000), and the nation-building project in France is probably better dated to the nineteenth rather than to the eighteenth century (e.g., Weber 1976). Nonetheless, the eighteenth century has a strong case as the founding period for what today would be the recognizably nationalist conception of territorial space. From this point of view, nationalism as a popular political project has its roots in the American and French Revolutions. They stimulated other nationalist projects as new states "invented" (Hobsbawm and Ranger 1983) or promoted (Wallerstein 1991) the nation as the "natural" territorial basis to statehood. With the decolonization of Europe's empires in the second half of the twentieth century, nationalism became a worldwide phenomenon.

The second question has been more specifically addressed in contexts other than England and France. Germany and Italy figure particularly prominently. These are cases, perhaps not coincidentally, in which statehood dates only from the mid-nineteenth century but which have had much longer cultural-territorial histories as putative nations. The emphasis is on (1) what can be called the "local life of nationhood" (Applegate 1990; Confino and Skaria 2002; Jones and Fowler 2008); (2) the relation of local and regional to national identities (Agnew 1995; Kaplan 1999; Núñez 2001; Jones and Fowler 2008); and (3) the "fluid" and "contested" identities of state borderlands (Kulczycki 2001; Agnew 2007; Hametz 2010; Walker 2011). The overall focus is on relating national identities to the geographical scales and contexts in which they are embedded rather than presupposing a nationalist "wave" that washes over a territory from either a center or the margins, wiping out all other identities in its path. In this view the national is always forged in and through "the local." Over time the very borders of the territory "at stake" can shift significantly, as in the German, Polish, and

Chinese cases (on China, see, e.g., Friedman 2008). In Germany, for example, the idea of *Heimat* (homeland) has connected local and regional communities to the nation. In particular, and following World War II, "by talking about *Heimat*, Germans found a way to talk about that which was so problematic to talk about, namely the nation" (Confino and Skaria 2002: 11). The nation's territory is not a simple block of space but a complex set of relationships between local, regional, and national levels of social practice and geographical imagination. Nationalism relates to territory, therefore, in more complex ways than most students of nationalism have tended to believe.

## Ethnic versus Civic Nationalism

According to the political theorist Bernard Yack (2001; 520), "A large part of the story of the emergence and spread of nationalism lies in the way that these two images of community, the nation and the people, have become entangled in our minds." Indeed, one of the major contemporary disputes about the nature of nationalism and whether there are "better" and "worse" kinds revolves around the interpretations given to the intersections between the two terms. On one side are those who distinguish between "ethnic" and "civic" nationalisms and on the other are those who fail to see the distinction or who see it as a false and misleading one. To the first group ethnic nationalism involves the exclusive identity of the people with the nation whereas civic nationalism involves the inclusive identity of the nation with the people. Thus, if ethnic nationalism is characterized by shared cultural loyalties, civic nationalism is all about shared political principles and institutions. Some writers, such as Greenfeld (1992, 1996), use the civic/ethnic dichotomy to distinguish more "democratic" (civic) from more "authoritarian" (ethnic) versions of nationalism. In this usage there is little if any ethical commitment to an idealized "civic nationalism." It is merely a taxonomic device to classify varieties of nationalism. This is helpful in pointing out, for instance, that some examples of nationalism, such as that in Israel (Berent 2010), are basically ethnic despite the claim to democratic-civic credentials that the state uses to justify itself. The "ethnicization" of some national identities in the face of terrorist threats from those putatively distinctive on ethnic if not on citizenship grounds also draws attention to the utility of the distinction for understanding how nationalism works in practice (e.g., Kostakopoulou 2008). Other commentators, however, have attempted to reconcile nationalism with liberalism by arguing for a "civic" nationalism, like that said to exist in the United States, France, or Britain (e.g., Tamir 1993; Viroli 1995). In this understanding, the "main characteristic of the democratic national idea [is]: the effort to transcend the level of concrete identities and ethnic solidarities through citizenship" (Schnapper 1998: 234). Yet, liberalism and the "communitarianism" implicit in nationalism are uncomfortable bedfellows. If the first appeals to the "needs" of the autonomous individual, the second insists in subordinating these to a particular group. In their incompatibility: "One recalls," says Zygmunt Bauman (1995: 551), "the Soviet rulers' proposition that the ultimate community goal, the abolition of the state, was to be achieved by radically increasing its coercive power. And one recalls also the consequences of that instance of double-thought."

But, as the second group tends to maintain, ethnic and civic types of nationalism both rest on claims to popular sovereignty on the part of nations that are necessarily exclusive and politicized. Even if they can be empirically distinguished in any particular case, and this is often doubtful, they share a common historical trajectory: that of popular sovereignty. As Yack (2001: 529) makes the point:

You need to assume the existence of [territorial] boundaries between peoples before you can exercise the principle of popular sovereignty. Therefore, you cannot use popular sovereignty to determine where the boundaries between peoples should lie. Popular sovereignty can help guide us in determining our political arrangements. It cannot help us decide how to determine the shape of our collective selves.

Nicholas Xenos (1996) makes a different but equally compelling point in challenging the meaningfulness of the dichotomy. He contrasts the concrete "patriotism" of city-dwelling with the abstract imposition of both civic and ethnic nationalism. The affection displayed for place in classical republican patriotism is that of the city not of the modern nation-state. Thus, those who argue from classical and early modern authors to justify a modern civic nationalism are guilty of misidentifying the object of patriotism (or belonging) articulated by such authors.

## Long-Distance Nationalism

Rather than simply a reflection of the association between a nation and its territory, the history of nationalism is also closely related to the experience of large-scale migration. With due regard to its peculiarities, Robert Wiebe (2002: 24) suggestively points to the linkage between migration and Irish nationalism, when following the Famine of the late 1840s: "While the Irish in Ireland buried the dead, nationalism survived by shifting its center of gravity across the Atlantic. In the years of O'Connell's ascendancy [over the Irish nationalist movement in the years before the Famine], the Irish in America had played only a minor role, cheering his cause and contributing money to it but otherwise simply watching from abroad. Now, as they took the initiative, they gave Irish nationalism its distinctive stamp: secular, public, and violent."

Typically, however, the influence of migration and more recent impacts of "space–time compression" due to the technological "shrinking" of the world are left out of both nationalist narratives and scholarly accounts of them (Mulligan 2005). In the stories of nationalists such external ties would undermine the seemingly natural connection between nation and territory; each begets the other. Scholarly accounts are similarly place-bound and often simply accept the claims of nationalist stories at face value. To the extent that the "long-distance national-ism" of "absent patriots" is taken seriously, it is as a novel phenomenon tied to the nationalist proclivities of groups of recent immigrants from formerly colonial countries to the countries of Western Europe and North America. This is undoubtedly an important feature of recent world politics (see, e.g., Goulborne 1991 on Sikhs and Guyanese in Britain, or Schiller and Fouron 2001 on Haitians in the United States), but its novelty is exaggerated and the long-standing relationship between long-distance migration, romanticism about the land and people "left behind," and nationalism is obscured. Long-distance nationalism did not arrive with the fax.

The American radical Tom Hayden (2002) is neither alone nor the first in adopting a romantic nativism in which his American "outside" disguises the fact that he is "Irish on the inside." All of the clichés of absent patriotism are present in his account, from the Irish sages who say that Irish culture is very ancient, older, of course, "than the English," and that the Irish soul is "like an ancient forest" to the "mystical courage" of the martyrs to the Irish cause. But this is not a joke. Rather, it is the essential core of the romanticism that inspires long-distance nationalism, even many generations and much intermarriage beyond the original migrants, many of whom often wanted to forget about where they came from. Of course, the "search for roots" in distant places need not always end up with the essentialized national identities that Hayden evokes. Catherine Nash (2002) shows nicely how investigations into personal genealogies can produce unsettling and complicated family pasts when the roots turn out to be less "purely" Irish than family lore might have suggested. Similarly, heritage tourism not only reproduces convenient national stories but also can offer local correctives that open to question dominant understandings of the national past particularly prevalent among absent patriots (Johnson 1999). If somewhat overstated, however, Ian Buruma's (2002: 14) commentary on Hayden's book captures what has often been at stake with the romantic nationalism of absent patriots: "Hayden is haunted by blood-thirsty ghosts. He is not alone. There are Sikhs in Toronto, Muslims in Britain and France, Jews in Brooklyn, and many others in far-flung places who seek to sooth ancestral voices by encouraging barbarism far from home. Some are prepared to die for their causes. Most are content to let others do the dying, while they work on their identities at home."

## Religion and Nationalism

There are cases where religion and nationalism have been almost complete partners, as with the Greek and other Orthodox Christian churches, Iranian Shi'ite Islam, Orthodox Judaism, and the state churches of England and other northern European countries, on the one hand, and powerful nationalist movements and sentiments, on the other. In England, for example, the Protestant Reformation and the threat to it from the Catholic states served to unify the English into a national enterprise that was lacking in those states where church and state did not become mutually supportive. But there are others, as in many Muslim and predominantly Roman Catholic countries, where religious identities either compete with national ones or have complex relations to them. In Italy, for example, from 1870 until 1929 the pope refused to recognize the Italian state because, in his view, it had usurped his temporal powers when it had annexed the papal territories of central Italy. Under threat of excommunication, active Catholics were required to abstain from any involvement in national politics and in the life of the nation.

At one time nationalism was seen as largely reflective of religious, linguistic, and other cultural cleavages. Obviously this is problematic in an evident empirical sense. Such cleavages often exist without generating nationalism. It is also problematic, however, because religion is frequently a banner for a wide range of differences and resentments that are only at most secondarily religious, in the sense of commitment to doctrines and beliefs: access to political power, availability of public offices, and so on (Harris 1990: 11). Indeed, and today, religious identities, particularly in the Muslim world, often cut across nationalist lines, except in the Iranian and Palestinian cases. The universalistic claims of Islam and Catholic Christianity have frequently coexisted uneasily with the particularistic claims of nationalist movements. Sometimes the character of religious belief, in the sense of popular as opposed to officially sanctioned belief, can also undermine national identities and nationalism in the interest of privileging local identities (see, e.g., on popular Catholicism in Italy, Carroll 1996).

Yet, there are two ways in which religion has intersected powerfully with nationalism down the years. The first is emphasized by Benedict Anderson (1983: 12) when he proposes that "nationalism has to be understood by aligning it, not with self-consciously held political ideologies [although I have challenged this assertion earlier], but with the large cultural systems that preceded it, out of which – as well as against which – it came into being." In this understanding, sacred languages such as Latin, Arabic, and Mandarin Chinese provided the core element to the civilizations that increasingly decomposed into "national" parts as vernacular languages replaced the sacred as the main media for popular literacy and public communication. Religion, by means of sacred languages, thus provided the common foundation (along with dynastic politics and, later, racial categories) upon which nationalism's "imagined communities" came to be imagined (e.g., on China, see Friedman 2008). The second has been religion's role in providing the material for the "tyranny of small differences" upon which many nationalist movements have relied to distinguish their nation from others. As Daniele Conversi (1994) has claimed, using even minor distinctions (in global terms) to define boundaries with the Other against whom you are defining yourself (e.g., the English for the Irish, the Germans for the French, the Pakistanis for Indians, etc.) is as if not more important to nationalist movements than is defining what makes you special without benefit of comparison and contrast. It is clear that religious differences have often played this role, for example in Irish, Welsh, and Scottish nationalism (Pope 2001).

## Gender and Nationalism

Nationalism is frequently seen as the most masculinist or male-dominated type of politics. Not only did women's roles in politics seem to decline along with the rise of nationalism (e.g., Radhakrishnan 1992), but also nationalist ideologies seem to rest on a peculiarly gendered division of political labor, with women allocated the role of nurturing the Motherland (or standing in for it symbolically as with the French national symbols of Joan of Arc (for the right) and Marianne (for the left)) by producing future generations, while men are given the directing role and charged with defending the homeland against or liberating it from its foreign enemies (Sharp 1996; Blom, Hagemann, and Hall 2000). In this understanding, and in the direst of circumstances, such as the bloody nationalist wars in the Balkans in the 1990s, women's bodies come to represent the very territory to be conquered or claimed and thus subject to rape and defilement (Skelsbæk 2001). More mundanely, the metaphor of the nation as a "family" has carried much weight, sometimes to obscure the degree to which patriarchy is operative at multiple geographical scales but often, as in the late nineteenth century, to refocus the social life of the nation around an idealized household with men and women holding quite different social roles (Eley 2000).

In the light of recent research, however, this perspective on gender and nationalism seems not so much incorrect as overstated. Matters seem much more complicated than it suggests. First of all, women have not been simply passive bystanders to and symbols for nationalist movements even when seemingly marginalized within them. As Catherine Nash (1997) shows with respect to Ireland, it was not just exceptional and "famous" women, such as Maud Gonne and Countess Markievicz, but also a multitude of "ordinary" women who played a key part in the political protests of the nineteenth- and early twentieth-century nationalist movements. At the same time, questions of gender, sexual, and national identity are never simply linear and additive. Male–female and sexual identity differences do not line up on a single axis of nationalist politics with men and women and gays and heterosexuals on opposite sides and with competing roles (Dowler 2002; Marston 2002; Luibhéid 2011). As Nash (1997: 123) concludes: "The history of Ireland and women's activism in contemporary Northern Ireland both point to the limitations of neat oppositions and single visions."

In the second place, sexual violence in the context of nationalist conflict, such as that directed at women in particular in the Balkans and elsewhere, seems related to the fear and advent of territorial partition and the collapse of social order rather than to nationalist politics *per se*. Mass rape is a long-standing weapon of war. It usually seems to occur in settings in which partition of contested territory is under way and/or social disorder is rampant, such as South Asia in 1947, the Balkans in the 1990s, and in the Congo and Rwanda since the mid-1990s, rather than because it somehow is directly connected to nationalist politics. As anthropologist Robert Hayden (2000: 33) plausibly claims:

> Partition . . . is not only a liminal state but a time when the state itself is liminal, and the questions of whose state it is, and how the population will be defined are open. . . . After these issues are settled, mass rape will no longer be likely, because either coexistence will have been reconstituted or the newly consolidated groups will have separated.

Finally, women who have organized themselves in political organizations have sometimes been major independent proponents of nationalism. In the United States, for example, in the years between the Civil War and World War I, women's organizations played a central part in generating American nationalism. Groups such as the Women's Relief Corps emerged in the aftermath of the US Civil War to insist adamantly that "patriotism knows no sex" (quoted in O'Leary 1999: 92; see also Rowbotham 1992). As O'Leary (1999) shows in detail, most members endorsed the idea of women's moral superiority to men and were opposed to limiting their work to serving veterans or staying within the bounds of domesticity. But just as they connected in the 1890s with the more partisan women's movement, they also became major sponsors of patriotic events such as Memorial Day, the campaign to fly the flag at every school, petitioned for flag-desecration laws, and lobbied to include the pledge of allegiance in the public (state) schools (O'Leary 1999: 97). In sum, it turns out that nationalism has not consistently discriminated on the basis of sex after all.

## Nationalism and Landscape

Tying the nation to territory has often involved identifying a prototypical landscape as representative of the collective identity. In this way the natural environment can be recruited for the national cause not only to naturalize the connection between nation and territory but also visually to communicate and reinforce identity with the nation. The physical images, buildings, monuments, and scenes encountered in everyday life come to provide a mundane or "banal" element to nationalism itself (Billig 1995; Grabham 2009; Webster 2011). The very familiarity of symbols seen on a daily basis makes the nation the "daily plebiscite" that Ernest Renan famously described it as being. Monumental spaces and other "places of memory" have been of particular significance in potentially bonding current residents to a common past (Till 2003). Through the landscape the memory of the nation is given concrete form as a reminder of what "we" have been through and why "we" need to remember.

More generally, however, a national landscape "imagery" is a visual technique that naturalizes particular images into a national narrative (Häyrynen 2000). Published and disseminated over long periods of time, these images make the national territory concrete as a distinctive block of space and as a result elicit shared values and meanings. If in some countries identification of a "national landscape" seems to have met with considerable success, in England, Finland, and Switzerland, for example, elsewhere this proved more elusive. In Switzerland after the founding of the modern federation in 1848, Alpine scenery not surprisingly provided both a geographical icon for the new state and, when combined with the image of virtuous peasants fruitfully tilling what soil there was, a "powerful symbol of republican will and cultural mediation" peculiar to Switzerland (Zimmer 2001). In Italy, however, attempts at using either Tuscan rural scenery or Roman ruins after unification to represent an idealized national landscape for the new nation-state came largely to naught (Agnew 2002: Ch. 3), though the Northern League, the avowedly regionalist movement in contemporary northern Italy, uses the image of the Alps to represent the largely lowland but less visually impressive and polluted region it claims (Huysseune 2010). The combination of fragmented political identities in a physically divided peninsula, strong church–state tensions, the ambiguous legacy of ancient Rome, and the political incoherence of both liberal and fascist regimes made crafting a national landscape ideal extremely difficult. Nationalism, therefore, is not invariably naturalized successfully through the creation of a national land-scape imagery.

## Conclusion

The memory of the New York City firefighters as giving up their lives for others on 9/11 has gained a powerful hold in American collective consciousness, particularly in media re-crea-tions. At the end of the day, it is sacrifice such as this, or interpreted as such, whatever any individual firefighter might have been thinking, that nationalism has to offer. It is also this focus on the sacrificial that other political ideologies find particularly problematic about nationalism. If its appeal still remains elusive to those of us who are not particularly attracted to it, we nevertheless understand that nationalism is far from a spent force. If anything, nationalism has achieved even greater success recently than anyone might have predicted ten or twenty years ago. From India to Ireland, Israel, and Indonesia, nationalism is a powerful element in everyday politics. It is simply banal. Understanding the contemporary world, therefore, requires understanding nationalism. And we should remember that in many places it is still deeply rooted, wired into the routines and ephemera of everyday life, omnipresent in stamps, banknotes, flags, and the monuments passed on a daily basis.

The poet and writer Patricia Storace (1996: 10) tells the story of Greek high school stu-dents who refused to read Vergil's *Aeneid*. "These particular students held it as dogma that the *Aeneid* was a cheap [Roman] imitation of the [ancient Greek] Homer, responding with a popular Platonism, present in both the ancient Greek preoccupation with sculpture and the modern Greek preoccupation with icons, that insisted there was one ideal original, and the rest of the genre was increasingly false and bloodless." The ideal original, of course, had to be Greek. Whether that Greek would recognize himself in modern Greece is, for the national-ist, entirely beside the point. The modern Greek sees no distinction. That's the miracle of nationalism.

## References

Agnew, J.A. (1995) The rhetoric of regionalism: The Northern League in Italian politics. *Transactions of the Institute of British Geographers*, 20, 156–172.

Agnew, J.A. (2002) *Place and Politics in Modern Italy*. Chicago: University of Chicago Press.

Agnew, J.A. (2007) No borders, no nations: Making Greece in Macedonia. *Annals of the Association of American Geographers*, 97, 398–422.

Agnew, J.A. and Corbridge, S. (1995) *Mastering Space: Hegemony, Territory and International Political Economy*. London: Routledge.

Anderson, B. (1991/1983) *Imagined Communities: Reflections on the Origins and Spread of Nationalism*, revised edition. London: Verso.

Anderson, J. (1988) Nationalist ideology and territory. In *Nationalism, Self-Determination and Political Geography*, ed. R.J. Johnston, D.B. Knight, and E. Kofman. London: Croom Helm.

Antonsich, M. (2009) On territory, the nation-state and the crisis of the hyphen. *Progress in Human Geography*, 33, 789–806.

Applegate, C. (1990) *A Nation of Provincials: The German Idea of Heimat*. Berkeley: University of California Press.

Banti, A.M. (2011) *Sublime madre nostra. La nazione italiana dal Risorgimento al fascismo*. Rome: Laterza.

Bauman, Z. (1995) Communitarianism, freedom, and the nation-state. *Critical Review*, 9, 539–553.

Bell, D. (2001) *The Cult of the Nation in France: Inventing Nationalism, 1680–1800*. Cambridge, MA: Harvard University Press.

Berent, M. (2010) The ethnic democracy debate: How unique is Israel? *Nations and Nationalism*, 16, 657–674.

Billig, M. (1995) *Banal Nationalism*. London: Sage.

Biorcio, R. (2010) *La rivincita del Nord. La Lega dalla contestazione al governo*. Rome: Laterza.

Blom, I., Hagemann, K., and Hall, C. (eds.) (2000) *Gendered Nations: Nationalisms and the Gender Order in the Long Nineteenth Century*. Oxford: Berg.

Breuilly, J. (1982) *Nationalism and the State*. New York: St. Martin's.

Brustein, W. (1996) *The Logic of Evil: The Social Origins of the Nazi Party, 1925–1933*. New Haven: Yale University Press.

Buruma, I. (2002) The blood lust of identity. *New York Review of Books*, April 11, pp. 12–14.

Carroll, M.P. (1996) *Veiled Threats: The Logic of Popular Catholicism in Italy*. Baltimore: Johns Hopkins University Press.

Cederman, L.-E., Wimmer, A., and Min, B. (2010) Why do ethnic groups rebel? New data and analysis. *World Politics*, 62, 87–119.

Chatterjee, P. (1986) *Nationalist Thought and the Colonial World: A Derivative Discourse*. Minneapolis: University of Minnesota Press.

Colley, L. (1992) *Britons: Forging the Nation, 1707–1837*. New Haven: Yale University Press.

Comaroff, J.L. and Stern, P.C. (1995) New perspectives on nationalism and war. In *Perspectives on Nationalism and War*, ed. J.L. Comaroff and P.C. Stern. London: Gordon and Breach.

Confino, A. and Skaria, A. (2002) The local life of nationhood. *National Identities*, 4, 7–24.

Conversi, D. (1994) Reassessing current theories of nationalism: Nationalism as boundary maintenance and creation. *Nationalism and Ethnic Politics*, 1, 73–85.

Conversi, D. (1999) Nationalism, boundaries, and violence. *Millennium*, 28, 553–584.

Conway, S. (2001) War and national identity in the mid-eighteenth-century British Isles. *English Historical Review*, 116, 863–893.

Dowler, L. (2002) Till death us do part: Masculinity, friendship, and nationalism in Belfast, Northern Ireland. *Society and Space*, 20, 53–71.

Dunn, J. (1979) *Western Political Theory in the Face of the Future*. Cambridge: Cambridge University Press.

Eley, G. (2000) Culture, nation and gender. In *Gendered Nations: Nationalisms and Gender Order in the Long Nineteenth Century*, ed. I. Blom *et al.* Oxford: Berg.

Friedman, E. (2008) Where is Chinese nationalism? The political geography of a moving project. *Nations and Nationalism*, 14, 721–738.

Gellner, E. (1983) *Nations and Nationalism*. Oxford: Blackwell.

Gentile, E. (2011) *Italiani senza padri. Intervista sul Risorgimento*. Rome: Laterza.

Ginsborg, P. (2010) *Salviamo l'Italia*. Turin: Einaudi.

Goulborne, H. (1991) *Ethnicity and Nationalism in Post-Imperial Britain*. Cambridge: Cambridge University Press.

Grabham, E. (2009) "Flagging the skin": Corporeal nationalism and the properties of belonging. *Body and Society*, 15, 63–82.

Greenfeld, L. (1992) *Nationalism: Four Roads to Modernity*. Cambridge, MA: Harvard University Press.

Greenfeld, L. (1996) The modern religion? *Critical Review*, 10, 169–191.

Hametz, M. (2010) Naming Italians in the borderland, 1926–1943. *Journal of Modern Italian Studies*, 15, 410–430.

Harmes, A. (2011) The rise of neoliberal nationalism. *Review of International Political Economy*, 17, 1–28.

Harris, N. (1990) *National Liberation*. Reno: University of Nevada Press.

Hastings, A. (1997) *The Construction of Nationhood: Ethnicity, Religion and Nationalism*. Cambridge: Cambridge University Press.

Hayden, R.M. (2000) Rape and rape avoidance in ethno-national conflicts: Sexual violence in liminalized states. *American Anthropologist*, 102, 27–41.

Hayden, T. (2002) *Irish on the Inside: In Search of the Soul of Irish America*. London: Verso.

Häyrynen, M. (2000) The kaleidoscopic view: The Finnish national landscape imagery. *National Identities*, 2, 5–19.

Hechter, M. (2000) *Containing Nationalism*. Oxford: Oxford University Press.

Hobsbawm, E. (1992) *Nations and Nationalism since 1780: Programme, Myth, Reality*. Cambridge: Cambridge University Press.

Hobsbawm, E. and Ranger, T. (eds.) (1983) *The Invention of Tradition*. Cambridge: Cambridge University Press.

Huysseune, M. (2010) Landscapes as a symbol of nationhood: The Alps in the rhetoric of the Lega Nord. *Nations and Nationalism*, 16, 354–373.

Johnson, N.C. (1999) Framing the past: Time, space and the politics of heritage tourism in Ireland. *Political Geography*, 18, 187–207.

Jones, R. and Fowler, C. (2008) *Placing the Nation: Aberystwyth and the Reproduction of Welsh Nationalism*. Cardiff: University of Wales Press.

Kaplan, D.H. (1999) Territorial identities and geographic scale. In *Nested Identities: Nationalism, Territory, and Scale*, ed. D.H. Kaplan and G. H. Herb. Lanham, MD: Rowman and Littlefield.

Kostakopoulou, D. (2008) How to do things with security post 9/11. *Oxford Journal of Legal Studies*, 28, 317–342.

Kulczycki, J.J. (2001) The national identity of the "natives" of Poland's "Recovered Lands." *National Identities*, 3, 205–219.

Luibhéid, E. (2011) Nationalist heterosexuality, migrant (il)legality, and Irish citizenship law: Queering the connections. *South Atlantic Quarterly*, 110, 179–204.

Mann, M. (1992) The emergence of modern European nationalism. In *Transition to Modernity: Essays on Power, Wealth and Belief*, ed. J.A. Hall and I.C. Jarvie. Cambridge: Cambridge University Press.

Marston, S.A. (2002) Making difference: Conflict over Irish identity in the New York City St. Patrick's Day Parade. *Political Geography*, 21, 373–392.

Meer, N., Dwyer, C., and Modood, T. (2010) Embodying nationhood? Conceptions of British national identity, citizenship, and gender in the "Veil Affair." *Sociological Review*, 58, 84–111.

Mortimer, E. (ed.) (1999) *People, Nation and State: The Meaning of Ethnicity and Nationalism*. London: I.B. Tauris.

Mulligan, A.N. (2005) Absence makes the heart grow fonder: Transatlantic Irish nationalism and the 1867 rising. *Social and Cultural Geography*, 6, 439–454.

Murphy, A.B. (2002) National claims to territory in the modern state system: Geographical considerations. *Geopolitics*, 7, 193–214.

Murray, S. (1997) *Not on Any Map: Essays on Postcoloniality and Cultural Nationalism*. Exeter: University of Exeter Press.

Nash, C. (1997) Embodied Irishness: Gender, sexuality and Irish identities. In *In Search of Ireland: A Cultural Geography*, ed. B. Graham. London: Routledge.

Nash, C. (2002) Genealogical identities. *Society and Space*, 20, 27–52.

Neocleous, M. (2003) Off the map: On violence and cartography. *European Journal of Social Theory*, 6, 409–425.

Núñez, X.-M. (2001) The region as *essence* of the Fatherland: Regionalist variants of Spanish nationalism (1840–1936). *European History Quarterly*, 31, 483–518.

O'Leary, C.E. (1999) *To Die For: The Paradox of American Patriotism*. Princeton: Princeton University Press.

Ó Tuathail, G. (2009) Placing blame: Making sense of Beslan. *Political Geography*, 28, 4–15.

Patriarca, S. (2010) *Italianità. La costruzione del carattere nazionale*. Rome: Laterza.

Peckham, R.S. (2001) *National Histories, Natural States: Nationalism and the Politics of Place in Greece*. London: I.B. Tauris.

Pope, R. (ed.) (2001) *Religion and National Identity: Wales and Scotland, c.1700–2000*. Cardiff: University of Wales Press.

Radhakrishnan, R. (1992) Nationalism, gender, and the narrative of identity. In *Nationalisms and Sexualities*, ed. A. Parker *et al*. London: Routledge.

Ragussis, M. (2000) Jews and other "outlandish Englishmen": Ethnic performance and the invention of British identity under the Georges. *Critical Inquiry*, 26, 773–797.

*La Repubblica* (2011) Le celebrazioni. Unità d'Italia, la Lega bufera. March 16.

Reynolds, S. (1984) *Kingdoms and Communities in Western Europe, 900–1300*. Oxford: Clarendon Press.

Roshwald, A. (2006) *The Endurance of Nationalism: Ancient Roots and Modern Dilemmas*. Cambridge: Cambridge University Press.

Rowbotham, S. (1992) *Women in Movement: Feminism and Social Action*. London: Routledge.

Said, E. (1993) *Culture and Imperialism*. New York: Knopf.

Scattergood, J. (2001) *The Libelle of Englyshe Polyce*: The nation and its place. In *Nation, Court and Culture: New Essays on Fifteenth-Century English Poetry*, ed. H. Cooney. Dublin: Four Courts Press.

Schiller, N.G. and Fouron, G.E. (2001) *Georges Woke Up Laughing: Long-Distance Nationalism and the Search for Home*. Durham, NC: Duke University Press.

Schnapper, D. (1998) Beyond the opposition: Civic nation versus ethnic nation. In *Rethinking Nationalism*, ed. J. Couture, K. Nielsen, and M. Seymour. Calgary: University of Calgary Press.

Schulze, H. (1994) *States, Nations and Nationalism: From the Middle Ages to the Present*. Oxford: Blackwell.

Sharp, J. (1996) Gendering nationhood: A feminist engagement with national identity. In *Bodyspace: Destabilizing Geographies of Gender and Sexuality*, ed. N. Duncan. London: Routledge.

Skelsbæk, I. (2001) Sexual violence and war: Mapping out a complex relationship. *European Journal of International Relations*, 7, 211–237.

Smith, A.D. (1999) *Myths and Memories of the Nation*. Oxford: Oxford University Press.

Smith, A.D. (2002) When is a nation? *Geopolitics*, 7, 5–32.

Storace, P. (1996) Marble girls of Athens. *New York Review of Books*, October 3, pp. 7–15.

Tamir, Y. (1993) *Liberal Nationalism*. Princeton: Princeton University Press.

Thrift, N. (2007) Immaculate warfare? The spatial politics of extreme violence. In *Violent Geographies: Fear, Terror, and Political Violence*, ed. D. Gregory and A. Pred. New York: Routledge.

Till, K.E. (2003) Places of memory. In *A Companion to Political Geography*, ed. J. Agnew, K. Mitchell, and G. Ò Tuathail. Oxford: Blackwell.

Viroli, M. (1995) *For Love of Country: An Essay on Patriotism and Nationalism*. Oxford: Oxford University Press.

Walker, M.A. (2011) Knowledge production and border nationalism in northern Mexico. *Nations and Nationalism*, 17, 168–187.

Wallerstein, I. (1991) The construction of peoplehood: Racism, nationalism, ethnicity. In *Race, Nation, Class: Ambiguous Identities*, ed. E. Balibar and I. Wallerstein. London: Verso.

Weber, E. (1976) *Peasants into Frenchmen*. Stanford, CA: Stanford University Press.

Webster, G.R. (2011) American nationalism, the flag, and the invasion of Iraq. *Geographical Review*, 1001, 1–18.

Wiebe, R. (2000) *Imagined Communities*: Nationalist experiences. *Journal of the Historical Society*, 1, 33–63.

Wiebe, R. (2002) *Who We Are: A History of Popular Nationalism*. Princeton: Princeton University Press.

Xenos, N. (1996) Civic nationalism: Oxymoron? *Critical Review*, 10, 213–231.

Yack, B. (2001) Popular sovereignty and nationalism. *Political Theory*, 29, 517–536.

Yiftachel, O. (2000) The homeland and nationalism. In *Encyclopedia of Nationalism*, vol. 1. New York: Academic Press, pp. 359–383.

Yiftachel, O. (2002) Territory as the kernel of the nation: Space, time and nationalism in Israel/Palestine. *Geopolitics*, 7, 215–248.

Zimmer, O. (2001) Forging the authentic nation: Alpine landscape and Swiss national identity. In *Modern Roots: Studies of National Identity*, ed. A. Dieckhoff and N. Gutiérrez. Aldershot: Ashgate.

# Chapter 15

# Object Lessons: From Batholith to Bookend

*Caitlin DeSilvey*

## Introduction

In January 2011 Adrian Lea presented a talk on "The Building Stones of Cornwall" to a gathering of the local history group in the village of Constantine, a former copper-mining and granite-quarrying settlement near Falmouth, England. During his talk Adrian told an intriguing story. In 2004 his family moved to Cornwall and bought an old farmhouse on the outskirts of Stithians (another village that grew up around the local granite industry). The house and garden required considerable work. Several years after he moved to the property, Adrian began to rebuild part of a failing Cornish "hedge" – a high, stone-faced earthen wall, seeded with wild plants and shrubs. As Adrian was working, he unearthed a strangely shaped piece of granite, about the size of a small loaf of bread, with two smooth faces that met in a right angle.

"Glad of a rest, I examined the stone carefully and put it to one side," he explained. "It was too good to remain as part of a hedge" (personal communication, April 12, 2011). Some time later, about two meters further along the hedge, he found a similar piece of granite, apparently identical to the first. To his surprise, when the two pieces were cleaned he discovered on one a small brass plate, with the inscription: "Granite from the Old London Bridge, London, England" (Figure 15.1). The two odd stones were a pair of bookends.

When he finished his story, Adrian passed one bookend around the audience assembled in the Women's Institute hall. The piece weighed several pounds; felt pads were still fastened on the bottom face of the stone to protect underlying surfaces. At some point these bookends had been incorporated into the hedge where Adrian found them, but when, and why? I had a hard time concentrating on the rest of Adrian's talk. I kept wondering about the other stories connected to those chunks of rock. Had they been extracted from one of the local

*The Wiley Blackwell Companion to Cultural Geography*, First Edition.
Edited by Nuala C. Johnson, Richard H. Schein, and Jamie Winders.
© 2013 John Wiley & Sons, Ltd. Published 2016 by John Wiley & Sons, Ltd.

**Figure 15.1** Brass plate on bookend.
Source: photo by Adrian Lea.

quarries? What was their structural contribution to the London Bridge? When the bridge was dismantled and sold for reconstruction in the Arizona desert, had these fragments been shipped to the United States as well? Was their final journey to Cornwall intentional or accidental? The story of the bookends set me off "constellating material histories" (DeSilvey 2007a); once I started, it was difficult to know where to stop.

For me, the bookends were potent objects – things that radiated potential paths of inquiry, speculative histories, complex and mobile geographies. For this reason I have decided to use these objects to structure this chapter – to bookend it, if you will, and to help the varied and occasionally divergent approaches I discuss line up more or less neatly in the middle, their spines turned out for examination. As others have noted, there is no singular or unified way of "doing" the cultural geography of material culture (Whatmore 2006; Cook and Tolia-Kelly 2010). A chapter on cultural geography's engagement with objects and things has, almost by necessity, to reckon with border-crossing, borrowed theories, tangled methodologies, and scrambled scales. It seems appropriate to approach this task by enlisting some objects to help me out. Adrian's granite bookends travel through the story (much as the story of a grounded cargo ship structures Cook and Tolia-Kelly's 2010 chapter in the *Oxford Handbook of Material Culture Studies*). Along the way, I form a speculative biography of these things – call it their "spatio-temporal life" (Hill 2006), their "socio-spatial biography" (Pike 2011) or, perhaps my favorite, their "geobiography" (Karjalainen 2003).

This chapter is grounded in an approach that understands an artifact as a process rather than a stable entity (DeSilvey 2006). In other words, "objects are not what they are made to be but what they become" (Thomas 1991: 4). In the course of this chapter, the bookends are variously revealed as geological formation, building material, structural component, symbolic artifact, heritage icon, waste matter, and personal possession. Their provisional identity depends on where they are in their geobiography and who is looking at them. Sometimes they are part of a vast assemblage; sometimes they are discrete and of a more modest size. They slide in and out of material and symbolic registers and occupy the nature/culture borderlands quite happily. This kind of promiscuous material thinking has become familiar in cultural geography over the last decade or so, fueled by engagements with theoretical work in other disciplines. Increasingly, geographers have been concerned to focus on "the processes whereby materialities achieve specific capacities and effects" (Anderson and Tolia-Kelly 2004: 672), with a language of "emergence" and "becoming" overwriting an emphasis on "inscription" and "construction." This chapter sets out to play with some of these different ways of making meaning in collaboration with materials and, in conclusion, makes the point that sometimes these approaches offer more in combination than they do in isolation.

## Formation and Extraction

Before the bookends could be bookends, they had to be part of the London Bridge. Before they could be part of the London Bridge, they had to be extracted from the earth. It was 1820 and the quarries on the Cornubian batholith (which stretches out beneath most of Cornwall and to the eastern edge of Dartmoor in Devon) were picking up their production of granite building stone to supply the increasing demand for material in the construction of bridges, harbors, lighthouses, and public buildings (Stanier 1999: 6). Quarrymen bored into existing joints in the batholith and then lifted the blocks with intricate systems of cranes and winches, which grew more sophisticated as the industry matured (Figure 15.2). Ten years earlier, civil engineer John Rennie had sourced most of the stone for the building of London's Waterloo Bridge from quarries in Cornwall's Carnmenellis district (which includes the villages of Constantine and Stithians). When it came time to replace the 600-year-old London Bridge, Rennie chose newly established quarries on Haytor, Dartmoor, to supply the bulk of the structure's exterior material (with blue-gray Aberdeen granite forming the interior). Supplies from Haytor and Aberdeen ran low, however and builders turned back to the Cornish quarries: an operation at Carnsew, near Penryn, supplied material for two of the bridge arches in 1828 (Stanier 1999: 129). The bookend granite is of a coarse-grained "salt-and-pepper" texture, with scattered black mica crystals and some reddish discoloration. According to local quarry workers, its characteristics are similar to those of the surface-lying field stones in the Carnmenellis district. Given the stone's composition and character, there is a reasonable likelihood that it originated at Carnsew, less than a mile away from the hedge in Stithians where the bookends were found 186 years later.

**Figure 15.2** A Cornish granite quarry.
Source: photo by Adrian Lea.

I discuss the likely origins of this stone to start us out on our exploration of different ways of approaching these particular objects as research subjects. The moment when the bookend granite transformed from "matter" to "material," on its way to becoming "thingly" (Ingold 2007), seems a reasonable place to begin, if not the usual point of departure for a cultural geographer. The granite under study here formed several hundred million years ago, its relatively large crystal structure suggesting a process of slow cooling within the emplacement of the molten batholith. Over time the stone acquired a set of physical properties that would condition its future enrollment in cultural projects. The Carnsew quarry stone was only used in the London Bridge on the condition that it would not be used below the high water mark, presumably because of concerns about weathering and durability. The material properties of the stone, its hardness and flexural strength, emerged out of processes of "growth and transformation" (Ingold 2007: 9); these processes did not stop once the stone became temporarily stabilized in the form of the London Bridge.

In recent years this sort of inquiry into process and material flux has begun to preoccupy some geographers (Anderson and Wylie 2009; Edensor 2011). When does matter become material? When does material become object? What would research that takes seriously the entwining of geological and cultural process look like? Doreen Massey (2006) opened out some of these questions in her "landscape provocations," and a study by James Housefield (2007) investigated the production of art objects that engage with themes of geologic time and fractured landscape. Other geographers have used the figure of the assemblage to call attention to the labor of "assembling and reassembling" contingent and heterogeneous sociomaterial practices (Anderson and McFarlane 2011: 125), as in Tim Edensor's examination of the "vital properties" of stone in the life history of a Manchester church (Edensor 2011: 239) or Gillian Rose's account of the "affective materiality" of a shopping mall and its role in the "assembling of building events" (Rose, Degen, and Basdas 2010: 344). In a related vein, Jane Bennett's theories of "animate materialism" (2010) have informed attempts to "set materiality free from its traditionally lumpen role" in geographical research and to open up investigation of the "turbulent, interrogative, and excessive" qualities and properties of matter (Anderson and Wylie 2009: 332). A similar orientation underlies Nigel Clark's recent work on the socio-geophysics of our unpredictable planet (2011). I mention these works here to suggest that they might help us attend to the margin where research on "materiality" shades into work on "material culture": the bookends are a product of both geophysical and human labor, though their apparent integrity and coherence can mask their complex history. All objects originate in raw matter, even as their functional and symbolic properties rise to the surface in their later lives. If such thinking makes it difficult to ascertain where the work of the physical geographer ends and the work of the cultural geographer begins, then perhaps it suggests that these internal disciplinary boundaries are more permeable than we are usually inclined to assume.

## Maintenance and Malfunction

When construction on Rennie's London Bridge ended in 1831, our bookend chunks were left lodged within one of the five massive elliptical arches (Figure 15.3). The new bridge increased the volume of traffic over the crossing; by 1896 it was possibly the busiest point in London, carrying an estimated 8,000 foot passengers and 900 vehicles each hour. One visitor noted that "The roar from the bridge comes to one at a distance like the rumble of remote thunder" (Coe 1896: 28). In 1902 the congestion on the bridge was so extreme that

**Figure 15.3** London Bridge, 1890.
Source: published with the permission of the Southwark Local History Library and Archive.

a decision was made to widen the structure, a development in which the American press took a prescient interest, with the *New York Times* reporting, "The Englishman is so conservative that it will surprise most Americans to learn that the London authorities are at last 'doing something' about the London Bridge problem" (*New York Times* 1902). Engineers used Dartmoor granite for the widening, but the foundations were not reinforced to bear the increased weight. Structural investigation in the 1920s found that the bridge was sinking by about an inch every eight years (Shepherd 1971: 115). The bridge's integrity was also challenged by the friction of the tidal river and the unanticipated weight of heavy automobile traffic: the investment of labor and resources required to maintain the structure in working order was considerable. It held together until the 1960s, when the City of London began to plan for the bridge's replacement. London Bridge was falling down (not for the first time in its long history – the children's song dates to the thirteenth century, when Queen Eleanor's diversion of bridge maintenance funds led to the bridge's deterioration and partial collapse).

This period in the history of the bridge (and, by extension, the history of the bookends) invites reflection on the significance of repair and maintenance, a topic of growing interest to geographers. Things require both cultural and practical work if they are to preserve their integrity as discrete and coherent entities, lest the "material flux" mentioned above take over and demote them to mere matter again. Stephen Graham and Nigel Thrift (2007) explore the means by which "the constant decay of the world is held off" and suggest that "things only come into visible focus as things when they become inoperable" (p. 2). Wilford (2008) makes a similar point in his study of post-Katrina New Orleans, where destruction made visible material orderings that usually went without notice. My own work on the fate of a Cornish harbor has exposed the investment of labor and resources required to achieve the provisional persistence of a structure threatened by sea swell and storm surge (DeSilvey

2012). And Jane Jacobs (2006), in her "geography of big things," considers the technical work involved in achieving the "de-materialisation" of a Glasgow highrise. Bridges, harbors, highrises, and houses are all transient entities; or, as Tait and While argue, "these objects are constantly *made* or performed, rather than existing naturally in the world" (2009: 735). This point also holds at a smaller scale, in the maintenance of household objects like sofas and tables. Gregson, Metcalfe, and Crewe (2009) suggest that practices of maintenance and repair drive the continual "becoming" of such objects. They show how, for example, the restoration of a family dining table, and the attempted erasure of blemishes and imperfections acquired through intensive use, discloses the social dynamics of one couple's cohabitation. They also point out that the neglect of repair and maintenance practices threatens the introduction of social, as well as physical, disorder. On London Bridge, the gradual emergence of an unplanned and unwanted speed bump at the sinking end of the structure surely generated expressions of both forms of disorder, as maintenance engineers struggled to smooth over the gap created by slow subsidence.

## Rescue and Reinscription

Now, the story gets a bit strange. In 1967 the Corporation of London, instead of dismantling the bridge and salvaging the material for other projects, decided to sell Rennie's London Bridge to the highest bidder. Corporation engineer Harold King was sent to the United States to meet with prospective buyers, where the majority of inquiries originated. After extended negotiations, the Corporation accepted an offer of $2,460,000 from Robert McCulloch, an American who had made his fortune in chainsaw manufacturing. McCulloch had recently invested in property in Arizona near "Lake" Havasu, a reservoir created by the construction of the Parker Dam on the Colorado River in the 1930s. Eager to attract investors to Lake Havasu City, McCulloch sought an attraction that would put his speculative settlement on the map. The numbered, dismantled bridge sections were hauled to Merrivale Quarry in Devon, where the outer face of the bridge stone was sawn off to be used as cladding for a concrete-framed reconstruction in Arizona (Stanier 1999: 130). The disassembled bridge material traveled through the Panama Canal to Long Beach, California, and then overland to Arizona. McCulloch had the bridge reconstructed in Lake Havasu City, where it would provide access to an artificial island; desert sand supported the arches during the installation. The Lord Mayor of London attended the bridge rededication ceremony in October 1971. Development rapidly crowded the banks of the canal which had been excavated under the completed structure, with an "English Village" shopping district and resort as the prime attraction (Figure 15.4). By all accounts "Merry Olde England" has seen better days; but the town still claims that the bridge (often referred to as the "World's Largest Antique") is Arizona's second most-visited tourist attraction, after the Grand Canyon.

With the rebirth of the bridge as a heritage tourist attraction, the cultural geographer reenters more familiar territory. In the first edition of this book, Nuala Johnson reviewed a substantial body of work on the "role of public sculpture and monumental architecture in . . . anchoring collective social memory" (2004: 316). In this case, granted, we have a simulacrum of an architectural icon anchoring a fabricated collective memory (if you can call it that) of a place called "England" – represented by a pastiche of faux-Tudor architecture, Union Jack iconography, an ersatz pub, and a decommissioned Routemaster bus-turned-snackbar. There is almost too much to work with here, but if we were to undertake a study, we might start with the relation between materiality, memory, and meaning. We could, after

**Figure 15.4** Artist's impression of London Bridge on location in Lake Havasu City, with the "English Village" in foreground, c. 1971.

Dydia DeLyser (1999), look at how people encountering the bridge project their own interpretations of its "authenticity" onto the structure. Or we could produce an "object-centered" account of how the politics of memory at this site is "materialized" through the presence of the bridge and negotiated through various attempts to capitalize on (or ignore) its iconic status (Hoskins 2007). We also might consider how memory is performed in relation to this object through embodied encounters (Marshall 2004) and ritual practices (Coleman and Crang 2002), such as the annual "Quit Rent" ceremony which, according to a plaque installed at the site, is reenacted every October under the bridge to symbolize London's friendship with Lake Havasu City: "The bridge provides a bond between two very different municipalities, the 2,000 year old English City and Lake Havasu City, established a few decades ago in the American southwest." The displaced bridge provides an opportunity to reflect on a range of geographical concerns, including expressions of nationhood and belonging, the construction of meaning through practices of tourism and travel, and the transitive properties of collective memory.

## Circulation and Consumption

While select slices of London Bridge performed their role as The World's Largest Antique in Arizona, remnant samples of bridge granite embarked on more mobile trajectories. When the cladding sections were shipped out, a large store of material was left behind at Merrivale Quarry; this deposit became the base for a thriving cottage industry in London Bridge souvenirs. Bookends, pen stands, paperweights, and ash trays made of "authentic" London Bridge granite were produced for home and export markets, with particularly robust trade in the US (Shepherd 1971). Masons at Merrivale and other regional quarries (including Hantergantick quarry, which provided the pier stone for the current London Bridge) transformed the remaining rock from scrap to desired commodity. The rock that would become Adrian's bookends was sawn, polished, packaged, and sent out for sale, perhaps making it as far as Arizona to join its material relations. Someone bought the pair of bookends (as a gift?), and they eventually found their way back to Cornwall. Other pairs begin to circulate in second-hand markets: a few appeared at auction houses; more sifted into junk shops and car-boot sales. A cursory e-bay search reveals several authentic pieces of London Bridge granite, of various sizes and styles of presentation, available for purchase at a modest reserve.

As the bookends take on a role in the unfolding story as discrete objects, they become available for study in different ways. Most obviously, they enter into more intimate, and intricate, systems of production, consumption, and use. While the study of the "social life of things" (Appadurai 1988) emerged out of work in anthropology and sociology, in recent years geographers have enlivened this literature with explicitly spatial approaches to "following" things as they move through social, economic, symbolic, and emotional circuits of significance. Such approaches, applied to our bookend case study, might lead to a multi-site ethnography of the constellation of relations linked to the bookends' production and consumption (Cook and Harrison 2007; Cook et al. 2004). Or research might take a more focused interest in the object as souvenir, as Ramsay (2009) does in her "following" of souvenir objects from Swaziland to the UK, attending to processual aspects of object agency and materiality as things are purchased, used, and displayed. In a similar study, Burrell (2011) examines the consumption of "Western" things by children in Poland. In this study, fragments of Western consumer culture take on an "enchanted" significance. It is possible to imagine that at one time a dedicated Londonophile living in Doncaster, or Des Moines, would have felt a comparable enthusiasm about owning a pair of bona fide London Bridge bookends.

Although most of the bookends were likely destined for private collections or second-hand retail spaces (Gregson and Crewe 2003), some of them may have entered into the more public spaces of the museum. A "museum geography" (Geoghegan 2010) of these objects could involve an examination of contingent curatorial practices of accession, inventory, and conservation (DeSilvey 2007b; Patchett and Foster 2008), a tracing of their connection to other collections and spatial contexts (Hill 2006), or a focus on the political and cultural "memory-work" that the objects are asked to perform (Hoskins 2007; Till 2005). These approaches flag up an issue of scale in relation to our bookends. In the previous section the granite fragment subsumed within a larger architectural feature lent itself to studies of monumental and symbolic registers of significance. As stand-alone artifacts, the bookends make available interpretations that focus more on the idiosyncrasies of emergent social and material relations. This scalar sorting is replicated outside geography, as larger artifacts fall under the remit of heritage studies or architectural history, while smaller objects tend to be shuffled into museum studies or archaeology. There is no clear boundary between these fields.

## Disposal and Dispossession

Moving on to another kind of field boundary, how did the bookends find themselves incorporated into a Cornish hedge in Stithians? There is something appealing about the thought that someone deliberately placed the bookends in the hedges as a kind of ritual act, returning a fragment of Cornish matter to its approximate origins (still assuming that these pieces were quarried down the hill at Carnsew and not 100 miles away on Dartmoor). I proposed this theory to Adrian, however; and he dismissed it as fanciful: "I think a previous occupant of our property simply wanted to get rid of the bookends and the hedge was a convenient spot" (personal communication April 13, 2011). Convenient, I suppose, but also a relatively elaborate way to dispose of an unwanted object. Perhaps there was some element of guilt involved, or a desire to hide the evidence of discard from the gift-giver.

The apparent disposal of the bookends, far from sealing off opportunities for further study, opens up a rich seam of possible research approaches, as geographers have begun to assert with an abundance of recent publications on the practice, poetics, and politics of "wasting" (Davies 2012; Crang 2010; Gregson 2007; Gregson and Crang 2010; Hawkins 2010; Sundberg 2008). Much of this work focuses on how practices of wasting, disposal, and divestment make visible the systems that we use to order our social worlds and establish value (Gregson, Metcalfe, and Crewe 2007a). If we could somehow interview the person who chose to discard the bookends in the hedge, we might discover that he/she disposed of these objects because the possession of them no longer (if it ever had) aligned with a desired self-narrative (Gregson, Metcalfe, and Crewe 2007b): London Bridge bookends give way to a designer vase, perhaps. But, as Kevin Hetherington has pointed out, disposal is about the "placing of absences"; and more often than not, this absence is only partly achieved. It is likely that before the bookends found their way to the hedge, they spent months or years in a state of "unfinished disposal" (Hetherington 2004) at the back of a closet or in a box in a shed, until they had become sufficiently "cooled" to be released (Gregson *et al.* 2007b: 684). Even once they passed this point, however, their stubborn materiality persisted and the possibility of return remained. In fact, the abandoned bookends only accrued another form of value in their discard (Crewe 2011).

One form of alternate value emerged through the bookends' enrollment as material for the previous round of hedge building, or repair. The bookends had slipped back into the category of "matter," shedding their symbolic, metonymic function to perform a more prosaic task – contributing to the structural integrity of a stone wall. Not quite the London Bridge, but important nonetheless. One could spin out a corollary research strand on the Cornish hedge as a vernacular regional artifact, perhaps engaging with the tradition of Sauerian cultural study (Jackson 2000) to inform a "reanimation" of local landscape, as Hayden Lorimer does in his paper on the lived geographies of a Cairngorm reindeer herd (2006). Lorimer's attention to the material relics of human and animal dwelling in the landscape – rock circles, ruined shelters, stone carvings – recalls geography's earlier preoccupation with "empiricism and materiality" but couples it with "critical scrutiny of how cultural topographies of inquiry now differ" (2006: 516). A sympathetic approach cast in relation to Adrian's hedge might consider the way that Cornwall's granite hedges both constrain and guide movement through the landscape as assemblages of material which sustain both ancient and contemporary patterns of land use and habitation.

## Salvage and Storytelling

We return to the beginning of our story, with Adrian's chance discovery of the bookends while rebuilding the hedge on his new property: "I can't imagine why anyone would want to dispose of such an important part of Cornwall's quarrying legacy – the bookends are one of my most prized possessions – and what are the chances of me finding them in my hedge?" (personal communication April 13, 2011). The story is clearly one that Adrian enjoys telling. It resonates with his interest in regional geology and also creates a link between his personal history and the history of the parcel of land where he now lives. One friend, aware of the significance of the bookend find, found another fragment of London Bridge granite (this one

**Figure 15.5** The rescued bookends.
Source: photo by Adrian Lea.

mounted on a wooden base) in a London junk shop and brought it back to Cornwall as a gift for Adrian. The first object draws in a parallel object, and a collection begins to form (Figure 15.5).

Adrian's relationship to the bookend lends itself to a study framed by the concept of "relational personhood" (Strathern 1988), which boils down to the assertion that people do not only make things but are made by them in turn (Miller 2008, 2009). Individuals construct their sense of self out of their relationships with material cultures, as well as their relationships with other people. In this instance, the bookends become a touchstone for an emerging identity based around Adrian's residence in Cornwall and his interest in the geological foundations of his adopted landscape. It would be possible to frame a study around the integration of these meaningful objects in Adrian's "home culture" (Blunt and Dowling 2006) or to explore the way that Adrian's enthusiasm for the study of regional geology expresses itself through his acquisition of appropriate specimens. Other geographers have explored similar themes in their investigation of the way that model railway enthusiasts (Yarwood and Shaw 2010) and industrial archaeology buffs (Geoghegan 2009) construct and maintain their unique self-identity in relation to specific material cultures. As Tolia-Kelly observes in her study of domestic material cultures in British Asian households, the meaning of such personalized objects is infused with the biography of their owner: "Their intrinsic value is limited, but their symbolic value shifts through time . . . These curios become treasures, they are revered through their reconstruction and in turn reconstruct their contexts of display" (2004: 325–326). With their exhibition in Adrian's home as prized possessions, the London Bridge bookends undergo yet another recontextualization, another chapter in their itinerant, intricate life-story.

## Conclusions

This chapter narrates a series of intervals and events in the geobiography of a pair of granite bookends; these intervals then open out to introduce a diverse range of different approaches to the study of objects and their material identities. We begin with a description of the formation and extraction of the bookends' granite and use this history to discuss geographical perspectives on the underlying instability and dynamism of ostensibly inert matter. We then follow the stone as it is incorporated in a built structure and explore the investment of labor required to maintain its durability as a cultural form. As the bridge undergoes a transformation to foreground its symbolic significance over its practical value, we encounter ideas about the way that material forms mediate the performance of cultural memory. The residual pieces of the bridge, re-crafted as souvenirs, present an opportunity to think about commodity geographies and the circulation of value. When the bookends shed their value as either economic or sentimental entities, we watch as their discard leads to their reincarnation as a material for use in a vernacular regional feature. This interval of incomplete disposal leads on to the rediscovery and revaluing of the objects as anchors for individual identity.

To the extent that these different approaches are compatible with each other, it is the bookends that makes them so. The presence of these objects in the chapter works, as I suggested at the outset, to hold together a set of often incongruent perspectives and philosophies and to keep them from tumbling off the shelf into chaos. The bookends provide an underlying coherence that allows the rest of the chapter to work on a principle of adjacency and conjecture, tracing connections that might otherwise be overlooked. There is no attempt here to restrict our study of the object to its significance as a symbol of social relations, though this is one of the aspects considered. Instead, the range of significant relations is expanded to encompass the geophysical, vocational, practical, and structural aspects of object identity as well. The approach also acknowledges, implicitly, the "wayward expressiveness" of matter (Kearnes 2003) and the potential presence of relations that are not legible to us, or available for study. An object-centered narrative of this kind allows us to play with different ways of making geographical meaning in collaboration with materials; the portrait of the bookends that we are left with is expansive and resolutely indeterminate, open to future transformations and appropriations.

## References

Anderson, B. and McFarlane, C. (2011) Assemblage and geography. *Area*, 43, 124–127.

Anderson, B. and Tolia-Kelly, D.P. (2004) Matter(s) in social and cultural geography. *Geoforum*, 35, 669–674.

Anderson, B. and Wylie, J. (2009) On geography and materiality. *Environment and Planning A*, 41, 318–335.

Appadurai, A. (ed.) (1988) *The Social Life of Things: Commodities in Cultural Perspective*. Cambridge: Cambridge University Press.

Bennett, J. (2010) *Vibrant Matter: A Political Ecology of Things*. Durham, NC: Duke University Press.

Blunt, A. and Dowling, R. (2006) *Home*. Abingdon: Routledge.

Burrell, K. (2011) The enchantment of Western things: Children's material encounters in late socialist Poland. *Transactions of the Institute of British Geographers*, 36, 143–156.

Clark, N. (2011) *Inhuman Nature: Sociable Life on a Dynamic Planet*. London: Sage.

Coe, F. (1896) *The World and Its People: Modern Europe*. New York, Boston, and Chicago: Silver, Burdett, and Company.

Coleman, S. and Crang, M. (2002) *Tourism: Between Place and Performance*. Oxford: Berghahn.

Cook, I. *et al.* (2004) Follow the thing: Papaya. *Antipode*, 36, 642–664.

Cook, I.J. and Harrison, M. (2007) Follow the thing: West Indian hot pepper sauce. *Space and Culture*, 10, 40–63.

Cook, I.J. and Tolia-Kelly, D.P. (2010) Material geographies. In *Oxford Handbook of Material Culture Studies*, ed. D. Hicks and M. Beaudry. Oxford: Oxford University Press, pp. 99–122.

Crang, M. (2010) The death of great ships: Photography, politics and waste in the global imaginary. *Environment and Planning A*, 42, 1084–1102.

Crewe, L. (2011) Life itemised: Lists, loss, significance and the impossibility of erasure. *Environment and Planning D: Society and Space*, 29, 27–46.

Davies, A.R. (2012) Geography and the matter of waste mobilities. *Transactions of the Institute of British Geographers*, 37 (2), 191–196.

DeLyser, D. (1999) Authenticity on the ground: Engaging the past in a California ghost town. *Annals of the Association of American Geographers*, 89, 602–632.

DeSilvey, C. (2006) Observed decay: Telling stories with mutable things. *Journal of Material Culture*, 11, 318–338.

DeSilvey, C. (2007a) Salvage memory: Constellating material histories on a hardscrabble homestead. *Cultural Geographies*, 14, 401–424.

DeSilvey, C. (2007b) Art and archive: Memory-work on a Montana homestead. *Journal of Historical Geography*, 33, 878–900.

DeSilvey, C. (2012) Making sense of transience: An anticipatory history. *Cultural Geographies*, 19 (1), 31–54.

Edensor, T. (2011) Entangled agencies, material networks and repair in a building assemblage: The mutable stone of St Ann's Church, Manchester. *Transactions of the Institute of British Geographers*, 36, 238–252.

Geoghegan, H. (2009) "If you can walk down the street and recognise the difference between cast iron and wrought iron, the world is altogether a better place": Being enthusiastic about industrial archaeology. *M/C Journal*, 12 (2), http://journal.media-culture.org.au/index.php/mcjournal/issue/view/enthuse (accessed October 19, 2012).

Geoghegan, H. (2010) Museum geography: Exploring museums, collections and museum practice in the UK. *Geography Compass*, 4, 1462–1476.

Graham, S. and Thrift, N. (2007) Out of order: Understanding repair and maintenance. *Theory, Culture and Society*, 24, 1–25.

Gregson, N. (2007) *Living with Things: Ridding, Accommodation, Dwelling*. Oxford: Sean Kingston Publishing.

Gregson, N. and Crang, M. (2010) Materiality and waste: Inorganic vitality in a networked world. *Environment and Planning A*, 42, 1026–1032.

Gregson, N. and Crewe, L. (2003) *Second-Hand Cultures*. Oxford: Berg.

Gregson, N., Metcalfe, A., and Crewe, L. (2007a) Moving things along: The conduits and practices of divestment in consumption. *Transactions of the Institute of British Geographers*, 32, 187–200.

Gregson, N., Metcalfe, A., and Crewe, L. (2007b) Identity, mobility, and the throwaway society. *Environment and Planning D: Society and Space*, 25, 682–700.

Gregson, N., Metcalfe, A., and Crewe, L. (2009) Practices of object maintenance and repair: How consumers attend to consumer objects within the home. *Journal of Consumer Culture*, 9, 248–272.

Hawkins, H. (2010) Turn your trash into . . . rubbish, art and politics: Richard Wentworth's geographical imagination. *Social and Cultural Geography*, 11, 805–826.

Hetherington, K. (2004) Secondhandedness: Consumption, disposal, and absent presence. *Environment and Planning D: Society and Space*, 22, 157–173.

Hill, J. (2006) Travelling objects: The Wellcome Collection in Los Angeles, London and beyond. *Cultural Geographies*, 13, 340–366.

Hoskins, G.C. (2007) Materialising memory at Angel Island Immigration Station, San Francisco. *Environment and Planning A*, 39, 437–455.

Housefield, J. (2007) Sites of time: Organic and geologic time in the art of Robert Smithson and Roxy Paine. *Cultural Geographies*, 14, 537–561.

Ingold, T. (2007) Materials against materiality. *Archaeological Dialogues*, 14, 1–16.

Jackson, P. (2000) Rematerializing social and cultural geography. *Social and Cultural Geography*, 1, 9–14.

Jacobs, J. (2006) A geography of big things. *Cultural Geographies*, 13, 1–27.

Johnson, N.C. (2004) Public memory. In *Companion to Cultural Geography*, ed. J.S. Duncan, N.C. Johnson, and R.H. Schein. Oxford: Blackwell, pp. 316–328.

Karjalainen, P.T. (2003) On geobiography. In *Place and Location: Studies in Environmental Aesthetics and Semiotics III*, ed. V. Sarapik and K. Tüür. Tallinn: Estonian Literary Museum, pp. 87–92.

Kearnes, M.B. (2003) Geographies that matter: The rhetorical deployment of physicality? *Social and Cultural Geography*, 4, 139–152.

Lorimer, H. (2006) Herding memories of humans and animals. *Environment and Planning D: Society and Space*, 24, 497–518.

Marshall, D. (2004) Making sense of remembrance. *Social and Cultural Geography*, 5, 37–54.

Massey, D. (2006) Landscape as a provocation: Reflections on moving mountains. *Journal of Material Culture*, 11, 33–48.

Miller, D. (2008) *The Comfort of Things*. Cambridge: Polity.

Miller, D. (2009) *Stuff*. Cambridge: Polity.

New York Times (1902) Widening London Bridge: New parapets being built in order to relieve the congested traffic. New York Times, October 5.

Patchett, M. and Foster, K. (2008) Repair work: Surfacing the geographies of dead animals. *Museum and Society*, 6, 98–122.

Pike, A. (2011) Placing brands and branding: A socio-spatial biography of Newcastle Brown Ale. *Transactions of the Institute of British Geographers*, 36, 206–222.

Ramsay, N. (2009) Taking-place: Refracted enchantment and the habitual spaces of the tourist souvenir. *Social and Cultural Geography*, 10, 197–217.

Rose, G., Degen, M., and Basdas, B. (2010) More on "big things": Building events and feelings. *Transactions of the Institute of British Geographers*, 35, 334–349.

Shepherd, C.W. (1971) *A Thousand Years of London Bridge*. London: John Baker.

Stanier, P. (1999) *South West Granite: A History of the Granite Industry in Cornwall and Devon*. St. Austell: Cornish Hillside Publications.

Strathern, M. (1988) *The Gender of the Gift: Problems with Women and Problems with Society in Melanesia*. Berkeley: University of California Press.

Sundberg, J. (2008) "Trash-talk" and the production of quotidian geopolitical boundaries in the USA–Mexico borderlands. *Social and Cultural Geography*, 9, 871–890.

Tait, M. and While, A. (2009) Ontology and the conservation of built heritage. *Environment and Planning D: Society and Space*, 27, 721–737.

Thomas, N. (1991) *Entangled Objects: Exchange, Material Culture, and Colonialism in the Pacific*. Cambridge, MA: Harvard University Press.

Till, K. (2005) *The New Berlin: Memory, Politics, Place*. Minneapolis: University of Minnesota Press.

Tolia-Kelly, D.P. (2004) Locating processes of identification: Studying the precipitates of re-memory through artefacts in the British Asian home. *Transactions of the Institute of British Geographers*, 29, 314–329.

Whatmore, S. (2006) Materialist returns: Practising cultural geography in and for a more-than-human world. *Cultural Geographies*, 13, 600–609.

Wilford, J. (2008) Out of rubble: Natural disaster and the materiality of the house. *Environment and Planning D: Society and Space*, 26, 647–662.

Yarwood, R. and Shaw, J. (2010) "N-gauging" geographies: Craft consumption, indoor leisure and model railways. *Area*, 42, 425–433.

# Landscapes

*The Wiley Blackwell Companion to Cultural Geography*, First Edition.
Edited by Nuala C. Johnson, Richard H. Schein, and Jamie Winders.
© 2013 John Wiley & Sons, Ltd. Published 2016 by John Wiley & Sons, Ltd.

Chapter 16

# Economic Landscapes

*Niall Majury*

## Introduction

Over the past decade scholarship within economic geography has drawn upon an increasingly pluralist, heterodox intellectual culture compared to the more "centered" forms of economic geography associated with constructing a regional science or accounting for industrial restructuring. As Peck put it, its practices and positions now encompass "spatial science and non-representational theory, neo-Marxism and new geographical economics, modelling and ethnography, feminism and poststructralism, and just about everything in between" (2005: 129). In the process what is understood as an economic landscape has been recast, theoretically reconstructed in terms that often bear little resemblance to ones of old. Neither agricultural hinterlands nor restructured industrial spaces are any longer privileged vantage points from which to approach disciplinary concerns. Encounters during the 1990s with poststructural methods (Graham 1991), postcolonial studies (Watts 1993), and feminist theories (Hanson and Pratt 1995) challenged "the impression that there is always only one story to tell, and that it is often economic, masculinist and white" (Barnes 1996: 41). With economic geography's cultural, relational, and institutional turns a virtue has been made of encounters with a multiplicity of theoretical and substantive concerns. A new kind of economic geography has emerged, one that promotes "the understanding of open systems, appreciation of context and qualitative techniques" (Amin and Thrift 2001: 5) and problematizes the place within economic geographic practice of formal mainstream economics and traditional Marxism (Amin and Thrift 2005). The "decentering" of the subdiscipline has generated much acrimony (Smith 2005; Hudson 2006; Harvey 2006), producing a fragmented form of pluralism (Barnes and Sheppard 2010) and considerable debate over future disciplinary directions. However, out of this have emerged explicitly variegated conceptions

*The Wiley Blackwell Companion to Cultural Geography*, First Edition.
Edited by Nuala C. Johnson, Richard H. Schein, and Jamie Winders.
© 2013 John Wiley & Sons, Ltd. Published 2016 by John Wiley & Sons, Ltd.

of "the economy," more complex, situated understandings of economic identities and relations, and insights into how capitalism transforms and evolves across time and space.

The task I was set in writing this chapter was to reflect on how an economic geographer would approach, theorize, and understand a landscape. Given the twists and turns the subdiscipline has traversed in recent years, this is not a straightforward task. A diversity of views over what constitutes economic geographic knowledge places the object of analysis – an economic landscape – in contention. However, to my mind this is indicative of a new-found intellectual vitality that characterizes the subdiscipline, challenging entrenched orthodoxies and questioning taken-for-granted categories. In this spirit, I will draw principally upon economic geographers' engagement with economic sociology – a strand of heterodox economic theory – to demonstrate that even though landscapes may appear legible only in economic, cultural, or political terms, they can in fact be read as the nexus of all sorts of relations and scales of praxis. At the heart of this approach is a rejection of the notion that "the economy" should somehow be thought of as always "a material ground out of which the cultural is shaped, or in relation to which it acquires its significance" (Mitchell 2002: 3). Rather "the economy" can be understood as a set of social practices that put in place a particular politics of calculation which operate as a series of boundaries, distinctions, exceptions, and exclusions (Callon 1998) that constitute "the economic" through time and space. This approach problematizes the conceptual terms by which we claim to know and understand "the economy" (e.g., capital, labor, market) and offers new inflections to geographers' sensitivity to space, place, and geographical circulation. This will be illustrated in relation to a landscape of contemporary capitalism that was until recently relatively overlooked by economic geographers – the landscape of owner-occupied residential housing.

A touchstone for economic geography's engagement with heterodox economic theories (and economic sociology in particular) was an article published in the *American Journal of Sociology* by Mark Granovetter in 1985 on of the social embeddedness of economic relations (cf. Amin and Thrift 1992; Grabher 1993; McDowell 1997; Storper 1997; Peck 2001; Gertler 2004). Granovetter challenged the prevailing Parsonian division of labor between economics and sociology (Parsons 1935a, 1935b), questioning the deference traditionally afforded neoclassical economics in establishing "the truth about markets" (Kay 2003). He took issue with their model of economic action, positioned outside of culture and politics, conceived narrowly as instrumental transactions among atomized actors. Granovetter, in contrast, conceptualized economic action as embedded in networks of personal relationships and broader social processes of norm making and institution building. This notion of embeddedness has given rise to a diverse program of research on the historical evolution of different "national" *varieties of capitalism*, exploring how the strategic behavior of firms and other actors is embedded in a range of institutional environments and the significance of this for the comparative advantage of particular regions in the global economy (Berger and Dore 1996; Hollingsworth and Boyer 1997; Hall and Soskice 2001). This approach to understanding *capitalism as a constructed system* drew attention to the ways in which actors, firms, and markets are constituted by and operate within particular configurations of cultural, political, institutional, and legal relations. National institutional archetypes and relatively bounded national economies were positioned relative to a spectrum that ranged between liberal market economies (an idealized form of American capitalism) and coordinated market economies (a stylized description of features of the economies of countries such as Germany and Japan). The *varieties* project has tended to be programmatic in nature, identifying and refining a set of propositions with regard to variation among national institutional spaces. While economic geographers share an analytic commitment to understanding differences in capitalist forms of organization over time and space, they have also, importantly, provided their own inflection by thinking about the (re-)production of variety in relational terms (Christopherson 2002; Bathelt and Gertler 2005; Clark and Wojcik 2007; Engelen and Grote 2009). Geographers have been more attuned to problematize the ontological status of national economic space (Agnew 1994), acknowledging that the spaces and scalar configurations of circuits of capital can no longer be assumed as pre-given (Amin 2002, 2004) and that there are systemic interdependencies between disparate national institutional spaces (Marston 2000; Brenner 2001). The "onshore" features of national institutional spaces are critically dependent on the webs of "offshore" relations within which they are embedded (Peck and Theodore 2007). For example, "if the rise of India and China, in particular, raises questions about 'new' varieties of capitalism that have hitherto barely been charted, it also throws into sharp relief the issue of the complex asymmetries and webs of connection that increasingly characterise the unevenly integrating global economy. Hence the need to think about variety in relational terms" (Peck and Theodore 2007: 766).

The *varieties* project has established a plausible analytical counter-narrative to free market discourse and associated "flat-earth" visions of the trajectory of economic restructuring under globalization (Friedman 2005). It has highlighted the significance of institutional embeddedness for understanding economic systems and their transformations. However, as Peck and Theodore (2007) have argued, economic geographers are moving beyond the pluralization of capitalism toward not only documenting differences in trajectories of development, but also calibrating connections and understanding the contingent relations that underpin apparent divergences and convergences. This entails examining the principles, dimensions, and micro- and macro- sources of capitalism's *variegation*. As economic geographers, distinctions among the landscapes of contemporary capitalism should not be conceived of in quantitative terms (i.e. on a continuum running from a utilitarian abstraction of the market towards "non-market" forms of coordination). Rather, distinctions should be drawn in terms of qualitative variegation (i.e., recognizing that markets assume diverse forms, cannot function autonomously, and are constituted through and coexistent with cultural, institutional, and political structures). As Krippner argues, "every transaction, no matter how instantaneous, is social in the broader sense of the term: congealed into every market exchange is a history of struggle and contestation that has produced actors with certain understandings of themselves and the world which predispose them to exchange under a certain set of rules and not another. In this sense, the state, culture and politics are contained in every market act; they do not variably exert their influence on some kinds of markets more than others" (2001: 112). Within a variegated approach, an important task for economic geographers is to deconstruct across time and space what passes for market structures and market relations, tracing the circulation and reception of the normative ideas and practices that are built into them and the practical, essential characteristics of state and non-state authority that underpin them. Geographies of supply and demand are not simply "out there," waiting to be invoked in the overdetermination of economic landscapes, but instead have had to be constructed, ideologically and institutionally. Formatting "the economy" puts in place a cultural politics of calculation, operating as a series of socio-spatial boundaries, inclusions, and exclusions, in which moral claims, arguments about justice and forms of entitlement, are forged. These situated logics and imperatives animate a geography of markets that is permanently "under construction."

## Housing and Homeownership

> Our house: hall mat, tan coir, from Noble Bros on the main road. On the wall to the left, a joined
> VW of coat pegs, red balls on black stalks, bought from Nobles', mounted by Harry, though
> unused as a rule, as too many coats impeded the opening of the front door; on the wall to the
> right, a mirror, moulded plaster frame, leaves and berries, a wedding present from my Aunt
> Mildred, my mother's younger sister. Through door to: dark-grey moquette armchair, one of two
> (the other faced it across the room), making up, with the three-seater settee beneath the window,
> the Chesterfield suite, from the Co-op on the instalment plan. Either side of the second chair, a
> radiogram, possibly from the Co-op too, probably on the instalment plan as well, a wedding
> present from my father, and an occasional table said to have been in Harry's family 'for genera-
> tions' . . . Whenever I attempted this mental inventory, I rarely even made it into the kitchen.
> So many things and so many still to buy. Every second day it seemed another delivery van arrived
> in the street: carpets for number 17, a wardrobe for number 10. (Patterson 2003: 23–24)

Housing, especially owner-occupied housing, embodies complex, politically and ethically charged entanglements between the materiality of housing, the meaning of home, and the mobilization of finance (Smith 2008; Smith and Munro 2008). While housing is not necessarily coterminous with "home," houses are objects of emotional investment and attachment, as illustrated in the above passage. It is taken from a novel set in a suburban street in Belfast constructed in the 1950s, summoning up a resident's mental inventory of her then newly acquired home: an interior space filled with everyday mass-produced objects, popular styles and fashions typical of homes within the neighborhood at the time, some bought on credit, yet many invested with emotional significance, markers of memory, identity, and sense of belonging. During the twentieth century, the materiality of "home" as housing, in particular owner-occupied housing within Anglo-American economies, became embedded within a wider system of mass production and mass consumption and the evolution of an associated stream of financial services (consumer and mortgage credit). A remarkable feature of the latter half of the twentieth century is the transformation of a minority form of housing tenure, homeownership, into the dominant one in the United States and United Kingdom. In 1900 around 10 percent of British and 45 percent of American households owned their own homes. By 2000 this had risen to around 70 percent in both countries. However, homeownership is a highly geared means of providing shelter, entailing households taking on record levels of debt. The risks associated with managing this financial obligation stretch out over typically 25–30 years. At the same time households assume responsibility for the maintenance, repair, and insurance of a property. Despite this, an increasing proportion of society has, until relatively recently, literally bought into the idea that owning your own home is "the done thing." In the process the drive to ownership has transformed the metropolitan geographies of British and American cities, fueling suburban expansion and (more recently) inner-city gentrification. In both countries it has been prescribed by acts of governance which prioritize discursively and materially home purchase over other forms of tenancy, casting renting as "dead money" associated with dependency and beset with problems associated with limited quality, condition, availability, and an uncertain future (given the possibility of stock transfers) (Gurney 1999; Flint 2003). Owner occupation has become a gateway to scarce public goods, such as safer neighborhoods, better schools, and enhanced local amenity. It has also become not only a housing strategy "of choice" but also an increasingly important investment strategy. Housing wealth is no longer just considered an asset accumulated during working life to either offset reduced income in old age or pass on to another generation. Financial deregulation, declining social support, and wage stagnation over the last twenty years have resulted in housing wealth being reconfigured as an active resource to be utilized by home-owners in meeting a wide range of welfare needs and consumer desires (Montgomerie 2007; Smith 2008; Langley 2008a).

The remainder of this chapter will explore how the idea of "homeownership" has been mobilized in the United States and enrolled within wider notions of "responsible citizenship" and socially sanctioned consumption norms. Over the twentieth century the idea, associated practices, and landscapes forged in its name became hallmarks of American prosperity and a template for economic development. Yet, as will shortly be illustrated, the stream of financial services and regime of valuation that was constructed to advance owner occupation as the cornerstone of a new objective market order put in place a particular politics of calculation which operated as a series of boundaries, distinctions, and exclusions. These transformed metropolitan geographies, fueling postwar suburban growth and the framing of wider political conflicts over property rights, the nature of citizenship, and distributive justice in particular ways. Only this year, in the wake of the "sub-prime crisis," the *Financial Times* (Braithwaite 2011) reported that though rates of home ownership in the United States had fallen to 66.5 percent in the last quarter of 2010, its lowest level for 12 years, the rate of decline was not uniform, with levels of ownership among white Americans falling to 74.2 percent and rates among African Americans to 44.9 percent. As will be highlighted in the remaining sections of this chapter, the growth of owner occupation may appear legible only in economic terms – the configuration of a market to finance a particular category of tenure – but in fact the construction of a market for owner-occupied housing can also be read as the nexus of all sorts of relations (economic, political, and cultural) and scales of praxis.

## Constructing a Market for Homeownership

Up until the 1920s just over two-fifths of US households were homeowners. Speculative building, subdividing (curbstoning), and self-building (from plan books or mail order kits) had characterized the rapid expansion of residential areas around the polluted, crowded centers of industrial cities. Advances in methods of mass production that had translated into impressive productivity gains in other sectors of the economy were confined in the residential construction industry to the production of pre-cut houses by mail order companies and the supply of prefabricated construction materials by lumber companies. The actual construction of houses was still dominated by small to medium-sized local construction firms and incremental self-building. Values of thrift, mutual aid, and self-reliance went into making these suburban landscapes, many of which were unplanned (Harris 1996; Hayden 2004). Mortgages, unless you were a farmer, were the exception rather than the rule as the terms of most made them prohibitive for many. They were provided by locally based financial institutions organized within regional markets for mortgages. These lending institutions required borrowers to put down between 46 and 54 percent of the purchase price of the property and typically offered it for a term of between three and five years (Freund 2007). Mortgages were not amortized, leaving borrowers with a huge lump-sum repayment at the end of the term of the loan or, more commonly, costly negotiations for second and third mortgages.

After the collapse of wages and property values in 1929, the Great Depression ushered in an unprecedented housing and credit crisis. By 1933 more than a thousand mortgages were being foreclosed each day and, by one estimate, approximately half of all US mortgages were delinquent (Hillier 2003). Homeownership appeared unsustainable, its legitimacy as a means of securing adequate shelter in question. However, it was in the midst of managing this crisis that an alliance of private and public interests forged a new national market for mortgage finance and positioned the promotion of homeownership at the center of wider initiatives to make sense of the Great Depression and engineer recovery through shoring up the purchasing power of industrial labor (Blyth 2002). Early Depression-era housing legislation was experimental in nature – emergency responses to the swift collapse of regional markets for mortgage finance and associated banking crises. The Federal Home Loan Bank Act (1932) introduced a framework for the regulation of local savings banks, providing participants in regional credit markets with federal loans to compensate for sudden fluctuations in their capital reserves. A year later the Home Owners' Loan Corporation (HOLC) was established to provide federal assistance to lenders to refinance delinquent mortgages. Both of these initiatives were significant in demonstrating the sorts of roles the state could play in supporting credit markets in general and housing finance in particular. Within the two-year period that HOLC was authorized to assist with refinancing delinquent mortgages, nearly one in every five mortgages in the United States came to be owned by it. Although these initiatives were only intended to assist *existing* homeowners, an influential network of land economists and real estate developers lobbied for measures to *extend* the market for residential mortgages, promoting a vision of economic growth centered on the growth of homeownership, residential construction, and associated consumption norms. Key to their vision was the widespread use of a more flexible and affordable mortgage instrument.

Constructing a new market for such a mortgage was contingent upon stabilizing the properties of the object or asset against which such loans would be secured – property or real estate. Policymakers drew upon the principles of land-use science to validate a means of governing land uses (i.e., through restrictive zoning and covenants) and to regularize valuation practices (i.e., property appraisal) across the country. In the first decades of the twentieth century in the United States the new science of land-use planning gravitated from a preoccupation with aesthetics (City Beautiful Movement) toward developing techniques, principally land-use zoning, to engineer the growth of orderly, efficient, healthy cities. The efforts of the National Conference on City Planning (NCCP, 1909) to popularize the idea of zoning as a means to promote "public welfare" quickly attracted the interest of the real estate industry and their national organization, the National Association of Real Estate Boards (NAREB, 1908). The involvement of the real estate industry in shaping land-use science quickly transformed a broad concern with determining "best uses" to ensure "public welfare" into a narrower focus on protecting property values (Weiss 1987). With support from the Department of Commerce under Herbert Hoover, NCCP and NAREB members sought to codify real estate practice as a scientific theory of the land market and create a professional culture and associated set of institutions. Important to this project was the Department of Commerce's support for a group of real estate economists based at the Institute for Research in Land Economics and Public Utilities (from hereon "the *Institute*") at the University of Wisconsin (Weiss 1989). Founded by Richard Ely in 1920, the *Institute* worked closely with planners, developers, and public officials to explore how land-use strategies, methods of valuation, and financing techniques could be adapted to reengineer the market for housing finance in a way that would promote mass participation in homeownership. The essential preconditions required to sustain such a market, they argued, were: the standardization of property appraisal practices; the widespread use of a more affordable, flexible mortgage instrument; and the adoption of land-use zoning ordinances and restrictive covenants to protect property values (Freund 2007). In 1921 NAREB established a formal affiliation with the *Institute*, collaborating in the publication of Ely's *Land Economics Series* of textbooks, materials that in time transformed real estate practice and college curricula nationwide.

The model of the urban property market advanced through the new science of land-use economics and promoted by the Department of Commerce awarded special status to residential land uses, and in particular privately owned, single-family dwellings. Model legislation circulated by the federal department to state and municipal governments in the 1920s promoted the assumption that a key measure of a well-designed zoning ordinance was the protection of single-family homes from "incompatible" development or populations. Rather than specify "compatible" uses, such legislation endorsed the assumption that local property owners were best qualified to assess what constituted the "character" of a neighborhood and determine the range of compatible uses that would not undermine property values. The intent and function of this exclusionary theory of zoning was presented by land economists as a scientific, technocratic means of managing urban growth; however, racial science figured prominently in its development, mirroring contemporary intellectual fashion as well as public debate about urban congestion (Kantor 1974) and immigration (Haney-Lopez 2006). In his manifesto for the zoning movement, Benjamin Marsh had argued in *An Introduction to City Planning: Democracy's Challenge to the American City* (1929) that zoning was "a means for preventing race deterioration" (p. 9). Given then commonplace white racial thinking about biological difference and racial hierarchy, land economists and real estate developers articulated and codified what they saw as common-sense rules about race and property: namely, the perceived threat of black occupancy to a neighborhood's property values. These arguments centered on economics and "the imperatives of the market," justifying in 1924 the inclusion within NAREB's code of ethics of a clause "forbidding members from introducing into a neighborhood "members of any race or nationality" whose presence "will clearly be detrimental to property values" (Freund 2007: 15). Though attempts to define occupancy by a racial minority as an "incompatible" land use were struck down by the Supreme Court (*Buchanan v. Warley*, 1917), by the 1930s a set of economic arguments took hold to justify racial residential segregation in terms of the (ostensibly) impersonal processes of a "free market" and the perceived threat racial difference posed to (mainly white) residential property values. This "market imperative" thinking was to have a profound influence on the network of academics, planners, financiers, and real estate developers that the Hoover and Roosevelt administrations drew upon to devise strategies to revive the mortgage market (Home Owners' Loan Corporation, 1933) and promote homeownership as a stimulus for economic recovery (Federal Housing Administration, 1938).

Beginning with the Home Owners' Loan Corporation (HOLC, 1933), the federal government enrolled the calculative practices that Ely's *Institute* had codified to begin to construct a qualitatively different market for privately owned houses, changing how people bought their homes and the means of determining who could participate in this market. Over the three years that the HOLC offered assistance to lenders to help refinance delinquent mortgages, it received 1.9 million applications (Hayden 2004). It financed just over half of these, translating the industry practices codified in Frederick Babcock's (1924) *The Appraisal of Real Estate* into a set of standardized procedures for property valuation. This included a range of metrics of evaluation based on the form and fabric of the house, as well as others that qualified its value in terms of the "character" of the neighborhood in which it was situated and "compatibility" of surrounding land uses. Whereas for decades restrictive covenants and the informal practices of real estate agents had segregated neighborhoods racially, the HOLC's system of appraisal reproduced segregation on the basis of economics rather than belief in racial differences. Its system of metrology simply assumed, among other things, that homes and neighborhoods occupied by minorities were worth less and their values were at best unstable, if not in decline. In 1935 the HOLC's appraisal procedures were put to work by the Federal Home Loan Bank System to assess not only applicants for HOLC financing, but also to rate and qualify the suitability for mortgage finance of whole metropolitan areas. Local estate agents and lending institutions were commissioned to apply their local knowledge and deploy HOLC property appraisal procedures to devise *Residential Security Maps*. These maps delineated the boundaries of districts and neighborhoods, ranking them on a scale from A (most desirable, therefore valuable) to D (in decline, therefore least valuable), delimiting spaces within each major metropolitan area of the United States according to their suitability for inclusion within a market for residential mortgage finance. As Jackson (1985) has detailed, these ratings were informed and guided by the explicit racial and ethnic calculus that had become embedded within the science of urban zoning, rewarding with high ratings the use of restrictive covenants and absence of "foreigners or Negros." Each ranking was color coded on the maps, with D-rated neighborhoods delimited in red, giving rise to the term "redlining," as they were deemed unsuitable for long-term investment. These maps were then put into circulation among planners, lending institutions and public officials as they worked toward reconstructing the market for homeownership.

With the creation of the Federal Housing Administration (FHA, 1938) and Federal National Mortgage Association (Fannie Mae, 1938), these appraisal technologies were enrolled in the task of a more ambitious project to extend homeownership to many through the construction of a federally insured national market for mortgage finance. The network of land economists and real estate developers centered on the *Institute*, NCCP, and NAREB successfully lobbied the Hoover and Roosevelt administrations for measures to reconstruct the market for residential mortgages around a more affordable, longer-term mortgage instrument, arguing it would act as an economic stimulus, promoting economic growth nationally through the growth of homeownership, residential construction, and the boosting of associated consumption norms (Freund 2006). They also drafted the legislation and staffed the new agencies. Frederick Babcock was appointed as the FHA's chief appraiser, who set about applying the scientific practice of land-use management that he had been instrumental in codifying to the task of developing a detailed underwriting manual or rule book to guide private lending institutions and FHA officials in determining which mortgage applications would be deemed ineligible for FHA support. Through the FHA and Fannie Mae the federal government undertook to insure private lending institutions against the risk of borrowers defaulting on FHA-approved loans and also created a national "secondary" market in which investors could trade mortgages originated in regionally segmented markets for housing finance. This government guarantee to insure lenders against the downside risk of FHA-approved or "prime" loans enabled lending institutions to offer more affordable mortgages with a smaller down payment (20 percent of the value of the property), longer term (initially over twenty years, then extended to thirty-five), fixed rate of interest, and amortization (i.e., borrowers pay off both principal and interest during the life of the loan).

However, this project to construct a new market for housing finance put in place a particular politics of calculation, codified in the FHA's underwriting manual, that configured the geography of "prime" lending in terms of a series of spatial boundaries, distinctions, and exclusions, framing the cultural and political relations that had long structured notions of race and residence within the narrow calculus of the operation of a "free market" and the impersonal forces of supply and demand. FHA-authorized procedures for lending by exclusion embodied a race- and gender-specific theory of "the market" for residential property in which those who were permitted and supported to go into debt through federal government guarantees were white (male) breadwinners (Hayden 2004). Racial exclusion was now constitutive of the formal rules governing the operation of the housing market nationwide. The success of New Deal initiatives in realizing the goal of extending homeownership to the majority of the population in the postwar years, fueling suburban growth, sustaining new consumption norms, and dramatically reworking the urban landscape, was achieved through exclusionary lending practices that openly and systematically discriminated against racial minorities, entrenching further racial segregation and inequality. Yet, from the FHA's perspective, segregation was a function or at worst a symptom of "a healthy free market for property" (Freund 2007: 119) financed (ostensibly) by private capital. Indeed, the rapid growth of American suburbs in the postwar period and associated decline of central cities appeared to validate this, in the process reconfiguring the white racial thinking that underpinned exclusionary practices. As the majority of whites became suburban homeowners, they increasingly came to view racial inequality itself through the purportedly neutral optic of "the market" – that is, the "natural" workings of market relations and the defense of hard-earned rights as homeowners. By the 1960s wealth was increasingly concentrated in the suburbs, where homeownership was seen as a prerequisite for full citizenship in the United States – a nation of homeowners and a landscape of suburban housing, quintessentially embodied in the neat, picket-fenced dwellings of the "sitcom suburbs" popularized in television shows such as *Father Knows Best* and *Leave it to Beaver* (Hayden 2004).

## Concluding Remarks: From Geographies of Prime to Sub-Prime Lending

The exclusionary practices that constituted the market for homeownership remained in place until the 1970s. Urban insurrection and the civil rights movement challenged the legitimacy of the social practices, forms of expertise, and institutions that determined what constituted FHA-approved "prime lending." Legislative initiatives such as the Civil Rights Act (1968), Community Reinvestment Act (1977), and Federal Housing Enterprise Safety and Soundness Act (1992) sought to reform the market by promoting homeownership for racial minorities and low-income groups. At the same time, fiscal pressures encouraged the Johnson administration to privatize Fannie Mae in 1968, designating it as a Government Sponsored Enterprise (GSE). Nevertheless, even though this arrangement recast government guarantees for Fannie Mae's market-making activities as only implicit, this proved sufficient to retain the participation of investors and private lending institutions in expanding the US market for housing finance, extending the spatial and social net of "prime lending" (Thompson 2009).

However, social technologies, such as FHA-approved appraisal and underwriting guidelines, are constituted as market devices through a process of *active* translation, in which they are continually circulated, interpreted, reworked, and extended (Callon and Munesia 2002). By the early 1990s Fannie Mae and private lending institutions had begun experimenting, combining traditional rule-based methods of assessing mortgage applications with statistical methods for calculating the likelihood of a borrower defaulting by utilizing consumer credit data (FICO scores). The enrollment of individualized consumer risk scores into the underwriting process enabled, to varying degrees, its automation and reconfiguration from a process of exclusion to one of calibrated *inclusion*. Rather than screen mortgage applications with the intention to exclude those who did not meet established criteria, lenders began to assess applications in terms of a continuum of degrees of "creditworthiness," along which the price and terms of a mortgage could be calibrated accordingly (Poon 2009). These practices evidenced generative capacities, enabling the risks of loan origination to be parceled off to institutional investors (such as banks, insurance companies, and pension funds) and sovereign investors (in particular China and Japan) in ever more creative ways, transforming "non-prime" into "sub-prime." The transition from low-risk exclusionary to high-risk inclusionary lending practices transformed not only the market for homeownership, but also the structure of capital markets in general, politicizing the character of calculability (Langley 2008b, 2009). As scholars have just begun to delineate within the contemporary context, what passes for market structures and market relations, the normative ideas and practices that constitute them, and the characteristics of state and non-state authority that underpin them are a matter of inquiry, not pre-given. The geographies of supply and demand, such as for housing finance, are not simply "out there," waiting to be invoked in the overdetermination of a particular economic landscape, but instead have to be constructed, forging moral claims, arguments about justice and particular forms of entitlement – a variegated geography of "worth" (Boltanski and Thevenot 2006).

## References

Agnew, J. (1994) The territorial trap: The geographical assumptions of international relations. *Review of International Political Economy*, 1 (1), 53–80.

Amin, A. (2002) Spatialities of globalization. *Environment and Planning A*, 34, 385–399.

Amin, A. (2004) Regulating economic globalization. *Transactions of the Institute of British Geographers*, 29 (2), 217–233.

Amin, A. and Thrift, N. (1992) Neo-Marshallian nodes in global networks. *International Journal of Urban and Regional Research*, 16, 571–587.

Amin, A. and Thrift, N. (2001) What kind of economic theory for what kind of economic geography? *Antipode*, 32, 4–9.

Amin, A. and Thrift, N. (2005) What's left? Just the future. *Antipode*, 37, 220–238.

Babcock, F. (1924) *The Appraisal of Real Estate*. New York: Macmillan.

Barnes, T. (1996) *The Logics of Dislocation: Models, Metaphors and Meanings of Economic Space*. New York: Guilford Press.

Barnes, T. and Sheppard, E. (2010) "Nothing includes everything": Towards engaged pluralism in Anglophone economic geography. *Progress in Human Geography*, 34 (2), 193–214.

Bathelt, H. and Gertler, M.S. (2005) The German variety of capitalism: Forces and dynamics of evolutionary change. *Economic Geography*, 81, 1–9.

Berger, S. and Dore, R. (eds.) (1996) *National Diversity and Global Capitalism*. Ithaca: Cornell University Press.

Blyth, M. (2002) *Great Transformations: Economic Ideas and Institutional Change in the Twentieth Century*. Cambridge: Cambridge University Press.

Boltanski, L. and Thevenot, L. (2006) *On Justification: Economies of Worth*. Princeton: Princeton University Press.

Braithwaite, T. (2011) US homeowners racial gap widens. Financial Times (online). http://www.ft.com/cms/s/0/064c4870-3a01-11e0-a441-00144feabdc0.html#axzz1d6yU9a8O (accessed October 22, 2012).

Brenner, N. (2001) The limits to scale? Methodological reflections on scalar structuration. *Progress in Human Geography*, 25, 591–614.

Callon, M. (1998) Introduction: The embeddedness of economic markets in economics. In *The Laws of Markets*, ed. M. Callon. Oxford: Blackwell, pp. 1–57.

Callon, M. and Munesia, F. (2002) Economic markets as calculative and calculated collective devices. *Organisation Studies*, 26, 1229–1250.

Christopherson, S. (2002) Why do national labor market practices continue to diverge in the global economy? The "missing link" of investment rules. *Economic Geography*, 78, 1–20.

Clark, G. and Wojcik, D. (2007) *The Geography of Finance: Corporate Governance in the Global Marketplace*. Oxford: Oxford University Press.

Engelen, E. and Grote, M. (2009) Stock exchange virtualisation and the decline of second-tier financial centres: The case of Amsterdam and Frankfurt. *Journal of Economic Geography*, 9, 679–696.

Flint, J. (2003) Housing and ethopolitics: Constructing identities of active consumption and responsible community. *Economy and Society*, 32, 611–629.

Freund, D. (2006) Marketing the free market: State intervention and the politics of prosperity in metropolitan America. In *The New Suburban History*, ed. K. Kruse and T. Sugrue. Chicago: University of Chicago Press, pp. 11–32.

Freund, D. (2007) *Colored Property: State Policy and White Racial Politics in Suburban America*. Chicago: University of Chicago Press.

Friedman, T. (2005) *The World is Flat: A Brief History of the Twenty-First Century*. New York: Farrar, Straus and Giroux.

Gertler, M.S. (2004) *Manufacturing Matters: The Institutional Geography of Industrial Practice*. Oxford: Oxford University Press.

Grabher, G. (ed.) (1993) *The Embedded Firm: On the Socioeconomics of Industrial Networks*. London: Routledge.

Graham, J. (1991) Fordism/post-Fordism, Marxism/post-Marxism: The second cultural divide. *Rethinking Marxism*, 4, 39–58.

Granovetter, M. (1985) Economic action and social structure: The problem of embeddedness. *American Journal of Sociology*, 91, 481–510.

Gurney, C. (1999) Pride and prejudice: Discourses of normalisation in public and private accounts of home ownership. *Housing Studies*, 14 (2), 163–183.

Hall, P. and Soskice, D. (eds.) (2001) *Varieties of Capitalism: The Institutional Foundations of Comparative Advantage*. Oxford: Oxford University Press.

Haney-Lopez, I. (2006) *White by Law: The Legal Construction of Race*. New York: University of New York Press.

Hanson, S. and Pratt, G. (1995) *Gender, Work and Space*. London: Routledge.

Harris, R. (1996) *Unplanned Suburbs: Toronto's American Tragedy, 1900–1950*. Baltimore: Johns Hopkins University Press.

Harvey, D. (2006) Editorial: The geographies of critical geography. *Transactions of the Institute of British Geographers*, 31, 409–412.

Hayden, D. (2004) *Building Suburbia: Green Fields and Urban Growth, 1820–2000*. New York: Vintage Press.

Hillier, A. (2003) Redlining and the Home Owners' Loan Corporation. *Journal of Urban History*, 29 (4), 394–420.

Hollingsworth, J.R. and Boyer, R. (eds.) (1997) *Contemporary Capitalism: The Embeddedness of Institutions*. Cambridge: Cambridge University Press.

Hudson, R. (2006) On what's right and keeping left: Or why geography still needs Marxian political economy. *Antipode*, 38, 374–395.

Jackson, K.T. (1985) *Crabgrass Frontier: The Suburbanization of the United States*. New York: Oxford University Press.

Kantor, H.A. (1974) Benjamin C. Marsh and the fight over population congestion. *Journal of the American Planning Association*, 40 (6), 422–429.

Kay, J. (2003) *The Truth About Markets*. London: Penguin.

Krippner, G.R. (2001) The elusive market: Embeddedness and the paradigm of economic sociology. *Theory and Society*, 30, 775–810.

Langley, P. (2008a) *The Everyday Life of Global Finance: Saving and Borrowing in Anglo-America*. Oxford: Oxford University Press.

Langley, P. (2008b) Sub-prime mortgage lending: A cultural economy. *Economy and Society*, 37 (4), 469–494.

Langley, P. (2009) Debt, discipline and government: Foreclosure and forbearance in the subprime mortgage crisis. *Environment and Planning A*, 41, 1404–1419.

Marsh, B. (1929) *An Introduction to City Planning: Democracy's Challenge to the American City*. New York: Marsh.

Marston, S. (2000) The social construction of scale. *Progress in Human Geography*, 24, 219–241.

McDowell, L. (1997) *Capital Culture: Gender at Work in the City*. Oxford: Blackwell.

Mitchell, T. (2002) *Rule of Experts: Egypt, Techno-Politics, Modernity*. Berkeley: University of California Press.

Montgomerie, J. (2007) Giving credit where it's due: Public policy and household debt in the United States, the United Kingdom and Canada. *Policy and Society*, 25 (3), 109–141.

Parsons, T. (1935a) Sociological elements in economic thought I. Historical. *Quarterly Journal of Economics*, 49, 414–453.

Parsons, T. (1935b) Sociological elements in economic thought II. The analytical factor. *Quarterly Journal of Economics*, 49, 646–667.

Patterson, G. (2003) *Number 5*. London: Penguin.

Peck, J. (2001) *Workfare States*. New York: Guilford Press.

Peck, J. (2005) Economic sociologies in space. *Economic Geography*, 81 (2), 129–175.

Peck, J. and Theodore, N. (2007) Variegated capitalism. *Progress in Human Geography*, 31 (6), 731–772.

Poon, M. (2009) From New Deal institutions to capital markets: Commercial consumer risk scores and the making of subprime mortgage finance. *Accounting, Organizations and Society*, 34, 654–674.

Smith, N. (2005) What's left? Neo-critical geography, or, the flat pluralist world of business class. *Antipode*, 37, 887–899.

Smith, S. (2008) Owner-occupation: At home with a hybrid of money and materials. *Environment and Planning A*, 40, 520–535.

Smith, S. and Munro, M. (eds.) (2008) *The Microstructures of Housing Markets*. London: Routledge.

Storper, M. (1997) *The Regional World: Territorial Development in a Global Economy*. New York: Guilford Press.

Thompson, H. (2009) The political origins of the financial crisis: The domestic and international politics of Fannie Mae and Freddie Mac. *Political Quarterly*, 80 (1), 17–24.

Watts, M. (1993) Development I: Power, knowledge, discursive practice. *Progress in Human Geography*, 17, 252–272.

Weiss, M.A. (1987) *The Rise of the Community Builders: The American Real Estate Industry and Urban Land Planning*. New York: Beard Books.

Weiss, M.A. (1989) Richard T. Ely and the contribution of economic research to national housing policy, 1920–1940. *Urban Studies*, 26, 115–126.

# Chapter 17

# Political Landscapes

*Nuala C. Johnson*

## Political Scenes

On a foggy morning in April 2010, the plane carrying Polish president Lech Kaczynski, his wife, and ninety-four other passengers and crew crashed on its approach to the regional airport at Smolensk in western Russia. Nobody survived. Kaczynski, along with numerous other Polish government officials – members of parliament, chiefs of the navy and army – were visiting Smolensk to commemorate the seventieth anniversary of the Katyn massacre, which had taken place in forests outside the town in 1940. The massacre of Polish officers by the Soviet secret police was one of the most notorious incidents of World War II, and has long been a source of tension between Warsaw and Moscow (Harding 2010). In the aftermath of the plane crash Poland and Russia agreed to construct a memorial at the site and the Russians erected a boulder for that purpose. Relatives of the deceased placed a plaque on the stone, which claimed that the Polish president and his entourage died while traveling to commemorate "the Soviet crime of genocide against prisoners of war, Polish Army Officers" (Kramer 2011). The governor of the Smolensk region, however, had the plaque removed and replaced with an alternative one that read: "In memory of the 96 Poles led by the president of the Republic of Poland, Lech Kaczynski, who died in a plane crash near Smolensk on April 10, 2010." Ostensibly the governor claimed that the plaque had been replaced because the original was in Polish and there was no Russian translation, while the replacement was in both languages. However, behind the linguistic claim also lay a political motive.

The Russians believed that there was an implied connection between the air crash and the Katyn massacre. The governor of Smolensk, Sergei Anufriev, claimed: "These are two absolutely different events, and there is no sense in imposing the idea that the second tragedy was a continuation of the first one" (quoted in Kramer 2011). While Polish sensitivities were

*The Wiley Blackwell Companion to Cultural Geography*, First Edition.
Edited by Nuala C. Johnson, Richard H. Schein, and Jamie Winders.
© 2013 John Wiley & Sons, Ltd. Published 2016 by John Wiley & Sons, Ltd.

aroused by this change of wording, it also reflected a wider unease among parts of the Polish population that Russian air traffic controllers were, at least partly, responsible for the air crash. The report commissioned by the Russians, however, placed all blame on the Polish pilots who, they alleged, ignored warnings from the air traffic controllers of the dangers of trying to land at Smolensk in thick fog. While this whole episode underscores the fragile state of the diplomatic territory between Poland and Russia, it more broadly draws attention to the continued role of historical consciousness in fashioning contemporary political landscapes.

If diplomatic relations were metaphorically cooling between Russia and Poland during the course of 2010–2011, there was something of a thaw taking place among the producers of the *Times Comprehensive Atlas of the World* published in 2011. HarperCollins, the publisher of the thirteenth edition of the atlas, showed large areas of the eastern and southern coasts of Greenland colored brown or pink, indicating that the permanent ice cap over the territory was covering a significantly smaller area of the landmass than had appeared in the 1999 twelfth edition of the atlas. The map suggested that approximately 300,000 sq. km, or 15 percent of Greenland's ice cover, had disappeared over that period. In a press release the publishers claimed: "This is concrete evidence of how climate change is altering the face of the planet forever – and doing so at an alarming and accelerating rate" (quoted in Vidal 2011). This bold statement about the thawing of the Greenland ice sheet immediately stimulated leading climate scientists to claim a blunder on the part of the cartographers at HarperCollins. Researchers at the Scott Polar Research Institute, University of Cambridge, asserted that the cartographic representation of a 15 percent permanent decrease in ice cover was "both incorrect and misleading . . . Recent satellite images of Greenland make it clear that there are in fact still numerous glaciers and permanent ice cover where the new Times Atlas shows ice-free conditions and the emergence of new lands" (quoted in Vidal 2011). Numerous other scientists backed up these claims and wondered if the cartographers had become confused between data on ice thickness and ice extent, thus producing a map which implied large-scale ice retreat. The publisher defended the data and the map on the grounds of their expert knowledge and their technical skill. A spokesperson assuredly declared: "We are the best there is. We are confident of the data we have used and of the cartography . . . Our data show that it has reduced by 15%. That's categorical" (quoted in Vidal 2011). They qualified their original explanation for this reduced ice cover by saying that climate change was a large part of the story, if not all. The scientific community, however, was quick to respond, insisting that there was not a 15 percent reduction in the ice cover, that this was an error. Mark Serreze, Director of the National Snow and Ice Data Center in Colorado, professed: "It was a case where, really, the [scientific] community came together really fast with both barrels blazing. Everyone had some real bad memories of this whole fiasco that had to do with Himalayan glaciers. No one wanted to see that again" (quoted in Barringer 2011). In a climbdown, HarperCollins conceded that it would be "urgently reviewing the depiction of ice in the atlas against all current research and available data, and we will work with the scientific community to produce a map of Greenland which reflects all the latest data" (quoted in Press Association 2011). A revised insert map, they promised, would be included in the Atlas.

While, at one level, this dispute was about the accuracy of cartographic representation, it was also a political battlefield between climate scientists, mapmakers, and skeptics of global warming. As Harley's (1989: 13) seminal work on critical cartography reminded us over two decades ago: "The power of the map-maker was not generally exercised over individuals but over the knowledge of the world made available to people in general ... The map is a silent arbiter of power." In the case of Greenland, for climate scientists, suggestions that they had provided data that exaggerated the extent of ice-sheet retreat had to be solidly rebuffed, while for the publisher reputation was critical. Monmonier (2011) suggests that the misleading representation of Greenland's ice-sheet cover arose because the publisher did not have the proofs of the map examined by external expert reviewers, but also because "the inherent persuasiveness of any map [lies] with a crisp appearance, a prestigious pedigree and the imprimatur of a large, well-known publishing house – traits that not only confer clout in the cartographic marketplace but invite overconfidence and hubris." In the case of HarperCollins all these factors may have shaped the direction of the dispute over the map. But this example speaks to the wider cultural contexts surrounding the adjudication of conflicts over the production and dissemination of information that is both environmental and political. The significance of the Greenland landscape in this case is not so much centered on the accuracy of conventional political messages, which have aroused controversy in other map images (for instance, Iran's defense of the use of Persian Gulf against any attempts by its neighbors to rename it Arabian Gulf), but the capacity of the map of Greenland to perform as a space in which environmental theories and disputes might be regulated or resolved.

While the visual interpretation of landscape has a long genealogy in geographical research (Cosgrove 1998; Duncan 1990) and continues to play a significant role in understanding the political power dynamics embedded in landscapes, scholarship in this field has extended to consider the relationships between ideas and practices of governmentality and biopower enacted through landscapes, particularly but not exclusively in colonial situations (Duncan 2007; Legg 2007; Nally 2011). There have also been extended analyses of the material production of landscapes in terms of process, movement, and action. Here the emphasis is firmly placed on treating landscape as a process rather than an object or image (Mitchell 2002), and in understanding, often from a neo-Marxist perspective, the evolution of particular types of landscape (e.g., textile towns) as the manifestation of unfolding struggles between different economic and political agents within the structure of capitalism (Mitchell 2003). Research into landscape practices and their unfolding through embodied performances, particularly in relation to everyday life, has been another fruitful line of inquiry into how the political intersects with the cultural. Practices such as hill walking, boating, and driving have been analyzed in relation to their role in structuring conduct within such landscapes, but also in relation to wider political questions about state and local planning, private and public regimes of health, and ecological questions surrounding environmentalism (Matless 1998; Lorimer and Lund 2003; Wylie 2005). Each of these approaches to understanding the politics of landscape overlaps and intersects in various ways. In the remainder of this chapter I seek to reflect on three arenas – nation, map, nature – where the cultural geographies of landscape reflect and refract with deeply political questions centered on identities and power hierarchies.

## Nation, Nominalism, and Landscape

Where ideas and expressions of nationhood have been concerned, the links between the cultural and the political have long been explored. Hobsbawm and Ranger's seminal (1983) work on the "invention of tradition" set the scene for a host of studies that have examined how particular landscapes can create and reflect a sense of common national identities (for an overview see Till 2004). Geographers have been particularly alert to the spatial foundations of nationhood through their examination of the idea of homelands (Penrose 2002) and the iconography of national landscapes (Daniels 1993; Johnson 1997; Matless 1998). More recently the contested practices of reproducing an idea of national identity have been addressed (Johnson 2003, 2012). The role of national elites and structural conditions (e.g., print capitalism, educational systems) vis-à-vis the agency of individuals has been the focus. Rather than taking a top-down perspective on the production of national landscapes, geographers have stressed the interrelatedness between elites and local populations in the fashioning of these spaces where "political identities and interests are structured geographically as the result of human agency in the places where people live" (Agnew 2002: 1). One avenue through which the dialectics of elite–popular conceptions of nationhood take shape is through linguistic geographies and the definition of national languages in the landscape. Let us pause to look at one particular example of this process.

Aberystwyth historically has been an important locale for the reproduction of Welsh linguistic national identity. The town's significance rests on its location and activism more than its size *per se*. With a population of around 15,000 people, the importance of this place resides in its position in the so-called Welsh-speaking heartland, where the presence of the university and its role as the headquarters for many Welsh nationalist organizations make it significant. Jones (2008: 326) highlights how the campaign in the late 1960s and early 1970s for a Welsh-medium hall of residence within the University College of Wales Aberystwyth "complicates the distinction made between nationalist leaders and followers." In a complex campaign that involved students, academic staff at the university, and Plaid Cymru (Welsh nationalist party) supporters, Jones (2008) concludes that the success of the action – the establishment of a mixed-sex Welsh-medium hall of residence in 1973–1974 – reveals how elites and ordinary members of the "nation" mobilized together and mutually constituted each other's desire to promote Welshness.

In a further study, Jones and Merriman (2009) examined the practices of popular forms of nation-building through an analysis of the bilingual road sign campaign in Wales. They take as their starting point Billig's (1995) thesis that nationalism resides in the mundane and the banal, reproduced through the everyday actions of individuals and groups. They suggest it is forged through iterative practices rather than being a "hot" or extreme ideology as suggested by Ignatieff (1993) through his image of "blood and belonging." In stressing the ordinariness or banality of nationalism, Billig's approach relocates the processes of nationalizing landscapes away from the exceptional toward the day to day. In their study of the landscape of road signs, Jones and Merriman (2009: 165) take further the idea that "nationalist discourses and practices are reproduced in *everyday* contexts." In so doing they demonstrate how mundane features such as English-language road signs across the Welsh landscape came to be viewed as expressions of centralized state power. These galvanized Welsh nationalists to forge a campaign of resistance to what they regarded as the embodiment of a wider British nationalism. The significance of language to Welsh identity has been well documented with the foundation of Cymdeithas yr Iaith Gymraeg (Welsh Language Society) in 1962, which drew together support for the language and its use in everyday life in Wales. The ubiquity of English road signs was one campaigning element of this organization's dissatisfaction with the status of Welsh within the landscape. In 1967 the campaign for bilingual road signs began, and involved a range of Welsh linguistic and nationalist organizations. The nature of the agitation stretched from official appeals to the Welsh Office for bilingualism in signage to the active defacing of English-only signs and the subsequent arrest of protesters. Monolingual signs were regarded, within the movement, as a linguistic injustice to the Welsh "nation" and a visible emblem of the superiority of English over Welsh. Moreover, different participants within the campaign had very different understandings of what constituted defacement. For the Welsh Language Society, English road signs were themselves defacement and a cultural defilement of the Welsh landscape, and hence were regarded as acts of vandalism toward Welsh identity. By contrast, for the broader political establishment in Wales and in Westminster, the tactic of daubing English-language signage was wholly condemned as vandalism. Consequently, there was a complexity to how the ordinary and mundane were understood and practiced by different groups inside and outside Wales. The state tended to view the possibility of bilingual signage in technical and scientific terms. How clear and safe would bilingual signage be? What fonts, colors, designs should be used on signage to minimize disruption or confusion among road users? By focusing on the technicalities of producing bilingual signs, the state distanced itself from the political significance of the linguistic composition of the signs. It seemingly made marginal the role of language in identity. The sign debate in Wales, however, was something wider than just the technicalities of dotting the landscape with bilingual signs and, for Jones and Merriman, underscored that the "everyday is particularly useful as a way of conveying the fluid inter-relationship between hot and banal nationalism" (2009: 172).

This case of Welsh nationalism highlights three broader themes about the significance of politics to landscape. First, linguistic geography continues to play a powerful role in identity politics in general and with respect to nationalist identity in particular. The provision of Welsh-only living spaces for students attending Aberystwyth University reinforces this claim. Second, landscape becomes an important vehicle through which linguistic geographies are expressed, debated, and challenged. The presence of visual symbols – road signs – that interact directly with the rhythms of everyday life across Welsh territory provoked diverse responses and actions on the part of the citizenry and the state. Third, by focusing on the intersections between banal and hot forms of nationalism, and between elite and ordinary members of "nations," we are better equipped to elide the tendency to treat the political and cultural refractions of identity in dualistic and separate ways.

## Paper Landscapes: Maps, Borderlands, and Zones of Contact

Borders, both material and metaphorical, form zones of contact, cooperation, and conflict between different political and cultural groupings. As Brenner and Elden (2009: 355) observe, "territory is best conceived as a historically and geographically specific form of political organization and political thought." Drawing on Lefebvre's tripartite division of space into "perceived, conceived, and lived," these three interrelated practices affect the everyday experience of people across the globe (Brenner and Elden 2009). From the paper landscapes of mapmakers to the material landscape of individuals and groups, borders are of significant import socioculturally as much as politically. This is perhaps most visible where control over territory is hotly disputed and a source of intense political conflict.

In Northern Ireland, at the height of the "Troubles" during the 1970s, for instance, strong mental maps of "no go" areas were maintained by Catholics and Protestants especially along the sectarian border zones. In west Belfast the Shankill–Falls divide profoundly affected the daily practices of local people, who would avoid entering or passing through each other's territory even when it represented the shortest route from home to work, for example; a "frontier zone" was effectively being established (Boal 2002). Such spatial strategies of avoidance not only developed from mental images of potential danger and hostility but found material expression in the landscape as physical barriers such as high walls and barbed wire fences were constructed to maintain divisions between what were seen as two "warring" communities. Described as "peace" walls, these structures are both reflective of but also structuring of relationships and practices of interaction between the Catholic and Protestant populations residing each side of these barriers. They act as agents of circulation and restriction by providing a frame of movement around which the two populations operate. As such, this type of division mirrors the claim that understanding borders requires a focus on the "complex and varied patterns of both implicit and explicit bordering and ordering practices" (van Houtum, Kramsch, and Zierhofer 2005: 2). In the case of west Belfast, the implicit ordering practice is one of separation and division reflecting what Newman and Passi (1998) claimed to be the social, personal, and symbolic roles of borders as much as the strictly physical or territorial ones. This bordering is not an international political boundary but it does mark a significant contrasting set of cultural allegiances and national identities in the landscape of Northern Ireland's capital city.

In Northern Ireland I have considered intra-state boundaries erected as part of the historical context of divided identities; but we can also look to the supranational scale to examine how cultural affinities extend beyond the borders of individual sovereign states. Although geographers have long been concerned with territory and its relationship with ideas of national identity in particular, supranational identities that have a territorial dimension have been far less well explored, apart from the emergence of the European Union (EU). One such case is the development of a "counter-cartography" as expressed in the mapping of the Arab Homeland in maps and atlases produced within the region and standing in contradistinction to maps produced externally denoting the Middle East and North Africa. The Arab Homeland as an entity emerged synchronically with the development of the pan-Arab movement of the mid-twentieth century and as a reaction against the perceived oppression of the Ottoman Empire in this part of the world. Culcasi (2011) in her analysis of atlases and maps produced within the Arab Homeland demonstrates the significance of territory and border delineation in constructing a transnational Arab identity. For instance between 1965 and 1986, the Egyptian Ministry of Education published a series of maps entitled *The Arab Atlas*. In these a political map titled the "Arab Homeland" appeared that demarcated this area from the remainder of Africa and Asia. Using thick red ink, borderlines identified who was in and who was outside of this cartographic imaginary. While the precise boundaries shifted with new editions of the atlas (e.g., Mauritania and Somalia were included in the third edition), the map implied a unified cultural landscape even though politically the homeland comprised numerous individual, sovereign states and amplified a pan-Arab political agenda.

Place names were also significant. In atlases published after 1952 the toponym Persian Gulf was replaced with Arabian Gulf, and the Arabic place name al-Quds was substituted for the Judaic-Christian one to name Jerusalem. While there are some variations in the maps produced to depict the "homeland" by the different states within the territory, they have all "helped to discursively create an Arab Homeland as a unified supranational Arab territory," and this idea of "homeland" does not passively exist in people's geographical imaginations "but it informs, frames and guides material geopolitics" (Culcasi 2011: 425). It does this in ways that move far beyond the paper landscapes of the atlas and into the lives of non-Arab peoples living within this area. Kurds, for instance, have been periodically subject to discriminatory practices, displacement, and murder as their absence from cartographic renditions of the region is mirrored by attempts to physically render them absent. If the political landscape of the pan-Arab world has found expression in maps at a transnational scale, the landscape of conflict in the Middle East, particularly between Palestine and Israel, has also had mapping at its ideological and geopolitical center.

Capturing ideas of a homeland territory by Palestinians and Israelis is ironically achieved through "mirror-image" maps (Wallach 2011). Both depict their homeland as virtually identical in shape and area, and thus the maps become rhetorical devices for staking their individual claims to territory and political identity. These maps portray a sliver-shaped zone lying between the River Jordan and the Mediterranean Sea, mirroring the borders of the British Mandate (1922–1948), and having the readily recognizable knife shape with the blade pointing in a downward direction. There is some difference in detail in the outline of these maps, with Israeli versions including the Golan Heights, which was occupied from Syria since 1967. Ostensibly, then, these maps look extremely similar in shape/territory but it is the coloring, nomenclature, and legend that offer visual clues about difference. These maps have entered into popular culture and everyday life as "logo-maps" by being reproduced on t-shirts, jewelry, and other objects as well as being used in weather forecasting broadcasts. They thus form an important part of a visual vocabulary, but as Wallach (2011: 359) points out, "What is unique to the Israel/Palestine conflict, however, is that the same 'logo-map' is used by two opposed national projects, and that the same 'geo-body' inhabits two nations." Unlike many other political conflict zones across the world, in this case both sides claim virtually the exact same national territory. Wallach (2011) has examined how the maps produced by each side in the conflict are invested with deep emotions, especially love and pain. He has analyzed how these maps enter everyday life in the Middle East and the affective worlds of its inhabitants by focusing on their use in the education systems, on memorials and stamps, and in weather reports.

In Palestinian textbook maps up to 2007, for example, no mention was made of Israel or Israeli cities and this was seen by Jews as an attempt to deny their right to exist and to use geography textbooks to reinforce this effort. Concomitantly from a Palestinian perspective, Israeli maps failed to mark the Palestinian territories under their military occupation. Indeed, tourism maps posted in London Underground stations in 2009 advertising Israel as a tourist destination were seen by Palestinian activists as attempts to erase Palestine from the cartographic register by including Gaza and the West Bank as parts of Israel. The posters containing these maps were eventually removed from the stations. The evocative as much as the representational, however, have given these maps their performative power. Wallach (2011) identified, for instance, the use of "Blue Box" maps from the 1920s. As emotional tools these "Blue Box" maps represented Israel and were placed on Zionist donation boxes, distributed by the Jewish National Fund (JNF). The JNF was the principal Zionist land-purchasing organization, and the maps highlighted the areas bought by the JNF as part of their resettlement program in the Middle East. The boxes were painted in the colors of Zionism, blue and white, and were distributed in Palestine and among the Jewish diaspora and promoted the idea of "land redemption" (Bar-Gal 2003). As Wallach (2011: 362) claims: "Dropping coins into the box and emptying it were performances of identity through which Jewish boys and girls, far beyond Palestine, developed an attachment to the map . . . These rituals and the emotional investment in the map transformed it into something of a sacred object." These maps, therefore, became reservoirs of vast visceral appeal in the popular consciousness of Jews throughout the globe.

By contrast, after 1948, a map representing Mandatory Palestine became part of the Palestinians' wider nationalist movement and entered into their popular culture through its use in stamps, memorials, stationery, jewelry, and logos. The landscape, in this expression of

Palestinian identity, is not just an abstract symbol but is performed "in visual, material and tactile ways" (Wallach 2011: 365). For example at memorials, erected to publicly commemorate Palestinians killed in the conflict, the map is regularly incorporated as a key feature of the site. Similarly a map of Palestine is also used in the private spaces of mourning among the families of those killed. An image of the map will often accompany a photograph of a deceased family member, thereby directly connecting their individual death and sacrifice with the larger political project of Palestinian nationalism. The map can function, therefore, to elicit a whole range of emotional responses, from grief and anger to determination and steadfastness in the pursuit of cultural and political goals. Both past and future political landscapes are embedded in the drama of the map and, as Wallach notes, "Even more than Israeli maps, the Palestine map is a performative statement of utopian vision. It is an idealized version of the historical homeland, seen through the nostalgia of loss and exile" (2011: 365). In this section I have suggested that the mental map of territory, as well as the material, paper landscape of the cartographic image, play crucial roles in the articulation and symbolization of border construction, border maintenance, and border conflict. They are thus important ingredients in structuring national and international geopolitical relations.

## Nature's Landscape and the Body Politic(s)

The natural landscape and ideas of nature have both historically and today acted as significant components in the cultural practices of political identity formation. As the dispute over the map of Greenland at the beginning of this chapter suggested, nature is often part of a wider political debate about human impact on the environment in general and, in this case, climate in particular. The *Times Atlas* purported to illustrate that the ice-covered landscape of Greenland had much reduced since the previous edition of the text, and this claim spoke to the larger scientific and deeply political question of the effect of human practices on "nature." Consequently, issues surrounding how human behavior might be modified collectively through international agreements, nationally through state policies, and locally through individual practices could all oscillate around the authenticity of this map's scientific claims. In the final section of this chapter I wish briefly to consider the interconnections between political and natural landscapes as a means of understanding how power relations and social and cultural identities are fashioned through everyday engagements with "nature."

William Cronon (1995) has reminded us how the coalescence of the ideas of the sublime, the frontier, and a national polity informed debates about the preservation of "wilderness" in the development of the American national park system. Offering a thoroughly cultural reading of the historiography of this process, Cronon has highlighted how political identities, such as individualism, were forged around landscapes that were seen to be the least contaminated by modernity and urbanism. As he presents it, it was the people of America who had most benefited from urban industrial capitalism who were also some of the most vocal proponents of both preserving and experiencing wilderness. Thus, from the mid-nineteenth century onward, tourism to sublime landscapes became part and parcel of the cultural and political experience of the wealthy and the urbane. Enormous estates built in the Adirondack mountains, for instance, became sites of recreation. They encapsulated the rejuvenating potential of the wild to reinvigorate these rich urban dwellers. They embodied the national frontier myth that the core of American political values was historically forged along the open wilderness. The national parks system therefore enabled these urban dwellers to experience emotionally and physically what they regarded as the natural antithesis of the superficial and ugly artificiality embodied in the modern city. The parks achieved this "idyllic" quality by employing landscape architects who designed the spaces to preserve the scenery by deploying various forms of concealment and screening of undesirable views, yet maintaining an infrastructure that was necessary for the comfort and convenience of the visitor. Thus, for instance, sanitary facilities and other utilities were hidden from public view by sequestering them through planting native species of tree or using large boulders to conceal them, thus offering the illusion that human intrusion on these landscapes was negligible (Colten and Dilsaver 2005). A vision of wilderness, therefore, could be preserved for visitors to the national parks and the visceral responses to these seemingly natural landscapes could be protected for the American public.

It is not only, however, in the public landscapes of national parks that nature has been politicized. In the more domestic landscapes of the suburbs, place-based identities can also be mobilized, expressed, and experienced. In their study of the suburban settlement of Bedford, 44 miles north of New York City, Duncan and Duncan (2004) have explored how these place-based identities deploy ideas of nature to create settings in which desirable social identities are protected, projected, and sometimes challenged. They claim: "A seemingly innocent appreciation of landscapes and desire to protect local history and nature can act as subtle but highly effective mechanisms of exclusion and reaffirmation of class identity" (2004: 4). Tracing the historical development of zoning laws and the evolution of this highly maintained pastoral landscape, Duncan and Duncan (2004: 5) have highlighted how sustaining a place of rolling hills, open meadowland, and dirt roads required immense labor and "highly sophisticated political organization" on the part of the residents. In this elite suburb, residents invest both immense financial and human capital to protecting the quality of the landscape. They achieve high social status through their aesthetic consumption practices, not least in their efforts to enhance and retain the beauty of the town. Underpinned by a romantic ideology, anti-urbanism, anti-modernism, and an intense localism, the residents affirm their individual and collective identities through their practices of protecting both nature and the historic dimensions of this built environment. The people of Bedford regard their local landscape as communicative of community identities and they see it as inculcating their political and moral values. Consequently, the residents are prepared to invest a lot of time and energy in its protection (Duncan and Duncan 2004).

Landscape preservation is primarily achieved through the vehicle of zoning laws and practices and Duncan and Duncan (2001) observe that they are ultimately highly exclusionary in Bedford. Over 80 percent of all land in the area is zoned for single-family houses on a minimum of four-acre lots, 95 percent for houses on one or more acres, and less than 1 percent for two-family dwellings or apartments. These conditions are justified on environmental and aesthetic grounds where the protection of beauty and "naturalness" is seen as unquestionably good, irrespective of the socially exclusionary consequences of such zoning policies. Alongside the valorization of the pastoral landscape, locals have also sought to preserve a small bit of "wilderness" in Bedford. The Mianus River Gorge Wildlife Refuge and Botanical Preserve was established in 1953 by five wealthy locals and became in 1964 the first Natural Historic Landmark in the United States; however, as Duncan and Duncan (2001: 400) point out, "Wilderness in Bedford is produced out of a class-based aesthetic that values both the pastoral and the picturesque." Although the residents' lives are intimately bound up with the global economic system – many have gained their wealth through urban industrial and financial market-generated means in New York City – their retreat to Bedford masks the interconnectedness between their income generation and their desire to reside in a picture-perfect colonial New England village. Nature and historical buildings are preserved here within a wider framework and act as positional goods for the residents. While Bedford may represent an extreme case of the aestheticization of political life in an American suburb, it is certainly not unique.

While "natural" landscapes are mobilized to engender social status and positional wealth through cultural capital as revealed in prosperous American suburbs, the display of "nature" can also be part of the political vocabulary of cities. Take, for example, botanical gardens. These institutions date back to the sixteenth century, originally established as physic gardens attached to medical faculties in university towns (for instance, Padua in Italy in 1545). They served to enhance trainee doctors' knowledge of the medicinal qualities of plants and fundamentally catered to a very specialized audience. However, by the eighteenth century, botanical gardens began to shift their focus away from being repositories of medicinal herbs and plants to being spaces to serve the interests of the science of botany. Moreover, by the nineteenth century they were firmly established as scientific spaces, designed to display plant taxonomy, exotic species, and arboretums and to serve a wider desire to encourage rational recreation among the general public and to educate the wider population on the workings of nature. As such botanical gardens became arenas in which there was an ambition to educate the public, regulate its behavior, and control the manner in which visitors might experience the natural world through these gardens. Despite such lofty ambitions, however, opening such gardens to the public free of charge provoked intense political debate in a variety of different cities. The Royal Botanic Garden Belfast, for instance, operated as a private limited company from its foundation in 1829. Access was restricted to shareholders, annual subscribers, and those who paid an entrance fee at the gate. This fee structure restricted access primarily to the city's middle classes, despite the founders' objectives for the gardens to act as an educative and recreational space for the working classes in this expanding industrial city. The gardens' proprietors acknowledged that wider public access was desirable "whereby public peace, loyalty and government are generally promoted" (quoted in Johnson 2011: 173), improving ultimately the moral status of the citizenry, and thus in 1865 free admission was introduced on Saturdays. The role of the gardens in Belfast was not just to provide a leisure space for the city's laboring classes but also to serve as a moral arena for the cultivation of civic pride and popular allegiance to local and national governance.

In Dublin too the botanical gardens in Glasnevin, founded by the Royal Dublin Society in 1795, served political as well as scientific ends. The Royal Dublin Society, a learned society composed mainly of a Protestant elite, obtained an annual government grant to subsidize the gardens. Dublin sought to have a garden of equal prestige to that at Kew in London. Improving Irish agricultural practices as well as developing systematic botany underpinned its foundation (Johnson 2007). As a publicly subsidized garden it was, from the outset, open to the public, but that public's behavior was, as in Belfast, to be strictly controlled. Moreover, one of the most controversial issues surrounding access related to opening the gardens to the public on Sundays. The Royal Dublin Society strongly resisted any attempts on introduce Sunday opening on the grounds of the sacredness of the Sabbath. For the city's predominantly Catholic population, however, such Sabbatarian views were inconsequential. More significantly, Sunday opening would benefit the city's working classes enormously as this was often their only day for recreation. Despite its huge opposition, eventually the Royal Dublin Society acquiesced to government and popular pressure and opened the gardens to the public on Sundays in 1861 (Johnson 2011). Such examples illustrate how the political was interspersed with the scientific and cultural in discussions about how these semi-public spaces would be accessed and used in the everyday lives of city-dwellers, and how these landscapes served an ideology of good citizenship and improvement in Victorian Britain and Ireland.

## Concluding Comments

In this chapter I have brought together at least three arenas in which landscapes become central to the expression, practice, and discussion of political identities at a variety of different scales. The significance of transnational political identities, forged through the maps of an Arab Homeland, speaks toward the efforts of a pan-Arab movement to create a unified political landscape that transcends the existence of independent sovereign states. The veneration of the natural landscape through the national park system in the United States celebrates the significance of the nationally bounded state. At the sub-state scale, the linguistic geographies of road signage in Wales indicate the prominence of ideas of nationhood within the larger spatial context of the United Kingdom. Finally, at the local scale of a suburb of New York City, social and political values become embedded in specific landscape practices that nurture a highly place-based identity despite the deep connections with a globalized world. Together these examples attest to the broader significance of political landscapes historically and in the contemporary world and to the interrelationships between different scales in the modulation of identities.

Moreover, this recent work carried out by geographers interested in the political suggests some wider ramifications for studies of landscape more generally. First, the visual continues to animate discussions of landscape, and while this has been greatly enhanced by a renewed interest in the performative, it is clear that there is an ontological cohesion between "looking and doing," especially in the political arena. For Poles and Russians, marking the site of the Smolensk air crash involved linguistic, ethical, and visual vocabularies that were not necessarily shared. Second, political geographers' recent move toward analyzing the everyday, mundane, and ordinary dimensions of people's day-to-day worlds has helped shift focus away from treating the political as an embodiment of the actions and attitudes of an elite, played out on the landscape. Indeed, it has moved the conceptual apparatus for understanding power away from the hierarchical toward a more flattened and variegated terrain of practice. With respect to understanding national identities, for instance, this emphasis on the everyday and the popular reveals how the reproduction of national cultures is embedded as much in the banal practices of the everyday (for instance, having the opportunity to speak a particular language or having access to a public garden) as in the manipulation of "culture" by the powerful in the state. Finally, these transformations have opened up a variety of new avenues of research that move beyond conventional conceptions of the political. The connections between scientific and cultural-political understandings of nature have widened the epistemological canvas across which different disciplines can reflect on how debates about natural landscapes are also intimately bound up with debates about our role within and as part of nature.

## References

Agnew, J. (2002) *Place and Politics in Modern Italy*. Chicago: University of Chicago Press.

Bar-Gal, Y. (2003) *Propaganda and Zionist Education: The Jewish National Fund, 1924–1947*. Rochester, NY: University of Rochester Press.

Barringer, F. (2011) Scientists want publisher to refreeze Greenland. New York Times. http://www. nytimes.com/2011/09/25/science/earth/25atlas.html (accessed October 22, 2012).

Billig, M. (1995) *Banal Nationalism*. London: Sage.

Boal, F. (2002) Belfast: Walls within. *Political Geography*, 21, 687–694.

Brenner, N. and Elden, S. (2009) Henri Lefebvre on state, space and territory. *International Political Sociology*, 3, 353–377.

Colten, C.E. and Dilsaver, L.M. (2005) The hidden landscape of Yosemite national park. *Journal of Cultural Geography*, 22, 27–50.

Cosgrove, D. (1998) *Social Formation and Symbolic Landscape*. Madison: University of Wisconsin Press.

Cronon, W. (ed.) (1995) *Uncommon Ground: Rethinking the Human Place in Nature*. New York: Norton.

Culcasi, K. (2011) Cartographies of supranationalism: Creating and silencing territories in the "Arab Homeland." *Political Geography*, 30, 417–428.

Daniels, S. (1993) *Fields of Vision: Landscape Imagery and National Identity in England and the United States*. Princeton: Princeton University Press.

Duncan, J.S. (1990) *The City as Text: The Politics of Landscape Interpretation in the Kandyan Kingdom*. Cambridge: Cambridge University Press.

Duncan, J.S. (2007) *In the Shadow of the Tropics: Climate, Race and Biopower in Nineteenth Century Ceylon*. Aldershot: Ashgate.

Duncan, J.S. and Duncan, N.G. (2001) The aestheticization of the politics of landscape preservation. *Annals of the Association of American Geographers*, 91, 387–409.

Duncan, J.S. and Duncan, N.G. (2004) *Landscapes of Privilege: The Politics of the Aesthetic in an American Suburb*. London: Routledge.

Harding, L. (2010) Polish president Lech Kaczynski killed in plane crash. Guardian. http://www.guardian. co.uk/world/2010/apr/10/poland-president-lech-kaczynski-killed (accessed October 22, 2012).

Harley, J.B. (1989) Deconstructing the map. *Cartographica*, 26 (2), 1–20.

Hobsbawm, E. and Ranger, T. (eds.) (1983) *The Invention of Tradition*. Cambridge: Cambridge University Press.

Ignatieff, M. (1993) *Blood and Belonging: Journeys into the New Nationalism*. London: BBC Books.

Johnson, N.C. (1997) Making space: Gaeltacht policy and the politics of identity. In *In Search of Ireland: A Cultural Geography*, ed. B. Graham. London: Routledge, pp. 151–173.

Johnson, N.C. (2003) *Ireland, the Great War and the Geography of Remembrance*. Cambridge: Cambridge University Press.

Johnson, N.C. (2007) Grand design(er)s: David Moore, natural theology and the Royal Botanic Gardens in Glasnevin, Dublin: 1838–1879. *Cultural Geographies*, 14, 29–55.

Johnson, N.C. (2011) *Nature Displaced, Nature Displayed: Order and Beauty in Botanical Gardens*. London: I.B. Tauris.

Johnson, N.C. (2012) A royal encounter: Space, spectacle and the Queen's visit to Ireland 2011. *Geographical Journal*, 178, 194–200.

Jones, R. (2008) Relocating nationalism: On the geographies of reproducing nations. *Transactions of the Institute of British Geographers*, 33, 319–334.

Jones, R. and Merriman, P. (2009) Hot, banal and everyday nationalism: Bilingual road signs in Wales. *Political Geography*, 28, 164–173.

Kramer, A.E. (2011) Poland and Russia spar over wording of memorial. New York Times. http://www. nytimes.com/2011/04/11/world/europe/11katyn.html (accessed October 22, 2012).

Legg, S. (2007) *Space of Colonialism: Discipline and Governmentality in Delhi, India's New Capital*. Oxford: Blackwell.

Lorimer, H. and Lund, K. (2003) Peak performance: Practicing walking on Scotland's mountains. In *Nature Performed: Environment, Culture and Performance*, ed. B. Szerszynski, W. Heim, and C. Waterton. Oxford: Blackwell, pp. 130–144.

Matless, D. (1998) *Landscape and Englishness*. London: Reaktion.

Mitchell, D. (2003) *The Right to the City: Social Justice and the Fight for Public Space*. New York: Guilford Press.

Mitchell, W.J.T. (2002) *Landscape and Power*. Chicago: University of Chicago Press.

Monmonier, M. (2011) Hubris came before the Times Atlas's fall. New Scientist. http://www.newscientist.com/article/dn21058–hubris-came-before-the-times-atlass-fall.html (accessed October 22, 2012).

Nally, D. (2011) *Human Incumbrances: Political Violence and the Great Irish Famine*. Notre Dame, IN: University of Notre Dame Press.

Newman, D. and Passi, A. (1998) Fences and neighbours in the postmodern world: Boundary narratives in political geography. *Progress in Human Geography*, 22, 186–207.

Penrose, J. (2002) Nations, states and homelands: Territory and territoriality in nationalist thought. *Nations and Nationalism*, 8, 277–297.

Press Association (2011) Times Atlas reviews Greenland map accuracy after climate change row. Guardian. http://www.guardian.co.uk/world/2011/sep/22/times-atlas-reviews-greenland-map (accessed October 22, 2012).

Till, K. (2004) Political landscapes. In *A Companion to Cultural Geography*, ed. J.S. Duncan, N.C. Johnson, and R.H. Schein. Oxford: Blackwell, pp. 347–364.

Van Houtum, H., Kramsch, O., and Zierhofer, W. (eds.) (2005) *B/ordering Space*. Aldershot: Ashgate.

Vidal, J. (2011) Times Atlas is "wrong on Greenland climate change." Guardian. http://www.guardian.co.uk/environment/2011/sep/19/times-atlas-wrong-greenland-climate-change (accessed October 22, 2012).

Wallach, Y. (2011) Trapped in mirror-images: The rhetoric of maps in Israel/Palestine. *Political Geography*, 30 (7), 358–369.

Wylie, J. (2005) A single day's walking: Narrating self and landscape on the South West Coast Path. *Transactions of the Institute of British Geographers*, 30, 234–247.

Chapter 18

# Landscapes of Memory and Socially Just Futures

*Derek H. Alderman and Joshua F.J. Inwood*

Erika Doss (2010: 2) has used the phrase "memorial mania" to describe the United States' growing "obsession with issues of memory and history and an urgent desire to express and claim those issues in visibly public contexts." The American landscape is increasingly populated with statues, monuments, museums, roadside shrines, historical plaques, public art installations, and other commemorative sites – permanent and temporary as well as spontaneous and planned. Similarly, David Lowenthal (1996) characterized society as "possessed" by a cult- or religious-like devotion to the past. Heritage has become a global industry that sells the past to promote tourism and development, feeding a rampant consumer appetite for things retro, restored, and reenacted. These activities signal an important transition in the construction of landscapes of memory, from a historically elite-dominated practice to one increasingly populist in terms of its participants and historical themes.

The popularization of commemoration, heritage tourism, and historic preservation offers insight into the shifting and contested boundaries of identity within contemporary society. How we imagine ourselves in the present is intimately linked to how we remember ourselves in the past. For some scholars, the invocation of heritage compensates for a sense of loss and dislocation brought on by market forces, mass migrations, and rapid technological transformation (Lowenthal 1996). For others the growing pace of commemoration results from "adamant assertions of citizen rights and persistent demands for representation and respect" by public groups, reflecting broader national debates over "who and what should be remembered" (Doss 2010: 2). By asserting these rights many groups are creating a memorial infrastructure that, while continuing the tradition of celebrating heroism and patriotism, also addresses wide-ranging legacies, including trauma, discrimination, anger, shame, and survival.

In short, it is an exciting time to study landscapes of memory, not only because of the growing volume of memorials and heritage sites but also because these manifestations speak

*The Wiley Blackwell Companion to Cultural Geography*, First Edition.
Edited by Nuala C. Johnson, Richard H. Schein, and Jamie Winders.
© 2013 John Wiley & Sons, Ltd. Published 2016 by John Wiley & Sons, Ltd.

to changes and tensions in contemporary society. While memory is ostensibly about the past, it is shaped to serve ideological interests in the present and to carry certain cultural beliefs into the future. The notion that what is remembered tells us as much about the present and future as the past is a major foundation of memory studies. Memory studies represent a vibrant interdisciplinary field and geographers have made major contributions by examining the role of landscape in the social construction and contestation of public memory (Till 2006). In this chapter we review the importance of landscape to the process and politics of remembering (and forgetting), provide a broad overview of current geographical work on memorial landscapes, and discuss two established frameworks for these landscape interpretations – narrative and arena. In the process we also identify new analytical possibilities within each approach and provide avenues for future research directions.

Before moving forward with our discussion, it is important to set out the perspectives that guide this chapter. Within the politics of identity, having a place in a nation's past is often essential to being heard and taken seriously and asserting that one belongs. It is little surprise, then, that the challenging and changing of commemorative landscapes have become strategies used by historically marginalized groups to reconstruct their public importance and articulate an alternative social future. Cultural geography increasingly seeks to make interventions into how landscapes mediate social relations and how they can be imagined in more just ways. It is within this intellectual and political context that we write, drawing ideas from other scholars and from our own research on the African American experience within the southeastern United States. Ultimately this chapter is meant to inspire scholars to actively engage with the politics of memory and landscape interpretation.

## The Importance of Landscape to Memory

Traditionally, cultural geographers spoke about the importance of "the past" in shaping the landscape rather than focusing on memory. It was assumed that this singular past could be uncovered by using landscape artifacts and other evidence to peel away different eras of human settlement and environmental modification. The past was given its own causal power, but there was little exploration of how people mediated the past or how ideas about history were themselves social products open to multiple interpretations. Two important works in the 1970s signaled a shift toward a critical analysis of memory within geography. For Lowenthal (1975), the landscape was not simply a product of past human actions but was a tangible symbol of people's attachments to the past. These attachments – rather than a direct reflection of all that had happened historically – represented selectively saved, altered, and even fabricated reconstructions of the past. Harvey (1979) also recognized that landscapes could just as easily hide as reveal what happened in the past, arguing that the Basilica of the Sacred Heart in Paris obfuscates rather than elucidates the bloody, revolutionary history of France. Harvey's study exposed the important political, myth-making role that monuments play within nations and the need to analyze the social relations and conflicts that create landscapes of memory.

The emergence of the "new" critical school of cultural geography in the 1980s and 1990s, which emphasized the symbolic and iconographic qualities of the landscape, created a fertile environment for further development of memory studies in geography. Cultural geographers increasingly focused on interrogating a landscape's many layers of meaning rather than simply uncover its layers of historical use. The discipline's growing dialogue with social theory exposed cultural geographers to the memory-related writing of other scholars in the social sciences and humanities. The French thinkers Maurice Halbwachs (1992/1951) and Pierre Nora (1989) were especially influential. Halbwachs argued for the collective nature of all memory – even personal memory – and how remembering the past was shaped as much by group interactions, social institutions, and cultural practices as by brain chemistry and individual psychology. Geographers were especially drawn to the work of Nora, who asserted that social interpretations of the past are constituted, in part, through the construction of "sites of memory" (or *lieux de mémoire*). These sites of memory consisted of physical, concrete places of commemoration as well as the non-material rituals and displays of memory.

Nora's ideas about the importance of materiality and spatiality to social memory meshed well with the way geographers were rethinking the power of landscapes. Rather than simply reflecting culture, landscapes, it was argued, participated in the reproduction of social life and cultural practices. As Johnson (1995: 51) asserted in the mid-1990s, the landscape is not simply the "incidental material backdrop" for memory but plays an active role in constructing the meaning of commemoration. In the years that followed, geographers have explored how memorials and heritage sites dialectically draw meaning from and give meaning to their surroundings. A major idea underlying this work is that landscapes of memory, like all cultural landscapes, have a normative power. They are important conduits for not just giving voice to certain visions of history but casting legitimacy upon them – a way of ordering and controlling the public meaning of the past. At the same time, because this normative power is not absolute, landscapes of memory hold the seeds of their unmaking and can become important sites for contesting and negotiating memory and identity (Schein 2003).

Memorials and heritage sites influence how people remember and value the past in part by creating a sense of authenticity, especially when the site is the scene of the historical event being remembered. Historical authenticity, however, is not an inherent condition but a socially constructed experience that relies upon an active preservation and even staging of the landscape and its artifacts. Creating tangible and believable connections with the past does not simply give the impression of "going back in time" but channels the public to invest in a history supportive of certain cultural myths and national values (DeLyser 1999). The occurrence of a significant event at a location does not necessarily guarantee the production of a landscape of memory, especially when the event is characterized by violence and tragedy. Some places of tragedy go through a process of sanctification in which people make them into sacred landscapes that serve as sites of pilgrimage. According to Till (2005: 15), "through the ritual of returning [to places of trauma], one may experience a transformative moment and confront personal and social hauntings." Other sites of tragedy, however, might be obliterated or simply never commemorated because of unresolved historical and political interpretations of the landscape and its past (Foote 2003). In these instances, the landscape serves as both the medium for representing memory and, because of its own complex material history, the very subject of what is remembered or forgotten.

Even when landscapes of memory do not mark the location of remembered historic events, they can give the past an everyday familiarity and spatial permanence that facilitate a shared sense of place and time. Commemorative street naming, for example, inscribes social ideas about the past into a city's daily vocabulary, both verbal and visual. In contrast to the banality of street names, other landscapes of memory influence people by being decidedly extraordinary. Government elites regularly construct iconic architecture, grandiose monuments, and lavish public ceremonies to inspire public identification with state-controlled memory, illustrating how the landscape serves as a stage for the performance of national tradition and identity (Hagen and Ostergren 2006). The landscape is also a constitutive stage for the memorial practices of everyday people. These vernacular performances – which range from tourist rituals to citizen protests – can reinforce or challenge official modes of remembering and, in some instances, reclaim forgotten histories and identities. Performance, whether in the form of evocative displays and demonstrations or mundane acts of bodily repetition and work, is of growing interest within cultural geography more generally and memory studies in particular (Hoelscher and Alderman 2004).

Landscapes of memory anchor and bring historical legitimacy to the identities of social groups, but they also serve as a conduit for debating what (and whose) view of the past should be remembered. Holocaust-related memorials at former Nazi concentration camps such as Auschwitz and Buchenwald are instructive here in light of the competing historical interpretations and claims projected onto them by various social and political stakeholders (Charlesworth 1994; Azaryahu 2003). Public commemoration is not simply about debating the appropriateness of remembering the past in a certain way; it also involves deciding where best to emplace that memory within the broader cultural landscape. Sometimes memorials become embroiled in controversy when antagonistic memories are perceived as infringing upon one another's symbolic space. As geographers have discovered in researching post-communist Central and Eastern Europe, monument removal and/or relocation are common during times of political revolution and regime change. Political leaders purge the landscape of old historical symbols and create (or restore) memorials supportive of the new ideological order, although these transformations can be fraught with conflict (Palonen 2008). "The removal of a monument from one place to another has profound impacts on the meaning of these places, as well as the meanings of the monument" (Dixon 2009: 86).

As the previous examples suggest, where we remember the past is important to how we remember. The location of a memorial may support, diminish, or even contradict the intended meanings of its creators. This is well illustrated in the context of recent efforts to celebrate the civil rights movement in the United States. Because of public opposition, African Americans have struggled and often been unsuccessful in placing monuments to the movement within the traditional core of memorial space in cities. For the most part, Main Street, the county courthouse, and city hall remain devoted to remembering white-dominated historical narratives. Many (but not all) of America's roadways named for Martin Luther King, Jr. are side streets or portions of roads located within poor, black areas of cities. The confinement of King's memory to marginal and degraded locations has, in many instances, changed the meaning of the commemoration from a point of racial pride to a reminder of continued inequality (Dwyer and Alderman 2008).

At work through landscapes commemorating the civil rights movement are considerations of not only the specific placement of memorials but also how they are situated with regard to broader race- and class-based patterns in cities and towns. In trying to elevate the historical reputation of King through road naming, African American activists frequently struggle to convince whites to remember the civil rights leader in places that challenge long-standing boundaries, even though challenging historically entrenched patterns of racial segregation is exactly the purpose of many street-naming campaigns. Ironically, the end result is landscape of memory that, while representing the movement as a settled part of the past, actually speaks to its unfinished nature and the ongoing African American struggle for racial justice. Memorial landscapes can be thought of as not only a product of social power but also a tool or resource for achieving it.

Finally, the social power of landscapes of memory is often realized through the broader political economy of cultural symbols and place promotion. Associations with the past can confer prestige, privilege, and status on social actors and groups – providing them a form of symbolic capital – while also having economic value. Neo-traditional urban development sells residents an invented, nostalgic image of community life that reinforces patterns of social and spatial exclusion (Till 1993). Tourism also perpetuates a commodified heritage that frequently neglects complex local histories and writes certain racial and class identities into the landscape while ignoring others (Johnson 1999; Inwood 2010). Although it is a difficult undertaking, some communities in the United States are developing heritage tourism landscapes that address ingrained racial disparities and promote reconciliation (Barton and Leonard 2010). In this respect, the landscape of memory holds out potential for it to be used for therapeutic purposes rather than simply for economic or social gain.

## Approaches and Possibilities

### Landscape as Narrative

Recognizing the great authority that the landscape casts upon certain visions of the past, geographers have shown significant interest in critiquing the historical discourses represented via the landscape. This leads to an analysis focused on the communicative medium of the landscape and the identification of the selective ways in which the past is retold through the form and content of memorials and heritage sites. The collective process of remembering is accompanied, simultaneously, by a process of forgetting – an excluding of other historical accounts from public consideration and recognition. The narrative approach mobilizes a series of characteristic questions in studying landscapes of memory. What is said and not said about the past? Whose history is remembered or forgotten? What does the differential treatment of histories and identities tell us about power relations and patterns of inequality within historical and contemporary societies? And to what extent do commemorative silences perpetuate these unequal power relations into the future? Motivating a critique of the historical narratives manifested within landscapes of memory is the fact that these stories can be internalized by members of the public in different and sometimes conflicting ways. Landscape representations of the past, while creating a collective sense of belonging and stability for some social groups, can be a source of alienation for other groups who are left out of these narratives. As Legg (2005) has argued in the context of anti-colonial struggles in India, the refusal to forget (or be forgotten) can be actively mobilized as a resource in the politics of identity and social change.

The emphasis placed on narrative analysis is derived, in part, from the "landscape as text" metaphor in cultural geography, which calls for a critical reading of the symbolic messages continually written into and read from landscapes. The textual metaphor has been criticized for privileging the visual aspects of the landscape over its aural and other dimensions. Geographers have tended to perpetuate this bias in their work on memory. Yet narratives can be spoken and heard as well as written and read. Speech acts are cultural performances that work to constitute and claim landscapes as well as narrate identity of oneself and others (Kearns and Berg 2002). The marginalization of the history of slavery and African Americans at antebellum plantation house museums in the southeastern United States is carried out on many fronts, but none more obvious than in the spoken words of tour guides and docents. Historically, these docents have been reluctant to even utter the words "slave" or "slavery" when discussing plantation history and have used euphemisms (e.g., servants) to describe the enslaved if they are mentioned at all. The term "symbolic annihilation" has been used to capture the manner in which the identities and histories of Africans and African Americans are made silent on the plantation landscape along with their painful racialized histories (Eichstedt and Small 2002). This racist narrating of the past has not gone unchallenged. Some African Americans have reclaimed their plantation heritage, producing counter-narratives that bring the slave struggle front and center within the retelling of the Old South. In Natchez, Mississippi, long famous for its tour of antebellum mansions, African Americans host a performance of gospel songs for visitors called *A Southern Road to Freedom* that defiantly recasts the meaning of the Civil War from a black perspective and enacts stories of oppression, resistance, and survival during slavery. The Natchez production demonstrates the great potential in studying music, chants, and even groans as part of the narrative landscape of memory (Hoelscher 2006). These sounds and speech acts take on a performative force that embodies and communicates representations of the past beyond sheer textuality and thus create a "contested space of political utterances" (Rose-Redwood 2008b: 875).

Geographers have devoted considerable attention to the role of memorials, monuments, and heritage sites in narrating and legitimizing certain hegemonic discourses about national identity (Foote and Azaryahu 2007). These discourses enact important ideas about who belongs in normative society, which has important implications for the selective narration of minority histories. Hegemony operates by acknowledging the needs and ideas of subordinate groups and then seeming to incorporate the interests of subordinate groups into the national collective identity, thereby giving the appearance that the interests of marginalized groups have been considered in the organization and maintenance of society. Within such a hegemonic social order, memorials and heritage sites narrate a more racially or ethically inclusive national history, but it is a story scripted to uphold dominant cultural ideas and values about society. For instance, Atlanta's Martin Luther King, Jr. National Historic Site and the surrounding Auburn Avenue community produce a set of discourses through their exhibits and tours that tell a story of the civil rights movement that silences and reframes the more radical chapters of Dr. King's life (such as his ideas about wealth redistribution) and uses his legacy to redeem, rather than question, the neoliberal democratic structure of US society. Stories of integration and national unity take precedence over addressing the continuing legacies of racism. Important in the case of King is how historical narratives inscribe the landscape at different scales, providing not only a national story of positive social change but also a means of marketing Atlanta as a "progressive" southern city (Inwood 2009). The case of the King Center notwithstanding, little work in geography has focused on the impact of neoliberalism and its emphasis on privatization, individualism, and a narrow sense of social responsibility on landscapes of memory, in general and specifically to giving voice to minority heritage narratives.

Despite the great emphasis that geographers have placed on the landscape as a medium for communicating narratives, there has been limited work on how historical stories are specifically configured through landscape design, creating what Azaryahu and Foote (2008) call "spatial narratives." A number of strategies exist for spatially configuring narratives, some of which facilitate the retelling of complex historical stories at various scales and from different social perspectives. Understanding the mechanics of arranging narratives in space could allow geographers to collaborate with and influence memory practitioners, planners, and entrepreneurs, thus creating an opportunity for challenging the production of hegemonic landscapes of memory. Geographers' familiarity with geospatial technology, digital humanities, social media, and Web 2.0 could be great assets in designing spatial narratives that allow the public to crisscross the memory terrain from different ideological and social points of view.

In focusing on the immediate period in which historical narratives are written into land-scapes, geographers have unnecessarily neglected "the pre and after-lives of [memory] sites" (Till 2006: 330). Future work might consider paying closer attention to the temporally dynamic nature of how memorials and heritage sites are produced and consumed by social actors and groups. Memorials and heritage sites are in a constant process of becoming as present social needs and ideological interests change. The term "symbolic accretion" is a very useful starting point for capturing the manner in which new narrations of the past can be appended to older memorial narratives and spaces (Dwyer 2004). To track engagements with landscapes of memory over time will require more emphasis on longitudinal studies of how historical narratives are (re)constructed at memory sites and how audiences (re)interpret and co-construct these stories through their own interpretations and stories, including family history (genealogy) and personal connections to larger historical events and themes. A search for ancestral homeland drives the decision of many African Americans to tour the slave castles of Ghana, and these tours are frequently narrated in anticipation of these "roots tourists."

As we adopt a dynamic narrative approach to landscapes of memory, it will be important to broaden our thinking about the nature of stories and how they affect people and places. Recently, Hoskins (2010: 260) encouraged us to consider how historical narratives function as "mobile circulatory markers of place" rather than static representations to be unpacked for meaning. He introduces the concept of "narrative economy" to characterize how memori-als and heritage sites are made and remade "through the exchange of stories that acquire value as they circulate and intersect," including stories that challenge official imperatives and "factual" accounts (Hoskins 2010: 260). Hoskins also reflected on how stories might work to recuperate the histories and identities of socially marginalized groups, but cautioned that a strict valuation of these narratives on the basis of representational accuracy and historical evidence could limit our ability to hear the very voices that have been historically silenced. He claimed: "A responsible heritage then is not one that rejects accuracy, but it is one that recognizes accuracy as just one among many components in a broader restorative truth" (Hoskins 2010: 272).

Achieving a restorative truth will lead to paying closer attention to *how* stories are nar-rated and the affective connection they create between people of the past and the present. For example, the mere factual mention of slavery at southern plantation sites does not neces-sarily encourage visitors to identify with and care about the enslaved. It is important to explore not only how stories move through landscapes, but also how these storied landscapes move people or inspire geographic-historical empathy (Modlin, Alderman, and Gentry 2011). Doss (2010: 376) argued for more than simply an outpouring of public feeling through memorials but the "channeling of fury into something passionate and progressive" and "pro-viding spaces and subjects that permit cultural and political creativity and prompt acts of 'good' citizenship."

A progressive narration of the histories of marginalized groups might also address the affective capacity of objects at heritage sites, recognizing that they "can be both 'subject to' and 'initiative of' discursive construction." The very physicality and materiality of an object can "afford it a communicative force that goes beyond what language can portray" (Hoskins 2007: 441). For example, visitors to the Slave Relic Museum in Walterboro, South Carolina, are allowed to hold shackles used during the transatlantic slave trade. The physical work of lifting the heavy shackles encourages a tactile and emotional engagement that, unlike the plantation site, refuses to forget that the enslaved existed and suffered, while also demonstrating the power of the visitor's corporeality in constituting and shaping narrative spaces with the museum (Alderman and Campbell 2008). Analyzing landscapes of memory as a narrative involves more than a detached, linear reading or listening. It also requires being sensitive to the embodied, multi-sensual ways that people experience memory and contribute to storytelling (Till 2008).

## Landscape as Arena

The multiple ways in which landscapes of memory can be authored/spoken, read/heard, and experienced have led many geographers to examine the politically contentious nature of remembering the past. Despite the popular impression that memorial landscapes are somehow frozen in time, they are perhaps better seen as open-ended, conditionally malleable systems. Public memory is under constant reconstruction and reinterpretation, but the process is not without constraints. People's ability to memorialize the past is limited by competition and sometimes conflict with other groups or individuals who might have alternative motivations or stories about the past. The struggle and negotiation over whose conception of the past will prevail in this circumstance constitute a politics of memory that can illuminate larger social conflicts.

The production of landscapes of memory is often controlled by social and political elites (Forest and Johnson 2002), but others may seek to turn the landscape into a site for struggle and resistance. There is increasing evidence that groups traditionally ignored in the memorialization process often build "sites of counter-memory" that challenge the dominant historical narratives that frequently exclude or misrepresent them (Legg 2005). Thus the metaphor of "arena" focuses on the capacity of memorials and heritage locations to serve as sites for social groups, with varying levels of power and social resources, to actively interpret and debate the meaning of the past as part of larger struggles over recognition and the legacies of discrimination and dispossession (Alderman 2010). Examining memorial landscapes as an "arena" recognizes the highly public and performative nature of these debates as actors and groups seek to influence collective decisions or policies, justify their claims to the past, and entice others to participate in the debate. The word arena often carries with it an image of formal confrontation, but it is important to note that resistance and conflict also come in more subtle, everyday forms that should not be ignored.

Geographers have devoted significant attention to commemorative landscapes of the southeastern United States as arenas for conflicts over regional and racial identity. Controversy in the South over the public display and meaning of the Confederate Battle Flag provides a good example. On the one hand, many white southerners see the flag as a symbol of their ancestors' heroic fight for independence during the Civil War. On the other hand, many African Americans view the flag as a symbol of racism and a commemoration of past efforts to preserve slavery and white supremacy. They argue that the mere presence of these memorials to the secessionist southern government not only marginalizes African Americans from any meaningful discussion of the region's history but also openly conflicts with their ongoing efforts to construct a more empowering image of black memory built upon civil rights. The end result has been the removal of the flag from many public places, but also an intensification of the intransigency of white Neo-Confederate activists, illustrating how memorial resistance can be enacted by members of hegemonic groups and not just the historically marginalized (Webster and Leib 2008).

Rose-Redwood (2008a) has rightly argued that the landscape cannot be reduced to a monolithic discussion of the dominance of elites and the resistance of the marginalized. Such a dualism blinds us to the multiple agendas and identities that are often at work in memorialization processes. As he found in examining the history of street naming in New York City, tensions and struggles over commemoration take place within both elite and marginalized groups as well as between them. In the case of Harlem, for example, recognition of the historical achievements of African Americans on street signs was carried out, but initially at the expense of remembering important women of color. When an outspoken African American female activist sought to build a monument in Savannah, Georgia, to retell the traumatic history of the transatlantic slave trade, she encountered intense resistance from fellow African Americans, including two male city officials (Alderman 2010). There is considerable room in geography to study landscapes of memory as arenas for debating gender identity and feminist politics (e.g., DeLyser 2008).

Given the important role that public commemoration plays in asserting the public visibility and legitimacy of marginalized groups and subgroups within the population, it is surprising that more geographers have not analyzed landscapes of memory from a social justice perspective. Commemoration, rather than a mere symbolic act, is a material practice that takes place within, and contributes to, larger geographies of socioeconomic opportunity and disparity. For example, the traditional neglect of African Americans within US collective memory has reflected and worked to justify a larger racial inequality in American life still felt far beyond memorials and monuments. In terms of procedural justice, geographers might consider exploring what factors limit the participation of marginalized groups in the decision-making process that drives public commemoration. In terms of distributive justice, geographers could shed more light on the social and spatially uneven ways that marginalized histories are positioned within the landscape and how this affects the meanings attached to these memories and their locations.

Any effort to bring greater fairness to the remembering of marginalized groups requires addressing the legacies of violence and trauma within societies. Public remembrance of violence is a necessary tool for facilitating social compensation to victimized groups and moral education among the larger society. Yet the process can be contentious for it involves identifying perpetrators, which requires assigning social responsibility to them, and identifying survivors, which for some means carrying past trauma into the present. Historical justice is a concept gaining traction among memory scholars who wish to use their work to facilitate the remembering of past injustices as part of the healing and reconciliation process. Studying the landscape as arena is not restricted to matters of dissonance and contest, which has tended to be the focus of much of the politics of memory-work in geography. The arena can also be conceived as a place of conflict resolution, recognizing "heritage spaces and landscapes as key sites for conciliatory civil society development through meaningful engagement with difficult histories" (Lehrer 2010: 269). As Johnson (2012) found in the commemoration of the Omagh bombing in Northern Ireland, memorials can be an important part of the peace and reconciliation processes in post-conflict societies, illustrating the redemptive potential of remembering and even forgetting past physical and psychological violence.

Truth and Reconciliation Commissions are potentially important arenas for coming to terms with these difficult histories. They have an important memory function by collecting personal recollections of violence and trauma and other evidence to produce a truth narrative that counters the institutionalized forgetting of injustices found in official histories. Plans to build public memorials or monuments to victims frequently result from these Commissions. Traditionally the United States has not hosted Truth and Reconciliation Commissions, although they are now growing in number, and it is appropriate that the first was held in 2005 in the southern city of Greensboro, North Carolina. In 1979, Greensboro was the site of a shooting of labor activists by the Ku Klux Klan – a massacre that local police contributed to and for which no one was held criminally liable. Because the Greensboro City Government openly opposed the Commission, the truth process resulted from grassroots activists who reworked historical territorial divisions in the city and created a public space that brought perpetrators, survivors, and community members together for purposes of transformation. The Commission asserted the need to have the shooting memorialized within Greensboro, but it also recognized how memories of this violence continue to inform structural racism and reproduce inequality and disenfranchisement in the city (Inwood 2012). Thus, landscapes of memory can be arenas for challenging and potentially redefining the lines of belonging for marginalized groups and are but one avenue activists can take in the continuing struggle for social and economic justice.

Greensboro is instructive of the importance of studying the politics of remembering injustice from the bottom up. Till (2005) has shown considerable interest in places marked by past acts of violence, calling our attention to the "memory-work" of activists, artists, and other citizens in Germany as they sought to represent the histories and legacies of National Socialism and the Holocaust. Memory-work is a useful yet underutilized concept in geography that, in addition to capturing the labor involved in building landscapes of memory, recognizes the political and cultural creativity needed to create public spaces through which citizens can debate their understandings of the past, question dominant regimes of memory, and work through historical losses and trauma. For Till (2008: 109), these memory-workers are hugely important to the future of memory studies: "by taking seriously artistic and activist place-based practice, not only do scholars have much to learn about memory theoretically and empirically; we can also begin building responsible research agendas that contribute to more socially just futures." In developing this responsible agenda, academic geographers will need to reflect further on the role of their own practices within the politics of memory and possibly identify opportunities for engaging and assisting memory-work. In seeking to build socially inclusive landscapes of memory, geographers will invariably become participants in the public memorial arena rather than simply onlookers.

## References

Alderman, D.H. (2010) Surrogation and the politics of remembering slavery in Savannah, Georgia. *Journal of Historical Geography*, 36, 90–101.

Alderman, D.H. and Campbell, R. (2008) Symbolic excavation and the artifact politics of remembering slavery in the American South: Observations from Walterboro, South Carolina. *Southeastern Geographer*, 48, 338–355.

Azaryahu, M. (2003) RePlacing memory: The reorientation of Buchenwald. *Cultural Geographies*, 10, 1–20.

Azaryahu, M. and Foote, K.E. (2008) Historical space as narrative medium: On the configuration of spatial narratives of time at historical sites. *GeoJournal*, 73, 179–194.

Barton, A.W. and Leonard, S.J. (2010) Incorporating social justice in tourism planning: Racial reconciliation and sustainable community development in the Deep South. *Community Development*, 41, 298–322.

Charlesworth, A. (1994) Contesting places of memory: The case of Auschwitz. *Environment and Planning D*, 12, 579–593.

DeLyser, D. (1999) Authenticity on the ground: Engaging the past in a California ghost town. *Annals of the Association of American Geographers*, 89, 602–632.

DeLyser, D. (2008) "Thus I salute the Kentucky Daisey's claim": Gender, social memory, and the mythic West at a proposed Oklahoma monument. *Cultural Geographies*, 15, 63–94.

Dixon, S. (2009) Mobile monumental landscapes: Shifting cultural identities in Mexico City's "*El Caballito.*" *Historical Geography*, 37, 71–91.

Doss, E. (2010) *Memorial Mania: Public Feeling in America*. Chicago: University of Chicago Press.

Dwyer, O.J. (2004) Symbolic accretion and commemoration. *Social and Cultural Geography*, 5, 419–435.

Dwyer, O.J. and Alderman, D.H. (2008) *Civil Rights Memorials and the Geography of Memory*. Chicago: Center for American Places at Columbia College.

Eichstedt, J. and Small, S. (2002) *Representations of Slavery: Race and Ideology in Southern Plantation Museums*. Washington, DC: Smithsonian Institute Press.

Foote, K.E. (2003) *Shadowed Ground: America's Landscapes of Violence and Tragedy*, 2nd edition. Austin: University of Texas Press.

Foote, K.E. and Azaryahu, M. (2007) Toward a geography of memory: Geographical dimensions of public memory and commemoration. *Journal of Political and Military Sociology*, 35, 125–144.

Forest, B. and Johnson, J. (2002) Unraveling the threads of history: Soviet-era monuments and post-Soviet national identity in Moscow. *Annals of the Association of American Geographers*, 92, 524–547.

Hagen, J. and Ostergren, R. (2006) Spectacle, architecture and place at the Nuremberg Party Rallies: Projecting a Nazi vision of past, present and future. *Cultural Geographies*, 13, 157–181.

Halbwachs, M. (1992/1951) *On Collective Memory*. Chicago: University of Chicago Press.

Harvey, D. (1979) Monument and myth. *Annals of the Association of American Geographers*, 69, 362–381.

Hoelscher, S. (2006) The white-pillared past: Landscapes of memory and race in the American South. In *Landscape and Race in the United States*, ed. R. Schein. New York: Routledge, pp. 39–72.

Hoelscher, S. and Alderman, D.H. (2004) Memory and place: Geographies of a critical relationship. *Social and Cultural Geography*, 5, 347–355.

Hoskins, G. (2007) Materialising memory at Angel Island Immigration Station. *Environment and Planning A*, 39, 437–455.

Hoskins, G. (2010) A secret reservoir of values: The narrative economy of Angel Island Immigration Station. *Cultural Geographies*, 17, 259–275.

Inwood, J.F.J. (2009) Contested memory in the birthplace of a king: A case study of Auburn Avenue and the Martin Luther King Jr. National Park. *Cultural Geographies*, 16, 87–100.

Inwood, J.F.J. (2010) Sweet Auburn: Constructing Atlanta's Auburn Avenue as a heritage tourist destination. *Urban Geography*, 31, 573–594.

Inwood, J.F.J. (2012) Righting unrightable wrongs: Legacies of racial violence and the Greensboro Truth and Reconciliation Commission. *Annals of the Association of American Geographers*, 192, 1450–1467.

Johnson, N.C. (1995) Cast in stone: Monuments, geography, and nationalism. *Environment and Planning D: Society and Space*, 13, 51–65.

Johnson, N.C. (1999) Framing the past: Time, space and the politics of heritage tourism in Ireland. *Political Geography*, 18, 187–207.

Johnson, N.C. (2012) The contours of memory in post-conflict societies: Enacting public remembrance of the bomb in Omagh, Northern Ireland. *Cultural Geographies*, 19 (2), 237–258.

Kearns, R. and Berg, L. (2002) Proclaiming place: Towards a geography of place name pronunciation. *Social and Cultural Geography*, 3, 283–302.

Legg, S. (2005) Sites of counter-memory: The refusal to forget and the nationalist struggle in colonial Delhi. *Historical Geography*, 33, 180–201.

Lehrer, E. (2010) Can there be a conciliatory heritage? *International Journal of Heritage Studies*, 16, 269–288.

Lowenthal, D. (1975) Past time, present place: Landscape and memory. *Geographical Review*, 65, 1–37.

Lowenthal, D. (1996) *Possessed by the Past: The Heritage Crusade and the Spoils of History*. New York: Free Press.

Modlin, Jr., E.A., Alderman, D.H., and Gentry, G.W. (2011) Tour guides as creators of empathy: The role of affective inequality in marginalizing the enslaved at plantation house museums. *Tourist Studies*, 11, 3–19.

Nora, P. (1989) Between memory and history: Les lieux de mémoire. *Representations*, 26, 7–25.

Palonen, E. (2008) The city-text in post-communist Budapest: Street names, memorials, and the politics of commemoration. *GeoJournal*, 73, 219–230.

Rose-Redwood, R. (2008a) From number to name: Symbolic capital, places of memory, and the politics of street renaming in New York City. *Social and Cultural Geography*, 9, 431–452.

Rose-Redwood, R. (2008b) "Sixth Avenue is now a memory": Regimes of spatial inscription and the performative limits of the official city-text. *Political Geography*, 27, 875–894.

Schein, R.H. (2003) Normative dimensions of landscape. In *Everyday America: Cultural Landscape Studies after J.B. Jackson*, ed. C. Wilson and P. Groth. Berkeley: University of California Press, pp. 199–218.

Till, K.E. (1993) Neotraditional towns and urban villages: The cultural production of a geography of "otherness." *Environment and Planning D: Society and Space*, 11, 709–732.

Till, K.E. (2005) *The New Berlin: Memory, Politics, and Place*. Minneapolis: University of Minnesota Press.

Till, K.E. (2006) Memory studies. *History Workshop Journal*, 62, 325–341.

Till, K.E. (2008) Artistic and activist memory-work: Approaching place-based practice. *Memory Studies*, 1, 99–113.

Webster, G.R. and Leib, J.I. (2008) The Confederate battle flag and the neo-Confederate movement in the South. In *The Neo-Confederate Movement in the United States*, ed. E. Hague, H. Beirich, and E. Sebesta. Austin: University of Texas Press, pp. 169–201.

Chapter 19

# Consumption and Landscape

*Mona Domosh*

The words landscape and consumption are both vernacular terms with common-sense meanings, meanings that on the surface do not seem to bind them together; but their genealogies hint at some points of overlap and congruence. Consumption refers technically to the act of consuming, but that consuming can consist of things like food or drink, or to the burning or using up of natural resources such as forests or coal. It also has a very particular meaning as a term in economics that refers to expenditures on goods and services as distinct from the production of those goods and services (Bennett, Grossberg, and Morris 2005). The word originated in the fourteenth century and was first used to refer to the wasting away of the body through disease, but its meaning shifted to the using up of materials in the sixteenth century and then in the early modern period to types of economic expenditures, coincident with the transition from a feudal to a capitalist order (Bennett *et al.* 2005). The term landscape as an expanse of rural scenery that could be seen from a single vantage point was originally a painterly term that referred to a particular way of representing space, and it too was first used in the early modern period with the transition from a feudal to a capitalist economic and social order (Cosgrove 1984). Later the word came to refer not just to a way of depicting a rural scene, but to the scene itself, and to the human-made spaces that are shaped in and through a society's economy and culture (Jackson 1984). In other words, the differing meanings contained within these two terms suggest some commonalities (both terms draw their contemporary meanings from the early modern period) and some overlap (both terms touch on issues related to the economy and economic class) that may not be immediately apparent from their everyday usage. In this chapter I draw on some of these commonalities and overlaps in order to highlight the ways in which landscape is consumed, and the ways in which consumption produces landscape.

*The Wiley Blackwell Companion to Cultural Geography*, First Edition.
Edited by Nuala C. Johnson, Richard H. Schein, and Jamie Winders.
© 2013 John Wiley & Sons, Ltd. Published 2016 by John Wiley & Sons, Ltd.

## The Visual Consumption of Landscape

More than a generation ago, Denis Cosgrove (1984) examined how the origins of the meaning of landscape as a concept that refers to a visual construct – a particular way of seeing (Berger 1972) – was already implicated in the notion of consumption. Cosgrove traced the idea of landscape to Renaissance Italy and early Georgian England, and to the ways in which the new elite classes whose power was based on commercial activities began to imaginatively reshape agricultural lands that had once been productive into landscapes that were meant to be visually consumed. In fifteenth-century Italy, a feudal system that was based on control over productive agricultural lands was shifting to a capitalistic system, and along with that shift came a different way to value land, not only for what it could produce in terms of agriculture and land rent, but also as a landscape, a scene to be enjoyed for its pleasures and for the prestige it accorded to those who knew how to "see" it (Cosgrove 1985). In other words, he showed how the idea of landscape was created within a very particular historical time and space, one where power relations were shifting. Creating, viewing, and appreciating the aesthetics of a landscape, whether *en plein air* or on canvas, became a form of class distinction (Bourdieu 1984). This new idea of landscape was materially reiterated and reproduced in paintings, maps, verbal accounts, and on the land itself, as merchants invested in estates that were made into visual landscapes, designed by a new profession, that of landscape architect.

Landscape as such was also predicated on a particular technology, a technology based on Euclidean geometry that allowed surveyors, landscape designers, and painters to create on the land and on canvas a perspective from which the scene could be viewed from one vantage point (Cosgrove 1985). This idea of landscape and its technologies reverberated throughout the new capitalistic world of Northern Europe and North America, taking on particular hues of place and time, but maintaining its connection to the consumptive habits of the elite and their newly found power over land (Cosgrove 1984). In Georgian England, for example, the emerging elite class of capitalists based in London began to invest some of their money in the countryside, building lavish country estates with surrounding parklands as a way of displaying their status and of legitimizing their wealth. These country estates lent an air of aristocratic prestige that London's financiers and merchants found enticing, particularly since land on these estates was not meant for agricultural work (as it would have been during feudalism), but instead for leisurely consumption. As Stephen Daniels (1988) suggests, landscape architects such as Capability Brown and Humphrey Repton built their careers around designing and devising technologies to create purely aesthetic landscapes that would express the gentry's power over land, and present a prospect unmarred by any reminders of agricultural labor. For example, Brown's aptly named invention, "the ha-ha" – a narrow ditch that acted as a fence for grazing animals – allowed an uninterrupted landscape view from the house out toward the parkland, while the artful placement of clumps of trees "enhanced the size of a park and the pleasure of running one's eyes possessively over its contours" (Daniels 1988: 45).

The visual consumption of landscape as a marker of class and other forms of identity continues today. In one of the most thorough analyses of landscape tastes and class identities in the contemporary United States, Nancy and James Duncan (2004) focused on the consumption of particular landscape forms that came to define the town of Bedford in Westchester County, New York, an affluent suburb of New York City. They identified three ways that Bedford's residents maintained their exclusionary landscape: first, an aesthetic based on notions of the pastoral, wilderness, and the New England village was incorporated into the town's zoning laws; second, environmentalism was used to give legitimacy to tax codes that protected open spaces; and third, historic preservation initiatives were used to prevent any new construction in the town. These three mechanisms of landscape governance and control, and the aesthetic they are based on, have effectively created an exclusionary community only affordable to the elite. For example, Duncan and Duncan (2004) documented how the theme of environmentalism worked to cloak the class and political motives behind certain tax codes that prevent any type of new housing "development" from occurring in Bedford, while the theme of historic preservation keeps out any "modern" intrusions into the manicured and museum-like "New England" village of Bedford (there was even a large protest over the installation of a traffic light in the town after a young driver was seriously injured when another driver failed to stop at the stop sign). In other words, the landscape of Bedford was continually being made and maintained according to a particular aesthetic that, while generally seen to be unquestionably "good" (who would question, for example, the environmentally friendly large open tracts of land?), was in fact working to exclude other classes of people from any participation in the use or visual consumption of this landscape.

In a similar way, but in a totally different context, geographers and others have shown how certain types of American and European landscapes such as gated housing communities have been transported through the world and are being consumed as symbols of modernity and high style (King 2004; Wu 2004). Geographers Choon-Piew Pow and Lily Kong (2007) show the ways in which the new upper classes in Shanghai are consuming the visual landscape as a marker of their newly found identities. Through analyses of real estate advertisements and interviews with residents of new gated communities in suburban Shanghai, Pow and Kong reveal the various themes that make these landscapes popular with the new urban bourgeoisie, themes that include social prestige, landscape exclusivity, and what they call "foreign chic" (Pow and Kong 2007: 147). The theme of foreign chic comes in many forms. Some developers hire Western architects, adopt Western architectural styles, and/or name their housing communities after well-known places in the West, such as Manhattan Garden, Rancho Santa Fe, Edinburgh Villa. Other developers deliberately borrow landscape motifs that "infuse their housing projects with 'enchanting' qualities of an imagined Western suburban lifestyle" (Pow and Kong 2007: 148), such as Western kitchens and appliances. Appeals to nature and natural scenery likewise attract buyers through their associations with the West and the pastoral aesthetic, but also draw on the significance of gardens in Chinese history. As Pow and Kong relate: "Real estate advertisements explicitly compare their interior landscaping to the classical Chinese gardens such as the Lion Forest Garden (*shizhilin*) and 'Humble Administrator's Garden' (*zhuozhenyuan*), both famous landmarks in Suzhou, a historic city in Jiangsu Province that is well-known for its elaborate gardens built by reclusive elites during the Ming and Qing dynasties" (2007: 146). The combination of foreign chic with the prestige associated through Chinese history with gardens and nature has made Shanghai's new gated "garden" communities a primary status symbol for the city's new elite, a visual landscape that is, by all accounts, being rapidly consumed.

## The Ways Landscapes are Commodified

Landscape as the embodiment of a particular aesthetic that is consumed by an elite class is a very specific way that landscapes are turned into commodities; other types of landscapes are subject to commodification on grounds that have little to do with aesthetics *per se*. Tourist landscapes are an obvious example of what geographers have called "place marketing," that is, the packaging and selling of places for commercial reasons. Tourism, from the days of the Grand Tour through Europe in the eighteenth century to today's package tours, is at its root a form of landscape consumption; even before tourists leave their houses they have been sold a particular place through advertisements, books, websites, and conversations. The tourist site itself is often reconfigured to meet expectations of the exotic, the beautiful, the authentic, or the historic. John Urry's now classic book *Consuming Places* (1995) makes very clear the role that the tourist gaze plays in shaping and reshaping particular landscapes; "environments, places and people," he writes, "are being regularly made and re-made as tourist objects" (p. 192). Ironically, it turns out of course that this commodification of landscapes often destroys the very qualities that tourists wanted to consume in the first place: the authentic is less so as places are packaged for commercial use, while the beautiful is hard to see with all of the other tourists blocking the view. The "something else" that tourists seek to consume may in fact turn out to be little different from what they have at home.

Taking this point further, some geographers have argued that the practices of tourism are fairly mundane and "normal." In other words, much of contemporary tourism involves activities not dissimilar to those conducted at home, and may in fact replicate and reaffirm landscapes of home. Commenting on packaged bus tours, Tim Edensor (2007) shows how the everyday and mundane are enacted: "Although it can never be totalizing, travel on the tour bus provides a distinct, familiar, mundane rhythm wherein a cosseted, quiescent body is seated in plush seating, calmed by the soft purr of the engine, shielded from glaring sunlight by tinted windows, and often informed by the commentary of the tour guide about the sights outside, a rhythm that includes intermittent movement outside the bus to gaze, photograph, eat and shop" (2007: 210). This everydayness of tourism is made possible by the fact that tourists are used to thinking of landscapes – even the ones at home – as commodities. In other words, geographers and others have argued that a good deal of postmodern urban developments and architecture are designed as commodities, as places not only built as settings for consumer activities, but also consumable themselves in terms of being marketed and packaged to attract customers.

The "normalizing" of landscapes as commodities is due partly to a fairly common strategy of urban economic development, what scholars have called the creation and selling of the entrepreneurial city (Hall and Hubbard 1998; Cronin and Hetherington 2008). In response to the economic and demographic declines of the late 1980s in many countries of the global North, city governments and non-governmental organizations (NGOs) began concerted efforts to rebrand their cities as creative, vibrant, and cultural centers, thereby promoting not only tourist visits, but also economic development. These cities in effect sold themselves to investors as sites of economic opportunity in terms of retail sales and service functionalities, and in turn their urban landscapes were turned into themed retail settings, festival marketplaces, historic attractions, and other spectacles of consumption. As a result, the landscapes of these entrepreneurial cities are composed of stage settings for consumption, designed to be viewed, performed in, and played with, at the expense of landscapes that are meant to provide a sense of community or experience (Zukin 2011). Steven Miles argues that the urban landscapes of many contemporary cities have been shaped primarily by "the need or at least the perceived need to reinvent the city as a service-driven entity in which image and perception takes precedence over familiarity and reality" (2010: 164). These contemporary urban landscapes for consumption are not limited to the West. Like Pow and Kong (2007), Miles uses the example of Shanghai to highlight the importance of architecture to the packaging and branding of cities, focusing on the incredible transformation of the Pudong region of the city, "an area of 350 square kilometers of land that is located on the east bank of the Huangpu River and which was once the home to run-down houses and farms and which now presents Shanghai's face to the rest of the world . . . a graphic physical manifestation of a market-driven philosophy" (Miles 2010: 78–79).

This branding, marketing, and selling of cities – through the construction of iconic architecture, festival settings, and shopping malls – has often been criticized for leaving little space for everyday life and authentic encounters. However, in their analyses of the spaces and functions of the Victoria and Alfred Waterfront Mall in post-apartheid Cape Town, South Africa, geographers Miriam Houssey-Holzschuch and Annika Teppo (2009) uncovered a far more complicated picture of the socio-spatial dynamic operating within the mall. What they found is that in a city experiencing rapid changes including an erosion of public space and the legacies of spatial and social racial segregation, the mall served not only as a "privately owned space devoted to consumerism," but also as a "place where racially and socially diverse people exert their 'right to the city' " (Houssey-Holzschuch and Teppo 2009: 352). In other words, the mall had become a place where people of different "races" actually came together in one public arena, albeit with visible and invisible boundaries that still separate people. The authors conclude that "the Waterfront mall undeniably offers a safe and accessible haven for expressing new social identities" (Houssey-Holzschuch and Teppo 2009: 371); the mall, in other words, provides one of the few spaces in the city where different "races" are allowed to express their identities to each other.

## How Consumption Produces (Real and Imagined) Landscapes

Although not everyone lives in sites that were designed for sale and where commodification is normalized as an everyday activity, we all do participate in consumption on a daily basis: we buy food, use electrical and gas power in our houses, ride our cars to work, and each of these daily acts of consumption, if traced backward to the site of production of that commodity, is linked to a complicated network of actions. These commodity chains, perhaps better referred to as commodity circuits, outline relationships between the sites of production, transfer, processing, and consumption. For example, most food items can be traced to an agricultural field or grazing area, other items to fishing villages on the coast; these raw food materials are then processed somewhere, shipped on trains, trucks, boats, or planes, and brought for sale at retail outlets from farmers' markets to large retail food chains. Geographers and others have documented the ways in which this linking of production with consumption highlights the complex political economies of consumption, and raises important questions with regard to such issues as ethical trade and sustainable production (Freidberg 2004, 2007; Schroeder 1995; Barnett et al. 2005; Popke 2009). What I want to focus on here are the ways in which examining *imagined* landscapes of production and consumption point to a different (though related) set of ethical and political questions.

For example, while the supermarket or the restaurant is the primary space for the purchase of food items, much of that food is produced in places quite far away. Creating imaginative geographies of those "exotic" landscapes can have profound effects on consumption practices and meanings. Sahar Monrreal (2008) has shown how the late nineteenth-century selling of Mexican food in the United States – particularly tamales – drew on and reinforced stereotypical images of the Mexican landscape and culture that positioned Mexico as part of the United States' informal empire. Similarly, Ian Cook (2004) demonstrates how imagined geographies of Jamaica and its historical imperial relationship to the United Kingdom shaped the ways that buyers, importers, and shoppers reacted to and participated in the consumption of papaya. Through an imagined scenario of a consumer in the market, Cook shows how seeing Jamaica listed as the place of origin of the papaya summoned images of an exploitative past of sugar cane production, in comparison to the relatively benign impacts of papaya: "A fifty-two acre farm in Jamaica. Where sugar cane used to be grown. The plantation's great house, sugar factory, and rum distillery in ruins at its centre. Traces of the agricultural, export-oriented society Jamaica was set up to be. But at least they weren't still farming sugar cane. That's a horrible business. Back breaking. Jamaica has needed to diversify exports for some time. Identifying niche markets. Overseas. For high value commodities. Like tropical fruits. Like papaya" (p. 647).

Like foodstuffs, clothing is another commodity readily associated in the consumers' mind with an imagined landscape of production. The anti-sweatshop campaigns of the past twenty years have raised awareness of the often abusive and always exploitative conditions of clothing production, an industry that relies on inexpensive human labor for its continued profitability. Most of these campaigns drew on images of women working in exploitative conditions in the maquilladoras of Mexico, and in factories in India, China, and Malaysia, while companies like American Apparel promote their products as "made in America" under fair working conditions, claiming that their advertisements feature not models but factory workers. Imagined landscapes of production can also be used in more subtle ways to promote other forms of consumption. For example, Gokariksel and Secor (2009, 2010) show how the Turkish veiling industry has been successful at transforming the explicit geopolitical meaning of veiling since 9/11 – its role in signifying Islamic piety and power – to a more nuanced set of meanings associated with fashion. It has done so by explicitly positioning its headscarves not as products of Islam *per se*, but as products of a cosmopolitan world (Gokariksel and Secor 2010). For example, the catalogue of the company SetrMS features women in headscarves, pants, and coats, posed in front of images of foreign cities and famous urban skylines. According to Gokariksel and Secor, these images "underline the idealized mobility of the SetrMS consumer, her ability to travel, to experience the goods of the world, and to fit in as a member of the cosmopolitan elite" (2010: 126). Yet at the same time, these companies are actively proclaiming their Islamic identity as part of what Gokariksel and Secor call Islamic capitalism, choosing names for their companies and writing mission statements that include explicit reference to Islamic law. Mustafa Karaduman, the chief executive officer of one of the largest of these companies, Tekbar, credits the success of his company to "the hard work and Islamic devotion and mission of its founders" and claims his company "has not received any loans from the state and has not benefited from any incentives because of its policy to avoid interest" (2009: 12). Thus women purchasing fashionable headscarves in Istanbul know that the scarf was produced under conditions and in spaces that satisfy Islamic law, creating an imagined pious landscape of production, while at the same time participating in a cosmopolitan and fashionable world.

## The Ways Landscapes are Literally Consumed

By linking the meanings of commodities with particular sites of production, the act of consuming food or clothing can be seen as productive of landscapes, imagined and real. But the act of consumption is also by definition a destructive act. The extractive industries of the world that fuel our economies and consumer habits (oil, natural gas, coal, and so on) are by their nature taking away parts of our landscapes, literally devouring whole sections of land and water. Modern methods of open-cast coal mining, for example, peel off layers of land to expose coal seams. In a more indirect but no less destructive manner, the consumption of energy and products that require energy for their use and/or production also destroy landscapes through their contributions to climate change. Recent estimates suggest that global warming will lead to sea-level rises of up to 2 ft by 2100, destroying most coastlines around the world, some of the most valued and valuable landscapes (IPCC 2007). This association of consumption with the destructive effects of global climate change and the politics surrounding it has turned the spaces of consumption into a political and ethical domain: are there ways to consume that are more "green" and sustainable? What do consuming practices signify to whom? As Bryant and Goodman argue, "The consuming body thus becomes the frontline as everyday acts – eating, bathing, shopping, or dressing, for example – are politicized" (2004: 344). Thus as global climate change has become the most significant public environmental issue, consuming acts are increasingly being "read" as political and ethical performances.

And as geographers and others note, these ethically driven performances of consumption, developed initially out of a concern with the destruction of landscapes often far removed spatially from the event itself, are often more related to the local, regional, and national frames in which they are performed. For example, Rachel Slocum (2004) has documented the ways in which the Cities for Climate Protection (CCP) campaign – a national movement in the United States with the goal of reducing energy consumption in urban areas – placed responsibility for climate change at the level of the individual consumer (instead of, for example, the local municipality) and worked therefore at promoting environmental education of consumers, assuming that this education would lead to "better" choices by individuals. Her examination of the ways this campaign unfolded in three cities – Minneapolis, Seattle, and Tucson – shows how everyday consumers making household decisions came to be judged as "good" urban citizens. But in the end, these campaigns made very little difference in overall energy consumption, since they targeted individuals instead of large-scale energy consumers, such as corporations and governments. What Slocum showed is that acting according to the politically correct norms of a particular place – individual consumers in, say, Minneapolis, making "wise" energy choices – may have little to do with the actual environmental effects of consumption.

Concerns over the environmental effects of consumption have also been taken up by corporations as ways of marketing products. If, for example, consumers are now interested in protecting coastlines and saving particular natural environments, then companies can use that desire to promote certain products that may in some ways be associated with those landscapes. Raymond Bryant and Michael Goodman (2004) document the ways in which corporations have drawn on what they call "edenic myth-making" in order to transform concerns over the destruction of the Amazonian region into particular icons that can be used to sell certain products as part of the "alternative" consumption movement. They argue that these corporations draw on common Western motifs associated with the natural environment: "This process occurs notably with reference to cultural resonant 'icons' such as 'wilderness' (an unsullied or original state of nature), 'jungle' (a threatening and chaotic place) or 'rainforest' (science, beauty and vulnerability)" ((2004): 350). One of the examples they draw on is a children's cereal called Amazon frosted flakes. The cereal box's decoration aligns images of the rainforest with "good" consumption (the words "envirokids" and "organic" are superimposed over lavish images of exotic animals and lush green landscapes) while the text (meant for the parents) leaves little to the imagination: "Right now, time is running out for our planet's rainforests, and the Amazon is being slashed and burned to make way for cattle farms . . . By putting Amazon flakes on your breakfast table, you've taken a big step towards preserving our planet's priceless genetic resources" (Bryant and Goodman 2004: 351). The message here is that somehow destructive environmental practices in the Amazon will be eliminated by buying and eating this cereal, although it is not clear what the direct link is between the cereal *per se* and better sustainable environmental practices. Nonetheless, turning the link between consumption and the destruction of landscape on its head – i.e., portraying products as somehow useful in sustaining and maintaining natural environments – has become a particularly lucrative form of marketing and selling commodities to consumers in the global North.

## Landscaping as Consumption

The destructive aspects of consumption are particularly apparent when considering the making of landscape itself as a form of consumption, in other words, examining the act of *landscaping*. The altering of natural environments to fit ideals of a domesticated nature is a long-standing cultural practice throughout the world. At the beginning of this chapter I focused on the ways in which the emerging bourgeoisie in early modern European cultures remade the countryside into vistas to be seen from particular vantage points, using this visual consumption of landscape as a sign of prestige and power. To construct these landscapes required large amounts of energy and the use of a range of technologies, including different forms of irrigation, water pumps, fertilizers, mowers, and reapers, all of which comprised a new form of consumption. And the art and science of landscaping was not limited to Europe. In ancient China, for example, the scholar-elite classes created secluded gardens within easy access of their homes in order to escape the turmoils of the city and have time and space to meditate alone (Tuan 1974). James Wescoat (1995; Wescoat, Brand, and Mir 1991) has examined the gardens of the Mughal empire as symbols of paradise and as technological feats, another form of landscaping that expressed power and status.

In the United States, the pastoral ideal of maintaining greenspace around one's house was derived from the English gentry of the eighteenth century, while the obsession with the main- tenance of a front and back yard composed of closely mowed grass can be traced to the introduction of games such as tennis, croquet, and golf from England just after the Civil War (Jenkins 1994, 1999). In the late nineteenth century the invention of the lawnmower and the marketing of grasses that could be readily grown in different climates contributed to the popularity of the lawn, though until the mid-twentieth century the luxury of owning a single- family house with enough space for a lawn was reserved for the upper classes. This changed in the mid-twentieth century when, as Dolores Hayden (2004) among others has shown, the majority of the homes built during the postwar housing boom in the United States were located in the suburban regions, and each home was meant to be surrounded by the green lawn, an ideal of domesticated nature that served many purposes. This large-scale adoption of the lawn as a norm of middle-class American life led to a mushrooming of consumer products required to maintain it.

As late as the 1930s lawncare texts told homeowners that weeds needed to be tolerated, and advised against using chemicals given that lawns were often the source of edibles, but much of this rhetoric changed during the World War II era (Robbins and Sharp 2003a; Robbins and Sharp 2003b). Beatriz Colomina has explored the ways in which the American lawn became both "a therapy for war and a form of war" (1999: 138). During the war the American government encouraged citizens to create victory gardens (growing vegetables for personal use) in order to free up agricultural products for the war effort. But even more so, the government promoted garden work as therapeutic in that it allowed for an escape from the everyday reminders of war that surrounded most citizens. But this therapy was not without its own violence. Colomina shows how advertisements for garden products as well as articles in journals such as *Better Homes and Gardens* used the rhetoric of battle to describe the importance of eradicating pests. Bugs, she argues, were "represented as enemy soldiers and flying insects as Japanese airfighters" (1999: 138). This discursive alignment of bugs with wartime enemies reached its apotheosis in the rhetoric concerning the Japanese beetle. Colomina quotes an article that appeared in *Life* magazine in 1944: "Japanese beetles, unlike the Japanese, are without guile. There are, however, many parallels between the two. Both are very small but very numerous and prolific, as well as voracious, greedy, and devouring. Both have single-track minds. Both are inscrutable " (1999: 138). With such rhetoric, it is not surprising that the way to fight lawn pests was portrayed as similar to military campaigns and tactics; in the case of the lawn, that meant chemical warfare, insecticides that had been used during the war to protect soldiers in the field. In this way, using chemicals to maintain a green lawn was a patriotic act, one that kept insects/enemies out of the United States.

After the war, with the proliferation of insecticides and the alignment of the perfect lawn with the "good" American citizen, consumption of lawncare products accelerated. This acceleration was exacerbated by three other forces. First, as I mentioned earlier, much of the postwar housing boom occurred in the suburbs, and therefore the sheer percentage of land cover dedicated to lawns increased rapidly. Second, the postwar economy relied on increased domestic consumption to replace wartime defense spending. Some of the companies that had produced tanks were now producing automobiles (making suburban expansion possible) and lawnmowers, while many defense contractors used their experiences with chemicals during the war to create new insecticides for the garden (Colomina 2007). And third, the imagery of the single-family middle-class house surrounded by its own yard came to be seen as an ideological weapon in the Cold War, both an antidote to and bulwark against communism and Soviet aggression. The single-family suburban house filled with domestic appliances and surrounded by a manicured lawn represented the ideals of capitalism and democracy: individualism, consumer choice, and prosperity, in distinction of course to the communist world, which was depicted as collective, constrained, and without consumer goods. As such, the daily activities of lawncare and the promotion of the consuming, middle-class lifestyle were figured as weapons to help fight the Cold War.

In recent decades, this now standardized ideal of middle-class American life – single-family housing with lawn – has come to characterize more and more of the American landscape. Robbins and Sharp estimate that 23 percent of all metropolitan land is under private turfgrass (2003a: 958), while the National Gardening Association tells us that the average household in the United States spent $351 on lawn and garden activities in the year 2011, totaling $29.1 billion (http://assoc.garden.org/). Although not quite on the same scale as the English estates of the eighteenth and nineteenth centuries, these relatively small gardens serve similar purposes: they act as expressions of class and gender, as spaces for recreation and meditation, and as ways to connect to the natural world. Like all forms of consumption, lawns and gardens – landscapes – express and shape individual, group, and national identities. As I have highlighted throughout this chapter, the idea of landscape as a way of seeing is a form of visual consumption, while the various practices of consumption often create (and at times destroy) real and imagined landscapes. Understanding American lawns and Chinese gardens, as much as understanding fashion and foodways, means exploring our collective and individual "dream worlds" of consumption (Williams 1982).

# References

Barnett, C., Cloke, P., Clarke, N., and Malpass, A. (2005) Consuming ethics: Articulating the subjects and spaces of ethical consumption. *Antipode*, 37, 23–45.

Bennett, T., Grossberg, L., and Morris, M. (eds.) (2005) *New Keywords: A Revised Vocabulary of Culture and Society*. Oxford: Blackwell.

Berger, J. (1972) *Ways of Seeing*. Harmondsworth: Penguin.

Bourdieu, P. (1984) *Distinction: A Social Critique of the Judgement of Taste*. Cambridge, MA: Harvard University Press.

Bryant, R. and Goodman, M. (2004) Consuming narratives: The political ecology of "alternative" consumption. *Transactions of the Institute of British Geographers*, 29, 344–366.

Colomina, B. (1999) The lawn at war: 1941–1961. In *The American Lawn*, ed. G. Teyssot. New York: Princeton Architectural Press, pp. 134–153.

Colomina, B. (2007) *Domesticity at War*. Cambridge, MA: MIT Press.

Cook, I. *et al.* (2004) Follow the thing: Papaya. *Antipode*, 36, 642–664.

Cosgrove, D. (1984) *Social Formation and Symbolic Landscape*. London: Croom Helm.

Cosgrove, D. (1985) Prospect, perspective and the evolution of the landscape idea. *Transactions of the Institute of British Geographers*, 10, 45–62.

Cronin, A. and Hetherington, K. (eds.) (2008) *Consuming the Entrepreneurial City: Image, Memory, Spectacle*. New York: Routledge.

Daniels, S. (1988) The political iconography of woodland in later Georgian England. In *The Iconography of Landscape*, ed. D. Cosgrove and S. Daniels. Cambridge: Cambridge University Press, pp. 43–82.

Duncan, J. and Duncan, N. (2004) *Landscapes of Privilege: The Politics of the Aesthetic in an American Suburb*. New York: Routledge.

Edensor, T. (2007) Mundane mobilities, performances and spaces of tourism. *Social and Cultural Geography*, 8, 199–215.

Freidberg, S. (2004) *French Beans and Food Scares: Culture and Commerce in an Anxious Age*. New York: Oxford University Press.

Freidberg, S. (2007) Supermarkets and imperial knowledge. *Cultural Geographies*, 14 (3), 321–342.

Gokariksel, B. and Secor, A. (2009) New transnational geographies of Islamism, capitalism and subjectivity: The veiling-fashion industry. *Area*, 41, 6–18.

Gokariksel, B. and Secor, A. (2010) Between fashion and tesettür: Marketing and consuming women's Islamic dress. *Journal of Middle East Women's Studies*, 6 (3), 118–148.

Hall, T. and Hubbard, P. (1998) *The Entrepreneurial City: Geographies of Politics, Regime and Representation*. Chichester: John Wiley & Sons.

Hayden, D. (2004) *A Field Guide to Sprawl*. New York: W.W. Norton.

Houssey-Holzschuch, M. and Teppo, A. (2009) A mall for all? Race and public space in post-apartheid Cape Town. *Cultural Geographies*, 16, 351–379.

International Panel on Climate Change (IPCC), Fourth Assessment Report (2007) http://www.ipcc.ch/publications_and_data/publications_ipcc_fourth_assessment_report_synthesis_report.htm (accessed October 23, 2012).

Jackson, J.B. (1984) *Discovering the Vernacular Landscape*. New Haven: Yale University Press.

Jenkins, V.S. (1994) *The Lawn: A History of an American Obsession*. Washington, DC: Smithsonian Institution Press.

Jenkins, V.S. (1999) "Fairway living": Lawncare and lifestyle from croquet to the golf course. In *The American Lawn*, ed. G. Teyssot. New York: Princeton Architectural Press, pp. 116–132.

King, A. (2004) *Spaces of Global Culture: Architecture, Urbanism, Identity*. New York: Routledge.

Miles, S. (2010) *Spaces for Consumption: Pleasure and Placelessness in the Post-Industrial City*. London: Sage.

Monrreal, S. (2008) "A novel, spicy delicacy": Tamales, advertising, and late 19th-century imaginative geographies of Mexico. *Cultural Geographies*, 15, 449–470.

National Gardening Association, (2012) http://assoc.garden.org (accessed December 4, 2012).

Popke, J. (2009) Geography and ethics: Non-representational encounters, collective responsibilities and economic difference. *Progress in Human Geography*, 33, 81–90.

Pow, C.-P. and Kong, L. (2007) Marketing the Chinese dream home: Gated communities and representations of the good life in (post-)socialist Shanghai. *Urban Geography*, 28 (2), 129–159.

Robbins, P. and Sharp, J. (2003a) The lawn-chemical economy and its discontents. *Antipode*, 35 (5), 955–979.

Robbins, P. and Sharp, J. (2003b) Producing and consuming chemicals: The moral economy of the American lawn. *Economic Geography*, 70, 425–451.

Schroeder, R. (1995) Contradictions along the commodity road to environmental stabilization: Foresting Gambian gardens. *Antipode*, 27 (4), 325–342.

Slocum, R. (2004) Consumer citizens and the cities for climate protection campaign. *Environment and Planning A*, 36, 763–782.

Tuan, Y.F. (1974) *Topophilia: A Study of Environmental Perception, Attitudes, and Values*. Englewood Cliffs, NJ: Prentice Hall.

Urry, J. (1995) *Consuming Places*. New York: Routledge.

Wescoat, J. (1995) From the gardens of the Qur'an to the "gardens" of Lahore. *Landscape Research*, 20, 19–29.

Wescoat, J., Brand, M., and Mir, N. (1991) Gardens, roads and legendary tunnels: The underground memory of Mughal Lahore. *Journal of Historical Geography*, 17, 1–17.

Williams, R. (1982) *Dream Worlds: Mass Consumption in Late Nineteenth-Century France*. Berkeley: University of California Press.

Wu, F. (2004) Transplanting cityscapes: The use of imagined globalization in housing commodification in Beijing. *Area*, 36 (3), 227–234.

Zukin, S. (2011) *Naked City: The Death and Life of Authentic Urban Places*. New York: Oxford University Press.

Chapter 20

# Landscape and Justice

## Tom Mels and Don Mitchell

## Introduction

### Gotland

Halfway into the nineteenth century, capitalism entered the seemingly peripheral countryside of Gotland, Sweden, rousing an acute awareness of how struggles over justice intertwined with struggles over geography and uneven development. British entrepreneurs had acquired and cleared extensive portions of woodland on the island and invested in sawmills for the export of timber, while the state sought to raise agricultural productivity and marketability through the legally endorsed redistribution of arable land. In a concomitant maneuver to transform customary outfields into capitalist space, vast, erstwhile common-access mires were privatized and reclaimed by Gotland's Mire Company, bringing together urban and mainland capitalists with key positions in Swedish politics, manufacturing, finance, the media, and international trade. Their capital was not only channeled into the physical geography of mire soils, but also circulated as variable capital through the bodies of a new working class of canal diggers. The emergence of a powerful capitalist class alliance, increasingly controlling rural assets and developing a system of wage labor, carried with it a whole new set of values that were widely disseminated through scientific reports, agricultural exhibitions, journals, newspaper articles, and a wealth of drainage maps. The forces of capitalist modernity thus seemed well on their way, having mobilized a range of material and discursive tactics aimed at "the systematic destruction and annihilation of all the non-capitalist social units which obstruct its development" (Luxemburg 2003: 350).

The advent of land reclamation materialized a move from a "world in which 'community' is defined in terms of structures of interpersonal social relations to a world where the community of money prevails" (Harvey 2010: 294). Yet the prospect of capitalizing Gotland's

*The Wiley Blackwell Companion to Cultural Geography*, First Edition.
Edited by Nuala C. Johnson, Richard H. Schein, and Jamie Winders.
© 2013 John Wiley & Sons, Ltd. Published 2016 by John Wiley & Sons, Ltd.

mires was a distressing experience for local people that could not pass unchallenged. After all, mirelands were places of ingrained use-value, shaped through customary fishing and hunting rights, haymaking, and a whole array of mutual obligations among farmers. Alienation from family land through deceit and violence, and widespread apprehension about what would happen to family property, were themes which the peasantry could readily link to entrenched moral geographies and histories encoded in local stories. Some of these held the cathartic promise of eventual justice through the recovery of access to the means of production (Palmenfelt 1994: 126). Disciplinary problems related to the locally recruited labor force were also rife. The supervisor's attitudes "gave rise to a strong and widespread resistance among those who were perfectly content with the supply of fodder, fish and game in their mires and frowned upon the uninvited 'gentlemen' who infringed upon their old boundaries" (Säve 1938: 191–192). Added to environmental degradation and the enormous costs involved in the land reclamation project, this engagement in cultural resistance against a new disciplinary regime of social regulation resulted in "lengthy court proceedings and trouble, which all for many years had a paralyzing effect on the endeavour's progress" (Fagraeus 1888: 58).

## Youngstown

On the other side of the world, and as the twenty-first century gains steam, Youngstown, Ohio's landscape has become iconic for the third time. By the end of the nineteenth century and through the first three-quarters of the twentieth, Youngstown was a quintessential steel town. Massive mills stretched 24 miles up and down the Mahoning Valley, coal smoke filled the air, tight-knit ethnic neighborhoods climbed the hills away from the river, even as land was set aside to create large landscaped parks around some of the deeper ravines (Linkon and Russo 2002). A whole, seemingly permanent, landscape was built. Home to Youngstown Sheet and Tube, Youngstown was one of the high-tech cities of its time. While class struggles always simmered just below the surface, and sometimes broke out into the open, and while divisions of race and ethnicity were keenly deepened and exploited by the mill owners and managers, smoke meant prosperity (Bruno 1999). Youngstown was an icon of mid-twentieth-century industrial might.

By the early 1980s, Youngstown had been totally deindustrialized. Youngstown Sheet and Tube (now part of New Orleans-based LTV) shuttered most of its mills in a single week in 1977. Other steel companies and associated businesses followed suit (Buss and Redburn 1983). The effect on the working people of Youngstown was, of course, devastating (even as many fought to preserve their livelihood; Camp 1995; Lynd 1982). Distress was everywhere apparent in the landscape; houses were abandoned (and arson soared), stores, bars, and schools rapidly closed. Even the old mills themselves were removed. By the beginning of the 1990s there was shockingly little evidence of steelmaking in the landscape (High and Lewis 2007). Perhaps no place better exemplified the ravages induced by footloose capital at the end of Fordism than Youngstown: the very absence of coal smoke now meant not a cleaner environment but the devastation of working-class livelihoods.

Now Youngstown is at the forefront of a global "shrinking cities" movement. Realizing that Youngstown will never be what it was during its industrial heyday, city officials are seeking to shrink its footprint, rationally planning a smaller city wherein some neighborhoods are abandoned altogether (and perhaps reverted to farmland), and others are more tightly focused around key institutions (a school, a church, a small shopping center). Efforts to attract new capital are focused almost solely on the small downtown and the area near the university. With these efforts Youngstown has become a model, its redevelopment strategies a focus of intense study and increasing emulation (Hassett 2008). If before it was icono-graphic, first of capitalist mass production and then of capital's unrelentingly violent restless-ness, the Youngstown landscape is now iconographic of what many take to be a revolutionary move in America: planning not for capital's local growth but for its ongoing retrenchment. Yet the city's success in attracting reinvestment downtown has come at the cost of a decreas-ing standard of living for most Youngstowners and a symptomatic ignorance of "the city's real problems: high unemployment, poverty, continued high crime rates, and the deterioration of Youngstown's neighborhoods." There are now more renters than homeowners in what used to be called the "City of Homes," and absentee landlordism is a growing problem. In that way, "shrinking cities" is little more than smoke and mirrors, and the remnants of the working class might have little to gain from this new reinvention of Youngstown's landscape (Center for Working-Class Studies at Youngstown University n.d.)

Our introductory examples confirm in different ways that justice and injustice are embed-ded in, maintained, and contested through the landscape. Land reclamation on Gotland was a story of primitive accumulation – epigrammatically put by Marx as "the historical process of divorcing the producer from the means of production" (Marx 1954: 668). Although Marx denounced the rhetoric of ethics and values as long as they were treated in isolation from materialist analysis, he "plainly condemn[ed] capitalism – for its oppressions and unfreedoms and also, . . . for its injustices" (Geras 1985: 85). Thus, his impassioned descriptions of primitive accumulation in terms of robbery and theft draw attention to the unjust ground-work of capitalism. As a case of primitive accumulation, the transformation of mire land-scapes implicated justice in a broad spatial sense, ranging from the discursive and material obliteration of customary practice, to efforts to discursively reappropriate the right to land, and on to experiences of environmental damage. In the more urban setting of Youngstown, a long history of investment, disinvestment, and reinvestment – of capital circulating through the built environment – has led to different levels of working-class power (and within the working classes, differential access to what power there is), and thus to vastly uneven out-comes. Many of those thrown out of work during Youngstown's deindustrialization found themselves stuck. The capital sunk in *their* landscape – their homes and churches and places of recreation – was essentially permanent; unlike the capital in the hands of LTV, it could not get up and go. It could only be devalued in place, destroyed as a precondition for new capital investment (Harvey 1982). Since the effects of any new investment, targeted to a shrunken footprint, are highly uneven, the landscape that results is not necessarily any more – or less – just than that which preceded it; but it does rearrange relations of power on the ground and transform the conditions of social struggle.

## Why Justice?

The landscapes of Gotland and Youngstown suggest an indissoluble link between landscape and justice, but the link is a complex one. "Justice" is an ideal; "landscape" is more than an ideal. The latter is the very material effect – the "spoor" Peirce Lewis (1975) called it – of social practice, as well as the basis for such practice. In its built form it is the world "as it really is" (Harvey 2001/1984), even as, through representation, the meanings such a world might take on can be highly varied and deeply powerful (Mitchell 1994; Duncan and Duncan 1988). The former, justice, is seemingly as immaterial as it is aspirational. As Engels once wrote:

Justice which is the organic, regulating, sovereign basic principle of societies, which has nevertheless been nothing up to the present, but which ought to be everything – what is that if not the
stick with which to measure all human affairs, if not the final arbiter to be appealed to in all
conflicts. (Quoted in Merrifield and Swyngedouw 1995: 1)

The three iconic forms of the Youngstown landscape can indeed be measured against this
stick: at each moment in its evolution, for example, the landscape calls up and makes solid
in its morphology, questions of equity: the just distribution of the spoils of capitalist development and the burdens – often bodily – of capitalist destruction. Neither the emplacement nor
the displacement of capitalist production can occur *except* in an already-existing landscape
which it then remakes, unevenly (Smith 1990). Similarly the mirelands: use-values were
embedded in the landscape and their (struggled-over) alienation, expropriation, or destruction
both required and advanced a reorientation of those use-values, who would benefit from
them, and who would lose: it required remaking the landscape and thus the very nature of
the space within which "justice" (of whatever sort) could or could not be achieved. In remaking the landscape, the capitalization of the mirelands transformed them from a customary
commons into a new kind of property. A new notion of "the good" was instantiated in and
through the landscape, which those behind the capitalization understood to be refracted
through notions of progress, modernization, economic development, and profit-making – a
very different sense of what constituted "good" and "right" than had operated before.

## Liberal Sticks

So what, then, is this "stick"? John Stuart Mill asserted in 1863 that:

Justice is the name for certain classes of moral rules, which concern the essentials of human well-
being more nearly, and are therefore of more absolute obligation, than other rules for the guidance
of life. (Quoted in Smith 1994: 23)

This merely specifies the question: what are these "classes of moral rules," and how are they
decided upon? David Smith (1994: 24) argues that "justice involves treating people right or
fairly, in a calculated way," and identifies two different forms. *Retributive justice* concerns
the fair imposition of penalties on those who commit crimes or otherwise sin against prevalent
norms, while *distributive justice* entails the fair allocation of divisible goods. Distributive
justice is usually further subdivided into the overlapping categories of *economic justice* (the
fair distribution of costs and benefits, including income), *social justice* (the fair distribution
of life chances, which includes economic considerations but also exceeds them), and *political
justice* (the fair distribution of power, rights, and liberties).

"Justice" can also be categorized as *procedural justice* (fair rules) and *substantive justice*
(fair outcomes). These two can be, and frequently are, contradictory: procedurally just practices can lead to substantively unjust outcomes and substantively just outcomes can be created
through procedurally unjust practices (Fainstein 2010).

Mainstream debate over principles, practices, and philosophies of justice is typically confined to questions of distribution and procedure (Smith 1994). Rawls' (1971) famous thought
experiment – wherein people find themselves at the dawn of society (in "the original position") and must divide up available goods without knowing precisely who will get to choose
their resulting share first and who last, and who thus parse out benefits as close to equally

as possible – is perhaps the classic statement of *distributional* justice. Arguing against Rawls, Nozick (1974) notes that goods to be shared out come from somewhere; they are produced. For Nozick, a just distribution is one in which people have rights in that which they produce. Nozick thus "considers 'just' a distribution in which individuals keep whatever goods they can accumulate through just production and just transfers" (Mansbridge 1995: 363).

Rawls' and Nozick's ideas are rooted in variants of liberalism, and as such incorporate particular notions of *procedural* justice. Rawls begins from an assumption that all members of society are free and equal, and as they seek to divide up goods, enter, as equal individuals, into contractual relations with one another. His ideas are thus rooted in the tradition of Locke, Rousseau, and Kant, if not so much in the utilitarian liberalism of Bentham or Mill (which is based in a single, universal principal: the stick against which all is measured is maximal utility). As free individuals, people may freely and rationally contract with each other; a procedurally just society is one in which such freedom is manifest. While Rawls exhibited faith that such free individuals would arrive at substantively just outcomes, it was not vital to his theory that they do so (Wenar 2008). The role for the state in this conception of justice is to establish the conditions by which people contract with each other, and to enforce the terms of resulting contracts.

For his part Nozick (1974) advanced a strong neo-Lockean libertarian position. He argues that any self-owning individual may use her own, or appropriate unused, resources, just so long as no other individual is made worse off by such use or appropriation (in other words, as long as minimal compensation for externality effects is made) (Vallentyne 2010). A procedurally just society, in this view, is one in which one is at liberty to use, or not, what is rightfully one's own in any way one pleases. If some become disadvantaged in the process, so be it; it was their action, or lack thereof, that induced this disadvantage. The only role for a state in such a system of justice is to guarantee the conditions of liberty. There is, in this view, little room for the sort of customary forms of justice (and distribution) that marked the preindustrial mirelands.

## Radical Sticks

There are innumerable variants on these liberal positions on distributive justice. More radical theorists, however, find them wanting because they ignore the unequal social relations of class, "race," and gender behind distribution. This leads to an uncritical acceptance of prevailing institutional contexts and exploitative relations of production. Against such liberal approaches, and without reducing the complexity and contradictions at the heart of different forms and meaning of justice, Iris Marion Young (1990: 15) positions "social justice" (understood as something more than only the just distribution of life chances, though this is a necessary condition) as the most encompassing form of justice, at least conceptually. She understands social justice to mean "the elimination of institutionalized domination and oppression. Any aspect of social organization and practice relevant to domination and oppression is in principle subject to evaluation by ideals of justice." Young (1990: 44) is not as concerned with individuals as she is with social groups, which are "defined not primarily by a set of shared attributes, but by a sense of identity." Social groups, she argues, "are not entities that exist apart from individuals, but neither are they arbitrary classifications of individuals according to attributes which are external to or accidental to their identities." That is to say, neither libertarianism nor contractualism is sufficient for understanding substantive possibilities for, and procedures of, justice, especially since "groups  .  .  .  constitute individuals" (Young 1990: 45). Individuals are not atomistic and ontologically prior to the groups of which they are a part. Custom – and solidarity – matters. Any theory of justice rooted in individualism (as is both Rawls' and Nozick's) is insufficient, as is any theory of justice that does not take into consideration already-existing inequalities and relations of power.

Social justice must be theorized in relation to the group (and the individuals in it), and for Young (1990) it must be theorized in relation to oppression – and, it ought to be added, in relation to the already-existing landscape and what it makes possible or impossible. Rawls' "original position" makes no sense because the world is always already here, and always already uneven, unjust. The libertarianism of Nozick is unacceptable to Young and other feminist philosophers, like Susan Okin (1989), because "all possession is socially constructed. Women [as a group] produce children through hard labor, but do not conclude they have property rights in their product" (Mansbridge 1995: 364). Women, of course, also labor in lots of other ways, frequently to find the products of their (re)productive labor expropriated by others; gendered divisions of labor (as just one example) mean already unequal access to power, and hence some in society, as groups, find themselves in *structurally* oppressive circumstances. As Young (1990: 50) puts it: "The freedom, power, status, and self-realization of men is possible precisely because women work for them." Similar arguments could be made about the structural privileges whites gain through the exploitation of black labor, and about much else besides.

### The Other Side of the Stick: Oppression

However, oppression in Young's (1990: 48–63) formulation has "five faces": not just exploitation, as we just described, but also marginalization, powerlessness, cultural imperialism, and violence. For Young (1990: 53), marginalization is different from exploitation in that the former begins not from appropriating the fruit of the labor of others but from excluding others from the very ability to productively labor at all. What Marx (1954) called "primitive accumulation," and what Harvey (2003) calls "accumulation by dispossession," relies on such marginalization. To the degree that mire-people were uprooted from their land, their labor made redundant, then to that degree they were marginalized from the rising system of production, at least until such time as their very presence as a laboring class (rather than as a class rooted in customary access to the resources of the landscape) had been assured.

Exploitation and marginalization are made possible by the development of powerlessness. But powerlessness exceeds the other two, especially in modern society, since "the labor of most people [not just the traditional working class] augments the power of relatively few" (Young 1990: 56). As importantly, powerlessness is manifest in other ways. For example, some factions of capital in Youngstown – those local capitals that had the bulk of their wealth "trapped" or "fixed" in the landscape of small shops or stores, for example – simply could not pick up and move as could the capital encapsulated in the plants and productive processes of LTV. "[T]he powerless," according to Young (1990: 56), "are situated so that they must take orders and rarely have the right to give them"; they are subject to rather than masters of the forces that shape social, political, and economic life.

Cultural imperialism is oppression of a different form. It "involves the universalization of a dominant group's experience and culture, and its establishment as the norm" (Young 1990: 59). In Fraser's (1987) view, such oppression means that some social groups are subject to, rather than controllers of, "the means of interpretation and communication in a society" such that groups differing from the norm find their experiences and ways of knowing "reconstructed largely as deviance and inferiority." Finally, oppression may manifest itself as violence. Young (1990: 61) points in this regard to "random unprovoked attacks on [people's] person or property," but the invocation of "random," as her discussion in fact makes clear, is misleading: oppressive forms of violence are *systemic*. They might be "low-level" "incidents of harassment, intimidation, or ridicule [conducted] simply for the purpose of degrading, humiliating, or stigmatizing group members," or they might be concerted campaigns against a targeted group, such as lynchings, gay-bashing, or mass rape, but in either case (which are differentiated by degree rather than kind), the violent acts are systemic and are facilitated by "the social context surrounding them, which makes them possible and even acceptable." To this sort of violence must be added another sort of systemic violence, a form that is especially important in relation to the landscape (Loyd 2009; Mitchell 2010): what anthropologists call "structural violence." Structural violence is "suffering [that] is 'structured' by historically given (and often economically driven) processes and forces that conspire – whether through routine, ritual, or, as is more commonly the case, the hard surfaces of life – to constrain agency" (Farmer 2003, 40; Galtung 1969), leading to premature and excess death, high rates of disablement or chronic illness, and the like.

## The Hard Surfaces of Life

Landscapes are "the hard surfaces of life" – the very place of (in)justice. Invoking Marx, Harvey (1996) argues for a theory of justice that understands that prevailing and conventional standards of social formations – including especially their geography – condition what is just and right. "Right can never be higher than the economic structure of society and its cultural development conditioned thereby" (Marx and Engels 1970: 19). In this view, as a *historical proposition*, the surplus value-producing, waged-labor relationship that is the very heart of capitalism – wherein a worker gives up for a set time the right to the use of her labor power *and that which it produces* in exchange for an agreed-upon wage – is perfectly just, even if, with Young, we might still call this "exploitation":

> The justice of transactions between agents of production consists in the fact that these transactions arise from the relations of production as their natural consequence. The legal forms in which these economic transactions appear as voluntary actions of the participants, as the expressions of their common will and as contracts that can be enforced on the parties concerned by the power of the state, are mere forms that cannot themselves determine this content. They simply express it. The content is just so long as it corresponds to the mode of production and is adequate to it. It is unjust as soon as it contradicts it. Slavery, on the basis of the capitalist mode of production, is unjust; so is cheating on the quality of commodities. (Marx 1981: 460–461)

Harvey's view is supported by passages such as this, revealing a tendency to relativize values, ethics, norms, and justice as having no independent transhistorical (or transgeographical) reach. However, Marx nevertheless condemns capitalism as unjust. While the former tendency typifies Marx's narrow conception of justice (measured only by prevailing standards), the latter suggests a far broader one, permeating his unqualified, normative critique of capitalist property rights, the appropriation of surplus value, and exploitation generally as "loot," "booty," "theft," "embezzlement," "usurpation," and "robbery." This broader view can also be found in Harvey's own formulations. Any sense of the historicity of justice is, claims

Harvey, tempered with arguments about what justice *could be* under other historical-geographic conditions. To achieve a *different kind* of justice, then, one would not attend (for example) merely to the question of "exploitation" – to what it is and why it is bad as measured against some eternal "stick" (an idealist effort) – but instead to the conditions under which *particular forms* of exploitation are advanced, and how they can be transformed so that some other way of living and producing can be achieved (a normative, historical-materialist effort) (Harvey 2009/1973: 137).

## The Politics of Landscape

The question of "where [and when and how] multiple forms of oppression coalesce" (Harvey 1996: 349) is thus a vital one. The material shapes and structures of landscape are not simply already given exterior surfaces. They are contested spatialities of ossified human labor, entwining, passing through, and refracting shifting practices and politics of meaning. The politics of landscape is profoundly performative in two senses. First, various forms of discourse are not only attempts to represent, convince, and be trusted, but are also ideologies in built form that help secure or contest particular social relations (Herod and Wright 2002), codes of conduct (Matless 1998), or both (Duncan and Duncan 2001). Second, capital also represents "itself in the form of a physical landscape created in its own image" (Harvey 1985: 43). More specifically, it "produces a geographical landscape . . . appropriate to its own dynamic of accumulation at a particular moment of its history, only to have to destroy and rebuild that geographical landscape to accommodate accumulation at a later date" (Harvey 1996: 412). The critique of uneven development thus necessarily feeds into a deeply political question about geography and justice: "how does the geographical configuration of the landscape contribute to the survival of capitalism?" (Smith 1990: 4). Such a critique is ultimately inspired by the aim to "illuminate the ways in which the resultant landscapes scream out for the resolution of social inequality" (Smith 1990: 243).

Such screaming inequalities are, however, frequently muted. Although material forms and signified landscapes by no means come out of the blue, landscapes easily become subjected to "an amnesia of genesis" (Schein 1997: 663). Rather than yielding themselves up, the historical geographies of (in)justice through which landscapes come to embody power struggle, toil, and labor power may to an extent, and for various reasons, be hidden behind a physical appearance of naturalness or seemingly neutral depiction or description: ideology in built form. Like space generally, the immediate perspicuity of landscape "is illusory and the secret of the illusion lies in the transparency itself" (Lefebvre 1991: 287). This is why critical geographers seek to unpack reified notions of normality, inevitable naturalness, or rationality through which landscapes appear as devoid of human labor, power relations, and political process, in order to trace the specific uneven conditions under which landscapes are materially and discursively produced (Mels 2002; Mitchell 1996). By extension – because this necessarily foregrounds the discursive and material workings of oppression and dominance – such a project means that landscape is unavoidably caught up in notions of justice and injustice.

## Landscape as Polity and Place of Justice

The struggle over primitive accumulation on Gotland offers a useful entry point to illustrate a recurring theme of work on landscape and justice, especially as developed by Kenneth

Olwig. Olwig's core contribution in this field revolves around struggles between landscape as the expression of a place-oriented logic on the one hand, and the rationalities of geometric, cartographic space on the other (Olwig 2002a). Each of these political landscapes emanates from divergent notions of political justice: the former on "that of custom centered on the particularity of place," and the latter on that of regular, universal law or "nature de-centered in universal space" (Olwig 2005: 299–300). Olwig explains that landscape can historically be traced back to "the sort of enclosed room-like area that is demarcated, for example, by the territories of historically constituted places, such as the German *Landschaft* polities" (Olwig 2002b: 3). Gotland was a Nordic *landskap* polity in this sense too, with principles of justice codified in its own medieval customary laws, but under constant threat of the centralized imperial ambitions of the Swedish and Danish state. Much later, in the wake of primitive accumulation, the abstract space of land reclamation maps, scientific knowledge production, and elite power ran into such place-oriented notions of justice and conventional practice, the particularistic vestiges of which were still felt in the nineteenth century.

With the help of empirical evidence from Europe and North America rather than Gotland, Olwig launched his findings at a kind of triple remove from earlier cultural geographies of landscape. First, he turned to notions of place and justice at a time when landscape was above all discussed in terms of abstract space and distanced way of seeing (Olwig 1996; cf. Casey 1997). Second, he relocated the politics *of* representation – broadly understood as discursive partiality of vision, text, and image – into a context of *political* representation, pertaining to the division of power and geographies of natural and customary law. Third, he coupled a strong sense of practice and performance to notions of representation, law, and justice (Olwig 2007, 2008, 2009).

Yet at the same time, with place as its ultimate point of return, this triple remove also entails a politicized preference for the justice of place and community, typical of the wider humanistic tradition in geography: "place is primary in terms of human historical and personal experience . . . It is the moral behaviour that arises through the sharing of common resources which has the greatest effect in building communities because it is rooted in the habitus of practice" (Olwig 2005: 318; Setten 2004). Hence the recurring emphasis on the contrast between place, custom, and convention on the one hand, and the rationality of cartographic space on the other hand: "The meaning of landscape, in practice, is thus very much a regional affair, with roots going deep into the identities of . . . historical regions . . . This is the landscape of place to which people become attached to history. Scenic space, by contrast, is the infinite space of the map and the drawn plan" (Olwig 2009: 203). As we have argued, for people on Gotland and in Youngstown, landscape was definitely more than a regional affair. They became "attached to history" not just through some secluded, rooted, and meaningful landscape of place, but rather through a restless network of extended social relations and spatial processes, producing those places as part of the uneven landscapes of capitalist space (smoke-filled or not).

An understanding of customary landscape from the perspective of ideology critique is less prepared to suspend the space–place dialectic. It draws out the politics of "customary" landscapes as implicated in, and developed through spatial experiences of, for instance, imperialism, anti-colonialism, and capitalism (Mels 2006). Amidst these uneven landscapes we thus find not only community politics but also social antagonisms of class, race, and gender – a concern which tends to disappear through the (strategic) "amnesia of genesis" in mainstream policymaking, as we argue next.

## European Conventions

Recent developments in European landscape governance reveal a certain decentralized penchant for landscape as a common resource, a place of community and customary rights, albeit in awkward tension with an outspoken top-down tactic to ensconce landscape in neoliberal space and an exclusionary version of justice. The former tendency speaks to a progressive politics of difference (Young 1990), while the latter turns that politics into a conservative defense of the status quo (Harvey 1996).

Thus, the European Landscape Convention of the Council of Europe promulgates the recognition in law of landscape as "an area, as perceived by people, whose character is the result of action and interaction of natural and/or human factors." The Convention obliges its "Contracting Parties" (states) "to recognize landscapes in law as an essential component of people's surroundings" and identities; "establish and implement policies aimed at landscape protection, management and planning"; create procedures for public participation in management and preservation; and "integrate landscape into . . . regional and town planning policies" as well as into policies covering other practices (agriculture, industrial development, and so on) that might affect the landscape (Déjeant-Pons 2006: 370).

The mandate for public participation is both particularly important in relation to normative visions of a just landscape, and particularly tricky. Beyond its recognition of local culture and lay knowledge, the Convention simultaneously supports an approach to procedural justice that prioritizes instrumental rationality through expert rule over the landscape. In the terms of the Convention, public participation in landscape policy and management "should not be seen as a substitute for official decision-making but as a complement to it. The objective is to draw into the decision-making process the views of all concerned groups of stakeholders, whether defined as local communities, residents, visitors, landholders, deprived groups, or specialists, alongside representative, democratically elected bodies" (Jones 2009: 234; cf. Olwig 2009). As attractive as that sounds, Jones (2009: 237–238) notes that "the Convention's own Explanatory Report recommends 'performing the evaluation [of the landscape] according to objective criteria first' (as if any criteria can be objective), and then comparing the findings with the various assessments of the landscape by people concerned and other interest groups." The problem with this is that, as others have shown (e.g., Aitken 2002), "expert discourses" usually dominate and effectively exclude – marginalize – those less than fluent in it (cf. Fainstein 2010). They can be a form of cultural imperialism which through its avowedly expert-led scientism serves to mask fundamental, substantive concerns since "conflicts concerning landscape values are often symptomatic of deeper-lying social conflicts" (Jones 2009: 248; see also Jones 1999).

With an accent on technocratic omnipresence of governance, authority, homogeneity, and integration, combined with a celebration of place-identity and difference, this contradictory message thus repeats key features of "justice" embedded in neoliberalizing space. In that sense the European Landscape Convention can be maneuvered to shore up the ongoing broadening of the neoliberal policy gamut and its discursive repertoire, including "the selective appropriation of 'community' and nonmarket metrics, the establishment of social-capital discourses and techniques, the incorporation (and underwriting) of local-governance and partnership-based modes of policy development and program delivery" (Peck and Tickell 2002: 390). Indeed, the selective appropriation of community in the Convention, combined with its paradoxical treatment of procedural justice, seems to leave little room for considerations of forms of oppression that tend to structure "justice" in capitalist landscapes. As large a step forward as the European Landscape Convention represents, then, it is not without its infirmities as a tool for developing a just landscape, justly arrived at (cf. Harvey 2009/1973: Ch. 3).

## Environmental Justice

Landscape politics does not only entail questions of social and economic justice as exemplified in struggles over access to resources, labor conditions, property, and the redistribution of land, as early land reclamation on Gotland makes clear. With its implications for land degradation, insect pests, and hydrologic and microclimatic changes, landscape politics – and practice – there also raised important environmental concerns. During the twentieth century, the few remaining mirelands on the island were of crucial importance in the social struggle over nature preservation. The latter involved not only local devotees who linked wetlands to customary livelihoods, material resource use, discourses and experiences of nature, but also well-known figures from the scientific elite in Sweden concerned with the preservation of species and habitats (Ohlsson 1961; Sernander 1941). The experiences on Gotland thus raise questions about environmental justice because the production of nature and environmental degradation brings together the qualities of landscape's biophysical nature with issues of social equity. The destruction of livelihood that marked Youngstown's deindustrialization, no less than the shrinking of its footprint that marks the contemporary landscape, are also centrally questions of environment. While the absence of smoke that deindustrialization brought might portend better health for some residents, it might also portend a new era of structural violence in the landscape, an era in which high rates of such environmentally linked diseases as diabetes, obesity, and asthma find new, though still uneven, grounds upon which to flourish (Mitman 2007).

Originating from relatively localized, activist struggles over the unequal exposure to pollution and risk in the United States, environmental justice has increasingly been co-opted internationally by mainstream environmental agendas in, for instance, government policy-making (Agyeman 2005; Heiman 2006). In geography, concern for environmental equity and justice has seen a rapid development during the past twenty years. Early formulations were based on fairly "simple geographies and spatial forms," preoccupied as they were with the documentation of distributional inequalities (Walker 2009: 615). A majority of research efforts concerned the mapping of hazardous sites, often revealing intentional environmental racism, but remained vulnerable to the same kind of limitations that continue to haunt distributional approaches to justice in the Rawlsian sense as spelled out in Harvey's (2009/1973) "liberal formulation" of locational or geographic justice. Reifying rather than seeking to explain distribution, these efforts ran the risk of obscuring the more shifting, dispersed, scaled, and less easily mapped landscapes of environmental inequality, stretching far beyond local proximities (Kobayashi and Ray 2000; Swyngedouw and Heynen 2003; Stanley 2009). Any such failure to transcend the local seemed liable to sustain deeply parochial ideals of justice – "militant particularisms" (to use David Harvey's [1996: 399] evocative phrase) that are not offset by a more "global sense of place" (Massey 1994).

During the past decade, sustained exposure to relational thinking about landscape and space and increasing receptivity to situated discourse have brought more nuanced epistemologies of environmental justice and inequality into sight. Concurrently, attention has increasingly shifted to the intersections between environmental justice, race, class, gender, and uneven landscapes of production and reproduction under capitalism (Katz 2008; Kurtz 2007;

Pulido 1996; Sundberg 2008; Walker and Bulkeley 2006). Explicitly linking environmental justice to economic and social justice, the sorts of oppressions that signal cultural imperialism and violence, and the politics of cultural recognition as pioneered by Fraser and Young, this move rerouted scholarly commitment from describing the hard surface patterns of life to deeper explanations of the processes and relations through which injustice is produced, sustained, and contested and from which these hard surfaces arise (Pulido 1994, 2000; Schlosberg 2002, 2007).

## Conclusion: Landscapes of Justice

Something like the European Landscape Convention seems unimaginable in a place like Youngstown, and imagining the American landscape, shot through as it is with so many forms of social, economic, and environmental injustice, as a series of regional *res publica* (as Olwig's recent work urges) seems even more remote. And yet, as George Henderson (2003: 196) insists, imagining such things – and struggling to put them into place – is precisely what is needed. What we need

> is a concept of landscape that helps point the way to those interventions that can bring about much greater social justice. And what landscape study needs even more is a concept of landscape that will assist the development of the very idea of social justice. To achieve this geographers and other landscape analysts will need to engage in a more sustained conversation with the disciplines of moral and political philosophy concerning the enumeration of basic human rights and modes of their defense. (Henderson 2003: 196)

Such a conversation has begun, perhaps best exemplified most recently by the conference on the Right to Landscape held in Cambridge in 2008. Bringing together an impressive array of legal scholars, landscape architects, architects, geographers, anthropologists, and human rights practitioners, the workshop debated the relationship between human rights and landscape and specifically sought "to collectively define the concept of the right to landscape and to generate a body of knowledge that will support human rights" (Cambridge Centre for Landscape and People 2010; quoted in Egoz, Makhzoumi, and Pungetti 2011: 2). This initiative has the potential to galvanize debate around questions of landscape, justice, and social activism in the same manner that the growing enthusiasm around the concept of the "right to the city" has. However, the old problem of local determination – "militant particularism" – remains with its attendant dangers, as the workshop participants were well aware. "Human Rights discourse itself is not free of political tensions, in particular the problematic notion of universalism versus cultural relativism" (Egoz et al. 2011: 6).

While the Right to Landscape workshop was quite cognizant of the representational aspects of landscape, it is apparent that any "concept of landscape that will assist the development of the very idea of social justice" must be more than cognizant of it; politics of representation – Fraser's and Young's politics of "cultural recognition" – must be worked right into the heart of studies of landscape and justice. Richard Schein (2006, 2009, 2012) has made the urgency of such a project apparent in his recent studies of the erasure and reclamation of alternative histories of racialized landscape in Lexington, Kentucky, and its surrounding countryside. Understanding both representational and morphological erasures in the landscape helps address the workings of cultural imperialism – the flip side of cultural recognition. This is an issue of aesthetics as well as one of physical space: "any definition of the beautiful landscape would have to include the full participation of all and the economic means to do so" (Henderson 2003: 197; Duncan and Duncan 2001, 2004).

Another way to put this is to say that landscape *is* the "stick." As the citizens of Gotland and Youngstown know only too well, landscapes are material and representational evidence of what the current state of justice is, and the foundation for what it can become.

# References

Agyeman, J. (2005) *Sustainable Communities and the Challenge of Environmental Justice*. New York: New York University Press.

Aitken, S.C. (2002) Public participation, technological discourses and the scale of GIS. In *Community Participation and Geographic Information Systems*, ed. W. Craig, T. Harris, and D. Weiner. London and New York: Taylor and Francis, pp. 357–366.

Bruno, R. (1999) *Steelworker Alley: How Class Works in Youngstown*. Ithaca: ILR Press.

Buss, T. and Redburn, F. (1983) *Shutdown at Youngstown: Public Policy for Mass Unemployment*. Albany: State University of New York Press.

Cambridge Centre for Landscape and People (CCLP) (2010) Home page. http://www.cclp.group.cam.ac.uk/ (accessed October 24, 2012).

Camp, S. (1995) *Worker Response to Plant Closings: Steelworkers in Johnstown and Youngstown*. New York: Garland.

Casey, E. (1997) *The Fate of Place: A Philosophical History*. Berkeley: University of California Press.

Center for Working-Class Studies at Youngstown University (n.d.) A renaissance for whom? Youngstown and its neighborhoods. http://cwcs.ysu.edu/about/news/renaissance (accessed October 24, 2012).

Déjeant-Pons, M. (2006) The European Landscape Convention. *Landscape Research*, 31, 363–384.

Duncan, J. and Duncan, N. (1988) (Re)reading the landscape. *Environment and Planning D: Society and Space*, 6, 117–126.

Duncan, J. and Duncan, N. (2001) The aestheticization of the politics of landscape preservation. *Annals of the Association of American Geographers*, 91, 387–409.

Duncan, J. and Duncan, N. (2004) *Landscapes of Privilege: The Politics of the Aesthetic in an American Suburb*. New York: Routledge.

Egoz, S., Makhzoumi, J., and Pungetti, G. (2011) The right to landscape: An introduction. In *The Right to Landscape*, ed. S. Egoz, J. Makhzoumi, and G. Pungetti. London: Ashgate.

Fagraeus, L. (1888) Om Gotland myrar. *Svenska mosskulturföreningens tidskrift*, 1, 58–61.

Fainstein, S. (2010) *The Just City*. Ithaca: Cornell University Press.

Farmer, P. (2003) *Pathologies of Power: Health, Human Rights, and the New War on the Poor*. Berkeley: University of California Press.

Fraser, N. (1987) Social movements vs. disciplinary bureaucracies: The discourse of social needs. CHS Occasional Paper No. 8, Center for Humanistic Studies, University of Minnesota.

Galtung, J. (1969) Violence, peace, and peace research. *Journal of Peace Research*, 6, 167–191.

Geras, N. (1985) The controversy about Marx and justice. *New Left Review*, 150, 47–85.

Harvey, D. (1982) *The Limits to Capital*. Chicago: University of Chicago Press.

Harvey, D. (1985) *The Urbanization of Capital*. Oxford: Blackwell.

Harvey, D. (1996) *Nature, Justice and the Geography of Difference*. Oxford: Blackwell.

Harvey, D. (2001/1984) On the history and present condition of geography: A historical-materialist manifesto. In *Spaces of Capital: Towards a Critical Geography*. New York: Routledge, pp. 108–120.

Harvey, D. (2003) *The New Imperialism*. Oxford: Oxford University Press.

Harvey, D. (2009/1973) *Social Justice and the City*. Athens: University of Georgia Press.

Harvey, D. (2010) *The Enigma of Capital and the Crises of Capitalism*. London: Profile Books.

Hassett, W. (2008) The "shrinking" strategy of Youngstown, Ohio. In *Building the Local Economy: Cases in Economic Development*, ed. D. Watson and J. Morris. Athens: Carl Vinson Institute of Government.

Heiman, M. (2006) Environmental justice. In *Encyclopedia of Human Geography*, ed. B. Warf. Thousand Oaks, CA: Sage.

Henderson, G. (2003) What (else) we talk about when we talk about landscape: For a return to the social imagination. In *Everyday America: Cultural Landscape Studies After J.B. Jackson*, ed. C. Wilson and P. Groth. Berkeley: University of California Press, pp. 178–198.

Herod, A. and Wright, M. (eds.) (2002) *Geographies of Power: Placing Scale*. Oxford: Blackwell.

High, S. and Lewis, D. (2007) *Corporate Wasteland: The Landscape and Memory of Deindustrialization*. Ithaca: ILR Press.

Jones, M. (1999) Landskapsverdier som konfliktpunkt i planlegging: Eksempler fra Trondheim. In *Landskapet vi Lever i: Festskrift til Magne Bruun*, ed. M. Eggen, K. Geelmyden, and K. Jørgensen. Oslo: Norsk Arkitekturforlag.

Jones, M. (2009) The European Landscape Convention and the question of public participation. In *Justice, Power, and the Political Landscape*, ed. K.R. Olwig and D. Mitchell. London: Routledge, pp. 231–251.

Katz, C. (2008) Bad elements: Katrina and the scoured landscape of social reproduction. *Gender, Place and Culture*, 15, 1–29.

Kobayashi, A. and Ray, B. (2000) Civil risk and landscapes of marginality in Canada: A pluralist approach to social justice. *Canadian Geographer*, 44, 401–417.

Kurtz, H.E. (2007) Gender and environmental justice in Louisiana: Blurring the boundaries of public and private spheres. *Gender, Place and Culture*, 14, 409–426.

Lefebvre, H. (1991) *The Production of Space*. Oxford: Blackwell.

Lewis, P. (1975) Common houses, cultural spoor. *Landscape*, 19 (2), 1–22.

Linkon, S. and Russo, J. (2002) *Steeltown U.S.A. Work and Memory in Youngstown*. Lawrence: University Press of Kansas.

Loyd, J. (2009) "A microscopic insurgent": Militarization, health and critical geographies of health. *Annals of the Association of American Geographers*, 99, 863–873.

Luxemburg, R. (2003) *The Accumulation of Capital*. London: Routledge.

Lynd, S. (1982) *The Fight Against Shutdowns: Youngstown's Steel Mill Closings*. San Pedro: Singlejack Books.

Mansbridge, J. (1995) Justice. In *A Companion to American Thought*, ed. R.W. Fox and J.T. Kloppenberg. Oxford: Blackwell, pp. 361–365.

Marx, K. (1954) *Capital: A Critique of Political Economy*, vol. 1. Moscow: Progress Publishers.

Marx, K. (1981) *Capital*, vol. 3. Harmondsworth: Penguin.

Marx, K. and Engels, F. (1970) *Selected Works*, vol. 3. Moscow: International Publishers.

Massey, D. (1994) *Space, Place, and Gender*. Minneapolis: University of Minnesota Press.

Matless, D. (1998) *Landscape and Englishness*. London: Reaktion Books.

Mels, T. (2002) Nature, home and scenery: The "official" spatialities of Swedish national parks. *Environment and Planning D: Society and Space*, 20, 35–54.

Mels, T. (2006) The Low Countries' connection: Landscape and the struggle over representation around 1600. *Journal of Historical Geography*, 32, 712–730.

Merrifield, A. and Swyngedouw, E. (1995) Social justice and the urban experience. In *The Urbanization of Injustice*, ed. A. Merrifield and E. Swyngedouw. London: Lawrence and Wishart, pp. 1–17.

Mitchell, D. (1996) *The Lie of the Land: Migrant Workers and the California Landscape*. Minneapolis: University of Minnesota Press.

Mitchell, D. (2010) Battle/fields: Braceros, agribusiness, and the violent reproduction of the California agricultural landscape during World War II. *Journal of Historical Geography*, 36, 143–156.

Mitchell, W.J.T. (ed.) (1994) *Landscape and Power*. Chicago: University of Chicago Press.

Mitman, G. (2007) *Breathing Space: How Allergies Shape Our Lives and Landscapes*. New Haven: Yale University Press.

Nozick, R. (1974) *Anarchy, State, and Utopia*. New York: Basic Books.

Ohlsson, A. (1961) *Lina myr*. Stockholm: LT förlag.

Okin, S. (1989) *Justice, Gender, and the Family*. New York: Basic Books.

Olwig, K.R. (1996) Recovering the substantive nature of landscape. *Annals of the Association of American Geographers*, 86, 630–653.

Olwig, K.R. (2002a) *Landscape, Nature and the Body Politic: From Britain's Renaissance to America's New World*. Madison: University of Wisconsin Press.

Olwig, K.R. (2002b) The duplicity of space: Germanic "Raum" and Swedish "rum" in English language geographical discourse. *Geografiska Annaler*, 84 B, 1–17.

Olwig, K.R. (2005) The landscape of "customary law" versus that of "natural law." *Landscape Research*, 30, 299–320.

Olwig, K.R. (2007) Are islanders insular? A personal view. *Geographical Review*, 97, 175–190.

Olwig, K.R. (2008) Has "geography" always been modern? *Choros*, (non)representation, performance, and the landscape. *Environment and Planning A*, 40, 1843–1861.

Olwig, K.R. (2009) The practice of landscape "conventions" and the just landscape: The case of the European Landscape Convention. In *Justice, Power, and the Political Landscape*, ed. K.R. Olwig and D. Mitchell. London: Routledge, pp. 198–212.

Palmenfelt, U. (1994) *Per Arvid Säves möten med människor och sägner: folkloristiska aspekter på ett gotländskt arkivmaterial*. Stockholm: Carlsson.

Peck, J. and Tickell, A. (2002) Neoliberalizing space. *Antipode*, 34, 380–404.

Pulido, L. (1994) *Environmentalism and Economic Justice: Two Chicano Struggles in the Southwest*. Tucson: University of Arizona Press.

Pulido, L. (1996) A critical review of the methodology of environmental racism research. *Antipode*, 28, 142–159.

Pulido, L. (2000) Rethinking environmental racism: White privilege and urban development in Southern California. *Annals of the Association of American Geographers*, 90, 12–40.

Rawls, J. (1971) *A Theory of Justice*. Cambridge, MA: Harvard University Press.

Säve, P.A. (1938) *Åkerns sagor: spridda drag ur odlingshävderna och folklivet på Gotland*. Visby: Ridelius Bokhandel.

Schein, R.H. (1997) The place of landscape: A conceptual framework for interpreting an American scene. *Annals of the Association of American Geographers*, 87, 660–680.

Schein, R. (2006) Digging in your own backyard. *Archivaria*, 61, 91–104.

Schein, R. (2009) Belonging through land/scape. *Environment and Planning A*, 41, 811–826.

Schein, R.H. (2012) Urban form and racial order. *Urban Geography*, 33 (7), 942–960.

Schlosberg, D. (2002) *Environmental Justice and the New Pluralism*. Oxford: Oxford University Press.

Schlosberg, D. (2007) *Defining Environmental Justice: Theories, Movements and Nature*. Oxford: Oxford University Press.

Sernander, R. (1941) Gotlands kvarlevande myrar och träsk. *Kungliga Svenska Vetenskapsakademiens avhandlingar i naturskyddsärenden*, 3.

Setten, G. (2004) The habitus, the rule and the moral landscape. *Cultural Geographies*, 11, 389–415.

Smith, D. (1994) *Geography and Social Justice*. Oxford: Blackwell.

Smith, N. (1990) *Uneven Development: Nature, Capital and the Production of Space*, 2nd edition. Oxford: Blackwell.

Stanley, A. (2009) Just space or spatial justice? Difference, discourse, and environmental justice. *Local Environment*, 14, 999–1014.

Sundberg, J. (2008) Placing race in environmental justice research in Latin America. *Society and Natural Resources*, 21, 569–582.

Swyngedouw, E. and Heynen, N.C. (2003) Urban political ecology, justice and the politics of scale. *Antipode*, 35, 898–918.

Vallentyne, P. (2010) Libertarianism. In *The Stanford Encyclopedia of Philosophy*, ed. E. Zalta. http://plato.stanford.edu/archives/fall2008/entries/libertarianism/ (accessed October 24, 2012).

Walker, G. (2009) Beyond distribution and proximity: Exploring the multiple spatialities of environmental justice. *Antipode*, 41, 614–636.

Walker, G. and Bulkeley, H. (2006) Editorial: Geographies of environmental justice. *Geoforum*, 37, 655–659.

Wenar, L. (2008) John Rawls In *The Stanford Encyclopedia of Philosophy*, ed. E. Zalta. http://plato.stanford.edu/archives/fall2008/entries/rawls (accessed October 24, 2012).

Young, I.M. (1990) *Justice and the Politics of Difference*. Princeton: Princeton University Press.

Chapter 21

# Rural Landscapes

*Paul Cloke*

## Landscape Perspectives

As I sit writing this chapter, I look out of my study window onto a rural landscape. From the Devon hillside village of Bishopsteignton, my gaze is drawn down past landmark trees, across the tidal estuary of the River Teign, and up again to the valley side beyond. Rolling topography and ancient field enclosures – frequently repatterned, recolored, and relit with diurnal and seasonal change – are intersected by narrow lanes and straggly footpaths. The ebb and flow of the river continuously refresh the scene, imposing alternative senses of time on what can seem timelessly pastoral. A picture-postcard? Yes, but so much more. This is where we walk our border collie, Ringo, where I ride my bike for exercise, and where I drive the car on my commute to work in the nearby city. This is where I am periodically enchanted by the affective capacity of bluebell woods, of the color and texture of birch and rowan, of the persistence and beauty of goldfinch, blue tit, and woodpecker, yet can remain relatively unaffected by the scenic presence of the view, or by the potential for hands-on proximity with nature in the performance of gardening. This is where the peaceful music of a summer evening is disrupted by the discordant, buzzy soundscape of lawnmower, strimmer, and chainsaw. This is where myriad cans, bottles, and other rubbish lazily discarded at the road-side from car windows are collected by the village outdoor art group and reshaped into aesthetically pleasing forms for display on the seafront in the summer. This is where I struggle with political and religious conservatism and social monoculturalism, and am struck by the vehemence of opposition to new housing developments, especially from those who occupy the previous rounds of development. This landscape, then, is gazed on, lived in, performed, and experienced in so many different ways. It combines and narrates the human and the non-human in diverse assemblages and in both representative and quotidian registers.

*The Wiley Blackwell Companion to Cultural Geography*, First Edition.
Edited by Nuala C. Johnson, Richard H. Schein, and Jamie Winders.
© 2013 John Wiley & Sons, Ltd. Published 2016 by John Wiley & Sons, Ltd.

My landscape will not be the same as your landscape, but yours too will reflect some of these complexities, these discontinuities, these *tensions* that are inherent in seeing, feeling, experiencing, and performing. As John Wylie (2007) has argued, the role of cultural geographers is not to suggest some all-embracing resolutions of these tensions (although some have tried!), but rather to permit the productive *stretching* of our understanding of landscape through exploration of the different perspectives on nature–culture assemblages enabled by distance and proximity, by observation and participation, and by the role of mind, body, and spirit. Over the years, cultural geographers have formulated a number of approaches to landscape, of which three are particularly relevant here. First, Sauer's (1963) "morphology of landscape" presented landscape as a cultural entity, as the product of human modification of nature. As such it could only be accessed through observational practices that enabled a reading of the "real" landscape rather than seeking out embedded meanings. As a leading proponent of this observational approach, John Fraser Hart (1995), tells us, with some intentional humor, "we need to learn to read the landscape, not just to see and react to it, but what we see is real, and no conceivable amount of sophistry can protect the Deep Thinkers from the reality of getting spattered, not inappropriately, if they get too close to the rear end of that bull" (pp. 24–25). This stark rebuttal of philosophical and interpretive argument seems a little old-fashioned, but the observational approach that underlies it is perhaps resonant in the recent interest in the scientific biogeographies of landscape (see, for example, Kent 2007). Second, later approaches in cultural geography have attempted to address the wider social and political contexts in which cultural landscapes have been constituted and expressed (Jackson 1989). Such approaches treat landscapes as ways of shaping the world and its meanings; as sites of iconography (Cosgrove and Daniels 1988) in which landscapes are symbolic of their enrollment within historical and material processes, and thereby have the capacity to mold ideas about, for example, race, gender, and morality. Access to iconography will often be via the reading of key cultural texts (Duncan and Duncan 1988) that write, portray, or otherwise act out landscape meaning. Third, phenomenological approaches have been used to examine the everyday lived experience of landscape (Ingold 2000; Wylie 2002a, 2005). Here, cultural geographers have used a reawakened interest in the embodied practices of being-in-the-world to explore how landscape can be perceived, performed, and dwelt. In this way, landscape is about feeling, emotional investment, and rhythms of involvement; it is both a site of cultural meaning and a sensorium of experience. As Wylie points out to us, landscape is thereby a ripe topic for non-representational (see Dewsbury *et al*. 2002), or perhaps more helpfully "more-than-representational" approaches (Lorimer 2005):

> The act of representing (speaking, painting, writing) is understood by non-representational theory to be *in* and *of* the world of embodied practice and performance, rather than taking place outside of that world  . . .  the world is understood to be continually in the making – processual and performative – rather than stabilised or structured via messages in texts and images. (Wylie 2007: 164)

Accordingly, the focus on embodied experience points away from already made representations of landscape and toward the practises of landscaping.

In the remainder of this chapter I briefly examine how *rural* landscapes have been differently understood in terms of history, cultural politics, performance, and assemblage. In using these categories I merely seek convenient pegs on which to hang different ways of stretching ideas about rural landscape, suggesting that the seemingly "distinct" approaches to landscape discussed above are not mutually exclusive but intersect and co-constitute in different ways. Rurality itself is a contested concept (Cloke 2003, 2006) variously denoting observable features of (non-urban) marginality, imagined geographies of social and natural spaces, and performative arenas of, for example, being-in-community and being-in-nature. However, the idea of "the rural" often does work as an assembler of ideas, discourses, and practices and remains a key category for the co-constitution of imagined and practiced space. As a consequence, the rural provides an interesting laboratory for stretching our understandings of landscape.

## Rural Landscape/History

This too is the last of England. The Solway estuary west of Carlisle is a desolate place of salt marshes, migratory birds, industrial relics and imperial ambitions. The Roman wall reached its limit at Maia (Bowness today) . . . African legionnaires were here a millennium before the Normans. The Brythonic (Welsh) kingdoms of Rheged and Strathclyde straddled both sides of this narrow firth. Norse settlers from Ireland and the Isle of Man spread through the region. The expansion of Northumbria led to new forms of cultural synthesis, as the Anglo-Scandinavian stone crosses at Gosforth and Dearham indicate. The Scots . . . contested the area for two centuries after the arrival of the Normans. In the nineteenth century, a canal and railway built by Irish labour attempted to link Carlisle with the sea. The past of this "corner of a corner of England," to adapt Hilaire Belloc, "is infinite and can never be exhausted." (Hayes 1998: 46)

Every rural landscape, as David Hayes reminds us, has its history, and for some this historical narrative is formative to their reading of the landscape. History works in the landscape at different scales. For example, Conzen's (1994) collection of essays on *The Making of the American Landscape* tackles the historical transformation of the landscape of an entire nation in terms of the forces of settlement and human shaping of the land over the past 10,000 years. The emphasis here is on how to read the clues in the landscape that provide a record of these changes. By contrast, the recent resurgence of interest in place names in Britain (Mills 2011) takes reading the landscape down to a much more local scale, arguing that names serve as linguistic fossils suggesting original landscape meanings that are not always apparent in their contemporary forms.

Such narratives promulgate an observational approach to the history of the landscapes concerned, but they also interact with and in some cases reinforce more nostalgic notions of these landscapes. Understandings of rural landscapes in Britain, for example, are beset by a marked tendency to assume that the immediate past landscape represents the organic heart of rural life which has been lost or threatened by subsequent changes. Raymond Williams (1985) suggests that history in the rural landscape is often a case of just looking back "over the last hill" (p. 9). Current rural life and landscape have changed radically since the 1940s. Yes, but residential settlement after 1900 and enclosure after 1861 were also pivotal markers of change, and then in the 1820s Cobbett was writing about happier times fifty years previously, and so on. Williams sees this deployment of history as a use of the immediate past as a stick with which to beat the present, and as evidence of a universal and persistent tendency toward nostalgia that inflects the reading of the landscape.

Murdoch *et al.* (2003) argue that understandings of the rural landscapes in Britain have largely been shaped by two historical discourses: *pastoralism* and *modernism*. Pastoralism is rooted in the Romantic movement of the eighteenth and nineteenth centuries (see Bunce 1994;

Short 1991), in which poets such as Wordsworth and Tennyson were active in giving cultural emphasis to the beauty and unspoilt nature of countryside landscapes – in contrast to the corrupted urbanism of the Industrial Revolution. Accordingly, rural landscapes became identified as that zone beyond industrialism; that space of nature that stands in pure contradistinction to the environmentally and morally degenerative impacts of industrialization. This rather elite intellectual idea was gradually put into practice by more popular movements of middle-class households in the twentieth century, first by visiting the countryside, and then by moving out of cities to live in suburbs and surrounding rural areas. Such moves perhaps represented an emotional escape from the dominant values of capitalism and a nostalgic embrace of dwelling amongst more traditional contexts of rurality. It can also be argued that the attraction of countryside landscapes is inseparable from their historical character, and that lament over countryside change includes a deep-felt regret over the loss of a human monument built up over the centuries by rural workers. As Scruton (1998) insists:

> The need that modern people feel for the countryside is not a need for fresh air and vegetation only; it is a need for another and older experience of *time* – . . . the time of the earth, in which people work at unchanging tasks and the pace is set by the seasons. (p. 320)

It takes little imagination to see that this sense of history in the landscape can be connected with the political conservatism of "old-fashioned values" through which rural landscapes come to represent the supposed heartland of nationalistic and jingoistic expression.

The second historical discourse underpinning the symbolic nature of rural landscapes is that of *modernism*, in which the very characteristics celebrated by Romanticism become symbols of backwardness and remoteness from the progress and excitement of urban living. In some ways, modernism can be linked to a flight by some from the countryside in search of urban progress. Even modernism, however, has helped to co-constitute some aspects of rural landscapes because of the increasingly important role of heritage as a response to modernity. Grant (1998), for example, has argued that modernity has been marked by a gradual dissolution of historic certainty and sustaining frameworks of belief. It is not so much about the loss of a past as the loss of a "tradition-saturated present" (p. 39), and so as compensation, modernity has fueled a heritage industry that self-consciously serves to reconstitute the place of history in culture. Rural landscapes offer many opportunities for such heritage, which in turn becomes emblematic of many landscapes. Heritage will often celebrate the aristocratic and the powerful, and can therefore carry with it implicit orthodoxies of power and control. Heritage can also increasingly be viewed in terms of performances – for example of engaging in living history, of volunteering in support of National Trust houses and gardens, and of visiting historic or heritage sites – and so can be seen to come alive in the experiences of particular practices of landscape.

Historic clues, linguistic fossils, pastoral symbolism, and the heritage that emerges as a response to modernity all have their place in the histories of rural landscapes. Time has its own affective voice, but is also the subject of highly commodified ventriloquy. The countryside is variously performed as ideological heartland, time-deepened dwelling place, and embodied practices of becoming. Memory and historical texts and images contribute to the making of this becoming rural world; living in a rural area or visiting countryside landscapes will involve repositories and sites of cultural meaning and an immanent sensorium of experience. In these and other ways, the practice of rural landscaping is being significantly touched by history.

## Rural Landscape/Cultural Politics

The classic cultural device used to reflect pastoralism and responses to modernism in English rural landscapes is that of some kind of rural *idyll* (Bunce 2003; Cloke 2003), suggesting a happy, healthy, and problem-free experience in communion with both a close-knit social community and an unsullied and therapeutic natural environment. This cultural template serves both to extol the virtue of rural land and life and to cloak any alternative narratives of rural problems (see Cloke *et al.* 1995, 2000). As Jo Little and Patricia Austin (1996) have pointed out, the idea of idyll is neither geographically nor culturally all-embracing as a descriptor of rurality; indeed, much more needs to be known about its precise importance in relation to how people perceive, practice, and experience being-in-the-rural. However, there is some evidence that idyllic rurality has contributed to the countryside becoming part of the national identity of England in its cultural "gluing together" of people with what might be regarded as their "natural" homelands or territories. As such, the rural idyll is connected up to the paraphernalia of the past (Mingay 1989) as well as to countless contemporary social practices.

The significance of the rural idyll lies partly in the ways in which it transports implicit ideologies amongst its iconography, and symbolizes the enrollment of rural landscapes into particular material and political processes in the production of cultural space. This ideological baggage has been detailed elsewhere (Cloke and Milbourne 1992), but in this context we can trace a few of the key connections that have been made. Rural landscapes have, for example, been imbued with meanings associated with *patriotism* (Short 1991), suggesting to some that the unsullied nature of the space conveys some kind of a nationalistic purity, or at least a cultural hearth of the nation. Rurality figures both practically as the site of conservative politics and symbolically in the "earthing" of nationalist politics (Winter 1996). The cultural politics of rural landscape as a site of patriotic conservatism sponsor at least two significant spaces of meaning. First, landscapes are endowed with qualities of unchanging preciousness that seem to demand *conservation* and protection from the ravages of new housing and infrastructural development. Second, rural landscapes are often associated with white *ethnicities* (Chakraborti and Garland 2004), representing both a contrast to multicultural cities and potentially a space in which people of other ethnicity experience unease, or out-of-placeness (Cresswell 1996). Rural idylls have also been recognized as shoring up traditional *gender* and *class* formations; the former through implicit assertion of patriarchal norms in gendered identity, domesticity, and familism (Little 2001); the latter in the celebration of aristocratic and elitist relations between the property paternalism and power of landowners and the deferential performance of their workers (Newby 1979; Newby *et al.* 1978).

These ideological associations have been accessed in many different ways, not least the interpretation of key symbolic texts such as paintings and photographs (see, for example, Berger 1972; Rose 1993) or advertisements (see, for example, Brandth 1995) in which particular class and gender relations are assumed. More recently, however, cultural geographers have attempted to deconstruct any too-easy reading of rural cultural texts. In two excellent examples, *Sylvanian Family* toys (Houlton and Short 1995) and *Postman Pat* books (Horton 2008a, 2008b) have been recognized as potential purveyors of the class, gender, and ethnic ideologies of the rural idyll, but have also been understood as far more complex practices in which playing with toys and reading and learning from books and associated filmic texts respectively can deconstruct as well as reinforce idylls. Here the representational texts become part of embodied performances of play and reading that can destabilize the production of meaning through the practices of its consumption.

It is important to acknowledge, then, that idyllic cultural constructions do not serve as automatic propaganda for the ideologies of idyll. We should also emphasize that other representative forms and texts directly oppose this idyll. For example, David Bell's (1997) research on the anti-idyll of horror movies set in American rural landscapes demonstrates that by no means all rural landscapes are portrayed as idyllic:

> From the 1950's onwards, small-town movies began to depict their settings as suffocating and repressive. As the huge upheavals of the 1960s were worked through in the cinematic medium, small towns and the countryside were increasingly portrayed as sites of contestation and decay, often embodied in those characters living there. (p. 106)

Similarly, dystopic qualities of rural landscapes have emerged, for example in: portrayals of animal disease, such as the outbreak of foot and mouth disease in Britain in 2001 (Convery *et al.* 2005) in which the sight and smell of the resultant funeral pyres of slaughtered cattle represented a clear contradiction of the usually happy and healthy iconography of the countryside; debates over the siting of nuclear waste dumps (Gowda and Easterling 1998) in which the marginality of native American landscapes recommends them for hazardous storage facilities that contravene any notions of a therapeutic and healthy landscape; and the use of rural areas for military purposes (Woodward 2004) resulting in the non-idyllic shaping of landscapes and environments through practices and discourses of militarism. Once again, however, these dystopic geographies of rural landscape do not stand separate from embodied practices of being in the world. As Ingrid Pollard records her unease as a black woman in the landscapes of the Lake District (Kinsman 1995), her photographs are more than a simple representation of the heritage and romanticism of the English rural landscape. Rather, they are a portrait of her own embodied practice of being in the rural world, and a recording of the sensorium of her unease as she performs and experiences this involvement. Similarly, when local farmers and vets record their impressions of the foot and mouth outbreak in their rural areas in the form of poetry (Nerlich and Döring 2005), these poems are more than a simple representation of the counterintuitive nature of funeral pyres in the rural landscape. Rather, these poems are an emotional investment in the lived experience of a countryside being destabilized and remade in processual fashion. As with history, the cultural-political web that shapes and is shaped by rural landscapes involves both sites of meaning and sensorial experiences that far exceed any simple reading of the landscape.

## Rural Landscapes/Performance

Performative understandings of rural landscape draw both on the concerns of feminist theory to take the body seriously and on the reinvigoration of phenomenological approaches that emphasize the role of the body in the creation, practice, and knowing of the world. Recent interest in non-representational ideas (Thrift 2008; Anderson and Harrison 2010) has pointed to the pre-cognitive knowings and practices of the body, and to its "other intelligences" or affective capacities. These conceptual fascinations have opened out new ways of exploring rural landscapes by exploring the performative practices through which we not only use and engage with landscapes but also experience landscapes in-the-making. As the countryside becomes increasingly commodified (Cloke 1993; Perkins 2006), the visibility of different ways of performing rural landscapes has become more evident. As well as involving walking, running, cycling, driving, riding, and other different mobilities, our performance of landscape is often a purposeful experience of, for example, farming, residing, visiting, exploring, leisure, exercise, hunting, hunt sabotage, bird-watching, and so on.

These performances can to some extent be scripted culturally, and will be articulated through particular forms of identity and practice, but they also unfold in the here-and-now, with landscape being made through involvement and experience. Tim Edensor (2001), writing about tourism, points to an interconnected series of ideas about performativity: the power of representation to conjure up particular anticipatory ideas about places and practices; the power of mediators to "stage" particular performances; and the importance of everyday habits and instincts that are unreflexive but provide common-sense understandings of what it is to be and become in a particular place or landscape. The unfolding of these ideas can be seen in research on adventure tourism in New Zealand (Cloke and Perkins 1998; Cater and Cloke 2007). Here, particular elite wilderness landscapes have taken on fresh identities through adrenalin-fueled pursuits such as bungee jumping, jet boating, and white-water rafting. What might otherwise be understood as landscapes to gaze upon, or walk through, have become something else in the experience of adventure tourists. In this example, Edensor's concerns find practical expression. Representational images and ideas abound as New Zealand in general, and the Queenstown area in particular, is commodified as the "Adventure Capital of the World." Specialist firms have been established to sell adventurous opportunities, providing both site access and equipment that serve as theater and props, and crew who become the co-actors and stagehands in the unfolding drama. However, these representations and stagings are part of, rather than separate from, the embodied practice of adventurous performance. Bungee jumpers, for example, were often unable to make sense of the unrepresentable and ineffable nature of their jump – but in this embodied practice, they encountered a landscape world that was corporeally in-the-making rather than already fixed, experienced in the knowing rather than reinforcing what was already known.

Adventure tourism is perhaps an extreme example of how practices of embodied landscaping help to unfold through performance, and a more everyday illustration can be found in the technologies and experiences of performing rural landscape through walking. Tim Edensor (2000) narrates walking as a being in the nature of the countryside, and as an enhancing of naturalness through embodiment. In his account, walking can be seen first as a reflexive practice which produces an awareness of the self and particularly of the body and the senses. Walking in rural landscapes can thus become an embodiment of beauty, freedom, and the picturesque, or of more dystopic characteristics. But walking is also an unreflexive practice, producing habitual and unintentional conventions of bodily demeanor that are not shaped by cultural norms, and it is also a means of reproducing and reinterpreting the places and spaces of landscapes. The sensory nature of embodied experience gives rise to a being-present and becoming-involved in the world, and produces cultural meanings and social relations along the way. Sensory experiences, then, not only inscribe meanings on the body, they also open out new sets of meanings which can be unfamiliar, unpredictable, and different.

These senses of walking as an opening out, a stretching, a becoming of landscape, have been narrated in an excellent study by John Wylie (2005) of walking on the English South West Coast Path. His purpose is not simply to record the practices and performances that lead to a landscape in-the-making, but also to use walking as a methodology for activating "a space and time within which I might engage with and explore issues of landscape, subjectivity and corporeality, in the context of their current discussion within cultural geographies and cultural theory more generally" (p. 234). Wylie's account embraces his attunement with those sensibilities that draw both on romantic and sublime configurations of landscape and self, and on the cultural politics of patriotism, gender, rurality, fitness, and so on. However, a substantial part of his project is to work through the domains of experience that are constructed through *affects* and *percepts*:

> In the context of coastal walking these terms connote configurations of motion and materiality – of light, colour, morphology and mood – *from which* distinctive senses of self and landscape, walker and ground, observer and observed, distil and refract . . . [A] percept is a style of visibility, of being-visible, a configuration of light and matter that exceeds, enters into, and ranges over the perceptions of a subject who sees. An affect is an intensity, a field perhaps of awe, irritation or serenity, which exceeds, enters into, and ranges over the sensations and emotions of a subject who feels. (p. 236)

Wylie's study, then, offers a post-phenomenological account of landscape as the interconnected materialities and sensibilities "*with which* we act and sense" (p. 245); his walking has practiced landscaping as a series of emergences, resonances, and interrelations, and his narrative of landscape is an outcome of its unfolding rather than an experience of presupposed notions of what a landscape is or what it means. His account of performing landscape therefore serves to stretch further our configuration of how history, cultural politics, and embodied sensitivity and sensibility come together within rural landscapes.

## Rural Landscape/Assemblage

Performative approaches render it impossible simply to regard rural landscape as a cultural construction in which human meaningfulness is imposed upon nature. While the active role of nature is implicit in both the historical attention to landscape evolution and in the idyllized extensiveness and beauty of the non-urban and the dystopia inherent in diseased animals or pollutant materials that are somehow out of kilter in the countryside, the contribution of non-humans becomes increasingly explicit in the unfolding resonances of performative practice. Over recent years, the understanding of nature–society relations has been transformed in various ways via the acknowledgment of the interrelationships between humanity and non-humanity. Bruno Latour's (1993) recognition of nature and society as a *hybrid collectif* led to a surge in human geographical attention to hybridity (Whatmore 2002) within nature and society by which the fabric of everyday living is seen to consist of relational achievements involving the creative presence of organic beings and technology as well as people. Initial attention was focused on how pluralities of interrelated achievements are mapped or expressed through *actor* (or *actant*) *networks* working toward particular ends. Such networks offer a fluid and plural vision of everyday life suggesting symmetry between humans and non-humans and a dynamic problematization of geographical proximity and distance in which networks can be connected across time and space without relying on temporally or spatially contiguous configuration. Rural landscapes can clearly be implicated in such networks. For example, "crops" of plants or trees are integral to networks based on farming or forestry in which their role goes far beyond that of a mere "resource," instead reflecting a creative capacity of growth and character that is essential to the overall relational achievement.

Networks, however, offer a particular perspective that can sometimes be unhelpful in addressing place-based aspects of rural landscapes. As Nigel Thrift (1999) has argued, while actor network theory does provide a convincing account of how all manner of things constantly combine and recombine in the formation of the functioning social world, this approach does not throw light on how these comings together can have particular qualities, or have particular qualities brought to them, that can contribute to the formation of places. Equally, networked models of nature–society relations, because of their insistence on the relational nature of agency, can strip individual actants of any peculiar qualities that might be translated as enchanting or vibrant (Bennett 2001, 2010). In their study of cetacean tourism in Kaikoura, New Zealand, Cloke and Perkins (2005) show how a particular rural place has become transformed because of the charismatic nature of whales and dolphins, whose performances have attracted many millions of visitors to the town. In a very real way, they conclude, the place and landscape of Kaikoura have been co-constituted by the presence and attractiveness of cetaceans.

An alternative formulation of the assemblage of landscape comes from the reformulation of Heideggerian ideas about dwelling, notably by Tim Ingold (1993, 1995). In one important sense, dwelling suggests the inhabitation of landscape:

> Dwelling is about the rich intimate ongoing togetherness of beings and things which make up landscapes and places, and which bind together nature and culture over time. (Cloke and Jones 2001: 651)

Ingold (2000) asserts that the landscape becomes meaningful through being inhabited, through processes of being immersed-in-the-world. Both people and environment are continually developing through mutual interaction, and "both cultural knowledge and bodily substance are seen to undergo continuous generation in the context of an ongoing engagement with the land and with the beings – human and non-human – that dwell therein" (p. 133). By this view, landscape is dwelling – not land, not nature, but rooted in corporeal human perception of the surrounding environment. It follows that landscape becomes known by those who dwell within it, by the skills of involved practice involving both long-standing cultural meaning and the performative sensorium.

These various skills of perceiving the dwelt environment have been variously explored by cultural geographers. Cloke and Jones (2001) narrate the example of a Somerset orchard in which apple trees are at the creative center of a time-thickened, place-forming series of practices – pruning, painting the pruning cuts, thinning the young apples, picking, and so on – that suggest an intimate fine-grained materiality of dwelling. As such the orchard evokes a rich, intense making of the world in which all manner of things fold and form and interact in particular formations. Here "the sensuous and tactile experience of generation and seasonality testifies to how human actants are embedded in landscapes, how nature and culture are bound together, and how landscape invariably has time-depth which relates the present to past futures and future pasts" (p. 664). By contrast, John Wylie's work on journeys – that of Scott and Amundsen to the South Pole (2002b) and that of his own to the top of Glastonbury Tor (2002a) – explores more immanent and haptic registers in which self and landscape are co-produced. In the former journey, for example, dwelt landscape becomes "a concrete and sensuous concatenation of material forces" (p. 251) in which polar explorers sought ways of becoming-polar through intimate dwelling with the environment. Whether in terms of time-deepened intimate ongoing togetherness or of a more immanent process of becoming intimate, these ideas about landscape as dwelling seem to offer considerable scope for stretching our understanding of the human/non-human assemblages that call landscape into being. In particular, the web of being-in-the-world suggested by dwelling approaches contrasts markedly with the more abstract relational agency of actor network theory, as illustrated by Ingold in his staged debate between the ANT (actor network theory) and the SPIDER (the dwelling perspective):

> But there you are surely wrong, exclaims SPIDER. The lines of my web are not at all like those of your network. In your world there are just bits and pieces of diverse kinds that are brought together or assembled so as to make things happen. Every "relation" in the network, then, is a connection *between* one thing and another. As such, the relation has no material presence. For the materiality of the world, in your view, is fully comprehended in the things connected. The lines of my web, to the contrary, are themselves spun from the materials exuded from my own body, and are laid down as I move about. You could even say they are an extension of my very being as it trails into the environment – they comprise, if you will, my "wideware." They are the lines *along* which I live, and conduct my perception and action in the world. (Ingold 2011: 91)

It is these lines along which we live, and this conduct of perception and action in the world, that hold such significant promise for innovative approaches to the understanding of rural landscapes.

## Resetting Landscape Perspectives

I have for now stopped gazing out onto the view beyond my window. Its beauty is two-dimensional, lacking depth of field and depth of engagement. The corporeality of sitting at the picture-window is constraining; it restricts the framing of the picture but also my capacity to sense and experience the scene. I am now out walking, with Ringo, down the hill to the river. He knows this well-worn route and his excess energy suggests excitement, anticipation, the prospect of freedom from the constraints of house and garden. The hill puts gradient under our feet and takes us past houses where UK Independence Party posters have recently been displayed, and from which "preserve us from new housing" petitions have been launched. The houses are significant to me because of these politics, but that's my self at work, a haunted marking of the landscape with memories of past reactions. I wonder what the Bishop of Exeter was like when he owned the village in 1086 – not much different in many respects is my guess.

Past the ancient fir tree, and into the soundscape of the school – the children are on half-term but their play-sounds are loud in my memory and continue to clash vitally with the fragrance of retirement that pervades much of the village. Down to the main road, past the roadside cans – I know that I should pick them up – but beyond the road is freedom; Ringo off the lead chasing his ball, through trees and into fields, over the railway footbridge to the river-beach. My attention is captured in these moments neither by pastoral beauty, nor by the inherent danger of gunshot in the distance, but by the technology of repeated interaction between me, dog, ball, and ball-throwing device (we call this "the wanger"). It is a time-honed skill to scoop up ball and deliver it several meters further down the path, avoiding hedge (and associated ball-searching) and field (and associated dog-trampling). Equally it seems to be written into Ringo's border collie DNA to eschew other sights, smells, and presences in order to concentrate on fetching and delivering the ball, reveling in the freedom of movement and the intensity of interaction. So we move in ball-throwing and chasing corridors through the landscape. And then to the river-beach. Why does Ringo run into the river after every wang of the ball? How come, despite the periodic interruption of Great Western along its riverside track, this seems a peaceful place for stopping and reflecting? Is this connected with the relics of old boats and vestiges of ancient shellfish industries? Is it the long views up to Dartmoor and down to the sea? Perhaps it is simply the performative sensorium of sky and river, boats and birds, dog and ball, friends and family, subjectivity and self; of movements, impressions, events, encounters, relations. And in this thought, I carry John Wylie's (2005) wise words with me:

> The movements, sensations, thoughts and encounters which animated the walk . . . and which equally animated me, were not an alien or fleeting facade, obscuring some underlying, authentic landscape, nor were they a tissue of significations infusing an in-itself mute landscape with meaning. (p. 245)

Perhaps, after all, I have unwittingly brought Tim Ingold on this walk with me, and through him I have unwrapped a landscape that interconnects the materialities and sensitivities with which we practice; maybe this, then, is my version of landscape as dwelling.

## References

Anderson, B. and Harrison, P. (eds.) (2010) *Taking-Place: Non-Representational Theories and Geography*. Farnham: Ashgate.

Bell, D. (1997) Anti-idyll: Rural horror. In *Contested Countryside Cultures*, ed. P. Cloke and J. Little. London: Routledge, pp. 94–108.

Bennett, J. (2001) *The Enchantment of Modern Life*. Princeton: Princeton University Press.

Bennett, J. (2010) *Vibrant Matter: A Political Ecology of Things*. Durham, NC: Duke University Press.

Berger, J. (1972) *Ways of Seeing*. Harmondsworth: Penguin.

Brandth, B. (1995) Rural masculinity in transition: Gender images in tractor advertisements. *Journal of Rural Studies*, 11, 123–133.

Bunce, M. (1994) *The Countryside Ideal: Anglo-American Images of Landscape*. London: Routledge.

Bunce, M. (2003) Reproducing rural idylls. In *Country Visions*, ed. P. Cloke. Harlow: Pearson, pp. 14–30.

Cater, C. and Cloke, P. (2007) Bodies in action: The performative geographies of adventure tourism. *Anthropology Today*, 23, 13–17.

Chakraborti, N. and Garland, J. (eds.) (2004) *Rural Racism*. Cullompton: Willand.

Cloke, P. (1993) The countryside as commodity: New rural spaces for leisure. In *Leisure and the Environment*, ed. S. Glyptis. London: Belhaven, pp. 53–67.

Cloke, P. (2003) Knowing ruralities. In *Country Visions*, ed. P. Cloke. Harlow: Pearson, pp. 1–13.

Cloke, P. (2006) Conceptualizing rurality. In *Handbook of Rural Studies*, ed. P. Cloke, T. Marsden, and P. Mooney. London: Sage, pp. 18–28.

Cloke, P. and Jones, O. (2001) Dwelling, place and landscape: An orchard in Somerset. *Environment and Planning A*, 33, 649–666.

Cloke, P. and Milbourne, P. (1992) Deprivation and lifestyles in rural Wales: 2. The cultural dimension. *Journal of Rural Studies*, 8, 359–371.

Cloke, P. and Perkins, H. (1998) Cracking the canyon with the Awesome Foursome: Representations of adventure tourism in New Zealand. *Environment and Planning D: Society and Space*, 16, 185–218.

Cloke, P. and Perkins, H. (2005) Cetacean performance and tourism in Kaikoura, New Zealand. *Environment and Planning D: Society and Space*, 23, 903–924.

Cloke, P., Goodwin, M., Milbourne, P., and Thomas, C. (1995) Deprivation, poverty and marginalisation in rural lifestyles in England and Wales. *Journal of Rural Studies*, 11, 351–365.

Cloke, P., Milbourne, P., and Widdowfield, R. (2000) Homelessness and rurality: Out of place in purified space. *Environment and Planning D: Society and Space*, 18, 715–735.

Convery, I., Bailey, C., Mort, M., and Baxter, J. (2005) Death in the wrong place? Emotional geographies of the UK 2001 foot and mouth disease epidemic. *Journal of Rural Studies*, 21, 99–109.

Conzen, M. (ed.) (1994) *The Making of the American Landscape*. New York: Routledge.

Cosgrove, D. and Daniels, S. (eds.) (1988) *The Iconography of Landscape*. Cambridge: Cambridge University Press.

Cresswell, T. (1996) *In Place/Out of Place: Geography, Ideology and Transgression*. Minneapolis: University of Minnesota Press.

Dewsbury, J.-D., Wylie, J., Harrison, P., and Rose, M. (2002) Enacting geographies. *Geoforum*, 32, 437–441.

Duncan, J. and Duncan, N. (1988) (Re)reading the landscape. *Environment and Planning D: Society and Space*, 6, 117–126.

Edensor, T. (2000) Walking in the British countryside: Reflexivity, embodied practices and ways to escape. *Body and Society*, 6, 81–106.

Edensor, T. (2001) Performing tourism, staging tourism. *Tourist Studies*, 1, 59–81.

Gowda, R. and Easterling, D. (1998) Nuclear waste and native America: The MRS siting exercise. *Risk: Health, Safety and Environment*, 9, 229–258.

Grant, R. (1998) History, tradition and modernity. In *Town and Country*, ed. A. Barnett and R. Scruton. London: Jonathan Cape, pp. 34–45.

Hart, J.F. (1995) Reading the landscape. In *Landscape in America*, ed. G. Thompson. Austin: University of Texas Press.

Hayes, D. (1998) Ozymandias on the Solway. In *Town and Country*, ed. A. Barnett and R. Scruton. London: Jonathan Cape, pp. 46–58.

Horton, J. (2008a) Producing *Postman Pat*: The popular construction of idyllic rurality. *Journal of Rural Studies*, 24, 389–398.

Horton, J. (2008b) *Postman Pat* and me: Everyday encounters with an icon of idyllic rurality. *Journal of Rural Studies*, 24, 399–408.

Houlton, D. and Short, B. (1995) Sylvanian families: The production and consumption of a rural community. *Journal of Rural Studies*, 11, 367–386.

Ingold, T. (1993) The temporality of landscape. *World Archaeology*, 25, 152–174.

Ingold, T. (1995) Building, dwelling, living: How people and animals make themselves at home in the world. In *Shifting Contexts: Transformations in Anthropological Knowledge*, ed. M. Strathern. London: Routledge.

Ingold, T. (2000) *The Perception of the Environment*. London: Routledge.

Ingold, T. (2011) *Being Alive: Essays on Movement, Knowledge and Description*. London: Routledge.

Jackson, P. (1989) *Maps of Meaning: An Introduction to Cultural Geography*. London: Unwin Hyman.

Kent, M. (2007) Biogeography and landscape ecology. *Progress in Physical Geography*, 31, 345–355.

Kinsman, P. (1995) Landscape, race and identity: The photography of Ingrid Pollard. *Area*, 27, 300–310.

Latour, B. (1993) *We Have Never Been Modern*. Hemel Hempstead: Harvester Wheatsheaf.

Little, J. (2001) *Gender and Rural Geography*. New York: Prentice Hall.

Little, J. and Austin, P. (1996) Women and the rural idyll. *Journal of Rural Studies*, 12, 101–111.

Lorimer, J. (2005) Cultural geography: The busyness of being "more-than-representational." *Progress in Human Geography*, 29, 83–94.

Mills, A. (2011) *A Dictionary of British Place Names, revised edition*. Oxford: Oxford University Press.

Mingay, G. (ed.) (1989) *The Rural Idyll*. London: Routledge.

Murdoch, J., Lowe, P., Ward, N., and Marsden, T. (2003) *The Differentiated Countryside*. London: Routledge.

Nerlich, B. and Döring, M. (2005) Poetic justice? Rural policy clashes with rural poetry in the 2001 outbreak of foot and mouth disease in the UK. *Journal of Rural Studies*, 21, 165–180.

Newby, H. (1979) *The Deferential Worker*. Harmondsworth: Penguin.

Newby, H., Bell, C., Rose, D., and Saunders, P. (1978) *Property, Paternalism and Power: Class and Control in Rural England*. London: Hutchinson.

Perkins, H. (2006) Commodification: Re-resourcing rural areas. In *Handbook of Rural Studies*, ed. P. Cloke, T. Marsden, and P. Mooney. London: Sage, pp. 243–257.

Rose, G. (1993) *Feminism and Geography*. Minneapolis: University of Minnesota Press.

Sauer, C. (1963) *Land and Life*. Berkeley: University of California Press.

Scruton, R. (1998) Conserving the past. In *Town and Country*, ed. A. Barnett and R. Scruton. London: Jonathan Cape, pp. 317–328.

Short, J.R. (1991) *Imagined Country: Society, Culture and Environment*. London: Routledge.

Thrift, N. (1999) Steps to an ecology of place. In *Human Geography Today*, ed. D. Massey, J. Allen, and P. Sarre. Cambridge: Polity.

Thrift, N. (2008) *Non-Representational Theory: Space, Politics and Affect*. London: Routledge.

Whatmore, S. (2002) *Hybrid Geographies*. London: Sage.

Williams, R. (1985) *The Country and the City*. London: Hogarth Press.

Winter, M. (1996) *Rural Politics*. London: Routledge.

Woodward, R. (2004) *Military Geographies*. Oxford: Blackwell.

Wylie, J. (2002a) An essay on ascending Glastonbury Tor. *Geoforum*, 33, 441–454.

Wylie, J. (2002b) Becoming-icy: Scott and Amundsen's polar voyages, 1910–1913. *Cultural Geographies*, 9, 249–265.

Wylie, J. (2005) A single day's walking: Narrating self and landscape on the South West Coast Path. *Transactions of the Institute of British Geographers*, 30, 234–247.

Wylie, J. (2007) *Landscape*. London: Routledge.

Chapter 22

# Seeing Seeing Seeing the Legal Landscape

*David Delaney*

[L]aw, rather than a mere technical add-on to a morally (or immorally) finished society, is, along of course with a whole range of other cultural realities from the symbolics of faith to the means of production, an active part of it.

(Geertz 1983: 218)

## Introduction

In this chapter I sketch out a critical culturalist conception of the legal that is more service-able to the aims of contemporary cultural geography than are other common approaches. Given the complexity and contestability of both the culture concept and the law idea, I first stipulate my understanding of these and their relation to each other. I then engage the practice of contemporary landscape theorization in light of the law-as-culture thematic. This is fol-lowed by an illustration concerning aesthetic nuisance litigation, which demonstrates the potential for braiding the themes of culture, law, and landscape in cultural geography. Readers interested in a deeper engagement with the increasingly rich literature on law and landscape would do well to start with work by Blomley (1998, 2007, 2010), Duncan and Duncan (2004), Mitchell (2008), and Olwig (2005, 2009), as well as to "follow the citations" in this chapter. For introductions to legal geography more generally see Blomley (1994), Blomley, Delaney and Ford (2001), Holder and Harrison (2003), and Delaney (1998, 2010).

## The Culture Question

Cultural geography is one of the more venerable subfields of the discipline of human geog-raphy. As a scholarly endeavor, it "raises questions about how we live in, experience and

*The Wiley Blackwell Companion to Cultural Geography*, First Edition.
Edited by Nuala C. Johnson, Richard H. Schein, and Jamie Winders.
© 2013 John Wiley & Sons, Ltd. Published 2016 by John Wiley & Sons, Ltd.

shape a particular environment, about what living in and reshaping that environment means to us" (Oakes and Price 2008: 1). But cultural geography is not only a profession or line of work, it is itself a cultural practice – one that is increasingly oriented toward seeing "seeing" the world. It was institutionalized at a time when the distinctions among the subfields seemed clearer and the concept of "culture" itself seemed more self-evident than is presently the case (Baldwin *et al.* 2006; Nuckolls 1998).

In the *Handbook of Cultural Geography* (2003) Anderson *et al.* deal explicitly with the slippery and polysemous character of "culture" and with the debates that this slipperiness has given rise to. They note (at least) five senses of "culture" commonly assumed by cultural geographers: the distribution of things, ways of life, meaning, doings, and power. In their book *Redefining Culture* Baldwin *et al.* (2006) survey the history and politics of the term across a range of disciplines and present a compendium of more than 300 scholarly definitions. Among the most common reference points are meanings, values, beliefs, customs, conventions, symbolic systems, modes of transmission and communication, sense-making, and interactions characteristic of distinctive "ways of life." The sense of "culture" that I will be assuming also locates "the cultural" as collective phenomena involving these kinds of things that are intermediate between the human universal and the individual or idiosyncratic. A core characteristic of the cultural, then, is the contingent collective responses to what may be universal features of human life, say, birth, sexuality, death, work – or, for geographers, ways of world-making (Delaney 2010). We might also fruitfully sidestep any ontological questions about culture and suggest that for the purposes of scholarship "the cultural" names a set of conventional but shifting questions that practitioners find it useful to pursue; that is, less a fact about the world and more a feature of the rhetoric of inquiry. While some cultural phenomena may evince relative stability over different time spans, the foci of cultural analysis are better understood in terms of dynamic, shifting configurations. Whatever else one might say about culture, it is *lived*, and as such, continuously revised in practice. It is this pragmatic, interpretive sense of culture that I take to underpin the project of cultural geography and, more specifically, a "culturalist" conception of "the legal."

## The Law Idea

"Law" and "the legal" can no more be defined uncontroversially than can "culture." As Mezey has written, "When law and culture are thought together, they are conceptualized as distinct realms of action and only marginally related to one another" (2001: 35). This seems to hold true in cultural geography. As a preliminary matter I will briefly survey some approaches to the legal which are commonly encountered in human geographical scholarship that, I feel, retain its "alien" character and render it less useful for these purposes. The first is a common-sense understanding whereby authors refer to some elements of law – say, rules, cases, practices – without problematizing or thematizing them. Readers are required to have no more specialized knowledge of law beyond any competent adult and there is no intention to reveal anything about law as such. A second approach takes an "internalist" perspective. It takes law seriously on its own terms as a complex, technical enterprise and adopts a lawyer's view of blackletter or positivist law. The law is taken to be what "The Law" says it is. Here one refers to cases, doctrines, or judicial procedures in a more sophisticated way than in common-sense approaches but, like them, remains generally uncritical. The bounds of debate over such things as "reform" are provided by the disciplinary concerns of traditional legal scholarship. Where an internalist perspective does not look outside of the conventional practices of law, a third common approach typically does not look sufficiently "inside" the legal and reduces what goes on there to the political. Unlike common sense and internalism, reductionist approaches may be strongly critical, but, speaking generally, what happens *within* the distinctive practices of the legal is either of no concern or is already positioned as political with no remainder. Reductionist approaches have a tendency toward viewing law in strongly instrumental and functional terms. This tendency may neglect important sociological, psychological, normative, or cultural aspects of the distinctively legal. Not every aspect of the social life of law is appropriately understood instrumentally or functionally. Moreover, insofar as the legal *is* necessarily about power, reductionist assumptions may mischaracterize *how* power works in and through the legal in non-instrumental and non-functional ways. Ironically, summarily reducing the legal to the political may impede clearer understanding of how the political itself happens.

Each of these ways of looking at law may have its appropriate purposes, but each is also limited for the purposes of cultural-geographical studies. In this chapter "the distinctively legal" refers to a distinct, complex set of practices, institutions, roles, discourses, mythologies, relationships, performances, normative commitments, and events that are centrally concerned with ruling, authority, dispute resolution, punishment, and so on. That is, "the legal" refers to what common sense and internalism conventionally designate as such, but the approach advocated here asks very different kinds of questions.

## Law and/as Culture

"The legal" is the object of study of numerous interdisciplinary tendencies. The operations of law can and should be interpreted in terms of its politics – struggles, contests, asymmetries of power – and in relation to the workings of political economy more generally. There are also vibrant projects of legal sociology, legal history, law and psychology, law and literature, law and gender studies, and law and geography. In the past twenty years there has also developed robust engagement with the cultural study of law (Coombe 1998, 2001; Sarat and Simon 2003; Rosen 2006).

The characterization of law-*as*-culture that I offer here is not intended to displace other conceptions of the legal. It is not the truth about law. It supplements other non-positivist approaches. My argument is simply that a more culturalist understanding would more comfortably and productively inform the work of cultural geographers. As Sarat and Simon have written, "treating law as a cultural reality means looking at the material structures of law to see it in play and at play, as signs and symbols, fantasies and phantoms" (2003: 13). The legal can readily be seen as an aspect or dimension of any collective social formation. In form and content it may reflect the distinctive preoccupations, commitments, anxieties, and contradictions of the social formation of which it is an important part. This, however, does not entail anything about the homogeneity of these worlds or any consensus regarding these values. On the contrary, if the legal is anything, it is a social site for the disclosure of dissensus, disputes, and the articulation of projects and counter-projects of cultural fabrication. The legal is implicated in *how* these preoccupations and contradictions are given expression, how they are realized, how they are contested, and so on. Cultural analysis of the legal discloses how – practically, pragmatically – salient dimensions of social power (power to, power over) are justified, challenged, rationalized, or legitimated. For cultural geographers such analysis can reveal effects in a range of world-making or geo-generative projects, for example, how spatialities, places, landscapes, nature, various socio-spatial processes and events are made meaningful in the official discourses of power. Law is, of course, a highly important system of meaning(-making). "Law is simply one of the signifying practices that constitute culture and, despite its best efforts, it cannot be divorced from culture. Nor, for that matter, can culture be divorced from law" (Mezey 2001: 46). Closer attention by cultural geographers to law can facilitate the comprehension of *how* such meanings are produced and variously and contentiously interpreted; how they are practically, performatively negotiated and navigated; how such meanings are invested with (or divested of) power; how alternative meanings are dismissed or subordinated; and, finally, why this matters for what matters to cultural geographers.

"Meaning" is one of the core themes of cultural analysis and cultural geographers have long been concerned with investigating the meanings of places and landscapes. But "meaning" means a lot of different things. It often refers to the affective significance of something *for* or *to* someone (see quote from Oakes and Price 2008 above). It can also often reference modes of discursivity. But legal meanings are distinctive and significant in a number of ways. As a lexicon or vocabulary legal discourse is continuous with ordinary language but at the same time it is highly specialized, complex, technical, and characterized by restricted social access. The law itself specifies who may speak authoritatively in the name of the law, and under what conditions and with what effects. In its more technical aspects legal language may effectively be a foreign language to those who are subject to it. Ordinary people may require the services of a professional "translator" (Cunningham 1992). Consider the basic idea of "rights" so prominent in modern, liberal legal regimes. Socio-legal scholars distinguish "ordinary rights consciousness" from expert or professional forms (Ewick and Silbey 1992; Mraz 1997). This distinction is both culturally contingent and highly significant for cultural analysis. Imagine a world otherwise, a world without lawyers and professional legal interpreters. Rights, in turn, are taken to refer to the social allocation of discretion, authority, and power. A culture of rights also implicates social presumptions and performances pertaining to how social actors respect or respond to the rights claims of others and, in cases of alleged "violation" or "infringement," how enforcement unfolds.

Among other important features of modern legal discourse is a strong tendency toward abstraction and dichotomization. In part as a consequence, legal discourse is characterized by a significant and ineradicable amount of indeterminacy. Legal discourse and rights discourse (and, therefore, "rights" themselves and how they operate in social life) are complex and ambiguous. The social, cultural life of rights is characterized by struggles over "meaning": semantic, syntactic, pragmatic; by struggles over the interpretive practices through which such ambiguities and indeterminacies are to be authoritatively resolved; and by struggles over the cultural grounds, narratives, and mythologies that are purported to provide foundation to these practical resolutions. These meaning-making practices are themselves highly significant *cultural* practices. Moreover, unlike other cultural meaning systems, such as those associated with art, religion, or science, law is not optional. It is pervasive and invasive. Everyone is required to participate. Everyone is required to abide by the law, *or else*. Here too we may note a set of distinctive cultural practices, rituals, mythologies, and magical incantations. Consider how cultural dispositions are made manifest in events such as hearings and trials; performances such as the giving of testimony, the signing of contracts; contingent cultural notions of evidence and proof; the calibration of notions of "objectivity" in relation to contested conceptions of "justice."

What we call "law" or "the legal" is at once a domain of culture, a site of cultural production or fabrication, a collocation of cultural events wherein other cultural concerns are worked on and provisionally worked out in accordance with culturally contingent modes and styles of validation and invalidation. Law-as-culture (popular and professional) is continuously implicated in social spatializations and respatializations; in the formation, maintenance, and revision of places; in the production and transformation of landscapes. Foregrounding cultural dimensions of the legal draws attention to the ways in which distinctive and contingent practices and projects are implicated in the social phenomena that cultural geographers in particular seek to investigate, interpret, explain, or criticize. This may be most obvious with respect to the production of "meaning." Law-as-culture highlights distinctive discursive and interpretive practices and the contingent hierarchical social organization of interpretive capacity. Because legal meanings are always *about* power, core questions about power and the production of geographies *of* power can be pursued by investigating how distinctively legal interpretive practices are organized, how rival interpretations are winnowed and prioritized. Insofar as legal signification is pervasive and comprehensive, the arrangements and social dynamics of the world – or life-worlds – can be better understood as cultural artifacts. Every centimeter of the world is over-coded with legal signifiers; every event that takes place does so within complex, ambiguous, shifting fields of legal meanings. These meanings may refer to how power is to unfold. Every landscape "item" – including embodied creatures – is the material referent of legal discourse. If, as Schein suggests, "the cultural landscape becomes the *discourse materialized*" (1997: 663), then perhaps landscapes become the materialization of the legal as such.

## The Practice of Landscape Theorization

While a culturalist take on the legal may be useful for many cultural-geographic projects, I suggest that it is particularly fruitful with respect to landscape studies. Just as cultural geography is itself a cultural practice, so is the more specific endeavor of landscape theorization.

As a cultural practice landscape theorization appears to be as vibrant as it ever was and much more diverse. It is particularly significant that one of the divergences between ordinary and professional understandings (as well as between traditional and "newer" cultural geographies) is associated with the problematization of *seeing* itself (Rose 2002; Nash 1996; Wylie 2007). Where ordinary and traditional conceptions of landscape define it as "the scene within the range of the observer's vision," or "a portion of the earth's surface that can be comprehended in a glance," contemporary views are more likely to be suspicious of the hegemony of vision, visuality, "the gaze" or, in Wylie's phrasing, "spectoral epistemology" (2006). Equally important, contemporary theorization gives much greater explicit attention to the *unseen*, or the operations on landscapes of what has *actively* been hidden, obscured, masked; or to what is not there to *be seen* at all. Wylie has written that "Landscape, as a particular type of visual representation, mystifies, renders opaque, distorts, hides, occludes reality" (2007: 69). Similarly, Mitchell claims that "the landscape itself is anything but self-evident . . . landscape *obscures*" (2008: 33). It also "conceals." Insofar as the task of much landscape theory in cultural geography is to "reveal" or disclose the hidden truths about landscape (Henderson 2003: 189) and to reveal the operations, conditions, and effects of power that are not discernable to the untrained eye of naïve observers, then a culturalist *legal* perspective can be quite useful. As Mezey notes, "law operates even when it appears not to, . . . legal ground rules are all the more effective because they are not visible as law" (2001: 48). This should be as applicable to landscape processes and practices as anything else. I will forego a recitation of the historical landmarks of post-Sauerian Anglophone cultural geography (see Henderson 2003; Wilson and Groth 2003). Instead I will simply list a handful of significant themes that more contemporary theorists have developed and debated. I will then briefly show how a culturalist notion of the legal comports with or furthers these thematic concerns.

In contrast with traditional practitioners, contemporary cultural geographers are more comfortable seeing landscapes as "duplicitous" (Daniels 1989), as marked by significant "tensions" (Cresswell 2003; Wylie 2007) or contradictions (Mitchell 2002; Till 2004). There is a much greater emphasis on regarding landscapes as having been "produced" (and not merely created) and greater interest in investigating the social and political-economic conditions, contests, and struggles through which production takes place. Some theorists argue that landscapes should be understood less as static "things" than as dynamic processes as such. "Landscapes are always in the process of 'becoming,' no longer reified or concretized – inert and there – but continually under scrutiny, at once manipulated and manipulable, always subject to change, and everywhere implicated in the ongoing formation of social life" (Schein 1997: 662). Indeed, Massey and others argue that landscape should better be understood as event (Massey 2006), practices, or doings (Cresswell 2003; Wylie 2007). Landscape is also frequently discussed in terms of discourses and textuality (Duncan and Duncan 1988; Duncan 1990). For Henderson, "Landscape as discourse is the idea that the landscape is an ideological expression, particularly one that aestheticizes power and subjugation" (2003: 182). The critiques of visuality not only problematize, relativize, and politicize the cultural acts of seeing (Rose 2002; Nash 1996; Cresswell 2003; Wylie 2007) but may be critical of the privileging of sight over other senses or modes of engaging with the world. Wylie advocates "increased attention to *tactile*, as opposed to *visual* landscape experiences" (2007: 166). In the following sections I will simply touch on some of the cultural-geographic themes I've mentioned and note how a culturalist conception of the legal might prove useful.

We can begin to sketch how these themes can be productively informed by a critical culturalist notion of the legal starting with the more traditional notion of landscape as "the visible, tangible scene" (Lewis 1979). This may align neatly with the notion of cultural geography as concerned with the elucidation of "the distribution of things" (Anderson *et al.* 2003). Clearly, legal phenomena are deeply implicated in the social determination of the hows and whys of what is where – as well as what it (landscape, world) *looks* like. It is incontestable that distinctively legal processes and events, such as those related to zoning, planning, land-use regulation, architectural review boards, building codes, conservation, and the broader official governance of space and place, strongly condition the appearance of things in the world. In our world nearly every "thing" is allowed, forbidden, mandatory, and/or regulated in some way. Every thing (and many no-things) has a distinctly legal significance.

Affirming the idea of landscapes as having been produced, we can examine the distinctly legal conditions of production and revision. Cases in point are the twentieth-century American landscapes of race and racialization: the ubiquity of race signage (Abel 2010), the manifest material inequalities that were reflected and reinforced through architectural practices and the socio-spatial organization of public facilities, the very presence and absence of categories of people in the lived-in landscapes. These are inextricable from the historical-legal metaphysics of racial categorization itself, such as the work of "the one drop rule." These landscapes were quite literally and deliberately *made* out of distinctively *legal* meanings.

The themes of landscape as process and culture as process are implicit in landscape as product. Landscapes are not produced once and for all. They are continuously re-produced, actively maintained, adjusted, and revised. Landscapes are lived and experienced, if not in some sense alive, at least "animated" (Rose and Wylie 2006). They are not passively interpreted as texts. Rather, the constitutive meanings are taken up by situated actors as instructions of a sort for how to navigate and engage them. Much of the dynamism of landscapes can be apprehended with reference to the social life of rights: how rights are continuously deployed by those who "have them" (through signs, walls, doors) as well as by how these deployments are responded to by others. Rights assertions, tacit or explicit, are most commonly confirmed by others; but they are occasionally disconfirmed or disregarded.

At a finer level of analysis such legal landscape processes resolve to legal landscape practices. We "do" landscape largely through how we do the legal. I will discuss property-as-culture in the following section. For now it is sufficient to note that we *do* landscape largely in accordance with how we are variously figured by law as, for example, "owner" (homeowner, landlord, employer, developer, and so on) and "non-owner" (stranger, neighbor, tenant, guest, employee); as legal specialist (police, park ranger, inspector, regulator), as "citizen" or "alien," and on and on. We do landscape as we do rights, duties, immunities, and powers. We buy and sell, we use, we destroy, we are displaced by others, we abide by regulations or we don't.

If we understand landscape as discourse (or in Schein's demonstration, a complex collocation of discourses [1997]), then the significance of specifically legal discourse is of profound importance to any adequate understanding of the hows and whys of landscape. But, again, beneath or behind common-sense recognition of "property," "sovereignty," or regulation is an enormous (but patterned) stock of cultural preoccupations, available narratives and counter-narratives of order and disorder, justice and injustice, freedom and coercion. These are not simple categorical distinctions. A cultural-geographic analysis of the workings of binaries such as these and the effects of their "imprints" on the landscape needs to be attentive to pervasive ambiguities, contradictions, or "tensions," and to how these are provisionally stabilized or suppressed in practice. This directs attention to the cultural practices of distinctively legal modes of argument and to projects oriented toward the expansion, contraction, and provisional finalization of legal meaning.

By this time the relevance of a culturalist conception of the legal to the theme of landscapes of power should be evident enough. Power itself is a cultural phenomenon and much of the life of social power is refracted through legal discourses, forms of consciousness, practices, and institutions. Much of this finds expression in "rights": claims and counter-claims, validations and invalidations. Rights give social expression and experiential form to wider culturally and historically specific power relations such as those pertaining to race, gender, sexuality, labor, class, citizenship, and so on. Lived fields of power are inextricable from contestable fields of legal meanings as these are concretized in landscapes.

## The Unseeable

Finally, we return to the theme of visuality. As mentioned, the cultural operations of the legal strongly condition what is to be seen in the landscape. But law-as-culture also strongly conditions how seeing happens and how visuality is socially, culturally organized. It allows us to ask: who sees how? We may (variously) "see" landscapes through (versions of) the public/private distinction. Seeing landscapes with and through legal consciousness tells us what is open or closed, what is mine, theirs, ours; what is forbidden, acceptable, dangerous. It tells us how we may and may not engage with the world and what the consequences of engaging one way or another might be. Where one might "see" landscape through ordinary, standard-issue legal consciousness, another may see it very differently through more specialized or professional versions of legal consciousness: as real estate, as regulated, as investment oppor-tunity, as "blight." How one sees the landscape through legal discourse plays recursively back on how one sees oneself. And if these observers are empowered to act in accordance with rights and obligations, they may act in, on, or with the landscape in ways that are profoundly consequential. Recall the distinction between ordinary and professional modalities of legal consciousness. Where the former *might* be servicable in apprehending a landscape and seeing "property," it is unlikely to structure seeing a landscape as having been produced by "the expansion of the public use doctrine" or "the application of the exception to the doctrine of changed conditions" or "the test for aesthetic nuisance." These differing ways of seeing seeing may have significant social and material effects. We might also investigate how some ways of seeing are valorized over alternative ways and how these become invested with power. As I will show below, we might see how visuality may be subordinated to other sensory modali-ties in ways that affect rights to landscape production.

Now, regard the nearest landscape. Can the number of legal traces or signifiers that con-stitute it – its "items," the terms of their assemblage, the ways in which these signifiers can be taken up and acted upon by differently situated people – even be counted? Is it plausible to assume that these form a coherent, unequivocal set that is immune to strategic interpretive restructuring? The answer to these questions is, of course, no. Any and every landscape as "made" is made meaningful by an open-ended store of such signifiers – not once and for all, but continuously. At a given moment such meanings may appear to have congealed to provide sufficient coherence and stability for the purposes of pragmatic prediction. But they are always vulnerable to (strategic) destabilization by one who sees things differently.

## Seeing Seeing the Landscape: Aesthetic Nuisance Litigation

Here is a suggestive illustration of what a cultural-legal geographic analysis of landscape might take into account. If, formally, property law organizes social relationships with respect to things, including abstract spaces, in terms of the lived discourses of rights, no-rights, duties, immunities, powers, and so on, it thereby also organizes social relations to landscapes as visual (and other perceptual and sensual) fields. It casts such perceptual relations in the dis-tinctive idioms of legal discourse and vests them with power. It is used to allocate rights, to determine what is where and what the world will look, smell, and sound like. The core "right to use" may be conditioned by those cultural concerns associated with the notion of aesthet-ics. For immediate purposes let's stipulate that this refers to *how seeing feels*. In some situa-tions an owner might exercise her right to use her property in such a way that results in what a non-owner regards as unsightly or ugly. Let's say she uses her front yard as a place to put junked cars, broken machinery and such. In many such situations a non-owner, say, a neigh-bor, will consider that he has no choice but to lump it (or mitigate it by planting a hedge or building a fence, thereby reconfiguring the landscape) so long as he understands that his offending neighbor "has the right" and that "having the right" presupposes the "right" to disregard the sensibilities of one's neighbors. However, a core maxim (or magical incantation; Allen 2008) of liberal property law discourse is *sic utere tuo ut alienum non laedas* (one should use one's own property in such a manner as not to injure that of another). Thinking through this maxim, *and seeing the landscape through it*, the offended neighbor (or his lawyer) might redescribe ugliness and the willful production of ugliness as a kind of "injuring": thus the uglifying neighbor actually does *not* "have the right," she "exceeds her rights." Further, he can come to feel that his own rights have been infringed or invaded. As a meaning-conferring practice the offended neighbor, or his lawyer, is activating the legal subdiscourse of tort, and more specifically nuisance. As suggested earlier, "nuisance" is both a word in ordinary language and a technical legal term. The divergences of these discursive registers and the constraints of translatability between them are (culturally) significant. With the assistance of his attorney the offended neighbor becomes transformed into the cultural figure "plaintiff" and renders the offender as "defendant." Now, each party may have an attorney to act as an informed proxy in a ritualized, adversarial encounter oriented toward persuading a judge and/or jury to interpret the specific landscape through their preferred arrangement of legal categories: the defendant does or does not "have the right," the plaintiff is or is not "injured," ugliness is or is not categorized as a legally cognizable "nuisance," the state may or may not demand the abatement of such nuisance, and so on. A plaintiff in these cases typically argues that the ugliness is not inert but effectively diminishes his own "right to use and enjoy" his own property and that in so reducing the sticks in his "bundle of rights" the neighbor has effectively taken this right (Coletta 1987; Dodson 2002). One also typically argues that proximity to ugliness reduces the economic value of property (Smith and Fernandez 1991). As refracted through the overlapping discourses of property and tort, the uglification of a landscape can be redescribed as a kind of theft.

Peering more deeply into the cultural practices of aesthetic nuisance litigation as they pertain to the conditions of landscape production, we can see that the outcomes of these cases – and so their material consequences – often turn on culturally specific metaphysical assumptions about human perception and the spatiality of perception. These assumptions, in turn, underpin conventional claims concerning the institutional distribution of state power and, thereby, claims about the legitimacy of state action. Aesthetic nuisance claims rest on the analogy of ugliness to more conventionally recognized (private) nuisances involving sound (loudness), smell (foul odors), and particulate matter. Our appreciation of the work of nuisance discourse on landscape practices may be enhanced if we recognize that experts in the law of nuisance themselves acknowledge that "nuisance law has been called 'contingent and unsummarizable,' 'a wilderness of law,' 'an impenetrable jungle,' 'a legal garbage can' full of 'vagueness, uncertainty and confusion,' 'a mystery,' 'a quagmire' and a 'mongrel' " (Halper 1998). Traditionally, and still most commonly, seeing the world is understood as a significantly different kind of experience than hearing or smelling it. Based on how the difference is conceptualized through legal discourse, visual affronts are most commonly excluded from the legal category of "nuisance" and therefore legally interpreted as not "injuring." Landscape practices that produce what plaintiffs may feel injured by (absent an aural or olfactory component) are categorized as "within the rights" of an owner. Such an understanding, of course, is a contingent cultural, historical (and, perhaps, political) way of seeing seeing. Acknowledging this allows *us* to more clearly see seeing seeing landscapes through the mediating technologies of legal discourses.

Among the reasons commonly given by judges for maintaining the legal distinction between aural and olfactory affronts on the one hand, and visual offenses on the other, is that where loud noises and foul odors cannot be avoided by people who are subjected to them, ugliness can be mitigated by simply not looking. The spatial metaphysics of this seems to be that noxious sounds and smells are understood as originating within the space of the defendant's control and as escaping, crossing boundaries, and invading the space of neighbors (thereby "infringing" rights), whereas sight is conceptualized as originating in the plaintiff's space and traveling outward toward the defendant's space. This understanding, in turn, renders the plaintiff at least partially responsible for his own "injury." This is also supported by the notion that the remedy is within the power of the plaintiff – don't look or, if possible, erect a barrier. Whereas we cannot *not* hear loud noises or smell foul odors, we *can* not look upon ugliness. But there is more. Insofar as there is a broad cultural disposition toward viewing vision as a "higher-order" sensory modality than hearing or smelling, there is a relatively easy elision from "sense" to "sensibilities" with respect to seeing. Indeed, aural and olfactory nuisances are not regarded as *aesthetic* at all. These are considered to be amenable to *objective* analysis whereas alleged visual nuisances are aestheticized and thereby rendered as *subjective*. As one judge in an aesthetic nuisance appeal put it,

> Aesthetic considerations are fraught with subjectivity. One man's pleasure may be another man's perturbation, and vice versa. What is aesthetically pleasing to one may totally displease another ... Judicial forage into such a nebulous area would be chaotic. Any imaginary good from doing so is far outweighed by the lurking danger of unduly circumscribing inherent rights of ownership of property and grossly intimidating their lawful exercise. This court has no inclination to knowingly infuse the law with such rampant uncertainty. (*Ness v. Albert*, 665 S.W. 2d, 1 at 4 [1984])

That is, seeing the legal landscape (and in so doing, not seeing "injury") is conditioned by the pragmatic operations of the (Cartesian?) object/subject epistemological distinction. Where ugliness is commonly regarded by judges as being "in the eye of the beholder," smelliness is not in the nose of the beholder but an objectively verifiable fact about the world. And, as is well known, some beholders are much more refined or sensitive than others. It follows from this – as a matter of obvious cultural logic – that the use rights of an owner ought not to be held hostage to the refined sensibilities (taste!) of her neighbors. Within the ritual cultural space of a courtroom, it also follows that judges are ill-equipped to validate or invalidate the discrepant sensibilities of neighbors.

Aesthetic nuisance cases, as cultural-legal-geographic events, begin with landscape practices – including the perception of these practices by others. They are organized around conventional authorized modes of adversarial contestation. Often enough these contests are "political" in the most fundamental sense. No doubt many of these political contests are most accurately understood in terms of conflicts between factions of capital, capital and labor, or inter-class struggles (between, say, affluent second-home owners in rural areas and local working people for whom "junked cars" are spare parts or inventory). But frequently the contests are not so easily shoehorned into our preferred analytic categories, and the more powerful party does not always win. Cases like this may suggest that *how* "ordinary people" see landscapes and their landscaping practices are strongly conditioned by rights consciousness; by conventional understandings of their own rights, the rights of others, the felt sense of being "injured," the possibility of remedy, and so on. Likewise, the mutability of legal categories is conditioned by historical-political shifts in the culture of seeing. Professional intermediaries translate these "naïve" understandings into the formal categories, syllogisms, maxims, and tests associated with nuisance. They participate in technical, adversarial competitions for the validation of made-meanings. Judges respond by activating cultural understandings of the spatiality of perception which underpin their understanding of their own capacity to intervene in the production and transformation of landscapes. Common-sense, internalist, and instrumental-functionalist perspectives on the legal miss this. They may thereby miss significant vectors and moments of contingency in the cultural processes of landscape production and collective habitation. If the cultural practices of cultural geography and professional landscape theorization are oriented toward helping us see how seeing-the-world happens, then a culturalist *legal* geographical "lens" can be quite handy for helping *us* see ("reveal," "disclose," or "unmask") *how* we see *how* we see.


## References

Abel, E. (2010) *Signs of the Times: The Visual Politics of Jim Crow*. Berkeley: University of California Press.

Allen, J. (2008) A theory of adjudication: Law as magic. *Suffolk University Law Review*, 41, 773–831.

Anderson, K., Domosh, M., Pile, S., and Thrift, N. (eds.) (2003) *Handbook of Cultural Geography*. London: Sage.

Baldwin, J.R., Faulkner, S.L., Hecht, M.L., and Lindsley, S.L. (2006) *Redefining Culture: Perspectives Across Disciplines*. Mahwah, NJ: Lawrence Erlbaum Associates.

Blomley, N. (1994) *Law, Space and the Geographies of Power*. New York: Guilford Press.

Blomley, N. (1998) Landscapes of property. *Law and Society Review*, 32, 567–612.

Blomley, N. (2007) Making private property: Enclosure, common right and the work of hedges. *Rural History*, 18, 1–21.

Blomley, N. (2010) Cuts, flows and the geographies of property. *Law, Culture and the Humanities*, 7, 203–216.

Blomley, N., Delaney, D., and Ford, R. (2001) *The Legal Geographies Reader*. Oxford: Blackwell.

Coletta, R. (1987) The case for aesthetic nuisance: Rethinking traditional judicial attitudes. *Ohio State Law Journal*, 48, 141–176.

Coombe, R. (1998) Critical cultural legal studies. *Yale Journal of Law and Humanities*, 10, 463–486.

Coombe, R. (2001) Is there a cultural studies of law? In *A Companion to Cultural Studies*, ed. T. Miller. Oxford: Blackwell, pp. 36–62.

Cresswell, T. (2003) Landscape and the obliteration of practice. In *Handbook of Cultural Geography*, ed. K. Anderson, M. Domosh, S. Pile, and N. Thrift. London: Sage, pp. 269–281.

Cunningham, C. (1992) The lawyer as translator, representation as text: Towards an ethnography of legal discourse. *Cornell Law Review*, 77, 1298–1387.

Daniels, S. (1989) Marxism, culture and the duplicity of landscape. In *New Models in Geography*, ed. R. Peet and N. Thrift. London: Unwin Hyman, pp. 196–220.

Delaney, D. (1998) *Race, Place and the Law: 1836–1948*. Austin: University of Texas Press.

Delaney, D. (2010) *The Spatial, the Legal and the Pragmatics of World-Making: Nomospheric Investigations*. London: Routledge.

Dodson, R. (2002) Rethinking private nuisance law: Recognizing aesthetic nuisance in the new millennium. *South Carolina Environmental Law Journal*, 10, 1–22.

Duncan, J.S. (1990) *The City as Text: The Politics of Landscape Interpretation in the Kandyan Kingdom*. New York: Cambridge University Press.

Duncan, J. and Duncan, N. (1988) (Re)reading the landscape. *Environment and Planning D: Society and Space*, 6, 117–126.

Duncan, J. and Duncan, N. (2004) *Landscapes of Privilege*. London: Routledge.

Ewick, P. and Silbey, S. (1992) Conformity, contestation and resistance: An account of legal consciousness. *New England Law Review*, 26, 731–750.

Geertz, C. (1983) *Local Knowledge: Further Essays in Interpretive Anthropology*. New York: Basic Books.

Halper, L. (1998) Untangling the nuisance knot. *Boston College Environmental Affairs Law Review*, 89–130.

Henderson, G. (2003) What (else) we talk about when we talk about landscape. In *Everyday America: Cultural Landscape Studies After J.B. Jackson*, ed. C. Wilson and P. Groth. Berkeley: University of California Press, pp. 178–198.

Holder, J. and Harrison, C. (2003) *Law and Geography*. Oxford: Oxford University Press.

Lewis, P. (1979) Axioms for reading the landscape: Some guides to the American scene. In *The Interpretation of Ordinary Landscapes*, ed. D. Meinig. New York: Oxford University Press, pp. 11–32.

Massey, D. (2006) Landscape as provocation. *Journal of Material Culture*, 11, 33–48.

Mezey, N. (2001) Law as culture. *Yale Journal of Law and the Humanities*, 13, 35–67.

Mitchell, D. (2002) Cultural landscapes: The dialectical landscape: Recent landscape research in human geography. *Progress in Human Geography*, 26, 381–389.

Mitchell, D. (2008) New axioms for reading the landscape: Paying attention to political economy and social justice. In *Political Economies of Landscape Change: Places of Integrative Power*, ed. J. Wescoat and D. Johnston. Dordrecht: Springer, pp. 29–49.

Mraz, J. (1997) Of law and the tears of things: Notes on the varieties of legal consciousness. *Political and Legal Anthropology Review*, 20, 101–114.

Nash, C. (1996) Reclaiming vision: Looking at landscapes and the body. *Gender, Place and Culture*, 3, 143–169.

Nuckolls, C. (1998) *Culture: A Problem That Cannot Be Solved*. Madison: University of Wisconsin Press.

Oakes, T. and Price, P.L. (2008) Introduction. In *The Cultural Geography Reader*, ed. T. Oakes and P.L. Price. London: Routledge, pp. 11–14.

Olwig, K. (2005) Law, polity and the changing meaning of landscape. *Landscape Research*, 30, 293–298.

Olwig, K. (2009) The landscape of "customary" law versus that of "natural" law. In *Justice, Power and the Political Landscape*, ed. K. Olwig and D. Mitchell. London: Routledge, pp. 11–32.

Rose, M. (2002) Landscape and labyrinths. *Geoforum*, 33, 455–467.

Rose, M. and Wylie, J. (2006) Animating landscape. *Society and Space*, 24, 457–479.

Rosen, L. (2006) *Law as Culture: An Invitation*. Princeton: Princeton University Press.

Sarat, A. and Simon, J. (2003) Cultural analysis, cultural studies and the situation of legal scholarship. In *Cultural Analysis, Cultural Studies and the Law*, ed. A. Sarat and J. Simon. Durham, NC: Duke University Press, pp. 1–36.

Schein, R. (1997) A place of landscape: A conceptual framework for interpreting an American scene. *Annals of the Association of American Geographers*, 87, 660–680.

Smith, G.P. and Fernandez, G.W. (1991) The price of beauty: An economic approach to aesthetic nuisance. *Harvard Environmental Law Review*, 15, 53–83.

Till, K.E. (2004) Political landscapes. In *A Companion to Cultural Geography*, ed. J.S. Duncan, N.C. Johnson, and R.H. Schein. Oxford: Blackwell, pp. 347–364.

Wilson, C. and Groth, P. (eds.) (2003) *Everyday America: Cultural Landscape Studies After J.B. Jackson*. Berkeley: University of California Press.

Wylie, J. (2006) Depths and folds: On landscape and the gazing subject. *Environment and Planning D: Society and Space*, 24, 519–535.

Wylie, J. (2007) *Landscape*. London: Routledge.

Chapter 23

# Aging

*Elizabeth A. Gagen*

## Introduction

In the original edition of the *Companion to Cultural Geography*, my contribution was a chapter entitled "Landscapes of Childhood and Youth" (Gagen 2004). In the new *Companion*, still residing in the section on landscapes, this chapter takes a different approach to age-specific identities, asking readers to think beyond the category of childhood and toward the relational process of aging. This orientation reflects a number of changes in cultural-geographic research on age. First, the literature on children's geographies has increased exponentially, creating a less homogeneous and arguably more contested subfield. Second, some critics are directing attention away from the narrow focus on one end of the age continuum and proposing that if we are interested in the socio-spatial processes through which age is constructed and experienced, then some sensitivity to intergenerational relationships and the relational process of aging ought to be valuable, if not necessary (Hopkins and Pain 2007; Vanderbeck 2007).

One of the outcomes of this critical intervention has been to bring into conversation two areas of geographical research which have traditionally operated as discrete subfields: geographies of the young and geographies of the old (Hagestad and Uhlenberg 2005). Influenced in part by developments in sociological and anthropological research, geographers have become increasingly interested in concepts such as intergenerationality, life course, and transitions. Dissatisfied with the notion that children and young people can be properly understood outside of their constitutive relationship with other family members and members of the wider community, many of whom are adults, geographers have looked to alternative conceptual frameworks for understanding age-based identities. In what follows, I look, first, at how emerging research in geography approaches the issue of aging and examine three related

*The Wiley Blackwell Companion to Cultural Geography*, First Edition.
Edited by Nuala C. Johnson, Richard H. Schein, and Jamie Winders.
© 2013 John Wiley & Sons, Ltd. Published 2016 by John Wiley & Sons, Ltd.

approaches to aging: intergenerationality, life course, and transitions. These three approaches are not necessarily distinct fields; indeed, they have more in common than separates them. They do, however, represent choices in the way geographers make sense of aging identities. I then look at the geography of aging, paying particular attention to cultural-geographic understandings of the spatiality of aging and the built environment.

## Intergenerationality, Life Course, Transitions: Alternatives to the Compartmentalization of Youth and Old Age

In a world where universals rarely apply, we can be sure of one thing: we are all aging. Our identities are shaped by the age we are, the age we appear to be, and the ideals and expectations that mediate our experience of biological age. In social science, the role of age in constructing identities has gained increasing attention alongside other markers of identity like race, gender, ethnicity, and sexuality (Bytheway 1995; Featherstone and Wernick 1995; Jamieson, Harper, and Victor 1997). The peculiarities of age and the aging process, however, have produced a complex set of traditions. What has become apparent over the last two decades, particularly in geography, is the disproportionate attention devoted to individuals at the lower end of the age spectrum. The rise of children's geographies has produced a rich literature on the spatialities of childhood and youth and continues to grow in range and depth. Geographies of old age, on the other hand, have received comparatively less attention (McHugh 2006).

While the study of aging has traditionally been wide ranging, incorporating health and social care professionals as well as social scientists from sociology, psychology, and planning, it has yet to take root in geography as squarely as some might like, particularly in social and cultural geography (Andrews and Phillips 2006). It is revealing that Graham Rowles' (1978) landmark ethnography of five elderly people, evocatively titled *Prisoners of Space?*, is yet to be surpassed in the geographical literature and is still a regular reference point in a subfield that struggles to gain critical mass. Revealing, too, is an examination of the contributors to Andrews and Phillips' (2006) multidisciplinary volume on *Ageing and Place*. While one might presume cultural geographers have much to contribute to such a collection, the limited presence of geographers in it is stark.

This is not to underplay the very significant work that some geographers have done on aging and the elderly (e.g., Warnes 1982, 1989; Joseph and Martin-Matthews 1993; Joseph and Chalmers 1995; Bartlett and Phillips 2000; Hodge 2008; Davies and James 2011). The point rather is that the work produced in geographical gerontology has tended to come from the traditions of demography, planning, and social policy. This point was taken up by Harper and Laws (1995) in their review of work on aging and geography in which they called for a fresh infusion of perspectives from cultural geography and social theory to enliven and broaden geographical encounters with aging. Fifteen years on, there has been a steady growth of research on aging, partly in response to shifting demographic patterns that are seeing a significant extension of life in the global North. The obvious repercussions this extension will have on pension provision, health care, housing, and infrastructure have produced understandable academic attention. However, given the cultural significance of old age in terms of identity, the aging body, emotional health, and segregation, cultural geographers still demonstrate only limited interest in the subject (there are, of course, exceptions; see McHugh 2003, 2007; Andrews *et al.* 2006; Milligan 2009). Indeed, as Andrews and Phillips (2006) note (see also Kearns and Andrews 2006), we are far more likely to find geographical attention brought to bear on aging issues by non-geographers in social gerontology than we are to find social and cultural geographers paying attention to the elderly.

Despite the relative inattention given to the elderly, aging as a *process* has come under recent scrutiny in geography. As mentioned above, the issue of aging as a relational process that affects identities across the life course has been summoned by a number of geographers who call for more intergenerational perspectives (Hopkins and Pain 2007; Vanderbeck 2007; Hopkins et al. 2011; Tarrant 2010; Holloway and Pimlott-Wilson 2011). To date, this call has emerged from researchers concerned primarily with children and young people rather than with the elderly. These interventions ask that we open up the study of aging to understand it as a process affecting identities across the generational continuum rather than something operating at the margins of age (Hopkins and Pain 2007). The charge is that not only has old age been relatively neglected, but so too have the so-called "middle years" of adulthood, which are equally affected by aging (Maxey 2009). Before examining the rationale for such an intergenerational approach to aging in geography, it is worth briefly reflecting on the way aging has been understood in the social sciences.

In the 1980s, an emerging trend in social theory challenged the accepted term "life cycle," which theorized aging as a sequential and predictable process through which individuals progressively moved between birth and death (Rossi 1985; Spencer 1990). "Envisaged as a series of fixed stages and roles through which every individual moved as they aged, this cyclical pattern was held to be repeated and to remain unchanged across the generation" (Hockey and James 2003: 11). Instead, sociologists, anthropologists, psychologists, and geographers adopted the term "life course" to evoke a more fluid and contingent process of aging. The shift from "cycle" to "course" conveyed a greater sense of aging as an unpredictable process, whereby changes are dependent on socio-spatial context and transitions themselves are understood to be variable, indeterminate, and incomplete.

With the shift to life course studies came renewed attention to the role that aging played in constructing identities. In the 1990s, when poststructural accounts of identity construction were complicating received understandings of racial, gender, sexual, and ethnic identities, the notion that identities were also fundamentally contingent upon age came under greater scrutiny. Indeed, Hockey and James (2003: 3) argue that age "has become one of the key bases for the production of social identity, acting as a way to classify and order the passing of time in an individual's life." However, in sociological accounts of aging, such as Hockey and James' (see also Jenkins 1996), time is taken to be the dominant register by which aging is understood. In geography, an appreciation of life course was further developed by Monk and Katz (1993), whose insistence on the importance of *space* in moderating the experience of time across the life course brought new complexity to the subject.

As life course and aging have become more widely interrogated, greater attention has been directed toward the transitions that punctuate the aging process (Henderson *et al.* 2007). Indeed, transitions have become *the* focal point for thinking through the process of aging. However, in geography, despite the developments in life course studies and work in critical gerontology, the transitions that have garnered most attention are those between youth and adulthood. In part, this focus is a legitimate response to the very real significance of youth transitions in the twenty-first century. Changes in the global economy and shifts in modern social and economic structuring, for example, have placed unparalleled pressures on young people transitioning to adult roles (McDowell 2003; Jeffrey and McDowell 2004). Such work builds on a rich tradition in sociology and cultural studies that examines the negotiations of working-class youth as they maneuver their way into adult labor markets (Hall and Jefferson

1976; Willis 1977). More recent work has broken out of this narrow focus on young working-class men, unpacking the spatial construction of youth transitions and the teenager (Valentine 2003; Weller 2006), examining transitions from youth to parenting (Bynner 2001; Thomson 2008), analyzing young people's transition to university (Hopkins 2006), and extending work on transitions to the global South (Punch 2002; Hampshire *et al.* 2011). This work presents a complex picture of transitions to adulthood for both young men and women. Moreover, rather than understanding transitions as absolute processes, whereby one identity is singularly replaced by another, this work demonstrates the incomplete nature of such transitions. As Punch (2002) argues, the transition to adult identities can be better understood as a "negoti-ated independence" that is ongoing rather than final.

Geographical work on transitions has brought attention to bear on important moments in the life course when identities require renegotiation. However, as Hopkins and Pain (2007) are keen to point out, the focus on childhood and youth in geography represents a skewed perspective on life course transitions. Along with others (Vanderbeck 2007; Maxey 2009), they call for a relational approach to aging which better accounts for the interactions and relations *across* generations that contribute to the mediation of social identities. By compart-mentalizing age groups and examining them as if they exist in discrete isolation from other generations, we neglect important features of identity. Geographies of childhood and youth, in particular, have been guilty of focusing disproportionately on the discontinuity between young people and adults (Kjørholt 2003; Vanderbeck 2007). The assumption of difference and divergence underpinned much early work on children's geographies, justifying the exclu-sive examination of childhood and youth as a category in opposition to, and frequently in conflict with, adults. While this separation is heuristically justifiable in some circumstances, it has meant that other forms of relations – perhaps less combative and more supportive – are missed in the analytic imperative to see generational difference.

In light of these recent calls to recognize intergenerational relations, one site that has come under increased scrutiny is the family. Parental identity and parent–child relations have been ongoing, if stuttering, concerns in geography (e.g., Aitken 2009 on fathering; Holloway 1998a, 1998b on mothering), as indeed has the negotiation of childcare relations within and outside of the family (Gregson and Lowe 1995; England 1996; Pratt 2004). In general, however, geographers have given family life only limited attention – particularly the personal and intimate relations that comprise family life (Valentine and Hughes 2011). While there are isolated examples of geographies of family life (e.g., Sibley 1995; Punch 2005, 2007), Valentine and Hughes describe the family as a "peculiar absent presence in the discipline of geography" (2011: 122). This lack of attention to the family is problematic, they argue, because despite reformulations of the form and structure of families in the late twentieth century, it still endures as a defining set of relationships in most people's lives (see also Cherlin 2009). Reciprocal relationships of care and support and affective personal relations still rely heavily on intergenerational interdependence. For this reason, the family – and, more impor-tantly, intrafamilial intergenerationality – ought to form a more central research focus in geography.

While not so widespread as in other social science disciplines, there is evidence that geog-raphers are increasingly adopting the framework of intergenerationality to make sense of everyday spaces and cultural reproduction within families. In the recent volume *Geographies of Children, Youth and Families* (Holt 2011), the first since Holloway and Valentine's (2000) defining text *Children's Geographies: Playing, Living, Learning*, there are five contributions devoted specifically to intergenerationality and the family. Elsewhere in geography, intergenerationality is being applied more widely to make sense of different sites of identity production. This work can be divided into three broad areas of interest. First, some useful work has highlighted the extent to which intergenerational relationships provide both material and emotional support (Valentine and Hughes 2011). In particular, the relationship between children, parents, and grandparents is being reformulated in ways that are spatially as well as generationally defined, as social, political, and economic change reformulate family structures, increase the occurrence of lone parents, and increase the importance of extended family (Harper 2005). This approach is taken up by Tarrant (2010) in a novel study of the importance of relational geographies of age in mediating the relationship between grandfathers and their grandchildren. A second strand of work looks at the transmission of values across generations and concludes that the conventional top-down direction of cultural transmission is not always evidenced. Such work points to the importance of site-specific research which can tease out the complex and fluid relationships that govern the negotiated transmission of cultural practices up, down, and between generations (Riley 2009; Hopkins et al. 2011; Besten 2011). Third, there is evidence that intergenerational relationships are transformed by migration and displacement. Work by Hampshire et al. (2011) in Ghanaian refugee camps and by Greenfields and Smith (2011) on Gypsy-Travelers' transition into housing suggests that displacement can fundamentally alter the way intergenerational relationships are forged.

Intergenerationality within families, including extended family, builds on a long-standing, if underdeveloped, trajectory of studying family life in children's geographies. However, there is a wider set of age relations that have yet to be squarely considered. In particular, Vanderbeck (2007) argues, the intergenerational relations of non-family life represent a significant gap in our understanding of relationships between age groups. There are huge discrepancies in the opportunities for interaction between non-familial age groups across different communities, due to the spatial segregation of age groups (see discussion below). However, there are also countless instances of interactions and relationships outside kinship structures that are forged across generations. There are relationships between children and their caregivers, teachers, sport instructors, Cub/Scout and Brownie/Guide leaders; intergenerational family friendships; community-based relationships with neighbors, and so on. All of these relationships can significantly enrich individual lives and build strong communities. Indeed, a growing literature in child development, parenting, psychology, and social work advocates relationships between adults and young people, particularly with regard to extra-familial mentoring (Galbo and Demetrulias 1996; Biddulph 1997; Rishel, Sales, and Koeske 2005; Chang et al. 2010). While many agree that such relationships are important, there is considerable work to be done in examining the way spatial structures facilitate or obstruct these relationships.

Before looking at the spatial structuring of age relations, it is worth noting that despite the recent embrace of intergenerationality as an explicit framework, there is research which predates the current enthusiasm for this approach but which did not necessarily use its explicit language. This is particularly true for work centered in the global South, where children's lives do not fit into Western conceptualizations of childhood as a period defined by leisure and education (Ansell 2005). In the global South, where children are more likely to be involved in paid and unpaid work, their lives are more immediately embedded in intergenerational responsibilities. As a consequence, there are numerous examples of geographic work which has been sensitive to intergenerational perspectives as a routine aspect of daily life. Elspeth Robson's (2000; Robson and Ansell 2000) work on young caregivers in Zimbabwe and South Africa powerfully demonstrates the ways in which young people are intimately involved in caring for family members. Likewise, Cindi Katz's (1991, 2004) work on social reproduction and environmental knowledge in a Sudanese village places children's experiences firmly in the context of their relationships with family and community. In looking at environmental knowledge acquisition, or rather, the erosion of opportunities for learning environmental knowledge, Katz's work exemplifies many of the ambitions of intergenerational work. This and other work on the global South demonstrates that age relations are deeply contextual and that such relations structure age-based identity and benefit from intergenerational understanding. It also reminds us, however, that the call for intergenerational approaches, while valid and timely, is not without precedent.

## Generations Apart: Age Ghettos and the Socio-Spatial Regulation of Age

Both children's geographies and geographies of older people have demonstrated that social discourses construct particular spaces as age appropriate (e.g., Holloway and Valentine 2000; Laws 1997). However, the primary tenor of this work is to understand the way in which socio-spatial discourses construct identities. Less work has been carried out on the *effects* such spatial constructions have on producing segregated landscapes. Moreover, the very notion of segregation has been reserved for discussions of race and ethnicity. As Vanderbeck (2007: 206) argues, "[w]hile geographers and other social scientists continue to vigorously debate how best to measure, conceptualize and understand racial and ethnic segregation, nowhere near the same energy has been applied to the study of age segregation, perhaps reflecting the extent to which certain kinds of age segregation are viewed as natural, inevitable or unproblematic." I would qualify this claim, however, by saying that those interested in older ages have been more engaged in the effects of age segregation than those studying youth.

Segregation, especially its isolating effect, has been a consistent theme among those studying older people. In geography, Rowles' (1978) vivid account of the acute loneliness felt by older people in US cities focused on their spatial isolation. More recent analysis demonstrates that state policies and private-sector developers conspire to produce an agist built environment that determinedly segregates older people and reifies agist attitudes (Laws 1993). While these analyses have yet to produce a systematic description of segregation, particularly at the neighborhood level (Vanderbeck 2007), there is extensive recognition that the spatial separation of older people from young generations is a widespread phenomenon, particularly in the United States, where retirement communities have a regional as well as urban geography (Gober 1985).

In the planning literature on how the built environment will accommodate the increasing number of people living longer, two camps have developed around the issue of the integration versus segregation of older communities (Rosenberg and Everitt 2001). On the one hand, advocates of integration (e.g., Riley and Riley 2000) argue that planners should provide support for older people to remain living among other generations. Proposals include building "in-law suites" as add-ons to single-family dwellings, deinstitutionalizing care facilities, providing more community-based care, and adapting and extending public transport systems to cater to older people with decreased mobility. These kinds of amendments can better support what has been termed "ageing in place" (Davies and James 2011). Alternatively, others have argued that older people frequently prefer a degree of age segregation (Hagestad and Uhlenberg 2005). Golant (1985), for example, argues that there is evidence to suggest that older people enjoy the shared experience of living with like generations and find comfort and security from living in environments that are specifically designed for their needs. Such environments can better provide health care, transport, and retail services; and while not suitable or indeed affordable for all, they should not be automatically ruled out in favor of integrated planning philosophies. While there is quantifiably greater support in the literature for integration as a goal of planning, there is clearly room for more research that explores the question of what older people want and need from the built environment (Rosenberg and Everitt 2001).

The ghettoization of childhood is less well developed in the literature, in part because it represents such a naturalized part of the built environment. Geographers have been among those to question construction of particular places and spaces as the "proper" place for children (Holloway and Valentine 2000; Gagen 2004). Valentine's (1996a, 1996b) pioneering work on the exclusion of children and young people from public space can be better understood in the wider context of the agist ideology that ghettoizes both older and younger groups. Children and young people are seen to properly belong in the home, in school, and in specialized urban environments like parks and playgrounds.

In terms of intergenerational contact, the increasing separation of spheres creates limits to interactions across generations which many have argued are counter to the wider social good. Such objections to the ghettoization of age groups can be traced back to the early work of Jane Jacobs in *The Death and Life of Great American Cities* (1961). Here, she argued that the segregation of children in specialized environments like parks and playgrounds was a regressive design feature of modern cities. It resulted in fewer opportunities for play because a child had to go or be taken there for a planned and purposeful period of "play" rather than relying on happenstance opportunities in more immediate environments. Of particular relevance here, she argued that such specialized environments offered far fewer opportunities for lessons in civic responsibility. On this latter point, she called for the positive surveillance afforded by casual street play, rather than the spatial segregation associated with sequestering children in playgrounds.[1] On the street, members of the wider public – shopkeepers, passersby, other parents – are invested in the well-being of children and more likely to intervene in disputes or watch over the safety of neighborhood children. She made a strong case for a kind of civic cultural reproduction whereby the shared use of street space allowed opportunities for civic values like respect and responsibility to be handed down via casual interaction. Reinforcing a point raised in more recent work, Jacobs argued that for this civic cultural reproduction to be effective, it had to be meted out by non-parental figures. Discussing the role of non-kin adults in supervising children, she argued:

> only from the ordinary adults of the city sidewalk do children learn – if they learn it at all – the first fundamental of successful city life: people must take a modicum of public responsibility even if they have no ties to each other. This is a lesson nobody learns by being told. It is learned from the experience of having other people *without ties of kinship or close friendship or formal responsibility to you* take a modicum of responsibility for you. . . . Such instruction must come from society itself, and in cities, if it comes, it comes almost entirely from the time children spend at incidental play on sidewalks. (Jacobs 1961: 108–109, emphasis in original)

The role of social and cultural reproduction is one of many arguments made in favor of generational integration. For Coleman (1982), the loss of intergenerational contact is felt in both directions: not only are children cheated out of important life experiences by not having exposure to non-parental adults, but adults and older people suffer from less contact with, and understanding of, children. For Thang (2001), there is evidence that contact with young people can have benefits on the mental and emotional well-being of older people. All this work suggests that an intergenerational perspective, as outlined above, might be useful not only for understanding the socio-spatial construction of age relations and identities, but also for providing material evidence for challenging age-segregated environments. Indeed, Thang's (2001) ethnographic account of a multigenerational institution in Japan that provides residential care for older people alongside a day-care facility for preschool children offers one example of a social program responding to the breakup of multigenerational living.

Other instances of interventions designed to bridge generational segregation are also increasing. One example that has gained recent exposure is the cohousing movement. Originating in Denmark, cohousing developments are intentional communities established to provide an alternative to single-family urban dwellings. They feature individual housing units, privately owned and managed, but supplemented by both indoor and outdoor communal spaces. Cohousing developments rely heavily on pooling household tasks like laundry, some cooking, and childcare. They are primarily an urban intervention designed to provide greater support and social interaction as an alternative to the perceived atomization of urban neighborhoods and, in particular, the nuclear family home (Williams 2005).

Much of the literature on cohousing has focused on non-kin support networks for working families, the sustainability objective of communal resources, and the safety of a pedestrian environment (Tchoukaleyska 2011). However, cohousing also offers an environment that explicitly fosters social interaction by allowing "those services traditionally assigned to individual households to transfer into the neighborhood. This enables resources and tasks to be shared amongst households thus easing individual burdens, promoting disadvantaged citizens and consolidating society" (Horelli and Vespa 1994, cited by Williams 2005: 201). Because of the explicit focus on sharing the burdens often felt specifically by working families with young children, cohousing has been disproportionately popular with families. However, within these developments, there is also ample opportunity to foster intergenerational relationships that have failed in traditional urban living arrangements. Cohousing developments frequently contain a mixture of housing from multi-bedroom family homes to single-occupancy apartments and attract both families and single adults, including older retired people. A 73-year-old single resident of the Springhill cohousing development in Gloucestershire, UK, is quoted as saying: "The shared meals are wonderful for a single, retired person like me – I don't have to cook for myself and there are interesting people to talk to. It's a much more natural way to live than alone on a street where you know no one" (*Guardian*, April 30, 2010). Cohousing developments are pitched as an alternative to urban living precisely because of the increased social interaction, and this engagement is frequently cited as being intergenerational.

For other people, multigenerational living arrangements are not a choice but a necessity. The financial crisis of the late 2000s and early 2010s created a more precarious labor market, which, combined with a lack of affordable houses, particularly in the US and UK, put enormous pressure on existing families and on young people entering the housing market. Other factors, including the blending of traditional nuclear families through divorce, remarriage, and shared custody; the increased longevity of dependent parents/grandparents; and the tendency of young adult children to remain in the family home for longer periods or return to it after a period away, have produced more instances of multigenerational family homes. In the US, 49 million individuals, or 16.1 percent of the population, currently live in multigenerational homes (Pew Research Center 2010). In Britain, the number of households with more than three generations has increased by 7 percent over the last five years to a total of 517,000, the highest number on record since the mid-nineteenth century (Dutta 2012). Among other things, this fact underscores the observation, long made by sociologists, that despite the emergence of many different ways of "doing" family, intergenerational connectivity is enduringly elastic in its ability to adapt to changing circumstances (Morgan 1996).

That multigenerational living is not always a choice but often a necessity is also a well-documented feature of life in the global South. As discussed above, significant work has demonstrated the complex intergenerational relations that emerge from caring responsibilities, forced migration, and changing patterns of social reproduction in the global South. Equally relevant to these dynamics, however, are the forced multigenerational households of the global South that emerge from profound financial, social, and medical need. Informal housing settlements in Brazil, the Philippines, and the Townships of South Africa, for example, represent instances of intergenerational living produced by chronic global inequalities (Huchzermeyer and Karan 2006).

These examples demonstrate both the continuities and differences produced by multigenerational living in the global North and South. While an emerging theme in family sociology and geography has begun to explore the changing role of grandparents in multigenerational living arrangements, in the global South, it has emerged from more acute circumstances. In southern Africa, for example, grandparents, grandmothers in particular, have been catapulted into caregiving roles in families affected by HIV/AIDS, especially where both parents have died. Indeed, Chazan (2008) argues that the role of grandmothers has been so widespread and effective that it has significantly lessened the burden of the epidemic for families. For grandmothers themselves, however, the effects on their health and pressures on their financial resources have been tremendous (Chazan 2008). Far from being an example of rescuing older people from a life of loneliness and retreat, as the story might be narrated in parts of the global North, these examples of multigenerational households demonstrate the hardship felt by older people taking on greater responsibility.

## Conclusions

The widening of geographical analysis from the so-called "bookend" generations to the ways in which individuals across the age continuum interact, find meaning from, and co-constitute each other is a welcome intervention. From the perspective of children's geographies, a greater appreciation of age relations has generated more research on families and intergenerational engagements and has done much to reorient interest away from the binary opposition that pitted children against adults. Indeed, an appreciation of life course, transitions, and intergenerationality opens up the narrow focus on single age groups to better appreciation of the processual and relational nature of identities more generally. Moreover, rather than focusing singularly on the temporal nature of age relations, geographers have much to contribute to understanding the *spatialities* of aging identities and the ways in which space facilitates or impedes intergenerational contact.

Aging has traditionally connoted something that happens only at the end of life, but a relational understanding of aging demands that we revise our thinking to approach it as a process happening across the generations. What is apparent in the literature, however, is that children and young people still receive far more academic attention than older generations when it comes to intergenerational interactions. While conceptually, intergenerationality and transitions ought to demand that older people are included, there is still much work to be done at the upper reaches of the age continuum. Holloway and Pimlott-Wilson (2011) caution that in our hurry to include adults in intergenerational studies, we should not extend our neglect of older people. I would add that while intergenerational concepts are valuable correctives within studies of aging, such work still requires understanding the age standpoint of individuals concerned. The compartmentalization of age groups has been a problematic feature of social science intent on studying aging as a relational process. Categories of age, nevertheless, remain a necessary foothold of any relational geography to come and continue to help us parse out the differential experiences of and responses to aging.

Since the reemergence of children's geographies as a major research focus in the 1990s, there have been significant overlaps between its dominant themes and approaches and those of cultural geography. The more recent focus on aging signals equally important entry points into existing debates in cultural geography. In particular, the imperative toward intergenerationality needs careful consideration from cultural geographers. While clearly valuable as a conceptual framework for understanding age relations, as a manifesto for living, it is more contested. This is particularly apparent in the example of multigenerational households. For some older and younger people, multigenerational living is a useful intervention into modern urban living, one that accommodates temporary financial strain, provides long-term care solutions for older people, and can alleviate childcare pressures on working parents. For others, however, it can represent an unwelcome solution to a problem born out of economic necessity and family loss. This is particularly evident when looking at examples of multigenerational informal housing in the global South.

The multigenerational family home – a long-standing feature of informal settlements in the global South and a reemerging site in the global North – represents a crucible of geographic and social processes that have long been of interest to cultural geographers. The home has become a site of intense research scrutiny over the past decade (Chapman and Hockey 1999; Miller 2001; Blunt and Dowling 2006). However, the *multigenerational* home has been given far less attention. If households in the global North continue to consolidate generations, we may see issues emerging that have previously been associated with informal communities in the global South. How, for instance, will multiple generations living together affect issues of privacy and the territorialization of domestic space?[2] How will people negotiate their material environment in a space of increased pressure over domestic resources? How will the coming together of generations affect social reproduction? What impact will multigenerationality have on sibling relations, parenting, and the division of household duties? How do relations beyond the family become complicated when the household contains multiple generations? Such questions are relevant to the established literature on the cultural geographies of the home but need particular scrutiny with regard to multigenerational living. We have rethought the home as a site and space, as a set of meanings and materialities, as a confluence of identities, meanings, and things. As the nature of households evolves, however, we need to understand how aging identities and intergenerational relations continue to reconfigure these domestic spatialities.

## Notes

1   This kind of surveillance is very different from the sort identified more recently by Cindi Katz (2005) as "hypervigilance" or "hyperparenting." As Katz documents, the response by many parents to the

perceived threats of global terror and insecurities that result from disinvestments in the social wage has taken the form of increased security measures. These include household surveillance strategies like "nannycams," webcams in childcare institutions, and heightened fear of public spaces. Such practices further reduce the likelihood of intergenerational interactions, especially in public space.

2  See Paula Meth's (in press) analysis of informal households in South Africa. Here she demonstrates that informal housing arrangements create particular anxieties for parents. Issues like privacy become acutely felt in close living quarters, particularly surrounding sexual behavior.

## References

Aitken, S. (2009) *The Awkward Space of Fathering*. Oxford: Routledge.

Andrews, G.J. and Philipps, D.R. (eds.) (2006) *Ageing and Place: Perspectives, Policy, Practice*. London: Routledge.

Andrews, G.J., Kearns, R.A., Kontos, P., and Wilson, V. (2006) Their finest hour: Older people and the historical geography of social life. *Social and Cultural Geography*, 7 (2), 153–177.

Ansell, N. (2005) *Children, Youth and Development*. London: Routledge.

Bartlett, H. and Phillips, D.R. (2000) The United Kingdom: Demographic trends, recent policy developments and care provisions. In *Ageing in East and West: Families, States and the Elderly*, ed. V.L. Bengston, K.-D. Kim, G.C. Myers, and K.-S. Eun. New York: Springer, pp. 169–189.

Besten, O.D. (2011) Negotiating children's outdoor spatial freedom: Portraits of three Parisian families. In *Geographies of Children, Youth and Families: An International Perspective*, ed. L. Holt. London: Routledge, pp. 136–150.

Biddulph, S. (1997) *Raising Boys*. London: Harper Thorsons.

Blunt, A. and Dowling, R. (2006) *Home*. Abingdon: Routledge.

Bynner, J. (2001) British youth transitions in comparative perspective. *Journal of Youth Studies*, 4 (1), 5–23.

Bytheway, J. (1995) *Ageism*. Buckingham: Open University Press.

Chang, E.S., Greenberger, E., Chen, C., Heckhausen, J., and Farrugia, S.P. (2010) Nonparental adults as social resources in the transition to adulthood. *Journal of Research on Adolescence*, 20 (4), 1065–1082.

Chapman, T. and Hockey, J. (1999) *Ideal Homes? Social Change and Domestic Life*. London: Routledge.

Chazan, M. (2008) Seven "deadly" assumptions: Unpacking the implications of HIV/AIDS among grandmothers in South Africa and beyond. *Ageing and Society*, 28, 935–958.

Cherlin, A. (2009) *The Marriage-Go-Round: The State of Marriage and the Family Today*. New York: Alfred A. Knopf.

Coleman, J.S. (1982) *The Asymmetric Society*. Syracuse: Syracuse University Press.

Davies, A. and James, A. (2011) *Geographies of Ageing*. Farnham: Ashgate.

Dutta, K. (2012) Beating the housing shortage: One home, three generations. *Independent* (online), April 8. http://www.independent.co.uk/news/uk/home-news/beating-the-housing-shortage-one-home-three-generations-7626973.html (accessed November 6, 2012).

England, K. (1996) *Who Will Mind the Baby: Geographies of Childcare and Working Mothers*. London: Routledge.

Featherstone, M. and Wernick, A. (eds.) (1995) *Images of Ageing: Cultural Representations of Later Life*. London: Routledge.

Gagen, E.A. (2004) Landscapes of childhood and youth. In *The Companion to Cultural Geography*, ed. J.S. Duncan, N.C. Johnson, and R.H. Schein. Oxford: Blackwell, pp. 404–418.

Galbo, J.J. and Demetrulias, D.M. (1996) Recollections of nonparental significant adults during childhood and adolescence. *Youth and Society*, 27, 403–420.

Gober, P. (1985) The retirement community as a geographical phenomenon: The case of Sun City, Arizona. *Journal of Geography*, 84 (5), 189–198.

Golant, S.M. (1985) In defense of age-segregated housing. *Aging*, 348, 22–26.

Greenfields, M. and Smith, D. (2011) Travellers, housing and the (re)construction of communities. In *Geographies of Children, Youth and Families: An International Perspective*, ed. L. Holt. London: Routledge, pp. 95–107.

Gregson, N. and Lowe, M. (1995) *Servicing the Middle Classes: Class, Gender and Waged Domestic Work in Contemporary Britain*. London: Routledge.

Hagestad, G. and Uhlenberg, P. (2005) The social separation of old and young: The root of ageism. *Journal of Social Issues*, 61, 343–360.

Hall, S. and Jefferson, T. (eds.) (1976) *Resistance Through Rituals: Youth Subcultures in Postwar Britain*. London: Hutchinson.

Hampshire, K., Porter, G., Kilpatrick, K., Kyei, P.O., Adjaloo, M., and Ampong, G.O.A. (2011) The search for belonging: Youth identities and transitions to adulthood in an African refugee context. In *Geographies of Children, Youth and Families: An International Perspective*, ed. L. Holt. London: Routledge, pp. 83–94.

Harper, S. (2005) *Ageing Societies*. London: Hodder.

Harper, S. and Laws, G. (1995) Rethinking the geography of ageing. *Progress in Human Geography*, 19 (2), 199–221.

Henderson, S., Holland, J., McGrellis, S., Sharpe, S., and Thomson, R. (2007) *Inventing Adulthoods: A Biographical Approach to Youth Transitions*. London: Sage.

Hockey, J. and James, A. (2003) *Social Identities Across the Life Course*. London: Palgrave.

Hodge, G. (2008) *The Geography of Ageing: Preparing Communities for the Surge in Seniors*. Kingston: McGill-Queen's University Press.

Holloway, S. (1998a) "She lets me go out once a week": Mothers' strategies for obtaining personal time and space. *Area*, 30, 321–330.

Holloway, S. (1998b) Local childcare cultures: Moral geographies of mothering and the social organisation of pre-school education. *Gender, Place and Culture*, 5 (1), 29–53.

Holloway, S. and Pimlott-Wilson, H. (2011) Geographies of children, youth, and families: Defining achievements, debating the agenda. In *Geographies of Children, Youth and Families: An International Perspective*, ed. L. Holt. London: Routledge, pp. 9–24.

Holloway, S. and Valentine, G. (eds.) (2000) *Children's Geographies: Playing, Living, Learning*. London: Routledge.

Holt, L. (ed.) (2011) *Geographies of Children, Youth and Families: An International Perspective*. London: Routledge.

Hopkins, P.E. (2006) Youth transitions and going to university: The perceptions of students attending a geography summer school access programme. *Area*, 38, 240–247.

Hopkins, P.E. and Pain, R. (2007) Geographies of age: Thinking relationally. *Area*, 39, 287–294.

Hopkins, P.E., Olson, E., Pain, R., and Vincett, G. (2011) Mapping intergenerationalities: The formation of youthful religiosities. *Transactions of the Institute of British Geographers*, 36, 314–327.

Huchzermeyer, M. and Karan, A. (eds.) (2006) *Informal Settlements: A Perpetual Challenge*. Cape Town: UCT Press.

Jacobs, J. (1961) *The Death and Life of Great American Cities*. New York: Random House.

Jamieson, A., Harper, S., and Victor, C. (eds.) (1997) *Critical Approaches to Ageing and Later Life*. Buckingham: Open University Press.

Jeffrey, C. and McDowell, L. (2004) Youth in comparative perspective: Global change, local lives. *Youth and Society*, 36, 131–142.

Jenkins, R. (1996) *Social Identities*. London: Routledge.

Joseph, A.E. and Chalmers, A.I. (1995) Growing old in place: A view from rural New Zealand. *Health and Place*, 1, 79–90.

Joseph, A.E. and Martin-Matthews, A. (1993) Growing old in ageing communities. *Journal of Canadian Studies*, 28, 14–29.

Katz, C. (1991) Sow what you know: The struggle for social reproduction in rural Sudan. *Annals of the Association of American Geographers*, 81, 488–514.

Katz, C. (2004) *Growing Up Global: Economic Restructuring and Children's Everyday Lives*. Minneapolis: University of Minnesota Press.

Katz, C. (2005) The terrors of hypervigilance: Security and the compromised spaces of contemporary childhood. In *Studies in Modern Childhood: Society, Agency, Culture*, ed. J. Qvortrup. London: Palgrave, pp. 99–114.

Kearns, R.A. and Andrews, G.J. (2006) Placing ageing: Positionings in the study of older people. In *Ageing and Place: Perspectives, Policy, Practice*, ed. G.J. Andrews and D.R. Phillips. London: Routledge, pp. 13–23.

Kjørholt, A.T. (2003) Creating a space to belong: Girls' and boys' hut-building as a site for understanding discourses on childhood and generational relations in a Norwegian community. *Children's Geographies*, 1, 261–279.

Laws, G. (1993) "The land of old age": Society's changing attitudes toward urban built environments for elderly people. *Annals of the Association of American Geographers*, 83, 672–693.

Laws, G. (1997) Spatiality and age relations. In *Critical Approaches to Ageing and Later Life*, ed. A. Jamieson, S. Harper, and C. Victor. Buckingham: Open University Press.

Maxey, L. (2009) Ageism and geographies of age. In *International Encyclopedia of Human Geography*, ed. R. Kitchin and N. Thrift. Amsterdam: Elsevier.

McDowell, L. (2003) *Redundant Masculinities? Employment Change and White Working-Class Youth*. Oxford: Blackwell.

McHugh, K. (2003) Three faces of ageism: Society, image and place. *Ageing and Society*, 22 (2), 1–21.

McHugh, K. (2006) Review of *Ageing and Place: Perspectives, Policy, Practice. Professional Geographer*, 58, 493–495.

McHugh, K. (2007) Generational consciousness and retirement communities. *Population, Space and Place*, 13, 293–306.

Meth, P. (in press) "I don't like my children to grow up in this bad area": Parental anxieties about living in informal settlements. *International Journal of Urban and Regional Research*.

Miller, D. (ed.) (2001) *Home Possessions: Material Culture Behind Closed Doors*. London: Berg.

Milligan, C. (2009) *There's No Place like Home: Place and Care in an Ageing Society*. Farnham: Ashgate.

Monk, J. and Katz, C. (eds.) (1993) *Full Circles: Geographies of Women Over the Life Course*. London: Routledge.

Morgan, D. (1996) *Family Connections: An Introduction to Family Studies*. Cambridge: Polity.

Pew Research Center (2010) *The return of the multi-generational family household. Pew Social and Demographic Trends Report*. Washington, DC: Pew Research Center.

Pratt, G. (2004) *Working Feminisms*. Philadelphia: Temple University Press.

Punch, S. (2002) Youth transitions and interdependent adult–child relations in rural Bolivia. *Journal of Rural Studies*, 18 (2), 123–133.

Punch, S. (2005) The generationing of power: A comparison of child–parent and sibling relations in Scotland. *Sociological Studies of Children and Youth*, 10, 169–188.

Punch, S. (2007) "I felt they were ganging up on me": Interviewing siblings at home. *Children's Geographies*, 5 (3), 219–234.

Riley, M. (2009) "The next link in the chain": Children, agri-cultural practices and the family farm. *Children's Geographies*, 7 (3), 245–260.

Riley, M.W. and Riley, J.W. (2000) Age-integration: Conceptual and historical background. *The Gerontologist*, 40, 266–270.

Rishel, C., Sales, E.S., and Koeske, G.F. (2005) Relationships with nonparental adults and child behaviour. *Child and Adolescent Social Work Journal*, 22 (1), 19–34.

Robson, E. (2000) Invisible carers: Young people in Zimbabwe's home-based health care. *Area*, 32 (1), 59–69.

Robson, E. and Ansell, N. (2000) Young carers in Southern Africa? Exploring stories from Zimbabwean secondary school students. In *Children's Geographies: Living, Playing, Learning and Transforming Everyday Worlds*, ed. G. Valentine and S. Holloway. London: Routledge, pp. 174–193.

Rosenberg, M. and Everitt, J. (2001) Planning for ageing populations: Inside or outside the walls. *Progress in Planning*, 56, 119–168.

Rossi, A. (1985) *Gender and the Life Course*. New York: American Sociological Association.

Rowles, G. (1978) *Prisoners of Space? Exploring the Geographical Experience of Older People*. Boulder: Westview Press.

Sibley, D. (1995) Families and domestic routines: Constructing the boundaries of childhood. In *Mapping the Subject: Geographies of Cultural Transformation*, ed. N. Thrift and S. Pile. London: Routledge, pp. 114–131.

Spencer, P. (ed.) (1990) *Anthropology and the Riddle of the Sphinx: Paradoxes of Change in the Life Course*. London: Routledge.

Tarrant, A. (2010) Constructing a social geography of grandparenthood: A new focus for intergenerationality. *Area*, 42 (2), 190–197.

Tchoukaleyska, R. (2011) Co-housing childhoods: Parents' mediation of urban risk through participation in intentional communities. *Children's Geographies*, 9 (2), 235–246.

Thang, L.L. (2001) *Generations in Touch: Linking the Old and Young in a Tokyo Neighbourhood*. Ithaca: Cornell University Press.

Thomson, R. (2008) Thinking intergenerationally about motherhood. *Studies in the Maternal*, 1 (1).

Valentine, G. (1996a) Angels and devils: Moral landscapes of childhood. *Environment and Planning D: Society and Space*, 14, 581–599.

Valentine, G. (1996b) Children should be seen and not heard? The role of children in public space. *Urban Geography*, 17 (3), 205–220.

Valentine, G. (2003) Boundary crossings: Transitions from childhood to adulthood. *Children's Geographies*, 1 (1), 37–52.

Valentine, G. and Hughes, K. (2011) Geographies of "family" life: Interdependent relationships across the life course in the context of problem Internet gambling. In *Geographies of Children, Youth and Families: An International Perspective*, ed. L. Holt. Oxford: Routledge, pp. 121–135.

Vanderbeck, R. (2007) Intergenerational geographies: Age relations, segregation and re-engagements. *Geography Compass*, 1, 200–221.

Warnes, A. (ed.) (1982) *Geographical Perspectives on the Elderly*. Chicester: John Wiley & Sons.

Warnes, A. (ed.) (1989) *Human Ageing and Later Life: Multidisciplinary Perspectives*. London: Edward Arnold.

Weller, S. (2006) Situating (young) teenagers in geographies of children and youth. *Children's Geographies*, 4 (1), 97–108.

Williams, J. (2005) Designing neighbourhoods for social interaction: The case of cohousing. *Journal of Urban Design*, 10 (2), 195–227.

Willis, P. (1977) *Learning to Labour*. London: Saxon House.

# Chapter 24

# Children/Youth

*Meghan Cope*

Think for a moment about the most mundane spaces of your own childhood – a bedroom, a school corridor, the backseat of a car, a secret fort. While young people's worlds occupy generally the same physical space as adults', the particular experiences of places that are used by, created by, or delimited for children and youth constitute a swirling set of overlapping and intersecting cultural meanings and performances. As with many groups designated as a category through social and cultural delineation (however problematic that designation may be), children and young people occupy and act upon space in diverse ways that cannot be easily generalized, particularly across regional and cultural contexts or through time. Simultaneously, those different regional and temporal contexts are characterized by varied constructions of what constitutes "childhood" and "youth"; that is, social definitions and expectations of being a young person are culturally defined through norms, traditions, laws, institutions, and daily routines. Perhaps because generalizations are so difficult to make, exploring young people's geographies has been a productive and lively area of inquiry in recent years, one that has achieved a level of maturity in its own right, though the field's depth and prospect for critical theorizing have lately been held up for critique (Horton and Kraftl 2006a, 2006b; Holt 2011; Vanderbeck 2008). Gagen (2004: 415) wisely noted that "as children's geographies reaches a critical mass, many of its advocates caution against partitioning the work in a discrete subfield, urging instead that it continues to reach across human geography's diverse interests." Thus, the key points of children's and youth geographies that are discussed here are particularly relevant for cultural geographers, such as landscapes, material culture, and social exclusion/inclusion. However, there is a great deal of exciting geographical scholarship on children/young people out there, of which this chapter provides only a small (but hopefully enticing) sample.

*The Wiley Blackwell Companion to Cultural Geography*, First Edition.
Edited by Nuala C. Johnson, Richard H. Schein, and Jamie Winders.
© 2013 John Wiley & Sons, Ltd. Published 2016 by John Wiley & Sons, Ltd.

As can be seen in other sections of this volume, the "critical turns" that geography has taken in the past few decades are deeply informed by analyses of *power* – economic power, social power, political power, biopower, and so on. Cultural geographers have been instrumental in this movement in no small part because the utility of a spatial perspective in understanding how power in its many forms is exercised, maintained, and challenged is clearer when we examine the *material and social landscapes* that are constructed to control certain groups and keep elites in power. Consider, for example, the many faces of adult power over young people, from physical control to economic and cultural dominance, and then think about how these many forms of power are substantiated through material landscapes. Evidence of adult power has been examined at multiple scales in children's geographies: as the regulation of the child's body (the smallest geographic "scale" [Colls and Horschelmann 2009]), the arrangement of home spaces and domestic boundaries, the politics of the street or play-yard, the institutional spaces of schools, the "warehousing" of young people in designated local spaces, or the concomitant time/space exclusions of those who are "under-age." Now, consider the many ways that children and young people contest, challenge, and otherwise *resist* these expressions of power – from toddlers' refusals to be strapped into strollers (pushchairs) to teens' hanging out in the local mall despite restrictions – and you may begin to see the rich potential for explorations of landscapes of power and resistance through the lens of childhood/youth. For all the vast variety of children's/youth geographies literature across age groups, genders, races, dis/abilities, nationalities, and cultural contexts, interest in issues of power (and the ways it is manifested in landscapes and material culture) has formed a cross-cutting thread of analysis. Thus, in this review, I call special attention to it as a foundational theme.

To organize the present discussion of new scholarship in children's geographies, while keeping the foundational themes of power, landscape, and material culture in the forefront, I call on several analytical constructs that are common in this literature: agency, identity, context, place, and discourse. These constructs are useful for understanding some of the rich empirical studies that have emerged in recent years and for helping us reflect on common, or divergent, patterns and processes. In effect, these constructs create a "bridge" between the routine, often taken-for-granted details of daily life and the fairly abstract theories of power and culture. For example, what could a neighborhood playground and a lunchbox have in common, conceptually? Based on some of the studies reviewed here, we will be able to identify a number of conceptual points: the ways that the playground and lunchbox both are sites of the performativity and discourses of parenting, represent age groupings (which are often contested by children themselves), could be seen as spaces of control (controlling types of play/types of foods, limiting/providing access to various experiences or foods), and can be used strategically by children and youth to challenge social expectations of their parents and other adults through refusals, transgressions, and negotiation. In this way, these analytical constructs serve as helpful devices through which we can identify connections among real-world actions, spaces, and materialities and bring our understanding of the cultural realm to a new level.

## A Short History of Children's Geographies

Open virtually any introductory chapter or paper on children's geographies and a common trajectory is traced in which several early influences are acknowledged. These include, for example, the work of James Blaut and David Stea (1971), who studied pre-literate 5- and

6-year-old children in multiple sites in Massachusetts and Puerto Rico, finding that they were quite capable of using aerial photos for geographic interpretation and drawing maps. Also frequently cited is the work of William Bunge and the Detroit Geographical Expedition (Detroit Geographical Expedition 1971), who coordinated participatory action research on issues of poverty and racial oppression and produced such radical pieces as first-person accounts of rat infestations by children and maps with titles such as "Where Commuters Run Over Black Children on the Pointes-Downtown Track." Roger Hart's (1979) work often makes an appearance in these introductions too, in which his painstaking ethnography with rural children in New England sets the stage for a long-standing interest in children's special places, hiding spaces, and creative outdoor play. Another important strand of research at this time revolved around children in cities, a trend reflected in Colin Ward's (1978) book *The Child in the City* and Kevin Lynch's *Growing Up in Cities* (1977), both of which combined assessments of the physical environment and children's interactions with those environments.

These five examples are important building blocks for much of what has followed in subsequent decades because they touch on several basic findings that continue to resonate with researchers. These findings include the ideas that children have more geographic sensibility than we typically give them credit for; that children experience oppression and exploitation through multiple subject positions, not just their youth (that is, also through race, class, gender, and so on); and that children have a capacity for creating meaningful spaces for play, reflection, socializing, travel, and practical life even when they are limited to operating in between or underneath the official spaces of the adult world, in places spanning the rural-to-urban spectrum. In contemporary children's/youth geographies, these findings align with the above-mentioned analytical constructs in the following ways. *Agency* refers to children's ability to have an effect on the world, through both creating meaningful spaces and resisting/conforming to broader power relations. *Intersectionality of identities* means that everyone holds multiple identities and subject positions, which combine in unique ways to influence that person's life. *Context* indicates the characteristics of one's surroundings and everyday lived experiences, both in the material, real-world sense and in terms of broader social-political-economic structures. *Place* refers to the differentiated and contested social-cultural meanings inscribed in sites and locations. Finally, *discourse* is constituted by the cultural narratives that are constructed, circulated, and constantly amended through media, communications, and landscapes.

Work on these themes proceeded in fits and starts during the 1980s, particularly in environmental psychology and in cognate disciplines such as sociology; but they show up again clearly in geography in the 1990s and early 2000s, when a renewed burst of attention to children and young people emerged. Key texts include M.H. Matthews' (1992) *Making Sense of Place*, multiple works by Stuart Aitken (1994, 1998, 2001), and several works in which Gill Valentine played a key role (Skelton and Valentine 1998; Holloway and Valentine 2000; Valentine 2004). Along with many special issues of journals and, indeed, entire journals devoted to young people's geographies (e.g., *Children, Youth and Environments*; *Children's Geographies*), these key texts helped to generate a vibrant subfield of geography that has now matured significantly. While examinations of particular experiences of young people in specific places continue to serve an important empirical base, children's/youth geographies are also becoming somewhat more theorized (though see Vanderbeck 2008 for critiques). Children's/youth geographers are contributing to other subfields' perspectives (e.g., children's political geographies [Bosco 2010], youth economic geographies, and so on). Other scholars are increasingly considering young people and the social construction of "childhood" in their work; and there is a growing strength in international perspectives tackling issues of transnationalism, migration, and cultural comparisons (Holt 2011; Hopkins 2010; Katz 2004; Panelli, Punch, and Robson 2007; Jeffrey 2010).

Many of these authors have been engaged with and contributing to what has become known as the new social studies of childhood (NSSC), an interdisciplinary movement centered on the argument that childhood/youth are *socially constructed*, not merely biological stages, and that the form and impacts of that social construction vary over time and place. The roots of this insight are commonly traced to the work of French historian Philippe Ariès (1962), who meticulously demonstrated that the notion of "childhood" is a fairly recent development of the modern era and one that is culturally specific. Thus, the conceptualization of childhood, similar to that of gender and race, can be seen as one that has some biological markers but is largely shaped and made meaningful by social and cultural practices. Once we understand childhood as a cultural construct, we can begin to identify ways in which the (supposed) "difference" of children and young people is reified, made more rigid and deterministic, or in the lingo of social theory, *essentialized*. When social differences are deeply embedded and assumed to be "natural," societies accept without question that, in this case, *childhood* constitutes certain expectations, that children themselves should have certain characteristics, behave certain ways, be in certain places (and not others), and so on. Therefore, being able to take a critical perspective on these topics first requires that we understand that age categories (specifically for this chapter, "childhood" and "youth") are created and reinforced by routine social and cultural practices, by institutions such as the family and schools, by legal and procedural frameworks (such as the age of majority, age of consent), and by the physical, material landscapes societies construct to manage and control children and young people (such as car-dependent suburbs that limit youth mobility, playgrounds that are designated for children but restrict their access to other public spaces, truancy and curfew laws that mandate young people's presence or absence in particular times and spaces). Although geographers' interactions with the new social studies of childhood are not entirely unproblematic (Horton, Kraftl, and Tucker 2008), the contribution of geographic perspectives to considerations of the social construction of childhood has been significant and is an ongoing topic of reflection.

## Landscapes of Childhood and Youth

Much of the scholarly exploration of children's spaces in recent years has been characterized by a focus on the intimate, small-scale, everyday sites of young lives. These sites have included spaces in the home, outdoor spaces of play, travel, or just "hanging out," spaces in schools and other institutions, commercial spaces, spaces of labor (which may or may not be in the home), spaces ranging from stereotypical idyllic rural "nature" to the equally stereotyped leftover rubble of abandoned city lots and spaces in which children are welcomed, barely tolerated, or violently prohibited. In studying young people's interactions with diverse spaces and landscapes, scholars frequently consider a common set of actions and influences that line up with agency, identity, context, place, and discourse. Often using creative and pathbreaking methodologies, especially participatory research practices (Cahill 2007; Hemming 2008; Higgins, Nairn, and Sligo 2007), children's geographers have explored many realms of childhood and youth. The variety and scope of these explorations are far too great to summarize or do any justice to here; but I provide a few examples to illustrate the themes of this chapter, which I hope are sufficiently tantalizing to encourage readers to explore this literature further.

First, young people's home spaces have been the subject of more investigation than is probably typical for other age groups, perhaps because *home* is a pivotal place for young people's daily lives, yet one that is often fraught with contradictions of comfort and angst, work and rest, opportunity and constraint, love and conflict, protection and violence. In one example, Aitken (1998) examined the fine-grained social-spatial accommodations that took place in families' homes upon the birth of a child and the ways that the minutiae of infant care related to a range of negotiation points for parents, from the physical layout of the home to the gender division of labor and employment outside the home. In another example, Sarah Holloway and Gill Valentine (2001), arguing that "home" has received less attention in *urban* geography due to the dominance of public spaces, examined British children's domestic use of information and communication technologies, specifically the Internet. They argued, with significant prescience, that the meanings and roles of home spaces for children were (and continue to be) in considerable flux with the introduction of new technologies that simultaneously broadened young people's worlds *and* potentially tethered them more securely inside domestic space. Tracey Skelton's (2000) work with teen girls in Wales demonstrated the tensions around home spaces – in this case where there was limited privacy or even wholesale exclusion from the home during certain hours of the day. Indeed, Evans and his colleagues (2009) found the following among 17-year-old rural white youth in New York, suggesting that home is a more conflict-ridden space than school in some circumstances:

> [t]he experiences of hassles and stressors throughout the day are not the same for low- and middle-income youth. Adolescents living in poverty experience significantly more hassles and stressors in their daily lives compared to middle-income youth. This is particularly true when they are with their families and issues of chaotic living conditions and lack of privacy are especially salient. (Evans *et al.* 2009: 171)

The experience of home is, thus, influenced by the positionality of young people and their particular intersections of identity, place, and context. Within the home, material space and control over it matter, too, in the intersection of cultural forces between adults and young people sharing home spaces, as Hopkins (who focuses on those aged 16–25 years) points out:

> [T]he nature of the space available to young people often changes during the course of the day as parents commonly determine what are adult spaces and adult times, creating a system that young people have to manage, negotiate, and may often contest . . . Furthermore, the spaces within the home and how these are used, controlled, and shaped by young people have important influences over how young people construct and contest their identities. (Hopkins 2010: 100–101)

All of these studies demonstrate that cultural context, social interactions, material characteristics, and public discourse matter greatly in studying the home spaces and family life of children and youth. Further, they also show that spaces hold diverse *meanings* for young people, which depend on their subjective experiences, identity positions, material conditions, and capacities for agency within a broader social framework. Finally, these studies illustrate the value of understanding the meaning of spaces from the viewpoints of young people, not merely their parents, teachers, or caregivers. That is, much of children's/youth geographies have been concerned with hearing directly from young people, not merely their adult proxies, and with learning from children first-hand to foster better understanding of youth perspectives. These commitments by researchers have generated a subfield of literature on the methodological, ethical, and research practice challenges of working with children that has, in turn, further enriched the broader discipline, particularly in the areas of participatory approaches and qualitative research methods (Aitken 2010; Cahill 2007; Cope 2009; Hemming 2008; Higgins *et al.* 2007; Valentine 1999).

"The street" is another landscape of childhood and youth that represents vast diversity in its characteristics and interpretations. Often employed as a catch-all phrase for multiple types of public spaces (hence the "scare quotes"), "the street" has been examined through the lens of children's/youth geographies with an eye on its public-ness and the deeply embedded cultural meanings therein. The question of just what constitutes "public" space is a subject of a long debate in geography that is beyond the scope of this chapter (see Mitchell 2003 for a framing of this debate). Suffice it to say that the ideals of open access and free discourse in public space of Western democracies are riddled with exceptions, exclusions, caveats, regulations, and locked gates, which are often based on the *identities* of potential occupants of public spaces as well as the *activities* people engage in. So, for example, in some places three elderly women could chat on a park bench and barely be noticed, while three young men doing the same thing on the same bench may be read as suspicious, criminal, or dangerous. Part of the ongoing challenge of critical cultural geographies, then, is untangling the webs of identity, power, and place represented by examples such as this one.

Just as with home spaces, both the social landscapes of power and the physical characteristics of public spaces (layout, materials, amount of litter, trees and natural elements, noise levels, smells, sitting areas, street furniture, and so on) contribute to the experiences of young people. First, "the street" serves an obvious role as a space for travel and mobility, though one that is often fraught with adult-induced tensions due to automobile traffic. Indeed, in most industrialized countries, street spaces have been "lost" for young people's use. This loss comes as a result of increased volumes of cars and land-use planning that designs automobile-centered landscapes, two factors that have effectively squeezed children and non-driving youth off the street and into the backseat, where the experience of mobility is vastly different from walking, cycling, or skateboarding (Romero 2010; Tillberg Mattsson 2002; Kerr *et al.* 2007). A wide stream of research on children's mobility has emerged in the past decade, some of it based on concerns about young people's access to public spaces and a great deal of it connected to fears of childhood obesity (Black, Collins, and Snell 2001; Fotel 2006; Karsten and Willem 2006; Mikkelsen and Christensen 2009; Pain *et al.* 2005). Linked to this loss of physical access to the street, media-fired panics about high-profile kidnappings have increasingly shunted young people into socially "safe" private spaces, primarily through the mechanisms of parental fear and shifting concepts of where children should or should not *be* (Valentine 1996; Carver, Timperio, and Crawford 2008). Thus, moving through, or even merely being on "the street," is characterized by constantly shifting (perceptions of) threats, prohibitions, and exclusions for children and youth, a landscape against which young people resist and transgress in various ways.

Even in a context of exclusion and threat, however, for many young people around the world, "the street" constitutes the most readily available play space or hang-out area (Matthews, Limb, and Percy-Smith 1998; Anderson 2010). Sidewalks, parks, city centers, plazas, shopping districts, and actual street spaces all have varying types of "affordances" (Kyttä

2004) that appeal to or repel children and youth of different ages, genders, sexualities, income status, nationality, dis/ability, and race. As Kristina Gibson (2011) found over several years of ethnographic work, these public spaces can also serve as home space for "street kids," a combination that often brings violence, fear, constant change, and varying forms of youth (dis)empowerment in which young people navigate complicated, often-clashing, institutional and cultural rules of police, outreach workers, gangs, street cultures, families, schools, and shelters.

Even quite small, mundane locations overlooked by adults can be imbued with rich, overlapping, and contradictory meanings among different groups or subcultures of young people; simultaneously, subcultures of young people may appropriate spaces strategically for their own occupation or expression (see Hopkins 2010 for excellent examples of youth subcultures and their geographies). For example, the space outside a corner store might constitute a convenient and comfortable space for one group of young people to hang out while representing a "tyrannical space" (Percy-Smith and Matthews 2001; Watt and Stenson 1998) of bullying and violence for others. A playground might be the site of unbridled joy for a group of 4-year-olds but turn into a space of exclusion for older teens shooed away by the toddlers' parents, even if both groups of young people only wanted to go on the swings (Jansson 2008). A public skateboard park may represent opportunity and excitement for some young people, while others feel excluded due to gender or disability and still others object to the "warehousing" of skateboarders in designated areas far away from the commercial areas of downtown retail and office spaces through practices of social exclusion, policing, and heavy surveillance (Flusty 2000; Woolley, Hazelwood, and Simkins 2011). These examples demonstrate the difficulty of generalizing about public spaces, youth subcultures, mobility, and leisure: the diversity of qualities of the spaces, the differential use of those spaces and associated material objects, and the societal assumptions or expectations about different bodies and identities result in the need for finely grained micro-geographies of cultural practices. This area of research represents fertile ground for cultural geographers – the combinations of power, landscape, and material culture that are manifested in contestations over public space (including cyberspace) are ripe for consideration and analysis.

It is quite common in children's and youth geographies that, having considered the home and "the street," we would turn to a third type of space that is highly influential in young people's lives: school. Indeed, school settings are richly textured spaces of cultural negotiation and identity formation. Children and young people spend a great deal of their waking hours at school, and schools gather young people together in large numbers such that peer cultures emerge in quite observable ways. Schools are simultaneously institutions with particular missions ("education," "control," "socialization") and the expression of adult goals. They represent the combination of physical buildings designed to direct the flow and behavior of young bodies and social practices of schedules, timed bells, inspections, rules, and punishments designed to discipline those bodies. At the same time, however, schools are sites of both generational cooperation and youth resistance. As Hopkins (2010: 184) notes, schools are "a place where young people learn much about the dominance of adults in society and the way in which power and control operate in society."

Considering in more depth the youngest population of children attending some form of school – those aged 0–4 years – Horton and Kraftl (2011) recently did a research project exploring the micro-geographies of a "Sure Start Children's Center" in England. Through creative interactions with 3- and 4-year-olds, as well as interviews with parents, the authors sought to capture a variety of preschoolers' views on the Center and to "emphasize the

importance of everyday, bodily, multisensuous, and affective registers in understanding the
success or otherwise of institutional spaces and policy contexts," including such experiences
as tears, laughter, and even one boy's comments that the Center was "pooey" (i.e., smelled
of baby-changing stations and, thus, was for *babies* and decidedly *not* for him). By calling
attention to even very young children's experiences of such institutional spaces and by demonstrating successful research methods for interacting with preschoolers, Horton and Kraftl
get at the heart of the contradictions of many schooling policies – for example, ones that use
strategic discourses of child-centeredness (for parents, administrators, politicians, the public)
while simultaneously structuring actual programs and sites so that they virtually *cannot* be
child-centered.

Looking at the spatialities of older children in school, Maryann Dickar's (2008) analysis
of "corridor cultures" identifies the hallways in a New York City charter high school with a
mostly black student body as a "thirdspace" (Soja 1996) in which binaries are challenged.
She says:

> While the exclave of the halls is an adaptation of local cultures, it does not mirror the streets and
> is not simply an inversion of the classroom. It pushes the limits of school policies but is not merely
> what the classroom is not. It is different, an alternative produced by students for themselves . . .
> Composing the exclave of the halls as a thirdspace helps explain the wide range of student
> responses to hall and academic culture, but it is important to emphasize that the halls are not a
> magical or idyllic space where students are free to explore a range of possibilities. It is part of the
> real world with rigid codes, social hierarchies, and symbolic and physical violence. (Dickar 2008:
> 80)

From Dickar's examination of students' appropriation of hallway spaces, we can return to
the analytical construct of *agency* by looking at the ways that young people actively construct
rules of operation in the halls, resist (with a high level of success) the efforts of teachers to
interfere with hallway "business," and create/maintain social rules of power around issues
such as heteronormativity, gender roles, social rank, reputations, clothing and material
culture, silencing, and fighting. We can also identify the negotiations of intersecting *identities*
woven into this discussion, with particularly heightened awareness of racial identity, gender,
sexuality, and social status. The *context* of the place, too, is tangible in Dickar's account, as
she describes not just the physical characteristics of the halls themselves but also the struggle
between adult expressions of power (bells, prohibitions on being late for class, teacher surveillance) and the teens' insistence on the halls as *their* space with *their* rules: "We in the
halls, Miss. You ain't got no weight" (Dickar 2008: 78). It is these tensions and power struggles that create the meaning of the hallways for both students and teachers; teachers were
complaisant in enforcing the late penalties, in part because their efforts were rebuffed, but
also because they valued preserving higher levels of control within the classroom and saw
some hallway freedoms as a price worth paying. Thus, the *discourse* surrounding high school
corridors – and, for that matter, preschools – simultaneously taps into and reflects larger
processes of social power, politics of control, and construction of (oppositional) youth
cultures.

The spaces of childhood and youth are not limited to those into which even quite small
bodies can squeeze themselves; rather, they include sites of cultural production and material
expressions of childhood/youth expectations through media and other mechanisms. As
Horton and Kraftl (2006b) remind us in earlier work, "even, or especially, the smallest,

*daftest*, most mundane, most throwaway, most humdrum, *everyday*, taken-for-granted things matter profoundly . . . an attention to material things might afford deeper or expanded apprehension of the everyday geographies of children and young people" (p. 73, emphasis in original). Take, for example, the study by Metcalfe and his colleagues (2008) of one of the most routine "spaces" of cultural production of childhood: the lunchbox. In this project, the authors "explore the ways in which the lunchbox may be considered as a space or 'container' into which various aspects of the school and the home – the public and the private – may be packed" (2008: 405). Metcalfe *et al.* take a three-pronged approach to the subject by (1) examining media and government anxieties about childhood obesity and diet; (2) considering the role of the lunchbox as an expression of parental "performance" and a connection between children and parents; and (3) doing direct ethnographic work with children in schools' dining areas to explore the relations between the contents of lunchboxes, patterns of consumption, peer cultures, and children's relationships. While at first glance the lunchbox may seem a laughably trivial geographic space, it is through attention to such routine, everyday practices as constitutive of cultures of childhood that we gain insight into much larger forces and processes in operation, including, as the authors point out, "the ways in which children themselves constitute identities, forge relationships and negotiate social and emotional boundaries" (Metcalfe *et al.* 2008: 412).

Other forms of cultural production and consumption that appear mundane yet are highly relevant to children's and youth geographies might include the design and marketing of toys. The normative discourses, values, and contradictions of toys became glaringly apparent for me one day when I came across a small advertisement for a toy produced by the company headquartered in the town I happened to live in at the time (Fisher-Price, based in East Aurora, New York). The promotional brochure included images of two young white girls playing with "Sweet Streets" toys (houses, cars, a street layout playmat, etc.) and a photo of a real neighborhood (Figure 24.1). The images, along with the accompanying text, contained

**Figure 24.1** Brochure for Fisher-Price® toys.
Source: © Fisher-Price, East Aurora, NY. Images of Fisher-Price product used with permission of Fisher-Price, Inc., East Aurora, NY 14052.

several prescriptive messages about gender – the toy was explicitly marketed to girls through both color-coding with pinks and purples and statements to parents and about ideal neighborhood spaces, as well as "American" values, domesticity, and class. The toys are purported to appeal to girls whether they live in a "city townhouse or a country cottage" and can function to "bring this big world down to size." Because I was engaged at the time in the Children's Urban Geographies project, a participatory research project with low-income, racially marginalized children in nearby Buffalo, New York (Cope 2008a, 2008b), I wondered what the children there would think of these images. I took the brochure to the after-school club where we were based and asked them to tell me what they saw, how the images made them feel, and so on.

They said it was "pretty," "looked like a nice place to live," and one commented: "it's the suburbs!" When I asked what makes it pretty, they said "it's light." I asked if their neighborhood looked like this advertisement, and they laughed and said no. "It's dull and dark," said Malia.[1] "Our streets are full of doggie doo-doo," said Jakob. I asked Malia if there was anything she could do about her neighborhood and she said no. "If I picked up the trash, they would just throw it down again." They also asked if this was where I lived, which, I had to admit, it probably was. Their reaction was, "Miss, you live in a beautiful place. I would like to own a house like that." I also asked them about the toy picture, if they thought it was supposed to be a neighborhood. Malia said that it looked sort of like a neighborhood but was missing shops, restaurants, barber shops, and malls.

This brief, admittedly merely illustrative, example hints at several important themes. First, we can see that the design and marketing of toys is a carefully strategic cultural production with layers of normative prescriptions, such as what girls should want to play with (dolls and dollhouses that can be safely "extended" to the street and community), what neighborhoods should look like, and what it takes for a street to be considered "sweet," complete with picket fence and American flag. Second, through the quick reactions of three children whose neighborhood bears little resemblance to the picture (see Figure 24.2), except perhaps in building materials, we can begin to interrogate ways that children themselves think about diverse representations of space (e.g. "light" or "dark"); how they negotiate their identities

**Figure 24.2** West Side, Buffalo, NY.
Source: photo by Meghan Cope.

in the face of dominant cultural expectations of gender, class, sexuality, and communities; and how they navigate through their own real spaces of urban disinvestment and racial segregation, having been presented with pretty images of spaces on the beneficiary side of those processes, that is, of wealthy white suburbs.

Finally, the children's comments hint at their own desires and longings for light and beauty, for streets without trash, while also showing their expectations of what constitutes a "neighborhood" as including shops and restaurants, as their own street does. In the course of conducting the Children's Urban Geographies project, my students and I were repeatedly struck by, and appreciative of, the children's ability to "read" real spaces and account for both the negatives and positives of those spaces, as well as their skills in deciphering representations of "ideal" spaces and their underlying messages. While this one small example is merely suggestive of future research, it does provide some evidence of how even quite young (8- to 10-year-old) children are savvy social observers and quite wise to the mixed messages of broader commercial and media representations, class processes, and cultural expectations.

## Conclusion

The review of recent research in geographies of childhood and youth presented here has primarily been organized around the broad themes of power, landscape, and material cultures, using key analytical constructs (agency, identities, context, place, and discourse) and specific types of spaces (home, public spaces, schools) to highlight the richly textured and varied landscapes of young people's interactions *and* the cultural construction of youth/childhood. The analysis of these spaces has hinged on documenting and accounting for what are often delicate and always-changing negotiations of power, knowledge, affect, and identity vis-à-vis peers, adults, institutions, and one's self. Common dichotomies of exclusion/inclusion, public/private, structure/agency, and child/adult become further blurred in critically examining young people's geographies, through the transgression of boundaries and the constant reworking of relations, whether purposeful or not. Here is where the importance of *context* – in a material sense, in a cultural sense, in a geographic sense – is highly relevant for understanding and translating the real-life experiences of young people to broader insights about childhood and youth. Simply put, by considering context, we are better able to make the leap from empirical to theoretical, from the concrete to the abstract realm, and back again, to shed light on how daily practices both *reflect* and *influence* social, economic, and political processes.

Cultural geography can continue to make significant contributions to the area of children's/youth geographies (and receive reciprocal scholarly benefits in return) by bringing expertise in several realms that are currently somewhat underdeveloped. First, the interweaving of social and material practices to produce cultural landscapes of childhood and youth could be greatly expanded, particularly with respect to two pressing themes: (1) how adult power is created and experienced in various landscapes of *control* (what about cyberspace? borders? workplaces? media? marketing? urban planning?); and (2) how young people themselves construct and influence cultural landscapes as knowledgeable and purposeful cultural actors. Second, cultural geographers could bring their expertise on nature/culture relations deeper into children's/youth geographies: many of the present studies on this topic focus on middle-childhood age groups' experiences of/productions of nature (e.g., forts, green space, edible schoolyards), while less is known of the intersections of nature and culture for the very young or for teens and young adults, for young people in the global South, for children of color, and so on. Finally, cultural geographers could make a major contribution by examining *peer* cultures of young people. While critiquing expressions of "adultism" in the broader culture holds seemingly infinite research possibilities, we must also consider ways to understand the relations within and among young people, not just between children and adults, as well as how these relations shape cultural productions of youth. As cultural geographers continue to explore the rich potential of children/youth topics, cultural geography itself will benefit from such endeavors through fresh insights, consideration of new research approaches, diverse viewpoints from young people and youth cultures, and theoretical frameworks emerging specifically from young people's geographies.

## Note

1 Names have been changed.

## References

Aitken, S.C. (1994) *Putting Children in their Place*. Washington, DC: Association of American Geographers.

Aitken, S.C. (1998) *Family Fantasies and Community Space*. New Brunswick: Rutgers University Press.

Aitken, S.C. (2001) *Geographies of Young People: The Morally Contested Spaces of Identity*. London: Routledge.

Aitken, S.C. (2010) Bold disciplinarianism, experimentation and failing spectacularly. *Children's Geographies*, 8, 219–220.

Anderson, J. (2010) *Understanding Cultural Geography: Places and Traces*. New York: Routledge.

Ariès, P. (1962) *Centuries of Childhood*. New York: Vintage.

Black, C., Collins, A., and Snell, M. (2001) Encouraging walking: The case of journey-to-school trips in compact urban areas. *Urban Studies*, 38, 1121–1141.

Blaut, J.M. and Stea, D. (1971) Studies of geographic learning. *Annals of the Association of American Geographers*, 61, 387–393.

Bosco, F.J. (2010) Play, work or activism? Broadening the connections between political and children's geographies. *Children's Geographies*, 8, 381–390.

Cahill, C. (2007) Doing research with young people: Participatory research and the rituals of collective work. *Children's Geographies*, 5, 297–312.

Carver, A., Timperio, A., and Crawford, D. (2008) Playing it safe: The influence of neighbourhood safety on children's physical activity: A review. *Health and Place*, 14, 217–227.

Colls, R. and Horschelmann, K. (2009) The geographies of children's and young people's bodies. *Children's Geographies*, 7, 1–6.

Cope, M. (2008a) Becoming a scholar-advocate: Participatory research with children. *Antipode*, 40, 428–435.

Cope, M. (2008b) Patchwork neighborhood: Children's urban geographies in Buffalo, New York. *Environment and Planning A*, 40, 2845–2863.

Cope, M. (2009) Challenging adult perspectives on children's geographies through participatory research methods: Insights from a service-learning course. *Journal of Geography in Higher Education*, 33, 33–50.

Detroit Geographical Expedition (1971) The geography of the children of Detroit. *Field Notes: A Series Dedicated to the Human Exploration of Our Planet*.

Dickar, M. (2008) *Corridor Cultures: Mapping Student Resistance at an Urban High School*. New York: New York University Press.

Evans, G., Vermeylen, F.M., Barash, A., Lefkowitz, E., and Hutt, R. (2009) The experience of stressors and hassles among rural adolescents from low- and middle-income households in the USA. *Children, Youth, and Environments*, 19, 164–175.

Flusty, S. (2000) Thrashing downtown: Play as resistance to the spatial and representational regulation of Los Angeles. *Cities*, 17, 149–158.

Fotel, T. (2006) Space, power, and mobility: Car traffic as a controversial issue in neighbourhood regeneration. *Environment and Planning A*, 38, 733–748.

Gagen, E. (2004) Landscapes of childhood and youth. In *A Companion to Cultural Geography*, ed. J.S. Duncan, N.C. Johnson, and R.H. Schein. Oxford: Blackwell, pp. 404–418.

Gibson, K. (2011) *Street Kids: Homeless Youth, Outreach, and Policing New York's Streets*. New York: New York University Press.

Hart, R. (1979) *Children's Experience of Place*. Oxford: Irvington.

Hemming, P.J. (2008) Mixing qualitative research methods in children's geographies. *Area*, 40, 152–162.

Higgins, J., Nairn, K., and Sligo, J. (2007) Peer research with youth. In *Participatory Action Research Approaches and Methods: Connecting People, Participation and Place*, ed. S. Kindon, R. Pain, and M. Kesby. London: Routledge, pp. 104–111.

Holloway, S.L. and Valentine, G. (2000) *Children's Geographies: Playing, Living, Learning*. London: Routledge.

Holloway, S.L. and Valentine, G. (2001) Children at home in the wired world: Reshaping and rethinking home in urban geography. *Urban Geography*, 22, 562–583.

Holt, L. (ed.) (2011) *Geographies of Children, Youth and Families: An International Perspective*. London: Routledge.

Hopkins, P. (2010) *Young People, Place and Identity*. London: Routledge.

Horton, J. and Kraftl, P. (2006a) Not just growing up, but *going on*: Materials, spacings, bodies, situations. *Children's Geographies*, 4, 259–276.

Horton, J. and Kraftl, P. (2006b) What else? Some more ways of thinking and doing "Children's Geographies." *Children's Geographies*, 4, 69–95.

Horton, J. and Kraftl, P. (2011) Tears and laughter at a Sure Start Center. In *Geographies of Children, Youth and Families: An International Perspective*, ed. L. Holt. New York: Routledge, pp. 235–249.

Horton, J., Kraftl, P., and Tucker, F. (2008) The challenges of "children's geographies": A reaffirmation. *Children's Geographies*, 6, 335–348.

Jansson, M. (2008) Children's perspectives on public playgrounds in two Swedish communities. *Children, Youth and Environments*, 18, 88–109.

Jeffrey, C. (2010) Geographies of children and youth I: Eroding maps of life. *Progress in Human Geography*, 34, 496–505.

Karsten, L. and Willem, V. (2006) Increasing children's freedom of movement. *Children, Youth, and Environments*, 16, 69–73.

Katz, C. (2004) *Growing Up Global: Economic Restructuring and Children's Everyday Lives*. Minneapolis: University of Minnesota Press.

Kerr, J., Frank, L., Sallis, J.F., and Chapman, J. (2007) Urban form correlates of pedestrian travel in youth: Differences by gender, race-ethnicity and household attributes. *Transportation Research Part D: Transport and Environment*, 12, 177–182.

Kyttä, M. (2004) The extent of children's independent mobility and the number of actualized affordances as criteria for child-friendly environments. *Journal of Environmental Psychology*, 24, 179–198.

Lynch, K. (1977) *Growing Up in Cities: Studies of the Spatial Environment of Adolescence in Cracow, Melbourne, Mexico City, Salta, Toluca, and Warszawa*. Cambridge, MA: MIT Press; Paris: UNESCO.

Matthews, H., Limb, M., and Percy-Smith, B. (1998) Changing worlds: The microgeographies of young teenagers. *Tijdschrift voor economische en sociale geografie*, 89, 193–202.

Matthews, M.H. (1992) *Making Sense of Place: Children's Understanding of Large-Scale Environments.* Hemel Hempstead: Harvester Wheatsheaf.

Metcalfe, A., Owen, J., Shipton, G., and Dryden, C. (2008) Inside and outside the school lunchbox: Themes and reflections. *Children's Geographies*, 6, 403–412.

Mikkelsen, M.R. and Christensen, P. (2009) Is children's independent mobility really independent? A study of children's mobility combining ethnography and GPS/mobile phone technologies. *Mobilities*, 4, 37–58.

Mitchell, D. (2003) *The Right to the City: Social Justice and the Fight for Public Space.* London: Taylor and Francis.

Pain, R., Grundy, S., Gill, S., Towner, E., Sparks, G., and Hughes, K. (2005) "So long as I take my mobile": Mobile phones, urban life and geographies of young people's safety. *International Journal of Urban and Regional Research*, 29, 814–830.

Panelli, R., Punch, S., and Robson, E. (2007) *Global Perspectives on Rural Childhood and Youth.* London: Routledge.

Percy-Smith, B. and Matthews, H. (2001) Tyrannical spaces: Young people, bullying and urban neighbourhoods. *Local Environment*, 6, 49–63.

Romero, V. (2010) Children's views of independent mobility during their school travels. *Children, Youth and Environments*, 20, 46–66.

Skelton, T. (2000) "Nothing to do, nowhere to go?" Teenage girls and "public" space in the Rhondda Valleys, South Wales. In *Children's Geographies: Playing, Living, Learning*, ed. S.L. Holloway and G. Valentine. London: Routledge, pp. 80–99.

Skelton, T. and Valentine, G. (1998) *Cool Places: Geographies of Youth Cultures.* London: Routledge.

Soja, E. (1996) *Thirdspace: Journeys to Los Angeles and Other Real-and-Imagined Places.* Oxford: Wiley-Blackwell.

Tillberg Mattsson, K. (2002) Children's (in)dependent mobility and parents' chauffeuring in the town and the countryside. *Tijdschrift voor economische en sociale geografie*, 93, 443–453.

Valentine, G. (1996) Children should be seen and not heard: The production and transgression of adults' public space. *Urban Geography*, 17, 205–220.

Valentine, G. (1999) Being seen and heard? The ethical complexities of working with children and young people at home and at school. *Ethics, Place and Environment*, 2, 141–155.

Valentine, G. (2004) *Public Space and the Culture of Childhood.* Aldershot: Ashgate.

Vanderbeck, R.M. (2008) Reaching critical mass? Theory, politics, and the culture of debate in children's geographies. *Area*, 40, 393–400.

Ward, C. (1978) *The Child in the City.* London: Architectural Press.

Watt, P. and Stenson, K. (1998) The street: "It's a bit dodgy around there": Safety, danger, ethnicity, and young people's use of public space. In *Cool Places: Geographies of Youth Cultures*, ed. T. Skelton and G. Valentine. London: Routledge, pp. 249–265.

Woolley, H., Hazelwood, T., and Simkins, I. (2011) Don't skate here: Exclusion of skateboarders from urban civic spaces in three northern cities in England. *Journal of Urban Design*, 16, 471–487.

Chapter 25

# Urban Landscapes

*Tim Bunnell*

Cultural geography's transatlantic revival in the 1980s came to be known as the "new cultural geography" and among its criticisms of the "old" was a perceived neglect of the urban. A more long-standing tradition of cultural geography, associated with Carl Sauer and the "Berkeley School," was cast as "dominantly rural and antiquarian," and new cultural geography distinguished itself as being, amongst a host of other things, "urban as well as rural," "contemporary as well as historical" (Cosgrove and Jackson, 1987: 95, 96). The intervening quarter century has seen the development of strands of work that were self-consciously defined in opposition to "traditional cultural geography" (Price and Lewis 1993: 1; e.g., Cosgrove 1983; Jackson 1989; Duncan 1990) as well as non-representational or more-than-representational approaches, which have, in turn, challenged the discursive and representational emphases of (no longer *new*) cultural geography (e.g., Thrift 1996; Rose 2002). Landscape has been a central concept deployed across cultural geography's various divisions and ruptures. The aim of this chapter is to demonstrate how diverse work on landscape in cultural geography can be drawn upon to engage critically with our increasingly urbanized (and decreasingly Atlantic-centered) world. In doing so, it also exemplifies the possibilities for a broadly inclusive urban cultural geography.

The empirical starting point is the city of Kuala Lumpur ("KL"), Malaysia, where I first carried out doctoral fieldwork in the 1990s. Examination of KL's urban landscapes in what follows is composed of three sections. The first revisits, re-views, and re-reads the urban landscape artifacts that formed the focus of that doctoral research, after a period of more than a decade. This entails considering insights from the iconographic and interpretive approaches that were still very much dominant in cultural geography at that time. The second section critically reconsiders such approaches in light of the subsequent rise to prominence of non-representational theory. While this section argues that work on landscape had in fact

*The Wiley Blackwell Companion to Cultural Geography*, First Edition.
Edited by Nuala C. Johnson, Richard H. Schein, and Jamie Winders.
© 2013 John Wiley & Sons, Ltd. Published 2016 by John Wiley & Sons, Ltd.

long been more-than-representational, there has clearly been a shift of emphasis toward the multi-sensorial, experiential, and affective dimensions of material landscapes. The implications of these new emphases for cultural geographical analyses are explored through the case of KL. The chapter's third section contributes to recent work that has sought to extend more-than-representational insights from embodied experience of material landscapes to analysis of various forms of landscape representation. Here the effects of the "travel" of KL landscape imagery and souvenir objects are used to explicate the potential rapprochement of these various approaches to urban landscapes.

## Re-reading the KL Skyline

In the 1990s, rapid economic development in many countries in East and Southeast Asia came to be glossed as miraculous. The Asian economic "miracle" (World Bank 1993) was most visibly marked in the rapid transformation of cities in the region, in the form of shopping malls, hotels, and, in particular, high-rise commercial buildings. The skyscraper has long been imagined as a "marker of modernity" (King 1996: 105) with its origins in technological developments pioneered in New York City and Chicago in the late nineteenth century. As such, the rash of skyscraping urban megaprojects in Asia at the end of the subsequent century – including buildings taller than anything ever constructed in North America – stoked fears in the West that the leading edge of modernity was shifting decisively eastwards. However, prevailing discourses of a specifically *economic* miracle, understood in terms of the diffusion of technologies, forms, products, and consumption practices from the West, did not do justice to cultural geographies of Asia's urban transformation. At the macro-level, booming "tiger economies" were viewed through orientalist cultural lenses that vacillated between imaginings of fabulous wealth on the one hand, and the terrible squalor of urban slums on the other. At a more micro-level, the visual similarity of tall buildings (and other landscape features) in Asian cities with putatively Western antecedents masked often very different cultural meanings given to them by both their proponents and everyday users. Iconographic and textual approaches that assumed centrality in new cultural geography in the 1990s held the promise of allowing such cultural meanings to be disclosed or "read" (e.g., Domosh 1989).

Mona Domosh showed how iconographic analysis, which had been brought into cultural geography through work on landscape and art history (Cosgrove and Daniels 1988), could be applied to material urban landscape forms such as tall buildings (Domosh 1989; see also Black 1996; and, in the context of Asia, Cartier 1999). Domosh provided a case study of iconographic landscape interpretation based on the late nineteenth-century construction of the New York World Building. The framework of interpretation suggested by Domosh may be extended to the very different context of contemporary Asia. In particular, following Domosh, the construction of a building such as the Petronas Towers in Kuala Lumpur could be understood in terms of macro-level explanations (as expressions of rapid economic growth and urbanization) as well as more micro-level explanations (as expressions of the preferences, egos, and ambitions of the building's proponents). However, as Domosh makes clear, it is also crucial to consider the interrelation of such macro- and micro-level explanations: "How can one determine the links between a particular landscape artifact, its socio-economic and aesthetic contexts and the actors who directly produced and/or created that artifact?" (Domosh 1989: 347).

The chief proponent of the Petronas Towers – and the Kuala Lumpur City Center (KLCC) megaproject of which it formed part – was the Malaysian prime minister, Dr. Mahathir

Mohamad. While the towers were designed by a high-profile international architect, César Pelli, a front cover of *Time* magazine in December 1996 identified Dr. Mahathir as the "master planner" who was "rebuilding Malaysia his own way." Political authority over the Federal Territory of KL had earlier been shifted directly to the Prime Minister's Department on account of Dr. Mahathir's personal interest in the development of KL, and he was recognized as having a penchant for "monumental" public works and mega-scale development projects (Cartier 1998). It was Mahathir who insisted that the original plans for a single KLCC tower became twin towers and that these should eclipse the height of any other skyscraper world-wide. The Petronas Towers overtook Chicago's Sears Tower as the tallest building in the world by means of 70m functionless spires. This, and the fact that the top four floors of the towers contained no rentable space, confirms that the building was more than merely an outcome of land prices and economic value; it was designed for symbolic reasons. As Mahathir himself put it, the KLCC project would serve to "put Kuala Lumpur on the world map" (see Bunnell 2004: 69).

While KLCC may reflect the symbolic intentions and idiosyncrasies of its main proponent, Dr. Mahathir was himself of course bound up in wider economic, cultural, and political processes. As his academic biographer Khoo Boo Tiek put it, Mahathir, like any other leader, was at once "representative" and "peremptory" (Khoo 1995: xxi). The ambition of marking Kuala Lumpur on world maps, for example, could be rationalized in the context of wider efforts to render cities "investible" (Sidaway and Pryke 2000) or attractive to mobile capital in an era of globalization. Developing Kuala Lumpur through a symbol of modernity, mean-while, chimed with many Malaysians' desire to shake off ingrained colonial (self-)perceptions of their economic backwardness, underdevelopment, or being "third world." Even the "Islamic" design of the Petronas Towers reflected wider cultural and ethnic politics. Although postcolonial Malaysia is officially composed of three main ethnic groups – Malays, Chinese, and Indians – the cultural and political supremacy of Malays (who are constitutionally Muslim) was heightened following racial riots in 1969. In addition to the New Economic Policy instituting affirmative action for Malays and groups deemed to be constitutionally indigenous (or *bumiputera*), a New Cultural Policy prescribed that national culture and identity be based on "the cultures of the people indigenous to the region" (cited in Tan 1992: 283). By the time Mahathir Mohamad became prime minister of Malaysia in 1981, the skyline of the national capital already included high-rise regionalist architecture with ostensibly Malay motifs and symbolism, in addition to more faceless international-style buildings. Islamization meant that Malay-ness was increasingly equated to being Muslim, so it was no surprise that the Petronas Twin Towers came to include ostensibly Islamic design features (work by cultural geographers on the often conflictual imprint of different groups on the urban landscape includes Caroline Mills' [1988] research on gentrification and David Ley's [1995] examination of contest between different diasporic groups over the removal of sequoia trees in suburban Vancouver).

While the symbolic intentions of a landscape artifact such as the Petronas Towers can be interpreted by relating the building and its chief proponent to wider processes, this clearly does not exhaust its meaning. Poststructuralist ideas brought into new cultural geography from literary theory gave rise to the idea that a landscape artifact, like any other cultural product, could be read as a "text" (Duncan and Duncan 1988; Duncan 1990). This opened the possibility that any given landscape could be read in multiple ways, including those that depart from or contest the original intentions of the "author." In the case of the Petronas Towers, even prior to completion the building had featured in a variety of representations which themselves expressed meanings that did not necessarily align with symbolic intentions. One Malaysian journalist, for example, noted how the tops of the building disappeared from view during the "haze" of 1997, such that the Petronas Towers effectively became "twin dipsticks" for air pollution levels in the city (see Bunnell 2004: 83). Such views or representations from "below" could express symbolic discontent with intended meanings of the building's proponents, and taking them seriously became a critical component of urban cultural geography's landscape interpretations (Bunnell 1999). This formed part of a wider shift in new cultural geography away from singular, authoritative meanings based on the elite view from "above," toward everyday views on and experiences of urban landscapes (Johnson 1995).

## The Skyscraper More-than-Representationally Reconsidered

The iconographic and textual analyses that dominated cultural geography at the time of the construction of the Petronas Towers have since been increasingly challenged by the rise of non-representational theory. Nigel Thrift's (1996) critique of representational thinking in human geography, and especially in the new cultural geography, from the mid-1990s challenged representational approaches with their persistent concern to extract, fix, and freeze-frame meaning, yielding only "dead geographies" (Thrift and Dewsbury 2000). Non-representational theory emerged as an umbrella term for various strands of work considering both life and thought as *practiced*. Some leading exponents of such work have explicitly stated that they are not keen on the concept of landscape. According to Tim Cresswell, for example, landscape "does not have much space for temporality, for movement and flux and mundane practice. It is too much about the already accomplished and not enough about the processes of everyday life" (Cresswell 2003: 269). Some have even wondered if the advent of non-representational geographies meant that the very term landscape was "beyond rescue" (Rose and Wylie 2006: 475). In contrast, however, there is also work in cultural geography which sees non-representational developments as an opportunity to (re)invigorate landscape theory (e.g., Merriman *et al.* 2008). Relatedly, notions of disciplinary succession in the form of a dichotomy between representational and non-representational theory have been cast as problematic and unhelpful. As such, it is perhaps preferable to think in terms of "more-than-representational" (Lorimer 2005) approaches to landscape and cultural geography in general.

A supposed rupture between no-longer-new cultural geography and non-representational approaches obscures important intellectual and scholarly continuities, including those involving the use and utility of the landscape concept. Iconographic and poststructuralist textual analyses have long considered the *effects* as well as the *meanings* of landscapes. The cultural materialist influence on new cultural geography meant that landscape was understood as more than merely a product, record, or representation of the social relations that gave rise to it. According to scholars such as Denis Cosgrove (1998), landscape is a "way of seeing" which gives rise to new identifications and subject positions through practices of viewing and spectatorship. Similarly, in Stephen Daniels' book, *Fields of Vision*, urban landscape representations, such as the view of St. Paul's Cathedral on the skyline of London, were hardly dead geographies – rather, they performed something in "articulating" contesting visions of national identity (Daniels 1993). In other words, there has long been work in new cultural geography which has understood landscape as playing an active role in the production of subjects in/through their worldly engagement, both material and textual (see also Matless

1998). Similarly, a key tenet of poststructuralist textual analysis was that landscape meanings were not merely to be read by skilled cultural geographers but rather that they gave rise to multiple, if not endless, readings as part of the everyday flow of things (Duncan and Duncan 1988).

We can find possibilities for the more-than-representational in the urban landscapes of Kuala Lumpur. Certainly, the Petronas Towers could be understood as a representation of either individual fantasies (of architects, for example, or their political paymasters), or of wider economic, political, and social forces. However, such new material landscapes and their representations also had performative force and subjectifying effects. This was about more than the symbolic intentions of proponents of mega-developments such as KLCC – presumed psychological effects of demonstrating to Malaysians, and especially ethnic Malays, that they "stand tall" in the world of nations – and had to do with a wider normative judgments about appropriate conduct in urban space (Bunnell 2004). The "normative landscape" (Cresswell 1996) of KL expresses codes for urban(e) living associated with an array of authorities: from management gurus to design professionals to social commentators and more conventional political figures and institutions. These sociocultural codes were associated with new ways of seeing and being, sights and sites enfolded into geographical subjectivities. This is not to say that KL-ites simply realized themselves in line with authoritative norms which were, in any case, dynamic and contested rather than set in stone, concrete, or any single text. Just as symbolic intentions were subject to popular and political reworking (cf. Pred 1995), appropriate conduct was often made known precisely in opposition to those who transgressed the boundaries of the normative landscape. Examples of unacceptable or inappropriate behavior covered *ad nauseam* in the press in the 1990s include undisciplined garbage disposal from high-rise residential blocks ("killer litter") and the "culture of rubbish" that had turned the Bukit Bintang shopping area into a "dump" (Bunnell 2004). Following established notions of "landscape as a verb" (Mitchell 1994), residents of KL as much as the city's material environment were bound up in ongoing landscaping processes.

While the epistemological rupture emphasized by advocates of non-representational theory may have been overstated, there is much to be gained from reconsidering KL's urban landscapes in light of recent and ongoing disciplinary developments. In the first place, the emphasis given to affective, embodied, everyday, even mundane, aspects of life suggests the importance of giving more attention to ground-level engagement with architecture and the urban landscape (see also Lees 2001). While new cultural geography-inspired approaches extended beyond top-down analysis of landscape artifacts such as the Petronas Towers by considering new ways of seeing and being, lived processes or practices of subjectification did not tend to be foregrounded empirically. And while there had been acknowledgment of how would-be authoritative meanings are subject to popular reworking, or how the normative landscape is transgressed, these were apprehended textually – in the form of alternative representations and analysis of media coverage – rather than by drawing upon (post-)phenomenological approaches. A shift toward non-representational work entails attending to the more-than-visual or multi-sensory ways in which ordinary people encounter, inhabit, and move through landscapes (see Merriman *et al.* 2008). Consideration of the ways in which landscape is sensed raises questions of time, rhythm, mood, and texture. We might now ask: What are the routines or time geographies through which the Petronas Towers is encountered? How is the building experienced at night-time (cf. Morris 2011)? What are the effects of lighting and illumination both in and of the building (cf. Edensor and Millington 2009)? How is it experienced haptically and affectively by people who variously clean, guard, maintain, manage, or carry out white-collar work within its offices? These are all questions that suggest ways into presenting – rather than representing – mundane experiences of this spectacular landscape form. Another route to more ordinary or everyday experience would be via decentering spectacular landscape artifacts altogether in favor of mundane urban forms or sites. As the product of less self-conscious symbolic intentions, these are more likely to be apprehended for what they are rather than for what they mean or represent.

More-than-representational emphases also give rise to – indeed, necessitate – new methodological strategies and practices. Cultural geographers have begun to shake off their "methodological timidity" in efforts to apprehend the sensuous, embodied, and creative aspects of social life (Latham 2003: 1993). Alan Latham's efforts to reframe research as "creative, performative practice" (p. 1994), for example, include use of diary photographs and diary interviews to get at transient, street-level experiences of urban space. Such ideas have, in turn, been incorporated into "walk-along" methods in which the researcher accompanies individuals (sometimes together with their friends and family members) in their routine use of urban public space (Rose, Degen, and Basdas 2010). Ethno-methodological research using video has been deployed to capture non-intentional and pre-cognitive knowledges for which verbal interviews or accounts that emerge from the conventional range of qualitative research methods are inadequate (Laurier and Philo 2006). There is also methodologically innovative work in cultural geography that more explicitly addresses issues of landscape, albeit mostly concerned with rural or countryside environments rather than with urban landscapes. Cultural geographers have made methodological use of the embodied experience of walking, either alone (Wylie 2005), or to capture the intercorporeal nature of moving through landscape as part of a group (Macpherson 2009). Work on the dynamic qualities of body–landscape encounters has given rise to methodological experimentation that could be extended from the British countryside to an increasingly urbanized wider world (e.g., Middleton 2010).

## Encountering the Travels of KL Landscapes

Non- or more-than-representational work has had profound implications for how we think about and conduct research on landscape as a portion of material space. In contrast, cultural geographers have given much less attention to what non-representational approaches might mean for landscapes as pictorial or material representations. However, Veronica della Dora (2009) has recently suggested possibilities for a reconceptualization of visual landscape representations, drawing upon theoretical work on materiality, performance, and mobility. Her suggestion is to treat landscape representations not simply as visual texts but as material objects with performative qualities or agency, and which, importantly, travel around. The main example that she gives of "traveling landscape-objects" concerns so-called raree-showmen who historically carried boxes of landscape representations from village to village in continental Europe and Great Britain. In the seventeenth century, the box contained objects that could be viewed by paying villagers and which formed the starting point for wondrous tales. By the nineteenth century, the development of optical devices allowed the cabinets to evolve into closed boxes with an eye-piece and a lens: "For a penny, sometimes even for half a penny, passers-by were allowed to peer, as through a round window, at a magical world in miniature, with fabulous cities, and distant, or legendary landscapes" (della Dora 2009: 336). The form of the boxes varied over time and space but one commonality was their ability to expand and reshape the geographical imaginations of paying audiences. This historical example has resonances that extend beyond Western Europe of the nineteenth century in that "we still travel the world in boxes" (p. 337). Today, as della Dora points out, it is magical "box" devices such as laptop computers and memory sticks that enable the circulation of places, including through Powerpoint projections at academic geography conferences.

Especially from the late twentieth century, urban landscapes have been transformed in ways explicitly designed to allow them to travel and to be experienced at a distance. Geographers of diverse subdisciplinary persuasions have been among a range of scholars to examine so-called imaging strategies. Although some of the classic exemplars of this literature are based on case studies of post-industrial cities in North America and Western Europe (e.g., Harvey 1989; Hubbard 1996), it is in Asia that the most spectacular material and symbolic landscape reworking has occurred over the past two decades (e.g., Chang 1997; Olds 2001). As has already been noted of the case of the KLCC project in Malaysia, such strategies frequently took the form of urban megaprojects, with a particular penchant for high-rise buildings such as the Petronas Towers. Efforts to produce a key urban-national landmark *building* were far from misplaced given dominant forms of visual imaging: "It focuses the lens of the journalist's camera, the eye of the camcorder, the direction of the mobile TV. It is always the image of the building – rarely the diffuse and ungraspable 'city,' and even less, the 'imagined community' of the nation – which is used to fix our gaze on the limited space of the rectangular screen" (King 1996: 102). The power and reach of images projected and disseminated through television (a clear twentieth-century descendant of the raree-man's box) and other electronic media clearly have the potential to allow a building to be experienced visually by many more people than are likely to encounter it directly in the city (King 2004). In Asia alone, there is a significant body of research detailing the real and symbolic production of urban landscapes meant for consumption at a distance (King 1996, 2004; Olds 1995, 2001; Bunnell 2004). The practices through which landscape representations are actually consumed, in contrast, have received very little attention, either from cultural geographers or from scholars of urban landscapes more broadly. This requires a shift from local sites (and sights) of production to more geographically extensive analyses of consumption at a distance.

It is now more than a decade since Don Mitchell's plea to landscape studies scholars in geography to resist the "lure of the local" (Mitchell 2001). Even at that time, Mitchell was able to identify "encouraging signs" that "some of the building blocks of a theory equal to the world we live in have begun to be assembled" (p. 270). His own well-established preference was for approaches that understood material landscapes as part of increasingly globalized processes of political economy (see Mitchell 1996). Concern for more-than-local aspects of landscape was also evident in Rich Schein's framework for landscape interpretation. Drawing upon Doreen Massey's conceptualization of places as "articulated moments in networks of social relations and understandings" (Massey 1993: 66), Schein sought to show how "a particular, identifiable cultural landscape in *this* place is related and connected to landscapes and social processes in *other* places" (Schein 1997: 662, emphasis in the original). While foregrounding "geographical connectivity" in landscape studies, however, the emphasis of such work was on how this particular place or landscape *here* is constituted through connections with *out there*. Similarly, in more recent work by cultural geographers on building "events," attention has been given to human and non-human assemblages that constitute "big things" such as high-rise apartment blocks (Jacobs 2006). The overwhelming focus, in other words, continues to be on how buildings, places, and landscapes are forged through extra-local connections – including the travels of architects (McNeill 2009) and flows of raw materials (Edensor 2010) as well as human mobilities – rather than on landscapes themselves as traveling objects.

In part, the propensity to approach urban landscapes as relationally constructed sites arises from ingrained methodological preferences. Work within and beyond cultural geography has tended toward what one urban scholar has referred to as "methodological territorialism" (Ward 2010: 479). Urban field sites or wider urban landscapes are examined as more or less territorially delimited units of empirical analysis, even while they are understood to have been constituted through wider networks and processes. Attention to local detail and specificity has long been a key strength of cultural geography and I am certainly not suggesting that this simply be abandoned in favor of more spatially extensive research practices. Rather, the point is that existing emphases need to be accompanied by – or to be complemented with – methodological strategies that enable the extra-local travels and effects of urban landscapes to be discerned. One way forward is to connect landscape studies to an emerging body of transdisciplinary urban studies work proposing multi-site ethnography (see Marcus 1998) as a means of examining the travels of urban policies (McCann 2011) and planning models (Gonzalez 2011). In addition, there is a well-established tradition of geographical scholarship that builds upon Arjun Appadurai's famous call to "follow the thing" (Appadurai 1986). Cultural geographers have already followed things ranging from tropical fruit (Cook 2004) to tourist souvenirs (Ramsay 2009), to material waste from "end of life ships" (Gregson *et al.* 2010). Such methodological practices demonstrate that relational understandings of urban landscapes can include consideration of where landscapes go to rather than merely where they came from.

The possibilities for "following the thing" in the case of Kuala Lumpur's urban landscape occurred to me long after my initial encounters and might more precisely be considered a case of "things following me." Even after moving on from research on KL and on tall buildings more generally, wherever I went – on vacation as well as in my research-related travels – KL seemed to follow me, particularly in the form of images of the Petronas Towers. Two brief accounts of such encounters will suffice here. The first was in Liverpool, UK, where research on elderly Malay ex-seafarers involved fieldwork beginning in August 2004 at a celebration of Malaysian independence (*Merdeka*) in the Toxteth part of the city (Bunnell 2008). Almost all of the entries in a drawing competition in which children designed posters representing Malaysia included images of the Petronas Towers. Encounters with the Petronas Towers in subsequent trips to Liverpool included: in a video recording of the Commonwealth Games held in Kuala Lumpur in 1998 which one of my informants insisted I watch while interviewing him; in numerous photograph albums of "roots" trips to Malaysia by descendants of ex-seafarers; on a postcard sent to the community clubhouse by a Malaysian woman who had previously studied in Liverpool; and even in the form of a souvenir on the mantelpiece in the living room of an elderly ex-seafarer.

Second, in fieldwork for research on post-tsunami Aceh, my Malaysian research assistant brought an almost identical miniature souvenir Petronas Towers to the one I had seen in Liverpool as a gift for an Acehnese man who had set up a small café with money earned from working in Malaysia. During the same trip to Aceh a student activist whom we interviewed came to meet us wearing a Petronas Towers t-shirt. None of these individual encounters in Aceh or Liverpool is particularly remarkable in its own right, especially given that all of the people associated with the landscape representations that I have noted were connected in some way or another to Malaysia. However, representations of KL landscapes have also followed me from places much less obviously connected to Malaysia. Knowing my one-time fascination with tall buildings, and the Petronas Towers in particular, some friends and colleagues have developed a habit of noting their own extra-KL encounters with the building. These include: images in investment brochures in Singapore; tourist advertisements in Solo in Indonesia and Vientiane in Laos; an exhibition of the world's tallest buildings in Shanghai and a postcard representation of the same from Melbourne, among many others. And this is not to mention the umpteen digital images, many of which are taken from stock photography sites (see Grabbauer 2010), that have been forwarded to me in the time since I stopped working on KL.

In each of these cases, the Towers are put to *work* (Mitchell 2003). The final step is to consider the effects and affects of landscape representations as they travel. There is a growing body of research in cultural geography and cognate fields, some of which has been referred to already, that provides clues as to how such an empirical investigation could proceed. In terms of landscape imagery such as the postcard pinned to a notice-board at the community clubhouse in Liverpool, Veronica della Dora's recent work has shown the importance of attending to "the materiality and substance of landscape representations and embodied aspects of viewing techniques" (della Dora 2009: 335). This might entail ethnographic work on visual encounters with the postcard, the conversations that it animates, memories that it evokes, and wider geographical imaginations that it sustains as it fades and curls up in the dusty building. Similarly, for souvenir objects such as the replica Petronas Towers that I encountered in Aceh as well as Liverpool, it is possible to draw upon work on the presence of such objects in everyday lives and the ways in which they create, unsettle, and/or rework geographical knowledges (Ramsay 2009). The point is to consider the geographical biographies of landscape images and representations, following these things so as to note their animating, enlivening, and affective qualities.

## Conclusion

I have used the landscapes of Kuala Lumpur – and the twin towers that form the focal point of that city's skyline – to trace and contribute to developments in work on urban landscape in cultural geography. This has moved from new cultural geography approaches that seek to understand what the building means or represents, to more recent non-representational work on how urban landscapes are experienced through embodied, multi-sensory encounters, and closed by suggesting possibilities to extend more-than-representational insights to landscape images and objects. But this is more than a chronological set of paradigm shifts. There are commonalities and complementarities in these varying approaches. As such, the intention has not been to show disciplinary succession in landscape studies but rather to consider the expanding range of its possible insights. There is little doubt that if I was to begin doctoral research in Kuala Lumpur again today, I would give less attention to iconographic and textual approaches and correspondingly more attention to everyday, embodied encounters with the landscape, both directly and through its "travels." However, this is not to suggest that earlier approaches were simply misplaced or should be replaced. There is recent work in cultural geography that has combined interpretive and experiential approaches effectively (Robertson 2007; Hawkins 2011). Susan Robertson, for example, considers urban infrastructure such as an elevated highway as at once something to be read as "a modernist marker" of the aspirations of a particular time and place, and as space experienced by mobile bodies (Robertson 2007).

That cultural geography has moved beyond the rural and antiquarian – leaving aside the issue of whether that association was valid in the first place – is beyond question. In addition, the importance of specifically *urban* landscapes appears set to continue to grow given the ongoing urbanization of the planet. Much of the action is taking place in regions of the world beyond the heartlands of academic knowledge production in North America and Western

Europe. Around half of the world's urban population now lives in Asia – and urbanization continues apace across much of that diverse region – yet cultural geographers continue to operate almost exclusively in Anglophone contexts, especially Britain. This brings us back, finally, to the question of cultural geography's Atlantic-centeredness. The largely unacknowledged Anglocentrism and regional specificity of what one might provocatively call transatlantic studies is surely problematic for any discipline that values cultural or contextual variation. To presume that analyzing urban landscapes in Britain or North America is sufficient for understanding "the urban" reduces developments in Asia and elsewhere to supposed Western antecedents – with a distinct whiff of modernization theory notions of progression. If cultural geography is to avoid a return to being cast as quaint and esoteric in an increasingly Asia Pacific-centered world, then a new generation of scholars will need commitment to learning languages other than English and acquiring cultural competencies often associated with area studies training. Ironically, this might proceed by looking at traditional Berkeley School forms of American cultural geography, which often emphasized overseas field-based empirical inquiry (Price and Lewis 1993). Such a move would enrich work on urban landscapes in cultural geography, whether focused on iconographic interpretation, on embodied experience, or on landscape-object travels – or, indeed, on some productive combination of them.

## References

Appadurai, A. (ed.) (1986) *The Social Life of Things: Commodities in Cultural Perspective*. Cambridge: Cambridge University Press.

Black, I. (1996) Symbolic capital: The London and Westminster Bank headquarters. *Landscape Research*, 21 (1), 55–72.

Bunnell, T. (1999) Views from above and below: The Petronas Twin Towers and/in contesting visions of development in contemporary Malaysia. *Singapore Journal of Tropical Geography*, 20, 1–23.

Bunnell, T. (2004) *Malaysia, Modernity and the Multimedia Super Corridor: A Critical Geography of Intelligent Landscapes*. London: RoutledgeCurzon.

Bunnell, T. (2008) Multiculturalism's regeneration: Celebrating *Merdeka* in a European Capital of Culture. *Transactions of the Institute of British Geographers*, 33 (2), 251–267.

Cartier, C. (1998) Megadevelopment in Malaysia: From heritage landscapes to "leisurescapes" in Melaka's tourism sector. *Singapore Journal of Tropical Geography*, 19 (2), 151–176.

Cartier, C. (1999) The state, property development, and symbolic landscape in high-rise Hong Kong. *Landscape Research*, 24 (2), 185–208.

Chang, T.C. (1997) From "instant Asia" to "multifaceted jewel": Urban imaging strategies and tourism development in Singapore. *Urban Geography*, 18 (6), 542–562.

Cook, I. *et al.* (2004) Follow the thing: Papaya. *Antipode*, 36 (4), 342–364.

Cosgrove, D. (1983) Towards a radical cultural geography. *Antipode*, 15, 1–11.

Cosgrove, D. (1998) *Social Formation and Symbolic Landscape*. Madison: University of Wisconsin Press.

Cosgrove, D. and Daniels, S. (eds.) (1988) *The Iconography of Landscape*. Cambridge: Cambridge University Press.

Cosgrove, D. and Jackson, P. (1987) New directions in cultural geography. *Area*, 19 (2), 95–101.

Cresswell, T. (1996) *In Place/Out of Place: Geography, Ideology and Transgression in England and the United States*. Minneapolis: University of Minnesota Press.

Cresswell, T. (2003) Landscape and the obliteration of practice. In *Handbook of Cultural Geography*, ed. K. Anderson, M. Domosh, S. Pile, and N. Thrift. London: Sage, pp. 269–281.

Daniels, S. (1993) *Fields of Vision: Landscape, Imagery and National Identity in England and the United States*. Cambridge: Polity.

della Dora, V. (2009) Travelling landscape-objects. *Progress in Human Geography*, 33 (3), 334–354.

Domosh, M. (1989) A method for interpreting landscape: A case study of the New York World Building. *Area*, 24 (1), 347–355.

Duncan, J.S. (1990) *The City as Text: The Politics of Landscape Interpretation in the Kandyan Kingdom.* New York: Cambridge University Press.

Duncan, J. and Duncan, N. (1988) (Re)reading the landscape. *Environment and Planning D: Society and Space*, 6, 117–126.

Edensor, T. (2010) Building stone in Manchester: Networks of materiality, circulating matter and the ongoing construction of the city. In *Re-shaping Cities: How Global Mobility Transforms Architecture and Urban Form*, ed. M. Guggenheim and O. Söderström. Abingdon: Routledge, pp. 211–230.

Edensor, T. and Millington, S. (2009) Illuminations, class identities and the contested landscapes of Christmas. *Sociology*, 43 (1), 103–121.

Gonzalez, S. (2011) Bilbao and Barcelona "in motion": How urban regeneration models "travel" and mutate in the global flows of policy tourism. *Urban Studies*, 48 (7), 1397–1418.

Gregson, N., Crang, M., Ahamed, F., Akhter, N. and Ferdous, R. (2010) Following things of rubbish value: End-of-life ships, "chocky-chocky" furniture and the Bangladeshi middle class consumer. *Geoforum*, 41, 646–654.

Grubbauer, M. (2010) The high-rise office tower as a global "type": Exploring the architectural world of Getty Images and Co, in M. Guggenheim and O. Soderstrom (eds) *Re-shaping Cities: How Global Mobility Transforms Architecture and Urban Form*. Routledge, Abingdon, pp. 63–80.

Harvey, D. (1989) From managerialism to entrepreneurialism: The transformation in urban governance in late capitalism. *Geografiska Annaler, Series B: Human Geography*, 71 (1), 3–17.

Hawkins, H. (2011) Dialogues and doings: Sketching the relationships between geography and art. *Geography Compass*, 5 (7), 464–478.

Hubbard, P. (1996) Re-imaging the city: The transformation of Birmingham's urban landscape. *Geography*, 81 (1), 26–36.

Jackson, P. (1989) *Maps of Meaning: An Introduction to Cultural Geography*. London: Unwin Hyman.

Jacobs, J.M. (2006) A geography of big things. *Cultural Geographies*, 13 (1), 1–27.

Johnson, N. (1995) Cast in stone: Monuments, geography and nationalism. *Environment and Planning D: Society and Space*, 13, 51–65.

Khoo, B.T. (1995) *Paradoxes of Mahathirism: An Intellectual Biography of Mahathir Mohamad*. Kuala Lumpur: Oxford University Press.

King, A.D. (1996) Worlds in the city: Manhattan transfer and the ascendance of spectacular space. *Planning Perspectives*, 11, 97–114.

King, A.D. (2004) *Spaces of Global Cultures: Architecture, Urbanism, Identity*. Routledge: London and New York.

Latham, A. (2003) Research, performance, and doing human geography: Some reflections on the diary-photograh, diary-interview method. *Environment and Planning A*, 35, 1993–2017.

Laurier, E. and Philo, C. (2006) Cold shoulders and napkins handed: Gestures of responsibility. *Transactions of the Institute of British Geographers*, 31, 193–207.

Lees, L. (2001) Towards a critical geography of architecture: The case of an ersatz colosseum. *Cultural Geographies*, 8 (1), 51–86.

Ley, D. (1995) Between Europe and Asia: The case of the missing sequoias. *Cultural Geographies*, 2 (2), 185–210.

Lorimer, H. (2005) Cultural geography: The busyness of being "more-than-representational." *Progress in Human Geography*, 29 (1), 83–94.

Macpherson, H.M. (2009) The intercorporeal emergence of landscape: Negotiating sight, blindness and ideas of landscape in the British countryside. *Environment and Planning A*, 41, 1042–1054.

Marcus, G.E. (1998) *Ethnography Through Thick and Thin*. Princeton: Princeton University Press.

Massey, D. (1993) Power-geometry and a progressive sense of place. In *Mapping the Futures: Local Cultures, Global Change*, ed. J. Bird, B. Curtis, T. Putnam, G. Robertson, and L. Tickner. New York: Routledge, pp. 59–69.

Matless, D. (1998) *Landscape and Englishness*. London: Reaktion.

McCann, E. (2011) Urban policy mobilities and global circuits of knowledge: Towards a research agenda. *Annals of the Association of American Geographers*, 101 (1), 107–130.

McNeill, D. (2009) *The Global Architect: Firms, Fame and Urban Form*. New York: Routledge.

Merriman, P., Revill, G., Cresswell, T., Lorimer, H., Matless, D., Rose, G. and Wylie, J. (2008) Landscape, mobility, practice. *Social and Cultural Geography*, 9 (2), 191–212.

Middleton, J. (2010) Sense and the city: Exploring the embodied geographies of urban walking. *Social and Cultural Geography*, 11 (6), 575–596.

Mills, C. (1988) "Life on the upslope": The postmodern landscape of gentrification. *Environment and Planning D: Society and Space*, 6, 169–190.

Mitchell, D. (1996) *The Lie of the Land: Migrant Workers and the Californian Landscape*. Minneapolis: University of Minnesota Press.

Mitchell, D. (2001) The lure of the local: Landscape studies at the end of a troubled century. *Progress in Human Geography*, 25 (2), 269–281.

Mitchell, D. (2003) Dead labor and the political economy of landscape: California living, California dying. In *Handbook of Cultural Geography*, ed. K. Anderson, M. Domosh, S. Pile, and N. Thrift. London: Sage, pp. 233–248.

Mitchell, W.J.T. (ed.) (1994) *Landscape and Power*. Chicago: University of Chicago Press.

Morris, N.J. (2011) Night walking: Darkness and sensory perception in a night-time landscape installation. *Cultural Geographies*, 18 (3), 315–342.

Olds, K. (1995) Globalization and the production of new urban spaces: Pacific Rim megaprojects in the late 20th century. *Environment and Planning A*, 27, 1713–1743

Olds, K. (2001) *Globalization and Urban Change: Capital, Culture and Pacific Rim Mega-Projects*. Oxford: Oxford University Press.

Pred, A. (1995) *Recognizing European Modernities: A Montage of the Present*. London and New York: Routledge.

Price, M. and Lewis, M. (1993) The reinvention of cultural geography. *Annals of the Association of American Geographers*, 83 (1), 1–17.

Ramsay, N. (2009) Taking-place: Refracted enchantment and the habitual spaces of the tourist souvenir. *Social and Cultural Geography*, 10, 197–217.

Robertson, S. (2007) Visions of urban mobility: The Westway, London, England. *Cultural Geographies*, 14 (1), 74–91.

Rose, G., Degen, M. and Basdas, D. (2010) More on "big things": Building events and feelings. *Transactions of the Institute of British Geographers*, 33, 334–349.

Rose, M. (2002) Landscape and labyrinths. *Geoforum*, 33 (4), 455–467.

Rose, M. and Wylie, J. (2006) Animating landscape. *Environment and Planning D: Society and Space*, 24, 475–479.

Schein, R. (1997) The place of landscape: A conceptual framework for interpreting an American scene. *Annals of the Association of American Geographers*, 87 (4), 660–680.

Sidaway, J.D. and Pryke, M. (2000) The strange geographies of "emerging markets." *Transactions of the Institute of British Geographers*, 25, 187–201.

Tan, S.B. (1992) Counterpoints in the performing arts of Malaysia. In *Fragmented Vision: Culture and Politics in Contemporary Malaysia*, ed. J.S. Kahn and F. Loh. Sydney: Allen and Unwin, pp. 282–303.

Thrift, N. (1996) *Spatial Formations*. London: Sage.

Thrift, N. and Dewsbury, J.D. (2000) Dead geographies, and how to make them live again. *Environment and Planning D: Society and Space*, 18, 411–432.

Ward, K. (2010) Towards a relational comparative approach to the study of cities. *Progress in Human Geography*, 34 (4), 471–487.

World Bank (1993) *The East Asian Miracle: Economic Growth and Public Policy*. New York: Oxford University Press.

Wylie, J. (2005) A single day's walking: Narrating self and landscape on the South West Coast Path. *Transactions of the Institute of British Geographers*, 30, 234–247.

# Chapter 26

# Domesticities

*Robyn Dowling and Emma R. Power*

Domesticities, as reflected in contemporary cultural geography and defined in this chapter, are the processes and sites through which people create senses of belonging, safety, security, and comfort. We use the plural rather than singular because domesticities are produced in myriad ways (homemaking, migration, imperialism), in diverse sites (houses, cars, colonial settlements), and across scales (home, city, national, transnational). For cultural geography, then, domesticities are of interest not only in and of themselves but also for the ways in which they illuminate the connections between identities, imaginaries, and geographies.

This pluralistic and processual understanding of domesticities is tangential to lay and scholarly uses of the term. In popular usage, domesticity connotes home and the domestic sphere – the sites of family, intimate relationships, and, frequently, the domain of women. Implicit in these definitions is the idea that domestic processes are separate from, and often inferior to, the worlds of work and men and that they operate at scales of the home and body rather than those of nation and globe. In scholarly terms, definitions of domesticity can be traced to the Neolithic term *domus*. Here, home was conceptualized as a place of culture in opposition to nature and wildness: the *agrios* (Hodder 1990). *Domus* was both a place and practice, referring literally to the house-as-home but also to the symbolic and material processes through which wildness was brought within the sphere of human influence through everyday practices around pottery, plants, and animals. At this early stage, *domus* was already strongly gendered and that included "mothering (women and children), nurturing (providing food), and caring (storage)" (Hodder 1990: 84) – a direct contrast with the masculine space and practices of *agrios*, which was associated with hunting, weapons, and death. The connection between culture and housing was formally recognized in early cultural geographers' efforts to record and map housing form. Informed by Sauerian approaches, Kniffen (1936), for example, developed a typology of American housing as a way of diagnosing cultural

*The Wiley Blackwell Companion to Cultural Geography*, First Edition.
Edited by Nuala C. Johnson, Richard H. Schein, and Jamie Winders.
© 2013 John Wiley & Sons, Ltd. Published 2016 by John Wiley & Sons, Ltd.

difference and diffusion across a landscape. Contemporary cultural geographers' engagement with domesticity both draws upon and exceeds these popular and historical definitions. Thus, this chapter begins with key theoretical currents in cultural geographers' understanding of domesticities, tracing the ways in which engagement with feminist, material culture, and postcolonial perspectives currently defines the term. It then considers domesticities through two lenses: domesticities in the house-as-home and domesticities beyond the house. Separately, these lenses encompass key geographical ideas; together, they encapsulate the spectrum of contemporary scholarship on domesticities.

## Theoretical Lineages

As we suggested in our discussion of *domus* above, theoretical articulations of domesticities have a long history. The dominant frameworks of twentieth-century human geography, however, often elided its importance. In Marxism, for example, domesticities are conceptualized in terms of the sphere of social reproduction in which labor power is reproduced and workers are fed, rested, clothed, and housed – a sphere which is, as elaborated by socialist feminists, tied to the sphere of production (Mackenzie and Damaris 1983). Domesticities in these frameworks are defined through, and practiced in, the private sphere, which, in turn, is separated from the public spheres of work and politics. With the "cultural turn" across the humanities and social sciences and the infiltration of postcolonial, poststructural, and feminist frameworks through cultural geography, conceptualizations of domesticities have broadened. Here, we elaborate on three key theoretical frameworks that conceptualize domesticity – feminism, postcolonialism, and material culture studies – and develop the concept of domestication as a unifying thread.

## Feminism

Feminist voices have perhaps been the loudest in understanding domesticities and, in particular, home. For feminist scholars, home is a key site in the daily lives of women and the reproduction of gendered identities and inequalities. The domestic sphere is socially constructed as, and can be in practice, the primary domain of women: childcare, housework, and other tasks of domestic labor, as well as management of household and family, take place within the home, often by women (Chapman 2004). These tasks, it is asserted, are central to the subordination of women in that they are culturally devalued and financially unvalued or undervalued. For instance, the notion of home as haven, as a sanctuary from society into which one retreats, may describe the lives of men for whom home is a refuge from work. It certainly does not, however, describe the lives of women for whom home is a workplace. For many women, home is also a space of violence, alienation, and emotional turmoil. Domestic violence, for example, constitutes the domestic sphere as unsafe and insecure. As lived experience, then, home can be oppressive for women.

The association of domesticity with a private sphere is strong but also criticized and reformulated from feminist perspectives (Pratt 2004). Empirically, scholars point out that the separation of public and private and the ascription of unique characteristics to each is class and race specific. Indeed, these "separate spheres" emerged out of unique historical and geographical circumstances where the separation of public and private served particular ideological, political, and economic purposes (Davidoff and Hall 2002). Moreover, the idea of separate spheres does not even hold empirically in the period from which it developed. For the English middle class of the eighteenth century, for example, men and women occupied both public and private life, such as women's involvement in the family business. Similarly, in nineteenth-century America, domestic intimacy was subject to significant societal evaluation and moral codes; the private sphere was governed by public norms. Domesticity, in the sense of a domestic sphere associated with women and the home, is constructed through connections with the public spheres of commerce and politics.

Feminists extend these empirical critiques theoretically to argue that the public and private are interdependent. Indeed, what is public has been defined through the exclusion of what is seen as private (Pateman 1989). It is here that the concept of domesticity is reformulated. Domesticity – sites and practices – is simultaneously public and private. Rather than being separated from public, political worlds, the domestic is constituted through the extra-domestic, and vice versa. Understanding domesticities, thus, requires as much attention to processes of commerce, imperialism, and politics as to household negotiations. Feminists have provided a number of compelling illustrations of this fluidity. Lesley Johnson's (1996) work on the housewife shows that experiences within the home, such as caring for children or older relatives, and relations with neighbors, are actually about creating citizens and modern subjects. Similarly, using the example of the domestic sphere in the nineteenth-century United States, Marston (2004) shows that the security and sanctity of the domestic sphere was justified materially and metaphorically to engage in national political debates. In feminist frameworks, then, domesticities are complex and connected to the constitution of gendered relations and identities.

## Postcolonialism

Postcolonial approaches to domesticity share feminism's concern with opening up the range of sites and social processes through which domesticity is experienced and produced. Postcolonial frameworks highlight the ways in which domestic ideologies, practices, and sites are linked to processes of imperialism, nationalism, and colonization, as well as to the racialization of identities (McClintock 1995). Within cultural geography, the work of Alison Blunt is most important here (1999, 2005). As Blunt explains, domestic ideologies and practices are central to colonizing processes, with impacts on both colonizer and colonized. On the one hand, material and symbolic domestic practices – the practice of making home and the gendered and racialized images of home – underpinned imperialism. On the other hand, homes within the colonial metropoles were constructed in light of imperialism. Domestic consumption practices and motherhood in Victorian Britain, for instance, reflected imperial ideas about racial purity (Blunt and Dowling 2006: 145).

Postcolonial framings of the contemporary era are more indirectly embedded in analyses of the ways in which domestic spheres are produced and maintained transnationally. A central postcolonial point – that senses of belonging and the practices that sustain them are produced as much beyond the home as within it – is used to examine the voluminous waves of migration that have occurred over the past thirty years. The term diaspora refers to the scattering of people across a number of sites, often transnationally. Diasporic domesticities are similarly transnational, both metaphorically and materially. Imaginaries of belonging, as sense of one's place in the world, are not tied to one "home" but to many for migrants. Material homes can also straddle more than one house, especially in the case of temporary migrants and business migrants. For these individuals, families and the domestic sphere are scattered across nations, termed "transnational households" for whom "there are two places of residence for the one household in two different countries" (Hardhill 2004: 386). Material cultures of home of British couples living in Dubai, for example, forge "home" in both Dubai and England (Walsh 2006). In the case of postcolonialism, then, two critical interventions in understanding domesticity are made: its imbrications with relations of power (e.g., imperialism, nationalism) and its multi-scalar character.

## Material Culture

Domestic practices and imaginaries proceed through relations with a more-than-human world. Various materials – bricks, wood, metals, and more – are used to create a house. In many approaches to domesticity, especially in Western culture, the achievement of belonging and the making of home are imagined as human accomplishments and in the realm of culture. More-than-human geographies of home examine the complexities of this relation and demonstrate home's dependence on non-human objects and actors, including "natural" elements such as water, air, and light. Home has also been examined as a site of cohabitation with non-human animals, from invited pets and companion animals that contribute to senses of home to uninvited pest species that threaten home as a safe and secure space (Franklin 2006; Power 2008, 2009a). Finally, the active materiality of home has been the subject of research with evidence that homemaking practices are influenced by the structures and designs of houses themselves (Miller 2002). This interest in the more-than-human has developed from an engagement with theories of materiality, including actor network theory, and notions of dwelling, which emphasize the embodied nature of homemaking and foreground the capacity of non-human others to productively shape and unmake home (Hitchings 2004; Power 2009a). Domesticity through a material culture lens, thus, highlights home as a more-than-human space and foregrounds the limits of human power in the material and imaginative production of home.

## Domestication

Our fourth theoretical lineage – domestication – is perhaps the least widely used across cultural geographies of domesticity but is also one with considerable conceptual purchase. We can think of domestication – in the broad sense of taming the wild or bringing the "other" into the frame of the powerful – across many of the examples we have introduced so far. British imperial rule in India, for example, involved the domestication of India, or its remaking through British eyes. The taming of spaces and places through domestic practices also has purchase at the urban scale, such as highlighted in Rowland Atkinson's (2003) "domestication by cappuccino," which denotes the colonization of inner cities by a new middle class. More generally, thinking domesticity through domestication further highlights intersections with relations of power. Cultural geographers have used the concept of domestication somewhat differently to describe the production of home as a human and "cultured" space. Humans have also, however, become physiologically and culturally domesticated through the making of home (Leach 2003). In this use domestication is a term and practice that is bound up with relations of power, particularly the extension of human power to the non-human world. Female sexuality and non-Western cultures have also been subject to these relations. Ideas about home, nature, and domestication have provided a foundation for racial hierarchies based on Western understandings of property, ownership, and possession. Anderson (1997), for example, shows that indigenous Australians have historically been constructed as "savages" as a result of their nomadic culture and perceived lack of fixed housing and agriculture, factors that suggest they are part of nature. In cultural geographies of domesticity, this inflection of domestication is important for its emphasis on the myriad processes of domesticating, the place of the more-than-human in domesticities, and relations of power.

These four theoretical lineages provide the scaffolding for contemporary cultural geographies of domesticity. Conceptually, they approach domesticity not in terms of dualism but in terms of interstices: nature–culture, public–private, power and identity. Similarly, they locate domestic practice both within and beyond the house-as-home. In what remains, we take a selective slice through this diverse literature to demonstrate the diversity of domesticity. We begin with the house-as-home – homemaking, spatial politics, and more-than-human achievements – and then move on to other scales.

## Domesticities at Home (1): Making the House-as-Home

Domesticity involves the making of houses into homes: domestic practice. Home does not simply exist but is made through everyday practices within and beyond the house-as-home. Research has attended to home as both an affective and a material space and shown that houses are made into homes through relations with and negotiations around objects, colors, furnishings, and textures, including the house itself (Miller 2002; Rose 2003; Young 2004). At its simplest, people choose items that they like and that create a sense of homeyness and belonging. Reflecting the dominant association between ideal "homey" homes and family/children in the contemporary Western imagination, objects that narrate social relations and familial connections have been shown to play a key role in achieving a sense of homeyness (Blunt and Dowling 2006). However, it is not simply the presence of these objects but the ways that they are used, arranged, and placed that is significant. In cohabiting households, the process of combining possessions and sharing decisions about the design and decoration of the house is an important way that houses are made into shared homes (Gorman-Murray 2006). Similarly, feelings of homeyness and familial connection emerge not just from the appearance and style of objects but through everyday practices that take place around these objects. For example, it is not simply the content of family photographs, but also the everyday practices that take place around photographs, such as looking at and sending them to relatives, that contribute to senses of belonging and familial connection (Rose 2003).

These relations are complex and multiple. Homemaking is not a one-way relation where people appropriate objects, furnishings, colors, and textures to achieve feelings of homeyness. Rather, homemaking is a multidirectional relation where the materiality of the house can challenge and disrupt residents' feelings of being at home. Miller's (2001, 2002) work on the relations of accommodation has been central in developing this understanding. Accommodation speaks explicitly to the materiality of homemaking, recognizing it as a multidirectional relation where people appropriate and change the dwelling place to suit their living patterns yet also change themselves and their living patterns to suit the house. Most interesting is the way that this understanding of homemaking stretches out the identity of the homemaker and the temporality of homemaking to recognize the ways that home is shaped by current and previous human residents as well as by the materiality of the house itself. These tensions and influences can be experienced in multiple, often banal ways. Miller (2001), for instance, describes how his feelings of homeyness are occasionally challenged and let down by the design of the house that he lives in. Although he likes the Arts-and-Crafts style that it represents, Miller finds it intimidating and challenging to furnish and decorate in a way that does not detract from the "creativity and style" of the original design. He also expresses a concern that the undesirable color scheme that the previous owners installed would appear, to visitors, as representing his own taste and style. It is here, when the materiality of home shapes everyday homemaking practice and the experience of being at home, that Miller identifies the material agency of the house itself.

Relations of accommodation are examined in recent research that explores how feelings of being at home are shaped by the materiality of the house, including house designs and furnishings. Dowling (2008) explores this relation through the experiences of people living in "open-plan houses": a house design in which family living spaces, dining area, and kitchens are co-located in one large room, typically at the back of a house. While some prefer open-plan living, others describe it as "blank" and experience anxiety that they cannot easily contain and supervise young children. This latter group often changed their living practices or the preferred layout of furniture to minimize the more problematic aspects of open-plan design. Gregson (2007) similarly highlights accommodation as an ongoing process of making the house feel homey and of adapting to undesirable and problematic aspects of the house. This adaptation involves a range of practices including acquisition, holding, sorting, and ridding and takes place over temporalities that range from the short to the long term. Moving into a new house, for example, is a stretched-out process where the new abode is gradually transformed into a home. In these relations the materiality of the house

> exerts effects on what we can do with it, place in it and on how it is possible to live in it and for what duration, particularly as our social relations change, as we age, (choose to) have children or not, keep animals or not and so on. (Gregson 2007: 34)

Furnishing and decorative choices, for example, can be influenced by the style and design of the house and existing furnishings. One of Gregson's participants explained how her choice of bathroom fittings and subsequent experience of the bathroom were determined by a sink that she saw and "had to have" (2007: 41). In this example the materiality of the house shapes the direction and nature of the resident's homemaking practices. The idea of accommodation has been an important tool in understanding domesticities and, in particular, the limits posed by the material environment of the domestic space. Such analysis has, however, been critiqued as exhibiting an overarching humanism because the notion of material agency that it develops is always bound up with the presence and activity of previous human residents and architects (Hitchings 2004). From this perspective, the material elements of home act as a sign that retains the presence and intent of previous residents, architects, and other significant people in the dwelling space but do not bring any capacities or properties independent of the people who designed, built, or lived in the house. This imaginatively places human agency at the center of homemaking.

Domesticity revolves around imaginaries of family and gender and, in particular, the nuclear family and the housewife. Home-based domestic practices are carried out by women in the process of "doing family": cooking, cleaning, and arranging are done not only in support of family life but also in the performance of familial and gendered identities. "Family," then, is made through relations within and beyond home, including these practices of homemaking. Andrey and Johnson (2010), for instance, discuss the pressure felt by mothers who are also involved in paid work away from home to vigilantly supervise children and be "available" in case of problems. Being "home for the kids" was an essential part of the way that some women maintained their "motherly" identity in the face of workplace demands (Andrey and Johnson 2010: 78). At the same time, an inability to participate in such vernacular activities can challenge gendered and familial identities. In his work on disability and homemaking, Imrie (2004) shows that housing designed around a normative body can be disabling for people who do not fit that norm. One participant, Ann, described how an inability to access kitchen cupboards and use the cooker was demoralizing as it challenged her identity as a mother.

Familial domesticities extend past, and draw from, worlds beyond the four walls of the house. Research about house-based domestic practices examines these imbrications and the ways that demands shaping the "public" sphere, including work, impact on home-based activities and relations. Recent examples of this work investigate the ways that contemporary challenges, such as flexible work and telework, are negotiated by homemakers (Andrey and Johnson 2010; Jarvis and Pratt 2006). The growing casualization of the workforce, increased proportions of dual-income households, and technologies that facilitate work from home are resulting in the increased interpenetration of paid employment and the domestic sphere. The time spent getting to work, flexible work practices that allow paid work to take place in the home, and extended work hours connect home to the temporal structure and demands of the workplace (Brannen 2005; Jarvis 2005; Kaufman-Scarborough 2006; Schwanen and Kwan 2008). People undertaking paid work in the domestic space illustrate the complexities of combining the temporalities associated with these conceptually separate spaces. Many experience the fragmentation of work time by the needs of children and domestic tasks. Where some workers try to maintain a separation between paid work and domestic tasks through strategies that include dressing in work clothes and working in an office-at-home, for others paid work is fit around the temporality of domestic and family demands, including the biological rhythms of children (Tietze and Musson 2002). These complex relations illustrate some ways that the practical interconnection of public and private are negotiated through the spatialities, materialities, and temporalities of home.

The ways that GLBQ subjects negotiate and challenge the heteronormativity of home through everyday homemaking similarly shows the stretching of domestic practices across private and public spheres (see especially Gorman-Murray 2006). For his participants the privacy of home was central to their sense of homeyness and acted as an antidote to their feeling of being out of place in spaces outside of home. Shared decisions between partners were also key in establishing and securing relationships, as were informed decisions to move house and more vernacular and regular choices around furnishings and home decoration. Renegotiating heterosexual norms around the use of space was also significant, with many couples emphasizing the importance of maintaining separate personal spaces within the home through private bathrooms and even bedrooms. In producing home as a couple's project yet also delineating the spatial boundaries of couples, understanding domesticity is expanded beyond the confines of heteronormativity.

Domestic practices also, however, take place beyond the home. Familial negotiations and the work of women in reproducing a family, for instance, occur across diverse sites such as the motor car. Dowling (2000) suggests that for women with children, the car is a "management tool" that they see as enabling them to be good mothers. Not only does it facilitate the mobility required to satisfy children's spatially dispersed activities, but it also became a site valued for its facilitation of domestic conversations. Rather than the home being the place in which children would share stories of their day, time spent in the car provided uninterrupted family time. Other urban spaces can also be domesticated, or made more home-like. These include non-traditional home spaces like prisons and sheltered accommodations, and also public spaces. In central Hong Kong, for example, Filipino domestic workers transform a public plaza into home, through cooking, reading, and writing letters to family in the Philippines (Law 2001). Interestingly, it is women's transformation and elongation of domestic spaces that figure prominently in this literature, perhaps indicative of women's more prevalent use of the domestic in oppositional ways or of researchers' continued blindness to links between domesticities and other social constructions like masculinity and childhood.

## Domesticities at Home (2): More-than-Human Domesticities

A second key area in cultural geographies of domesticity examines the more-than-human nature of home and domestic practice, highlighting the ways that non-humans are active in homemaking. This new area of research intersects and extends research into the materialities of contemporary domesticities by productively drawing it together with posthumanist ideas. Posthumanism is a conceptual approach that examines the interplay of human and non-human agency in world-making, effectively decentering the human agent. Where earlier work showed that home is imagined as a human space and site of culture in opposition to nature (e.g., Fiske, Hodge, and Turner 1987; Wilson 1992), this more recent research has foregrounded the complexity and multi-directional nature of homemaking, drawing attention to the more-than-human nature of home and domestic practice. Supported by a focus on the practices and materialities of homemaking, this research has made four key contributions. First, it has shown that the idea of home as a place of culture is not "natural" but rather imaginatively and materially produced through ongoing practices that separate home from nature and the outside. Second, it has demonstrated that despite home's appearance as a place of culture it is materially connected to and dependent upon non-human natures. Third, this work has begun to unsettle and decentralize the position of the human homemaker by highlighting home as a site of cohabitation with active non-human animals. Finally, it has foregrounded the numerous more-than-human agencies at play in the making of home, demonstrating that non-living objects such as light and water play a key and active role in the production of home.

A first step in this research has been to unsettle academic and popular framings of the house/home as a human place separate from nature, non-humans, and the "outside." It has done so by demonstrating that this separation is not natural or essential. Rather, research has shown that dualistic nature/culture frameworks imaginatively and materially inform the design and construction of the house-as-home and are (re)produced in everyday homemaking activities. Cleaning practices are one way that people effect these divisions in home, removing pestilent organisms and ridding the house-as-home of the bodily outputs of companion animals (Douglas 1966; Ger and Yenicioglu 2004). Housing structures and technologies help to consolidate this separation. For example, climate-control technologies such as air conditioning modify and standardize the house's internal environment and contribute to a sense of home as distinct and secure against a more unruly, variable external environment (Shove 2003). Similarly, invisible networks that supply water and electricity to the house-as-home facilitate a view of home as operating independently of environmental rhythms and constraints. Electric lighting, for instance, allows the house-as-home to operate outside the diurnal rhythms of daylight and darkness (Hinchliffe 1997; see also Kaika 2004). These practices reproduce and normalize the dominant perception of home as a space distinct from nature.

A second area of research expands the focus on the material production of home as a space of culture by demonstrating home's connection to, and reliance on, "natural" processes and spaces. Most notably, Kaika (2004) uses water as a vehicle to demonstrate this reliance and connectivity. Water is essential to the construction of home as a comfortable, clean space. It is essential for the cleansing of home and self; and cultures of home and self-care have co-evolved with the availability of clean, cheap, and readily accessible water (see also Shove 2003). Nonetheless, water is contrastingly imagined as separate and part of nature. Kaika shows that this construction is overcome by the social and material production of water as a purified and domesticated commodity. It is "abstracted, dammed, channelled, stored, distilled and chlorinated" (Kaika 2004: 274), shifting geographically and conceptually from the country (nature) to the city and ultimately the home. "Dirty" water, by contrast, is removed from home. Water's invisibility within home is spatially guaranteed through building and design practices that hide this essential infrastructure within wall cavities and below ground. Electricity production and supply is similar, distancing home from pollutive outputs and contributing to senses of home as an autonomous space with clearly controlled borders (Hinchliffe 1997). The ideological and conceptual construction of home as a space distinct from non-human natures contrasts with its material dependence on nature and natural processes. This paradox of the modern home means that home contains the seeds of its own undoing, as it constitutes nature as an uncanny presence with the potential to emerge and disrupt nature/culture separations and, with them, residents' sense of homeyness (Kaika 2004).

A third area of research broadens understandings of home in different ways, examining home as a site of cohabitation with non-human animals including pests and companion animals and challenging the humanism of existing geographies of home through recognition of a distinctly more-than-human agency (Franklin 2006; Power 2009a). Animals, both invited and uninvited, cohabit the house-as-home and significantly shape meanings of home and homemaking practices. Companion animals influence diverse homemaking practices, including "housing choice and design, furnishing and the internal configuration of space" (Franklin 2006: 154). They actively co-define the nature of the companionate relation as well as the form of the house, both disrupting and opening up new ways of living home. Smith (2003), for example, recounts her experiences of "becoming animal" as she learns to cohabit with rabbit ways of living. Dogs similarly change the ways that people think about home and practice homemaking, from influencing relations of family (Power 2008) to shaping furniture choices and cleaning practices (Gregson 2007). Uninvited animals also significantly impact home. In Australia, native common brushtail possums frequently dwell in the ceiling and wall cavities of the house-as-home, leaving at dusk and returning at dawn and traveling across rooftops, squealing and fighting. This presence not only impacts human residents' sleep patterns but also, in this settler context, shapes senses of homeyness and belonging to the nation and disrupts senses of the house-as-home as a secure, comfortable, and safe space (Power 2009a).

A final area of research explores the ways that non-living objects, elements, and materials are active in homemaking. This developing area of research expands Miller's (2002) notion of "accommodation," highlighting domesticities as more-than-human achievements that emerge through ongoing entwinements with more-than-human, more-than-living entities and hence also reflect the qualities, capacities, and properties of diverse other-than-human actors. Braun reflects on how an entity such as water might be understood:

Water flows. It reacts with certain chemicals and dissolves others. Often these dissolved chemicals are invisible, and diffuse rapidly and uncontrollably. Water evaporates when warmed, condenses when cooled, and, as any homeowner in Minneapolis knows, expands when it freezes. It obstructs movement and enables movement. It serves as a pathway for viruses and bacteria, but is also used to cleanse. It seeps into porous materials, but flows across those that are nonporous. (2005: 645–646)

Similarly, developing a materiality of luminosity, Bille and Sørensen (2007: 265) foreground the ways that light is "manipulated and used in social and material practices" that utilize its capacity to "reveal or conceal aspects of material and social life." Light is used as a material in architecture to "hide 'faults' and illuminate places in a house, and thus ultimately to transform spaces" (2007: 271). It can also be used to create atmosphere, including a sense of homeyness (Dowling 2008: 545; see Young 2004 on the role of color in real estate decisions). Sound can similarly create and delineate places, as well as disrupt and disturb. Noise can affect the value of residential areas and both support and challenge residents' sense of autonomy in the domestic space (Atkinson 2007). House structures are also significant. The rhythms of aging and decay that affect the physical structures of home shape the temporalities and practices of homemaking as they demand the response of human inhabitants (Power 2009b). Such insights offer opportunities to rethink cultural geographies of home in ways that foreground the materiality of domestic space and its entwinement with broader cultures and practices of home.

## Domesticities and Colonization

Domestic ideals and objects are part of colonizing processes at urban, national, and transnational scales, as we outlined in our discussion of the concept of domestication. Below, we provide examples of each of these. At the scale of the city, domesticity can be understood as part of class colonization processes. In particular, visions of middle-class domesticity inform the design of housing and neighborhoods for working-class and racially diverse populations, just as they have in imperializing processes. In postwar suburban Sydney, for example, public (social) housing was constructed to address a severe housing shortage amidst a rapidly increasing population. To receive housing, however, potential residents were assessed according to standards of middle-class domesticity (see Morgan 2006). In particular, they were required to demonstrate that they were able to live in a respectable manner, which entailed not only the ability to pay rent but also the display of appropriate neighborly behavior and certain standards of housing maintenance and aesthetic requirements like maintaining gardens. Renters were subject to inspections after occupancy, and adherence to these standards was assessed. These norms, as Morgan shows, were particularly onerous for Aboriginal applicants and an important element of the colonization of Aboriginal peoples in urban Australia. Lauster and Tester (2010) demonstrate the mobilization of middle-class ideals of domesticity in a very different context: the eastern Arctic. Canadian national standards on domestic crowding, they argue, reflect middle-class norms in delimiting the maximum number, gender, and age of housing occupants. Moreover, these standards have been used in various disciplining processes in the eastern Arctic since the 1960s, requiring Inuit families not only to live in houses (rather than tents or igloos) but also to transform culturally specific sleeping arrangements. The mobilization of culturally, racially, and class-specific norms of domesticity within cities, then, is one instance of domestication as colonization.

Domesticities have also been central to projects of nation building and the colonization of indigenous peoples and spaces they might entail. In Australia and other colonial nations, domestication, inflected as the culturing of a nature perceived as wild and threatening, is a key way that the unfamiliar and unsafe have been made familiar and safe – as home. In Australia such narratives can be traced to the words and practices of early European settlers. The diaries of Governor Phillip, the first Governor of the colony, situate the domestication of the unfamiliar land and people as an essential act of colonization.

> There are few things more pleasing than the contemplation of order and useful arrangement, arising gradually out of tumult and confusion; and perhaps this satisfaction cannot anywhere be more fully enjoyed than where a settlement of civilised people is fixing itself upon a newly discovered or savage coast. The wild appearance of the land entirely untouched by cultivation [ . . . ], are the first objects that present themselves [ . . . ]. But by degrees large spaces are opened, plans are formed, lines marked, and a prospect at least of future regularity is clearly discerned, and is made more striking by the recollection of former confusion. (Phillip and Auchmuty 1970: 69)

On a more vernacular level, these ideals influenced the making of the house-as-home and the production of domestic gardens, relations that Holmes (1999: 152) describes as a "ritual of habitation" through which British settlers to Australia "established themselves in a foreign landscape." These more-than-human projects involve intensive and ongoing engagements between people and non-human animals and plants. From the early days of the colony when land was claimed through inhabitation by domestic livestock and land subdivision and survey followed the movements of sheep and sheepherders (Meinig 1962) to the contemporary processes of quarantine that maintain the nation as a secure and perceptibly unified space (Muller *et al.* 2009), practices of domestication have been a process of colonization connected to Western notions of civilization and private property.

Finally, domesticities are part of colonizing processes transnationally. In cultural geography, much attention has been focused on the ways in which imperial power relies upon imagined and material homemaking practices and the domestication of imperial subjects. As Blunt summarizes in relation to the establishment of British homes in India, they were "essential not only for the reproduction of legitimate imperial rulers, but also for the reproduction of the domestic, social and moral values legitimating imperial rule" (Blunt and Dowling 2006: 145). Links between home and imperialism, then, are myriad, especially vis-à-vis the centrality of representations of home in the imperial imagination. Similarly, the domestication of empire was critical in achieving the hegemony of imperial rule. Exhibitions in London like the Ideal Home Exhibition, for example, brought the materials and peoples of places outside London figuratively and literally out of the realm of "exotic others" and into the domestic sphere (Blunt and Dowling 2006). Finally, domesticating the colonies was important in colonizing processes. Alison Blunt (2005) has demonstrated the ways that the making of home by British women in India under British rule was a tangible and visible element of the colonizing process. Domesticating empire was certainly contested, and in this respect domesticity became central to resistance to imperial rule as well (see Blunt 2005). In sum, definitions, discourses, and practices of domesticity were essential to the politics of imperialism and colonizing processes.

## Conclusion

This chapter has illustrated the ways in which contemporary cultural geographies of domesticity highlight the making of domestic spaces as a more-than-human, multi-scalar, multi-dimensional, and power-laden process. Looking forward, this understanding gives cultural geographies of domesticity an important role in engaging with, and understanding, a climate-changing world in which long-held constructions of nature and culture will be challenged, geopolitical relations shift, and meanings of home altered. For example, cultural geographies of domesticities are well positioned to play a key role in public debates and interventions in household sustainabilities (Lane and Gorman-Murray 2011). Research in domesticities has an important role in examining these changes, as well as in contributing to a force for change by identifying opportunities for adaptation. At the household scale, such research has commenced, albeit in early stages, as cultural geographers begin to grapple with the intersections between everyday household practices and (un)sustainable living (Dowling and Power 2011) and to highlight the role of the household as a crucible for change (Gibson *et al.* 2011). Perceptions of home as a site that is autonomous of nature may be challenged by these changes and may play an important role in prompting more sustainable household practice. Research may also focus on charting links, however tangential, between various modes of domesticity and resilience and adaptation of communities across the world. It might, too, suggest the importance of remaining alert to any colonizing impulses that may inhere in mobilizing domesticity to these ends. Future research in this field, then, offers exciting possibilities for modes of domestication appropriate in a carbon-free landscape.

## References

Anderson, K. (1997) A walk on the wild side: A critical geography of domestication. *Progress in Human Geography*, 21 (4), 463–485.

Andrey, J. and Johnson, L.C. (2010) Being home: Family spatialities of teleworking households. In *Family Geographies: The Spatiality of Families and Family Life*, ed. B.C. Hallman. Ontario: Oxford University Press, pp. 68–87.

Atkinson, R. (2003) Domestication by cappuccino or a revenge on urban space? Control and empowerment in the management of public spaces. *Urban Studies*, 40 (9), 1829–1843.

Atkinson, R. (2007) Ecology of sound: The sonic order of urban space. *Urban Studies*, 44 (10), 1905–1917.

Bille, M. and Sørensen, T.F. (2007) An anthropology of luminosity: The agency of light. *Journal of Material Culture*, 12 (3), 263–284.

Blunt, A. (1999) Imperial geographies of home: British women in India, 1886–1925. *Transactions of the Institute of British Geographers*, 24, 421–440.

Blunt, A. (2005) *Domicile and Diaspora: Anglo-Indian Women and the Spatial Politics of Home*. Oxford: Blackwell.

Blunt, A. and Dowling, R. (2006) *Home*. London: Routledge.

Brannen, J. (2005) Time and the negotiation of work–family boundaries. *Time and Society*, 14 (1), 113–131.

Braun, B. (2005) Environmental issues: Writing a more-than-human geography. *Progress in Human Geography*, 29 (5), 635–650.

Chapman, T. (2004) *Gender and Domestic Life: Changing Practices in Families and Households*. Basingstoke: Palgrave.

Davidoff, L. and Hall, C. (2002) *Family Fortunes: Men and Women of the English Middle Class, 1780–1850*. London: Routledge.

Douglas, M. (1966) *Purity and Danger: An Analysis of Concepts of Pollution and Taboo*. London: Routledge and Kegan Paul.

Dowling, R. (2000) Cultures of mothering and car use in suburban Sydney: A preliminary investigation. *Geoforum*, 31 (3), 345–353.

Dowling, R. (2008) Accommodating open-plan: Children, clutter and containment in suburban houses in Sydney, Australia. *Environment and Planning A*, 40, 536–549.

Dowling, R. and Power, E.R. (2011) Beyond McMansions and green homes: Thinking household sustainability through materialities of homeyness. In *Material Geographies of Household Sustainability*, ed. R. Lane and A. Gorman-Murray. Farnham: Ashgate.

Fiske, J., Hodge, B. and Turner, G. (1987) *Myths of Oz: Reading Australian Popular Culture*. North Sydney: Allen and Unwin.

Franklin, A. (2006) "Be[a]ware of the dog": A post-humanist approach to housing. *Housing, Theory and Society*, 23 (3), 137–156.

Ger, G. and Yenicioglu, B. (2004) Clean and dirty: Playing with boundaries of consumer's safe havens. *Advances in Consumer Research*, 31, 462–467.

Gibson, C., Head, L., Gill, N. and Waitt, G. (2011) Climate change and household dynamics: Beyond consumption, unbounding sustainability. *Transactions of the Institute of British Geographers*, 36 (1), 3–8.

Gorman-Murray, A. (2006) Gay and lesbian couples at home: Identity work in domestic space. *Home Cultures*, 3 (2), 145–168.

Gregson, N. (2007) *Living with Things: Ridding, Accommodation, Dwelling*. Oxford: Sean Kingston Publishing.

Hardhill, I. (2004) Transnational living and moving experiences: Intensified mobility and dual career households. *Population, Space and Place*, 10, 375–389.

Hinchliffe, S. (1997) Locating risk: Energy use, the "ideal" home and the non-ideal world. *Transactions of the Institute of British Geographers*, 22, 197–209.

Hitchings, R. (2004) At home with someone nonhuman. *Home Cultures*, 1 (2), 169–186.

Hodder, I. (1990) *The Domestication of Europe: Structure and Contingency in Neolithic Societies*. Oxford: Blackwell.

Holmes, K. (1999) Gardens. *Imaginary Homelands: The Dubious Cartographies of Australian Identity*, 61, 152–162.

Imrie, R. (2004) Disability, embodiment and the meaning of the home. *Housing Studies*, 19, 745–764.

Jarvis, H. (2005) Moving to London time: Household co-ordination and the infrastructure of everyday life. *Time and Society*, 14 (1), 133–154.

Jarvis, H. and Pratt, A.C. (2006) Bringing it all back home: The extensification and "overflowing" of work: The case of San Francisco's new media households. *Geoforum*, 37, 331–339.

Johnson, L. (1996) "As housewives we are worms": Women, modernity and the home question. *Cultural Studies*, 10 (3), 449–463.

Kaika, M. (2004) Interrogating the geographies of the familiar: Domesticating nature and constructing the autonomy of the modern home. *International Journal of Urban and Regional Research*, 28 (2), 265–286.

Kaufman-Scarborough, C. (2006) Time use and the impact of technology: Examining workspaces in the home. *Time and Society*, 15 (1), 57–80.

Kniffen, F.B. (1936) Louisiana house types. *Annals of the Association of American Geographers*, 26 (4), 179–193.

Lane, R. and Gorman-Murray, A. (ed.) (2011) *Material Geographies of Household Sustainability*. Farnham: Ashgate.

Lauster, N. and Tester, F. (2010) Culture as a problem in linking material inequality to health: On residential crowding in the Arctic. *Health and Place*, 16, 523–530.

Law, L. (2001) Home cooking: Filipino women and geographies of the senses in Hong Kong. *Ecumene*, 8 (3), 264–283.

Leach, H.M. (2003) Human domestication reconsidered. *Current Anthropology*, 44 (3), 349–368.

Mackenzie, S. and Damaris, R. (1983) Industrial change, the domestic economy and home life. In *Redundant Spaces in Cities and Regions*, ed. J. Anderson, S. Duncan, and R. Hudston. London: Academic Press, pp. 157–176.

Marston, S. (2004) A long way from home: Domesticating the social production of scale. In *Scale and Geographic Inquiry: Nature, Society and Method*, ed. E. Sheppard and R. McMaster. Oxford: Blackwell, pp. 170–191.

McClintock, A. (1995) *Imperial Leather: Race, Gender and Sexuality in the Colonial Context*. London: Routledge.

Meinig, D.W. (1962) *On the Margins of the Good Earth: The South Australian Wheat Frontier, 1869–1884*. Chicago: McNally.

Miller, D. (2001) Possessions. In *Home Possessions: Material Culture Behind Closed Doors*, ed. D. Miller. Oxford: Berg, pp. 107–121.

Miller, D. (2002) Accommodating. In *Contemporary Art and the Home*, ed. C. Painter. Oxford: Berg, pp. 115–130.

Morgan, G. (2006) *Unsettled Places: Aboriginal People and Urbanisation in New South Wales*. Adelaide: Wakefield Press.

Muller, S., Power, E.R., Suchet-Pearson, S., Wright, S. and Lloyd, K. (2009) "Quarantine matters!": Quotidian relationships around quarantine in Australia's northern borderlands. *Environment and Planning A*, 41, 780–795.

Pateman, C. (1989) *The Disorder of Women: Democracy, Feminism and Political Theory*. Stanford: Stanford University Press.

Phillip, A. and Auchmuty, J.J. (1970) *The Voyage of Governor Phillip to Botany Bay*. Sydney: Angus and Robertson in association with the Royal Australian Historical Society.

Power, E.R. (2008) Furry families: Making a human–dog family through home. *Social and Cultural Geography*, 9 (5), 535–555.

Power, E.R. (2009a) Border-processes and homemaking: Encounters with possums in suburban Australian homes. *Cultural Geographies*, 16 (1), 29–54.

Power, E.R. (2009b) Domestic temporalities: Nature times in the house-as-home. *Geoforum*, 40 (6), 1024–1032.

Pratt, G. (2004) *Working Feminism*. Philadelphia: Temple University Press.

Rose, G. (2003) Family photographs and domestic spacings: A case study. *Transactions of the Institute of British Geographers*, 28 (1), 5–18.

Schwanen, T. and Kwan, M.-P. (2008) The Internet, mobile phone and space–time constraints. *Geoforum*, 39 (3), 1362–1377.

Shove, E. (2003) *Comfort, Cleanliness and Convenience: The Social Organization of Normality*. Oxford: Berg.

Smith, J.A. (2003) Beyond dominance and affection: Living with rabbits in post-humanist households. *Society and Animals*, 11 (2), 181–197.

Tietze, S. and Musson, G. (2002) When "work" meets "home": Temporal flexibility as lived experience. *Time and Society*, 11 (2/3), 315–334.

Walsh, K. (2006) British expatriate belongings: Mobile homes and transnational homing. *Home Cultures*, 3 (2), 123–144.

Wilson, A. (1992) *The Culture of Nature: North American Landscape from Disney to Exxon Valdez*. Oxford: Blackwell.

Young, D.J.B. (2004) The material value of color: The estate agent's tale. *Home Cultures*, 1 (1), 5–22.

# Natures/Cultures

*The Wiley Blackwell Companion to Cultural Geography*, First Edition.
Edited by Nuala C. Johnson, Richard H. Schein, and Jamie Winders.
© 2013 John Wiley & Sons, Ltd. Published 2016 by John Wiley & Sons, Ltd.

# Chapter 27

# Choosing Metaphors for the Anthropocene: Cultural and Political Ecologies

*Paul Robbins*

During the very hot summer of 2003, the otherwise staid and conservative science journal *Nature* splattered the following on its editorial page: "Welcome to the Anthropocene" (Editorial 2003). This was to introduce an essay that urged scientists to communicate about the ecologically unprecedented world in which we find ourselves, one in which 83 percent of the earth's land surface has been influenced or altered by humanity (Center for International Earth Science Information Network 2011). The concept of a fully transformed world has been in circulation for more than a decade, but the term "Anthropocene" was most famously proposed by chemist Paul Joseph Crutzen (2002) to be assigned to the current geological epoch (vis-à-vis previous periods, e.g., the Pliocene or Miocene epochs, millions of years ago) because human activities have come to have significant global impact. Taken to include the whole gamut of human impacts on the earth, including deforestation, greenhouse gas emissions, and so on, Crutzen suggests the period started roughly 200 years ago, when James Watt designed the steam engine in 1784.

In this sense, the Anthropocene is a *metaphor*, a clever use of language to invert our perspective about human life and environmental order. To announce the Anthropocene is to suggest that it was *as if* humanity was a single planetary force, comparable to plate tectonics, the rock cycle, and other earth-scale systems. The power of this metaphor is startling. Rather than passengers riding through a vast concatenation of planetary forces over millennia, human beings are centered here as the architects of the earth's (runaway) socio-environments. As such, the term is a *cultural* artifact, an expressive, almost playful symbolic inversion that re-signs the meaning of earth history and people as planetary agents.

Alternative metaphors are necessarily available, of course, including people as a cancer on the earth, or people as stewards. The difference between each of these metaphors is important, insofar as each – if taken seriously – holds very different *political* implications.

*The Wiley Blackwell Companion to Cultural Geography*, First Edition.
Edited by Nuala C. Johnson, Richard H. Schein, and Jamie Winders.
© 2013 John Wiley & Sons, Ltd. Published 2016 by John Wiley & Sons, Ltd.

By directing attention to certain capacities and implying both blame and ideals and goals, these contending metaphors are bound up with normative implications for the control and redistribution of resources, the ability, authority, or obligations of certain people or groups to act or restrain action. The Anthropocene conveys both a cultural and political ecology, therefore.

Of course, the relationship between humans and non-humans has always been something of an elephant – as the old cliché goes – as viewed by blind men. It is polymorphous and complex enough to be seen in many ways at once, with a result being a proliferation of disagreements over what exactly the true nature of that relationship is. In this chapter, I briefly review several of the dominant metaphors in geography that have sought to encapsulate the relationship between humans and the non-human world, showing how each opens interesting views on the problem while closing down others. These metaphors are the stuff of the research field of cultural ecology and political ecology. The former field works to explain human adaption to physical environments and vice versa (see especially Steward 1972; Ellen 1982; Netting 1986; Turner 1989), while the latter field seeks to merge the "concerns of ecology and a broadly defined political economy" (Blaikie and Brookfield 1987: 17; see also Neumann 2005; Peet, Robbins, and Watts 2010; Robbins 2012). Each field seeks to further examine the concepts and languages that are used to describe these complex relationships, even while each field proliferates new metaphors at the same time.

By *metaphor*, I mean the insertion of a core concept or image that stands in place of the complex, indeterminate, and myriad relationships people have with one another and with non-humans. I further intend to suggest that the use of metaphor in this role is not only ubiquitous but ultimately necessary. This is because there is no way to practically and effectively describe and know the world in total. Instead it is far more succinct and powerful to think about it *as if* it were a "system," a "network," or a set of "functions." This assumes that our understanding of nature is always approximated through culture, by the invocation and grafting of meaning on our place in the world. This is not to say, however, that our relationships with the world are unknowable and cannot be sorted by experiment, experience, or empirical measurement. Rather, it simply must be admitted that the history of ideas shows the significance of *culture* in setting the terms for how we interpret and understand this relationship. More than this, as I will suggest here, each such metaphor – by obscuring and revealing parts of these complex relations – has profound implications for the adjudication of disputes, the imposition of power, and the justification of control. As such, each metaphor is also inevitably and profoundly *political*.

And when thinking about "nature," such metaphors do seem to proliferate! While some of these metaphors must be seen as more problematic (or even dangerous) than others, it is not the intention here to debunk them in pursuit of a single superior view. Instead, I hope to emphasize that these reflect the difficulty of the enterprise of analyzing society–nature relations in any field, whether it is called environmental geography, cultural ecology, or political ecology. I hope also to stress the many insights that emerge from the effort geographers have taken from the very start of their craft to come to grips with this question and the many efforts described here reflect the energy and creativity of that undertaking.

Though the diversity of accounts is too great to capture totally, several dominant themes are reviewed here, all of which share the unevenly realized ambition of achieving explanatory symmetry between people and the non-human world. First among these are accounts of nature and society that stress the determinant and driving effects of environmental influences over the emergence of cultural and social differences worldwide ("determinism"). A related theme stresses the ecologically functional qualities of various facets of human culture and society ("functionalism"). A radical reversal and response to these approaches is reflected in socio-environmental thinking that stresses human ingenuity and productive alteration of the environment ("adaptation"). More recent metaphors for human–environment relationships stress the *mutuality* of people's influence on the environment and vice versa. Preferred in many current environmental sciences, one such metaphor is that of the "coupled system," which highlights feedbacks and complex equilibria. More *ad hoc* and inductive approaches are based in "network" thinking, which stresses the way people and things become entangled in changing relationships. Each of these opens a window onto the way humans are inter-twined with the non-human world around (and within) them, but as will be argued here, each contains and conveys political implications that are often highly problematic and admit-tedly partial. I present these in the hope that critical engagements with the logic of previous geographic investigations can help lay the foundation for us to write our way into a new vocabulary for the Anthropocene.

## Society from the Soil: The Specter of Evolutionism and Determinism

Amongst these metaphors, perhaps the most persistent concept is determinism, an idea simul-taneously so compelling and so profoundly problematic that it seems neither to go fully away, nor to ease in its dangerous influence over development policy and geopolitics (Robbins 2012). As early as the 1880s, many geographers came to understand their role as tracing "the interaction of man in society and so much of his environment as varies locally" (Mackinder 1887: 143). This perspective would take many forms but chief amongst these was the effort to unravel the apparent mystery of European hegemony on the world stage. How did Europe come to rule Africa and Asia? To answer this, classical determinists, including Friedrich Ratzel and Ellsworth Huntington, posited that "advanced" cultures were those which had earliest agricultural civilization. As Halford Mackinder (1887: 157) explains, "certain conditions of climate and soil are needed for the aggregation of dense populations. A certain density of population seems necessary to the development of civilization." By implication, the contem-porary distribution of "civilization" must be explained by the distribution of good climates and soil. An image of cultural evolution is offered here, of a kind of footrace between discon-nected places, all progressing toward advancement, with those well endowed with agricultural surpluses receiving a kind of "head start" and so coming out "on top."

There is some interesting analysis that might be leveraged from this way of seeing the nature–culture relationship. In the early work of Ellen Churchill Semple, for example, we can find careful reconstruction of the diverse economies around the Mediterranean, whose need for varying forest products encouraged complex systems of trade (Semple 1919). The distri-bution of tree species, controlled in part by climatic limits, unquestionably conditioned the direction and flow of wood and resin-dependent economies. We might call this a "soft" determinism that provides some useful insights.

And on its face, this sort of metaphor serves an apparently liberal agenda. This logic may be mobilized, notably, for a certain kind of anti-racist argument. In its most contemporary iteration, Jared Diamond's *Guns, Germs, and Steel* (1997), an effort is made to explicitly stress that the people of the world are genetically identical in almost every regard and that the "superior" position of some places over others cannot be accounted for by race, and must instead be the historic inheritance of deeply geographic factors: soils, rainfall, growing seasons, isolation and connectivity.

Unfortunately for the determinists, however, evidence for these mechanisms and histories has consistently proven harder to assemble than to assume. Early in the development of determinism, and with mounting frustration, its advocates came to bemoan the limits of the available data (Brigham 1915). Seeking clear connections between specific places and specific types of people, researchers were met with diversity amongst groups, similarities between cultures, and terrific contradictions as to the direction of environmental influences (cold weather or disease being "good" for social development in some cases and "bad" in others). Evidence of high civilization in poor climates proliferated. Archaeology continued to unseat assumptions, moreover, as the development of agriculture was found to independently emerge in many places and at early dates, especially in places considered "unsuited" *a priori* by Eurocentric thinkers (most notably tropical Southeast Asia).

In such an account, the historical role of slavery and colonialism vanishes and the dominance of Asian, Indian Ocean, and trans-African economies prior to 1492 must be carefully ignored to sustain this argument (Abu-Lughod 1989; Blaut 1992, 2000; Frank 1998). Regrettably, moreover, even the most laudable anti-racist arguments embedded in determinism carry with them the taint of colonial logics. The metaphor imposes on us a false choice, which the classic determinist Ellsworth Huntington posed as "Race or Place," in language that exposes the very pejoratives and hierarchical class logics it appears to spurn:

> [I]t is only in adverse climates that we find the "cracker" type of "poor white trash" developing in appreciable numbers. If white men lived thousands of years in Egypt, it seems probable that a large proportion of them would degenerate to this type. (Huntington 1915: 33–34)

If people are "backwards," the determinists ask, and you reject racism, then you must accept the accidental influence of the environment in accounting for Anglo-European ascendance. In such a unilinear evolutionary view of society, successful or advanced civilization is assumed, *a priori*, to be that of Western Europe (and its later colonies in North America and Australia) and these must be used as the yardstick of progress and civilization against which all other socio-natures are judged, and from which all other advances emerge. In this sense, determinism is a socio-natural metaphor rooted in what James Blaut describes as the "colonizer's model of the world" (Blaut 1993). Thus, the return of deterministic thinking, not only in popular books (Landes 1998), but especially in the circles of international development (Gallup 2003), must be considered politically loaded. It must also be considered a model profoundly out of step with the dawning notion that human influence on the earth may be more important than the reverse flow of the earth's environments over people.

## Hardwiring: Functional Materialism and Biosocial Thinking

Another set of metaphors that tend to "naturalize" (following Castree 2005) social relationships for human society and culture comes in the forms of cultural materialism and sociobiology. Cultural materialism, more precisely described as Darwinian ecological anthropology (Symons 1989), provides explanations for contemporary cultural practices by appealing to the functional advantages they provide, or may have provided in times gone by, leading to their *selection* over time, in human populations and cultures. Made famous by anthropologist Marvin Harris, such an approach has been used to explain, for example, that aversion to pork in some religious traditions developed over deep historic time from the health complications of pig-keeping and eating in some environments (Harris 1974). Its most excessive speculations are notorious, as where Aztec ritual sacrifice was speciously explained as providing missing proteins in Native American diets (Winkelman 1998).

In a similar way, sociobiology, more recently, has stressed how elements and capacities of the human body – especially the human brain – emerged through selective evolutionary processes. Here, explanations for contemporary social interactions, like those governing relations between genders, or cultural practices like ethnic nepotism, lie deep in the genetic history of *Homo sapiens* (Alcock 2001).

While these are theories of a kind, they are also metaphors, in that they invite us to hold one thing, an element of culture, as another: a selected trait. These metaphors "naturalize" in the sense that characteristics of culture that are historically and geographically contingent and socially complex are explained by virtue of species survival, natural selection, and hardwired influences. This holds important political implications. Specifically, since they stress deeply structured conditions for contemporary society, things far outside of the direct control of people in their individual lives, they provide a powerful antidote to moralistic and choice-driven ways of thinking about human culture.

Consider the increase in overall body mass of individuals in contemporary society, an "obesity epidemic" with important health and healthcare implications. Viewed from the realm of free-choice and moral decision-making, it is quite easy to blame obesity and the health problems associated with it on the poor individual habits and choices of overweight people. "Fat" people, in such a moral narrative, become bad people, with political implications that largely evacuate social or collective-level obligations for their condition and welfare. In contrast, the position of some from evolutionary biology or sociobiology is that the human body evolved under trying conditions millennia ago under conditions where fat – a key building block of an overall healthy human body – was in scarce supply. Designed to crave and store fat during good times in order to offset scarcity during lean times, the human body is hardwired to consume fat. This is argued to lead to a problem under environmental conditions – specifically the modern food economy – where fat is plentiful (Power and Schulkin 2009). This means that only collective ways of coordinating the availability and circulation of differing kinds of food stand in the way of otherwise natural tendencies. Put simply, individuals aren't entirely to blame.

The empirical veracity of such an explanation is, needless to say, hard to adjudicate. It is certain in general terms that evolution has acted on the human mind and body with implications for sociability and behavior. This is both intuitive and undeniable. That a specific condition like obesity can be racked up to evolution, however, is nearly impossible to prove. Notably, in the case of obesity the actual historical trajectory of human body mass since the Pleistocene and into the twentieth century is empirically contested and technological and cultural influences are numerous (Guthman 2011). As Andrew Vayda suggests, many previous critiques of Darwinian ecological anthropology hold for sociobiology, therefore, that "it has no rigorous central core . . . and is united mainly by its 'practitioners'' common commitment to a flawed, cardboard Darwinism whereby some current utility of behavior is declared its raison d'être" (Vayda 2009: 147). It's a good story, in other words, but demands more evidence than current arguments typically provide.

Perhaps the more important issue is that, like other metaphors for nature and society, this one holds implications for action, struggle, coalition, and blame. By approaching obesity from one metaphor or the other, we effectively obfuscate a prior and concomitant question: is obesity a "problem" and whose problem is it? As Julie Guthman observes, a "crisis" of this sort is already a product of "particular ways of measuring, studying, and redressing the phenomenon so that existing assumptions about its causes, consequences and solutions are built into existing efforts to assess it independently as a problem" (Guthman 2011: 23). "Naturalizing" and functional explanations of this kind cannot be easily separated from assumptions about blame and responsibility that they either support or challenge, therefore. And by directing attention in one direction, toward either individual or evolutionary culpability, what other potentially culpable players and forces are left off the table? As Guthman further argues, in a radically changing global environment, where the international food economy confronts endocrine-disrupting chemicals (with the capacity to fully transform human hormone systems and so human metabolism), this urge to naturalize problems has dangerous shortcomings. Attending to the hardwired and internal drivers of contemporary outcomes risks distracting us from the structured political economy of the environment. Like determinism, for better and for worse, functionalism and biosociology are political metaphors with troubling implications for emerging global ecologies.

## Adaptation: The Politics of Environmental Adjustment

Ironically, these efforts to investigate the ecological immersion and genesis of cultural practices and social conditions, often described as cultural ecology (Netting 1986), served to proliferate empirical descriptions that stressed the remarkable flexibility of human beings and socio-environmental practices. As researchers explored the historical ecologies of "traditional" communities searching to document signs of universal environmental influences, they were often confronted with contingent and widely varying practices (Alland 1975). Far from hardwired, in other words, human cultures and societies, including and especially those practices rooted in interactions with the non-human world (interactions with animals, resources, landscapes, and so on), often proved pliable and responsive to an ever-changing world.

   The resulting tension, between the urge toward universal environmental explanations and the proliferation of evidence of socio-environmental dynamism, presented a demand for an alternative metaphor, one ecological in character but which stressed flexibility rather than determinacy. The favored metaphor, one very much in ascendance in this era of global environmental change, is *adaptation*. Though it contains a necessary hint or connotation of evolutionary process and selection, a stress on adaptation differs radically from that on function insofar as it focuses on learning and cultural modification within and between communities and generations, rather than phylogenetic or transgenerational selected inheritance (Ellen 1982).

   The value of this shift in emphasis is that it directs attention more to cataloguing, and less to explaining, the wealth of socio-environmental practices evident across groups and over history. Adaptation research stresses the inventiveness of people: New Guinea farmers create unique forms of mounded cropping in the face of complex temperature and moisture regimes (Waddell 1972), squatter households in urban Tijuana innovate complex ways to reuse water in the face of scarcity (Meehan 2012), forest dwellers in the Amazon transform whole soil ecosystems to promote and sustain communities (WinklerPrins and Barrera-Bassols 2004). That such adaptations *work* (or function, though only in a general sense), is more critical than why they emerged. Coincidence, contingency, and unintended consequences may all account for a specific adaptation, but the tendency to adapt becomes paramount.

   The relevance of adaptation for living amidst global change emerges from precisely this explanatorily agnostic, cataloguing effort. Rather than stress the roots of human practices, such an approach essentially *assumes* the universal tendency for people to adjust, and instead stresses the variability of the ability to do so in the face of new environmental challenges, including sea-level rise, water scarcity, and climatic extremes. The explosion of literature and policy initiatives that follows from this metaphoric configuration is extensive and daunting. Defining adaptation as "a process, action or outcome in a system (household, community, group, sector, region, country) in order for the system to better cope with, manage or adjust to some changing condition, stress, hazard, risk or opportunity" (Smit and Wandel 2006: 282), the imperative becomes understanding and reinforcing those things that allow people and communities to adjust to change. Whether that means promoting new hunting strategies for native Arctic communities facing climate change (Berkes and Jolly 2002), or flood-proofing urban coastal populations (Kirshen, Knee, and Ruth 2008), adaptation encourages a view of human beings adjusting to the upheavals of the Anthropocene.

Yet, precisely like previous metaphors for understanding humans within the environment, this too carries political freight. Directing attention to responses to an environment that comes prior to human communities and adjustments, adaptation necessarily directs attention away from the economic, social, and political arrangements that condition the transformations of the environment to which communities must adapt. Externalizing the very socio-ecological crises driven by previous iterations of human action (e.g., greenhouse gas emissions, biodiversity impacts, proliferation of waste), focus is shifted to "saving" or "helping" vulnerable communities (e.g., in the Arctic) rather than to the socio-ecological systems – often occurring far away, in places with greater concentrations of wealth – that produce vulnerability. Adaptation, though focused ostensibly on celebrating human potential and the improvement of socio-environmental conditions, holds potentially regressive political implications in a world where the economic industrial capacity to transform the environment may outpace efforts to adjust.

## Systems: Cybernetic Simplifications and Technical Control

The metaphor of "coupled systems" follows from the same tradition of ecological analysis. Here, symmetry between human and non-human is organized by treating environment and humanity as discrete "systems," linked together into a larger systemic whole (Hall and Fagen 1956). Operationalized through analyses that depend heavily on modeling, systems are essentially understood to consist of discrete variables and elements (e.g., trees, soil, farmers, crops, prices) in predefined relationships (e.g., when demand for agricultural land rises, the coverage of forest declines). By tying these together in a cascading set of quantitatively understood relationships, predictions and proscriptions can be made about how changes at one end of the system (an increase in prices or a change in policy) might indirectly impact conditions at the other end (decreasing forest cover and carbon stocks).

A conceptual model like this, in which the world is composed of interacting systems, is naturally attractive for geographers. This is, first, because universal mathematical concepts and relationships, including equilibrium and feedbacks, can be applied to all manner of things, conditions, and people in the world. The symmetry of this approach is elegant, insofar as people, trees, monkeys, and carbon all enter a systemic mix, interacting through modeled interactions. Moreover, the approach draws adherents seeking influence over policy and decision-making. Its utility, in the words of coupled-system scientists, is "directed to the overarching mission of sustainability science – provisioning humankind while reducing the threats to the earth system ... or those in which the human subsystem maintains the delivery of ecosystem services that society values from the environmental subsystem" (Turner, Lambin, and Reenberg 2007: 20669).

There are necessary silences and lacunae in adopting a systems perspective, and the shortcomings of the approach have been exhaustively detailed. The simplifications required for modeling typically exclude critical but hard-to-quantify relationships (Robbins 2012). So too, systems thinking is rooted to cybernetics (self-regulation) in a way that has "constrained the type of behavior researchers expect from the ... environment" by forcing the assumption, *a priori*, that certain features, like positive and negative feedback and equilibrium, are always present (Inkpen 2004: 115–116). Finally, starting from a *coupled* system assumes an ontological distinction between environment and society that undermines efforts to blur the distinction.

But the broader political implications of systems metaphors exceed these shortcomings. Their procedural characteristics and requirements tend to reproduce a narrow technocratic agenda, an ideology of control (following Gregory 1980), that coincides with logics of state and expert power. Transformations necessary for the reduction of complex things into "variables" and the collapse of complex interweavings into "states" and "relations" are similar to the sorts of categorical reductions and measurements demanded for government census and control. These James Scott (1998) calls "state simplifications" or *techne*, a form of knowledge distinct to state power and contrasted to other, practical, and immersed forms of popular and local knowledge (or *metis*). Such analytical reductions, insofar as they are inevitably exceeded and evaded by the behavior of real-world socio-environments, typically result in disaster when used as a guide for control, the very goal that underpins their existence. The underlying notion that understanding system dynamics can allow a lever on change in this way suits the logic of master control congruent with state power. So too, the stated or assumed goal that rendering the socio-environment as a coupled system can deliver the "ecosystem services that society values" (as per Turner *et al.* above) presupposes a known and shared value, something the divisive political history of struggle over the environment draws into question.

Consider the example of coupled-systems research to determine the stocks of carbon in Amazonian forests and modeling efforts to predict how changes in land management and control might work to maintain them (Geoghegan *et al.* 2010). Such research, so appropriately and elegantly keyed to the crises and concerns of the Anthropocene, reflects the strengths of the systems metaphor. Policy, prices, trees, and carbon are all metricized in such a way to show how tugging on one thread inevitably pulls on another. At the same time, however rooted a meta-technics of system logic, the approach underlines the colonial hubris of control ideology; the model invites regional policy scenarios where land tenure is shifted by the throw of a switch, to control the flow of carbon from the landscape, with asymmetrical implications for justice, access, and sovereignty of local forest communities. The political ecological patterns of control and exclusion emerging from such a model are underpinned by the politics of the systems metaphor itself.

## Networks: Entering a Labyrinth of Objects

Seeking a language less loaded with control and teleology, but maintaining a stress on connectedness, recent discussions of nature/culture have become inflected with the metaphors of assemblages or networks. Made most prominent by the work of Bruno Latour, and sometimes referred to as actor network theory (ANT), this approach is one that insists on an observer/ researcher effort to catalogue the associations and connections at work on a topic of concern or controversy (Latour 2005). ANT is closely associated with a number of other metaphors (Robbins and Marks 2009) all concerned with evoking the status of the non-human in the social and political lives of people (Braun and Whatmore 2010). These metaphors include *assemblages*, a term borrowed from the work of philosopher Gilles Deleuze (Deleuze and Guattari 1987), along with *hybrids* (Whatmore 2002) and *companion species* (Haraway 2003), among others.

The uses of this cluster of metaphors are highly varied, but they share two core habits. First is the insistence on describing a set of relationships between diverse and heterogeneous things, including people, objects, animals, chemicals, and so on. Second, such an approach is characterized by an emphasis on the dynamic effects that the elements have on one another, and their ongoing mutual transformations. "It's the work, and the movement," Latour suggests, "and the flow, and the changes that should be stressed" (2005: 143). In this sense, a network is perhaps the most self-admittedly metaphoric of human/environment metaphors. As Latour insists, networks do not exist in the world, out there somewhere to be discovered. Rather, a network is the characteristic of the observer's description: their *text*. "A good ANT account is a narrative or a description or a proposition where all the actors *do something* and don't just sit there" (2005: 128).

The power and attraction of such an approach are undeniable. In coming to terms with complex and intractable environmental histories, as where the Florida Everglades have undergone a century-long struggle over their status, control, and condition, it is enormously helpful to adopt a metaphoric approach that forces you to census and track all of the people (local gator-hunters, outlaws, and developers) and non-people (alligators, dredging boats, mangroves) that together constitute their "entanglement." In this vein, for anthropologist Laura Ogden, the region of the Everglades is a territory of *landscape assemblages* "constituted by humans and non-humans, material and semiotic processes, histories both real and partially remembered" (Ogden 2011: 35).

In an Anthropocene of emerging and dynamic connections, all demanding entirely novel descriptions, such an approach certainly seems powerful. Precisely like systems thinking, the emphasis is here on the diversity of players and their mutual influence on one another. Unlike the systems metaphor, the entanglements tracked through networks have no predefined trajectory, no tendency toward balance or systemic feedbacks, and no single currency (e.g., carbon, or energy) that mathematically threads them together.

But like all human–environment metaphors, and despite its evident utility, the network necessarily possesses political implications. By insisting on explanations that are *ad hoc*, notably, with each unique network not reflecting more "general" conditions, ANT eschews structural explanations that might point toward the role of elite power, institutionalized habits, and the asymmetry of different players within an assemblage. In practical terms, this means that most ANT explanations of things like scientific controversies focus heavily on experts in labs or in the field, the non-humans with which they immediately interact, and the historical chains of citation that come to constitute the truth about a changing environment (Latour 1999). Such explanation, it has been observed, "brackets the issues of power, funding, and institutional momentum" (Rudy 2005: 118) that are so deeply influenced by the broader circulation of capital and power. If we consider the question of global climate change, notably, this difference has stark implications for where to focus attention, criticism, and political leverage.

In terms of advocating explicit political change in the way the world operates to address such problems, this cluster of metaphors also conveys a specific vision, as where a liberal "parliament of things" is proposed to constitutionally reorder the division of powers that governs how humans and non-humans are represented in a more democratic fashion (Latour 2004). As Wainwright (2005: 118) observes, "These metaphorical powers are presented with no analysis of the barriers that exist to their actual existence and no discussion of how they might come into being." They necessarily disguise, in other words, the habituated, repetitive, and *structured* impediments to more transparent, equitable, and sustainable socio-environmental relationships. A world of networks is imagined as one of *ad hoc* symmetries, to be negotiated by deliberative collective decision-making. Whether the Anthropocene is actually governed solely by such horizontal relations and amenable to polite parliamentary procedure is not an uncontroversial assertion.

## Choosing Environmental Metaphors for the Anthropocene

This short discussion has by no means exhausted the list of metaphors that circulate around environmental questions. Instead, it has been my intention to point to a few such metaphors that have held currency in recent years and, in the process, to underline a key theme; each such metaphor is a cultural expression and a necessary simplification that allows certain kinds of insights into how people interact with the world around them. Inevitably, moreover, these metaphors carry with them assumptions and categorical definitions that predefine and profoundly influence how to make decisions, inform policy, set priorities, or allocate resources and decision-making authority.

Given the imperatives surrounding the real problems facing the socio-environment – unprecedented biodiversity decline, climate change, sea-level rise, water scarcity – it is possible that this suite of language, in its diversity, still is useful. The juxtaposition of one thing standing in place of another has long been recognized in geography as theoretically productive. As Barnes and Duncan (1992: 10) note, these metaphors produce "all manner of effects: incredulity, a smirk or, after sufficient time, a Nobel Prize winning novel or theory of physics . . . In this sense metaphor provides a bridge for understanding the development or formulation of theory."

Even so, the risk of metaphor lies on the flip side of that coin. Developing into an ossified artifact through repetitive habit of use, metaphors can, in a sense, die and "become equivalent to the literal" (Barnes and Duncan 1992: 11). By forgetting their partiality and their roots in language, metaphors become mistaken for the real or total. Here, their political implications become magnified, insofar as they are accepted as true, rather than as creative simplifications.

Which returns us to the Anthropocene itself, a metaphoric insistence that people are like forces of geology. Gloomy, anti-historic, non-contextual, and aggressively scientistic, it places an emphasis on the power of earth science and tacitly asserts global actions far from daily life. Compare this metaphoric assertion with one that casts the earth as a "rambunctious garden," in the words of Emma Marris (2011). Though anthropogenic (implying experiments with new ecologies), such an alternative metaphor is not anthropocentric (insisting on a dominant human agent of change). Playful and loaded with possibilities for local action, moreover, it implies a far different kind of political agenda.

One cannot assert one of these metaphors as superior to the other in a universal sense, of course, but juxtaposing them to one another represents a kind of political and cultural methodology. Reviewing the history of geographic thought relative to people and environment, therefore, encourages us to think differently about human/nature. What may yet result from such an exercise is the promulgation of new languages associating humans and non-humans, in order to jar loose the assumptions of ossified metaphors and evaluate them in urgently political terms. That work remains.

# References

Abu-Lughod, J.L. (1989) *Before European Hegemony: The World System A.D. 125–1350*. Oxford: Oxford University Press.

Alcock, J. (2001) *The Triumph of Sociobiology*. Oxford: Oxford University Press.

Alland, A. (1975) Adaptation. *Annual Review of Anthropology*, 4, 59–73.

Barnes, T.J. and Duncan, J.S. (1992) Introduction: Writing worlds. In *Writing Worlds: Discourse, Text, and Metaphor in the Representation of Landscape*, ed. T.J. Barnes and J.S. Duncan. New York: Routledge, pp. 1–17.

Berkes, F. and Jolly, D. (2002) Adapting to climate change: Social-ecological resilience in a Canadian Western Arctic community. *Conservation Ecology*, 5 (2).

Blaikie, P. and Brookfield, H. (1987) *Land Degradation and Society*. London and New York: Methuen.

Blaut, J.M. (1992) *1492: The Debate on Colonialism, Eurocentrism, and History*. Trenton, NJ: Africa World Press.

Blaut, J.M. (1993) *The Colonizer's Model of the World: Geographical Diffusionism and Eurocentric History*. New York: Guilford Press.

Blaut, J.M. (2000) *Eight Eurocentric Historians*. New York: Guilford Press.

Braun, B. and Whatmore, S.J. (eds.) (2010) *Political Matter: Technoscience, Democracy, and Public Life*. Minneapolis: University of Minnesota Press.

Brigham, A.P. (1915) Problems of geographical influence. *Annals of the Association of American Geographers*, 5, 3–25.

Castree, N. (2005) *Nature*. New York: Routledge.

Center for International Earth Science Information Network (2011) Last of the Wild Project. http://sedac.ciesin.columbia.edu/data/collection/wildareas-v1 (accessed October 28, 2012).

Crutzen, P.J. (2002) The "anthropocene." *Journal de Physique IV France*, 12 (10), 1–5.

Deleuze, G. and Guattari, F. (1987) *A Thousand Plateaus: Capitalism and Schizophrenia*. Minneapolis: University of Minnesota Press.

Diamond, J. (1997) *Guns, Germs, and Steel: The Fates of Human Societies*. New York: W.W. Norton.

Editorial (2003) Welcome to the Anthropocene. *Nature*, 424(6950), 709.

Ellen, R. (1982) *Environment, Subsistence and System: The Ecology of Small Scale Social Formations*. Cambridge: Cambridge University Press.

Frank, A.G. (1998) *ReOrient*. Berkeley: University of California Press.

Gallup, J.L. (2003) *Is Geography Destiny? Lessons from Latin America*. Washington, DC: Inter-American Development Bank.

Geoghegan, J., Lawrence, D., Schneider, L.C. and Tully, K. (2010) Accounting for carbon stocks in models of land-use change: An application to Southern Yucatan. *Regional Environmental Change*, 10 (3), 247–260.

Gregory, D. (1980) The ideology of control: Systems theory and geography. *Tijdschrift voor Economische en Sociale Geografie*, 71 (6), 327–342.

Guthman, J. (2011) *Weighing In: Obesity, Food Justice, and the Limits of Capitalism*. Berkeley: University of California Press.

Hall, A.D. and Fagen, R.E. (1956) Definition of system. *General Systems Yearbook*, 1, 18–28.

Haraway, D. (2003) *The Companion Species Manifesto: Dogs, People, and Significant Otherness*. Chicago: Prickly Paradigm Press.

Harris, M. (1974) *Cows, Pigs, Wars, and Witches: The Riddles of Culture*. New York: Random House.

Huntington, E. (1915) *Civilization and Climate*. New Haven: Yale University Press.

Inkpen, R. (2004) *Science, Philosophy and Physical Geography*. New York: Routledge.

Kirshen, P., Knee, K. and Ruth, M. (2008) Climate change and coastal flooding in Metro Boston: Impacts and adaptation strategies. *Climatic Change*, 90 (4), 453–473.

Landes, D. (1998) *The Wealth and Poverty of Nations: Why Some are So Rich and Some so Poor*. New York: W.W. Norton.

Latour, B. (1999) *Pandora's Hope: Essays on the Reality of Science Studies*. Cambridge, MA: Harvard University Press.

Latour, B. (2004) *Politics of Nature: How to Bring the Sciences into Democracy*. Cambridge, MA: Harvard University Press.

Latour, B. (2005) *Reassembling the Social: An Introduction to Actor-Network-Theory*. Oxford: Oxford University Press.

Mackinder, H.H. (1887) On the scope and methods of geography. *Proceedings of the Royal Geographical Society*, 9, 141–160.

Marris, E. (2011) *Rambunctious Garden: Saving Nature in a Post-Wild World*. New York: Bloomsbury.

Meehan, K. (2012) Greywater and the grid: The diverse economies of water. Unpublished MS.

Netting, R.M. (1986) *Cultural Ecology*. Prospect Heights, IL: Waveland Press.

Neumann, R.P. (2005) *Making Political Ecology*. London: Hodder Arnold.

Ogden, L. (2011) *Swamplife: People, Gators, and Mangroves Entangled in the Everglades*. Minneapolis: University of Minnesota Press.

Peet, R., Robbins, P. and Watts, M. (2010) *Global Political Ecology*. London: Routledge.

Power, M.L. and Schulkin, J. (2009) *The Evolution of Obesity*. Baltimore: Johns Hopkins University Press.

Robbins, P. (2012) *Political Ecology: A Critical Introduction*. Oxford: Blackwell.

Robbins, P. and Marks, B. (2009) Assemblage geographies. In *Geographies of Difference*, ed. S. Smith, S. Marston, R. Pain, and J.P. Jones III. Thousand Oaks, CA: Sage.

Rudy, A.P. (2005) On ANT and relational materialisms. *Capitalism Nature Socialism*, 16 (4).

Scott, J. (1998) *Seeing Like a State: How Certain Schemes to Improve the Human Condition Have Failed*. New Haven: Yale University Press.

Semple, E.C. (1919) Climatic and geographic influences on ancient Mediterranean forests and the lumber trade. *Annals of the Association of American Geographers*, 9, 13–40.

Smit, B. and Wandel, J. (2006) Adaptation, adaptive capacity and vulnerability. *Global Environmental Change: Human and Policy Dimensions*, 16 (3), 282–292.

Steward, J.H. (1972) *Theory of Culture Change: The Methodology of Multilinear Evolution*. Urbana: University of Illinois Press.

Symons, D. (1989) A critique of Darwinian anthropology. *Ethology and Sociobiology*, 10 (1–3), 131–144.

Turner, B.L. (1989) The specialist-synthesis approach to the revival of geography: The case of cultural ecology. *Annals of the Association of American Geographers*, 79 (1), 88–100.

Turner, B.L., Lambin, E.F. and Reenberg, A. (2007) The emergence of land change science for global environmental change and sustainability. *Proceedings of the National Academy of Sciences of the United States of America*, 104 (52), 20666–20671.

Vayda, A.P. (2009) *Explaining Human Actions and Environmental Changes*. Lanham, MD: Alta Mira.

Waddell, E. (1972) *The Mound Builders: Agricultural Practices, Environment, and Society in the Central Highlands of New Guinea*. Seattle: University of Washington Press.

Wainwright, J. (2005) Politics of nature: A review of three recent works by Bruno Latour. *Capitalism Nature Socialism*, 16 (1), 115–122.

Whatmore, S. (2002) *Hybrid Geographies: Natures Cultures Spaces*. London: Sage.

Winkelman, M. (1998) Aztec human sacrifice: Cross-cultural assessments of the ecological hypothesis. *Ethnology*, 37 (3), 285–298.

WinklerPrins, A.M.G.A. and Barrera-Bassols, N. (2004) Latin American ethnopedology: A vision of its past, present, and future. *Agriculture and Human Values*, 21 (2/3), 139–156.

# Chapter 28

# Biotechnologies and Biomedicine

*Bronwyn Parry*

## Introduction

Throughout my career I have worked almost exclusively on the social, economic, and ethical issues that surround the emergence of what are thought of as new biotechnologies: techniques and tools for genetically engineering and cloning plants and animals, for culturing tissues or cells *in vitro*, or for sequencing and reordering genomes, to name but a few. In discussing my work, the question that I am most frequently asked, often by somewhat mystified interlocutors, is, "What has biotechnology got to do with geography?" From their perspective I can see how the confusion arises – they see biotechnologies as intimately connected to biology and the life sciences, whilst our discipline remains confined, in their rather limited geographical imaginations, to the study of rocks and rivers. How then could the two possibly relate to each other?

For me, however, the relationship between geography and biotechnology is both a very evident and significant one. The word "geography" derives from the Greek, a combination of *geo* or *gaea* meaning "earth," and *graphein* meaning "to write." Geographers are therefore popularly understood as those who study and write about the earth: its features, inhabitants, and phenomena. Whilst this is the received definition, I have always interpreted the lexical underpinnings of the word geography in a somewhat different way. For me, geography is not how we write *about* the earth, its features or inhabitants, but rather the study of how the earth and our relations to it are *themselves* being written and rewritten over time. In this context "biotechnologies," which are by simplest definition a fusion of biology and technology, provide the very means through which this progressive rewriting and reinvention of nature can be realized.

There is absolutely no doubt that biotechnologies have, in recent decades, allowed nature to be engineered in wholly unanticipated ways. It is though essential, in my view, to see this

*The Wiley Blackwell Companion to Cultural Geography*, First Edition.
Edited by Nuala C. Johnson, Richard H. Schein, and Jamie Winders.
© 2013 John Wiley & Sons, Ltd. Published 2016 by John Wiley & Sons, Ltd.

as a part of a much longer trajectory of productive, or even playful, engagement with nature. Activities such as cross-breeding plants or animals, or using biological processes to accelerate or alter existing production techniques (the use of yeast in brewing, for example), have very long histories, histories that persistently challenge or disrupt romantic conceptions of the existence of a priorly innocent or unmediated nature. When was it ever thus? For as long as humankind and nature have existed they have been involved in a collaborative process of productive coevolution, the parameters of which have been dictated only by reference to the tools available to effect it.

Understandings and definitions of what constitutes "biotechnology" have, consequently, also been subject to constant revision. What began with simple experiments in procedures like fermentation has culminated in the creation of entities as exotic as chimeras, such as human–animal hybrid embryos. Despite this shifting landscape it remains clear that at least three sets of relations to our natural world are fundamentally transformed by our engagement with, and applied use of, these technologies: the epistemological, the economic, and the ethical. However, as we shall see, even these are not altered in consistent or even predictable ways. My aims in this short chapter, then, are first, to give a sense of how biotechnologies themselves have advanced over the past century, second, to reveal how profoundly they have altered our understandings of, and relationships with, the natural world, and finally, to reveal their immanent capacity to rewrite our relations to nature in even more dramatic ways than previously envisaged in the years to come. I do this through three short case studies: the first on agricultural biotechnology, the second on stem cell applications, and the third on the cutting-edge frontier of biotechnology in the twenty-first century: synthetic biology.

## Agricultural Biotechnology

The term *biotechnologie* was first coined by the Hungarian agricultural engineer Karl Ereky as early as 1919 (Ereky 1919: 5). Ereky's goal was to sweep away the existing peasant economy in Hungary by revolutionizing agricultural production. Farming on an industrial scale was the model he championed, providing, by way of demonstration, an agro-industrial pig-rearing enterprise of a vast size capable of processing 100,000 pigs per year, the largest such operation in Europe at that time. As the historian Robert Bud (1993: 34–35) explains, for Ereky the pig was not simply an animal but rather an *arbeitsmachine*: a processing machine useful for "converting carefully calculated amounts of input into meat output." Ereky, very cleverly, realized that he could accelerate this conversion rate through the application of yet other biological tools, by using modified yeast as a cheap and cost-effective animal protein feed, for example. Biotechnology provided, in this conception, the means by which "raw materials could be biologically *upgraded* into socially useful products" (Ereky 1919: 9, my italics). He was not alone in pursuing such endeavors. As Bud (1993: 38–40) notes, within the decade Professor William Perkin, Jr. of Manchester University and colleagues at the Pasteur Institute had developed a technique for combining oil, acetylene, coal, natural gas, and other natural materials to catalyze synthetic rubber, whilst Alexander Fleming had distilled antibiotics from cell cultures in a powerful demonstration of the potential applications of biotechnology in medicine and health care.

Whilst these early attempts at "upgrading" nature through active recombination or industrial refinement of its constituent elements met with some success, they pale into insignificance beside the qualitative leap in capacity that was invoked by the molecular revolution. Crick and Watson's work on the structure of DNA was to usher in the science of genetic engineering with which biotechnology became so closely intertwined in the decades from 1970 onwards. A rather narrower definition of the term biotechnology began to dominate at this time: one that characterized it as directed primarily at genetic modification. The capacity to effectively "reconstruct" nature by inserting or deleting genes at will or by splicing genetic sequences from one organism into other, unrelated ones to create "transgenic" plants and animals was historically unprecedented, marking an epochal shift in our relations to biology and our capacity to engineer it for productive ends. The entities that were manufactured out of this process – such as herbicide-resistant soya or pest-resistant cotton – would fundamentally alter the political economies of agricultural production in ways in which Ereky could only have dreamed.

As David Harvey has noted (1991: 229), capitalism has been characterized by continuous efforts to shorten turnover times in production and consumption to enable goods to circulate through the economy with greater efficiency. The more demand that is created for a product, the more of it that can be sold, but only if it can be produced quickly enough to satisfy that demand. That goal has been achieved historically through the implementation of a host of innovative technical "solutions" devised to *speed up* the dynamics of production and consumption. The creation of the conveyor belt, which enabled assembly-line methods of production in Fordist factories, and built-in obsolescence in product manufacturing are two such examples. Advanced biotechnologies have been called upon to perform similar work in the burgeoning agri-food industrial complex: to "*speed up*" existing biological processes to generate entirely new biologies for economically productive purposes. This has been done with the explicit intention of improving efficiency within this sector of the capitalist economy. It is a simple equation: the faster or more efficiently a product (in this case a maximally efficient organism) can be "turned out," the greater the profit margin for the manufacturer. There is perhaps no more pertinent example of how contemporary biotechnology achieves this end than that of the genetically modified salmon, which currently awaits approval by America's Food and Drug Administration (FDA).

The fish, an Atlantic salmon, has been genetically engineered by the American company AquaBounty. Normally the salmon do not make growth hormones in cold weather and only feed intensively in the summer and spring. The existing genetic makeup of this salmon has, however, been augmented with DNA from two other species, the Pacific Chinook salmon and an eel-like species called an ocean pout (Zoarces americanus). The growth hormone gene from the former and the genetic on-switch to feed all year round from the latter combine to make the genetically modified salmon feed continually, allowing it to reach market size in 16 to 18 months instead of the usual three years. If allowed to go on growing, it can reach disproportionate sizes. Its development has evoked a number of complex responses which mirror those that have attended the manufacture of other engineered organisms, such as transgenic crops or cloned animals for example Dolly the sheep or the Oncomouse™. Each has raised a set of, as yet, unanswered questions about our epistemological, ethical and economic relations to these entities that I shall now outline.

## Epistemologies, Ethics, and Economics of Contemporary Biotechnologies

If we think of this modified salmon as a particular example of a nature "rewritten," then it behoves us to step back and think of how we come to know these entities; of how our accounts of such rewritings are generated; of what themes become dominant within these accounts and thus within the historiography of biotechnology. Perhaps the most common reading is that which suggests that biotechnology has been employed by humans to act upon a preexisting and immutable nature in ways that are not only historically unprecedented, but which also *threaten* the essential "naturalness" of nature. The presentation of the story about genetically modified crops such as GM maize provides a good example of this: plants, which are somehow assumed to have remained largely unchanged for centuries are then said to have their fundamental genetic makeup altered by the application of new biotechnologies. This work is undertaken by humans who themselves are presented as behaving in a particularly "masculinist" way: acting upon a passive natural world, dominating it, intervening in its construction in a deliberately proactive manner, doing things to it expediently, for their own benefit, to obtain a "mastery" of it. Such readings have, in turn, conditioned public response to biotechnology and its products, stoking controversy and evoking fears about the Frankensteinian monstrosities that result when one "plays God" with nature. Indeed, as if to demonstrate the power of such imaginaries, AquaBounty's genetically modified salmon has been recently described as a "Frankenfish."

It is particularly important when assessing the novelty and potential impacts of biotechnologies to establish what is and is not new in their mode of application. It is important to remember, for example, that the ability to combine genetic traits in novel ways through the use of technology is neither new nor unprecedented; such outcomes have long been achieved through controlled cross-breeding of species. What *is* unprecedented is the ability to create animals or plants that are genuinely *transgressive* – the "glow in the dark" lawn seed that was created by splicing genes for luminescence from fish into lawn seed being a particularly relevant example. There are several things about these entities that individuals find disturbing. They seem, at least at this moment in history, to be what Freud would call "uncanny": simultaneously familiar but also oddly strange. Their "supernatural" character creates a kind of cognitive dissonance within the experiencing subject, who is often both attracted and simultaneously repulsed by their paradoxical nature.

The ethical arguments that have been marshaled against genetically modified plants and animals speak directly to these epistemological concerns. The Frankenfish has been constructed in public debate and by those who protest its existence as an abomination the production of which is not only morally offensive, but also simultaneously risks "polluting" the essential and apparently immutable "naturalness" of the world into which it is released. The debate that surrounds the risks presented by genetically modified organisms including animals and crops, such as pest-resistant maize has, perhaps as a consequence, become highly polarized in recent years. Those who protest their development argue that the ingestion of such foods poses health risks that, whilst identifiable and considerable, remain largely underresearched by national governments who act in service to powerful corporate interests and the wider project of neoliberalization of trade. Advocates of agricultural biotechnology conversely argue that genetically engineered crops and animals provide an efficient and safe means through which to meet the consumption needs of a burgeoning global population.

Arguments about the prospective economic utility of new biological entities have been evoked not only to rationalize their development but also to legitimate the construction of new regimes of commodification and regulation to govern their use. The United Nations Convention on Biological Diversity (UNCBD), for example, endorses an unashamedly utilitarian definition of biotechnology, arguing that it comprises "any technological application that uses biological systems, living organisms, or derivatives thereof, [or which] makes or modifies products or processes for specific use." Biotechnologies generate economic value from biological materials by drawing upon two of their inherent qualities – their "plasticity" and their "vitality." The capacity of living material to be radically altered in its very constitution, to undergo a series of shocks, rearrangements and manipulations and to adapt to, and survive, those changes *intact* is key to the success of the experimentation that underpins the operation of contemporary bioscience. It is this that has allowed biotechnologists to creatively remodel organisms, to produce from them new "manufactures of nature" that, as we shall see, could become constructed both socially and economically as marketable and patentable "products."

It is, however, perhaps the *generative* capacity of biological entities – their inherent ability to reproduce – that provides the real engine of productivity in the biotechnological realm. For whilst it is desirable to be able to create a novel biological entity – such as a stem cell line – it is the ability to continually reproduce that product technologically within the confines of the laboratory that has proven to be so economically productive. The sociologist of science Catherine Waldby (2000: 33) has argued that what she calls "biovalue" is actualized "wherever the generative and transformative productivity of living entities can be instrumentalised along lines that make them useful for human projects: science, industry, medicine, agriculture and other areas of technical culture" and is specifically created by harnessing "the surplus of invitro vitality produced by the biotechnical reformulation of living processes" (2002: 310). An excellent example of this can be found in the case of tissue engineering, to which I shall shortly turn.

As any Marxist would remind us though, this surplus "biovalue" can only be secured if private rights of ownership to these "reformulated entities" can be successfully prosecuted and defended. It was not immediately evident in the early 1970s, when modern biotechnologies emerged how it would be possible to exert any kind of monopolistic claim over biological organisms as they were then considered, in law, to constitute part of the freely available and commonly owned heritage of all the earth's citizens. This impediment was overcome in 1980 when a claim for a patent on a biologically engineered organism was first successfully prosecuted in the US Supreme Court in the case of *Diamond v. Chakrabarty*. Chakrabarty, who then worked for the General Electric Corporation, had applied for a patent on a bacterium that he had constructed in the laboratory from four previously unassociated plasmids. The bacterium was designed to consume crude oil and was intended to have commercial application in remediating oil spills. The application for patent was initially rejected by a lower court on the grounds that the bacterium was a "product of nature" and a living organism, both of which were considered to lie constitutionally outwith the scope of patentable subject matter. However, in later granting the patent on appeal, the Supreme Court of the United States determined that the plasmid was in fact "a nonnaturally occurring manufacture or composition of matter – a product of human ingenuity" and thus eligible for patent protection.

It was not only whole engineered organisms that became eligible for patent protection but also elements of these organisms that had been altered technologically. As Kathleen McAfee (2003) has noted, the double reductionism inherent in molecular biology, which sees complex biological entities stripped down to a series of "discrete units" such as genes and plasmids, has served to legitimate a similarly reductive approach to the economization of these "units." Each are now constructed and marketed as individuated commodities capable of being bought and sold, packaged and patented separately, rather than as an indivisible part of the whole complex assemblage of an organism. The right to patent engineered whole organisms and their constituent parts that was established by the US Supreme Court in the Chakrabarty case could conceivably have remained restricted to the US legal jurisdictions to which its judgments pertain. However, with the rise of neoliberalism came demands to "harmonize" existing systems of national regulation (for example in the realm of intellectual property rights [IPR]) in order to facilitate the creation and operation of globally expansive spaces of trade and exchange and regimes of capital accumulation. These demands were met in 1994 when all member states of the General Agreement on Tariffs and Trade (GATT, later the World Trade Organization [WTO]) were required to become signatories to a new agreement on Trade-Related Intellectual Property Rights (TRIPs). This agreement adopted, as one of its central tenets, the right to patent modified living organisms that had been established in the Chakrabarty case.

With the globalization of this new regime of IPR law came the capacity to secure defensible patents over modified biological material in many different national jurisdictions and to extend the commodity form to a host of biological resources than had previously been considered economically inalienable. The vitality of both the engineered organisms and the regulatory regimes to which they have given rise has sparked some visceral fears – fears of *excess*. We have seen that there came, first, a fear that the entities that modern biotechnology had spawned would escape containment and proliferate into the wild, contaminating an existent and seemingly pristine nature. This fear was, with the introduction of the TRIPS regime, compounded by another: that the desire to profit from the development of these "unnatural" entities would morph and warp into an excessive interest in securing new ways and means of privatizing and commodifying them for financial gain. This tendency, it has been argued by those who oppose biological patents, has been evidenced in the promulgation of overly robust regimes of IPR protection, such as the GATT TRIPs agreement. These, they argue, have similarly "overproliferated" into the previously uncontaminated regulatory domains of sovereign states that have historically rejected the patenting of life forms, imposing on them a system of regulation that they neither believe in ideologically, nor support.

These concerns have been accompanied by others – most notably that biological patents would take no account of the contributions made by those whose biological materials or resources formed the basis of these biotechnological inventions. The appropriation of samples of genetic and biochemical materials from rainforest plants, animals, and seeds and crops modified over many generations by indigenous communities and their subsequent use in commercial bioscience prompted protesters and academics in developing countries to argue that this bio-prospecting constituted a new form of "bio-colonialism." Activists such as Vandana Shiva, for example, argued that these activities are nothing more than an exploitative form of biological resource extraction. Demands that such inequities be remedied prompted the creation of counterbalancing legislation, notably, under the Convention on Biological Diversity, of what are known as Access and Benefit Sharing regimes. These are designed to ensure that the "donors" of the genetic and biochemical materials that form the basis of marketable products receive a percentage of the value of the profits that accrue from their sale.

The later cases of John Moore and Henrietta Lacks, whose bodily materials were retained without their consent for use in pharmaceutical and stem cell development, led to calls that benefit sharing be extended to include human "donors" (Parry 2008). Such cases had more far-reaching effects however, forcing wider and more profound epistemological reassessments: of whether the concept of "ownership" should extend to human biological materials; of how rights to biotechnological inventions might conceivably be ordered in the future; and of what impact the ability to reengineer ourselves would have on conceptions of the relationship between the human and the technological, the natural and unnatural, in the twenty-first century. These concerns, which were first evoked in relationship to agricultural biotechnology, were to acquire significantly more purchase in the late twentieth century as the project of engineering ourselves began to come to full fruition.

## Medical Devices and Tissue Engineering

The term biotechnology, as we have seen, has been associated historically with technologies designed to reengineer plants and animals employed in agriculture and the biosciences. The definitions of biotechnology elaborated throughout the twentieth century from that first developed by Ereky to later elaborations offered by the UNCBD exemplify this. Both suggest that it encompasses any technology that employs a biological system or living organisms to make or modify new products or processes, particularly when those products or processes are themselves biological. The concepts of acceleration and enhancement are often centrally implicated in these endeavors. The use of yeast to accelerate brewing or the insertion of a gene to enhance resistance to pests in crops both provide familiar examples of the ways in which biology is applied to biology in a multiplicatory fashion in order to speed up, refine or enhance existing organisms to improve their longevity or their sustainability.

Over the past twenty years though, a curious reorientation of biotechnology has occurred, although it is one rarely acknowledged by its practitioners. For during this period we began to see a shift in the object of biotechnologies' interest – from a discreet and, to an extent, disassociated natural world "out there" to the intimate landscape of our own lived bodies. Technological mechanisms such as the pacemaker and the artificial heart, stents, and replacement knee and hip joints have all revealed the promise that these devices hold for performing the work that is central to this new biotechnological project: that of refining and enhancing, in this case human organisms, and improving their longevity and, yes, even their sustainability. They may not qualify as biotechnologies, I hear you cry, as they remain simply technological (mechanical) interventions that have no iterative relationship to biology – they are neither themselves biological nor do they have any organic relationship to the organism in which they are inserted, remaining forever foreign to it.

But what then are we to make of the most recent advances in tissue engineering? Let us take by way of example the process of generating a heart for transplant that has been renovated and, more importantly, "personalized" through the applied use of bioactive scaffolds and nanotechnology. This revolutionary technique involves taking a donor heart and decellularizing it by chemically stripping away all the flesh, cells and DNA that it contains. What is left after this process is a kind of "ghost heart" – just the inner "scaffold" of collagen that gives the heart its structure. This structure is then immunologically inert. Hydrogels, which are technologically engineered compositions of polymers that promote cellular attachment, molecular responsiveness, and biocompatibility, are then applied to the scaffold to enable the heart to be "reseeded" with stem cells extracted from the prospective recipient. These stem cells are then prompted to differentiate into the cells the organ needs to function. Within days they can be seen to be grouping together to create new heart tissue that populates the scaffold of the ghost heart and begins "beating" instinctively. This new heart is a thoroughly recombinant construct; a hybrid of tissue and technology that, due to its tailoring, can be implanted in the recipient without any risk of an immunological response. It is not rejected as it is not understood by the body to be foreign; it has become, by virtue of this process of technologization, rather ironically, thoroughly "naturalized." Scientists are now even employing nanotechnology to construct novel engineered scaffolds capable of mimicking the nanostructure of the tissues in the body, a competency, once secured, that would obviate even the need for the collagen "ghost heart."

What is our reaction to these assemblages or indeed to being, *ourselves*, biotechnologically engineered organisms? If we consider this question in relation to the three axes of interest I set out earlier – the epistemological, ethical, and economic – we arrive at some, perhaps surprising, conclusions. In the early 1990s we saw the emergence of a number of accounts of the implications that these kinds of technoscientific advancements might have for the very question of what it means to be "human." Francis Fukuyama (2003) began by diagnosing the arrival of a new and, to him, disturbing epoch of "posthumanism" in which the world is increasingly populated by cyborgian figures that are a dystopic concoction of man and machine. As Jamie Lorimer (2009: 348) has noted, this is an "apocalyptic" reading of events, one in which these biotechnological interventions threaten to again "pollute" some essential (and essentialized) humanism, one that existed in a much more hygienic, hermetically sealed, nostalgically revered ontological realm in which, as Lorimer puts it, "humans were humans and nature natural." Other theorists, such as Donna Haraway (1990), view the figure of the cyborg in a more optimistic light, regarding these technologies as affording historically unprecedented opportunities to create new posthuman entities, the enhanced capacity of which will, triumphantly, exceed humanity's inherently limited "natural" potential.

Geographers such as Bruce Braun (2008) and Sarah Whatmore (2002; Whatmore and Hinchcliffe 2008; Braun and Whatmore 2010) have intervened in this debate in very important ways. They have done so by revealing the considerable intellectual labor that has been invested historically in generating and maintaining the (purported) ontological distinctiveness of the human. This has been evidenced in what Braun describes as the "anxious differentiations" made between humans and animals and the organic and the inorganic in support of the "classical" fiction that each are unquestionably distinct from the other, and on which the whole concept of humanism rests.

What they describe as a more "relational ontology" seeks to do two things in this context – the first is to decenter humans from the heart of the narrative about how relations between nature and society are progressively made and remade. Nature in this conception is no longer viewed as merely "the receptacle for human strivings" (Braun 2008: 668), but rather an "active co-conspirator" in the construction of new, more politically egalitarian biologies. The second related aim is to actively disrupt the ontological security of the distinctions that have been constructed historically between the human, animal and technological. Rather than insisting that assemblages such as the reseeded ghost heart be seen as either one kind of thing or another, this reading would understand the hybrid heart, and indeed the "posthuman" into which it is inserted, as the lively, vital product of a collaborative and democratic engagement between each.

This certainly seems to be how these entities will be viewed by their recipients if we take the reception of other biomedical devices as a case in point. Interestingly, whilst engineered agricultural entities have attracted much disapprobation and ethical concern, very little has been expressed in relation to this project of self-engineering. Although the insertion of the first artificial hearts and animal organs were met with a degree of public revulsion (expressively characterized by Gail Davies [2006] as "the yuck factor"), concerns over the "unnaturalness" of such techniques have, in the intervening years, progressively melted away, apart from, perhaps, at the extreme margins where practices such as pre-implantation genetic diagnosis (PIGD) invoke concerns about eugenics. In general, however, individuals around the world have actively embraced the dream of reengineering and enhancing our "petty selves" in the production of much more idealized constructs – informational, material, and technological hybrids. Out of this desire emerges what the sociologist of science Carlos Novas (2006) calls "a political economy of hope," in which individuals actively sponsor and become engaged in all manner of research and technological development directed toward realizing their own "biovalue." They do this, as sociologist Nikolas Rose argues, in accordance with their role as good "biological citizens" of the neoliberal order, as "prudent yet enterprising individuals, actively shaping his or her life course through acts of choice" (Rose 2008: 134).

Recent research, that I have begun to undertake with Nikolas Rose, reveals the ways in which the project of maintaining and enhancing the body through biotechnological means can become a source of profit and shareholder value in the rapidly expanding global market for medical devices. The global corporation Medtronics, which was issued with the most patents on new medical devices between 1969 and 1998, had a revenue income from sales of devices of US$12.9 billion in 2007 yet still lagged well behind the world-leading company, Johnson and Johnson, with sales of US$21.7 billion (Rosen 2008). Both form just part of a global market worth US$500 billion in 2010, the growth of which has been driven not only by demand in developed countries but also amongst the aspiring and newly wealthy elites of the tiger economies of India and China. The ethical normalization of this "rewriting" of human construction and capacity that is suggested by the phenomenal growth in this market has been amplified recently by those scientists whose breakthroughs provide the means by which such dreams are realized. Professor Molly Stevens, one of the world's leading tissue regeneration scientists, was asked in interview whether she had ever felt that people may consider the application of her techniques as an example of humans "playing God" or creating "Frankenstein"-like entities. Her response was: "I think what we are doing is fairly straightforward: what we are doing is designing materials to help the body to repair itself or to detect disease and there is not really anything very Frankenstein about that" (Stevens 2011). Perhaps we could conclude then that we become less concerned about tampering with nature when the nature that stands to profit from the intervention is our own.

## Synthetic Biologies: Constructing the Future

So where, in conclusion, does that leave biotechnology now at the turn of the twenty-first century? The experiments that I have outlined here in the fields of agricultural biotechnology and in human repair and enhancement have been highly successful, becoming, over time, increasingly sophisticated in nature. They are, however, about to be completely overshadowed in both scope and implication by the project upon which scientists are now embarking. The emergent field of synthetic biology is set to provide the means through which to realize that most ambitious of all biotechnological fantasies: the ability to construct artificial organisms from "the ground up," to a design of one's own choosing. An illustrative example might provide a useful case in point. In 2010 Craig Venter, the US geneticist and venture capitalist, announced that, following a ten-year and US$40 million investment, his team of twenty scientists had succeeded in creating the first "artificial life form": a bacterium containing a synthetically constructed genome. How was this done and what are the epistemological, ethical and economic implications of this development?

In order to create a synthetic genome, it is first necessary to remove DNA from an existing organism and to deaggregate it into genetic sequence code. This code, which might be thought of as a script, is then edited to create a new "blueprint" or "recipe" for a novel genome. Using the tools of organic chemistry and molecular biology, scientists are then able to synthesize the constituent elements of the proposed genome from the newly scripted code. In this way they can begin to *manufacture* genomes (and thus organisms) chemically and *in vitro*. This process is a continuation of earlier biotechnological projects but it is distinguished from them in one important respect: the aim of synthetic biology is not to "rewrite" an existing nature, but rather to "author" new ones *de novo*. Ventner employs informational metaphors to try to capture the profound technological and epistemological transformations that this scientific breakthrough, which has been described as a "defining moment in the history of biology and biotechnology," will inevitably induce. Describing the converted cell as "the first self-replicating species we've had on the planet whose parent is a computer," he legitimizes its creation by arguing that in "writing new biological software and creating new species, we can create new species to do what we want them to do, not what they evolved to do" (cited in Wade 2010).

The full ramifications of the development of synthetic and artificially generated organisms must await the attentions of future researchers. However, two sets of pressing issues, one ethical and the other economic, will already pique the interest of a new generation of economic and cultural geographers. While Ventner and other scientists provide us with new tools of biological authorship, we may yet find that we know not what we write. We may have acquired the capacity to make ourselves and nature up as we go along, but whether our ability to assess and accommodate the ethical consequences of this *agencement* will keep pace with this, still remains in question. Some of the ethical concerns that have been raised echo those that have attended the development of other biotechnologically produced entities. These include concerns that humanity is overstepping important and long-standing ontological boundaries in manufacturing life forms that have no natural correlates or in creating entities that we may not ultimately have the capacity to control. As the Oxford ethicist Julian Savulescu reminds us, "Ventner is creaking open the most profound door in humanity's history, potentially peeking into its destiny. He is not merely copying life artificially . . . or modifying it radically by genetic engineering. He is going towards the role of a God in creating artificial life that could never have existed naturally." His colleague David Magnus, director of Stanford University's Center for Biomedical Ethics, has other concerns about the unauthorized use of synthetic biology, asking: "What's to stop terrorists from buying pieces of DNA and fitting them together into a vicious pathogen?" (Sample 2010: 1).

Perhaps the most serious ethical implications of synthetic biology, though, may arise in relation to its commercial use. The applications for synthetic organisms are potentially myriad, ranging from use in biofuel production to malarial vaccines. The desire to protect the productive capacity of these new inventions has seen Ventner and others successfully secure patents on these manufactured life forms. This has sparked renewed debate and speculation about the potentially destructive "anti-commons" effect that such legislation could have on this fledging enterprise. As Rai and Boyle (2007) have noted, there is considerable historical evidence, including evidence from virtually every important industry of the twentieth century, that broad patents on foundational research can dramatically slow growth. As they remind us, the specter of broad patents loomed large in the fledgling computer hardware industry until the US government effectively forced licensing of the AT&T transistor patent as well as patents obtained by Texas Instruments and Fairchild Instruments on integrated circuits. No such actions have, however, been taken in relationship to patents on the foundational biological technologies that will underpin future innovation in synthetic biology.

Privatization of resources has in neoliberal economies been proffered as a remedy for the commonly perceived "tragedy of the commons" (Hardin 1968), in which multiple stakeholders, none with an absolute interest in the resource they share, all seek to maximize their self-interest to the ultimate depletion, or despoliation, of the resource in question. Ownership here becomes an ameliorative – a means of securing effective oversight and control of resource use. In a direct challenge to this epistemological position, Heller and Eisenberg (1998) have argued that the dramatic proliferation of intellectual property rights, such as patents in biomedical research, suggests a different tragedy: an "*anti-commons*" in which people underuse scarce resources because too many owners block each other's use.

A more redemptive political ideology and set of practices is now, though, being proffered in response – one that offers a more hopeful reading of the way in which access to the "building blocks of biology" may be constructed in the future. In this reading modified biological materials and information would remain as "foundational resources" that innovators can draw upon and utilize in constructing these new biotechnological inventions and life forms. Drawing on the principles of "open-source" access, pioneered in the digital informational economy (see Kelty 2008), recent global initiatives have attempted to support the generation of a creative biological commons by realizing the concept of "open-source biology." The developmental biologist Drew Endy of Stanford University has, for example, argued that synthetic biology would advance more rapidly if scientists could employ standardized biological parts, much as regular engineers do. To this end he has created the BioBricks Foundation, which has constructed a catalogue of such parts that are now freely available to all in the scientific community to facilitate open innovation.

The essence of the open-source concept is at work here: what is provided with open access is not the product itself, but rather the enabling technology – the equivalent of the source code. Those who agree to the terms of sharing have rights to use this enabling technology and to make and commercialize products from it, royalty free. In return they agree to feed back into the public domain the further refinements they have made to the enabling biotechnology for others to employ. Whether or not Endy's experiment is ultimately successful only time will tell; however, it at least suggests ways in which the political economy of biotechnology in the twenty-first century might be creatively reworked to elicit more just and equitable outcomes for all those involved in its progressive evolution. The more complex question, of how conceptions of our own role within this biotechnologically enhanced posthuman realm that these advances in biotechnology will bring, whether as author or subject of this latest and most dramatic rewriting of natural relations, awaits further resolution but will undoubtedly provide fecund ground for geographical research for many years to come.

## References

Braun, B. (2008) Environmental issues: Inventive life. *Progress in Human Geography*, 32 (5), 667–679.

Braun, B. and Whatmore, S.J. (eds.) (2010) *Political Matter: Technoscience, Democracy and Public Life.* Minneapolis: University of Minnesota Press.

Bud, R. (1993) *The Uses of Life: A History of Biotechnology.* Cambridge: Cambridge University Press.

Davies, G. (2006) Mapping deliberation: Calculation, articulation and intervention in the politics of organ transplantation. *Economy and Society*, 35 (2), 232–258.

Ereky, K. (1919) *Biotechnologie der Fleisch-, Fett-, und Mitcherzeugung im land-wirtschaftlichen Grossbetriebe.* Berlin: Parey.

Fukuyama, F. (2003) *Our Posthuman Future: Consequences of the Biotechnology Revolution.* New York: Picador.

Haraway, D. (1990) *Simians, Cyborgs, and Women: The Reinvention of Nature.* London: Routledge.

Hardin, G. (1968) The tragedy of the commons. *Science,* 162, 1243–1248.

Harvey, D. (1991) *The Condition of Postmodernity.* London: Blackwell.

Heller, M. and Eisenberg, R. (1998) Do patents deter innovation? The tragedy of the anticommons in biomedical research. *Science,* 280, 698–701.

Kelty, C. (2008) *Two Bits: The Cultural Significance of Free Software.* Durham, NC: Duke University Press.

Lorimer, J. (2009) Posthumanism/posthumanistic geographies. In *International Encyclopaedia of Human Geography,* vol. 8, ed. R. Kitchin and N. Thrift. Oxford: Elsevier, pp. 344–354.

McAfee, K. (2003) Neoliberalism on the molecular scale: Economic and genetic reductionism in biotechnology battles. *Geoforum,* 34 (2), 203–219.

Novas, C. (2006) The political economy of hope: Patient's organisations, science and biovalue. *Biosocieties,* 1 (3), 289–305.

Parry, B.C. (2008) Entangled exchange: Reconceptualising the characterisation and practice of bodily commodification. *Geoforum,* 39 (3), 1133–1144.

Rai, A. and Boyle, J. (2007) Synthetic biology: Caught between property rights, the public domain, and the commons. *PLoS Biology,* 5 (3), e58. DOI: 10.1371/journal.pbio.0050058

Rose, N. (2008) *The Politics of Life Itself: Biomedicine, Power, and Subjectivity in the Twenty-First Century.* Princeton: Princeton University Press.

Rosen, M. (2008) Global medical device market outperforms drug market growth. WTN News, June 2. http://wtnnews.com/articles/4790/ (accessed October 29, 2012).

Sample, I. (2010) Craig Ventner creates synthetic life form. *Guardian,* May 20.

Stevens, M. (2011) Interview, "The Life Scientific," BBC Radio 4, November 14. http://www.bbc.co.uk/iplayer/episode/b0174gk0/The_Life_Scientific_Molly_Stevens/ (accessed October 29, 2012).

Wade, N. (2010) Researchers say they created a "synthetic cell." *New York Times,* May 20.

Waldby, C. (2000) *The Visible Human Project: Informatic Bodies and Posthuman Medicine.* Abingdon: Routledge.

Waldby, C. (2002) Stem cells, tissue cultures and the production of biovalue. *Health,* 6 (3), 305–323.

Whatmore, S. (2002) *Hybrid Geographies: Natures, Cultures, Spaces.* London: Sage.

Whatmore, S. and Hinchcliffe, S. (2008) Hybrid geographies: Rethinking the "human" in human geography. In *Environment: Critical Essays in Human Geography,* ed. K. Anderson and B. Braun. London: Ashgate.

Chapter 29

# Animal Geographies

*Jamie Lorimer and Krithika Srinivasan*

## Introduction

Animal geography has developed and differentiated since its revival as a subdiscipline in the 1990s. Self-proclaimed animal geographers are not as common as some might have expected, but an increasing number of academics now consider the "more-than-human" dimensions of social and spatial practices (Whatmore 2006), exploring various non-human agencies and the risks and responsiblities these pose to established ways of thinking and acting. There has also been a growing interest in "animating" the discipline to appreciate the embodied and affective dimensions of everyday life. Knowledges and practices that were previously only associated with non-human animals are now center-stage in the established field of "non-representational geographies" (Thrift 2007). Outside of geography there has been a significant growth in the multidisciplinary field of animal studies, which builds on prior work in philosophy on questions related to animal ethics. Animal-related books, journals, and degree programs are increasingly commonplace across many of the humanities and social sciences.

In this chapter we will trace a genealogy of work in animal geography that has emerged in the last decade. We will take as our point of departure a trinity of scholarly collections and reviews of the field that were published around the millennium (Philo and Wilbert 2000; Wolch and Emel 1998; Wolch, Emel, and Wilbert 2003). Our aim is to identify the rich and plural character of the subdiscipline by mapping the different forms of animal geography that have emerged from the diverse ways in which geographers have become and continue to be interested in animals. Having reviewed these forms, we discuss some of the implications of the more-than-human turn in the discipline, some of the surprising absences in the current work, and suggest some opportunities for future research. Our aim is to present an overview, illustrated with indicative examples.

*The Wiley Blackwell Companion to Cultural Geography*, First Edition.
Edited by Nuala C. Johnson, Richard H. Schein, and Jamie Winders.
© 2013 John Wiley & Sons, Ltd. Published 2016 by John Wiley & Sons, Ltd.

## Forms of Animal Geographies

We can disaggregate recent animal geography according to Philo and Wilbert's (2000) useful distinction between work concerned primarily with either "animal spaces" or "beastly places." The first category describes research examining the geographies of how people relate to animals and what these relations tell us about the characteristics of different human groups and processes. The focus here is on people rather than animals. The second category describes work concerned more with the bodies, ecologies, and lived experiences of animals themselves, focusing especially on the practical, ethical, and political implications of their interactions with humans. These are not discrete categories – there is a growing body of work that looks at both animal spaces and beastly places – but this distinction offers a useful heuristic for classification.

### Animal Spaces

Geographers have taken Lévi-Strauss' famous advice that animals are "good to think with" to explore the various ways in which animals are spaced and ordered by people. These authors have come from a range of theoretical positions and are impelled by diverse political ends. Here we identify four broad strands of this work.

The first has continued to explore the structures, discourses, and practices that set up associations between socially disempowered human groups and specific animal "others" in order to constitute and sustain the simultaneous marginalization of both. Here the treatment of animals has been variously connected to practices of exploitation, commodification, patriarchy, alienation, and racism. For example, in her ongoing work on the histories of the classification of civilization, race, and animality in Australia, Kay Anderson (2006) draws on posthumanist and critical race theory to document how the colonial (and postcolonial) subjugation of Aboriginal people was legitimated by their discursive animalization as wild savages. Colonial science located Aborigines in proximity to animals and ranked them at the bottom of a linear, teleological scale of civilization. The perceived failure of Aboriginal peoples to respond to colonial efforts toward their development only served to confirm their animal status and legitimate their marginalization through socially and ecologically disastrous policies.

A second strand of work on animal spaces is associated with a vibrant strand of neo-Marxist and postcolonial political ecology. Here writers have explored how the treatment of animals under contemporary forms of capitalism and/or neocolonialism demonstrates the socially unjust and ecologically damaging character of neoliberal modes of political economy and emerging forms of free-market environmentalism. For example, in her extensive research on the production, processing, and consumption networks associated with the global seafood industry, Becky Mansfield traces the range of practices through which fish and fishing are commodified, marketed, distinguished, and regulated under contemporary forms of global capitalism (e.g., Mansfield 2003). Documenting declines in fish stocks, she notes the inadequacies of modes of market-based environmental regulation and the tendency toward overexploitation in capitalist modes of resource use (Mansfield 2006). Her argument – alongside other political ecologists exploring animals (and other non-humans) as resources (e.g., Franklin 2007) – is that fish tell us something new about capitalism, while attending to the biophysical properties of animals helps explain the different ways in which their bodies are (or are not) subsumed to the logic of capitalist accumulation (Bakker and Bridge 2006). Here, for example, the history of animal domestication and exploitation can be linked to the malleability or intractability of their bodies, behaviors, and genomes.

Similar concerns with power and exploitation characterize a growing body of work in political ecology on animal conservation. For example, in her investigation of "crocodile crimes" in the postcolonial politics of conservation in Zimbabwe, JoAnn McGregor (2005) traces conflicts between the understandings of animals held by international scientists and marginal local fishermen. Documenting the dangerous consequences for fishermen of reclassifying crocodiles as a conservation concern and the livelihood implications of criminalizing their crocodile killing, she notes the challenges posed by unequal postcolonial power relations in creating space for internationally significant biodiversity. The themes explored in McGregor's work resonate with research examining the commodification of animals in the postcolonial economies of ecotourism. Here the growing demand for spectacular and/or touching encounters with charismatic animals like elephants and whales is presented as leading to large-scale ecological transformation and the perpetuation or invention of exploitative and neocolonial forms of political economy (e.g., Duffy and Moore 2010).

A third strand of work, informed more by Foucault's later writings on governmentality, has examined what the ordering of animals in (largely Western) societies tells us about late modern forms of biopower and biopolitics. This approach examines knowledge practices that seek to govern human and non-human life at the level of the population. For example, in their work on agriculture, Lewis Holloway, Carol Morris, and their fellow researchers (e.g., 2009) have traced the growth and consequences of genetic and genomic-based science for the conduct of pedigree livestock breeding. They identify shifting power relations and the emergence of novel forms of value, as well as tensions between genetic and more traditional modes of evaluating and governing livestock. Drawing on Foucault-inspired actor network theory, Holloway traces the role of technologies like robotic milking machines in the performance of this ordering.

A concern with biopolitics also characterizes recent work examining the practices of animal biosecurity, such as those associated with the governance of animal and zoonotic diseases (Enticott 2008), invasive species (Barker 2008), and risky predators (Buller 2008). This research examines what these practices tell us about the place of risk and the management of uncertainty in contemporary modes of anticipatory governance and political economy. Other authors have drawn on similar poststructuralist theory to explore the biopolitics of animal welfare (Buller and Morris 2003) and biodiversity conservation (Dempsey 2010), identifying the "material assemblages" of texts, technologies, and classification schemes that establish distinct regimes for governing which animals live and under what conditions. Focusing on cows, Lorimer and Driessen (2011) provide a review of these prevalent modes of non-human biopolitics – outlining the differences between agriculture, welfare, conservation, and biosecurity. They go on to document the biopolitics of "rewilding" and "dedomestication," which are emerging as new modes of governing non-human difference in nature conservation.

Finally, an established strand of work has continued to explore the cultural politics of representing animals, examining what tensions between different claims to authority tell us about the place of science and other forms of expertise in contemporary and historical social contexts. For example, in their work on the "animal landscapes" of twentieth-century British otter hunting and wildfowling, David Matless and his fellow researchers demonstrate how arguments over human conduct in relation to animals were linked to the growing power of scientific studies of populations, the declining authority of traditional forms of animal knowledge associated with rural elites, and the "varying abilities of field sports to restyle themselves as modern" (Matless, Merchant, and Watkins 2005: 191). This interest in the politics of nature resonates with a growing body of work at the interface of human geography and the sociology of science that explores the importance of vernacular ecological knowledge and the role of "amateurs as experts" in the conduct of natural history and wildlife conservation (e.g., Ellis and Waterton 2005). These authors draw primarily on ethnographic and participatory research to document situations in which animal scientists must work with and give ground to multiple epistemic communities.

Perhaps as a consequence of the non-representational turn in cultural geography, there has been a decline in the type of geographical research examining textual representations of animals that was so popular during the cultural turn of the late 1990s. However, strands of this work persist in efforts to explore the "more-than-representational" (Lorimer 2005) dimensions to animal imagery and other media. For example, Jamie Lorimer (2010b) has explored the different "affective logics" through which elephants are evoked in moving imagery, contrasting elephant imagery configured around sentimentality, sympathy, curiosity, and disconcertion. This work seeks to supplement a concern with the meanings of animal representations with a critical assessment of the affective force of moving imagery, examining how the multi-sensory qualities of different animal media are mobilized and to what ends.

## Beastly Places

If the first body of work reviewed above is characterized by a concern for what human–animal interactions tell us about people and their practices, a second strand of work in animal geography has been more concerned with the agencies and lived experiences of animals, especially those animals in close interaction with people. This research seeks to understand how animals affect the lives of humans and, in turn, how humans impact the lives of animals. Very often, these animal geographies set out to challenge Cartesian understandings of animals as insentient objects and instrumental resources, and aim to develop means to improve human relations with animals.

A small part of this work is aligned with wider developments in "critical animal studies" (Twine 2010) and animal ethics (Palmer 2011). Here certain trans-species animal properties (like the capacity to suffer) are used as universal criteria for ethical and political critique and practice. These principles are systematically applied in all contexts that are of a similar nature, rather than permitting ethical decisions to be made at the levels of the individual or particular relationships. Such work often argues for the complete ethical and political reconceptualization, in theory and practice, of how humans currently relate to animals (see Hobson 2007). Within geography, the focus has mainly been on critically examining specific domains of human–animal interaction. For instance, Jody Emel (1998) offers an empirical critique of discourses around wolf-hunting in the United States, describing how hunting was valorized as vermin control and a masculine sport, even while opposition to hunting was delegitimized as bourgeois and elitist. More recently, David Lulka (2009) has explored the involvement of the American Kennel Club in the governance of canine breeding, using theoretical work on form and formlessness to unpack the ethical complexities of contemporary human–dog interactions, especially the management of dog reproduction to achieve narrow breed identities. To a lesser extent, there have been efforts to construct alternative models of inter-species justice, for instance by calling for the ethical recognition of animal individuals, or by suggesting that the hitherto purely human urban spaces should be equally accessible as habitats for non-human animals (e.g., Wolch 2002).

However, in geography, this type of work has largely been supplanted by writing that adopts relational approaches and that goes under the rubric of "more-than-human geographies." Here, the emphasis is on mapping and theorizing specific forms of non-human difference and situated human–animal relationships. In general, the work seeks to develop an understanding of human–animal interactions as modes of relating in which the principal agents and forms of expertise are "more-than-human." Humans and animals are understood to become what they are through situated and embodied interactions, rather than being determined in advance. With regard to ethics, it is argued that decision-making should be contingent on the particularities of individual circumstances and human cognitive and emotional complexity. Rather than advocating a radical reconceptualization of ethics and politics, this work tends to focus on what is perceived to be possible within existing economic, moral, and political frameworks.

Conceptually, these relational animal geographies have drawn on and developed strands of poststructuralist, phenomenological, and vitalist philosophy. One early trajectory in this work saw the extension and development of actor network theory (ANT) to animals, recognizing their agencies in the practices of everyday life. For example, Sarah Whatmore and Lorraine Thorne (2000) draw on ANT in their work on the "spatial formations of wildlife exchange" in global biodiversity conservation. Here they use Latour's conceptual vocabulary of networks and non-human agency to examine how the bodies and lives of elephants are shaped by two very different modes of ordering. In spite of its relational ontology and popularity in geography, authors like Whatmore and Thorne found ANT to be unsatisfactory for describing and engaging with animals. They note its tendency to flatten out forms of non-human difference especially between sentient and non-sentient non-humans and its inadequacy in engaging with specific animal competencies (Risan 2005). Further work, informed in part by these deficiencies, has developed approaches drawn from ethology, phenomenology, and vitalist philosophy to document specific forms of non-human difference and the material exchanges associated with multi-species interactions.

Here the recent writings of Donna Haraway (2008) on "companion species" have been especially influential. Haraway focuses on relationships between people and dogs, including her own experience as a dog agility racer. Drawing on a range of animal science, she traces the entangled histories of the two species as well as the multiple ways in which contemporary people and dogs become what they are in relation to each other. For example, she reflects on the forms of care and inter-species communication necessary for successful agility racing. She traces how the characteristics of her canine companion Cayenne are linked in part to long histories of working animal breeding. For Haraway these shared pasts and conjoined lives present important contemporary and future-oriented responsibilities to people to live well with animals. She is skeptical of claims for universal animal rights and a politics of animal liberation, noting the dependence of domesticated animals on human care. She instead presents and appeals for modes of human–non-human companionship aiming toward the flourishing of modes of non-human difference. While Haraway's work has been criticized, it continues to exert a substantial influence on more-than-human geographies, leading to a burgeoning literature that focuses on themes of care, companionship, and conviviality.

For example, both Jamie Lorimer (2010a) and David Lulka (2004) have drawn on Haraway and Deleuze in their work on biodiversity conservation. Their respective accounts develop scientific work on elephant and bison ecology and ethology to challenge forms of conservation that manage the lives of these animals toward fixed models of genetic difference or pristine wildness. Instead they propose "lively biogeographies" that seek to demonstrate what conservation stands to gain from attending to the beastly places of animals and their lively abilities to adapt to human relations. Similar work has sought to enliven the geographies of biosecurity, for example by examining relations of adaptation and accommodation in the management of invasive species (Barker 2008).

One of the main contributions of this relational approach has been to highlight the beastly places of animals that are often excluded by prevalent and powerful binary geographies of nature that establish clear spaces for people and wildlife. For example, a range of recent writing has sought to challenge prevalent modern urban geographies that tend to exclude animals from the city. Steve Hinchliffe, Sarah Whatmore, and their fellow researchers (2005) document "living cities" characterized by inter-species relations of "conviviality." Drawing on empirical investigations of the political ecologies of water voles, black redstarts, and peregrine falcons that make their homes in UK cities, they document distinct urban ecologies inhabited by urbanized animals that have learned to live amidst high human populations in disturbed habitats that are generally neglected by conservationists. This work develops earlier appeals by animal geographers for a "trans-species urban theory" (Wolch, West, and Gaines 1995) and argues for an open-ended form of urban governance that is sensitive to the as yet unknown ways in which animals adapt to their local environments. Similar challenges to modern spatial binaries can be found in work that challenges the pervasive nationalization of wild animals as either "alien" or "native," instead recognizing long histories of species movement and forms of human companionship (Warren 2007).

On the domestic front, geographers have examined the beastly places and associated geographies of responsibility associated with agriculture and pet keeping. For example, as part of a larger project developing new techniques for governing animal welfare, Mara Miele (2011) has explored the complexities of researching the emotional lives of animals and the potential of inventing indices of animal happiness (in this case, chickens) for shifting consumption habits. Similarly, Rebecca Fox (2006) undertakes an ethnography of human–pet relationships in Britain to demonstrate how the binary division between human and animal is troubled when people recognize and respect the subjectivity and individuality of their pets. Departing from this emphasis on companionship, care, and conviviality is some literature that looks at the harmful aspects of human interactions with animals. For instance, Buller and Morris (2003) examine the paradoxes inherent in discourses and practices of care associated with animal welfare, while Kathryn Yusoff (2012) argues that attention to the relationships of violence that underlie biodiversity loss might help reconfigure more benevolent relations. Such work, however, remains marginal in geography so far.

Methodologically, more-than-human animal research in geography, anthropology, and other cognate disciplines has sought to conjoin ethnographic and ethological methods of participant observation to develop techniques for research in a multi-species context. There has been a strong focus on proximal encounters between research participants and their animal subjects. Popular spaces for research include laboratories, parks, houses, and various field sites. Human–animal encounters are understood as comprising processes of "learning to be affected," in which the human (and sometimes animal) participants develop the skills to tune into the different ways of being performed by their partner animal. This endeavor has stimulated methodological innovation. For example, Eric Laurier and his co-researchers have developed new video methodologies for witnessing and analyzing human–animal encounters. Their research features a range of empirical projects documenting practices as varied as fly-fishing and dog walking (e.g., Laurier, Maze, and Lundin 2006). Other researchers have experimented with techniques for animating the archive to recount more-than-human historical geographies. For example, Hayden Lorimer (2006) offers archival and performative methods for witnessing the shared "herding memories" of humans and animals entangled in the practices of reindeer herding in Scotland. In very different empirical contexts, Laura Ogden (2011) and Jamie Lorimer and Sarah Whatmore (2009) offer techniques for mapping the embodied historical geographies of alligator and elephant hunting in the Florida Everglades and Sri Lanka, respectively.

Research concerned with the beastly spaces of animals' geographies has produced a sizable volume of work investigating different human–animal relations, often based around detailed case study material. This has helped identify a range of different ontologies. In short, we would suggest there are at least four ways of conceiving animals within contemporary animal geographies: (1) concern about *animal genetics and genomics* dominates critical work exploring the consequences of biotechnology for biodiversity and animal breeds; (2) work that adopts an overtly political approach to animal welfare tends to engage with *animals as individual beings*, focusing on lived experience and sentience; (3) work that examines conservation figures *animals as members of populations of either species or breeds* whose aggregate survival and flourishing are paramount; (4) a further body of work conceives of animals as vehicles for the expression of both valuable and risky processes, ranging from decomposition to infection to evolution. Animals therefore figure as *genes*, *individuals*, *species*, or *breeds* and as *agents of ecological processes*.

This ontological diversity can lead to subtle, often hidden, tensions within the field, particularly when they are associated with contradictory ways of thinking about the ethical and political status of animals. There is much more work to be done here, but some recent research has sought to acknowledge this ontological multiplicity and the tensions between divergent approaches. For example, in their writings on wildlife conservation Lorimer (2010a) and Lulka (2004) have examined the tensions between genetic, individual, species, and process-based ontologies. They identify scenarios that pit the life and welfare of individual animals against the future of the species or the stability of the ecosystems that they live in. These include programs for culling, breeding, rewilding, or cloning, or even wildlife research. Such ontological politics is also at the heart of debates around whether domestic animals such as cattle and sheep are better off being bred and raised for human purposes (Palmer 2011). Similarly, in their work on biotechnology and animal breeding, Gail Davies (2010), Carol Morris and Lewis Holloway (2009), and others have examined the ontological ambiguity and resulting ethical problems associated with various modes of postgenomic animal science that are uncertain about what determines animal behavior and experience.

A shift from animal to more-than-human geographies has accompanied a gradual broadening in the taxonomic scope of animal geographies research. For example, in recent years there has been a widening focus away from a subset of useful, risky, or charismatic birds and mammals to consider the spaces and places for plants and trees (Head and Atchison 2009), fish (Bear and Eden 2011), and insects (Bingham 2006). This taxonomic generosity can be linked to a nascent body of work in more-than-human geography that seeks to explore the agency of inorganic matter (Clark 2011). Here rocks, water, atmosphere, and sunshine figure as actors whose agency forces us to rethink inanimate figuring of the "geo-" in geography and geopolitics.

## Conclusions

In this chapter we have provided a short review of trends in animal geography in the last decade. We have identified the growth of a rich, vibrant, and heterogeneous subdiscipline that is characterized by diverse objectives and draws on multiple theoretical frameworks. We have differentiated this work according to critical intent and the relative prominence afforded to animal agency and identified vibrant strands of research documenting animal spaces and beastly places, as well as a growing interest in developing concepts and methods for tracing the entanglement between the two. Animal geography has matured as a subdiscipline in the last decade in conversation with the broader flourishing of the multidisciplinary field of animal studies. It has expanded and perhaps it has fragmented. However, this multiplicity is an asset. Taken as a whole, the body of work reviewed above demonstrates the important contribution that geographers are making to animal studies. To conclude, we would like to briefly reflect on some of the wider implications of this work, as well as some emerging opportunities for future research.

First, as several commentators have noted, the challenge presented by recent work in animal studies to the familiar modern divide between the human and the animal poses some far-reaching questions about the coherence and desirability of the category "human geography" (Whatmore 2006). Here the exclusion of humans from the category animals – and thus the necessity of a distinct non-human animal geography – reveals the persistence of the discipline's humanist history. The advent of the label more-than-human goes some way toward reordering this disciplinary division, but it is early days. Looking ahead, we see great potential in the growing enthusiasm for intra-disciplinary biogeographical research bringing social scientists into conversation and collaboration with natural scientists (Whatmore 2009). Some commentators have argued that with the advent of more-than-human geography, certain strands of cultural and animal geography might even be returning to their zoogeographical roots, albeit with perhaps a more sophisticated understanding of political dynamics (Braun 2003).

This enthusiasm for questioning the humanism of human geography can also be detected in the growing interest in non-human agency in strands of the discipline – like political ecology and urban studies – that have traditionally been skeptical of the utility and consequences of such moves. For example, Karen Bakker (2010) has appealed for researchers working on resource geographies to consider the difference that non-human (including animal) difference makes to the operations of political economic practices. Here political ecologists have revisited Marx's theories of metabolism and the subsumption of nature to explore how the beastly spaces of animal (and plant) bodies, genomes, and lived environments help shape and are shaped by economic practices. We anticipate interesting new work in this area, especially in emerging research critically examining the modes of lively biocapital associated with recent developments in capitalist animal experimentation and biotechnology (Rajan 2006). Perhaps the divide in environmental geography between structuralist and relational approaches to the politics of nature (see Castree 2002) is easing, with the emergence of new theoretical approaches and research collaborations.

Finally, if we situate animal geographies within the wider field of animal studies we can note the surprising lack of engagement in the burgeoning geographical work on human–animal relationships with analytical philosophy. While Jonathan Murdoch (2003) briefly discusses Singer's and Regan's work on animal ethics in his reflections on geography's "circle of concern," there is limited work in geography that draws from and develops

Anglo-American animal philosophy and animal ethics. Much of the animal geography writing that follows the relational route emerges from critiques of the inadequacies of older work on animal ethics (especially Peter Singer's [1975] utilitarian approach and Tom Regan's [1983] rights approach). However, subsequent developments in animal ethics, both by other authors (e.g., Rollin 2006) and by Singer (2006) and Regan (2001) themselves, have been more or less overlooked. These recent writings build upon, modify, and often address many of the lacunae observed in older work. They offer nuanced positions on the ethics of human–animal relationships, with which animal and more-than-human geographies could usefully engage (see for example Palmer 2011).

## References

Anderson, K. (2006) *Race and the Crisis of Humanism*. London: Routledge.

Bakker, K. (2010) The limits of "neoliberal natures": Debating green neoliberalism. *Progress in Human Geography*, 34, 715–735.

Bakker, K. and Bridge, G. (2006) Material worlds? Resource geographies and the "matter of nature." *Progress in Human Geography*, 30, 5–27.

Barker, K. (2008) Flexible boundaries in biosecurity: Accommodating gorse in Aotearoa New Zealand. *Environment and Planning A*, 40, 1598–1614.

Bear, C. and Eden, S. (2011) Thinking like a fish? Engaging with nonhuman difference through recreational angling. *Environment and Planning D: Society and Space*, 29, 336–352.

Bingham, N. (2006) Bees, butterflies, and bacteria: Biotechnology and the politics of nonhuman friendship. *Environment and Planning A*, 38, 483–498.

Braun, B. (2003) Nature and culture: On the career of a false problem. In *A Companion to Cultural Geography*, ed. J. Duncan and N. Johnson. Oxford: Blackwell, pp. 151–179.

Buller, H. (2008) Safe from the wolf: Biosecurity, biodiversity, and competing philosophies of nature. *Environment and Planning A*, 40, 1583–1597.

Buller, H. and Morris, C. (2003) Farm animal welfare: A new repertoire of nature–society relations or modernism re-embedded? *Sociologia Ruralis*, 43, 216–237.

Castree, N. (2002) False antitheses? Marxism, nature and actor-networks. *Antipode*, 34, 111–146.

Clark, N. (2011) *Inhuman Nature: Sociable Living on a Dynamic Planet*. London: Sage.

Davies, G. (2010) Captivating behaviour: Mouse models, experimental genetics and reductionist returns in the neurosciences. *Sociological Review*, 58, 53–72.

Dempsey, J. (2010) Tracking grizzly bears in British Columbia's environmental politics. *Environment and Planning A*, 42, 1138–1156.

Duffy, R. and Moore, L. (2010) Neoliberalising nature? Elephant-back tourism in Thailand and Botswana. *Antipode*, 42, 742–766.

Ellis, R. and Waterton, C. (2005) Caught between the cartographic and the ethnographic imagination: The whereabouts of amateurs, professionals, and nature in knowing biodiversity. *Environment and Planning D: Society and Space*, 23, 673–693.

Emel, J. (1998) Are you man enough, big and bad enough? Wolf eradication in the US. In *Animal Geographies: Place, Politics and Identity in the Nature–Culture Borderlands*, ed. J. Emel and J. Wolch. London: Verso, pp. 91–118.

Enticott, G. (2008) The spaces of biosecurity: Prescribing and negotiating solutions to bovine tuberculosis. *Environment and Planning A*, 40, 1568–1582.

Fox, R. (2006) Animal behaviours, post-human lives: Everyday negotiations of the animal–human divide in pet-keeping. *Social and Cultural Geography*, 7, 525–537.

Franklin, S. (2007) *Dolly Mixtures: The Remaking of Genealogy*. Durham, NC: Duke University Press.

Haraway, D.J. (2008) *When Species Meet*. Minneapolis: University of Minnesota Press.

Head, L. and Atchison, J. (2009) Cultural ecology: Emerging human–plant geographies. *Progress in Human Geography*, 33, 236–245.

Hinchliffe, S., Kearnes, M.B., Degen, M. and Whatmore, S. (2005) Urban wild things: A cosmopolitical experiment. *Environment and Planning D: Society and Space*, 23, 643–658.

Hobson, K. (2007) Political animals? On animals as subjects in an enlarged political geography. *Political Geography*, 26, 250–267.

Holloway, L., Morris, C., Gilna, B. and Gibbs, D. (2009) Biopower, genetics and livestock breeding: (Re)constituting animal populations and heterogeneous biosocial collectivities. *Transactions of the Institute of British Geographers*, 34, 394–407.

Laurier, E., Maze, R. and Lundin, J. (2006) Putting the dog back in the park: Animal and human mind-in-action. *Mind, Culture, and Activity*, 13, 2–24.

Lorimer, H. (2005) Cultural geography: The busyness of being "more-than-representational." *Progress in Human Geography*, 29, 83–94.

Lorimer, H. (2006) Herding memories of humans and animals. *Environment and Planning D: Society and Space*, 24, 497–518.

Lorimer, J. (2010a) Elephants as companion species: The lively biogeographies of Asian elephant conservation in Sri Lanka. *Transactions of the Institute of British Geographers*, 35, 491–506.

Lorimer, J. (2010b) Moving image methodologies for more-than-human geographies. *Cultural Geographies*, 17, 237–258.

Lorimer, J. and Driessen, C. (2011) Bovine biopolitics and the promise of monsters in the rewilding of Heck cattle. *Geoforum*. DOI: 10.1016/j.geoforum.2011.09.002

Lorimer, J. and Whatmore, S. (2009) After "the king of beasts": Samuel Baker and the embodied historical geographies of his elephant hunting in mid-19th century Ceylon. *Journal of Historical Geography*, 35, 668–689.

Lulka, D. (2004) Stabilizing the herd: Fixing the identity of nonhumans. *Environment and Planning D: Society and Space*, 22, 439–463.

Lulka, D. (2009) Form and formlessness: The spatiocorporeal politics of the American Kennel Club. *Environment and Planning D: Society and Space*, 27, 531–553.

Mansfield, B. (2003) From catfish to organic fish: Making distinctions about nature as cultural economic practice. *Geoforum*, 34, 329–342.

Mansfield, B. (2006) Assessing market-based environmental policy using a case study of North Pacific fisheries. *Global Environmental Change*, 16, 29–39.

Matless, D., Merchant, P. and Watkins, C. (2005) Animal landscapes: Otters and wildfowl in England 1945–1970. *Transactions of the Institute of British Geographers*, 30, 191–205.

McGregor, J. (2005) Crocodile crimes: People versus wildlife and the politics of postcolonial conservation on Lake Kariba, Zimbabwe. *Geoforum*, 36, 353–369.

Miele, M. (2011) The taste of happiness: Free-range chicken. *Environment and Planning A*, 43, 2076–2090.

Morris, C. and Holloway, L. (2009) Genetic technologies and the transformation of the geographies of UK livestock agriculture: A research agenda. *Progress in Human Geography*, 33, 313–333.

Murdoch, J. (2003) Geography's circle of concern. *Geoforum*, 34, 287–289.

Ogden, L. (2011) *Swamplife: People, Gators, and Mangroves Entangled in the Everglades*. Minneapolis: University of Minnesota Press.

Palmer, C. (2011) *Animal Ethics in Context*. New York: Columbia University Press.

Philo, C. and Wilbert, C. (2000) *Animal Spaces, Beastly Places: New Geographies of Human–Animal Relations*. London: Routledge.

Rajan, K.S. (2006) *Biocapital: The Constitution of Postgenomic Life*. Durham, NC: Duke University Press.

Regan, T. (1983) *The Case for Animal Rights*. Berkeley: University of California Press.

Regan, T. (2001) *Defending Animal Rights*. Champaign: University of Illinois Press.

Risan, L.C. (2005) The boundary of animality. *Environment and Planning D: Society and Space*, 23, 787–793.

Rollin, B.E. (2006) *Animal Rights and Human Morality*. New York: Prometheus Books.

Singer, P. (1975) *Animal Liberation: A New Ethics for Our Treatment of Animals*. New York: Random House.

Singer, P. (2006) *In Defense of Animals: The Second Wave*. Oxford: Blackwell.

Thrift, N. (2007) *Non-Representational Theory: Space, Politics, Affect*. London: Routledge.

Twine, R. (2010) *Animals as Biotechnology: Ethics, Sustainability and Critical Animal Studies*. London: Earthscan.

Warren, C.R. (2007) Perspectives on the "alien" versus "native" species debate: A critique of concepts, language and practice. *Progress in Human Geography*, 31, 427–446.

Whatmore, S. (2006) Materialist returns: Practising cultural geography in and for a more-than-human world. *Cultural Geographies*, 13, 600–609.

Whatmore, S. (2009) Mapping knowledge controversies: Science, democracy and the redistribution of expertise. *Progress in Human Geography*, 33, 587–598.

Whatmore, S. and Thorne, L. (2000) Elephants on the move: Spatial formations of wildlife exchange. *Environment and Planning D: Society and Space*, 18, 185–203.

Wolch, J. (2002) Anima urbis. *Progress in Human Geography*, 26, 721–742.

Wolch, J. and Emel, J. (1998) *Animal Geographies: Place, Politics, and Identity in the Nature–Culture Borderlands*. London: Verso.

Wolch, J., Emel, J. and Wilbert, C. (2003) Reanimating cultural geography. In *Handbook of Cultural Geography*, ed. K. Anderson. London: Sage, pp. 184–206.

Wolch, J.R., West, K. and Gaines, T.E. (1995) Transspecies urban theory. *Environment and Planning D: Society and Space*, 13, 735–760.

Yusoff, K. (2012) Aesthetics of loss: Biodiversity, banal violence and biotic subjects. *Transactions of the Institute of British Geographers*, 37 (4), 578–592.

# Chapter 30

# Food's Cultural Geographies: Texture, Creativity, and Publics

*Ian Cook, Peter Jackson, Allison Hayes-Conroy, Sebastian Abrahamsson, Rebecca Sandover, Mimi Sheller, Heike Henderson, Lucius Hallett, Shoko Imai, Damian Maye, and Ann Hill*[1]

## Introduction

It's February 2012. You're going to the AAG annual conference in New York in a couple of weeks' time. You want to find out first-hand about the latest research on food geographies. Maybe you're brushing up an undergraduate module in which food plays a major part. Maybe you're in the early stages of putting together a research proposal with food at its heart. Maybe you're a faculty member, or a student, or someone else attending that conference. You know that food is more than just an area of geographical inquiry. It offers rich, tangible entryways into almost any issue in which you might be interested. You're on the conference website, searching for food sessions and for papers with food as a keyword. The result? Fifty sessions and 187 papers. You're spoilt for choice. There's so much going on. The Chicago AAG conference six years earlier had only six food sessions and forty-four food papers. Those numbers were much easier to manage. Recent years, it seems fair to say, have witnessed an explosion in geographical research on food.

This chapter is about emerging cultural geographies of food. It has eleven authors. We all work on food. Most of us are geographers. Some of us call ourselves cultural geographers. This chapter is the result of a collaborative blog-to-paper process that, last time, led to an experimental, fragmented, dialogic text (Cook *et al.* 2011).[2] This is a more straightforward, single-voiced, text. It's based on two characterizations of cultural geography written by Phil Crang (2010) and John Wylie (2010) to mark the twentieth anniversary of the publication of Peter Jackson's (1989) *Maps of Meaning*. Their papers sparked and orientated our online discussions. Neither Crang's nor Wylie's papers, however, discussed, or even mentioned, food's cultural geographies. That was fine. What was fascinating to us were the ways in which they described the vast, interconnected, and fragmentary field of contemporary cultural

*The Wiley Blackwell Companion to Cultural Geography*, First Edition.
Edited by Nuala C. Johnson, Richard H. Schein, and Jamie Winders.
© 2013 John Wiley & Sons, Ltd. Published 2016 by John Wiley & Sons, Ltd.

geography as sharing certain vitalities, orientations, sensibilities, styles of thought, and practices. These shared elements included a "stress . . . on the affective, emotive and praxis-based aspects of life" (Wylie 2010: 213); a "desire for different types of writing, methods, formats and 'outputs' " (Wylie 2010: 213); a working through of the "tension between the significant and the insignificant, the small and the mighty, the trivial and the momentous" (Crang 2010: 195); and an interest in developing the kinds of "creative writing, . . . photography and video, . . . site-specific art, etc." that could help to improve "the relatively low profile of the [wider] discipline" (Wylie 2010: 213).

We recognized all of these elements from the work that we know and do. Food has become an important medium for exploring new practices, methods, outputs, and textures of a more praxis-based geography. Food is often researched precisely because it can help to vividly animate tensions between the small and intimate realms of embodiment, domesticity, and "ordinary affect" (Stewart 2007) and the more sweeping terrain of global political economy, sustainability, and the vitality of "nature." Food's cultural geographies, like cultural geography more broadly, can be "best characterized by powerful senses of texture, creativity and public engagement" (Crang 2010: 197). This is what we hope to illustrate, add to, rework, and reflect upon below.

## Texture

Perhaps the most common starting point in any "geographies of food" discussion is the fact that food, like other commodities, links consumers with unknown and distant others, creating connections "from farm to fork" (Jackson, Ward, and Russell 2006) and "between field and plate" (Stassart and Whatmore 2003). Looking at how food becomes displaced, circulated, and performed in different sites, such work focuses on the ways in which the production, marketing, and storying of food products is folded into consumer behavior in complex, and often surprising, ways. However, such work could be, and is becoming, more attuned to physicality, the senses, embodiment, affect, and materiality – what Crang (2010) calls "texture." First, this new focus has evolved because the location of "field" and "fork" is being questioned. Practices of transforming things into food – such as harvesting, transportation, retail, marketing, and cooking – apprehend the body of the eater in a reciprocal exchange which makes a linear conception of those transformations problematic (Roe 2006). In short, the field is on the plate just as much as the plate is in the field. Second, this attention to "texture" emerges because mapping these transformations has chiefly involved tracing out and following chains that, somewhat surprisingly, end abruptly before the food is ingested (e.g., Cook *et al.* 2004). Thus, recent work has suggested a need to suspend the conceptual boundaries that separate food from the eating body (Abrahamsson and Simpson 2011) and to pay attention to the physicalities and materialities of food and the ways in which these connect with bodies through eating, or otherwise physically engaging, with food (Mol 2008).

One mode through which food geographies may attend to such physicalities is by focusing on the feelings that food–body relationships produce. There is a growing recognition of "hidden geographies" undergirding the food system, where "food links up with ideas, memories, sounds, visions, beliefs, past experiences, moods [and] worries, all of which combine to become material – to become bodily, physical sensations" (Cook *et al.* 2011: 113). Paying attention to such visceral feelings (Hayes-Conroy and Martin 2010) allows geographers to broaden the task of "following food." Both ends of the production/consumption process have had little attention to these bodily, physical experiences. In Cook *et al.*'s (2004) "Follow the thing: Papaya," before the fruit is shipped, a picker describes "cleaning" the fruit in fungicides which eventually results in latex burns with "blistered fingertips and thumbs hurting so much" (p. 657). Whether at the point of production, consumption, or in between, paying attention to what food, and food systems more broadly, *do* to bodies upon being touched, tasted, ingested, smelled, heard, or seen (e.g., Mann *et al.* 2011) reveals the visceral physicality of bodily engagement with food.

Such a venture into the body is, of course, accomplished along a different path from, and with different goals than, nutrition or medical science versions of "following" food in the body. The objectives can be diverse, but center on feelings as significant drivers of food-relevant cultural behavior and cultural (re)production. Here, both bodies and food are recognized as social agents, or at least as possessing "agentic" qualities. Allison Hayes-Conroy and Jessica Hayes-Conroy (2010) argue, for example, that "the body" is not a holistic container that passively awaits food but, rather, actively engages with ingested stuff in different, sometimes surprising ways. Thus, just as there are complex geographies of, for instance, the transportation of food, there are equally complex, and often hidden, geographies of the eating body. These geographies are not necessarily pre-discursive or unarticulated but, rather, are acted upon and worked with in certain practices. In other words, while there may be patterns and tendencies to food–body relationships, we can mold our bodies to feel food or to respond to various kinds of food in new and different ways.

In her work on the political ecology of things, Jane Bennett (2007) argues against the anthropocentrism of commodity-chain analysis. The study of food primarily as a resource for human consumption, she argues, fails to engage seriously with food's "agentic capacities" as vital matter. Attention needs to be paid, she suggests, both to the physical capacities of food itself and to the ways in which these capabilities intersect with practices of production, consumption, aesthetics, and morality. These ideas are perhaps best illustrated by recent work on the art and science of cheese-making, where protein bundles, fatty acids, and metabolic enzymes all contribute to the lively materiality of the finished product. In Heather Paxson's (2011) work, for example, the process of artisan cheese-making is understood as involving a balance of aesthetic creativity and intuition combined with accurate measurement, meticulous record-keeping, and scrupulous hygiene. It is a process that brings together cross-sensory apprehension (of taste, smell, and touch) with reasoned analysis, combining "quasi-mystical" elements with an acknowledgment of market-based tastes and commercial calculation. Other apparent dichotomies are challenged in Annemarie Mol's (2009) work on consumer-citizens. Exploring how contemporary food advertising depicts the pleasures of health and fairness, Mol argues that we should not oppose pleasure-seeking consumers with socially responsible citizens. Instead, we should search for alternative models of the consumer-citizen that bring together the expression of "private" pleasures and public goods: "healthy and yummy," "fair and delicious."

In addition to research that attends to a diversity of feelings at one particular point along the food chain, there is also fascinating work that attends to one type of feeling (codified as an emotional category or sensation-based category) across a commodity chain. Benson and Fischer (2007), for example, focus on desire, explicitly as a described emotion and implicitly as a bodily feeling, which guides (and connects!) distinct practices of broccoli production and consumption and works both for and against the "hegemonic constellations" of the global food trade (p. 800). Such work invites us to consider how food exists within a complex and contradictory cultural politics in which the often "hidden" domain of feeling acts as a central driver of both business-as-usual and the possibility of a different and better system. For a cultural geography of food, paying attention to such an embodied cultural politics could offer a way to maintain a critical edge and remain relevant to today's diverse and growing struggles over the politics of food. Indeed, while some have sensibly worried that a focus on feeling/affect or mundane/other-than-representational might take us further from a critically oriented cultural politics of food and bodies (e.g., Crang 2010; Jacobs and Nash 2003), thinking through desire (or other named feelings) could indicate a way to merge seemingly disparate calls to attend, on the one hand, to the sensibilities of the everyday, non-representational, or affective realm (perhaps the realm of unintentional performance) and, on the other, to the representational realm in which intentional performativity allows for planned and collective forms of (cultural political) resistance. The ways in which Benson and Fischer (2007) think through desire clearly shows the stitching of relations between the physical, the affective/emotive, and the cognitive realms; such work invites cultural geographers interested in "texture" to link up with those writing on other experiential aspects of food systems on all points along the food chain.

Perhaps particularly important here would be to attend to the texture of environmental justice issues in food systems, such as the effects of agrochemicals on workers, mentioned above, or farmworker hunger and strife (e.g., see Harrison 2006, 2008; Alkon and Agyeman 2011). More broadly, it's also important to ask how linkages between texture and politics, such as Mol's (2009) appreciations of consumer-citizenry, and the Hayes-Conroys' arguments about visceral politics (Hayes-Conroy 2008; Hayes-Conroy and Hayes-Conroy 2010), can be drawn into food-based projects intended to study and motivate progressive eco-social action. How can the provision of sensory/bodily experiences of food encourage the connection of political ideas and bodily feelings at all points along the food chain? As Rachel Slocum (2011: 318) has recently argued, this kind of connection requires an acknowledgment of both the "radical particularity" of food experiences and the ways in which power and social divisions materially impact people's bodily relations with food.

## Creativity

The texture of food and its precarious position between sustenance and garbage make it a powerful creative medium (Kirshenblatt-Gimblett 1999, 2007), both in the (un)intentional domestic food practices mentioned above and in the work of chefs and artists. Cultural geographers of food have begun to pay attention to a range of everyday and specialist creative food practices which bring together and experiment with foods' materialities, agentic capacities, and visceral politics. We want to begin our discussion of such creative food geographies in the worlds of celebrity chefs, their restaurants, cookbooks, and re-creations of (inter)national culinary traditions (see Bardhi, Ostberg, and Bengtsson 2010; Lindenfeld 2007). This is where emphases on the artistic aspect of cooking as a performance of culinary culture are perhaps most commonly found.

Chefs' work operates across materials, people, and money, including flows of representations, advertising, and commodity networks. Chefs often work in/on the various kinds of relations and distances between the origins of different "ethnic" foods and the locations where they prepare and serve food. This position affects not only the aesthetic presentation of meals but also the entire style or philosophy of creating a space for serving food to customers. Often, chefs have to represent whole nations, populations, and cultures by their culinary art and skills (Cook *et al.* 2008). Shoko Imai (2010), for example, discusses the work of Nobuyuki Matsuhisa, a Japanese chef running more than twenty restaurants worldwide, who has created his own "Nobu-style" Japanese food using the essence of Latin American flavors. Matsuhisa worked in many places and countries and established his own way of cooking by negotiating and interacting with his customers, adapting his techniques and knowledge accordingly, and using ingredients obtained locally and from long distances. Imai (2010) argues that Matsuhisa and his "Nobu-style" food perform this story, allowing him to express himself and make himself distinguished, to establish his own brand, and to support its "authenticity" (see Cook, Crang, and Thorpe 2000).

These professional forms of culinary creativity can feed into popular food culture via TV shows, cookbooks, chef-branded foods and equipment, and "eating out" experiences. They also feed into less overtly creative practices of food consumption in the domestic settings, mundane practices, and routinized behavior of everyday life where "feeding the family" is often the priority (though see Finch 2007). Recent work has emphasized the significance of family practices, examining the dynamic processes through which families are created and reproduced, revealing the multiple ways of "doing family" in contemporary social life (see Jackson 2009 for a review). Here, paying attention to the textures of food and the interface between the rational and non-cognitive allows for a greater understanding of the subtleties and vagaries that inform choices about shopping, cooking, eating, and waste disposal.

Awareness of the non-cognitive effects of dealings with food and its technologies acknowledges that these can shape ideas and actions (Crouch 2003). Food, for example, is performed through many everyday acts that highlight the materialities of what we eat and the social and economic networks shaping and informing our food choices. These kinds of everyday, creative food practices have provided the raw materials for performance art that taps into a long feminist tradition exploring our gendered relationships with food. Bobby Baker's performances, for example, bring together slices of beef, flour, treacle, other foodstuffs, and her own body and experiences – on stage, and in "real" domestic spaces like her own kitchen – to celebrate and protest against women's (her) "daily life" (Aston 2000). Caroline Smith, in contrast, dresses as Mertle – a 1950s housewife modeled on celebrity chef Elizabeth Craig – to encourage strangers to confess their eating habits, peculiarities, and secrets in one-to-one sessions. She then draws on these confessions in an on-stage monologue which shows how food is less a fuel for our bodies and more a reflection of our anxieties and desires (Groskop 2009). Both Baker and Smith, then, work with food memories, emotions, narratives, and food itself to create with their audiences visceral, bitter-sweet appreciations of its central role in – primarily women's – everyday lives.

These staged performances are the tip of an iceberg when it comes to artists' engagements with food, its materialities, visceral politics, and geographies. As the 2010 "Uneven Geographies" art exhibition in Nottingham vividly illustrated, works of art can help to make "the obscure and labyrinthine causalities of globalisation more visible and legible, and its human consequences more proximate and affective" than is possible via traditional forms of academic writing (Farquharson 2010: 4). No food-based work was included in the exhibition; but, we argue, the food-based work of artists Shelley Sacks, Lonnie Van Brummelen and Siebren De Haan, and Kate Rich clearly fits its remit. Sacks' social sculpture "Exchange Values: Images of Invisible Lives," for example, used the dried, cured, and stitched skins from twenty boxes of St. Lucian bananas, and the recorded voices of their growers telling visitors about their lives and work, to create a social-sculptural "space for imagination" that was intended to provoke discussion about hidden relations between producers and consumers in contemporary capitalism (see Cook *et al.* 2001 for a detailed description). Van Brummelen and De Haan's (2007) film/publication/installation "Monument of Sugar" was made from cheap subsidized European beet sugar that they purchased in Nigeria (where it undermines the growth of sugar cane), packed and shipped back to Europe "to turn the flow around": this sugar import was only legally permissible because it was a "work of art." Finally, "artist-grocer" Rich's "Feral Trade" project is made out of social networks through which she encourages in-person commodity chains. Through these commodity chains, small batches of coffee, sweets, cola, and other foods are direct from their producers, with each set of transactions, travels, handovers, and import documentation logged on her feraltrade.org website. In each case, carefully chosen foods became key artist materials, their physical qualities, malleability, legal status, and agentic and visceral capacities helping to shape both the work and the ways it could generate affective appreciations of the complexities of trade.

This brings us to the final point we want to make about creativity and the cultural geographies of food: the potential for cultural geographers to put into creative practice our appreciations of food's textural qualities; to work with, like, and/or as "artists"; and to gain academic and popular recognition for the work that this approach produces (Wylie 2010; Crang 2010; Cook and Tolia-Kelly 2010; Regine 2011). What is encouraging are the ways in which the academic concerns we have outlined in this chapter intersect with recent creative food work involving psychogeography, mobile locative art, and expanded dramaturgy. Take, for example, the 2007–2010 "Urbanibalism" project, based in Amsterdam and working in an explicitly geographical way with edibles in cities. A 2010 workshop was framed as an experiment in performance art and had an immediate geographical appeal: the "stomach as compass is an expedition and convivium that orientates by eating, or eats to orientate" (Mass and Pasquinelli 2010). This workshop situated itself between food strategies during wartime (and in times of scarcity) and an expected food shortage in the future. For participants, it highlighted the many edibles that exist in our immediate environment. Urbanibalism's artists also developed an android app called Boskoi with which foragers could map, and perform, the city as an edible space, allowing them to add information on where to find wild apples, rosehips, nuts, fungi, and so on.

There are lots of similar initiatives – urban and guerrilla gardening, dumpster diving, etc. – being taken in many urban environments and not necessarily by artists working on food but, rather, by groups of people with different concerns (political, economic, social, environmental) who want to perform cities as edible spaces. Displacing the notion of performance from "art" to "doing," "enacting," or "practicing," this emphasis on performance with respect to food speaks to the ways in which things are done, practiced, lived, as food. Geographers, performers, artists, audiences, and publics seem now to be coming together in new ways, potentially extending the creative edges of food geographies into more engaged and engaging contexts. Under these circumstances, the question for us is, *what can cultural geography (or social theory more generally) bring into creative practice that is distinctive, research-based, historically informed, and maybe even transformative?*

## Publics

These creative engagements with the textures of food have the potential to generate new conceptions of the political, new ethical engagements with agri-food systems, and new forms of activism. They also have the potential to show that public cultural geographies can do more than increase public understandings of geography as a discipline (Wylie 2010) and/or to engage publics in academic research through collaboration with museums, broadcasters, and other public institutions (Crang 2010; see Fuller 2008 and Fuller and Askins 2010 for reviews). We are excited by the prospect of geographers working with publics not only like/ as artists but also like/as activists. Therefore, in this final section, we concentrate on work by cultural and other geographers who have explicitly aimed to appreciate, critique, perform, and transform diverse public geographies of food.

Let us start with the sweeping terrain of the "global food crisis." Recent food price spikes and related concerns about the sustainability of food systems have led to the reemergence in international policy contexts of a discourse on "food security" (MacMillan and Dowler 2012; Mooney and Hunt 2009). Food geographers have begun to respond to these concerns by cultivating new scripts for the "drama of food" (Belasco 2008), critiquing dominant public policy discourses and highlighting the spatial contradictions and tensions inherent in food–society relations and politics. David Nally (2011) shows, for example, how food security is constructed from a narrow neoliberal viewpoint, which he terms "a neoliberal truth regime" (p. 49). This regime presents global markets, agrarian biotechnologies, and multinational corporate initiatives as the "structural preconditions" to alleviate hunger. Nally (2011) highlights the interdependency between abundance and scarcity and the way that the modern food regime relies on overproduction in some places and underproduction in others. Lucy Jarosz (2011) also shows how scaled definitions of food security have been used to serve neoliberal ideology, linking individuals to global modalities of governance that emphasize the instrumentality of agricultural productivity in development strategies.

As Jarosz, Nally, and others powerfully show, geographers have important roles to play in public debates about food security. Their work reveals how scale can be used to justify political actions and support ideological objectives on the grounds of "moral responsibility." It challenges claims that food-chain resilience can be best achieved via market liberalization and risk management. The challenge now for food geographers, however, is how to make these new food scripts more "public" – i.e., how to find ways to enter and inform public debate. To date, geographical critiques challenging neoliberal discourse of food security have not really entered public debate. They exist instead alongside a "public world" championed by social movements (e.g., La Via Campesina) and non-governmental organizations (e.g., Oxfam) that explicitly challenge and espouse alternative food security visions, advocating, for instance, food sovereignty, food rights, and agro-ecological approaches over market solutions. Some "public food scholars" are influential in these debates. Raj Patel (http://raj-patel.org/), a writer, activist, and academic, is notable here, often using blogs and other social networking platforms to communicate ideas and challenge convention. Food security, thus, symbolizes one "at large" debate where geographers can creatively collaborate in future with social and political organizations, journalists, and activists to inform public discourse.

In recent years, critiques of global agribusiness have proliferated in the new media ecology of Web 2.0. More critiques are now more widely accessible than ever before. Equally important, an explosion of user-generated content has, to a significant extent, democratized debate (see Graham and Haarstad 2011). These critiques have pressured corporations to develop more ethical trading practices and generated new kinds of "affective pull" to engage wider publics in food justice campaigns. Seeds of their activist potential can be traced to the early 2000s, when researchers found UK food industry interviewees admitting that a relentless stream of media exposés of poor pay and working conditions had been "'the driving force' behind the adoption of ethical trade standards by supermarkets" (Freidberg 2004: 516; Hughes 2005). Exposés continue to be produced; but their critics have argued that by repeatedly "showing how crappy and messed up our world is, how exploitative and degenerative its ruling class, [and] how grotesque its economic system" (Merrifield 2009: 382), they produce a disempowering fatalism among both activists and potentially concerned consumers. In response, new forms of cultural activism have emerged that aim both to shame corporations into action and to imaginatively engage consumers in trade justice campaigning in visceral, affective, and playful ways (Cook and Woodyer 2012).

Many examples of food-based cultural activism are showcased in the grocery department of Ian Cook *et al.*'s followthethings.com, a "complex and elaborately composed research centre" designed to resemble an online store (Kneip 2009: 177). Click its bag of "mixed nuts," for example, and you can watch and read about a short, animated film called "The luckiest nut in the world," which left children humming a song performed by an animated, guitar-playing American peanut about the World Trade Organization's role in the unfair international nut trade (Cook *et al.* 2011). Click its oven-ready chicken and you can find and read about a TV series documenting the efforts of a celebrity chef to convert low-income consumers and big UK supermarkets to both the taste and ethics of organically raised chickens. Both pages document these examples' impacts on viewers, corporations, and/or food policy and the effects of both their subversion and deployment of TV genres (e.g., eccentric kids' cartoons and reality TV) and their subsequent use in NGOs' trade justice and animal welfare campaigns. followthethings.com is one of a number of experiments that draw upon the public, collaborative potentials of Web 2.0 both to document and to encourage new forms of food (and wider commodity) activism for progressive eco-social change.[3]

These arguments take us full circle to a body of research that adopts performative understandings of "diverse economic" relations in which researchers recognize and take responsibility for "their constitutive role in the worlds that exist, and their power to [help] bring new worlds into being" (Gibson-Graham 2008: 614; Cameron 2011). This literature is critical of both realist understandings of research as truth finding and of theoretical understandings of capitalism as a single monolithic system. It argues that what we might call "alternative economic geographies" are not an alternative to this monolithic system but are internal to it, fracture it, exist in abundance, can be researched and made public, and, as such, can inspire and show others how to bring new diverse economic worlds into being. It employs theory less to confirm what we already know about domination and oppression and more to "help us see openings, to provide a space of freedom and possibility" in an approach "that welcomes surprise, tolerates coexistence, and cares for the new" (Gibson-Graham 2008: 619). And it bypasses the individualized consumer at the center of so much research and policy to concentrate on the "we" of community members and their/our collective necessities and responsibilities (DeLind 2011; Hill 2011).

Within this body of work, considerable efforts have been made to research and make public "possible food economies" outside agribusiness-driven production–consumption relations, economies that are cultivated through ethical concerns over how to survive well with others and how to generate and redistribute social surplus (Holloway *et al.* 2007; Gibson-Graham, Cameron, and Healy forthcoming). Work in this vein has also begun to draw on a hybrid research collective (HRC) approach in which the researcher identifies as but one actant in the research process working with other actants to bring about transformative change (Gibson-Graham and Roelvink 2009; Roelvink 2008). As Hill (forthcoming) demonstrates in her research on communal gardening projects in the Philippines, HRC actants may include community or lay-researchers, YouTube films, songs, web-based training tools, gardens, community groups, and whatever gathers around particular concerns such as malnutrition or broadening the economy. This body of research suggests that understandings of texture, creativity, and activism are not only what we should take into our research if we want to make a positive difference in the world, but also what we should look for when choosing what to study in the first place.

## Conclusions

You're back in front of that computer now. The results from your online search of the AAG conference program are still on screen. There are 187 papers on food geographies. You've read this paper now. It's not an attempt at a comprehensive review of that work; such a task would be too big. What it has tried to do is to tie together a field of food–cultural geographies that aims to be both orienting and generative of new work for its readers. We cannot avoid Lévi-Strauss' now seeming cliché that "food is good to think with." We find that it is particularly good at helping us to advance, and make diverse connections within, cultural geography's more-than-materialist musings. It is particularly good, for example, at helping us think sensitively through non-dualistic approaches/language for describing the world (e.g., biosocial, more-than-representational, minded bodies, visceral politics) and at helping us dissolve oppositions like public/private, internal/external, and artistic/intellectual. We hope that this chapter has conveyed this point in a number of ways.

Doubtless, the explosion of academic interest in food geographies is a mirror to the explosion of public interest in, and public discourse about, all kinds of food matters. We believe that the kinds of cultural geographies outlined above can play a key role in helping these public debates to not be boxed into ways of thinking about food and the food–body relationships dictated by the dominant industrial food system, its corporations and government allies. We do have to be cautious, however. When discussing the activist potential of such work, we have to ask how genuinely "transformative" it can be and if and how it can have more than local and transitory impacts vis-à-vis wider and longer-lasting social movements. We know that we have to better understand the ways in which its appreciations of materiality and affect might (re)connect in meaningful ways with the wider inequalities and injustices of the current agri-food system (what is called "scaling up" and "scaling out" in the language of alternative food networks). But we also need to continue discussing these issues, to involve more people in these discussions, and to widen these debates. Performative methods and the new media ecology of Web 2.0 can help us do so, and this chapter can play its part in this process. Each section has been copied onto a separate page on the blog that we used to write it. Each page can be commented on. So, let's keep the conversation going at foodculturalgeographies.wordpress.com.

## Notes

1 Ian Cook (Geography, University of Exeter), Peter Jackson (Geography, University of Sheffield), Allison Hayes-Conroy (Geography and Urban Studies, Temple University), Sebastian Abrahamsson (AISSR, Amsterdam University), Rebecca Sandover (Geography, University of Exeter), Mimi Sheller (Culture and Communication, Drexel University), Heike Henderson (Modern Languages and Literatures, Boise State University), Lucius Hallett (Geography, Western Michigan University), Shoko Imai (Area Studies, University of Tokyo), Damian Maye (Countryside and Community Research Institute, University of the West of England), and Ann Hill (Economics and Government, Australian National University).

2  The discussions on which this chapter is based can be found at http://foodculturalgeographies.word-press.com.
3  See, for example, sourcemap.com/ and wikichains.com.


# References

Abrahamsson, S. and Simpson, P. (2011) The limits of the body: Boundaries, capacities, thresholds. *Social and Cultural Geography*, 12 (4), 331–338.

Alkon, A.H. and Agyeman, J. (eds.) (2011) *Cultivating Food Justice: Race, Class and Sustainability*. Cambridge, MA: MIT Press.

Aston, E. (2000) "Transforming" women's lives: Bobby Baker's performances of "daily life." *New Theatre Quarterly*, 16, 17–25.

Bardhi, F., Ostberg, J. and Bengtsson, A. (2010) Negotiating cultural boundaries: Food, travel and consumer identities. *Consumption Markets and Culture*, 13 (2), 133–157.

Belasco, W. (2008) *Food: The Key Concept*. New York: Berg.

Bennett, J. (2007) Edible matter. *New Left Review*, 45 (May/June), 133–145.

Benson, P. and Fischer, E.F. (2007) Broccoli and desire. *Antipode*, 39, 800–820.

Cameron, J. (with C. Manhood and J. Pomfrett) (2011) Bodily learning for a (climate) changing world: Registering differences through performative and collective research. *Local Environment*, 16 (6), 493–508.

Cook, I. *et al.* (2001) Social sculpture and connective aesthetics: Shelley Sacks's "Exchange Values." *Ecumene*, 7 (3), 337–343.

Cook, I. *et al.* (2004) Follow the thing: Papaya. *Antipode*, 36 (4), 642–664.

Cook, I. *et al.* (2008) Geographies of food: Mixing. *Progress in Human Geography*, 32 (6), 821–833.

Cook, I. and Tolia-Kelly, D.P. (2010) Material geographies. In *Oxford Handbook of Material Culture Studies*, ed. D. Hicks and M. Beaudry. Oxford: Oxford University Press, pp. 99–122.

Cook, I. and Woodyer, T. (2012) Lives of things. In *Companion to Economic Geography*, ed. E. Sheppard, T. Barnes, and J. Peck. Oxford: Wiley-Blackwell.

Cook, I.J., Crang, P. and Thorpe, M. (2000) Regions to be cheerful? Culinary authenticity and its geographies. In *Cultural Turns/Geographical Turns: Perspectives on Cultural Geography*, ed. I. Cook, D. Crouch, S. Naylor, and J. Ryan. Harlow: Longman, pp. 109–139.

Cook, I., Hobson, K., Hallett IV, L., Guthman, J., Murphy, A., Hulme, A., Sheller, M., Crewe, L., Nally, D., Roe, E., Mather, C., Kingsbury, P., Slocum, R., Imai, S., Duruz, J., Philo, C., Buller, H., Goodman, M., Hayes-Conroy, A., Hayes-Conroy, J., Tucker, L., Blake, M., Le Heron, R., Putnam, H., Maye, D. and Henderson, H. (2011) Geographies of food: Afters. *Progress in Human Geography*, 35 (1), 104–120.

Crang, P. (2010) Cultural geography: After a fashion. *Cultural Geographies*, 17 (2), 191–201.

Crouch, D. (2003) Spacing, performing and becoming: Tangles in the mundane. *Environment and Planning A*, 35 (11), 1945–1960.

DeLind, L. (2011) Are local food and the local food movement taking us where we want to go? Or are we hitching our wagons to the wrong stars? *Agriculture and Human Values*, 28 (2), 273–283.

Farquharson, A. (2010) Foreword. In *Uneven Geographies*, ed. A. Farquharson and J. Waters. Nottingham: Nottingham Contemporary, pp. 3–4.

Finch, J. (2007) Displaying families. *Sociology*, 41, 65–81.

Freidberg, S. (2004) The ethical complex of corporate food power. *Environment and Planning D: Society and Space*, 22 (4), 513–531.

Fuller, D. (2008) Public geographies I: Taking stock. *Progress in Human Geography*, 32, 834–844.

Fuller, D. and Askins, K. (2010) Public geographies II: Being organic. *Progress in Human Geography*, 34 (5), 654–667.

Gibson-Graham, J.K. (2008) Diverse economies: Performative practices for "other worlds." *Progress in Human Geography*, 32 (5), 613–632.

Gibson-Graham, J.K. and Roelvink, G. (2009) An economic ethics for the Anthropocene. *Antipode*, 41 (1), 320–346.

Gibson-Graham, J.K., Cameron, J. and Healy, S. (forthcoming) *Take Back the Economy, Anytime, Anyplace*. Minneapolis: University of Minnesota Press.

Graham, M. and Haarstad, H. (2011) Transparency and development: Ethical consumption through Web 2.0 and the internet of things. *Information Technologies and International Development*, 7 (1), 1–18.

Groskop, V. (2009) Deliciously dark. *Guardian*, June 19. http://www.guardian.co.uk/lifeandstyle/2009/jun/19/mertle-food-eating-secret-caroline-smith (accessed October 30, 2012).

Harrison, J.L. (2006) "Accidents" and invisibilities: Scaled discourse and the naturalization of regulatory neglect in California's pesticide drift conflict. *Political Geography*, 25 (5), 506–529.

Harrison, J.L. (2008) Lessons learned from pesticide drift: A call to bring production agriculture, farm labor, and social justice back into agrifood research and activism. *Agriculture and Human Values*, 25 (2), 163–167.

Hayes-Conroy, A. (2008) Taking back taste: Feminism, food, and visceral politics. *Gender, Place, and Culture*, 15 (5), 461–473.

Hayes-Conroy, A. and Martin, D.G. (2010) Mobilizing bodies: Visceral identification in the Slow Food Movement. *Transactions of the Institute of British Geographers* NS, 35, 269–281.

Hayes-Conroy, J. and Hayes-Conroy, A. (2010) Visceral geographies: Mattering, relating, and defying. *Geography Compass*, 4 (9), 1273–1283.

Hill, A. (2011) A helping hand and many green thumbs: Local government, citizens and the growth of a community-based food economy. *Local Environment*, 16 (6), 539–553.

Hill, A. (forthcoming) Growing community food economies in the Philippines. PhD thesis, Australian National University.

Holloway, L., Kneafsey, M., Venn, L., Cox, R., Dowler, E. and Tuomainen, H. (2007) Possible food economies: A methodological framework for exploring food production–consumption relationships. *Sociologia Ruralis*, 47 (1), 1–19.

Hughes, A. (2005) Responsible retailers? Ethical trade and the strategic re-regulation of cross-continental food supply chains. In *Cross-Continental Food Chains*, ed. N. Fold and B. Pritchard. London: Routledge, pp. 141–154.

Imai, S. (2010) Nobu and after: Westernized Japanese food and globalization. In *Food and Social Identities in the Asia Pacific Region*, ed. J. Farrar. Tokyo: Sophia University Institute of Comparative Culture. http://icc.fla.sophia.ac.jp/global%20food%20papers/pdf/3_4_IMAI.pdf (accessed October 30, 2012).

Jackson, P. (1989) *Maps of Meaning*. London: Routledge.

Jackson, P. (ed.) (2009) *Changing Families, Changing Food*. Basingstoke: Palgrave Macmillan.

Jackson, P., Ward, N. and Russell, P. (2006) Mobilising the commodity chain concept in the politics of food and farming. *Journal of Rural Studies*, 22 (2), 129–141.

Jacobs, J.M. and Nash, C. (2003) Too little, too much: Cultural feminist geographies. *Gender, Place and Culture*, 10 (3), 265–279.

Jarosz, L. (2011) Defining world hunger: Scale and neoliberal ideology in international food security policy discourse. *Food, Culture and Society*, 14 (1), 117–139.

Kirshenblatt-Gimblett, B. (1999) Playing to the senses: Food as a performance medium. *Performance Research*, 4 (1), 1–30.

Kirshenblatt-Gimblett, B. (2007) Making sense of food in performance: The table and the stage. In *The Senses in Performance*, ed. S. Banes and A. Lepecki. London: Routledge, pp. 71–91.

Kneip, V. (2009) Political struggles within the market sphere: The internet as a "weapon." In *Political Campaigning on the Web*, ed. S. Baringhorst, V. Kneip, and J. Niesyto. Bielefeld: Transcript Verlag, pp. 173–198.

Lindenfeld, L. (2007) Visiting the Mexican American family: Tortilla soup as culinary tourism. *Communication and Critical/Cultural Studies*, 4 (3), 303–320.

MacMillan, T. and Dowler, E. (2012) Just and sustainable? Examining the rhetoric and potential realities of UK food security. *Journal of Agricultural and Environmental Ethics*, 25 (2), 181–204.

Mann, A.M., Mol, A.M., Satalkar, P., Savirani, A., Selim, N., Sur, M. and Yates-Doerr, E. (2011) Mixing methods, tasting fingers: Notes on an ethnographic experiment. *HAU: Journal of Ethnographic Theory*, 1 (1), 221–243.

Mass, W. and Pasquinelli, M. (2010) Maag als Kompas (Stomach Compass) Expedition. urbanibalism. org, October 8. http://www.urbanibalism.org/maag-als-kompas-stomach-compass-expedition (accessed October 30, 2012).

Merrifield, A. (2009) Magical Marxism. *Environment and Planning D: Society and Space*, 27, 381–386.

Mol, A. (2008) I eat an apple: On theorizing subjectivities. *Subjectivity*, 22, 28–37.

Mol, A. (2009) Good taste: The embodied normativity of the consumer-citizen. *Journal of Cultural Economy*, 2, 269–283.

Mooney, P. and Hunt, S. (2009) Food security: The elaboration of contested claims to a consensus frame. *Rural Sociology*, 74 (4), 469–497.

Nally, D. (2011) The biopolitics of food provisioning. *Transactions of the Institute of British Geographers*, 36 (1), 37–53.

Paxson, H. (2011) The "art" and "science" of handcrafting cheese in the United States. *Endeavour*, 35, 116–124.

Regine (2011) Architecture of Fear – a conversation with Trevor Paglen. we-make-money-not-art.com, November 21. http://www.we-make-money-not-art.com/archives/2011/11/trevor-paglen.php (accessed October 30, 2012).

Roe, E. (2006) Things becoming food and the embodied, material practices of an organic food consumer. *Sociologia Ruralis*, 46 (2), 104–121.

Roelvink, G. (2008) Performing new economies through hybrid collectives. PhD thesis, Australian National University.

Slocum, R. (2011) Race in the study of food. *Progress in Human Geography*, 35 (3), 303–327.

Stassart, P. and Whatmore, S. (2003) Metabolizing risk: Food scares and the un/re-making of Belgian beef. *Environment and Planning A*, 35 (3), 449–462.

Stewart, K. (2007) *Ordinary Affects*. Durham, NC: Duke University Press.

Wylie, J. (2010) Cultural geographies of the future, or looking rosy and feeling blue. *Cultural Geographies*, 17 (2), 211–217.

Chapter 31

# Environmental Histories

*Robert M. Wilson*

As Gerry Kearns aptly noted in the last edition of *A Companion to Cultural Geography* (2004), at one time nearly all geography was environmental history. Many early key works in the discipline addressed the relationship between people and the environment over time. Most of these scholars used an evolutionary framework to explain such connections, with the environment as the causal agent. Beginning in the 1920s, Carl Sauer and other early cultural and historical geographers switched this formulation, making culture the driving force in human–environment relations (Sauer 1965/1925). In Sauer's formulation, culture was active and nature was inert, like a lump of clay, sculpted by the actions of a cultural group. Despite their many differences, neither approach – that giving agency to the environment and that giving agency to humans – saw non-human nature as having an active role. Modern approaches in environmental history largely differ from these earlier environmental determinists or cultural geographers by seeing both humans and non-human nature as active, influencing, though by no means determining, social action.

The degree to which cultural geographers, historical geographers, and historians have focused on this relationship between humans and non-human nature has changed over time and varied by scholar. Certainly among cultural geographers in the 1990s and early 2000s, the role of culture predominated. Influential works during this period, such as Bruce Braun's *The Intemperate Rainforest* (2002), showed the idea of nature or wilderness as cultural constructions. The notion that non-human nature was an active, sculpting force was largely absent. Indeed, such works questioned our ability to ascertain the contribution of non-human nature to the development of landscapes or in influencing human society. Inherent in these studies was also a profound skepticism of the natural sciences. This skepticism posed a quandary for other environmental historians who sought to show non-human nature as an actor or believed science could serve as a tool to critique environmental destruction.

*The Wiley Blackwell Companion to Cultural Geography*, First Edition.
Edited by Nuala C. Johnson, Richard H. Schein, and Jamie Winders.
© 2013 John Wiley & Sons, Ltd. Published 2016 by John Wiley & Sons, Ltd.

Demonstrating nature as an active force required making truth-claims, however partial, about the way the non-human world operated (Cronon 1994; Demeritt 1994a, 1994b). Without science as a guide, environmental histories were somewhat adrift. Was environmental history simply telling stories about the cultural construction of nature?

The high tide of cultural constructionism did not last long, and cultural geographers embraced it far more than historians doing environmental history. Many insisted on a role for a material, active non-human nature, while recognizing people's role in culturally constructing environmental knowledge. Partly due to this dual recognition, environmental historians embraced the idea of *hybridity*. This concept, more than any other, dominated work in environmental history in the disciplines of geography and history during the first decade of the twenty-first century. Rather than seeing wilderness as purely "natural" or cities as purely "cultural," environmental historians saw them as complicated hybrid landscapes. Studying such places required environmental historians to embrace messy, unpure spaces. Such landscapes, in the words of historian Richard White, "are where we spend our lives, and, as much to the point, where most wild creatures spend theirs" (2010: 188).

The degree of engagement with social theory became one of the primary divisions among those practicing environmental history. During the past twenty years, cultural geographers have embraced critical theory, especially theoretical perspectives from Marxism, poststructuralism, feminism, and postcolonialism. In general, most historians practicing environmental history have eschewed social theory. Indeed, one prominent environmental historian, J.R. McNeill, has gone so far as to claim that many historians, especially environmental historians, were "refugees" from theory (2003: 36). The use of theory was also modest, to non-existent, for many geographers practicing environmental history trained in historical geography (for instance, see Colten 2005; Wilson 2010; Wynn 2007). This difference is key to understanding the different trajectories in environmental history: while many historical geographers and historians sought to advance *historiographic* debates, cultural geographers studying historical environmental topics sought to advance *theory*.

Another key difference between environmental historians and cultural geographers was the place of narrative in their work. Environmental historians sought to tell stories about the past with richly drawn characters, protagonists, and narrative arcs. In the early 1990s the historian William Cronon wrote what has become a classic essay about the role of narrative in environmental history and history more generally (1992). While recognizing the then-prevalent criticisms of narrative by poststructuralists, Cronon vigorously defended the form, arguing that despite its faults, narrative was a primary form people used to make sense of, and to care about, the past. More recently, the influential historian of fire Stephen Pyne has gone even further, saying that all good academic writing, environmental history included, is a form of creative non-fiction. His book, *Voice and Vision: A Guide to Writing History and Other Serious Nonfiction* (2009), is a how-to volume on using the staples of creative writing – dramatizing, plotting, and characterization – for writing scholarly prose. These environmental historians and some historical geographers, thus, place a premium on writing stories about society–nature entanglements in the past and publishing scholarly books written in a manner accessible to non-academic audiences.

What follows is a brief examination of key themes addressed by environmental historians over the past decade or so. In this review I include contributions by geographers and historians. In some cases, scholars in the two disciplines have examined similar themes while drawing on different concepts, theories, and historiographies. In others, geographers and historians have been part of a cross-disciplinary dialogue. This chapter tilts heavily toward work by North American environmental historians, mostly because I know this literature best. Already, the literature on North American environmental history is vast.[1] For those interested in the environmental history of other parts of the world, there are excellent review articles and survey volumes for non-North American regions (McNeill 2003; Miller 2007).

## Managing Nature

One of the overriding themes in environmental history since the inception of the field has been a focus on the management of nature. Of course, humans have "managed" nature in some sense since they domesticated fire; and certainly all agriculture is a form of environmental management. By management, I mean the development of state-based natural-resource management, especially in the nineteenth century, to oversee such resources as timber, water, oil and minerals, and wildlife. Some of the leading works that influenced the early generation of environmental historians addressed this topic. Samuel Hays' *Conservation and the Gospel of Efficiency* (1959) is the best-known example. In it, he addresses the rise of conservation in the United States as a movement heavily influenced by business interests seeking to extend the application of efficiency in factories to the management of the natural world. Early conservationists' ceaseless use of terms such as efficiency, waste, and production suggests they saw nature increasingly through a corporate lens. Other important works from the 1970s through 1990s addressed the role of state agencies in managing nature. Such agencies included the US Bureau of Reclamation and its role in developing water resources in the western United States (Worster 1985; Pisani 2002; Reisner 1986); the US Forest Service's role in managing National Forests (Hirt 1994); and the US National Park Service's role in protecting sublime spaces for tourists (Runte 1997; Sellars 1997).

Many of these works were top-down histories focused on the management of rivers, forests, and wilderness from the point of view of the managers themselves. Recent work on the United States and Canada, by contrast, demonstrates how local people contested the imposition of such state management on the landscapes where they lived and worked in the late nineteenth and early twentieth centuries (Braun 2002; Jacoby 2001; Kosek 2006; Loo 2006; Sandlos 2007; Spence 1999; Warren 1997). These subaltern voices, as geographers might call them, were silenced in the official histories of these agencies and the areas they managed. Early conservationists saw such people often as poachers and squatters resisting the efficient, enlightened use of natural resources. To locals, the arrival of state-led resource management often seemed as just another form of colonialism and a tactic of dispossession. This story is familiar to many geographers, especially political ecologists who have studied such processes in the global South for decades (Agrawal 2005). Environmental historians have shown how such resistance also occurred in the United States, Canada, and other developed countries at the inception of state-led environmental management.

Another divergence from earlier work in environmental history is an emphasis on the disconnect between the attempt to control nature and the often unruly, complicated outcomes of these efforts. Nancy Langston's pivotal book, *Forest Dreams, Forest Nightmares* (1996), examined how foresters sought to create an orderly, efficient forest in the intermountain western United States but, instead, created havoc as trees sickened and died under their care. Langston shows how these elite, university educated foresters profoundly misunderstood the crucial role of wildfire in semi-arid forest ecosystems, with disastrous results. Langston (2003) extended this perspective into a study of attempts of the US Fish and Wildlife Service (FWS) to manage riparian areas in the region. In my own book, *Seeking Refuge: Birds and Landscapes of the Pacific Flyway* (2010), I examine the efforts for the FWS to manage migratory birds in western North America while coping with powerful corporate farmers and federal irrigation agencies with which wildlife refuges shared the landscape. In all of these works, non-human nature is an active force influencing human actions and reacting to human developments. In contrast to Sauer's formulation, here, nature is not inert but an actor with important, albeit limited, agency.

## Environmental Politics

Closely allied with research on environmental management and governance is the literature on the history of environmental politics. Environmental history is, in large measure, an outgrowth of the environmental movement, so it is not surprising that the field's practitioners focus their attention on the politics of this movement and its antecedents. Again, Samuel Hays' *Conservation and the Gospel of Efficiency* is a crucial text for explaining the development of conservation. His classic, *Beauty, Health, and Permanence* (1987), has also had a profound influence on the field, and many environmental historians have adopted his basic framework for understanding the development of environmental concern in the United States. Conservationists, according to Hays, were concerned primarily with production, while environmentalists were fundamentally occupied with issues of consumption. As average incomes rose and the country became more suburban after World War II, American environmental politics turned less to making production more efficient and less wasteful and more to improving quality of life. Postwar Americans expressed concern about the increasing array of toxic chemicals, such as DDT and other pesticides bombarding the environment. Rachel Carson, Barry Commoner, and other popularizers of the science of ecology showed how such chemicals made their way through the food chain into humans. This knowledge led to a new conception of humans as interrelated to their surrounding environment. Marril Hazlett (2003) calls this new understanding the "ecological body." Linda Nash (2006) sees such understandings as the modern variant of an eighteenth- and nineteenth-century view of bodies as porous and the health of individuals as interconnected to that of the countryside (see also Valenčius 2002).

The rise of new environmental ideas coincided with, and was partly the result of, the rise of tourism and outdoor recreation. As the twentieth century progressed, increasing numbers of Americans, especially middle-class North Americans, experienced nature, not through work, but through outdoor leisure pursuits such as hiking, backpacking, skiing and snowboarding, boating, and climbing. As Paul Sutter shows in *Driven Wild* (2002), by the 1920s, those who sought to protect wilderness were as concerned about roads and automobiles defiling wild spaces as they were about the effects of logging, mining, and dam construction on the same areas. David Louter's *Windshield Wilderness* (2006) demonstrates how the US National Park Service constructed roads to frame particular views of the environment to cater to tourists traveling in comfort by car or camper. When Americans visited national or state parks, they often hiked on trails, camped in campgrounds, and took shelter in lodges constructed by the Civilian Conservation Corps (CCC), a popular agency created as part of President Franklin Roosevelt's New Deal program to combat the Great Depression. The CCC housed and employed young men, putting them to work on conservation projects around the country. Neil Maher's *Nature's New Deal* (2007) argues that the CCC democratized conservation ideals while laying the groundwork for the rise of the environmental movement.

The CCC's emphasis on providing recreation amenities for Americans foreshadowed the sorts of quality-of-life concerns that would animate the environmental movement of the 1960s and 1970s. While the CCC physically altered the landscape to benefit those seeking outdoor recreation, Brent Olson (2010) shows how the Outdoor Recreation Review Commission in the United States tried to make landscape on federal lands "legible" to resource managers and more conducive to management. He also demonstrates how traditional conservation agencies used many of the same tools and governance strategies employed to manage resources like timber to govern recreational spaces. These scholars, especially Sutter and Maher, complicate Hays' identification of World War II as the dividing line between conservation and environmentalism. They show, instead, how the concerns of environmentalists appeared much earlier than previously thought. Finally, historian and geographer Joseph Taylor takes a highly critical look at the emergence of outdoor recreation in *Pilgrims of the Vertical* (2010). Using the burgeoning rock-climbing culture in Yosemite National Park as a case study, he shows how a specific form of outdoor recreation became a vehicle for constructing masculine identities. Moreover, revered rock climbers such as Yvon Chouinard used the sport to fashion an environmental ethic that privileged recreational forms of interacting with nature.

In a series of books and articles, historian Adam Rome has sought to trace *where* and *when* environmentalism itself emerged. In *The Bulldozer in the Countryside* (2001) Rome shows how environmental concern arose in the blossoming postwar suburbs. Not only were suburbanites the sorts of people who visited state and national parks, growing numbers of them also became increasingly dissatisfied with the effect of sprawl and pollution in their neighborhoods. While many scholars have noted the postwar era as the crucible for the development of environmentalism, Rome (2003) goes further to define the 1960s as the pivotal decade in the formation of the movement. Environmentalism in this period emerged from an unlikely mixture of groups – traditional liberals, the counterculture, and middle- and upper-class white women. Liberals supported environmentalism as a part of an effort to extend the purpose of government to preserving healthy air, water, and landscapes for the public welfare. Those in the counterculture, especially the more radical, saw the deteriorating environment as yet one more example of capitalism run amuck. Saving the Earth was, thus, part of a larger revolutionary project to overthrow a system that fostered inequality, stifled free expression, and perpetuated neocolonial wars in Vietnam. Finally, middle- and upper-class white women, many of whom were well educated but barred from using their skills and knowledge in the workforce, funneled their energies into preserving the environment. They rallied in support of Rachel Carson, who demonstrated in *Silent Spring* that toxins sprayed on the land made their way into the breast milk of mothers, and ultimately, into infants. For these women, protecting the environment was a way to ensure the welfare of their homes and the families within them. Finally, Rome (2010, 2013) has turned his attention to Earth Day, the largest public demonstration in US history, as both the culmination of years of environmental activism and a meeting-ground for many activists where they helped foster the skills that enabled them to continue to push for stricter environmental legislation throughout the decade.

By far, the most ambitious book about postwar environmentalism and the society it helped create is Michael Bess's *The Light-Green Society* (2003). The book addresses the development of environmentalism in France, but his basic claims about the roots of environmentalism and its effects apply to other industrialized democracies as well. Was environmentalism a success? In one sense, no, Bess suggests. Clearly, the more radical goals of environmentalists never materialized. Neither France nor any of the other countries in western Europe, North America, or Japan are remotely sustainable. Yet in another sense, environmentalism has been very successful. "Green" ideas permeate these societies. Most people support recycling, and even corporations need to discuss their concern for the environment and make efforts to reduce their impact, even if these efforts are often just tokens.[2] Hence, Bess's characterization of these societies as "light green." Citizens of France and other countries in the global North have largely proved unwilling to fundamentally challenge industrial, consumer society. Whether this era is a transitional phase to an era of sustainability or a momentary blip on the road to environmental ruin remains to be seen.

## The *Longue Durée*: Transnational and World Environmental History

Nature does not adhere to artificial human borders, so neither should the studies by environmental historians. Yet many environmental historians still undertake their research within national frameworks (Sutter 2002; White 1999). The work by world environmental historians is an exception to this trend. These historians and geographers have been willing to extend their analysis over the *longue durée* to illuminate connections historical studies at smaller spatial scales and shorter time periods are unable to do. Also, the current interest in globalization has led environmental historians to examine the political, economic, and environmental roots of the phenomenon, following its networks and stretching their work across borders.

Even before environmental history existed as an identifiable field, geographers had developed a global vision for studying the relationship between nature and society over the long term. The seminal edited collection *Man's Role in Changing the Face of the Earth* (Thomas 1956), and its sequel four decades later, *The Earth as Transformed by Human Action* (Turner *et al.* 1993), examined from multiple perspectives how humans had modified the environment. The major influence for the first volume was the nineteenth-century polymath George Perkins Marsh, whose *Man and Nature* (2003/1864) served as one of the founding texts of conservation (see also Wilson 2005a). Marsh was also a proto-environmental historian who sought to explain the demise of civilizations in environmental terms from a global perspective (Lowenthal 2000; Sutter 2002).

Environmental historians have also sought to show how an environmental-history perspective illuminates the emergence of the modern world (Wilson 2005b). The father–son pair of William and J.R. McNeill produced *The Human Web* (2003), one of the most ambitious works of world environmental history. Using the web as a metaphor, they examined the grand pattern of human history from our origins as a species to the present. At the beginning, they explain, human communities were loosely connected to one another. Over time, however, these webs of connections tightened through transportation and exchange, not just of goods and ideas but also diseases. The McNeills take pains to show that this interconnectedness was not preordained; the development of the web emerged through fits and starts. In *The Unending Frontier* (2003) John Richards argues that human impact on the world's biota and flora was magnified after 1500 for a number of reasons: the increasing dynamism of European societies, new developments in human organization, and the growth of state and private institutions. Land use intensified in many regions, particularly in areas where agricultural societies displaced hunter-gatherers. Biological invasions brought new plants and animals into ecosystems far from the ones in which they evolved. Overharvesting and habitat destruction led to the drastic reduction or outright extinction of species such as dodos, bison, and some species of whales. The emergence of industrial societies after the early modern period intensified this process while spawning new problems, such as the development of large-scale pollution from factories and growing cities. J.R. McNeill continues this story in *Something New Under the Sun: An Environmental History of the Twentieth Century* (2000).

## Landscape, Bodies, and Disease

The idea of hybridity is most evident in the vibrant environmental-history literature on disease and bodies. Disease has long figured prominently in the field, such as in Alfred Crosby's *The Columbian Exchange* (1972) and *Ecological Imperialism* (1986), as well as proto-environmental histories such as William McNeill's *Plagues and Peoples* (1976). At the time of their release, these studies provided a radical take on human history, arguing that pathogens played a pivotal role in shaping the course of historical events. Crosby, in particular, showed how contagious diseases became part of imperial projects and facilitated European colonialism. J.R. McNeill extends these insights even further in *Mosquito Empires* (2010a). In the early decades of colonialism in the Caribbean, he suggests, Europeans held an advantage over indigenous peoples who had no immunity against measles, smallpox, and other diseases Europeans brought with them. Later, however, Europeans proved susceptible to yellow fever, a disease spread by mosquitoes who themselves had arrived as inadvertent stowaways on trading ships from Africa. Over time, locals raised in the tropics, regardless of race, developed resistance to the diseases. The political significance of this resistance, McNeill argues, became apparent when Europeans sought to crush Caribbean rebellions. When they sent soldiers from overseas to quell disturbances, the men died in droves since they lacked the locals' immunity. With his nuanced social and environmental analysis, McNeill demonstrates the geopolitical significance of tropical diseases.

Most research on disease and environmental history has not focused on diseases at this scale; but they do situate disease, health, and bodies within larger social contexts. This is a departure from the cultural approaches to bodies informed by Michel Foucault and Judith Butler that have thrived in history and cultural geography in recent decades. This new environmental history of bodies and landscapes has sought to show the material and ecological connections between bodies and environments, without becoming crudely materialist. It has sought to unite histories of health and environment through geographical analyses of landscapes, bodies, disease, and toxins. Conevery Valenčius (2002) and Linda Nash (2006) argue that from the colonial period in North America until the late nineteenth century, EuroAmerican settlers saw powerful connections between themselves and the surrounding landscape. When evaluating land for settlement, for example, they drew on a geography of health in which some landscapes fostered well-being while others diminished it. In particular, early settlers worried about miasmas – foul-smelling vapors emanating from swamps and bogs. In turn, this worry led to a devaluing of wetlands, which as Ann Vileisis shows (1997), were already despised landscapes by early settlers. Nash argues that the germ theory of disease replaced these earlier understandings with one that saw bodies as separate from landscapes. Disease came from within rather than outside bodies. Only with the rise of pesticides and their pervasive application on American farmland and suburbs did Americans once again begin to see their bodies as connected to the environment (Nash 2006; Hazlett 2003).

Noxious substances permeating vulnerable bodies is the main focus of Nancy Langston's *Toxic Bodies* (2010) and Brett Walker's *Toxic Archipelago* (2010). Much as Rachel Carson demonstrated fifty years ago, Langston and Walker show how toxic chemicals permeate our world and accumulate in our bodies. Langston, though, goes even further. Using insights from epigenetics, she shows how synthetic hormones such as Diethylstilbestrol (DES) affected the expression of genes. Such hormones led to the development of breast cancer and increased the likelihood of birth defects. Most disturbingly, she shows how these effects manifest themselves with minimal exposure. The *timing* of exposure to these chemicals mattered even more than the dosage. These changes could be passed on through generations, and fetuses in the womb were especially vulnerable. Langston deftly travels across scales – human cells, human bodies, and the surrounding landscape – to create an environmental history that breaks down simple divisions between bodies and larger environments. Similarly, Walker tells a story of Japan's industrialization and modernization through the poisoned bodies of its citizens, and to a lesser degree, its animals.

For all of these authors, disease emerges not primarily from the body or the landscape but through connections between the two. In *Breathing Space* (2007), an environmental history of allergies in the United States, historian Gregg Mitman makes this case forcefully, arguing that allergies are not a thing but a relationship. Mitman vividly shows how changes to the landscape fostered conditions suitable for the spread of allergens. In New Orleans, allergy and asthma rates increased, especially in poorer sections of the city, where deteriorating housing, environmental toxins, and substandard medical care left the population vulnerable to these ailments. For a brief period in the 1960s and 1970s, fewer people suffered from the disease as the federal government made a concerted effort to reduce poverty and deal with pollution. But as neoliberalism eroded these government safeguards, allergy rates crept up again. Mitman reaches the conclusion that the ultimate cause of allergies and asthma in New Orleans and cities like it is not a specific allergen but poverty itself.

## Urban Environmental History, Urban Political Ecology

Through the early 1990s, some scholars complained that environmental history was largely concerned with rural areas and wilderness. That is no longer the case. Over the past decade, the environmental history of cities and their relationship with their surrounding hinterlands has been the source of innovative work in the field. Examples of leading early research included the groundbreaking work by Joel Tarr (1996) and Martin Melosi (2000) on the consequences of urban industrialization and the development of urban sanitation. William Cronon's *Nature's Metropolis* (1991) examined the relationship between Chicago and its hinterland, though said relatively little about nature within the city limits. Such works were praised for their attention to urban nature but were later seen as inattentive to power relations and how poor and working-class groups contested these developments.

Later work by environmental historians tried to rectify these omissions. The most ambitious of the new urban environmental histories are Matthew Klingle's *Emerald City: An Environmental History of Seattle* (2007) and Michael Rawson's *Eden on the Charles: The Making of Boston* (2010). These works examine how the development of the city, the modification of the environment, and the "production" of nature in the form of city parks and infrastructure fostered inequality. "Humans wield power over one another," Klingle writes, "with nature as their instrument." Historical geographer Craig Colten (2005) and historian Ari Kelman (2003) also show how people wielded power over others as they transformed nature in New Orleans. Colten's book, *Unnatural Metropolis*, examines how residents, businessmen, and planners made New Orleans habitable amid a location susceptible to flooding by the Mississippi River, damage by hurricanes, and a haven for tropical diseases. He shows

convincingly the degree of environmental manipulation required to make the city habitable
– a topic too often overlooked by urban geographers and historians. Arn Keeling (2004,
2005a, 2005b) examines the role of pollution in Canadian urban development and the ways
that municipal governments and industries developed pollution abatement strategies in the
late nineteenth and twentieth centuries, while Jeremy Bryson (2012) shows how polluted
former industrial sites (known as brownfields) became sites of gentrification in the late twentieth century. Finally, Richard Walker shows the long history of urban park creation and
struggles over environmental justice in the San Francisco Bay area (Walker 2007).

Urban political ecology also addresses the role of nature in the city. Though not only
focused on urban nature in the past, many of the leading practitioners of urban political
ecology have done historical studies. Chief among them is Matthew Gandy, who, in *Concrete
and Clay* (2002), examines the environmental history of New York City through a number
of case studies including the city's acquisition of water, the development of Central Park, and
the fight by Harlem Latinos in the 1970s for social justice and protection from air pollution.
Maria Kaika (2005) examines how new sources of water were incorporated into the urban
fabric, allowing cities to grow but also fostering the alterations and development of new
"private" spaces in the home such as bathrooms. Indeed, water is a leading topic among
urban political ecologists (Heynen *et al.* 2006). Though both historians and urban political
ecologists study the relationship between nature and society in the city, their approaches
diverge in significant ways, illustrating the different ways they employ theory and use narrative. Urban political ecologists, reflecting approaches in human geography, employ social
theory to frame their studies, relying on insights from Marxist-informed political economy,
actor-network theory, and psychoanalytic theory. In contrast, urban environmental historians
tend to eschew social theory and frame their work to consider historiographic debates in
urban history and American or Canadian history more generally (for those studying North
American cities).

## Animals

Finally, environmental historians have produced a fascinating array of studies on the history
of animals. The anthropologists Lévi-Strauss once said that "animals are good to think with."
Studying them not only sheds light on the history of animals but on human history, too. Since
the inception of the field, environmental historians have used animals as key topics to study
society–environment relations. William Cronon's *Changes in the Land* (1983), for example,
examined how colonists changed the environment of New England during settlement and
the effects of these transformations on Native peoples. He also, however, shows, as does
Alfred Crosby (1972, 1986), how domestic animals such as cows, pigs, and horses aided
colonists in their settlement as the created "neo-Europes."

Predators, and wolves in particular, have elicited much attention from environmental
historians (Dunlap 1988). In *Vicious: Wolves and Men in America* (2004), Jon Coleman
(2004) asks why did Americans hate wolves so much but now revere them? Like nature writer
Barry Lopez (1978), historian Tom Dunlap (1988), and geographer Jody Emel (1998) before
him, Coleman reflects on the brutality Americans have rained down on predators through
most of the country's history. Only recently have many Americans learned to appreciate the
animals, a fact he attributes to the waning connections that Americans have toward livestock
(the sometime prey of wolves) and the growing dependence on cattle as industrial products.
The everyday brutality toward livestock in our food system has ironically enabled Americans

to appreciate better wild predators such as wolves, coyotes, and cougars. Coleman shows how deep-seated myths about wolves and seeing predators as a threat to livestock (which were also property) are at the root of Americans' wolf hatred. Yet in *The Lost Wolves of Japan* (2005), Brett Walker demonstrates how such hatred and the urge for extermination can emerge in very different cultures without a long history of aversion to predators. In early-modern Japan, wolves were revered creatures, celebrated by poets and pilgrims to Shinto shrines. With the arrival of livestock and the adoption of Western agricultural methods in the late nineteenth century, though, Japanese and American advisors undertook a concerted, and ultimately successful, campaign to expunge wolves from the islands. To achieve industrial progress, the Japanese, in essence, sacrificed wolves on the "bloody altar of modernity" (Walker 2005: 157).

Alfred Crosby showed how animals served as tools for colonists, especially in settler societies. Recent scholarship has both deepened and challenged his argument. Virginia DeJohn Anderson in *Creatures of Empire* (2004), for example, provides a nuanced study of animals in colonial America. Her work deepens our understanding of the colonial experience by showing how many disputes between Indians and colonists centered around domestic animals and colonists' use of them. Colonists often let their pigs roam freely beyond settlements, and in the process, they often devoured Indian crops. Colonists saw Indian killings of pigs or other domestic animals as the destruction of property. Given the centrality of domestic animals in colonial economies, more conflicts emerged as these new settlers encroached on Indian land to secure pasture for their animals. Like Crosby before her, Anderson, thus, sees animals as central to colonialism. Yet for Pekka Hämäläinen (2003, 2010), animals are not necessarily creatures of empire. Like any technology, other groups can adopt particular tools and use them to their advantage. No Native group in the Americas better illustrates this point than the Comanches in the eighteenth and nineteenth centuries. Before the arrival of the Spanish and their horses, the Comanches were a small, relatively inconsequential tribe. After adopting the horse, they used this animal to extend their territory and create an empire on the southern Great Plains, one so powerful that it was able to keep European powers at bay for decades before finally being conquered by Americans in the 1860s.

## Conclusion

This chapter is but a small sampling of the cutting-edge research in environmental history. Other important topics include histories of food consumption and production (Freidberg 2009; Vileisis 2007; Walker 2004), race and gender (Chiang 2008; Wilson 2011), oceans (Reidy 2009; Rozwadowski 2005), rivers (Armstrong *et al.* 2009; Evenden 2004, 2006a, 2009; Pritchard 2011), and energy (Huber 2011; Nye 1998; Sabin 2005). Over the past three decades, environmental history has become an influential and vast field with contributions from historians, geographers, and natural scientists. Its fluorescence shows no signs of abating, partly because our concern with the history of the relationship between people and the environment is driven by current environmental problems. Since the development of the field, environmental history has always responded to environmental crises and had a relationship, albeit an uneasy one sometimes, with the environmental movement.

There is tremendous popular interest in the subject of environmental history, as evidenced by the colossal success of Jared Diamond's *Guns, Germs, and Steel* (1997) and *Collapse* (2005). Though Diamond has been affiliated with the Department of Geography at the

University of California-Los Angeles for nearly a decade and has been a plenary speaker at an annual meeting of the AAG, his work has elicited indifference and outright hostility from many geographers.[3] Part of this resistance comes from his raising of the specter of environmental determinism, and with it, a dark chapter in the discipline's past (see Livingstone 1992, 2010; McNeill 2010b). In a rare sympathetic review of Diamond's recent books, historical geographer Matthew Evenden acknowledges the weaknesses of Diamond's work, especially his inattention to culture, but praises Diamond for his attention to often-neglected regions in world histories, such as New Guinea, and clear, compelling literary prose. He adds that Diamond writes world-encompassing historical geographies of the sort that geographers rarely write (though see the notable exceptions in the discussion of world environmental history above). Evenden concludes:

> [Diamond's book provides] broad interpretations to think productively with and against, runs contrary to a host of scholarly conventions and opens discussion about the public understanding of geography and history. Its evident popular success also challenges us to reflect upon the relative unpopularity of most academic work and why that is so. One need not approve of Diamond's work to read it with profit. (Evenden 2006b: 870)

Though some environmental histories have found a non-scholarly audience (Cronon 1991; Andrews 2008), cultural geographers, whether focusing on environmental topics or not, often write works that have little appeal outside the academy. If environmental works such as Diamond's are going to be challenged, they must be done so with rich, critical, and above all, literary books that engage scholars and non-scholars alike.

Though less commonly mentioned by geographers or historians critiquing Diamond's work, another point of trepidation about his books involves his use of evolutionary theory.[4] Diamond's training is as an evolutionary biologist, not a historian or historical–cultural geographer. Cultural geographers expunged evolutionary ideas from their work long ago; so when someone from the subfield reads a work, such as Diamond's, that is dependent on them, their unease should not be surprising. The virtue of Diamond's engagement with evolutionary theory, however, is that he shows human societies, landscapes, and the species themselves as historical. Still, the approaches of cultural geographers and evolutionists like Diamond seem largely incompatible.

A way out of this impasse comes from Edmund Russell, an environmental historian and historian of science and technology. In a provocative article and brilliant book (Russell 2003, 2011), he outlines a research program he calls evolutionary history, which links evolutionary insights from biology with cultural ones from history. He argues that humans have modified evolution in populations of people and other species, human-directed evolution has changed human history, human and non-human populations have coevolved, and evolutionary history can help us understand the past better than either history or biology alone. In particular, he notes, historians, and other scholars from the humanities and social scientists such as cultural geographers, can contribute to this field by examining the economic, political, and cultural factors that have affected selection pressures on organisms over time. He illustrates his ideas with wide-ranging examples, such as how poaching elephants for ivory in Africa has led to elephants with smaller tusks and how the use of pesticides produced pesticide-resistant insects and weeds. Russell avoids the somewhat crude determinism of Diamond's work by seeing humans as cultural beings using evolution, purposely or inadvertently, to alter human and non-human life through time (see also Worster 2010).

A discussion of evolutionary history is a suitable place to end this essay. The discipline of geography emerged in the nineteenth and early twentieth centuries as one reliant on environmental ideas to explain the relationship between society and the environment in the present and past. Cultural and historical geography under Carl Sauer challenged this paradigm, seeing landscapes as products of predominantly cultural forces. New cultural geographers, especially those working on historical topics, turned their attention to representation and generally shunned concepts from the natural sciences. Russell's work provides a provocative template for reuniting cultural geography with the natural sciences that does not see human actions or their history as determined by the environment, or nature as merely a cultural construction, but rather humans and the environment as coevolving through a process of evolution by natural selection and by the selective pressures of humans that are at once biological but very cultural, too.

## Notes

1   Blackwell recently published a lengthy companion to the environmental history of just the United States (Cazaux-Sackman 2010). Matthew Evenden and Graeme Wynn (2009) survey work by historians and geographers on Canada's environmental history.
2   Some scholars, such as Ted Steinberg (2009), sees this tokenism as an example of green neoliberalism in which environmental protection is reduced to a consumer matter best achieved through individual buying decisions rather than collective political action.
3   In September 2003, *Antipode* published a review symposium where five geographers roundly criticized *Guns, Germs, and Steel*. Andrew Sluyter, for instance, called the book "junk science." Anthropologists have also been highly critical of the book (McAnany and Yoffee 2010). Environmental historian J.R. McNeill (2010a) is slightly more generous.
4   Noel Castree (2009) reflects on the lack of engagement with evolutionary theory in human and environmental geography.

## References

Agrawal, A. (2005) *Environmentality: Technologies of Government and the Making of Subjects*. Durham, NC: Duke University Press.

Anderson, V.D. (2004) *Creatures of Empire: How Domestic Animals Transformed Early America*. New York: Oxford University Press.

Andrews, T.G. (2008) *Killing for Coal: America's Deadliest Labor War*. Cambridge, MA: Harvard University Press.

Armstrong C., Evenden M. and Nelles, H.V. (2009) *The River Returns: An Environmental History of the Bow*. Montreal: McGill-Queen's University Press.

Bess, M. (2003) *The Light-Green Society: Ecology and Technological Modernity in France, 1960–2000*. Chicago: University of Chicago Press.

Braun, B. (2002) *The Intemperate Rainforest: Nature, Culture, and Power on Canada's West Coast*. Minneapolis: University of Minnesota Press.

Bryson, J. (2012) Brownfields gentrification: Redevelopment planning and environmental justice in Spokane, Washington. *Environmental Justice*, 5, 26–31.

Castree, N. (2009) Charles Darwin and the geographers. *Environment and Planning A*, 41, 2293–2298.

Cazaux-Sackman, D. (ed.) (2010) *A Companion to American Environmental History*. Oxford: Blackwell.

Chiang, C. (2008) *Shaping the Shoreline: Fisheries and Tourism on the Monterey Coast*. Seattle: University of Washington Press.

Coleman, J. (2004) *Vicious: Wolves and Men in America*. New Haven: Yale University Press.

Colten, C. (2005) *Unnatural Metropolis: Wresting New Orleans from Nature*. Baton Rouge: Louisiana State University Press.

Cronon, W. (1983) *Changes in the Land: Indians, Colonists, and the Ecology of New England*. New York: Hill and Wang.

Cronon, W. (1991) *Nature's Metropolis: Chicago and the Great West*. New York: W.W. Norton.

Cronon, W. (1992) A place for stories: Nature, history, and narrative. *Journal of American History*, March, 1347–1376.

Cronon, W. (1994) Cutting loose or running aground? *Journal of Historical Geography*, 20.1, 38–43.

Crosby, A. (1972) *The Columbian Exchange: Biological and Cultural Consequences of 1492*. Westport, CT: Greenwood Press.

Crosby, A. (1986) *Ecological Imperialism: The Biological Expansion of Europe, 900–1900*. New York: Cambridge University Press.

Demeritt, D. (1994a) The nature of metaphors in cultural geography and environmental history. *Progress in Human Geography*, 18.2, 163–185.

Demeritt, D. (1994b) Ecology, objectivity and critique in writings on nature and human societies. *Journal of Historical Geography*, 20, 22–37.

Diamond J. (1997) *Guns, Germs, and Steel: The Fates of Human Societies*. New York: W.W. Norton.

Diamond J. (2005) *Collapse: Why Societies Choose to Fail or Succeed*. New York: Penguin.

Dunlap T.R. (1988) *Saving America's Wildlife*. Princeton: Princeton University Press.

Emel, J. (1998) Are you man enough, big and bad enough? Wolf eradication in the US. In *Animal Geographies: Place, Politics and Identity in the Nature–Culture Borderlands*, ed. J.R. Wolch and J. Emel. New York: Verso, pp. 91–116.

Evenden, M. (2004) *Fish Versus Power: An Environmental History of the Fraser River*. New York: Cambridge University Press.

Evenden, M. (2006a) Precarious foundations: Irrigation, environment, and social change in the Canadian Pacific Railway's eastern section, 1900–1930. *Journal of Historical Geography*, 32, 74–95.

Evenden, M. (2006b) Twenty-first century magic. *Journal of Historical Geography*, 32, 864–870.

Evenden, M. (2009) Mobilizing rivers: Hydro-electricity, the state and the Second World War in Canada. *Annals of the Association of American Geographers*, 99, 845–855.

Evenden, M. and Wynn, G. (2009) "54:40 or fight": Writing within and across boundaries in North American environmental history. In *Nature's End: History and the Environment*, ed. P. Warde and S. Sorlin. London: Palgrave, pp. 215–246.

Freidberg, S. (2009) *Fresh: A Perishable History*. Cambridge, MA: Belknap Press of Harvard University Press.

Gandy, M. (2002) *Concrete and Clay: Reworking Nature in New York City*. Cambridge, MA: MIT Press.

Hämäläinen, P. (2003) The rise and fall of Plains horse cultures. *Journal of American History*, 90, 833–862.

Hämäläinen, P. (2010) The politics of grass: European expansion, ecological change, and indigenous power in the Southwest borderlands. *William and Mary Quarterly*, 67, 173–208.

Hays, S.P. (1959) *Conservation and the Gospel of Efficiency: The Progressive Conservation Movement, 1890–1920*. Cambridge, MA: Harvard University Press.

Hays, S.P. (1987) *Beauty, Health, and Permanence: Environmental Politics in the United States, 1955–1985*. New York: Cambridge University Press.

Hazlett, M. (2003) Voices from the *Spring: Silent Spring* and the ecological turn in American health. In *Seeing Nature Through Gender*, ed. V. Scharff. Lawrence: University Press of Kansas, pp. 103–128.

Heynen, N., Kaika, M. and Swyngedouw, E. (2006) *The Nature of Cities: Urban Political Ecology and the Politics of Urban Metabolism*. New York: Routledge.

Hirt, P. (1994) *Conspiracy of Optimism: Management of the National Forests Since World War II*. Lincoln: University of Nebraska Press.

Huber, M. (2011) Enforcing scarcity: Oil, violence and the making of the market. *Annals of the Association of American Geographers*, 101, 816–826.

Jacoby, K. (2001) *Crimes Against Nature: Squatters, Poachers, Thieves, and the Hidden History of American Conservation*. Berkeley: University of California Press.

Kaika, M. (2005) *City of Flows: Modernity, Nature, and the City*. New York: Routledge.

Kearns, G. (2004) Environmental history. In *A Companion to Cultural Geography*, ed. J. Duncan, N. Johnson, and R. Schein. Oxford: Blackwell, pp. 194–208.

Keeling, A. (2004) Sink or swim: Water pollution and environmental politics in Vancouver, 1889–1975. *BC Studies*, 142/43, 69–101.

Keeling, A. (2005a) Urban waste sinks as a natural resource: The case of the Fraser River. *Urban History Review*, 34, 58–70.

Keeling, A. (2005b) Saskatoon's sewer: Pollution and the South Saskatchewan River. *Saskatoon History Review*, 19.

Kelman, A. (2003) *A River and Its City: The Nature of Landscape in New Orleans*. Berkeley: University of California Press.

Klingle, M. (2007) *Emerald City: An Environmental History of Seattle*. New Haven: Yale University Press.

Kosek, J. (2006) *Understories: The Political Life of Forests in Northern New Mexico*. Durham, NC: Duke University Press.

Langston, N. (1996) *Forest Dreams, Forest Nightmares: The Paradox of Old Growth in the Inland West*. Seattle: University of Washington Press.

Langston, N. (2003) *Where Land and Water Meet: A Western Landscape Transformed*. Seattle: University of Washington Press.

Langston, N. (2010) *Toxic Bodies: Hormone Disruptors and the Legacy of DES*. New Haven: Yale University Press.

Livingstone, D. (1992) *The Geographical Tradition: Episodes in the History of a Contested Enterprise*. Oxford: Blackwell.

Livingstone, D. (2010) Environmental determinism. In *The Sage Handbook of Geographical Knowledge*, ed. J. Agnew and D. Livingstone. New York: Sage.

Loo, T. (2006) *States of Nature: Conserving Canada's Wildlife in the Twentieth Century*. Vancouver: University of British Columbia Press.

Lopez, B. (1978) *Of Wolves and Men*. New York: Scribner.

Louter, D. (2006) *Windshield Wilderness: Cars, Roads, and Nature in Washington's National Parks*. Seattle: University of Washington Press.

Lowenthal, D. (2000) *George Perkins Marsh: Prophet of Conservation*. Seattle: University of Washington Press.

Maher, N.M. (2007) *Nature's New Deal: The Civilian Conservation Corps and the Roots of American Environmentalism*. New York: Oxford University Press.

Marsh, G.P. (2003/1864) *Man and Nature*. Seattle: University of Washington Press.

McAnany, P.A. and Yoffee, N. (2010) *Questioning Collapse: Human Resilience, Ecological Vulnerability, and the Aftermath of Empire*. New York: Cambridge University Press.

McNeill, J.R. (2000) *Something New Under the Sun: An Environmental History of the Twentieth Century*. New York: W. W. Norton.

McNeill, J.R. (2003) Observations on the nature and culture of environmental history. *History and Theory*, 42, 5–43.

McNeill, J.R. (2010a) *Mosquito Empires: Ecology and War in the Greater Caribbean, 1620–1914*. New York: Cambridge University Press.

McNeill, J.R. (2010b) Sustainable survival. In *Questioning Collapse: Human Resilience, Ecological Vulnerability, and the Aftermath of Empire*, ed. P.A. McAnany and N. Yoffee. New York: Cambridge University Press, pp. 355–366.

McNeill, J.R. and McNeill, W. (2003) *The Human Web: A Bird's-Eye View of World History*, New York: W.W. Norton.

McNeill, W. (1976) *Plagues and Peoples*. New York: Anchor.

Melosi, M.V. (2000) *The Sanitary City: Urban Infrastructure in America from Colonial Times to the Present*. Baltimore: Johns Hopkins University Press.

Miller, S.W. (2007) *An Environmental History of Latin America*. New York: Cambridge University Press.

Mitman, G. (2007) *Breathing Space: How Allergies Shape Our Lives and Landscapes*. New Haven: Yale University Press.

Nash, L. (2006) *Inescapable Ecologies: A History of Environment, Disease, and Knowledge*. Berkeley: University of California Press.

Nye, D.E. (1998) *Consuming Power: A Social History of American Energies*. Cambridge, MA: MIT Press.

Olson, B. (2010) Paper trails: The Outdoor Recreation Resource Review Commission and the rationalization of recreational resources. *Geoforum*, 41, 447–456.

Pisani, D.J. (2002) *Water and American Government: The Reclamation Bureau, National Water Policy, and the West, 1902–1935*. Berkeley: University of California Press.

Pritchard, S. (2011) *Confluence: The Nature of Technology and the Remaking of the Rhône*. Cambridge, MA: Harvard University Press.

Pyne S. (2009) *Voice and Vision: A Guide to Writing History and Other Serious Nonfiction*, Cambridge, MA: Harvard University Press.

Rawson, M. (2010) *Eden on the Charles: The Making of Boston*. Cambridge, MA: Harvard University Press.

Reidy, M. (2009) *Tides of History: Ocean Science and Her Majesty's Navy*. Chicago: University of Chicago Press.

Reisner, M. (1986) *Cadillac Desert: The American West and its Disappearing Water*. New York: Penguin.

Richards, J. (2003) *The Unending Frontier: An Environmental History of the Early Modern World*, Berkeley: University of California Press.

Rome, A. (2001) *The Bulldozer in the Countryside: Suburban Sprawl and the Rise of American Environmentalism*. New York: Cambridge University Press.

Rome, A. (2003) "Give earth a chance": The environmental movement and the sixties. *Journal of American History*, 90, 525–554.

Rome, A. (2010) The genius of Earth Day. *Environmental History*, 15, 194–205.

Rome, A. (2013) *The Genius of Earth Day: How a 1970 Teach-in Unexpectedly Made the First Green Generation*. New York: Hill and Wang.

Rozwadowski, H. (2005) *Fathoming the Ocean: The Discovery and Exploration of the Deep Sea*. Cambridge, MA: Harvard University Press.

Runte, A. (1997) *National Parks: The American Experience*. Lincoln: University of Nebraska Press.

Russell, E. (2003) Evolutionary history: Prospectus for a new field. *Environmental History*, 8, 204–228.

Russell, E. (2011) *Evolutionary History: Uniting History and Biology to Understand Life on Earth*. New York: Cambridge University Press.

Sabin, P. (2005) *Crude Politics: The California Oil Market, 1900–1940*. Berkeley: University of California Press.

Sandlos, J. (2007) *Hunters at the Margin: Native People and Wildlife Conservation in the Northwest Territories*. Vancouver: University of British Columbia Press.

Sauer, C. (1965/1925) The morphology of landscape. In *Land And Life: A Selection from the Writings of Carl Ortwin Sauer*, ed. J. Leighly. Berkeley: University of California Press, pp. 315–350.

Sellars, R.W. (1997) *Preserving Nature in the National Parks: A History*. New Haven: Yale University Press.

Spence, M.D. (1999) *Dispossessing the Wilderness: Indian Removal and the Making of the National Parks*. New York: Oxford University Press.

Steinberg, T. (2009) *Down to Earth: Nature's Role in American History*. New York: Oxford University Press.

Sutter, P. (2002) *Driven Wild: How the Fight against Automobiles Launched the Modern Wilderness Movement*. Seattle: University of Washington Press.

Tarr, J.A. (1996) *The Search for the Ultimate Sink: Urban Pollution in Historical Perspective*. Akron: University of Akron Press.

Taylor III, J. (2010) *Pilgrims of the Vertical: Yosemite Rock Climbers and the Nature of Risk*. Cambridge, MA: Harvard University Press

Thomas, W.L. (ed.) (1956) *Man's Role in Changing the Face of the Earth*. Chicago: University of Chicago Press.

Turner II, B.L., Clark, W.C., Kates, R.W., Richards, J.F., Mathews, J.T. and Meyer, W.B. (1993) *The Earth as Transformed by Human Action: Global and Regional Changes in the Biosphere over the Past 300 Years*. Cambridge: Cambridge University Press.

Valenčius, C.B. (2002) *The Health of the Country: How American Settlers Understood Themselves and the Land*. New York: Basic Books.

Vileisis, A. (1997) *Discovering the Unknown Landscape: A History of America's Wetlands*. Washington, DC: Island Press.

Vileisis, A. (2007) *Kitchen Literacy: How We Lost Knowledge of Where Food Comes from and Why We Need to Get It Back*. Washington, DC: Island Press.

Walker, B. (2005) *The Lost Wolves of Japan*. Seattle: University of Washington Press.

Walker, B. (2010) *Toxic Archipelago: A History of Industrial Disease in Japan*. Seattle: University of Washington Press.

Walker, R. (2004) *The Conquest of Bread: 150 Years of Agribusiness in California*. New York: New Press.

Walker, R. (2007) *The Country in the City: The Greening of San Francisco Bay Area*. Seattle: University of Washington Press.

Warren, L.S. (1997) *The Hunter's Game: Poachers and Conservationists in Twentieth-Century America*. New Haven: Yale University Press.

White, R. (1999) The nationalization of nature. *Journal of American History*, 86, 976–986.

White, R. (2010) From wilderness to hybrid landscapes: The cultural turn in environmental history. In *A Companion to American Environmental History*, ed. D.C. Sackman. Oxford: Wiley-Blackwell, pp. 183–190.

Wilson, R.M. (2005a) Supersized history. *Journal of Historical Geography*, 31, 563–567.

Wilson, R.M. (2005b) Retrospective review: *Man's Role in Changing the Face of the Earth*. *Environmental History*, 10.

Wilson, R.M. (2010) *Seeking Refuge: Birds and Landscapes of the Pacific Flyway*. Seattle: University of Washington Press.

Wilson, R.M. (2011) Landscapes of promise and betrayal: Homesteading, reclamation, and Japanese American incarceration during the Second World War. *Annals of the Association of American Geographers*, 101.2, 424–444.

Worster, D. (1985) *Rivers of Empire: Water, Aridity, and the Growth of the American West*. New York: Pantheon.

Worster, D. (2010) The living earth: History, Darwinian evolution, and the grasslands. In *A Companion to American Environmental History*, ed. D. Sackman. Oxford: Wiley-Blackwell, pp. 51–68.

Wynn, G. (2007) *Canada and Arctic North America: An Environmental History*. Santa Barbara: ABC-Clio.

# Chapter 32

# Science Wars

*David N. Livingstone*

"A perceptible flurry in the dovecote." So reported Jerry Fodor in the *London Review of Books* on November 29, 2007. He was responding to a series of attacks he had sustained from readers of a provocative piece entitled "Why Pigs Don't Have Wings," which he had published in the *Review* a month earlier. But even at that stage, he had no idea of the torrent of abuse to which he would subsequently be subjected when his latest book, co-authored with Massimo Piattelli-Palmarini, appeared in 2010 under the daring title *What Darwin Got Wrong*. What had started as a flurry of ruffled feathers became an avalanche of abuse. Another science war had broken out. Pondering on one or two recent clashes like this over Darwinism opens up a range of matters that geographers interested in the spaces of scientific culture might find illuminating.

## A Couple of Cautionary Tales

Jerry Fodor is State of New Jersey Professor of Philosophy at Rutgers University with a huge reputation as perhaps the world's leading philosopher of mind. What catches my interest here, however, is not his contributions to subjects like the modularity of mind, the semantics of counterfactuals, mental states, and the asymmetric causal theory of reference, but rather the furore over his interventions in the Darwin debates. It all began when he had a go at evolutionary psychology's penchant for turning to Darwinian adaptationism to explain just about everything from why we like music (apparently because singing strengthened bonds between hunter-gatherer groups) to modern management problems (supposedly because our minds evolved to survive on the African plains two or three hundred thousand years ago, and not to make us happy in twenty-first-century Manhattan). Fodor dismissed such accounts as entertaining, but fictional, "just-so stories" (Fodor 2007). Along the way he paused to

*The Wiley Blackwell Companion to Cultural Geography*, First Edition.
Edited by Nuala C. Johnson, Richard H. Schein, and Jamie Winders.
© 2013 John Wiley & Sons, Ltd. Published 2016 by John Wiley & Sons, Ltd.

inspect the idea of adaptation itself and came to the conclusion that the notion of nature selecting *for* particular traits was deeply problematic. To Fodor, nature – being the mindless kind of thing that it is – cannot "select" traits in anything like the way pigeon breeders select for their purposes those chicks with desirable variations. Why? Because pigeon fanciers have minds, and – well – nature doesn't. Hence his suspicion that the fundamental Darwinian metaphor is pretty wrong-headed.

It was not too long before missiles were lobbing in. A skirmish was under way. All sorts of scribblers – philosophers, historians of science, biologists, even a musician – felt the need to have a say. These of course included some of the usual suspects from the ranks of the High Darwinians: Dan Dennett, Jerry Coyne, Phil Kitcher. The former – Dennett – wondered what could have driven Fodor "to hallucinate" so wildly; the latter two – Coyne and Kitcher – found the argument "incoherent." Testy talk to be sure; but not yet open warfare of the fire-at-will variety. That had to wait till *What Darwin Got Wrong* hit the bookshelves.

In the meantime Fodor plugged away at his critique, this time in the pages of *Mind and Language*. The following February, 2008, it carried his "Against Darwinism," a title that left no doubt about his conclusion. Here, in rather more technical philosophy-speak, Fodor deployed a critical distinction between intensional and extensional propositions to ground his conviction that, like such states as believing, desiring, and the like, "selecting for" requires a capacity to make certain judgments – a mental facility of precisely the kind that nature doesn't have. The details need not detain us here; suffice to say that it led Fodor from just being down on evolutionary psychology to having severe "doubts about the whole adapta-tionist enterprise" (Fodor 2008: 2). Of course this did not mean that Fodor gave "the slightest reason to doubt the central Darwinist theses of the common origin and mutability of species"; it's just that he was now convinced that the standard pan-adaptationist explanation of evo-lutionary change could not do the job required of it (Fodor 2008: 23). So far so good.

In turn this article became the launching pad for *What Darwin Got Wrong*. The philo-sophical arguments here were fundamentally those Fodor had already articulated, but these thoughts were supplemented by a good deal of detail from experimental biology provided by his co-author. In large part the scientific case consisted in fleshing out the implications of Gould and Lewontin's (1979) insights on spandrels and expanding on certain developments in gene regulation, epigenetics, evolutionary development biology (so-called "evo-devo"), and the resurgence of interest in morphological laws. Fodor prosecuted the conceptual case against Darwin in a more leisurely and expansive way but the conclusion remained firm: "Familiar claims to the contrary notwithstanding, Darwin didn't manage to get mental causes out of his account of how evolution works. He just hid them in the unexamined analogy between selection by breeding and natural selection" (Fodor and Piattelli-Palmarini 2010: 162). A remarkable appendix, in which the authors provided a catalogue of what they con-sidered to be extraordinary "just-so" stories from celebrated advocates of evolutionary psy-chology in one shape or another, topped off the volume.

Judging by the reviews you would think the sky had fallen in. As Richard Lewontin (2010) put it in the *New York Review of Books*, "The circulation of the proof copy of *What Darwin Got Wrong* . . . has resulted in a volume of critical comment from biologists and philosophers that has not been seen since 1859. No week has passed that a manuscript expressing bewil-derment or outrage from a biologist or philosopher of science has not arrived on my desk or desktop." He further explained: "While *What Darwin Got Wrong* may have been designed *pour épater les bourgeois* and to forcibly get the attention of evolutionists, when two accom-plished intellectuals make the statement 'Darwin's theory of selection is *empty*,' they generate an anger that makes it almost impossible for biologists to give serious consideration to their argument."

So, then, a sampling of the invective. Courtesy of Douglas Futuyma (2010), readers of *Science* were told that the authors of *What Darwin Got Wrong* were "Two Critics Without a Clue." Samir Okasha (2010: 5), in the *TLS*, declared that the book "is the sort of thing that gives philosophy of science a bad name." Ned Block and Philip Kitcher (2010) regretted "that two such distinguished authors have decided to publish a book so cavalier in its treatment of a serious science, so full of apparently scholarly discussions that rest on mistakes and confusions – and so predictably ripe for making mischief." Writing in *Nature*, Massimo Pigliucci (2010: 354) pronounced the book's arguments "sterile and wrong-headed," while Jerry Coyne (2010a: 1, 6, 5) accused the authors of being "biologically uninformed," "wilfully ignorant," and making "claims that are simply silly." Neil Spurway (2010: 12), a physiologist, proclaimed that they "are not just arrogant and obfuscating; they are dangerous." Now to be sure, a few voices were raised in support. Mary Midgley (2010), writing in the *Guardian*, thought the book very timely and judged it to be "an overdue and valuable onslaught on neo-Darwinist simplicities." Philip Ball (2010), a science writer, told the readers of the *Sunday Times* that their insistence that natural selection was ripe for reassessment "should not be seen as scientific heresy or capitulation to the forces of unreason." And the linguist Norbert Hornstein (2010: 384), noting that much of the criticism to which Fodor and Piattelli-Palmarini were subjected had "misconstrued what they were saying," thought their argument was "pretty powerful." But these were far and away the exception.

So, then, why all the venom? The answer is not hard to find. Even the most cursory inspection exposes an underlying set of anxieties rotating around the so-called culture wars between science and religion, in this case over such *bêtes noires* as creationism and intelligent design. As Fodor (2011) himself later ruefully remarked, "Almost (but not quite) all the reviews were hostile, not to say hysterical. The blogs were alight with anonymous contumely. Various commentators suggested, pretty explicitly, that we had gone off our respective rockers . . . We had stumbled into the Culture Wars, from which no voyager returns unbesmirched." To get properly on track here, we need to record Fodor and Piattelli-Palmarini's views on religion. They describe themselves as "card-carrying, signed-up, dyed-in-the-wool, no-holds-barred atheists" (Fodor and Piattelli-Palmarini 2010: xv). That seems fairly clear. Nevertheless, again and again, interlocutors felt the need to cast the whole issue into the arena of science-and-religion. Daniel Dennett had already explained that there was a label for people like Fodor who don't swallow the claim that natural selection is a persuasive way to ground a theory of natural teleology: "we call them creationists," he declared. Those who aren't convinced that what he calls "Darwin's strange inversion" can provide an exhaustive account of the human mind or that natural selection is *the* explanatory "universal acid" that can deliver purposeless purpose, designer-less design, and the like, he calls "mind creationists" (Dennett 2009: 10062).

Shortly afterwards, the Harvard philosopher Peter Godfrey-Smith (2010) was worrying that Fodor and Piattelli-Palmarini had rehashed an "old argument, beloved of creationists." Readers of the *American Scientist* learned from the Chicago historian of science Robert Richards that the authors had orchestrated "a medley of contradictions that can delight only the ears of creationists and proponents of intelligent design." He hammered the point home with a concluding rhetorical flourish – presumably as a cautionary parable – drawn from the Wilberforce–Huxley legend in which Huxley is supposed to have retorted that he "would rather have a monkey as his ancestor than be connected with a man who used great gifts to obscure the truth" (Richards 2010). Just exactly how he thought this relevant was left for readers to infer. But I guess that wasn't too difficult. Even those reviewers who did largely concentrate their energies on the book's arguments included throw-away allusions to fundamentalist obscurantism. In almost the first breath of his review, the philosopher John Dupré (2010) declared that the book "has been, and will continue to be, picked up by the fundamentalist enemies of science." And Simon Conway Morris (2010), a leading palaeontologist, was concerned that although the authors would be "horrified" by the comparison, "the tenor of their argument is uncomfortably reminiscent of 'Intelligent Design'." Of course I'm not claiming that such observations are themselves false; I've no doubt they are true enough. It's rather that, because Darwin is such an iconic figure, in disputes over the explanatory power of natural selection, guilt by association counts in some quarters for a great deal.

Comparable anxieties could easily be elaborated. Just one more. Michael Ruse was perhaps the most forthright. Writing in the *Boston Globe* he concluded: "like those scorned Christians, Fodor and Piattelli-Palmarini just cannot stomach the idea that humans might just be organisms, no better than the rest of the living world . . . Christians are open in their beliefs that humans are special and explaining them lies beyond the scope of science. I just wish that our authors were a little more open that this is their view too" (Ruse 2010). Naturally enough Fodor (2011) didn't take too kindly to that. "Well none of that is remotely our view," he observed; "there's not a scintilla of text in our book (or elsewhere) to support the accusation of creeping theism . . . Short of trial by fire, water, or the House of UnAmerican Activities Committee, what must one do to prove one's bona fides?" And indeed the very first two sentences of their book ran: "This is not a book about God; nor about intelligent design; nor about creationism. Neither of us is into any of those" (Fodor and Piattelli-Palmarini 2010: xv).

Given the way in which *What Darwin Got Wrong* found itself catapulted into the maelstrom of a science–religion war, a dogfight that its authors clearly had no intention of engaging, their conclusion that the "howl of reflexive Darwinism" drowned out almost all serious attention "to the structure of the arguments or to their repercussions" is hardly surprising (Fodor and Piattelli-Palmarini 2011: 189). But mistaken targets, misconstrued intentions, and misplaced scorn are the sure signs of a culture war, as Keith Bennett, palaeoecologist, colleague, and recipient of a Royal Society Wolfson Merit Award, also recently discovered. His experience, which can be rehearsed in rather shorter compass, uncovers yet other dimensions of science wars. In 2010 he was invited by the *New Scientist* to publish a keynote lecture he had given at the International Palaeontological Congress that summer at Imperial College London. The other keynote speaker was to be Niles Eldredge. The piece made the front cover of the magazine. It presented evidence he'd gathered over many years to assess the role of adaptation to environment in evolutionary history. "Major climatic events such as ice ages," he observed, "ought to leave their imprint on life as species adapt to new conditions." Was that the case? Bennett didn't think so. His conclusion was that pan-adaptationism may turn out not to be the major driver of evolutionary change that has routinely been assumed. As he put it, "the connection between environmental change and evolutionary change is weak, which is not what might have been expected from Darwin's hypothesis" (Bennett 2010: 29, 30). In its place he proposed that evolution is non-linear and that the causes of macroevolutionary change lie in the "chaotic" dynamics of the relationship between genotype and phenotype.

From the blogs one could be forgiven for thinking that the Inquisition was gearing up again. Jerry Coyne verged on the apoplectic. A sample of his vocabulary should be enough to give a rough sense of his tone: "stupid," "thoughtless," "hogwash," "moron," "drivel," "ludicrous," "ignorant." As for Bennett's Wolfson Award, that only induced Coyne (2010b) to "weep for the Royal Society, which seems to have fallen on hard times." Soon the blog that Coyne himself runs on his website "Why Evolution is True" was mainlining vitriol. On the very day he posted his attack, forty-two comments were logged. One thought Bennett's piece "appalling" and worried that "it would be misinterpreted in the wrong corner"; another found it "sad and pathetic"; yet another speculated that Bennett had been "bitten by a Post-modernist" and warned that "those bites can get infected"! The list could go on: "ignorant," giving "fuel to creationists"; "completely misguided." A day or two later, Coyne (2010c) gave his readers another fix under the title "*New Scientist* defends bad science." Sixty comments followed in another adrenalin-rush of scorn. Many complained about the follies of science journalism; some claimed, missing the irony that blogs themselves are not subject to peer review, that Bennett's ideas wouldn't get a hearing "in a 'real' science journal" that uses proper expert evaluation.

To get some perspective on this gush of protest, which reveals something of an electronic herd instinct, two observations need to be recorded. First, Graham Lawton (2010), the com-missioning editor, contacted Coyne with the following observation: "if Bennett is so hope-lessly wrong, why was he ever invited to give that keynote (alongside Niles Eldredge)? Why did the symposium even take place? Bennett was not the only one to question the primacy of natural selection in macroevolution. Why does the Royal Society support his work? . . . I was at Bennett's talk; the room was full of learned and eminent people. He took a few questions but there were no howls of protest like yours. What am I to make of this?"

Second, in light of the accusations over the absence of peer reviewing, it's worth remarking that a few years earlier, Bennett had presented similar arguments at the Royal Society itself and published them in its *Philosophical Transactions*. Here he laid out evidence for his con-viction that species persisted unchanged over "multiple glacial–interglacial oscillations" and therefore that "stasis exists despite considerable environmental change." This led him to conclude that it could "well be the crucial insight that evolution, after all, has rather little to do with environmental change" (Bennett 2004: 299, 301). Evolution might well be driven by mechanisms that are non-adaptive. Commentators at the Royal Society displayed no con-tempt at the thought but engaged calmly and constructively with the proposal. One pointed out that environmental selection was only one element in Darwin's arsenal, another that natural selection should not be abandoned but expectations about links between evolution and environmental change revised. Bennett agreed.

These fresh dispatches from the trenches of the Darwin combat zone highlight a number of issues of interest to cultural geographers with an eye on the role of science in society and its engagement with other domains of cultural life. Three stand out.

## Reterritorializing Battlelines

The rumpus over *What Darwin Got Wrong* amply reveals that in disputes over scientific claims there are deeper cultural forces at work. In this case, critics were determined to find a science–religion vendetta where it was not. This realization requires a reterritorialization of both battlelines and enemy forces. What was originally presented as a biophilosophical reevaluation of natural selection's role in evolutionary explanation was routinely pitched into the quagmire of the science–religion culture brawls. Despite protestations to the contrary from Fodor and Piattelli-Palmerini, interlocutors persisted in allying them with causes far removed from their own interests. This meant that their arguments were rarely addressed head-on. Indeed, their location outside what they called The Guild of Professional Biologists, on whose territory they had apparently trespassed, was regularly resorted to by reviewers as a substitute for careful engagement with their proposals. The great blooming buzzing confusion, as William James might have put it, surrounding debates about the science curriculum, creationism, evolutionary naturalism, and intelligent design made many readers color-blind to the real target they had in their cross-hairs. To them the lines of battle were simply in different places.

Of course efforts to make a science–science spat into a science–religion clash up the stakes enormously, not least when zealots presume to know exactly what side of the fence the angels are on and when they have no doubts where the frontier lies between enlightenment and ignorance, civilization and barbarism. On closer inspection, however, these moralizing sightlines are anything but clear. Terry Eagleton has remarked on this kind of maneuver in a biting aside on Dennett's *Breaking the Spell: Religion as a Natural Phenomenon*: "One gathers . . . that he thinks that the invasion of Iraq was fine if it only could have been better managed." This, Eagleton reckons, raises the suspicion that not every evolutionary "iconoclast is radical in any other sense of the word" (Eagleton 2010: 39). Marilyn Robinson advertises something similar when she remarks on the ways in which certain evolutionary social scientists blithely translate costly acts of human self-sacrifice into the mere outcome of a kind of algorithmic calculation intended to bring payoffs for the altruist (Robinson 2010). And Jon Marks exposes another instance where moral cartographics cut clean through the conventional territorial lines of the science wars, when he identifies an evolutionary psychologist who "believes that the IQ of indigenous Africans is genetically set at about 70, that is to say, about the level of a mildly retarded European, and that this is the result of natural selection for over-sexuality and under-intellectuality" (Marks 2012: 306). Lest we are tempted to dismiss this case as an embarrassing aberration, he reminds us that "the first generation of Darwinists were willing to sacrifice the full humanity of the non-European races of the world in order to score rhetorical points against the Biblical traditionalists" (Marks 2012: 298). Indeed.

Remappings of this stripe have far-reaching implications – beyond the contemporary horizon – for those interested in the historical geography of scientific culture too. For they alert us to the ways in which debates over science are multi-factorial. The eager reception of Darwinism in nineteenth-century New Zealand, for example, cannot be understood without attending to what local enthusiasts perceived to be the imperialist implications of a Darwinian mindset for the future of Maori–settler relations. The application of a rigorous natural selection and survival-of-the-fittest mechanism to human races, no less than to rabbits and rats, lent scientific legitimacy to the colonial politics of Maori dispossession (Stenhouse 1996, 1999). In this part of the world, the flourishing of Darwinism – as a conceptual variety of invader species – depended no less on imperial ideology than on experimental science. In the American South it was different. Here, among the naturalists who congregated at the Charleston Museum of Natural History, Darwinism was repudiated. Why? Because it was seen to give sustenance to those urging that the human species was of monogenetic origin and thus that racial differences were literally only skin deep (Stephens 2000). In fact the politics of abolitionism, according to some, was precisely what motivated Darwin's whole enterprise in the first place (Desmond and Moore 2009). In cases like these, debates over Darwinism strayed well beyond the narrow confines of biological evolution. So, new maps of the territory are pretty obviously needed.

As for the presumptive cartography of the science–religion warzone, retrospective assumptions of conflict are likely to lead us far astray. The fate of John William Draper's *History of the Conflict between Religion and Science* (which came out in 1874) in Turkey is instructive here. This work, translated into Ottoman Turkish by the litterateur Ahmed Midhat, has recently been scrutinized by Alper Yalcinkaya who shows how, in this setting, the so-called conflict between science and religion was marshaled in the cause of a struggle between religion and religion. Midhat, it appears, stage-managed Draper's theory to present it as a contribution to the clash between Islam and Christianity by drawing attention to hints in Draper's text of a more positive stance toward science among Muslim writers and thereby to develop an apologia for Islam's greater compatibility with science compared to Christianity. Whether it was praising the contributions of the so-called "Saracens," identifying the scientific potentials in Islamic fatalism, or retrieving the insights of Averroes, Midhat used Draper to exonerate Islam and at the same time to confirm "the conflict between Christianity and science, thus providing Ottoman Muslims with a weapon against the missionaries" (Yalcinkaya 2011: 166). Such reterritorializing of zones of conflict opens up new lines of inquiry for which conventional campaign maps provide no guidance.

Comparable stories could be canvassed from elsewhere. What presented itself as a religious campaign against Henry Drummond's evolutionism in Victorian Scotland, for example, was more to do with internecine rivalry between Highlander and Lowlander. What was at stake were fears about the erosion of traditional Gaelic culture in the face of modernizing currents of thought at the turn of the nineteenth century (Wood 2011). Then there is the dismissal of figures like the theologian-chemist James Woodrow from his post at Columbia Seminary and the geologist Alexander Winchell from his chair at Vanderbilt during the 1870s and 1880s over evolution. These particular spectacles were immortalized in Andrew Dickson White's famous catalogue of scientific martyrdom (White 1896). But again it turns out not to have been just so simple. On closer inspection these intrigues had to do with anxieties of various stripes about the implications of modern scientific rationality for race relations between black and white in the wake of the American Civil War (Livingstone forthcoming).

Collectively, what these stories indicate is that the landscapes of science wars often need to be resurveyed and the battlelines redrawn. The zone needs to be reterritorialized and the interests of the conflict cartographers unmasked. What we need are maps that fruitfully complicate ideologically laden binaries by locating scientific controversies in the cultural conditions of their making.

## Theaters of Engagement

The different fate of Keith Bennett's querying of pan-adaptationism as an evolutionary mechanism in different arenas highlights the significance of what might be called "theaters of engagement" in scientific disputes. What can be said and – no less important – what can be heard, in different venues, is critical here. Plainly the expert audience that gathered in Lecture Theatre 1.31 of Imperial College London on the morning of Friday July 2, 2010, to hear Bennett's keynote speech in the session on macroevolution and the modern synthesis heard neither the idiocy nor the illogicality of the kind that Jerry Coyne found written all over the published version that appeared in a popular science journal. Similarly, participants in the Royal Society's discussion symposium on "The Evolutionary Legacy of the Ice Ages" in May 2003, whose contributions were published in the *Philosophical Transactions* the following year, engaged with Bennett's proposals in a conspicuously less hectic way than did Coyne's online "Evolution is True" blog-tribe. Different theaters of engagement for sure.

These scenarios connect in significant ways with the role of what I call "speech spaces" in scientific culture (Livingstone 2007). Crucial here are the ways in which settings both enable and constrain spoken communication. This is because there are intimate connections between *location* and *locution* in human communication. The implications are far-reaching. Miles Ogborn, for example, has advertised something of how speech, as an embodied performance of selfhood, exerted hefty racial power in the law courts of early eighteenth-century Jamaica. In a space that stipulated that slaves could not give evidence against their masters, profound questions arose over "what sort of truth . . . the enslaved, or the 'negro,' [could] be expected to speak" (Ogborn 2009: 15; Ogborn 2011). So far as scientific exchange is concerned, Diarmid Finnegan has inspected the speech protocols of two separate arenas – Exeter Hall and the Edinburgh Philosophical Institution – in mid-Victorian Britain. For the former, he has compellingly shown how the "reputation and regulation" of this speech space "shaped pronouncements about the relations between science and evangelical religion" (Finnegan 2011a: 47). The genteel "platform science" of the latter was no less "conformed to local expectations and customs, and reconfigured . . . according to agendas forged elsewhere" (Finnegan 2011b: 154, 155). This kind of analysis pinpoints the ways in which scientific speech was carefully managed in different discursive settings.

Because settings place limits on what can be said and heard, scientific discourse operates differently in public spaces and in camera, in formal gatherings and in private salons, in conferences and consultations, in courtrooms and clinics. In all these theaters of engagement different operational tactics, codes of behavior, communication conventions, and so on, pertain. And individuals moving between these spaces adjust their idiomatic forms – code-switching – to suit the setting because, to use Peter Burke's words, they are "performing different 'acts of identity' according to the situation in which they find themselves" (Burke 2004: 6).

Cultivating a sensitivity to formal and informal rules of engagement in different theaters of operation is critical to getting a handle on some high-profile spectacles in the history of scientific culture wars. Take the infamous altercation between Darwin's "bulldog" Thomas Henry Huxley and Archbishop Samuel – Soapy Sam – Wilberforce at the 1860 meeting of the British Association for the Advancement of Science over Darwin's recently published *Origin of Species*. What did that tussle amount to? Attending to whether or not rhetorical decorum was breached during that row is fundamental to interpreting the event. Matters of etiquette were certainly in the minds of those who later reflected on the occasion. Frederick William Farrar, for example, recalled that what Wilberforce said was neither vulgar nor insolent, but flippant, not least when he seemed to degrade women by pondering whether anyone would be willing to trace their descent from an ape through their *grandmother*. Everyone, as he recalled it, thought that the bishop "had forgotten to behave like a gentleman" and that Huxley "had got a victory in the respect of *manners* and *good breeding*" (Lucas 1979: 327). And yet, while later writers placed Huxley on the side of civility, at the time both the *Athenaeum* and *Jackson's Oxford Journal* thought he was the more ill-mannered of the two. So . . . did the bulldog bite the bishop, or did the bishop badmouth the bulldog? It all depends on the informal communicative regime that governed the speech space that June afternoon.

Of course violating discursive protocol can be a deliberate tongue-tactic. At the infamous 1874 Belfast meeting of the British Association, John Tyndall's taunting speech provoked precisely the reaction he wanted. "Every pulpit in Belfast thundered of me," he gleefully confided to a close friend (Barton 1987: 116). So when a local almanac railed against the "very bad taste" he had exhibited in his address, and when William MacIlwaine (1874–1875: 82) told the Belfast Naturalists' Field Club that same winter that his speech was "a violation of the rules of good taste" and nothing short of "reprehensible," there is reason to suspect that this was exactly what Tyndall had intended.

To make sense of public controversies over scientific issues – whether revolving around Darwinian evolution or to do with divisive topics from climate change to genetically modified crops, from laser-guided weapon systems to stem cell research – the specific theater of engagement for any particular skirmish is a primary point of hermeneutic departure.

## Trading Zones

Presumptions of warfare between scientific findings and philosophical commitment, or religious belief, or ethical conviction and the like don't map well onto the shifting lines of cultural history. But more. They miss the range of "trading zones" that have characterized science's relations with human culture in different times and places. The idea of the "trading zone," as an anthropological tool, has been mobilized to describe something of the processes by which different cultures have been able to exchange commodities despite their differences in language, social relations, and so on. Peter Galison has deployed this notion in his investigations of how physicists and engineers from different traditions went about collaborating with each other to develop radar and particle detectors. The metaphor of a trading zone helped explain how transactions could take place, and how rules of transaction could be elaborated, even when the partners "ascribe utterly different significance to the objects being exchanged" (Galison 1997: 783). Here I use the term in a rather looser sense to refer to those arenas of engagement, those spaces of transaction, where the interface between science and other realms of cultural life has facilitated fruitful intellectual commerce.

The one-dimensional cartographers of bellicosity typically annihilate "trading-zone" spaces in their depictions of the relations between scientific enterprises and religious cultures. As such they miss the fertility of questions like "Why Were the First Anthropologists Creationists?" which Jonathan Marks posed and imaginatively answered in a 2010 issue of *Evolutionary Anthropology*. He turns first to the German anthropologist Rudolph Virchow, who rejected human evolution. Instead of presuming Whiggish foreclosure on such matters, he begins with what from a contemporary perspective might be thought a provocation: "In a dualistic framework that pits evolutionism against creationism – abstracted from time, culture, and nuance – one is tempted to see Virchow as a closed-minded representative of the old ways . . . In short, as an old fool, precisely as he was portrayed by Ernst Haeckel, the leading spokesman for German Darwinism." That judgment, he argues, is woefully shallow. Presumptions that Virchow's rejection of the fossil evidence for evolution sprang from "backward-looking" creationism fails to take into account ways in which certain strands of nineteenth-century German creationist science could spring from anything other than "stupidity, intellectual conservatism, or religiosity" (Marks 2010: 222). In fact, a creationist explanation of human origins was widely adopted by early anthropologists because they were appalled at Ernst Haeckel's ultra-Darwinism, which undermined the psychic unity of the human species. That had nasty moral consequences. And at the same time it eroded the very foundations on which the whole science of ethnology was erected. Here a fertile historic "trading zone" between political ideology, moral philosophy, religious conviction, and anthropological inquiry lies exposed. Marks, moreover, intends his analysis as a contemporary parable. In the midst of today's science wars he insists that "it is possible to reject the racism of Philippe Rushton or James Watson, the evolutionary psychology of Steven Pinker, or the fanaticism of Richard Dawkins, and yet not be a creationist" (Marks 2010: 226).

In Darwin's own writings such trading zones are not hard to discern. And in this context two are worth mentioning. First, it is now well known that Darwin culled many of his metaphors from the prevailing political context of the time. Janet Browne (1996), for example, has noticed this and disclosed the profoundly imperial tone that pervaded a great deal of biogeographical writing in the Darwinian mode. This is hardly a surprising state of affairs given that a vast array of bio- and zoogeographical data were gathered by colonial officials. And as James Moore has shown, Darwin fastened on the language of colonization to depict the spread of plants and animals, and again and again in the *Origin of Species* has "his colonists 'beat,' 'conquer,' and 'exterminate' the 'aborigines' and 'natives'" (Moore 2005: 117).

Second, careful exegesis of his writings has revealed something of the extent to which Darwin made use of theological categories of understanding to attack special creation and shore up his own theory of evolution by natural selection. According to Stephen Dilley, "theology provided epistemic aid to evolution by its use of unbroken law and perhaps also shaped the content of evolution by endorsing a naturalized means of biological change" (Dilley 2012: 35. Seeing theology as "a handmaiden and accomplice to Darwin's science," not least when employed in an "artfully ambiguous" way, transgresses presumed firing-lines and exposes an exchange zone of significant intellectual commerce (Dilley 2012: 29, 33 also Brooke 1985; Richards 1997).

Transgressive trading-zone cartography could surely be extended. H. Allen Orr (1996) has written of the ways in which champions of Darwinian expansionism like Daniel Dennett attempt to "intimidate humanist opponents [by] rattling the saber of science" and thus ally themselves with the "armies of Progress" against "the mushy poets." Whatever the accuracy of that diagnosis, there is no doubt that such campaign tactics pay scant attention to dealings across the divide. As Diarmid Finnegan (2009) has pointed out, projects as diverse as Derrida's anti-essentialist posthumanism, Deleuze and Guattari's biophilosophy, Homi Bhabha's deployment of mimicry and hybridity, and Foucault's archaeological inquiries all stand in Darwin's long shadow. Such interchanges, of course, are not always edifying or beneficial. The serpentine criss-crossings of biology and ideology – whether to do with imperial dogma, racial supremacy, eugenic policy, *laissez-faire* economics, Soviet agronomy, or gender relations (Alexander and Numbers 2010) – reveal zones of exchange more akin to an intellectual black market.

## Wider Domains

In large part I have dwelt here on the Darwinian controversies as a means of saying something about how cultural geographers might tackle "science wars" more generally. The list of arenas of conflict is extensive: confrontations over scientific realism and anti-realism, racial history and genetic mapping, climate change and global warming, bio-informatics and the circulation of human tissue, ethnicity and intelligence, medical technology and transhumanism. This is just a sample of the regions which, I imagine, could profitably be inspected to see if resurveying the terrain might be enlightening. Certainly there seem to be *prima facie* grounds for suspecting that there is more going on than meets the eye in many groves of contemporary scientific culture. Disputes over the testing of vaccines and the use of body parts in biomedicine certainly stray well beyond even the most liberal self-circumscribed conception of "pure science" (Reid-Henry 2010; Parry 2008). The so-called "hockey stick" controversy in debates about global warming, over the technical accuracy of reconstructed thousand-year-long temperature records from proxies, shows just how culture-soaked scientific predictions and their policy use can be (Holland 2007). As for advances in neuroscience, the stakes come into sharp focus when one advocate announces in a scientific paper that "we have no more free will than a bowl of sugar" and that "the criminal justice system will need to adjust accordingly" (Cashmore 2010: 4503). Reterritorializing battlelines, inspecting the dynamics of different theaters of engagement, and identifying unexamined trading zones might prove useful tactics in these arenas too.

## Acknowledgments

For enlightening conversations and insightful commentary about this chapter I am extremely grateful to John Agnew, Keith Bennett, Diarmid Finnegan, Jerry Fodor, Nuala Johnson, Frances Livingstone, Justin Livingstone, Jon Marks, and Philip Orr.

## References

Alexander, D.R. and Numbers, R.L. (eds.) (2010) *Biology and Ideology from Descartes to Dawkins*. Chicago: University of Chicago Press.

Ball, P. (2010) Review of *What Darwin Got Wrong*. *Sunday Times*, February 21.

Barton, R. (1987) John Tyndall, pantheist: A rereading of the Belfast address. *Osiris*, 2nd series, 3, 111–134.

Bennett, K.D. (2004) Continuing the debate on the role of Quaternary environmental change for macroevolution. *Philosophical Transactions of the Royal Society of London, Series B*, 359, 295–303.

Bennett, K.D. (2010) The chaos theory of evolution. *New Scientist*, 208 (2782), 28–31.

Block, N. and Kitcher, P. (2010) Misunderstanding Darwin. Boston Review, March/April. http://bostonreview.net/BR35.2/block_kitcher.php (accessed October 30, 2012).

Brooke, J.H. (1985) The relations between Darwin's science and his religion. In *Darwinism and Divinity*, ed. J. Durant. New York: Oxford University Press, pp. 40–75.

Browne, J. (1996) Biogeography and empire. In *Cultures of Natural History*, ed. N. Jardine, J.A. Secord, and E.C. Spary. Cambridge: Cambridge University Press, pp. 305–321.

Burke, P. (2004) *Languages and Communities in Early Modern Europe*. Cambridge: Cambridge University Press.

Cashmore, A.R. (2010) The Lucretian swerve: The biological basis of human behavior and the criminal justice system. *Proceedings of the National Academy of Sciences*, 107, 4499–4504.

Coyne, J. (2010a) The improbability pump. The Nation, May 10. http://www.thenation.com/article/improbability-pump?page=full (accessed October 30, 2012).

Coyne, J. (2010b) Can *New Scientist* get any worse on evolution? http://whyevolutionistrue.wordpress.com/2010/11/05/can-new-scientist-get-any-worse-on-evolution/ (accessed October 30, 2012).

Coyne, J. (2010c) *New Scientist* defends bad science. http://whyevolutionistrue.wordpress.com/2010/11/09/new-scientist-defends-bad-science/ (accessed October 30, 2012).

Dennett, D. (2009) Darwin's "strange inversion of reasoning." *Proceedings of the National Academy of Sciences*, 106 (Supplement 1), 10061–10065.

Desmond, A. and Moore, J. (2009) *Darwin's Sacred Cause: Race, Slavery and the Quest for Human Origins*. London: Allen Lane.

Dilley, S. (2012) Charles Darwin's use of theology in the *Origin of Species*. *British Journal for the History of Science*, 45 (1), 29–56.

Dupré, J. (2010) Review: *What Darwin Got Wrong*. TPM: The Philosophers Magazine, 50 (July 23). http://www.thephilosophersmagazine.com/index.php/TPM/issue/view/TPM-50 (accessed November 5, 2012).

Eagleton, T. (2010) *Reason, Faith, and Revolution: Reflections on the God Debate*. New Haven: Yale University Press.

Finnegan, D. (2009) Darwin, dead and buried? *Environment and Planning D*, 42, 259–261.

Finnegan, D. (2011a) Exeter-Hall science and evangelical rhetoric in mid-Victorian Britain. *Journal of Victorian Culture*, 16, 46–64.

Finnegan, D. (2011b) Placing science in an age of oratory: Spaces of scientific speech in mid-Victorian Edinburgh. In *Geographies of Nineteenth Century Science*, ed. D.N. Livingstone and C.W.J. Withers. Chicago: University of Chicago Press, pp. 153–177.

Fodor, J. (2007) Why pigs don't have wings. *London Review of Books*, 29 (20), October 18.

Fodor, J. (2008) Against Darwinism. *Mind and Language*, 23, 1–24.

Fodor, J. (2011) From the Darwin wars. Unpublished MS.

Fodor, J. and Piattelli-Palmarini, M. (2010) *What Darwin Got Wrong*. New York: Picador.

Fodor, J. and Piattelli-Palmarini, M. (2011) *What Darwin Got Wrong: Updated Edition, with a New Afterword*. New York: Picador.

Futuyma, D.J. (2010) Two critics without a clue. *Science*, 328, 293.

Galison, P. (1997) *Image and Logic: A Material Culture of Microphysics*. Chicago: University of Chicago Press.

Godfrey-Smith, P. (2010) Letter. *London Review of Books*, 32 (15), August.

Gould, S.J. and Lewontin, R.C. (1979) The spandrels of San Marco and the panglossian paradigm: A critique of the adaptationist programme. *Proceedings of the Royal Society of London, Series B, Biological Sciences*, 205, 581–598.

Holland, D. (2007) Bias and concealment in the IPCC process: The "hockey-stick" affair and its implications. *Energy and Environment*, 18, 951–983.

Hornstein, N. (2010) An outline of the Fodor & Piattelli-Palmarini argument against natural selection. *Biolinguistics*, 4, 382–384.

Lawton, G. (2010) Blog post. http://whyevolutionistrue.wordpress.com/2010/11/09/new-scientist-defends-bad-science/

Lewontin, R. (2010) Not so natural selection. *New York Review of Books*, May 27.

Livingstone, D.N. (2007) Science, speech and space: Scientific knowledge and the spaces of rhetoric. *History of the Human Sciences*, 20, 71–98.

Livingstone, D.N. (forthcoming) *Dealing with Darwin: Place, Politics and Poetics in Religious Engagements with Evolution*. Baltimore: Johns Hopkins University Press.

Lucas, J.R. (1979) Wilberforce and Huxley: A legendary encounter. *Historical Journal*, 22, 313–330.

MacIlwaine, W. (1874–1875) Presidential address. *Proceedings of the Belfast Naturalists' Field Club*, 81–99.

Marks, J. (2010) Why were the first anthropologists creationists? *Evolutionary Anthropology*, 19, 222–226.

Marks, J. (2012) Evolutionary ideologies. In *Pragmatic Evolution: Applications of Evolutionary Theory*, ed. A. Poiani. Cambridge: Cambridge University Press, pp. 297–312.

Midgley, M. (2010) Review of *What Darwin Got Wrong*. *Guardian*, February 6.

Moore, J. (2005) Revolution of the space invaders: Darwin and Wallace on the geography of life. In *Geography and Revolution*, ed. D.N. Livingstone and C.W.J. Withers. Chicago: University of Chicago Press, pp. 137–159.

Morris, S.C. (2010) Mindless evolution. Big Questions Online, August 17. http://www.bigquestionsonline.com/columns/simon-conway-morris/mindless-evolution (no longer active).

Ogborn, M. (2009) Francis Williams's bad language: Historical geography in a world of practice. *Historical Geography*, 37, 5–25.

Ogborn, M. (2011) The power of speech: Orality, oaths and evidence in the British Atlantic world, 1650–1800. *Transactions of the Institute of British Geographers*, 36, 109–125.

Okasha, S. (2010) Whites and blues. *Times Literary Supplement*, March 16.

Orr, H.A. (1996) Dennett's strange idea. Natural selection: Science of everything, universal acid, cure for the common cold . . . Boston Review. http://bostonreview.net/BR21.3/Orr.html (accessed October 30, 2012).

Parry, B. (2008) Entangled exchange: Reconceptualising the characterisation and practice of bodily commodification. *Geoforum*, 39, 1133–1144.

Pigliucci, M. (2010) A misguided attack on evolution. *Nature*, 464, 353–354.

Reid-Henry, S.M. (2010) *The Cuban Cure: Reason and Resistance in Global Science*. Chicago: University of Chicago Press.

Richards, R.J. (1997) Theological foundations of Darwin's theory of evolution. In *Experiencing Nature*, ed. P.H. Theerman and K.H. Parshall. Dordrecht: Kluwer Academic Publishers, pp. 61–79.

Richards, R.J. (2010) Darwin tried and true. *American Scientist*, 98 (3), May/June. http://www.americanscientist.org/bookshelf/pub/darwin-tried-and-true (accessed October 30, 2012).

Robinson, M. (2010) *Absence of Mind: The Dispelling of Inwardness from the Modern Myth of the Self*. New Haven: Yale University Press.

Ruse, M. (2010) Origin of the specious. Boston Globe, February 14. http://articles.boston.com/2010-02-14/ae/29329727_1_natural-selection-darwinism-evolutionary-theory (accessed October 30, 2012).

Spurway, N. (2010) Review of *What Darwin Got Wrong. ESSSAT – News*, 20 (4), 7–12.

Stenhouse, J. (1996) "A disappearing race before we came here" : Doctor Alfred Kingcome Newman, the dying Maori, and Victorian scientific racism. *New Zealand Journal of History*, 30, 124–140.

Stenhouse, J. (1999) Darwinism in New Zealand, 1859–1900. In *Disseminating Darwinism: The Role of Place, Race, Religion, and Gender*, ed. R.L. Numbers and J. Stenhouse. New York: Cambridge University Press.

Stephens, L.D. (2000) *Science, Race, and Religion in the American South: John Bachman and the Charleston Circle of Naturalists, 1815–1895*. Chapel Hill: University of North Carolina Press.

White, A.D. (1896) *A History of the Warfare of Science with Theology in Christendom*. New York: Appleton.

Wood, D.M. (2011) Debating science and religion: Towards a comparative geography of public controversy, 1874–1895. PhD thesis, Queen's University Belfast.

Yalcinkaya, M.A. (2011) Science as an ally of religion: A Muslim appropriation of "the conflict thesis." *British Journal for the History of Science*, 44, 161–181.

# Circulations/Networks/Fixities

*The Wiley Blackwell Companion to Cultural Geography*, First Edition.
Edited by Nuala C. Johnson, Richard H. Schein, and Jamie Winders.
© 2013 John Wiley & Sons, Ltd. Published 2016 by John Wiley & Sons, Ltd.

Chapter 33

# From Global Dispossession to Local Repossession: Towards a Worldly Cultural Geography of Occupy Activism

*Matthew Sparke*

Occupy Wall Street (OWS) activism in 2011 suddenly tied global cities associated with the boom times of financial globalization to a world of discontent linked to global dispossession. Doing so most novelly within the affluent urban control centers and partially privatized public spaces of American capitalism, the direct action of the OWS encampments and associated protests also made a global capitalist class – the so-called 1 percent – a new focus for global critique. As Naomi Klein explained in a speech to OWS activists at Zuccotti Park, there was an important political–geographic shift made manifest in this critique: a shift from a geography of blaming territories – wealthy nation-states – to targeting transnational geographies of class domination. "It seems as if there aren't any more rich countries," she underlined. "Just a whole lot of rich people. People who got rich looting the public wealth and exhausting natural resources around the world. The point is today everyone can see that the system is deeply unjust and careening out of control" (Klein 2011). Here, I want to argue that this shift was also very much a cultural–geographic shift too, partly because of how it reframed and communicated concerns about global class domination through local place-based action, but also because of how it simultaneously made clear the worldwide resonance and relays of the activism in articulating new communities of cross-border and cross-cultural solidarity. Critical awareness about the global system careening out of control was thereby spreading from places in the global South, where it had long been obvious, to places of former plenty and complicity. "The world has come to Occupy Wall Street," noted Andy Kroll, in an article that went on to document the multiple cross-cultural connections articulated by and in the new global–local ties:

> Mayssa Sultan, an Egyptian American . . . , says her compatriots decided to support the occupation after hearing that Occupy Wall Street had taken inspiration from the Tahrir Square

*The Wiley Blackwell Companion to Cultural Geography*, First Edition.
Edited by Nuala C. Johnson, Richard H. Schein, and Jamie Winders.
© 2013 John Wiley & Sons, Ltd. Published 2016 by John Wiley & Sons, Ltd.

revolution. "The voices being heard at Occupy Wall Street and all the other occupied cities around the country are very similar to Tahrir," she says, "in that people who don't have work, don't have health care, are seeing education being pulled back, they are trying to make their voices heard." (Kroll, 2011)

It is now textbook teaching that cultural geography in the age of globalization must explore how the cultural politics of place embody global ties and tensions (Domosh *et al.* 2009). The text and texture of local landscapes need, thus, to be read against the context of global–local interdependencies; and when used to transcend scale-limited analysis, cultural geography can contribute to wider efforts to reimagine the spatial scope of ethics, activism, and politics more generally (e.g., Featherstone *et al.* 2012; Massey 2011; Newstead, Reid, and Sparke 2003; Panelli 2007; Popke 2006). Professional geographers, though, by no means hold a monopoly on this trans-local reimagination of ethico-political space (Barnett 2010). Thus, although she is more widely seen as a global justice activist, it is testament to Klein's cultural–geographic skill that her speech in Zuccotti Park highlighted the global geographies of dispossession that formed the back-story to the protestors' local, lower-Manhattan geography of repossession. Likewise, Mayssa Sultan, the Egyptian-American activist quoted by Kroll, reframed the occupation of Wall Street as a local site of activism that was both inspired by and inspiring of other efforts at global resistance. Such critical moves towards contextualizing local repossession amidst broader struggles against global dispossession do not represent a rejection of the strategy of occupying and culturally recoding particular public spaces. Indeed, Klein praised the protestors precisely for turning a center of financial calculation and control into a fixed spatial target of local direct action. At the same time, however, like Sultan, Kroll, and many others, the rest of Klein's argument also effectively urged her audience to see this target in more global terms, to see it as a control center of global processes of dispossession. Reflecting on these activist efforts at contextualization, this chapter explores what contexts, cultural discourses, and power relations, and thus what space-spanning geo-graphies of resistance a worldly cultural geography of Occupy activism might encompass.[1]

Another way of summing up the aim here is as a question: namely, how best can cultural geographers learn from and contribute to the critical cultural work of Occupy activists and allies who themselves reflect on the multiple local meanings, diverse global ties, and thus complex geo-graphical layerings of activist space? There are many useful academic examples to draw on in this respect, examples that also indicate ways around some of the most common intellectual pitfalls (for a longer review of geographies of resistance, see Sparke 2008). Critical geographers have shown that it is possible to study "convergence spaces" of activism and transnational grievance in ways that avoid romanticizing place-based resistance or interpreting it through managerial and governmental frameworks that obscure the relational construction of militant particularism (Featherstone 2003, 2005; Koopman 2008; Massey 2011; Routledge 2003). They have suggested that "accumulation by dispossession" works as a term for describing a shared concern of contemporary global justice movements (Harvey 2005), but only insofar as the analysis of dispossession dynamics stretches from the economic appropriations of neoliberalization to associated forms of sexual, racial, and xenophobic dispossession as well (Gilmore 2007; Harvey 2010; Pulido 2006, 2007; Winders 2007; Wright 2005, 2006). They have shown that we can simultaneously denaturalize dispossession through relational comparisons and through efforts to map counter-topographies of transnational struggle (Katz 2005; Hart 2006, 2007; McKittrick 2006; Sundberg 2007; Wainright 2007). Finally, they have collaboratively explored the serious economic, peda- gogic, and community-building lessons of sharing non-neoliberal truths about dispossession without losing sight of the humor and solidarity that can animate the "alter-geopolitical" war on error (Datta *et al.* 2010; Koopman 2011; Sparke *et al.* 2005; Wills 2004; Routledge 2003, 2012).

Based on these critical theoretical lessons, cultural-geographic readings of how local repos- session relates to global dispossession can clearly go in diverse directions, or at least they should (Sparke 2007a). Nonetheless, there are challenges that come with using clunky catego- ries such as the "global" and "local." Seen as spatially contained absolutes or as a form of scalar-turned-causal hierarchy, these terms risk reconsolidating a simple binary opposition of economic base (the space of dispossession) and cultural superstructure (the place of repos- session). They also may be mistaken for implying a top-down "impact" model of globalization that makes place-based resistance seem either useless or, alternatively, an idealistic incarnation of global revolutionary spirit. Relatedly, they might be used to impute immodest truth-claims about the immediate (and thus unmediated and ultimately unproven) purchase of globally universalizing ideas on local events (Barnett 2011). Here, by contrast, the more modest aim is to problematize these sorts of pre-Occupy assumptions – pre-occupations, we might call them – by instead examining how the global and local are interwoven in seven particular "problem spaces" that Occupy activism has brought into focus.

While Wall Street was the initial problem space targeted by US protestors, their adaptation of Arab Spring anti-authoritarianism and their diverse arguments against inequality and financial authoritarianism in the United States made clear that the problems at issue stretched far and wide from lower Manhattan to multiple lives foreclosed on by economic distress and dispossession (see, for example, the "We Are the 99%" blog at http://wearethe99percent. tumblr.com/). Diverse accounts of the suffering of the 99 percent indicated that the spatially fixed focus for OWS was tied to far-reaching concerns with all the inequalities and injustices associated with the fall-out from the failed spatial fix for global finance in the US housing boom-turned-bust (on the latter, see Harvey 2010). For the same reasons, the targeting of other centers of business-class authority took off across the United States and in many other parts of the world, a take-off everywhere that revealed the wide contemporary resonance of the critique of the 1 percent in a time of global economic crisis for the 99 percent. Reflecting on this global spread of Occupy activism, it is possible, therefore, to trace ties between what can usefully be labeled the (1) target space, (2) everywhere space, and (3) time-space of the movement. These ties have, in turn, opened up new kinds of (4) shared space, (5) teaching space, and (6) affect space that transform the problems into opportunities. These newly opened spaces have themselves made it possible to reexamine and remake another sort of problem space – namely (7) a utopian space for imagining alternatives. To be sure, all the labels used here to distinguish these seven problem spaces only begin to communicate the complexities of communication and representation that comprise the cultural geographies of each space. Catachresis (the effortful over-stretching of a word's meaning and application) is inherent in all such naming, and the labels involved might initially seem overly telegraphic rather than geographic. The suggestion in what follows, however, is that they at least serve as signposts for the kinds of interpretive and translational work that needs to be done by a geography of Occupy activism that aspires simultaneously to the catachrestic articulation of "worldly" and "cultural" as geo-graphy.

## (1) Target Space

Near the start of her Zuccotti Park speech, Naomi Klein told the protestors that she thought their spatial strategy of occupation was an important innovation in progressive struggle. She argued that the focus on the fixed target of Wall Street was giving the movement a sustained hold on the popular imagination that previous anti-neoliberal street protests sometimes lacked. Making her comparison with the anti-WTO protests in Seattle in 1999 and similar subsequent events, she noted that she was still "proud to have been part of what we called 'the movement of movements'." However, she continued:

> there are important differences too. For instance, we chose summits as our targets: the World Trade Organization, the International Monetary Fund, the G8. Summits are transient by their nature, they only last a week. That made us transient too. We'd appear, grab world headlines, then disappear. And in the frenzy of hyper patriotism and militarism that followed the 9/11 attacks, it was easy to sweep us away completely, at least in North America. Occupy Wall Street, on the other hand, has chosen a fixed target. (Klein 2011)

Similar target talk was also used in *The Nation* by John Nichols, who underlined the political value of naming and shaming Wall Street as a way of addressing "the heart of the matter."

> *The target is right.* This has been a year of agitation, from Wisconsin to Ohio to Washington. It has seen some of the largest demonstrations in recent American history in defense of labor rights, public education, public services. But all those uprisings attacked symptoms of the disease. Occupy Wall Street named it. By aiming activism not at the government but at the warren of bankers, CEOs and hedge-fund managers to whom the government is beholden, Occupy Wall Street went to the heart of the matter. (Nichols 2011)

At one level, these points about Occupy being focused on the correct spatial target were very simple. The targeting was proving meaningful to broad audiences because it was zeroing in directly on the financial agents of dispossession. By creating a fixed spatial focus for protest, it additionally gave the protestors staying power, allowing their criticisms to be heard for more than just one news cycle, although an argument can be made that the legacies of anti-neoliberal organizing still endure in older summit cities such as Seattle (Sparke 2011). Practically, and very geographically on the ground, the targeting of Wall Street pointed directly to financial industry class interests, the interests of the 1 percent, that more normally elude systemic criticism thanks to unaccountable and aspatial talk about invisible market forces and abstract economic imperatives. This form of targeting could also travel, of course. By making particular places rather than individuals or corporations or summit meetings the targets, however, it represented a significant innovation in global justice activism.

For all the same reasons, the praise for the protestors' targeting was not shared by *The Economist*. Always keen to signal market expertise in its attempts to promote pro-market policy (and expand its market share amongst business weeklies in the United States), the magazine issued an editorial in October 2011 that sought to suggest OWS was, in fact, spatially off-target. "In more than one sense," it judged, "the protest can seem misplaced. Some of the biggest financial firms left Wall Street for midtown Manhattan years ago" (*The Economist* 2011). This claim on empirical exactitude was itself a bit beside the point. It did not address the much wider movements of financial firms out of Manhattan altogether, the transfer of back-office work and data storage to New Jersey, the expansion of hedge fund and derivatives trading in Connecticut, and so on. Nor did it even begin to broach the much more profound global shifts in the geography of financial calculation to non-American market centers in Asia and Europe. But a certain wariness about these same global markets and whether they might yet get "spooked" still meant that in the end *The Economist* acknowledged that the cultural–geographic targeting of Wall Street could potentially achieve results. "With more muscle behind them, the protesters could yet change the world," it declared, albeit adding a 1-percent lament that "the shift might not be to any*one's* advantage" (*The Economist* 2011, emphasis added). In other words, while it sought to diminish the targeting of Wall Street as inaccurate, even *The Economist* concluded that the spatial fix for the protests might generate results.

Implicit in all this target talk and target assessment, something more complex was at work too. The cultural geography of the target as a problem space was by no means a simple geography of blame, much to the chagrin of far-right reactionaries who depicted the protestors as a demonic "Flea Party" mob ruining the Tea Party's more nationalistic and xenophobic reasons for hating Wall Street cosmopolitans such as George Soros (e.g., Coulter 2011). Advocates for Occupy, instead, turned the target space into a problem space by repeatedly underlining Wall Street's links to processes of dispossession in *other* places beyond lower Manhattan, including other places abroad as well as in the United States. Like so many of the activist arguments reported out of Zuccotti Park, Nichols and other critically minded commentators wanted to join up the dots between centers of financial expropriation and all the other places, the unreported real-world geographies of the 99 percent, experiencing austerity, foreclosure, unemployment, and diminished social citizenship rights. For the same reason, their target talk was quite distinct from the post-9/11 militarization of public discourse in "the age of the world target" (Chow 2006). Comments such as Klein's directly tied praise of the targeting to the quite different desire of global justice activists to recover from "the frenzy of hyper patriotism and militarism that followed the 9/11 attacks." This, then, was actually a reversal and replacement of the usual militarization of thinking found in popular target-talk in news on sports and business. Normally, this talk is associated with place-particularizing uses of metaphors such as "targets of opportunity" (Weber 2005) or masculinist ideas about penetrating and mastering place (Sparke 1995). By contrast, the reversal represented by Klein's usage recalled the original defensive idea that Samuel Weber suggests lies latent in any appeal to targets, an idea that is tied to the fact that what makes a target significant in the first place is the way in which it is linked up through a set of network relations to other people and places.

Weber acknowledges that the verb "targeting" implies that the particularities of time and space can "be transformed from media of alteration and dislocation into conditions of self-fulfillment and appropriation" (2005: 5). Against this, he suggests that in the end, targets tend to resist such singularizing spatial subsumption (Sparke 2008). Indeed, even military targeting ends up having to come to terms with the trans-local interspatial relationalities that make targets "opportunities" for attack in the first place. As Derek Gregory (2011) has shown with his detailed cultural geographies of the US air war, Pentagon planners have been compelled by the network logic of targeting to expand their bombing runs, drone attacks, and cyber hits into a globally expansive, border-crossing, and networked "everywhere war." By contrast, the global spread of Occupy activism has articulated a critique of vulnerability everywhere. Camping out in cities across the world, this targeting has also clearly crossed borders and gone global. Instead of creating global kill-chains that put "warheads on forehcads," though, it has sought to imagine and construct new sorts of global care-chains across the everywhere space of shared discontent with dispossession. It is to this articulation of everywhere space as a problem space for solidarity and activism that we now turn.

## (2) Everywhere Space

While the border-crossing aspect of the Occupy movement unnerved *The Economist* and other business commentators, it simultaneously heartened many progressive activists. Rebecca Solnit put it like this:

> If what's been happening locally and globally has some of the characteristics of an uprising, then there has never been one quite so pervasive – from the scientists holding an Occupy sign in Antarctica to Occupy presences in places as far-flung as New Zealand and Australia, São Paulo, Frankfurt, London, Toronto, Los Angeles, and Reykjavik. (Solnit 2011)

Such commentary on the global spread of Occupy protests was itself widespread, frequently taking the form of online photo galleries featuring multinational, multi-lingual, multi-colored, and multi-issue protestors rallying in the name of the 99 percent (e.g., *The Guardian* 2011). For Solnit herself, this global scope of the protests presented a useful response to the "so what now?" questions being asked by less sympathetic observers and policymakers.

> Surely the only possible answer to the tired question of where Occupy should go from here . . . is: everywhere. I keep being asked what Occupy should do next, but it's already doing it. It is everywhere. (Solnit 2012)

This hopeful geographic reimagination of everywhere space as the future may not have fully answered the questions about alternatives – something I return to below in the reflections on Occupy's utopian space. Nor did it acknowledge the geographic unevenness in the intensity of activism – that it was more urban than suburban or rural, more coastal than middle American, and more American than planetary. However, the articulation of "everywhere" as the all-encompassing geography of resistance was nevertheless a common meme of commentary, including commentary by less optimistic observers too. The US electoral pollster Nate Silver, for example, published an article on his *New York Times* blog entitled "The Geography of Occupying Wall Street (and Everywhere Else)" (2011). Here, the invocation of "everywhere" accompanied an analysis of protestor numbers across the United States, documenting that the largest Occupy protests in October 2011 were happening "far from Wall Street itself" on the West coast. "Despite Occupy Wall Street's name," Silver concluded, "its energy seems to be coming from the left coast."

Two wider forms of cultural–geographic accountability have followed efforts to denote the everywhere space of Occupy. The first concerns the global inspirations and transnational solidarities that originally enabled the movement to take place (and thereby remake the cultural geography of place) in New York City. The second involves mapping where the movement has subsequently moved, using media reports and crowd-sourcing on the world wide web.

On the first, it is now well known that the original call to bring a tent to Wall Street on September 17, 2011, itself came across the border from Adbusters, a culture-jamming anti-capitalist, or at least anti-commodification magazine based in Vancouver, Canada. The

Adbusters blog further underlined the internationalism of its call by asking: "Are your ready for a Tahrir moment?" (*Adbusters* 2011). This question undoubtedly reflected a longer history (and wider cultural geography) of cross-border culture-jamming in the netroots globalization of global cities (Huse 2007). More than this, however, it further reflected the international collaboration involved in actually organizing the practicalities of OWS. As Kroll explained it, this planning process involved a diverse group of activists who met at an artist's space near Wall Street on the fourth floor of 16 Beaver Street to talk about global transformation:

> There were New Yorkers in the room, but also Egyptians, Spaniards, Japanese, Greeks. Some had played a part in the Arab Spring uprising; others had been involved in the protests catching fire across Europe. (Kroll 2011)

While the planning had the considerable involvement and experience of local New Yorkers to draw on, including the organizing lessons of New Yorkers Against Budget Cuts, it thus involved other global justice activists with experience from uprisings all over the globe. In Kroll's assessment, this involvement was key.

> [The] international spirit would galvanize Occupy Wall Street, connecting it with the protests in Cairo's Tahrir Square and Madrid's Puerta del Sol, the heart of Spain's populist uprising. Just as a comic book about Martin Luther King Jr. and civil disobedience, translated into Arabic, taught Egyptians about the power of peaceful resistance, the lessons of Egypt, Greece, and Spain fused together in downtown Manhattan. (Kroll 2011)

Beyond describing the internationalism of Occupy's global inspirations and reverberations, the cultural geography of charting everywhere space took a more detailed cartographic form in online mapping efforts. *Huffington Post*, *Mother Jones*, *The Guardian*, *AlJazeera*, and even the GIS company ESRI took up this challenge, adding diverse sources of information and formats to the "User Map" of "attendee" occupations on the website of Occupy Wall Street.[2] As a mix of crowd-sourced and journalism-based online maps, these cartographies of everywhere space dramatically documented the space-spanning spread of Occupy activism, both nationally and internationally. Most tellingly perhaps (but also most fleetingly), the sites based on geo-data from Twitter and Facebook captured the popular fascination with Occupy in a way that pictured it as zeitgeist ghosting across the everywhere space of online social media (rather than across embodied space on the ground). Cravify.com offered its audience a map of global Occupy-related tweets. Its creator, Humphrey Flowerdew, explained that he was more interested in the technology than the politics of the resulting maps; but he still testified to the global (and comparative) perspectives on everywhere space produced by the online mapping. "If you zoom out to the whole world and see the tweets coming out of America and the Western world and compare those to the tweets coming out of Asia," he said, "it's interesting to see the perspective people take. And those are different than [the tweets coming] from South America and Africa . . . It conveys the worldwide nature of it" (Kessler 2011). Adding a historical sensibility to this zoom-lens enframing of everywhere space, *Huffington Post*'s map allowed viewers to watch the movement's increasing popularity over time – as indexed by geo-tagged Facebook "Likes" mapped on the website collective-disorder.com. "Click the play button on the map," said the *Huffington Post* page, "to view the movement's growth from October 3 through November 9." As a cartographic coda, the

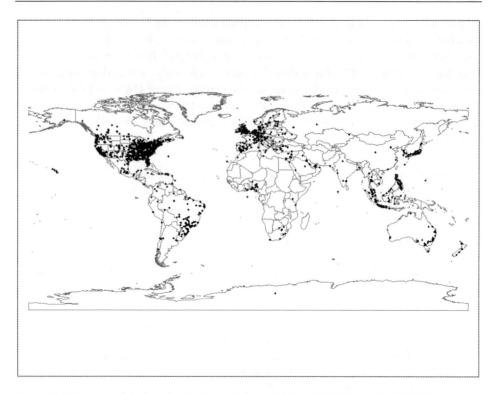

**Figure 33.1** Occupy-related geolocated tweets from October 15 to November 5, 2011.
Source: specially reformatted for this publication by Josef Eckert with the permission of the UW Social Media Lab (see also Eckert 2012).

online wiki world map Open Street Map subsequently included a whole series of entries mapping particular encampments in particular cities but also deleting them when protestors were evicted.

Geographers studying the rise of crowd-sourced cartography and the so-called "geoweb" have already played a role as participant-observers in this online mapping of everywhere space. Alan McConchie, a geography PhD student at the University of British Columbia, developed a blog entitled "Mapping Mashups" dedicated to listing online Occupy map sites; and Josef Eckert, a geography PhD student at the University of Washington, helped create a color-coded, user-friendly Google map of OWS.[3] Eckert also worked with colleagues in the Social Media Lab at the university to create a more rigorous global mapping of Occupy-related geolocated tweets from October 15 to November 5, 2011 (Figure 33.1). This ongoing mapping of everywhere space promises to make useful interventions in disciplinary debates over participatory geovisualization, the geoweb, and the possibilities for democratizing access and authority in crowd-sourced geographic information science (Elwood 2008, 2010). Key here are questions about how the volunteered aspects of the data (and the variations in forms of crowd "volunteering" involved) shape the status of the resulting maps as both geography and information (Goodchild 2007; Sparke 2010). Important, too, though, are other, more cultural–geographic questions about the optics, inclusions, and exclusions of the public mapping of everywhere space through the mediated and technologically trained "gaze" of the geoweb (cf. Wilson 2011).

Most obviously, there are the contrasts between the deliberate and open geocoding work of activists and the unaccountable private mapping of the protests by businesses providing maps to police and security agencies. The protestors' online maps can be seen as an innovation in counter-mapping, a new case of a surveyed population reworking the gaze of surveillance and thereby adding an interruptive and counter-hegemonic perspective that is *from* and *of* as well as *on* the crowd (Sparke 1998, 2010). The crowd-sourced Occupy mappings may also be seen as a contribution to the cartography of the commons, another example of using online maps to imagine newly public, political, and economic possibilities of place (St. Martin 2009). In addition, however, there are all sorts of exclusions to consider at the same time. Digital divides both within countries and internationally mean that only certain publics can freely participate in these innovations in participatory mapping. The technology, too, has neoliberal and radically individualizing aspects to it, linking the Occupy mappings with a wider genre of choice-maximizing online maps that allow one (including aspiring one-percenters too, no doubt) to see city space as a series of personalized shopping and recreational sites. Cravify.com, for example, seems to have moved on in this way to locating property, furniture, and electronics for rent and sale.

Juxtaposed to the all-encompassing enframing of individualized geographic choice are all the blank spots on online maps when they are zoomed up to enframe global space. Some of these blank spots on Occupy maps are significant because they indicate real disconnects between Occupy activism and other protest movements against dispossession (whether these be Maoists fighting land grabs in India, Palestinians resisting Israeli occupation, or Chinese migrant workers protesting labor conditions and sub-citizenship in the PRC's factory zones). In the Palestinian case, as in the cases of many indigenous groups demanding decolonization around the world, the disconnect with ongoing efforts at surviving hegemonic forms of occupation, and all their associated forms of exceptionalist mismapping (Gregory 2004), is as tragic as it is ironic. Nevertheless, in certain sites, Occupy activists overcame this disconnect and debated the implications of occupying "already occupied" land. "Seattle is already occupied Duwamish land," stated the poster of those demanding the decolonization of Occupy Seattle. In response, on Oct 19, 2011, the local General Assembly passed a declaration stating both that "the term 'occupation' has been used by imperialists to colonize indigenous lands" and that "the term 'occupation' has also been reclaimed by militant workers of color from Latin America (Oaxaca, Buenos Aires, South Korea, China among other places) to describe their occupation of factories, schools and neighborhoods, to strike back against the oppressive forces led by racism and capitalism. It is in this context that we use the term 'occupy'" (Black Orchid Collective 2011).

In yet other cases, the blank spots on the online maps of Occupy activism may have indexed the Western-centrism of the mapping itself. Most problematically, many of the online maps seemed to under-represent Occupy-associated protests in the global South. This appeared to be more a problem with the *Mother Jones* news-media-sourced mapping than with other maps like *The Guardian*'s that featured more direct crowd-sourcing and social-media feeds. Nevertheless, it was still a missed mapping (if not a mis-mapping) of both the heterogeneity and history of everywhere space. It missed the many inspirations for the Occupy movement found in the global South. It missed the great relevance and resonance of ongoing global-South critiques of austerity and the structural violence of financialized neoliberalization. It also missed the ways in which many of these critiques of 1 percent rule had already started imagining the global South as an inclusive everywhere space of 99-plus percentages long before the financial crisis of 2008–2012 (Sparke 2007b). This, for example, was how Vandana Shiva had described the global South back in 2005 in her scathing critique of Thomas Friedman's flat-world vision of globalization: a critique that pointed to the exclusivity and privilege that brought Friedman's flatness into view and that therefore argued that the flat world was really just an extreme 0.1 percent worldview ignoring the sweeping diversity of everywhere space. "Friedman presents a 0.1% picture," she argued, "and hides 99.9%" (Shiva 2005).

No doubt many other such imaginings of everywhere space – "a shared and common world," Shiva called it – can be identified amidst all the long-standing and ongoing critiques of Washington Consensus neoliberalism in the global South (e.g., Adiga quoted in Roy 2012: 546). However, while such worldly cultural geographies of the 99 percent clearly preexisted the Occupy movement and while they were not always well represented in online mappings, in 2011 they were suddenly much more resonant in places of former privilege and plenty. This resonance is probably why the concept–metaphor of everywhere space was suddenly in circulation as a way of articulating newly shared vulnerability. As foreclosure, unemployment, and economic anxiety continued for so many Americans and as the European economy flat-lined, Friedman-style geoeconomic myths about global flatness started to look as unconvincing to New Yorkers and Londoners as they had long looked to farmers and slum dwellers in India. The millennial marketing of the level playing field and the false image of prosperity and inclusion created by easy credit in American and European housing markets no longer matched an era of increasing alienation, exclusion, and struggle. There was, in this sense, a time-space to ideas about repossessing everywhere space; and it is to this time-space that I now turn.

## (3) Time-Space

As commentators attempted to make sense of the global take-off of Occupy protests, the explanation of changing times proved pivotal in understanding the expanding everywhere space of discontent. An editorial in London's *New Statesman* put it like this:

> London is one of 951 cities to witness protests in recent days. From Amsterdam to Athens, Berlin to Bogotá, Tokyo to Toronto, people have taken to the streets to protest against inequality and injustice. Leading the way are the disaffected young. The . . . new *événements*, unlike the antiglobalization protests that shook Seattle and Genoa a decade ago, enjoy the sympathy of the political mainstream. The last wave of protests took place at a time of easy credit, cheap oil and low unemployment; the current wave accompanies the largest fall in living standards since the 1920s. (*New Statesman* 2011)

Similarly, in her own reflections on why the Occupy movement was resonating more powerfully in the United States in 2011 than the global justice movement had in the first decade of the new millennium, Naomi Klein emphasized that the times had changed:

> The biggest difference a decade makes is that in 1999, we were taking on capitalism at the peak of a frenzied economic boom. Unemployment was low, stock portfolios were bulging. The media was drunk on easy money. Back then it was all about start-ups, not shutdowns. [And] while the good times rolled, taking on an economic system based on greed was a tough sell, at least in rich countries. (Klein 2011)

In 2011, by contrast, in the new period after the financial crash, after the bailouts for the banks, and amidst all the ongoing suffering of economic crisis, critical arguments about the dangers of market fundamentalism now seemed to make sense everywhere. Everywhere that is, except inside the institutions of the Wall Street–Washington axis and, thus, inside a White House where, in the words of political scientist Wendy Brown (2011), "the colossal failure of the Obama presidency to place even a light rein on neoliberal deregulation" now seemed so conspicuously out of sync with a historic moment of suffering. It was precisely this failure of neoliberal policymaking that was, in turn, making it possible for formerly middle-class Americans to see their acute class vulnerability, and thus, to articulate, albeit with populist percentile labels, the new need for a class politics in and for the 99 percent (Ehrenreich and Ehrenreich 2012).

At the same time, quite literally so, the anxieties of the rich themselves seemed to reflect acknowledgement of the problems and protests spreading everywhere. This at least was how Mike Davis saw the global situation in the Fall of 2011:

> What was inconceivable just a year ago, even to most Marxists, is now a spectre haunting the opinion pages of the business press: the imminent destruction of much of the institutional framework of globalization and undermining of the post-1989 international order. (Davis 2011)

For Davis, the time-space of imminent institutional breakdown represented a global specter newly haunting globalized capitalism. It was, in other words, a cultural–geographical rescaling of *The Communist Manifesto*'s nineteenth-century European specter in a twenty-first century time of instability everywhere. Such an argument, like those of Klein and the *New Statesman*, obviously emphasized the ties between the timing and the newly global scope of the problems and protests. Yet the carefully historicizing approach taken by Davis was by no means a simple epochal invocation of planetary end times, nor a zeitgeist announcement that ignored historical antecedents and comparisons. Davis, in fact, highlighted the transnational ties of protests past, including precursor occupations of US campuses and public spaces in the 1960s. He therefore traced the parallels between these predecessor protests (with their international inspirations in insurgencies in Asia and Latin America) and the trans-Atlantic inspirations of Occupy activism, the *indignados* in Europe with their own inspirational interlinkages with uprisings on the other side of the Mediterranean in Egypt and Tunisia.

However, Davis also was at pains to emphasize that this time, the times were different too. The crises of capitalism so common and brutal in the developing world were now being visited on former places of privilege and plenty, making it clear that critiques that had long issued out of the global South increasingly applied everywhere. "In 1968," he noted,

> few of the white youth protesting in Europe (with the important exception of Northern Ireland) and the United States shared the existential realities of their counterparts in countries of the South. Even if deeply alienated, most could look forward to turning college degrees into affluent middleclass careers. Today, in contrast, many of the protesters in New York, Barcelona and Athens face prospects dramatically worse than those of their parents and closer to those of their counterparts in Casablanca and Alexandria. Some of the occupiers of Zuccotti Park, if they had graduated ten years earlier, might have walked straight into $100,000 salaries at a hedge fund or investment bank. Today they work at Starbucks. (Davis 2011)

In other words, the time-space of Occupy activism seems to have been widely shaped by increasing unemployment and, in the United States and Europe, by a newly disturbing mix of underemployment and debt amongst populations that, up until 2008, had been deeply invested (culturally and psychologically as well as monetarily) in the landscapes of fictitious capital. Indeed, following the thread of Harvey's historical–geographical arguments about the parallels between the 1968 protests and the Paris Commune – parallels, he suggests, having to do with the failures of both US suburbanization and Haussmanization to fully secure political quiescence with a spatial fix for fictitious capital (Harvey 2010: 171) – we might even see the specific time-space of Occupy activism as tied to the fate of former US homeowners "who now live in tent cities because [the time-space] logic [of the global debt market] went haywire" (Harvey 2010: 190; see also Harvey 2011, 2012).

Other recent work suggests that today's global cultural geographies of unemployment and housing are still deeply divided and defined by class, caste, race, ethnicity, and sex (Hunter 2010; Jeffrey, 2010; Rankin 2012). Colonial conceits about waste still also structure how these time-spaces of waiting are described (Gidwani 2008). For related reasons, the bureaucratic metric of unemployment can itself reinforce North–South divisions insofar as its statistical counting and political–economic significance developed out of the experience of Fordist capitalism in rich countries, an experience that always remained elusive in the poor-country communities that saw postcolonial possibility eclipsed by the neocolonial vicissitudes of "wageless life" and structural adjustment (Denning 2010; Sparke 2012). To the extent that the rise of Occupy activism reflects the development of "wageless life" everywhere, however, including the emergence of an educated but underemployed "precariat" in global cities such as New York, it further underlines how the convergence space of contemporary protest simultaneously instantiates a convergence in time: a convergence time-space, then, of precarious life everywhere.

### (4) Shared Space, (5) Teaching Space, and (6) Affect Space

Social theorist Judith Butler argued in the wake of 9/11 that instead of the militarism that followed terrorism, an alternative response could have been developed around global mourning and reflection on shared vulnerability (2004). Moving on from that age of the world target with a reversal and replacement of militaristic targeting, it now seems that another aspect of the global convergence in Occupy activism may well be a renewed concern with just such shared vulnerability (Vrasti 2012). Conceptually, we might, therefore, see the intersection of Occupy's target space, everywhere space, and time-space in the new opportunities for political engagement it has made possible amidst global vulnerability. This is what seems to have been happening in embodied ways on the ground in the shared space, teaching space, and affect space of the encampments and associated protests.

Many blogs, photographs, and anecdotes testify to how Occupy activism has brought very different communities together to share their common sense of dismay and discontent with dispossession. Occupy thereby created what Solnit suggests is a shared space,

> a space in which people of all kinds can coexist, from the homeless to the tenured, from the inner city to the agrarian. Coexisting in public with likeminded strangers and acquaintances is one of the great foundations and experiences of democracy, which is why dictatorships ban gatherings and groups. (Solnit 2012)

To be sure, other recent US attempts to organize against dispossession – union rallies against neoliberal reforms in Wisconsin, for example, or the huge one-day protests against the dehumanization of US immigrants (Pulido 2007) – have also created shared spaces. These struggles have shown that organizing can go in more legislative and electoral directions, as well as into local cultural geographies of hybridized place-making (Smith and Winders 2008). The spaces of Occupy activism, however, have mobilized highly heterogeneous publics to share in and thereby produce cross-difference debating forums (Buell 2011). With union support and the collaboration of academics, community activists, housing activists, and all sorts of environmental activists, they have created shared spaces of radical democratic possibility (Laclau and Mouffe 1985; Massey 1995). But, as Jodi Dean (2011) has argued, they are shared in agonistic ways that go beyond electoral coalition politics, beyond conventional capitalistic constructions of consumer democracy, and even beyond abstract concepts of democracy as an inherently empty place. Filling places with argumentative campers, Occupy activism has instead offered a kind of communal rebuke to the consumerism and individualism of the neoliberal city and a reaffirmation of the shared meanings of place for citizen conversations rather than the consumption demanded by capital.

Meaning in the shared spaces of Occupy activism has been articulated in turn by the shared sounds of the "human microphone" through which the protestors have sought to overcome police bans on electronic amplification. It was also a constitutional feature of the elaborately and effortfully democratic General Assemblies through which Occupy encampments sought to self-govern. Having taken part in some of these in Oakland, Solnit celebrated the sharing across difference that was made possible politically.

> Once, for instance, I was in a breakout discussion group that included Native American, white, Latino, and able-bodied and disabled Occupiers, and in which I was likely the eldest participant; another time, a bunch of peacenik grandmothers dominated my group . . . Everyone showed up; everyone talked to everyone else; and in little tastes, in fleeting moments, the old divides no longer divided us and we felt like we could imagine ourselves as one society. This was the dream of the promised land – this land, that is, without its bitter divides. (Solnit 2012)

It is true that not all Occupy encampments lived up to such high hopes for shared space (Bliss 2012). Camps that expanded quickly could not protect everyone inside from violent co-campers. In certain sites, women complained of assaults at camps, although this was something seized on and over-exaggerated by right-wing commentators eager to depict mob violence (Seltzer 2012). In a rather different case of ongoing divides, Seattle students complained that local Occupy events were not attracting activists of color because they were not addressing racial dispossession. In other venues, anti-racist activists were more cautious in their criticism, attuned to how communities of color were especially hard hit by foreclosures and aware of the economic reasons keeping many African Americans away from joining the shared spaces of the camps (Miah 2012). Meanwhile, others, such as the African-American radio host Tavis Smiley, took up the big question provoked by the protests and began explicitly exploring the links between economic and racial inequality on his popular PBS shows (tavissmileyradio.com). This kind of take-up showed in turn that Occupy activism was opening up new teaching spaces. Even its failures were proving to be teaching moments both at General Assemblies and beyond. At the 2011 Cascadia critical geography conference in Seattle, for example, an energetic final session led to all sorts of teaching notes being gathered on the questions provoked by the activism (Figure 33.2). Closer to Wall Street itself, Lisa

**Figure 33.2** An Occupy teaching space at the sixth annual Cascadia Critical Geography conference at the University of Washington, Seattle.
Source: photo by kind permission of Magie Ramirez

Duggan in the New York University Department of Cultural and Social Analysis created much media interest by offering a new eighty-student course entitled "Cultures and Economies: Why Occupy Wall Street? The History and Politics of Debt and Finance" (Kral 2012). It may still be rather removed from a "co-revolutionary politics" with ordinary workers and more disenfranchised students; but in these sorts of educative experiments, we can perhaps witness "the intellectual wing of the alienated and discontented . . . deepen[ing] the ongoing debate on how to change the course of human development" (Harvey 2010: 241).

The passion for learning about Occupy activism also reflected the passionate feelings animating the occupations themselves. Affect was, in this sense, felt everywhere; and, just as in many prior protests against neoliberal rule in wealthy countries, the sensuous solidarities helped to turn Occupy events into enactments of a kind of embodied as well as "made for media" ethics (cf. Routledge 2012). When Naomi Klein began her speech at Zuccotti Park, for example, she started with the three simple words: "I love you." Partly, she jested, this was just so she could hear the human microphone repeat it back to her; but it also captured the wider spirit of caring, empathy, and sympathy that was felt at so many encampments across the United States and the world. "Compassion is our new currency" was an indicative message scrawled on a pizza-box lid in Zuccotti Park, a sign saying so much so fast about replacing heartless circuits of financial dispossession with circles of solidarity in repossession. Tracing the inspirations for such affect-based solidarity back to 2001 and Argentinean appeals to *politica afectiva*, Solnit (2012) also declared that "our operating system should be love; we are all connected; we must take care of each other." For some activists, these shared feelings even turned into romantic love; and on Valentine's Day 2012, *The Guardian* ran a story about these Occupy-inspired relationships under the title: "Occupy romance: 'I remember watching her march up to Goldman Sachs'" (Saro-Wiwa 2012).

Others, nevertheless, warned against the space of affect becoming a problem for the activism. Chris Hedges, for example, wrote a hotly debated article about the co-optation of

Occupy affect by what he saw as the hypermasculinist "lust" and self-aggrandizing ambitions of Black Bloc anarchists. "The Black Bloc movement is infected with a deeply disturbing hypermasculinity," he wrote.

> This hypermasculinity, I expect, is its primary appeal. It taps into the lust that lurks within us to destroy, not only things but human beings. It offers the godlike power that comes with mob violence. Marching as a uniformed mass, all dressed in black to become part of an anonymous bloc, faces covered, temporarily overcomes alienation, feelings of inadequacy, powerlessness and loneliness. It imparts to those in the mob a sense of comradeship. It permits an inchoate rage to be unleashed on any target. Pity, compassion and tenderness are banished for the intoxication of power. (Hedges 2011)

This critique undoubtedly overstated anarchist investment in violence and also over-exaggerated the extent of what Black Bloc violence there was as a metastasizing influence within Occupy activism. For many Occupy activists, it also represented a kind of betrayal of the anarchic engagement and joy they experienced in the General Assemblies and other ago-nistic moments of collective direct action (Vrasti 2012). Nonetheless, Hedges' concern with affect becoming the basis of co-optation and capitulation to hegemonic sentiment had some wider significance and, thus, also echoed arguments by others, such as Mike Davis, who underlined the capacity of reactionary populists (such as Marine Le Pen and Geert Wilders in Europe and the Tea Party movement in the United States) to mount a "reoccupation" of protest space from the far right.

In a different register, a concern with affect as a problem space was raised by the philoso-pher Slavoj Žižek. "One of the great dangers the protesters face," he noted, "is that they will fall in love with themselves." Against this, Žižek argued,

> The protesters should fall in love with hard and patient work – they are the beginning, not the end . . . While it is thrilling to enjoy the pleasures of the "horizontal organization" of protesting crowds with egalitarian solidarity and open-ended free debates, . . . the open-ended debates will have to coalesce . . . in concrete answers to the old Leninist question, "What is to be done?" (Žižek 2011)

Notwithstanding the impatience one finds in Žižek's own high-speed experiments with psy-choanalytic theories of pleasure and *jouissance*, his practical Leninist question points in a useful direction (and one in which psychoanalytic ideas about dream-work are also quite salient). It points, in short, to the importance of considering the utopian space of Occupy activism as a worldly and culturally contested problem space; and it is with a consideration of this problem space that these reflections now conclude.

## (7) Utopian Space

> What would happen if an anti-capitalist movement were constituted out of a broad alliance of all the discontented, the alienated, the deprived and dispossessed? The image of all such people everywhere rising up and demanding and achieving their proper place in economic, social and political life is stirring indeed. (Harvey 2010: 240)

It was with these Occupy-anticipating words that David Harvey summed up his own response to Lenin's question in his 2010 book on the global financial crisis. "The dream," he says a few pages later, "would be a grand alliance of all the deprived and dispossessed everywhere" (2010: 247). By linking what has gone on to become the Occupy meme of everywhere space with this dream image of an inclusive global struggle for repossession by the world's dispossessed, Harvey was here anticipating questions we might ask about the utopianism of Occupy activism. Following Harvey's own dialectical approach, the problem space of this utopianism needs to be considered in the context of his other well-known argument about neoliberalism being a project of capitalist class domination that represents itself as a globally inclusive utopia (Harvey 2005). As I and other critical geographers have argued too, this neoliberal utopianism tends to be characterized by a series of contradictory cultural-*cum*-political geographic dreamscapes that combine, albeit unstably, incorporative geoeconomic aspirations about globalization with ongoing geopolitical assertions about defending national position, property, and place (Roberts *et al.* 2003; Sparke, 2005, 2007c, 2013). A key question in this respect, therefore, concerns how precisely the utopian space of Occupy activism differs from the disabling double visions of neoliberal utopianism. How are the dreams of reoccupying public space as shared and radically democratic space different from the contradictory fantasies of flat-world incorporation and enclaved privilege that tend together to fill the business pages?

One way of making the distinction, and of thereby opening up the utopian space of Occupy activism to further empirical enquiry and reflection, is to suggest that the protests have themselves enacted a kind of critical cultural dream-work on the displacements of neoliberal dreamscapes. In Wendy Brown's (2011) account, this work is figured as enabling a "return of the repressed res-publica" that neoliberal fantasists try to deny and do without. This is also how Žižek suggested the protestors were working.

> They are dismissed as dreamers, but the true dreamers are those who think things can go on indefinitely the way they are, just with some cosmetic changes. They are not dreamers; they are the awakening from a dream that is turning into a nightmare. They are not destroying anything, but reacting to how the system is gradually destroying itself. We all know the classic scene from cartoons: the cat reaches a precipice but goes on walking; it starts to fall only when it looks down and notices the abyss. The protesters are just reminding those in power to look down. (Žižek 2011)

As readers familiar with Žižek's Lacanian-inspired philosophical imaginary know well, this cartoon trope is a common feature of his critiques of post-1968 consumer compensating ideologies of the real, what Stathis Gourgouris (2007) calls Žižek's "realism." But it is no less meaningful for being recycled here to describe the "get-real" effect of Occupy activism as a kind of counter-hegemonic dream-work. A key point in this respect is the argument that Occupy activism is utopian in its open questioning and in its anticipation of other better futures, not in offering a narrowly stipulated set of policy demands. Žižek thereby underlined that the utopian space of Occupy activism must not be given up for quick-fix policy solutions. "Yes, the protests did create a vacuum," he went on, "a vacuum in the field of hegemonic ideology, and time is needed to fill this vacuum in a proper way, as it is a pregnant vacuum, an opening for the truly new" (although this metaphor of pregnancy might also be read as feminizing the space of utopian possibility as something that Lacanian man has always already filled with the truly seminal).

Naomi Klein also pointed to the dangers of co-optation and the importance of preserving the utopianism of Occupy activism's openness. But, replacing Lacanian language with more Leninist practicality, she pushed the dialectical argument back in the other direction too, by insisting that what also should distinguish this utopia in the end must be its ongoing articulation with practical resistance and alternatives to the realities of neoliberalism. "The key," she insisted, is "in the combination of resistance and alternatives":

> A friend, the British eco- and arts activist John Jordan, talks about utopias and resistance being the double helix of activist DNA, and that when people drop out and just try to build their utopia and don't engage with the systems of power, that's when they become irrelevant and also when they are extremely vulnerable to state power and will often get smashed. And at the same time if you're just protesting, just resisting and you don't have those alternatives, I think that that becomes poisonous for movements. (Klein and Marom 2012)

Other experienced voices on the left have been making similar points – on the one hand, celebrating the open and anticipatory opportunities made possible by imagining Occupy space as utopian space yet on the other, maintaining that the movement needs to plan for the long haul with more hard work on building links to other social movements and more effort at organizing alternatives that link to ongoing struggles against dispossession. "To succeed," says David Harvey (2012: 162), "the movement has to reach out to the 99 percent." This is also how Noam Chomsky put it (with his characteristic sensitivity to the US-specific implications of utopian space in a country founded on so many utopian myths about freedom):

> The Occupy movement really is an exciting development. In fact, it's spectacular. It's unprecedented; there's never been anything like it that I can think of. If the bonds and associations that are being established at these remarkable events can be sustained through a long, hard period ahead – because victories don't come quickly – this could turn out to be a very significant moment in American history. (Chomsky 2011)

Adding a global overview with his own iconoclastic verve, Mike Davis initiated a review of everywhere's utopian space with a similar mix of excitement and warning about the work ahead. First came the thrill of utopian anticipation:

> The electrifying protests of 2011 – the ongoing Arab spring, the "hot" Iberian and Hellenic summers, the "occupied" fall in the United States – inevitably have been compared to the *anni mirabiles* of 1848, 1905, 1968 and 1989. Certainly some fundamental things still apply and classic patterns repeat. Tyrants tremble, chains break and palaces are stormed. Streets become magical laboratories where citizens and comrades are created, and radical ideas acquire sudden telluric power. *Iskra* becomes Facebook. (Davis 2011: 5)

Yet next came a series of sobering diagnostic questions from Davis about the challenges that must distinguish this space of everywhere activism:

> But will this new comet of protest persist in the winter sky or is it just a brief, dazzling meteor shower? For the moment, the survival of the new social movements – the occupiers, the *indignados*, the small European anti-capitalist parties and the Arab new left – demands that they sink deeper roots in mass resistance to the global economic catastrophe . . . It's a frighteningly long road just to reach the starting points of earlier attempts to build a new world. But a new generation has at least bravely initiated the journey. (Davis 2011: 5)

It is, indeed, a frighteningly long road ahead. But that a road ahead exists at all can be attributed to the work of Occupy activists and their global counterparts in upturning the false utopianism of neoliberal globalization and dreaming of making the repressed res-publica of politics a newly meaningful and embodied public place (Brown 2011). Doing so by fashioning local geographies of repossession, the target spaces, everywhere spaces, and time-spaces of Occupy activism have created a whole new suite of shared spaces, teaching spaces, and affect spaces. In the process, the ties and tensions between all six of these problem spaces create the possibility of an ongoing, iterative movement between fixing protests in space and opening them up in newly plural, participatory, and agonistic ways. In this ongoing and radically democratic dialectic, there lies a deep utopian impulse that is distinguished as much by its diagnosis of what is wrong with neoliberal utopias as by its anticipation of a better future. A worldly cultural geography can play a critical role in enabling this democratic dialectic, helping us to understand why the symbolic appeal of targeting Wall Street helped Occupy activism to take place around the world. Remembering that top-down vertical repossession can also lead to a reactionary politics of place, passion, and patriarchy and mapping the utopian imagining of spaces of resistance as they keep proliferating horizontally around the world, we can connect the catachreses of "worldly" and "cultural" with the local geographic imagination of global justice.

## Acknowledgments

I would like to thank the graduate student co-organizers of the sixth annual Cascadia critical geography conference for sowing the seeds of this chapter with their comments and engagements with Occupy activism in Seattle. I am also especially grateful to Mona Domosh, Joe Eckert, Monica Farias, Sara Koopman, Stephen Young, and Jamie Winders for their thoughtful feedback on earlier drafts of this chapter.

## Notes

1   For more on the responsibilities to the non-local implied by the "graphematic" spelling of geo-graphy with a hyphen, see Sparke (2005, 2007a).

2   See http://motherjones.com/politics/2011/10/occupy-wall-street-protest-map, http://www.guardian. co.uk/news/datablog/interactive/2011/oct/18/occupy-protests-map-world, http://www.aljazeera.com/ indepth/spotlight/occupywallstreet/2011/10/201110317294664881.html, http://www.esri.com/news/ maps/2011/occupy-wall-street-map/index.html, and http://occupywallst.org/attendees/ (accessed October 16, 2012).

3   See http://mappingmashups.net/occupymaps/ and http://maps.google.co.uk/maps/ms?msid=2112719 15139781289500.0004ae1be3e667fbd27d5&msa=0&ll=40.709237,-74.01048&spn=0.0011, 0.001475 (accessed October 16, 2012).

## References

Adbusters. (2011) #OCCUPYWALLSTREET: A shift in revolutionary tactics. http://www.adbusters.org/ blogs/adbusters-blog/occupywallstreet.html (accessed October 16, 2012).

Barnett, C. (2010) Geography and ethics: Justice unbound. *Progress in Human Geography*, 35 (2), 246–255.

Barnett, C. (2011) Theory and events. *Geoforum*, 42, 263–265.

Black Orchid Collective. (2011) Decolonize Occupy Seattle! http://blackorchidcollective. wordpress.com/2011/10/22/decolonize-occupy/ (accessed October 16, 2012).

Bliss, S. (2012) Reflections of an insider: Occupy's growing pains. CounterPunch. http://www. counterpunch.org/2012/03/15/occupys-growing-pains/ (accessed October 16, 2012).

Brown, W. (2011) Occupy Wall Street: Return of a repressed res-publica. *Theory and Event*, 14 (4), 2011 Supplement.

Buell, J. (2011) Occupy Wall Street's democratic challenge, *Theory and Event*, 14 (4), 2011 Supplement.

Butler, J. (2004) *Precarious Life: The Power of Mourning and Violence*. New York: Verso.

Chomsky, N. (2011) If we want a chance at a decent future, the movement here and around the world must grow. http://www.alternet.org/story/152933/noam_chomsky_speaks_to_occupy%3A_if_we_ want_a_chance_at_a_decent_future,_the_movement_here_and_around_the_world_must_grow/ (accessed October 16, 2012).

Chow, R. (2006) *The Age of the World Target: Self-Referentiality in War, Theory, and Comparative Work*. Durham, NC: Duke University Press.

Coulter, A. (2011) "Occupy Wall Street" [Hearts] Wall Street. October 19. http://www.anncoulter.com/ columns/2011-10-19.html (accessed October 16, 2012).

Datta, K., Evans, Y., Herbert, J., May, J., McIlwaine, C., and Wills, J. (2010) *Global Cities at Work: New Migrant Divisions of Labour*. London: Pluto Press.

Davis, M. (2011) Spring confronts winter. *New Left Review*, 72, 5–15.

Dean, J. (2011) Claiming division, naming a wrong. *Theory and Event*, 14 (4), 2011 Supplement.

Denning, M. (2010) Wageless life. *New Left Review*, 66, 79–97.

Domosh, M., Neumann, R.P., Price, P.L., and Jordan-Bychkov, T.G. (2009) *The Human Mosaic: A Cultural Approach to Human Geography*. New York: Macmillan.

Eckert, J. (2012) Geolocating the #Occupy movement – surprising results and the importance of scale, *Social Media Lab @ UW*. http://somelab.net/2012/03/geolocating-the-occupy-movement-surprising- results-and-importance-of-scale/ (accessed October 16, 2012).

*The Economist*. (2011) Not quite together. The Economist, October 22.

Ehrenreich, B. and Ehrenreich, J. (2012) The making of the American 99 percent. *The Nation*, January 2, pp. 19–21.

Elwood, S. (2008) Volunteered geographic information: Future research directions motivated by critical, participatory, and feminist GIS. *GeoJournal*, 72, 173–183.

Elwood, S. (2010) Geographic information science: Visualization, visual methods, and the geoweb. *Progress in Human Geography*, 35 (3), 401–408.

Featherstone, D. (2003) Spatialities of transnational resistance to globalization: The maps of grievance of the intercontinental caravan. *Transactions of the Institute of British Geographers*, 28, 404–421.

Featherstone, D. (2005) Towards the relational construction of militant particularisms: Or why the geographies of past struggles matter for resistance to neoliberal globalization. *Antipode*, 37, 250–271.

Featherstone, D., Ince, A., Mackinnon, D., Strauss, K., and Cumbers, A. (2012) Progressive localism and the construction of political alternatives. *Transactions of the Institute of British Geographers*, online pre-publication.

Gidwani, V. (2008) *Capital Interrupted: Agrarian Development and the Politics of Work in India*. Minneapolis: University of Minnesota Press.

Gilmore, R. (2007) *Golden Gulag: Prisons, Surplus, Crisis, and Opposition in Globalizing California*. Berkeley: University of California Press.

Goodchild, M. (2007) Citizens as sensors: The world of volunteered geography. *GeoJournal*, 69 (4), 211–221.

Gourgouris, S. (2007) Žižek's Realism. Essay commissioned as part of the DVD release of the film *Slavoj Žižek: The Reality of the Virtual*, produced by B. Wright and Olive Films.

Gregory, D. (2004) *The Colonial Present: Afghanistan, Palestine, and Iraq*. Oxford: Blackwell.

Gregory, D. (2011) The everywhere war. *Geographical Journal*, 177 (3), 238–250.

*The Guardian*. (2011) Occupy movement goes global – in pictures: Occupy Wall Street protests are linking up with other Occupy movements around the world. October 15. http://www.guardian.co.uk/world/gallery/2011/oct/15/occupy-wall-street-movement-global (accessed October 16, 2012).

Hart, G. (2006) Denaturalizing dispossession: Critical ethnography in the age of resurgent imperialism. *Antipode*, 38, 975–1001.

Hart, G. (2007) Changing concepts of articulation: Political stakes in South Africa today. *Review of African Political Economy*, 111, 85–101.

Harvey, D. (2005) *A Brief History of Neoliberalism*. Oxford: Oxford University Press.

Harvey, D. (2010) *The Enigma of Capital and the Crises of Capitalism*. Oxford: Oxford University Press.

Harvey, D. (2011) The Party of Wall Street Meets its Nemesis. Socialist Worker, October 28. http://socialistworker.org/blog/critical-reading/2011/10/29/david-harvey-occupy-wall-stree (accessed October 16, 2012).

Harvey, D. (2012) *Rebel Cities: From the Right to the City to the Urban Revolution*. New York: Verso.

Hedges, C. (2011) Black Bloc: The cancer in Occupy. http://www.alternet.org/occupywallst/154028/black_bloc%3A_the_cancer_in_occupy?page=entire (accessed October 16, 2012).

Hunter, M. (2010) *Love in the Time of AIDS: Inequality, Gender and Rights in South Africa*. Bloomington: Indiana University Press.

Huse, T. (2007) *easyCity: Neoliberal Urbanism and Spectacle*. Unpublished Master's thesis, University of Oslo.

Jeffrey, C. (2010) *Timepass: youth, class, and the politics of waiting in India*. Stanford, Calif.: Stanford University Press.

Katz, C. (2005) Partners in crime? Neoliberalism and the production of new political subjectivities. *Antipode*, 37, 623–631.

Kessler, S. (2011) Occupy Wall Street global map is a bird's-eye view of discontent. http://mashable.com/2011/10/17/occupy-wall-street-social-media-maps/ (accessed October 16, 2012).

Klein, N. (2011) Occupy Wall Street: The most important thing in the world now. http://www.alternet.org/occupywallst/152647/occupy_wall_street%3A_the_most_important_thing_in_the_world_now/ (accessed October 16, 2012).

Klein, N. and Marom, Y. (2012) Why now? What's next? Naomi Klein and Yotam Marom in conversation about Occupy Wall Street. http://www.thenation.com/article/165530/why-now-whats-next-naomi-klein-and-yotam-marom-conversation-about-occupy-wall-street (accessed October 16, 2012).

Koopman, S. (2008) Imperialism within: Can the master's tools bring down empire? *ACME: An International E-Journal for Critical Geographies*, 7 (2), 283–307.

Koopman, S. (2011) Alter-geopolitics: Other securities are happening. *Geoforum*, 42 (3), 274–284.

Kral, G. (2012) NYU establishes Occupy Wall Street course. http://www.thenation.com/blog/165699/nyu-establishes-occupy-wall-street-course (accessed October 16, 2012).

Kroll, A. (2011) How Occupy Wall Street really got started: Meet the international activists who lit the fuse for the populist protest movement that's sweeping the world. http://motherjones.com/politics/2011/10/occupy-wall-street-international-origins (accessed October 16, 2012).

Laclau, E. and Mouffe, C. (1985) *Hegemony and Socialist Strategy: Towards a Radical Democratic Politics*, trans. W. Moore and P. Cammack. London: Verso.

Massey, D. (1995) Thinking radical democracy spatially. *Environment and Planning D: Society and Space*, 13 (3), 283–288.

Massey, D. (2011) A counterhegemonic relationality of place. In *Mobile Urbanism: Cities and Policy-Making in the Global Age*, ed. E. McCann and K. Ward. Minneapolis: University of Minnesota Press, pp. 1–28.

McKittrick, K. (2006) *Demonic Grounds: Black Women and the Cartographies of Struggle*. Minneapolis: University of Minnesota Press.

Miah, M. (2012) African Americans and the Occupy Movement: A convergence of realities. *Race and Class*, January/February, 2–4.

*New Statesman*. (2011) It is time for governments to stand up for the 99 per cent. http://www.newstatesman.com/uk-politics/2011/10/society-income-governments (accessed October 16, 2012).

Newstead, C., Reid, C., and Sparke, M. (2003) The cultural geography of scale. In *The Handbook of Cultural Geography*, ed. K. Anderson, M. Domosh, S. Pile, and N. Thrift. London: Sage, pp. 485–497.

Nichols, J. (2011) The 99 percent rise up. *The Nation*, October 31.

Panelli, R. (2007) Time-space geometries of activism and the case of mis/placing gender in Australia. *Transactions of the Institute of British Geographers*, 32, 46–65.

Popke, J. (2006) Geography and ethics: Everyday mediations through care and consumption. *Progress in Human Geography*, 30, 504–512.

Pulido, L. (2006) *Black, Brown, Yellow and Left: Radical Activism in Los Angeles*. Berkeley: University of California Press.

Pulido, L. (2007) A day without immigrants: The racial and class politics of immigrant exclusion. *Antipode*, 39, 1–7.

Rankin, K. (2012) Subalterneity, ethnography, and praxis. *Annals of the Association of American Geographers*, 102 (2), 508–510.

Roberts, S., Secor, A., and Sparke, M. (2003) Neoliberal geopolitics. *Antipode*, 35 (5), 886–897.

Routledge, P. (2003) Convergence space: Process geographies of grassroots globalization networks. *Transactions of the Institute of British Geographers*, 28, 333–349.

Routledge, P. (2012) Sensuous solidarities: Emotion, politics and performance in the clandestine Insurgent Rebel Clown Army. *Antipode*, 44 (2), 428–452.

Roy, A. (2012) Afterword: Entrepreneurs of millennial capitalism. *Antipode*, 44 (2), 545–553.

Saro-Wiwa, Z. (2012) Occupy romance: "I remember watching her march up to Goldman Sachs." *The Guardian*, February 14. http://www.guardian.co.uk/world/2012/feb/14/occupy-movement-valentines-day (accessed October 16, 2012).

Seltzer, S. (2012) How right-wing smears against Occupy exploit victims of rape in the Movement. http://www.alternet.org/story/154257/how_right-wing_smears_against_occupy_exploit_victims_of_rape_in_the_movement?utm_source=feedblitzandutm_medium=FeedBlitzRssandutm_campaign=alternet_all (accessed October 16, 2012).

Shiva, V. (2005) The polarized world of globalization. *Global Policy Forum*, May 10. http://www.globalpolicy.org/component/content/article/162/27674.html (accessed October 16, 2012).

Silver, N. (2011) The geography of occupying Wall Street (and everywhere else). *New York Times* Five Thirty Eight blog, October 17. http://fivethirtyeight.blogs.nytimes.com/2011/10/17/the-geography-of-occupying-wall-street-and-everywhere-else/ (accessed October 16, 2012).

Smith, B.E. and Winders, J. (2008) "We're here to stay": Economic restructuring, Latino migration and place-making in the US South. *Transactions of the Institute of British Geographers*, 33, 60–72.

Solnit, R. (2011) Occupy your heart. *Tom Dispatch*, December 22. http://www.tomdispatch.com/archive/175483/ (accessed October 16, 2012).

Solnit, R. (2012) Why the media loves the violence of protesters and not of banks. http://www.alternet.org/media/154235/why_the_media_loves_the_violence_of_protesters_and_not_of_banks/?page=entire (accessed October 16, 2012).

Sparke, M. (1995) Writing on patriarchal missiles: The chauvinism of the Gulf War and the limits of critique. *Environment and Planning A*, 26 (7), 1061–1089.

Sparke, M. (1998) A map that roared and an original atlas: Canada, cartography and the narration of nation. *Annals of the Association of American Geographers*, 88 (3), 464–495.

Sparke, M. (2005) *In the Space of Theory: Postfoundational Geographies of the Nation-State*. Minneapolis: University of Minnesota Press.

Sparke, M. (2007a) Acknowledging responsibility for Space. *Progress in Human Geography*, 31 (3), 7–15.

Sparke, M. (2007b) Everywhere but always somewhere: Critical geographies of the global South. *Global South*, 1 (1), 117–126.

Sparke, M. (2007c) Geopolitical fear, geoeconomic hope and the responsibilities of geography. *Annals of the Association of American Geographers*, 97 (2), 338–349.

Sparke, M. (2008) Political geographies of globalization (3): Resistance. *Progress in Human Geography*, 32 (1), 1–18.

Sparke, M. (2010) The look of surveillance returns. In *Classics in Cartography: Reflections on Influential Articles from Cartographica*, ed. M. Dodge. New York: Wiley, pp. 373–386.

Sparke, M. (2011) Global geographies. In *Seattle Geographies*, ed. M. Brown and R. Morrill. Seattle: University of Washington Press, pp. 48–70.

Sparke, M. (2012) Ethnography, affect, geography, and unemployment. *Annals of the Association of American Geographers*, 102 (2), 510–515.

Sparke, M. (2013) *Introducing Globalization: Ties, Tensions and Uneven Integration*. Oxford: Wiley-Blackwell.

Sparke, M., Brown, E., Corva, D., Day, H., Faria, C., Sparks, T., and Varg, K. (2005) The World Social Forum and the lessons for economic geography. *Economic Geography*, 81 (4), 359–380.

St. Martin, K. (2009) Toward a cartography of the commons: Constituting the political and economic possibilities of place. *Professional Geographer*, 61 (4), 493–507.

Sundberg, J. (2007) Reconfiguring north–south solidarity: Critical reflections on experiences of transnational resistance. *Antipode*, 39, 144–166.

Vrasti, W. (2012) Precarious states. Paper presented at the meetings of the International Studies Association, San Diego.

Wainright, J. (2007) Spaces of resistance in Seattle and Cancun. In *Contesting Neoliberalism: Urban Frontiers*, ed. H. Leitner, J. Peck, and E. Sheppard. New York: Guilford Press, pp. 179–203.

Weber, S. (2005) *Targets of Opportunity: On the Militarization of Thinking*. New York: Fordham University Press.

Wills, J. (2004) Campaigning for low paid workers: The East London Communities Organization (TELCO) Living Wage Campaign. In *The Future of Worker Representation*, ed. W. Brown, G. Healy, E. Heery, and P. Taylor. Oxford: Oxford University Press, pp. 264–282.

Wilson, M. (2011) "Training the eye": Formation of the geocoding subject. *Social and Cultural Geography*, 12 (4), 357–376.

Winders, J. (2007) Bringing back the (b)order: Post-9/11 politics of immigration, borders, and belonging in the contemporary US South. *Antipode*, 39, 920–942.

Wright, M. (2005) The paradoxes of protests: The Mujeres de Negro of northern Mexico. *Gender, Place and Culture*, 12 (3), 277–292.

Wright, M. (2006) *Disposable Women and Other Myths of Global Capitalism*. New York: Routledge.

Žižek, S. (2011) Occupy first. Demands come later. http://www.guardian.co.uk/commentisfree/2011/oct/26/occupy-protesters-bill-clinton (accessed October 16, 2012).

# Chapter 34

# Political Moves: Cultural Geographies of Migration and Difference

*Rachel Silvey*

The last two decades have witnessed a burgeoning of cultural-geographic studies of migration. Indeed, in a recent review of migration studies, population geographer Russell King (2012: 143) points out that not only have cultural geographers been major contributors to recent studies of migration but also that "migration geographers . . . [have become] some of the key protagonists of the new cultural geography, and their papers have contributed an ever-increasing share of the contents of the leading journals in human geography since the mid-1990s." This expansion of interest is a response to both empirical changes in global migration and shifts in theoretical priorities in geography and cognate fields. As places and "cultures" have grown increasingly interconnected across space and as growing absolute numbers of migrants have traveled to rising numbers of places in increasingly complex patterns, the migrant has emerged as a key figure embodying, enacting, and representing the fears and hopes attached to globalization. The cultural politics of migration, thus, have required attention not only to the spatial demographies of migration but also to the social processes of meaning-making in relation to citizenship, borders, identities, and labor markets, as well as discourses and histories of racialization and gender relations. Through attention to migrants' lived geographies, recent research brings to life the political dimensions of migrants' cultural geographies. In this chapter, I argue that cultural geography, and in particular feminist cultural geography, offers conceptual tools that have been especially illuminating for the rapidly changing lived politics of migration.

The chapter is organized around three main themes.[1] First, it traces concepts of control and dominance in migration studies, examining cultural-geographic approaches to political-economic structures, state policies, labor markets, and the securitization practices and disciplinary discourses that underpin heightened surveillance and everyday policing of migrants. Second, the chapter focuses on subjectivities and the ways migrants as embodied subjects

*The Wiley Blackwell Companion to Cultural Geography*, First Edition.
Edited by Nuala C. Johnson, Richard H. Schein, and Jamie Winders.
© 2013 John Wiley & Sons, Ltd. Published 2016 by John Wiley & Sons, Ltd.

work out their social locations in socio-spatial terms – themes I illustrate with examples of migration research on religion and "intimate labor." Third, the chapter explores cultural migration scholarship in terms of geographies of im/migrant justice. Drawing inspiration from the work of migrant-rights activists, it outlines some practices already under way that offer promising directions for future migration research and advocacy. Across these themes, I pay special attention to feminist migration scholarship, which is vital to breaking new ground in the conceptualization of each organizing concept.[2]

## Structuring Migration and Controlling Migrants

The majority of Anglophone scholarship on migration is centered on European and North American immigration processes, and, as such, much of it is underpinned, albeit often implicitly, by the view that migration is driven and limited by the imperatives of empire. However, scholarship on migration that starts from postcolonial places, feminist sensibilities, and anti-imperialist agendas challenges the idea that global migration inequalities *originated* in colonial and imperial command centers. Rather, such work finds promise in approaching the "tensions of empire" (Cooper and Stoler 1997) as multi-directional encounters in which colonized actors and places – and, indeed, migrants – play important roles in the making of metropolitan core economies and identities as well as the other way around. Tracing imperial engagements as rooted not only in domination but also in negotiated social relations allows scholars to understand new geographies of migration (e.g., growing South–South global flows or the rising numbers of children of immigrants who return to the "homeland" of their parents). In addition, it shifts attention away from understanding global migration systems as determined entirely by the logics of global capitalism and toward the ways that migrants themselves have forged, countered, adopted, and reworked the meanings and implications of migration at specific historical conjunctures.

Critics of cultural approaches to migration have argued that some work pays inadequate attention to the materiality and inequality of migration systems. While some early work may have been guilty of this charge, most recent studies of cultural migration geographies are emphatically committed to understanding material inequalities as at least one important aspect of migration processes. However, rather than approaching structures of dominance and control as pre-given or unidirectionally imposed, cultural approaches tend to examine inequalities as always-in-the-making and always relationally produced. When oppression is understood as a process and as shifting sets of meanings rather than as predetermined or "natural" social hierarchies, research agendas expand and conclusions may offer surprises (e.g., King 2012; Blunt 2007).

Early feminist migration research tended to examine gender through a critique of patriarchy, which was understood as the general sociocultural privileging of the masculine over the feminine. Attention to patriarchal structures allowed early feminist work to insert questions of power and culture into studies of migration. The earliest feminist migration research understood that patriarchy took different social-geographic forms, yet it also demonstrated that women and men were pushed and pulled into migration in patterns that are gendered. Moreover, gendered inequalities in migration evidenced similar trends across places undergoing similar economic development processes. In some of the first work to parse out gender in relation to the New International Division of Labor, for example, "third world" women's growing rural–urban migration was understood to be prompted by increasing foreign direct investment and light manufacturing in export-processing zones. From this perspective, global capitalism was understood to work in tandem with patriarchal cultures of labor valuation and discipline to produce the offshoring and feminization of low-wage factory labor. These processes tended to be represented independently of social actors and outside the context of cultural negotiation. For example, work in this area examined gender cultures of women's presumed inherent manual dexterity or docility in terms of the ways these ideas were manipulated and subsumed by global capitalist expansion.

More recent feminist work has examined migrants' gendered and embodied labor and social relationships as operating both in concert and *in tension* with the hegemonic political-economic policies and pressures of globalization. Filipina domestic workers in Rome and Los Angeles, for example, work as "servants of globalization" who both build and respond to global networks of social reproduction (Parreñas 2001).[3] Migrant domestic workers subsidize the social-reproductive needs of the families and nations where they work and rely upon other, lower-paid women to take on the reproductive labor loads necessary to sustain their own families back home. Feminist geographers examine these interlocking systems of gendered and racialized labor migration as not only structured by but also necessary for and structuring of processes unfolding at global, national, regional, household, and bodily scales (Mattingly 2001; Mountz and Hyndman 2006). Attention to the interactions of processes across the multiple scales that shape migration and to the ways that social differences are reinforced or reworked in these encounters provides a lens onto subjects and scales that until recently have been overlooked or conceived as analytically parenthetical in migration studies (Blunt 2007; Nagar *et al.* 2002). Understanding the household, for example, as a site not just of gender-neutral resource-sharing but also of gendered hierarchies and unequal divisions of resources and labor allows feminists to see intra-household gender divisions of labor and power as worthy of study in themselves and as central to the production of migration inequalities and gendered contestations at broader scales of analysis (Lawson 1998; Lawson and England 2005).

The liberalization of trade barriers and the tightening of controls on labor migration in recent decades have reverberated through gendered and racial/ethnic labor segmentation processes to affect the everyday lives of migrants and their employers. Cultural-geographic attention to these processes asks how a myth such as gender neutrality is maintained, what interests such a myth serves, and how people understand and circulate the myth. Rather than reinforcing, for example, the myth of *homo economicus*, critical migration work insists on examining the economy and its gendered power relations as social processes always under construction and the migrant worker as a gendered subject rather than a universal laboring subject. In global cities, for example, gendered divisions of migrant labor are constitutive of the cosmopolitan urban. As Saskia Sassen (2003: 45) puts it, "In the day-to-day work of the leading service complex dominated by finance in the case of a city like New York, a large share of the jobs are low paid and manual, many held by women and immigrants." Global cities, and the financial service sectors within them, accumulate unforeseen concentrations of wealth, while the lifestyles of urban affluence rely upon the work of low-income immigrants.

Households and cities depend upon the work of migrants, whether as immediate labor or as remittance earners. Immigrant labor markets, and the inequalities that characterize them, are produced through discourses of relative skill, expertise, and entitlement that produce perceived and material valuations attached to particular bodies and work (Hanson and Pratt 1988, 1995). Migration inequality is, thus, structured by the political economy of neoliberal urbanization in connection with the controlling discourses of gender and difference. In this vein, the "cultures" of migrants tend to be conceived primarily as arenas of exploitation (in Marxist feminist work) and subjection (in Foucauldian feminist work), emphasizing the connections between political-economic structures and discursive pressures. While such perspectives help us understand the controlling discourses and policies that make the conditions under which migrants live their everyday lives, they have done less to contribute to understanding the complexity of the cultural struggles at the heart of how migrants make decisions, choose partners, raise their children, or define their problems and desires.

The Philippine state, perhaps the best studied "labor export state" (Rodriguez 2010), illustrates this last point, as the Philippine government's Overseas Employment Agency is actively involved in the cultural work of recruiting, training, and placing workers abroad. The billions of dollars sent by Filipino migrants each year are hard earned. As a "labor brokerage state" that expects its nationals working abroad to send remittances home, the Philippine government shifts the burden and responsibility of national debt and development away from itself and onto transnational worker-citizens. Such a process requires cultural work on the part of everyone involved. For some workers, a major element of the cultural work of overseas labor migration is the painful, extended family separation it requires. Indeed, even upon reunification, migrants often characterize their family relationships as haunted by the trauma of separation (Pratt 2012). The "labor export state," in the interests of ensuring an energetic labor force with high rates of successful contract completion, trains migrants to manage their sadness about family separation and loneliness. In the process, the state contributes to the discourse of the ideal worker as individualized, hard-working, and accommodating and manipulates ideologies of motherhood in particular to reframe overseas separation as ideal maternal self-sacrifice for the sake of the children and nation. As this case of the Philippines shows, both women and men – whether migrating to new employment opportunities, displaced through land grabs, or immobilized in refugee camps – experience uneven and often contradictory gender consequences of their mobility.

Nation-states implement immigration policies that, like economic policy more generally, smuggle gendered hierarchies into practice. That smuggling, however, is never a neat process. Even when the gender dimensions of nation-building projects are explicit (e.g., in the case of Singapore) (Yeoh and Willis 1999), the cultural practices are messy in practice (e.g., Mills 1999). For instance, the Chinese Exclusion Act of 1882 ostensibly excluded all Chinese people from the United States equally; but when immigration officials implemented the policy, their prejudices came into play:

> What were enforcement officials to do, for example, when confronted with affluent Chinese merchants attempting to bring wives with them to the United States? Or the widows of merchants who had inherited their husbands' businesses? Or the wives of laborers returning from a visit to China? Congress with its preconceptions of Chinese women as prostitutes, who had already been barred by the Page Act had failed to envision any such possibilities. Worse yet, as enforcement personnel struggled to fill the gaps in the 1882 laws, they found themselves permanently lodged between a rock and a hard place, as conflicts among and between patriarchal assumptions about the sacred unity of husband and wife, racist principles of maximum exclusion, and classist notions of merchant superiority, rendered almost every decision a "vexatious" one. (Letter from San Francisco Customs Collector, August 13, 1883, Record Group 85, Entry 134, Box 2, discussed in Calavita 2006: 251)

Such "vexatious" processes reveal more than could simple attention to the law as text. Indeed, Calavita's research on the Chinese Exclusion Act is "fundamentally a study of what law-in-action – and the unexpected social realities it encountered and the irresolvable dilemmas it confronted – can tell us about the hidden assumptions of the lawmakers' hegemonic worldview and the tangled logics that permeated those assumptions" (p. 253). The meanings of laws over which people struggle in often unanticipated ways are their "cultures," which not only come into conflict through migration and its regulation but also are revealed and produced through these very contestations and the exclusions to citizenship that they bring with them. The sense of white masculine privilege and class entitlement that law-makers carried with them through the Chinese Exclusion Act, thus, came to life in the practical implementation of immigration law.

Feminist migration geographers have taken up similar queries to ask what this grounded, lived complexity of migration politics tells us about how to theorize the state more generally. Within geography, Alison Mountz (2010) centers her recent book on the "geographical margins of sovereign territory: on islands, in airports, at sea, and in offshore detention centers where authorities and migrants encounter each other" (p. xvii). She offers an ethnographic account of geography's intertwining with law to show how bureaucrats actively perform, embody, police, and construct the spaces in which refugees make asylum claims. Her work focuses on places that are "stateless by geographic design" where asylum claimants are stigmatized as "bogus." The book's attention to the everyday intimate encounters between officials and migrants contributes to "seeing the state" and migration as complex social negotiations that are never entirely predetermined yet feed into (re)producing global geopolitical hierarchies. Mountz shows how the Canadian state's regulatory geographies shift in response to events, such as the entry into Canadian territory of unregistered boats filled with migrants smuggled from overseas. State officials frame such entries as crises of sovereignty, and their efforts to "stem the tide" of asylum claimants in Canada reverberates in the daily lives of migrants. In this way, Mountz's work exemplifies the feminist priority to understand migration as shaped by the connections between people's personal, embodied, and intimate lives and the political, abstract, and public realms and forces in which they are entwined.

Paralleling Mountz's emphasis on lived migration politics, Brenda Yeoh and Shirlena Huang (1999) examine the relegation of migrant domestic workers to the margins of "civil society" in Singapore, asking what this position implies for Singapore's nation-building project. Their findings, based on detailed interviews with migrant workers, dovetail with those of many researchers who argue that the exclusion of temporary workers from formal citizenship status intersects with less formal social processes of othering to further stigmatize and ostracize them. Media reports often mention immigrant workers' "cultural difference" as a code for racialization. In Singapore, as elsewhere, racialized migrant workers' "cultures" are denigrated as indolent, immoral, dirty, and disruptive and, as such, deemed threatening to the society's moral order and national security. Contemporary cultural geography examines how this "cultural difference" manifests in practice and how particular invocations of "culture" as an othering device do political work.

The politics of culture also figure prominently in migration research on national securitization campaigns and their increasingly palpable echoes "beyond the border" (Gilbert 2012). Emily Gilbert (2007) has written about the emergent concern with biopolitics at the regional scale in neoliberal times. In a study of the Security and Prosperity Partnership (SPP) of North America, signed by Canada, Mexico, and the United States in 2005, she argues that the emphasis on *trilateral* "partnership" as a discourse "signals a new political rationality . . . [that] promotes a divisive and striated regional [tri-national] space that will help perpetuate the ongoing tensions around illegal immigrants and undocumented workers in North

America" (p. 77). Gilbert interrogates the political culture that nominally subscribes to the ideals of democracy, freedom, and liberty yet, in practice, contributes to the hardening of borders *around* "Fortress North America" and the differentiation of mobility rights *within* national borders (p. 93). Biometric surveillance techniques launched in the name of regional and national security serve to ease travel restrictions for elites, while making it increasingly difficult for temporary or undocumented migrants to move anywhere or inhabit any space other than workplaces (also see Sparke 2005).

Airports are another key site within which cultural geographies of mobility politics come to life in terms of not only social stratification but also affect more generally. As Peter Adey (2008) has shown, the architecture of airports is designed to control mobility flows and the affect of travelers. He describes an affective climate of fear characterized by official ongoing efforts to calculate risk. An affective climate can overtake real events and have material effects, such as an airport's closure. To make his case, Adey draws on Massumi's (2005: 9, as cited in Adey 2008: 448) observations about the false anthrax alarm at the Montreal Airport in 2005:

> [Q]uick, close the airport! The airport must be closed just in case, to assuage the fear. The closure of the airport induces fear. Men in white decontamination suits descend. Police are brought in for crowd control. Far-flung airports with originating flights due to land are affected. The media amplify the alarm in real-time with live news bulletins. The fear of the disruption has become the disruption.

For Adey (2008: 448–449), this situation suggests that we may need "to consider whether it is at the level of the affective register that new regimes of power are being directed over life on the move." In his view, the affective register is potentially a more important focus for understanding mobility politics than is the body. In contrast, a feminist reading would emphasize the deep imbrication of affect and the body and examine how distinctive embodiments of affect refract the production of racial, national, and gendered differences in migration.

As a whole, recent cultural geographies of migration are characterized by shifting conceptions of domination and control. In particular, early feminist research contributed to understanding migration as shaped not only by capitalism but also by gender. It identified the role of patriarchal power in shaping the control of women's labor in both the home and workplace. Over the years, studies have increasingly come to view gender and power relations more generally as negotiated and contested rather than imposed and have shown power's multi-directional and multi-sited nature. For migration studies, this shift is evident in new approaches to migrants as not only objects of broader processes but also active participants in the making of the landscapes they inhabit and the places through which they travel. The ability of differently positioned subjects to shape or control migration trajectories is increasingly seen as influenced by individual and collective embodiment, invocations of biopolitical power, and the affective registers that animate spaces of im/mobility. As the next section discusses, similar shifts have taken place in the conceptualization of migrant subjectivities.

## Migrant Subjectivities

Researchers have long argued that the study of migration should be enriched through deeper engagements with social theory (see, e.g., White and Jackson 1995; Graham and Boyle 2001), and recent years have witnessed an efflorescence of precisely such work. Whereas in 1999,

Victoria Lawson and I (Silvey and Lawson 1999) argued that migration studies needed to move beyond static notions of culture, question the ideological moorings of its theories, and foreground the politics of difference, today, the literature effectively does all of this and more. Indeed, in addition to taking seriously the voices of migrants, cultural geographers have provided critical ethnographies of migration that critique the ethnocentrism, masculinism, and economism that haunts theories of migration. Taking inspiration from poststructural, postcolonial, and feminist theoretical work, there have been vibrant exchanges exploring migration as cultural production (or a "cultural event," as McHugh 2000 would call it) shaped through "alternative modernities," "body politics" (as distinct from Foucauldian biopolitics), the performative production of gender and difference, the politics of intimate labor, and religious subjectivities. This section takes up briefly each of these aspects of cultural production.

Gidwani and Sivaramakrishnan (2003) argue that circular migrants in some regions of India are participating in global flows of material consumption and capital intensification in ways that contribute to sometimes subtle but nonetheless transformative politics. They argue that people in three relatively globally linked Indian regions have translated "global modernity" into "alternative regional modernities" (p. 186). As "rural" villages have grown increasingly interwoven into "urban" labor markets through circular migration and as modern forms of consumption and desire travel more rapidly and intensively along rural–urban corridors, regions are not simply bulldozed by global capitalism. In fact, in these three regions of India, historically marginalized people have mobilized what Gidwani and Sivaramakrishnan call counterhegemonic practices. In the past poor, lower-caste, and tribal people were tied to their villages and dependent on patrons. Through recent circular labor migrations, however, they have forged "regional spaces for cultural assertion," becoming "bearers of 'cosmopolitan' lifestyles" (p. 200). They have changed their "body politics," including their styles of dress, manner of speaking, diet, comportment, and adornment, all in ways the rural elite have interpreted as threats to their dominance. While the authors refuse a naïvely celebratory account of the political potential of such "cultural assertion," they nevertheless see in these migrants' actions a meaningful "reworking of modernity" that classical Marxist and marginalist accounts of migration (and, indeed, Foucauldian biopolitical analyses) would tend to ignore.

Similarly, Jamie Winders (2011) conceptualizes the remaking of migrant geographies as material, discursive, and institutional processes in which migrants themselves play active roles. Latino migration to the American South is a rapidly growing phenomenon with rising numbers of recent immigrants from Mexico, Guatemala, and El Salvador building "communities . . . buying homes, and establishing business, social networks, and political groups" (p. 345). Winders views migrants' cultural interpretations of place as a key part of the remaking of the US South, noting that many migrants, though they live side by side with long-term residents, may not experience their new "neighborhoods" as definable, meaningful spaces. Many feel "both placeless and place-bound, unmoored [from Latin America] and tightly bound [to their work and limited daily travel to and from work] – but above all, not part of the local community or neighborhood" (p. 347). Discursively, Winders's work not only calls into question "the neighborhood" as an identifiable scale with shared meanings across groups of residents but also queries the historical legibility of the South as a region. As new residents challenge hegemonic understanding of what "the South" means, "southern geographies and identities are being materially and discursively *re-placed* through immigration and immigration experience" (p. 351, italics mine). Finally, institutionally, she argues, geographers have much to offer the conversations about immigration to the South precisely because of the discipline's attention to place-making as a dynamic social process.

Place-making is also deeply intertwined with religion and religious subjectivities. Migration research that deals with religion has tended to subscribe to a notion of "culture" as malleable, such that places of worship and religious subjectivities are produced not only by religious institutions but also in relation to fellow co-religionists and diasporic reworkings of religious sensibilities. Migrants' spiritual lives allow them to imagine alternative cartographies of power beyond the material. Indeed, many migrants view their practices of worship as capable of meaningfully transporting them beyond wherever their physical bodies may be. Prayer, as well as fasting, according to one migrant worker I interviewed, allows migrants to imagine that they can "get out of *this place* . . . and get closer to God" (Silvey 2009). Religious co-affiliation can also mean that groups of migrants may feel affinity and provide support for one another, despite differences in status or class backgrounds (Johnson 2010). Of course, religion is also often deployed in ways that deepen divisions between groups; and migrants are not able to harness religion everywhere in the same way. Nonetheless, through religious practice migrants in some instances report achieving subjective transcendence of the everyday, the material, and the embodied nature of their existence.

Cultural geographers have also explored the circuits across space in which migrants' subjectivities are made and communities are produced (McKay 2005). Migrants make meanings across places, and the meanings they ascribe to their destinations are bound up with those they ascribe to "home." Jean-François Bissonnette (2012) studies agricultural laborers who migrate from Java to oil-palm plantations in West Kalimantan, Indonesia. The male migrants he interviews narrate notions of idealized masculine strength and tenacity that, he finds, contribute to their willingness to endure harsh working conditions, low wages, and cramped dormitory accommodation in Indonesia. The social reproduction of their labor before and after their stints on the plantation is provided by wives and mothers "back home"; and from the plantations they imagine their origin villages as places of leisure, rest, and rejuvenation. Their romanticized views of their home villages reflect their own gendered positions in both origin and destination sites and are fantasies that emerge *along with and through* their migration away from home.

Migration is, thus, emotionally charged and often brings with it sets of anxieties for migrants and the communities in which they settle. In his detailed research on Indonesia's infamous export-processing island of Batam, Johan Lindquist (2009) takes migrants' (and tourists') emotions as his starting point and, in so doing, opens up distinctive theoretical terrain for understanding the social dynamics at work in such hypercapitalist border zones. His book offers a vivid, textured sense of Batam as a place where people produce and respond to an "emotional economy" that they forge in the context of the dizzying transformations taking place in the political-economic landscape. The book transports readers into the intimate, alienating, dangerous, wishful, and disappointing everyday worlds and lived cultural geographies of residents and visitors in Batam to illustrate how their specific cultural understandings of shame (*malu*), sojourning (*merantau*), and wildness (*liar*) affect their motivations and interpretation of migration and return.

Migrants' own interpretive framings and subjectivities are also important in the growing body of research that grapples with migrants' "intimate labor" (Boris and Parreñas 2010). Intimate labor is "work that involves embodied and affective interactions in the service of social reproduction," including care work, domestic work, sex work, and marriage migration. This labor is valued and coded in geographically specific ways that influence migratory experiences and the regulation of migration. For feminist and cultural migration scholars, attention to intimate labor provides insight into informal, relational, embodied, and affective dimensions of migration as a process inflected by gender, race, ethnicity, class, and nationality. For example, for migrants from the Philippines settling in rural Japan with their new Japanese husbands, migration involves doing the cultural work of becoming an "ideal traditional Japanese bride and daughter-in-law" (*oyomesan*) (Faier 2009: 161). Such cultural work requires that Filipina migrants adjust not only their language but also their bodily comportment, daily household work habits, and child-raising techniques. Faier finds that Filipina women's desires for mobility, glamor, and financial security come into productive tension with the ambivalence and longing that residents in a low-income, marginalized rural area of Japan (Central Kiso) felt toward the cosmopolitan, wealthy, and modern Japanese nation. When migrants and local residents worked out their desires in their everyday relationships, the meanings of both Japaneseness and Filipinaness changed. The encounters between embodied subjects became key arenas within which migration took on cultural meanings (see also Constable 2007 and Friedman and Mahdavi 2011 on rethinking migration through intimate labor). In the case of Filipinas in Japan, such relationships were shaped by inequalities and compromises; and some Filipinas ran away from their husbands and local communities to escape what they experienced as intolerable situations. Beyond running away, however, as the next section discusses, migrants around the world have developed a wide range of other strategies to confront and hopefully change that which they view as intolerable.

## Migrant Activism and Diverse Tactics

In a global context in which the regulatory regimes and surveillance tactics directed at low-income migrants appear ever-strengthening, it is heartening to see migrant-rights advocates working to expand recognition of migrants' entitlement and rights. A volume edited by Monica Varsanyi (2010) focuses on the ways that migrant-rights advocates in the United States have begun to make claims, particularly at the local scale, to oppose employer-sanction laws, to disallow city police from serving as arms of national immigration enforcement, to legalize day-laborer markets, and to resist various other anti-immigrant policies and ordinances. As federal and state immigration governance in the United States is devolved to local and municipal officials, activists have responded by "taking local control" (Varsanyi 2010). Some organizations have demanded that cities and states declare their territories "sanctuaries" for undocumented migrants, marking out spaces where immigration status does not affect access to health care, social services, public education, or employment protections. All of this activism indexes heated cultural/political struggles over who belongs in the nation, what sorts of entitlements and claims are/should be linked to formal citizenship, what constitutes or should constitute citizenship, and which scales of government are responsible for determining or enacting various aspects of service provision or legal regulation tied to immigration.

Cultural geographers have much to add to these conversations about the scales of immigration policy and the possibilities of migrant-rights activism. From a cultural-geographic perspective, political economies and landscapes of rights are socially produced. Citizenship at the national scale is shot through with ethical ambiguities that are lived out and confronted at local scales. For instance, urban activists in the United States organized efforts to create Cities of Refuge in the late 1960s to defend the rights of soldiers unwilling to fight in Vietnam and later to protect Central American refugees in the US from deportation. Most recently, they have focused on providing sanctuary spaces to undocumented immigrants in the US and Canada. Each of these movements mobilized sanctuary as a form of urban citizenship; and in each case, social movements were at the forefront of reshaping the definition of political membership (Ridgley 2010).

Ridgley's study of sanctuary space refuses to romanticize or overstate the material implications of Cities of Refuge for any of the social groups they intended to protect, defend, and support. Nonetheless, her work makes clear that to make the emergent and hopeful trajectories of sanctuary movements more material, researchers and activists must attend

> not simply to the forms of law and authority that shape immigration policy . . . but the everyday practices [and refusals] of immigration law enforcement . . . If an alternative is to be found that can loosen the hold the legitimacy of migration controls have on our political and geographic imaginations, it may well have to come from the subtle interventions of those who are refusing their everyday enforcement. (2010: 147)

Ridgley attends to insurgent forms of urban citizenship as expressions of emergent political potential rather than completed accomplishments. Her work, thus, provides an important example to help cultural geographers in their efforts to understand both how cultural hegemonies operate and how counterhegemonic cultural forms may take on meaning and power, even if only fleetingly. Indeed, rather than asking only how migrants are controlled by state regulations, border policing, political-economic pressures, or predominant discourses, we must also ask how alternative geographies of migration are being imagined and sometimes practiced. Such counter-mappings offer interventions into the cultural politics of nationalistic and xenophobic hegemony and clues to the development of more hopeful immigration futures.

One activist research project provides especially exciting possibilities for a future of migrant justice. Migrant remittances have become big business in recent decades, in some cases composing a larger percentage of the national income of recipient states than any other form of foreign direct investment (e.g., El Salvador, Philippines). Banks and private wire-transfer companies have cashed in on the bonanza, regularly charging extremely high rates (ranging from 10–20 percent per remittance) for use of their services and annually costing immigrant workers billions of hard-earned dollars worldwide.[4] Like remittance companies, payday loan outlets charge usurious rates for their services, deliberately setting up shop in neighborhoods with high proportions of low-income and immigrant residents. Activists have organized opposition campaigns to fight what they view as predatory lending practices, launching campaigns for "remittance justice" and taking companies such as Western Union to task for unfair banking and business practices.

One such organization, TIGRA (Transnational Institute for Research and Action), has developed a service and an associated technological tool to support remittance justice. As it states on its webpage, "TIGRA connects immigrants with the best ways to send money home. Through our Fair Remittance Standards, we accredit LOW-COST and SOCIALLY-RESPONSIBLE money transfer companies committed to supporting the communities they serve . . . We then use our Remit4Change platform to promote those providers throughout our network of 1400+ immigrant associations" (http://transnationalaction.org/). One scholar involved in this activism/research (Gibson 2012) is researching cultures of banking and finance to understand political uses and manipulations of "risk," "liability," and "debt." As she develops a praxis-oriented genealogy of the financial cultures of migrant remittances, she may be contributing not only to understanding how landscapes of immigrant inequality are socially produced but also to envisioning and enacting cultural geographies of justice for immigrants.

In similar fashion, activists in four major Canadian cities have developed an organization called "No One is Illegal" in response to their critique of the Canadian nation-state's taken-for-granted authority to determine membership in the nation. Among other things, No One is Illegal demands

> an end to all deportations and detentions; the implementation of a full and inclusive regularization program for all non-status people; access without fear to essential services for all undocumented people; the recognition of indigenous sovereignty; an end to the exploitation of temporary workers; an end to all imperialist wars and occupations; [and] an end to the use of Security Certificates and secret trials. (http://toronto.nooneisillegal.org/demands)

In this way, the group links the injustices directed at undocumented immigrants in Canada to the unjust treatment of First Nations groups and unjustified military interventions around the world, creating what Cindi Katz (2001) calls a countertopography that can point the way to more just futures.

## Conclusion

Pointing to connections among disenfranchised groups or even relying on a discourse of rights is not enough to transform the practices of surveillance and policing, the political economies of inequalities, or the historically deep social divisions and stereotypes that contour the daily geographies of migration in which many around the world live their lives. As this chapter has shown, cultural geographies of migration not only reflect but also are embedded in the production of geographies of difference that work across scales from the body to international borders and that are cross-cut by race, class, gender, and other forms of social differentiation. All of these geographies work through and upon political-economic systems that create multi-scalar social, political, and economic inequalities that drive many migration patterns. Nonetheless, the instances of activism discussed in the previous section shape and reshape the places, possibilities, and subjectivities of migrants and those with whom they live, and do so in potentially profound ways.

Cultural geographers are in an ideal position to explore these productions and transformations of place, political and social possibilities, and subjectivities associated with migration. From the ways that migrants make place at scales from the private bedrooms of domestic workers to the transnational and diasporic spaces of community, acts of migration are bound up with cultural geographies of home, neighborhood, city, nation, as well as the spaces in between. From the everyday acts of struggle and resistance of immigrants fighting for fair wages, equal treatment, and the right to be recognized as part of "the public" in their new homes to large-scale political activism of immigrant groups in their receiving and sending communities, migration generates cultural geographies of political possibilities that raise new questions about belonging, borders, the nation, and "the people" across spaces and scales. Finally, from the ways that migration reconfigures gendered, racialized, and classed hierarchies and formations to the ways that migrants themselves change local cultural practices and identities in their new and former abodes, migration and its related processes transform the subjectivities, identities, and senses of self and others for migrants, as well as for those they join in new places and leave behind, at least temporarily, at home. For all these reasons and in all these ways, migration politics *are* cultural politics and, as such, rich ground for cultural geographers of all stripes.

## Notes

1  Of course, none of these organizing concepts is the sole or primary purview of cultural geography as a subfield. Rather, each provides a lens onto the dynamic processes and cultural struggles through which migration takes on specific meanings, patterns, and force.

2  This chapter is a partial, positioned review; so there are undoubtedly important cultural geographies of migration not included here. Equally importantly, although I have organized this review around the themes of control, subjectivity, and activism, these themes interact and overlap across migration geographies and theoretical traditions; and the placement of a particular article or book in a discussion of any one conceptual category is intended to invite readers to think across and beyond this literature, not to delimit the scope of any specific project.

3  Reproductive labor is the work required to create labor power as opposed to commodities or products. It can include education, childcare, biological reproduction, sex work, and domestic work.

4  According to the World Bank (2008), "If the cost of sending money home to your family decreased by 5%, the developing world would have an extra $16 billion per year to spend on sustainable development, infrastructure improvements, education and financial literacy projects."

## References

Adey, P. (2008) Airports, mobility, and the calculative architecture of affective control. *Geoforum*, 39 (1), 438–451.

Bissonnette, J.-F. (2012) Envisioning agribusiness: Land, labour and value in a time of oil palm expansion in Indonesia. Unpublished PhD dissertation. Department of Geography and Program in Planning, University of Toronto.

Blunt, A. (2007) Cultural geographies of migration: Mobility, transnationality and diaspora. *Progress in Human Geography*, 31 (5), 684–694.

Boris, E. and Parreñas, R.S. (eds.) (2010) *Intimate Labors: Cultures, Technologies, and the Politics of Care*. Stanford: Stanford University Press.

Calavita, K. (2006) Collisions at the intersection of gender, race and class: Enforcing the Chinese Exclusion Laws. *Law and Society Review*, 40, 249–282.

Constable, N. (2007) *Maid to Order in Hong Kong: Stories of Migrant Workers*, 2nd edition. Ithaca: Cornell University Press.

Cooper, F. and Stoler, A. (eds.) (1997) *Tensions of Empire: Colonial Cultures in a Bourgeois World*. Berkeley: University of California Press.

Faier, L. (2009) *Intimate Encounters: Filipina Women and the Remaking of Rural Japan*. Berkeley: University of California Press.

Friedman, S. and Mahdavi, P. (2011) Rethinking intimate labor through inter-Asian migrations: Insights from the Bellagio Conference. *Asian and Pacific Migration Journal*, 20 (2), 253–262.

Gibson, M. (2012) Banking on remittances: Migration and development desires in the Philippines. Unpublished MA thesis, Department of Geography and Program in Planning, University of Toronto.

Gidwani, V. and Sivaramakrishnan, K. (2003) Circular migration and the spaces of cultural assertion. *Annals of the Association of American Geographers*, 93 (1), 186–213.

Gilbert, E. (2007) Leaky borders and solid citizens: Governing security, prosperity and quality of life in a North American partnership. *Antipode*, 39 (1), 77–98.

Gilbert, E. (2012) Harper's border deal expands the national security state. http://rabble.ca/news/2012/02/harpers-border-deal-expands-national-security-state, February 1 (accessed October 30, 2012).

Graham, E. and Boyle, P. (2001) Editorial introduction. (Re)theorising population geography: Mapping the unfamiliar. *Population, Space and Place*, 7, 389–394.

Hanson, S. and Pratt, G. (1988) Reconceptualizing the links between home and work in urban geography. *Economic Geography*, 64 (4), 299–321.

Hanson, S. and Pratt, G. (1995) *Gender, Work and Space*. New York: Routledge.

Johnson, M. (2010) Diasporic dreams, middle class moralities and migrant domestic workers among Muslim Filipinos in Saudi Arabia. *Asia Pacific Journal of Anthropology*, 11 (3/4), 428–448.

Katz, C. (2001) On the grounds of globalization: A topography for feminist political engagement. *Signs: Journal of Women in Culture and Society*, 26 (4), 1213–1234.

King, R. (2012) Geography and migration studies: Retrospect and prospect. *Population, Space and Place*, 18, 134–153.

Lawson, V. (1998) Hierarchical households and gendered migration: A research agenda. *Progress in Human Geography*, 22 (1), 32–53.

Lawson, V. and England, K. (2005) Feminist analyses of work: Rethinking the boundaries, gendering, and spatiality of work. In *A Companion to Feminist Geography*, ed. L. Nelson and J. Seager. Oxford: Blackwell, pp. 77–92.

Lindquist, J. (2009) *The Anxieties of Mobility: Development and Migration in the Indonesian Borderlands*. Honolulu: University of Hawai'i Press.

Mattingly, D.J. (2001) The home and the world: Domestic service and international networks of caring labor. *Annals of the Association of American Geographers*, 91 (2), 370–386.

McHugh, K. (2000) Inside, outside, upside down, backward, forward, round and round: A case for ethnographic studies in migration. *Progress in Human Geography*, 24 (1), 71–89.

McKay, D. (2005) Reading remittance landscapes: Female migration and agricultural transition in the Philippines. *Danish Journal of Geography*, 105 (1), 89–99.

Mills, M.B. (1999) *Thai Women in the Global Labor Force: Consuming Desires, Contested Selves*. New Brunswick: Rutgers University Press.

Mountz, A. (2010) *Seeking Asylum: Human Smuggling and Bureaucracy at the Border*. Minneapolis: University of Minnesota Press.

Mountz, A. and Hyndman, J. (2006) Feminist approaches to the global intimate. *Women's Studies Quarterly*, 34 (1/2), 446–463.

Nagar, R., Lawson, V., McDowell, L., and Hanson, S. (2002) Locating globalization: Feminist (re)readings of the subjects and spaces of globalization. *Economic Geography*, 78 (3), 257–284.

Parreñas, R.S. (2001) *Servants of Globalization: Women, Migration and Domestic Work*. Stanford: Stanford University Press.

Pratt, G. (2012) *Families Apart: Migrant Mothers and the Conflicts of Labor and Love*. Minneapolis: University of Minnesota Press.

Ridgley, J. (2010) Cities of Refuge: Citizenship, legality and exception in US sanctuary cities. Unpublished PhD dissertation. Department of Geography and Program in Planning, University of Toronto.

Rodriguez, R.M. (2010) *Migrants for Export: How the Philippine State Brokers Labor to the World*. Minneapolis: University of Minnesota Press.

Sassen, S. (2003) Strategic instantiations of gendering in the global economy. In *Gender and U.S. Immigration: Contemporary Trends*, ed. P. Hondagenu-Sotelo. Berkeley: University of California Press, pp. 43–60.

Silvey, R. (2009) Fieldnotes. Section available on request from author.

Silvey, R. and Lawson, V. (1999) Placing the migrant. *Annals of the Association of American Geographers*, 89 (1), 121–132.

Sparke, M. (2005) A neoliberal nexus: Economy, security and the biopolitics of citizenship on the border. *Political Geography*, 25 (2), 151–180.

Varsanyi, M. (ed.) (2010) *Taking Local Control: Immigration Policy Activism in U.S. Cities and States.* Stanford: Stanford University Press.

White, P. and Jackson, P. (1995) (Re)theorising population geography. *International Journal of Population Geography*, 1, 111–123.

Winders, J. (2011) Re-placing southern geographies: The role of Latino migration in transforming the South, its identities, and its study. *Southeastern Geographer*, 51 (2), 342–358.

World Bank (2008) *The Malaysia–Indonesia Remittance Corridor.* http://siteresources.worldbank.org/INTAML/Resources/Malaysia-Indonesia.pdf (accessed October 30, 2012).

Yeoh, B. and Huang, S. (1999) Spaces at the margins: Migrant domestic workers and the development of civil society in Singapore. *Environment and Planning A*, 31 (7), 1149–1167.

Yeoh, B. and Willis, K. (1999) "Heart" and "wing," nation and diaspora: Gendered discourses in Singapore's regionalisation process. *Gender, Place and Culture*, 6 (4), 355–372.

Chapter 35

# Mappings

*Jeremy W. Crampton*

## Introduction

Just north of the Bayshore Freeway in San Francisco stands an unprepossessing building known simply as "Building 45." From ground level the blue-sided two-story building appears unremarkable, apart from the generous number of disabled parking places. If you view it from above, however, the building yields a secret. The whole of the roof is covered in solar panels. So are other buildings nearby, and across Charleston Road to the north. In fact, what you're looking at (should you be able to peer at these buildings from the air) is the largest commercial array of solar panels in the United States.

Building 45 holds other secrets too. In fact, it is dedicated to enabling people to peer at the earth. On its second floor a team of programmers and engineers led by John Hanke are engaged in what *Wired* magazine calls a "cartographic revolution" (Ratliff 2007). Building 45 is the location of Google's "Geo" products such as Google Maps, Earth, StreetView, and Panoramio. More recently Google added user-generated mapping capabilities called My Places, in which users can create and share maps with each other using a simple file format known as KML or Keyhole Markup Language. Using a KML file you can post your customized map, email it to friends, use it in a Twitter message, or post it on Facebook. If you want to mark the position of Building 45 or any other spot on earth (and Google claims it provides over 60 percent coverage of the world's populated areas), you can create one of those iconic Google pushpin markers. These you can then embed in your website.

This chapter will return to the mystery of "Keyhole" below, but first will address the "cartographic revolution" that comprises much more than *Wired* magazine might expect in its focus on the technical aspects of Google Earth. That cartographic revolution incorporates yet extends beyond the changing technical nature of map production, to take into account

*The Wiley Blackwell Companion to Cultural Geography*, First Edition.
Edited by Nuala C. Johnson, Richard H. Schein, and Jamie Winders.
© 2013 John Wiley & Sons, Ltd. Published 2016 by John Wiley & Sons, Ltd.

map consumption, the manner in which we understand maps as imbricated with and implicated in our everyday social, political, and economic lives; as knowledge that is integral to
cultural processes; as a critical component of the very systems of meaning that are both mold
and mirror of our cultural practices.

## Cartographic Revolutions

Until fairly recently it was an unquestioned assumption among scholars that mapping was
a human universal – maps were created by almost all societies and could be found deep into
human history. Archaeological findings from prehistoric Europe, ancient China, South
America, Australasia, and Africa have all been interpreted as maps or at least proto-maps. In
the first English-language textbook on cartography by the Austro-Hungarian émigré Erwin
Raisz, a stylized "Time Chart" is offered, tracing the spread of cartography from antiquity
to modern maps (Raisz 1938). Raisz fought for the Austro-Hungarian Empire in World War
I, emigrated to the United States in 1923, and made his career at Columbia (where in 1927
he offered one of the first cartography classes) and then Harvard University (Yacher 1982).
The father of American cartography, Arthur Robinson said that Raisz was the "foremost
geographical cartographer in America" (Robinson 1970: 189) and his textbook shaped the
field for many years until Robinson's own influential postwar textbook (Robinson 1953).

Raisz's Time Chart presented a progressivist and presentist history of mapping achievements. It starts with a significant claim: "the making of maps antedates the art of writing"
(Raisz 1938: 7). Over time maps get more accurate, and with few exceptions the West is in
the vanguard. Similar narratives of the progression of mapping, usually told as a story adrift
from any sociopolitical events such as colonialism or state power, can be found in other classics such as Bagrow (1964), Brown (1949), and to a lesser extent in Robinson himself.

In response, the historical geographer J. Brian Harley and the historian of cartography
David Woodward set out to establish a history that would be "cartography without progress,"
in the words of Edney (1993). Their still-ongoing *History of Cartography*, conceptualized in
1977 during long walks in Devon (Woodward 1992), draws on cultural geography, anthropology, and the power of maps, as well as history, as their agenda-setting essay outlined
(Harley and Woodward 1987). However, it shares with those earlier histories the idea of
mapping as a universal; something that is common to both prehistoric cultures and late capitalist societies. Harley could not restrain himself from speculating along the very same lines
as Raisz: mapping "precedes both written language and systems involving number" (Harley
1987: 1).

In recent years this cultural universality has been challenged by those who understand the
history of mapping alongside the history of the state. Thus for Wood, maps are of relatively
recent origin (post-1600 CE); although there are scattered precursors, the vast majority of
mapping has occurred with the rise of (and in the service of) the modern state (Wood and
Fels 2010). (Here Wood has a traditional view of the state as a spatially bounded container,
itself an idea that is receiving increased attention from geographers.) Similarly, James C. Scott
argued that government needs to make its concerns "legible," for example through cadastral
(property) mapping (Scott 1998), and those who have taken up Foucault's outline of "governmentality" have mined a rich seam of mapping as governmental technology. On these
views, then, mapping and geographic information systems (GIS) are not universals but have
a very clear purpose as a component of state power and sovereignty. It is only with the modern
state that mapping realizes its true history.

## Sovereignty and Knowledge: The Emergence of Modern Mapping

How, then, did modern mapping emerge? In this section we shall briefly trace some of the key historical moments, not so much as a sequence of dates but under three general ways to approach maps. The first is *mapping as material form*, or what Robinson classically called "the look of maps" (Robinson 1952). The materiality of mapping is a long-standing interest of cartographers, and includes the design or appearance of maps as well as their mode of production, who has access to them, and the diversity of map types ("cartodiversity"). Geographic information systems also need to be designed and there are lots of places where you can get good advice (e.g., Esri's Mapping Center blog [http://www.esri.com/]) on how to best do this. Finally, there has been some effort on how to design maps for the web, although the best practitioners remain the small custom cartography companies rather than academic scholars.[1]

Second, we will consider *mapping as knowledge(s)*. Here we will deploy a key insight of work on theories of cartography over the last twenty years; maps are not just reflective of knowledge but actively create knowledge – what Foucault once said was the question of how they "thought out space" (Foucault 1984: 244). Mapping is an active process of intervention in the world and there is an important historicity or genealogy to the knowledges created in and around mapping. These knowledges do not act in isolation but exist as networks of power relations. Think of them like the news media. News stories report on what has happened but they choose what to report on and how to frame the narrative. In effect, some maps are like CNN, some are like the Fox Network, and some are like the BBC.

Third, we will consider *mapping as practice and performance*. How are maps and mappings used and experienced? What are the effects of mappings, politically, economically, and culturally? Further, how have emerging practices of mapping challenged traditional authoritative mapping institutions, for example through crowdsourcing? How have these changed and reflected back on the materiality of maps and the forms of knowledge creation? This question then asks how maps change the world in practice.

These three topics are fundamentally intertwined and invite us to reflect on maps' historicity or genealogy, not just as a sequence of events but as situated within a larger sociopolitical context. Thus, the study of maps and GIS in this manner has been the subject of *critical cartography and GIS*, which seeks to unpack the assumptions behind mapping. Mapping's "political turn" encompasses questions of map activism, of decision-making, and crucially of maps as "technologies" of the state (Branch 2011). But state concerns are not new and have been a central narrative in the emergence of modern cartography through to the machinations of "Keyhole."

Mapping is a sense-*creating* process as much as a sense-*making* process. Up until about the nineteenth century this was often understood to center on the natural (or God-given) world. But like its cognate disciplines such as geography, geometry, and natural history, this was not just a matter of description but of categorizing and placing objects of inquiry into a structured framework. If this meant mapping as knowledge, it also had a distinct normative and even teleological meaning, with the map performing ways of being.

The Greek writer Herodotus in his *Histories* (written around 430 BCE) attempted a coherent narrative not just of wars but of the world in which he lived. In a pattern that would be repeated, there was a distinct geography to his knowledge, with increasingly weird and monstrous races away from the centers of learning (Athens and Alexandria). At one point he (somewhat skeptically) provides information on the Neuri, a race of werewolves (Hdt.

4.105). Although people were sometimes described as occupying particular locales, these were not political borders in the modern sense.

But it is perhaps the work of Pliny the Elder and his *Natural History* (first century CE) that is the first serious effort to geographically account for human diversity. Pliny's account was written at a time of increasing exploration (particularly after Alexander the Great), just as the blossoming maps of the fifteenth and sixteenth centuries were. But it was also a time when writers grappled with nature's diversity and wondrousness and attempted to account for it. The "Plinian Races" had huge impact in medieval thought and mapping in particular, describing as he did monstrous people such as the "blemmyae" (headless people with eyes in their chests), "sciopods" or shadow-foots whose name derived from the fact that their legs were fused together with one large foot under which they could shelter if they lay on their backs, the "cynocephali" (dog-heads), and Arimaspi or one-eyed people (Friedman 1981). These strange peoples were again often located at a distance both spatially (e.g., in India) and culturally, far from where normal peoples were (Winlow 2009). Taking their cue from ancient writers and biblical stories (e.g., the Nephilim or giants mentioned in Genesis 6:4), medieval maps delighted in placing these human monsters around the margins of the maps.

Monstrousness is a theme also found in both medieval and later (eighteenth-century) writings. However, in the latter case it took place under a different register; if for Pliny the wonders and monsters were against nature, for eighteenth-century writers they were also a transgression against human laws. Thus the abnormal and the delinquent had a little bit of the monster in them that had to be either suppressed or medically treated.[2] As we shall see, maps of abnormality were very popular throughout the nineteenth and early twentieth centuries.

Medieval maps, known as mappae mundi (world maps) or T-in-O maps from their shape, understood the world in proto-race ways. Following another chapter in Genesis (10), which describes how the three sons of Noah (Shem, Japheth, and Ham) peopled the earth, medieval maps showed the world in three divisions, populated by three major groupings of people (Asians, Europeans, and Africans), which could later be interpreted as races. These three peoples were not necessarily meant to be equivalent. Drawing on a theory of multiple origins known as polygenism, they were understood to be hierarchical, with some at the top (Europeans) and others lower down (Asians and Africans). Noah's curse of his son Ham in Genesis (9:25), along with the fact that Ham was allocated to Africa, provided grounds not only for prejudice against Africans but was also often used to justify their slavery.

As Winlow has discussed, the establishment of evolutionary theories in the nineteenth century served to redouble efforts on mapping human racial types as part of a whole concern with human characteristics, population density, migration, and especially language and religion (Winlow 2009). The famous map by Gustaf Kombst (2nd edition, 1856), for example, showed various racial groupings allotted into distinct geographical territories (see Figure 35.1). These maps were made as part of a discourse that was concerned with the distribution of populations (often, as in Kombst, to compare the state of "pure" races with encroachments from other lesser races). This was by no means a nineteenth-century prerogative and many of its geo-race ideas made headway well into the twentieth century – and found friendly reception in geography, anthropology, and biology. The American lawyer Madison Grant, for example, whose racist book *The Passing of the Great Race* (Grant 1932) was indicative of mainstream race science prior to the war, was a longtime councilor on the American Geographical Society (AGS). As an associate of Isaiah Bowman, the AGS Director between 1915 and 1935, Grant had earlier published his work in the flagship journal of the AGS, the

**Figure 35.1** Ethnographic map of Europe according to Gustaf Kombst. In *The Physical Atlas of Natural Phenomena* by Alexander Keith Johnston (2nd edition, 1856).
Source: David Rumsey Map Collection. Used by permission of David Rumsey.

*Geographical Review* (Grant 1916). Grant's was a true biological racism, and his maps in *GR* and his book unhesitatingly drew distinctions between the three European races (Nordic, Mediterranean, and Alpine) and "Negroid" and "Mongoloid" races. He argued some countries were more affected by throwbacks with "Neolithic" traits. Even Britain, with its generally admirable Nordic type (blond, blue-eyed, with flowing hair), sometimes yielded evidence of a less-developed trait. Who can fail to observe, writes Grant, "on the streets of London the contrast between the Piccadilly gentleman of Nordic race and the Cockney costermonger of the old Neolithic type?" (Grant 1932: 27).

## Thematic Maps and State-istics

As populations-as-race came to the forefront of governmental concern, new forms of mapping were introduced to deal with the problem. In the late eighteenth century, thematic descriptions of one specific topic rather than the multiple features of a topographic landscape were mapped for the first time. These maps (known as thematic maps) were made not just for the sake of it, but rather to address a burgeoning problem. By the mid-nineteenth century most of the types of thematic maps in use in today's GIS had been invented. The well-known choropleth map, for instance, was first used in 1826. It was used to depict a crisis in education and shows the ratio of (male) children in school compared to population of regions in France. Its author, Baron Charles Dupin, wished to identify what was then called *la France obscure* and *la France éclairée* (uneducated and educated parts of France) (Dupin 1827).

There was tremendous contemporary interest in this map and it was much copied by his contemporaries in what Beirne (1993) calls a "social cartography" that helped invent certain kinds of people, mostly deviants or abnormals (Hacking 2002; Foucault 2003b). These choropleth maps (they were not called that then; the term was invented in 1938 by J.K. Wright: see Crampton 2009) were instrumental in framing a spatial discourse of norms and abnormals. Alongside the maps came a slew of statistical measures, again familiar to us today, such as the "normal distribution" developed by Adolphe Quetelet in his "social physics" (Hacking 1990). Many of today's GIS geostatistical measures came out of work in ecology in the early twentieth century. These statistics were critical as the very etymology of the term indicates: they were "state-istics" (Shaw and Miles 1979), that is, statistics for the state.

The point to consider then is how mapping and the production of certain kinds of knowledge have been imbricated with governmental projects – a question that involves but is not limited to the state. How do maps frame our understanding of spatial distributions such as race, and how as a practice do they create and promote certain forms of knowledge and not others? For instance, J.K. Wright's work in the early twentieth century has left a tremendous but largely unexamined legacy in geography, and specifically mapping and GIScience. Wright brought together a conception of space that could be modeled as points, lines, and areas. This schema today underlies GIS and vector data models of points, lines, and polygons. What is at issue here, then, is how practices of mapping have "thought out space" (Foucault 1984: 244). Instead of points, lines, and polygons, which is not a particularly everyday understanding of the world, perhaps maps should involve a more experiential aspect of our lives (maps as practices)? Or perhaps with its emphasis on hard and fast lines, the map has supported the idea of clear territorial borders, when in fact the real world is more diversified and spatially transitional?

## Returning to Keyhole

Now we can return to the question of the "Keyhole" in Google's KML. The Keyhole referred to is the name of a series of secret reconnaissance ("spy") satellites launched by the US government since the 1960s. It is also the name (Keyhole, Inc.) of a company that developed Earth Viewer, a virtual digital earth. Keyhole was acquired by Google in 2004 and renamed Google Earth (Crampton 2008). Prior to the purchase, Keyhole, Inc. was funded in part by the Central Intelligence Agency's venture capital company In-Q-Tel, which was set up in 1999 to fund technology that would advance the agency's intelligence mission. The CEO of Keyhole, Inc. was John Hanke, whom we met in Building 45. (Hanke left Google in 2010.) Prior to its buyout the main client of Keyhole was the National Geospatial-Intelligence Agency (NGA), a geographic intelligence agency about the same size as the CIA.

These interconnections show that government and mapping have had, and continue to have, an intimate relationship. In this it is not unique as there are other disciplines with a government (and military) legacy, such as physics (the Manhattan Project), computer science (DARPA and the invention of the Internet), the health and life sciences, and anthropology (Wakin 1992; Price 2008). These relations may go mostly unexamined, although in the case of the latter they recently prompted the major American anthropological association to issue a statement on research and the military intelligence community (Peacock et al. 2007). Similar concerns were raised in geography concerning participatory mapping expeditions to Mexico by academics in North America who had military ties (Bryan 2010). Nevertheless the legacy of involvement in geography is longer than most, given the way that states have mapped terrain for warfare and empire (Driver 2001). In this sense, then, mapping is a technology of government. This is not to reduce mapping to being only an element of government, but rather to identify a project that has not yet been completed: tracing the genealogy of mapping and the state. Nonetheless, there have been some important contributions (Hannah 2000; Edney 1997; Schulten 2001).

## The Possibilities of "Counter-Mapping"

We noted above that the term "Keyhole" provides an insight into both where mapping/GIS have come from (technology of government) and where it may be heading. We do this by examining the exciting potential of creating and sharing mappings, personal geographies, creative projects, and explorations with each other. Traditionally the big mapping projects (Ordnance Survey, US Geological Survey, even Lewis and Clark) were in the service of government – Scott's idea of the state making itself visible in order to govern it properly. This meant in turn a "trickledown" model from state and local government to the citizen. If you wanted, say, the plat map of your property, you would go to City Hall and obtain it (sometimes for a price) at the Planner's Office. Similarly, if you wanted an aerial or satellite image, you could go to a federal agency like the National Oceanic and Atmospheric Administration (NOAA) or the USGS. Over the past few years a rather different model of mapping has started to emerge. It is still very nascent (and unfortunately goes by a long list of clunky names like "volunteered geographic information" and the "spatial geoweb"), but the idea is clear: enable open-source data creation and sharing. A rather more evocative way to think about it is "counter-mapping." If the state is mapping and performing surveillance, we citizens are counter-mapping.

Counter-mapping uses tools and data that are *open source*, meaning three things:

1   Anyone is free to obtain them.
2   Anyone is free to change them (i.e., rewrite the code).
3   Anyone is free to distribute them.

"Free" means free to (*libre*) and often (but not necessarily) financially free (*gratis*).

The story of the rise of counter-mapping is a fascinating one. One critical moment occurred in late 2004 when Paul Rademacher was driving around in San Francisco trying to find a new place to live. He was balancing the well-known Craigslist of properties (originally a hard copy but now also online) and a stack of maps. As he drove around with piles of printouts and maps, Rademacher thought, "Wouldn't it be better to have one map with all the listings on it?" (Ratliff 2007: 157). His timing was excellent. On February 8, 2005, Google Maps went online and within only a matter of hours programmers had reverse engineered it so that their own content, rather than Google's, would appear on the maps (Roush 2005). What this meant was that Google Maps had been hacked – not by mischievous troublemakers but by people who wanted to use Google's well-designed maps to display and share their own data. The result was a website called housingmaps.com (still going today), where you can look at a Google map, plug in your price-range rent, and find available properties. Or you can look at a particular area and see what's available.

> One Thursday night, [Rademacher] posted a link to the demo on craigslist, and by the next day thousands of people had already taken it for a spin. "I had no idea how big it would be," he says. (Ratliff 2007: 157)

Google at this point could have closed the door on Rademacher and the other early mappers. It watched – and instead decided to officially open up its maps, releasing the Google Map API in June 2005. Its decision was soon vindicated. In the early fall of 2005, Hurricane Katrina struck the mainland of the United States, and millions of people used Google to visualize and look at the affected areas. While the government agency NOAA posted hundreds of freshly flown aerial imagery, these were on clunky or obscure websites and the public gravitated to Google Earth, where the images were overlaid as updates on the background. Perhaps significantly, the government itself began using Google Earth rather than their own usual channels. Rademacher's own story completes the circle: Google hired him.

While Google has provided some of the tools and resources that are often associated with this movement, and has done much to popularize mapping (Google Earth has supposedly been downloaded over a billion times), we should not forget that it is not open source. Google is a huge company – worth over US$200 billion (i.e., as big as Wal-Mart). And although its API (the application program interface which allows people to combine their data onto Google Maps) has been used in countless ways to make interesting map mashups and web map services, it is at the end of the day a for-profit enterprise (annual revenues of US$30 billion in 2010). The same goes for Esri, the private company that sells the popular ArcGIS software. Although its financials are not publicly available, it is often estimated as having about a third of the multi-billion dollar GIS market.

What this means is that Google and Esri control the data, in terms of what they'll allow you to create and join to their maps, how your maps will look (basically like all other Google maps, for instance), and how you may distribute, reproduce, sell, or not sell them. Essentially, they are in the same position as sovereign states with the added incentive to make a profit (they sometimes get labeled "Big GIS" for this reason). At any time they could alter their business model, close down or charge for their API, or suspend their data exchange services. (Esri has a useful one at arcgis.com.) On January 1, 2012, users got a taste of what this means when Google started charging for use of its Google Maps API over 25,000 hits per day. The new charges meant that some companies found themselves looking at hundreds of thousands of dollars in fees.

What this means, then, is that we need to go beyond Keyhole. Fortunately there are now many open-source alternatives that are robust enough to handle the traffic of even the busiest users, while also being user-friendly enough to let individuals master them. There are tools that provide open-source GIS (PostGIS), data mapping and visualization (GeoCommons), map design (Carto CSS), and tile renderers (Mapnik and TileMill). (If you look closely at Google Maps you'll see that it does not deliver one huge map but rather a series of tiles, and that as you zoom in these are replaced by smaller, more detailed tiles. This tiling helps to deliver rapid-response maps over the Internet. In fact it is a common experience that Google Maps will display more quickly over the Internet than Esri ArcMap installed on your local machine!)[3]

Perhaps the most ambitious project of all, however, is OpenStreetMap (OSM). This was founded in 2004 with the goal of providing a complete map of the world that is open source and copyright free. The challenge here is enormous because to achieve that goal, OSM cannot be based on any other maps (because they are copyrighted). Therefore it is built up mile by mile from the tracks of volunteers using their GPS units to record the route of highways, roads, paths, railroads, and so on. Currently, OSM is a Creative Commons Attribution-ShareAlike 2.0 (CC-BY-SA) license, which means that anybody is free to use it as long as they acknowledge it and provide the same license to end-users.[4] By the end of 2011,

OpenStreetMap had acquired and geolocated 2.7 billion coordinates, 121 million routes, and had half a million registered contributors. OSM basemaps now appear in a wide number of places (including Esri products), and are available for the iPhone, iPad, and Android phones and tablets.

To contribute to OSM you need a GPS unit, a web browser, and access to the Internet. Then, by traveling along routes that are not in the database, your GPS can collect information about the location and shape of the route. (You can do as much or as little as you like – you do not have to do the whole M1 or Route 66, for example!) You can travel how you like – by foot, bicycle, train, ferry, or ski lift. You can also map places or locations of interest to you, from the mundane (traffic lights, emergency phone boxes) to the more exotic (air gondolas and cross-country ski routes). Once you have your data, you upload it to OSM using a small text file in the GPS universal format (.gpx) from your web browser. The final step is to symbolize your data using the vast number of feature symbols already existing, or by making up a new one if it is not already present. More recently, OSM has been able to utilize data imported from aerial imagery.

When OSM was first launched many people worried that it would not be accurate. Some of this worry was a genuine concern to build the best map of the world possible. Other criticism of it and the open geodata movement was hard to disambiguate from vested interests. (Jack Dangermond, Esri CEO, once remarked he would not like to rely on open data to find where to dig for a pipe.) To test its accuracy Muki Haklay compared OSM in the UK to the gold standard of mapping, the Ordnance Survey (OS). In general, he found that OSM data are comparably accurate: on average within 6 meters of the position recorded by the OS (Haklay 2010). This does not make OS redundant, but, given its close control over data and licensing, OSM provides quality data where OS is not an option. One example might illustrate its usefulness. Following the 7.0-magnitude Haiti earthquake of January 2010, aid agencies rushed to assist the Haitian people, many of whom lost their homes in the earthquake. International aid was, however, significantly hampered by a lack of good maps of the country (including where the relief camps were). In the hours and days following the disaster, OSM mobilized users and coordinated available data (some providers such as GeoEye also relaxed restrictions on their commercial satellite imagery).[5] As a result a useful and open-source map of the affected areas was produced.

OSM is clearly a major initiative. Its success – like that of Wikipedia but without the same dependency on donations – derives from its thousands of volunteers. Its full usefulness has still to be realized, although as a well-designed copyright-free basemap with lots of detail it is appearing in more and more applications. In fact, technically it has no single design or look: it can be "rendered" with any number of symbolization schemes, or the data can be imported into GIS as shapefiles and designed how you like. If a map has no particular design, is the question of the "look of maps" solved or only deepened? This is a question that has not yet been much studied in cartography, particularly when it comes to optimal design for mobile devices and tablets.

Satellite companies have long played an important role in the production of geographical knowledge. Whether these have been unclassified research satellites (e.g., the Landsat series) or the secret Corona and Keyhole spy satellites of the Cold War (Cloud 2002), they provide data in quantities that no terrestrial sensor could achieve. Until recently these too were the province of wealthy or paranoid governments (US, China) due to their cost. However, today private satellite companies are major players. Their available resolutions are also not too different from the (presumed) resolution of government spy satellites. GeoEye, mentioned above, can provide images from space that can pick out objects as small as .41 meters across or the size of home plate on the baseball field. (The United States does limit commercial providers from releasing imagery beyond .50 meter resolution, and a provision of American law known as the Kyl-Bingaman Amendment prohibits high-resolution imagery of Israel from being released.)

Although this imagery is very useful, it is also costly. The manufacture, launch, and maintenance of a GPS satellite costs hundreds of millions of dollars. Therefore, another aspect of the open geodata movement has focused on developing inexpensive methods to collect "remote sensing" imagery using some rather classic tools: helium balloons and kites. In the United States one notable effort has emerged around the Public Laboratory for Open Technology and Science (PLOTS). Using simple and inexpensive materials (string, weather balloons, a tank of helium from the local hardware/DIY store) anyone can, with a bit of trial and effort, collect higher-resolution imagery than is available from commercial or government sources. Additionally, imagery can be recollected as often as needed. PLOTS is open source and community driven and came to prominence during the BP oil spill in the Gulf of Mexico in the summer of 2010. Local residents, concerned about the effects of the oil on sensitive marine ecosystems (and sources of income), teamed with PLOTS to monitor the spill. Although each image taken covers only a small piece of territory, the PLOTS mapknitter (a free online web-based tool) can "stitch" the images together to make a coherent image. These can be exported as georeferenced TIFF images (for import into GIS) or simple JPEGS. Depending on the sensor installed below the balloon, it is also possible to collect imagery in different parts of the spectrum. PLOTS members have experimented with thermal imagery and multispectral imagery, which has a number of applications (for example, assessing the health of vegetation). Others have used these methods to make 3D models of the environment to assess stream erosion or build digital models of buildings in a neighborhood, campus, or city (see Figure 35.2).

## Conclusion

Maps are both opportunity and threat. Today mapping and location technologies are helping to produce all sorts of surveillance possibilities, whether it be your mobile phone, unmanned aerial systems (UAS or drones), or humanitarian relief in Afghanistan using open-source tools. This centrality of mapping to modernity deserves our most sustained investigation as scholars, geographers, and map users. Unfortunately, instead of being grasped in its richness, mapping and cartography are often regarded as a legacy of a more technocratic age. This has sometimes acted to dissuade interest in mapping within academia, at a time when its transformational possibilities are greater than ever. (For example, the number of maps published in geography journals has been on the decline for some time, and cartography and GIS are underrepresented among women and minorities.) Part of the reason for this neglect has surely been the result of the legacy of postwar cartography and its emphasis on smaller, technicist questions divorced from sociopolitical issues. A prime mantra of many cartographers is that maps are – and should be – the View from Nowhere, that is, free of all politics. The primary goal of this chapter has been to sketch out a different view; namely, in what way maps are political.

There is a final consideration, however. If mapping and cartography are to realize their transformational potential, sometimes known as the "democratization" of cartography (Gorman 2011), access to mapping technologies and participation in mapping activities

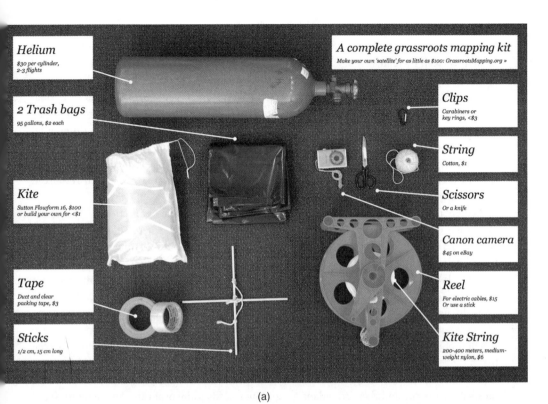

(a)

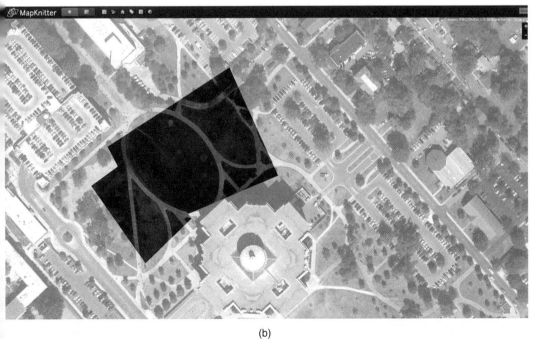

(b)

**Figure 35.2** Typical DIY equipment needed for balloon-mapping (top). Balloon imagery of the University of Kentucky campus being stitched together (bottom).
Source: Public Laboratory for Technology and Science. (CC-BY-SA) Public Lab contributors.

remain the province of the few. While costs have significantly lowered (a balloon mapping kit costs less than $100), participatory mapping, like much of the content on the Internet, is being produced by relatively small numbers of people. Known as the "long tail" or the 80:20 rule (where 80 percent of the content is created by 20 percent of the users), this phenomenon can be observed at work in projects as diverse as Wikipedia, OpenStreetMap, and locational Tweeting (only some 1–4 percent of Tweets are georeferenced). Despite the mantra about the "democratization of mapping," then, the reality is more complex. In the past this differential access was often known as the digital divide, but, as Haklay argues, it is perhaps better to think of "digital inequalities" in the same sense as we think about social inequalities. Indeed, the likelihood of an area being well mapped correlates with the area being well resourced (not socially deprived).

Haklay has conceptualized a hierarchy of involvement, from data collection to "participatory science" to what he calls "extreme" collaborative science, where those involved are co-creators of the very goals of the project (Haklay 2012). All this assumes, however, that people participate in the first place. This has many implications, including the fact that people studying Twitter or OSM are subject to significant bias. Not only are just 4 percent of Tweets georeferenced, but any fair summary of Twitter would have to conclude it is a collection of teens discussing Justin Bieber and Lady Gaga (they have around 20 million followers each; in fact, about 20 percent of Twitter users account for 98 percent of followers). There is also a geographical inequality of Twitter members (see data at http://twittercounter.com). Given that a range of entities are interested in analyzing Twitter (Hillary Clinton being the latest to express an interest in it to predict social uprisings), this is obviously problematic. Research on social networks and their attendant geographies needs to incorporate the "network bias" at stake here, that is, not everyone is equal. In that sense, there is demonstrably no "democracy" of the geoweb.

In an era when the state shows no signs of slowing its geosurveillant capacities (Crampton 2007), the classic mantra "map or be mapped" still has much power, but it might reasonably be rethought today as "only connect."

## Notes

1   Custom cartography companies often draw on strong academic mapping programs. Axis Maps, for instance, was founded by cartographers from Wisconsin–Madison and Middlebury College.
2   For more on this, see Foucault (2003a), especially the lecture of January 22, 1975.
3   PostGIS: http://postgis.refractions.net/; Mapnik: http://mapnik.org/; TileMill: http://mapbox.com/tilemill/; Carto CSS: http://developmentseed.org/blog/2011/feb/09/introducing-carto-css-map-styling-language/. One company's story, that of real estate company StreetEasy, is narrated here with these and many other useful links and details: http://bit.ly/xB7oUY.
4   In 2012 OSM switched to the Open Database License ODbl 1.0, which codifies its open data status (see http://opendatacommons.org/licenses/odbl/).
5   A time-lapse video of the OSM Haiti map from one week prior to the earthquake to twelve days afterward is available here: http://www.youtube.com/watch?v=OF-JuFxhDT8.

## References

Bagrow, L. (1964) *History of Cartography: Revised and Enlarged by R.A. Skelton*. London: C.A Watts.

Beirne, P. (1993) *Inventing Criminology: Essays on the Rise of Homo Criminalis.* Albany: State University of New York Press.

Branch, J. (2011) Mapping the sovereign state: Technology, authority, and systemic change. *International Organization*, 65, 1–36.

Brown, L.A. (1949) *The Story of Maps.* New York: Bonanza Books.

Bryan, J. (2010) Force multipliers: Geography, militarism, and the Bowman Expeditions. *Political Geography*, 29, 414–416.

Cloud, J. (2002) American cartographic transformations during the cold war. *Cartography and Geographic Information Science*, 29, 261–282.

Crampton, J.W. (2007) The biopolitical justification for geosurveillance. *Geographical Review*, 97, 389–403.

Crampton, J.W. (2008) Keyhole, Google Earth, and 3D worlds: An interview with Avi Bar-Zeev. *Cartographica*, 43, 85–93.

Crampton, J.W. (2009) Rethinking maps and identity: Choropleths, clines and biopolitics. In *Rethinking Maps*, ed. M. Dodge, R. Kitchin, and C. Perkins. London: Routledge.

Driver, F. (2001) *Geography Militant: Cultures of Exploration and Empire.* Oxford: Blackwell.

Dupin, P.C.F. (1827) *Forces productives et commerciales de la France.* Paris: Bachelier.

Edney, M.H. (1993) Cartography without "progress": Reinterpreting the nature and historical development of mapmaking. *Cartographica*, 30, 54–68.

Edney, M.H. (1997) *Mapping an Empire: The Geographical Construction of British India, 1765–1843.* Chicago: University of Chicago Press.

Foucault, M. (1984) Space, knowledge, and power. In *The Foucault Reader*, ed. P. Rabinow. New York: Pantheon, pp. 239–256.

Foucault, M. (2003a) *Abnormal: Lectures at the Collège de France (1974–1975).* New York: Picador.

Foucault, M. (2003b) *Society Must Be Defended: Lectures at the Collège de France, 1975–76.* New York: Picador.

Friedman, J.B. (1981) *The Monstrous Races in Medieval Art and Thought.* Cambridge, MA: Harvard University Press.

Gorman, S. (2011) Democratizing GIS through participatory accessibility. *geoiQ blog.* http://blog.geoiq.com/ (accessed October 31, 2012).

Grant, M. (1916) The passing of the great race. *Geographical Review*, 2, 354–360.

Grant, M. (1932) *The Passing of the Great Race or the Racial Basis of European History.* New York: Scribner's Sons.

Hacking, I. (1990) *The Taming of Chance.* Cambridge: Cambridge University Press.

Hacking, I. (2002) *Historical Ontology.* Cambridge, MA: Harvard University Press.

Haklay, M. (2010) How good is volunteered geographical information? A comparative study of OpenStreetMap and Ordnance Survey datasets. *Environment and Planning B: Planning and Design*, 37, 682–703.

Haklay, M. (2012) Citizen science and volunteered geographic information: Overview and typology of participation. In *Volunteered Geographic Information, Public Participation, and Crowdsourced Production of Geographic Knowledge*, ed. D.Z. Sui, S. Elwood, and M.F. Goodchild. Berlin: Springer.

Hannah, M. (2000) *Governmentality and the Mastery of Territory in Nineteenth-Century America.* Cambridge: Cambridge University Press.

Harley, J.B. (1987) The map and the development of the history of cartography. In *Cartography in Prehistoric, Ancient, and Medieval Europe and the Mediterranean*, ed. J.B. Harley and D. Woodward. Chicago: University of Chicago Press, pp. 1–42.

Harley, J.B. and Woodward, D. (eds.) (1987) *Cartography in Prehistoric, Ancient, and Medieval Europe and the Mediterranean.* Chicago: University of Chicago Press.

Peacock, J., Albro, R., Fluehr-Lobban, C., Fosher, K., McNamara, L., Heller, M., Marcus, G., Price, D., and Goodman, A. (2007) AAA Commission on the Engagement of Anthropology with the US Security and Intelligence Communities. American Anthropological Association.

Price, D.H. (2008) *Anthropological Intelligence: The Deployment and Neglect of American Anthropology in the Second World War*. Durham, NC: Duke University Press.

Raisz, E. (1938) *General Cartography*. New York: McGraw-Hill.

Ratliff, E. (2007) The whole earth, catalogued: How Google Maps is changing the way we see the world. *Wired*, 15, 154–159.

Robinson, A.H. (1952) *The Look of Maps: An Examination of Cartographic Design*. Madison: University of Wisconsin Press.

Robinson, A.H. (1953) *Elements of Cartography*. New York: John Wiley & Sons.

Robinson, A.H. (1970) Erwin Josephus Raisz, 1893–1968. *Annals of the Association of American Geographers*, 60, 189–193.

Roush, W. (2005) Killer maps. *Technology Review*, 108, 54–60.

Schulten, S. (2001) *The Geographical Imagination in America 1880–1950*. Chicago: University of Chicago Press.

Scott, J.C. (1998) *Seeing Like a State: How Certain Schemes to Improve the Human Condition Have Failed*. New Haven: Yale University Press.

Shaw, M. and Miles, I. (1979) The social roots of statistical knowledge. In *Demystifying Social Statistics*, ed. J. Irvine, I. Miles, and J. Evans. London: Pluto Press.

Wakin, E. (1992) *Anthropology Goes to War: Professional Ethics and Counterinsurgency in Thailand*. Madison: University of Wisconsin Press.

Winlow, H. (2009) Mapping race and ethnicity. In *The International Encyclopedia of Human Geography*, ed. N. Thrift and R. Kitchen. Oxford: Elsevier.

Wood, D. and Fels, J. (2010) *Rethinking the Power of Maps*. New York: Guilford Press.

Woodward, D. (1992) A Devon walk: The history of cartography. In *A Celebration of the Life and Work of J.B. Harley, 1932–1991 [17 March 1992]*. London: Royal Geographical Society, pp. 13–15.

Yacher, L. (1982) Erwin Josephus Raisz 1893–1968. In *Geographers: Biobibliographical Studies*, ed. G.J. Martin. New York: Continuum, pp. 93–98.

# Chapter 36

# Landscape, Locative Media, and the Duplicity of Code

*Andrew Boulton and Matthew Zook*

Amid the buzz and clatter of the diner, Nancy checks her phone; Sid should be here soon. Two hours ago he checked in at the grocery store on the way home from the office, and his Tweet from 34 seconds ago indicates that he is "heading into town with @nancyt." She opens the Places app on her phone to monitor his progress, and is horrified to note that two of her least favorite high school friends are right here in the Country Kitchen of all places. Time for a quick exit. She looks around; Bebe with her distinctive blond hair is sitting at the bar, but a brunette, not the redheaded Sheila, sits beside her. Safely in the street outside, she takes out her phone again, and unblocks Sheila's Facebook profile. That explains it: 361 profile pictures of her grinning face, the most recent mobile upload showcasing her "new look <3." Nancy needs a new plan, so checks her coupons app: a Mexican restaurant 0.2 miles away has a happy hour special, she notes; two seconds later she is perusing its four star user rating and a glowing review by "Herbert_Garrison," a recommended reviewer with 36 Urbanspoon contributions to his name. Looks good. She taps for walking directions, updates her status, and texts Sid the change of venue as she checks in.

## Introduction

Spurred by the rapid coming of age of the geoweb, in the form of consumer digital mapping and locational services, geographers are taking a reinvigorated interest in critical questions around cartographic representation and practice (Crampton 2009a, 2009b; Goodchild 2007). User-generated or crowdsourced mappings entail the enrollment of new publics in cartographic practices as diverse as natural disaster mapping and recreational geocaching, and as banal as checking in to locations and sharing locationally referenced photographs. In tandem, the role of digital technologies more generally in remediating the production of space (Crang,

*The Wiley Blackwell Companion to Cultural Geography*, First Edition.
Edited by Nuala C. Johnson, Richard H. Schein, and Jamie Winders.
© 2013 John Wiley & Sons, Ltd. Published 2016 by John Wiley & Sons, Ltd.

Crang, and May 1999) has captured the attention of growing numbers of scholars concerned with the agency of software code to shape everyday lives and places (Thrift and French 2002; Fuller 2008; Kitchin and Dodge 2011). This body of research focuses on the "automatic production" (Thrift and French 2002) of space via practices ranging from the policing of access and mobility through congestion pricing and CCTV surveillance, to the "software sorting" classifications (Graham 2005) that differentiate between individuals based on postal code origin and credit score.

These two strands of research overlap most notably in the context of the increasingly ubiquitous phenomenon of locative media technologies; that is, the smartphones, online maps, and proliferating layers of geographically referenced content that are fundamentally imbricated with contemporary experiences in and representations of place. The scenario presented in the opening vignette is commonplace within more privileged parts of the urbanized world, perhaps hackneyed in its familiarity. But just as significant as the spatial and class contours of these technologies – the uneven geographies of digital divides (Zook 2010) and technological inclusion/exclusion – are the behind-the-screens processes that mediate ostensibly straightforward engagements with locative media. In short, critical attention is increasingly directed to the technological, political, and social "innards," in the phraseology of Nigel Thrift (2011: 8), beneath the smooth "surface in continuous motion" on which digitally mediated social life is (s)played out. It is this software-mediated layer of everyday life that shapes our social interactions in important ways, even as it invites, even encourages, us to ignore it.

Metaphors of revealing innards, of unmasking deeper, more basic understandings of the work that code – software, the digital – does in the world, highlight fundamental questions of epistemology: how do we know (in) a world of apparent fluidity and multiplicity, continuous motion and indeterminacy? It is paradoxical that a key enabling technological layer of this superficial fluidity is packed away in the black boxes (sometimes literally) of the computers and cell phones that mediate our access to and experiences of the always-already digitally augmented world. When we talk about landscape we are talking about material places and ways of seeing that are (re)produced through computer screens, cell phones, traffic management, circulations of images and discourse, geospatial surveillance, and myriad other more or less insidious and more or less taken-for-granted manifestations of code's work. When we talk about subjectivity and experience we are talking about identities and perceptions that are coproduced with or reconfigured by digital technologies in various kinds of ways: whether through engagement in the witting theatricality of social media, or the unwitting individuation and software-sorted unevenness of, for example, border security, credit approval, and the digitization of bodies (Graham 2005; Crang and Graham 2007; Amoore and Hall 2009).

This chapter outlines some of the implications of code in the context of cultural geographies in general and cultural landscapes in particular. We first argue that the coding of landscapes should not be viewed simply as a discrete and highly technical series of practices involved in the programming of specific high-tech systems and spaces, but rather as a more diffuse set of subjective processes and practices enrolling individuals in more or less obvious ways in the writing of cultural landscapes. The often obscure(d) ways in which code works through landscape points to the need to (re)politicize its work in ordering and reflecting social lives, rather than accept it as an innocent or uncomplicated actor. Interrogating the duplicity of code re-places software as commensurable with and intrinsic to broader understandings of the ways in which landscape works as an actually existing material thing, and as a way of seeing (Schein 1997) and being seen: new visualities/visibilities.

Building upon these ideas, we next review and reflect on the ways in which geographers are beginning to understand locative technologies as constitutive of remediated regimes of visuality entailing particular subjects and objects of a coded gaze. In particular, we reflect on the ways in which the God's eye view of place afforded by interfaces such as Google Earth provides an intoxicating yet duplicitous landscape experience. The technology embedded within twenty-first-century consumer electronics promises to extend creativity and even authorship, albeit within tightly coded parameters and in concert with the simultaneous proliferation of new forms of self-surveillance.

We then turn to questions of positionality, and how locative technologies work to produce particular kinds of coded subjects. Far from a ubiquitous and uniform experience, digital mapping technologies and the digital landscapes they produce guide and code subjects toward specific experiences. Coded subjects are trained in the new regimes of visuality that multiply and highlight particular representations of places even as software may work to smooth out, or overlook entirely, the breadth and diversity of lay knowledges. Finally, we evoke code's role in the recombination of multiple discourses and temporalities into indeterminate presents and thereby in shaping memory and memorialization. The traces left by geotagged photographs, commentary, and other annotations offer fragmentary echoes of the past that are desequenced and incorporated into temporally flattened digital landscapes. Echoing Mike Crang and Penny Travlou (2001) on ancient Athens, the digital past becomes present-again, "available as a resource to be taken up and through which present actions can occur" (p. 173).

The goal of this chapter is to recognize that locative digital technologies are (increasingly) significant actants in everyday life, constitutive of and constituted by everyday places, and tied up with ways of knowing/being-in-the-world. This approach speaks to the need for the further mainstreaming of locative media within a broader cultural geographic framework. Doing so is crucial to understanding the complex ways in which these locative digital technologies remediate the production of space, landscape, and subjectivity.

## Coded Landscapes and the Duplicity of Code

We can think of software code most basically as a series of rules or processes that do work upon particular data inputs and (thus) on the world. Geographers have theorized the role of code in a variety of ways, often focusing on its capacity to produce or "transduce" particular types of spaces – often high-tech spaces of mobility such as the airport but also spaces of the household and the farm – through reiterative processes (Kitchin and Dodge 2011). This apparent autonomy of code is signaled by Thrift and French's (2002) concept of the automatic production of space, emphasizing the extent to which so much of "the background" of everyday life is transduced by the "absent presence" (p. 311) of software. Although such work stresses the agentive quality of code's transduction or remediation of space, geographers also note its contingency, indeterminacy, and irreducibly social character. There is a recognition, then, that code does not simply work in deterministic ways but changes according to contexts, toward the production of what Martin Dodge and Rob Kitchin (2005) differentiate as exceptional "code/spaces" in which "code *dominates* the production of space" (p. 198, original emphasis) versus "coded spaces" in which code is part of, but incidental to, the production of space. As a heuristic continuum, rather than a deterministic binary, the distinction signals that there may be qualitative differences between spaces in which code exercises different levels of autonomy, or, alternatively, where code is more or less central to the calling-into-being of spaces.

This code/space versus coded space distinction highlights the variable nature of code's mechanisms of action and how its presence is not always obvious, visible, or traceable to an origin, author, or explicit ideological moment: its absent presence (Thrift and French 2002). To the extent that code delimits or scripts behaviors – from requiring the following of accepted procedures at electronic checkouts to pre-screening risky airline passengers – it frequently does so at a distance, disciplining bodies to mundane, unquestioned, depoliticized practices. More ominously, Thrift (2011) argues that the construction of an apparently smooth surface of motion relies on:

> a whole host of techniques which are designed to *sink into the background and to be background*: conceal innards, eliminate dead links . . . eliminate all traces of where the medium derived from [*sic*] (p.8, emphasis added)

This idea that code conceals the conditions of its creation and power – even as it engenders new social relations and potential practices – points to the *duplicity* of code: that is the inherent articulation between code's visibility and masking, transparency and deception (cf. Daniels 1989), potential and foreclosure. The concept of duplicity highlights the complex ways in which code works to produce space and, by doing so, defines the boundaries of knowledge production, codifies the meanings of place, and delimits a field of potential practice even as it activates remediated temporal and spatial horizons for experience. Echoing Thrift's (2011) observation, it is, then, the obviousness (Mackenzie 2002: 6) or apparent naturalness of code's spaces in which its duplicity inheres.

The question thus becomes one of how the power of code and its duplicity work to reconfigure landscape as a way of seeing, and with what effects. Working from an evocative God's eye fantasy, then Vice President Al Gore imagined an interactive museum exhibit where a world of knowledge would, literally, be in the palm of the user's hand: that is, the globe would be manipulated using a special glove:

> Imagine, for example, a young child going to a Digital Earth exhibit . . . she sees Earth as it appears from space. [She] zooms in, using higher and higher levels of resolution, to see continents, then regions, countries, cities, and finally individual houses, trees, and other natural and man-made objects. Having found an area of the planet she is interested in exploring, she takes the equivalent of a "magic carpet ride" through a 3-D visualization of the terrain. (Gore 1998)

While the specific mechanics of manipulation were a little off, Gore's prediction/fantasy is a rather accurate description of the present character of Google Earth: zoomable, rotatable, three-dimensional imaging, overlaid with (potentially) limitless layers of information. And such capabilities are not the preserve of research institutions, museums, or even any longer of home computer users, but are readily accessible even on mainstream mobile devices. Increasingly, augmented reality applications layer spatial data, in real time, not on archived or stock imagery but on live imagery via a device's cameras, producing digitally enhanced landscapes via the ever present, yet ever veiled, work of code.

## New Visualities, New Visibilities: Objects of a Coded Gaze

While the technologies by which coded landscapes come into being may be new, powerful visual representations of landscape have long existed. For Cosgrove (1984) the "landscape idea" emerged out of the capitalist transition in sixteenth-century Italy. In this genealogy particular landscape visions/representations are products of (and in turn productive/affirmative of) particular sets of social relations: they are socially constructed, assertive claims to meaning in which the viewer is positioned in a particular relation to the scene s/he surveys. As Lesley McCormack (1991) has shown, such claims, in early modern England – as in nineteenth-century America in the guise of county atlases (Conzen 1984) – often centered around claims to ownership, legitimacy, authenticity, and the assertion of local embeddedness on the part of wealthy landowners of/for whom landscape maps were made.

There is a common epistemological thread linking the emergence of mass-consumption analog maps and landscape imagery – for example, in the form of the ubiquitous bird's eye views of industrializing America – and the emergence of contemporary locative media representations. Both are implicated in broader ideological and social impulses. Both are made more powerful by the participation of a large public. Both place the viewer in a particular position of comprehension of, participation in, and power over the scene/screen (see Schein 1993).

How can we think about this God's eye view of landscape – Donna Haraway's oft-cited "God trick" (1988) – afforded by interactive, slippery, zoomable, inhabitable digital maps such as Google Earth? What kind of regime of visuality does such a view entail? Following Gillian Rose (2006) and others, we take visuality to refer to a regime of seeing: how seeing is structured, how "we are able, allowed, or made to see, and how we see this seeing and the unseeing" (Foster 1988: ix).

Kingsbury and Jones (2009) offer the analogy of a "digital peep box" as one means of interpreting the regime of visuality associated with Google Earth, and argue that:

> the peep-box faces stand in for Google Earth's digital pictures and bit-maps, the cellophane represents Google Earth's "atmospheric lights" and "clear blue skies," while the peephole mimics the interface between users and the 3D scene. (p. 505)

But peeping is a voyeuristic, passive, often furtive act subject to the individual predilections of the viewer. Thus, while a peepshow is viewed through a private viewing slot and is situated at the margins of polite society, Google Earth/Maps is very much rated PG – naked sunbathers and other objects of the "erotics of ogling" (p. 505) excepted. Google Earth is viewed/displayed openly and without shame on a crisp, backlit screen. Moreover, the idea of voyeurism does not capture adequately the texture of the interactive, immersive experiences afforded by such digital earths, nor make mention of the hard-coded rules of the game that script the very spontaneity and excitement of ogling as a consumer experience.

Perhaps the digital peep-boxes of virtual earths are epiphenomenal to the structuring forces of the cultural landscape at work underneath the digitally transduced surface. The landscape appears as a shiny, phantasmagorical aura of twinkly screens (Kingsbury and Jones 2009), an almost-thereness distracting from the actually-there machinations of (something like) "authoritarian capitalism" ruthlessly ruling the roost through forms of "distraction" and "control" that automatically produce a carefully commoditized Dionysian "creativity" (Thrift 2011: 12). While such a view emphasizes the transductive power of code, it is overly restrictive toward agency as it precludes the possibility of critical consumption of software-derived products. Alongside peeping exists the real possibility that specific iterations of locative media can work as drivers of various forms of unanticipated improvisation and change, as asserted so suggestively in numerous locative art experiments. For example, the Loca: Set

To Discoverable project – pushing highly personalized messages to cell-phone users based on peer-to-peer surveillance of their movements – explicitly seeks to open a dialogue about the broader implications of a ubiquitous post-Orwellian surveillance logic (www.loca-lab.org). Thus, arguably unlike the pre-scripted passivity of the peep-box, the contents of digital earths, the 3D scenes of Google Earth, are amenable to user input, to changing visual perspective, to zooming, pausing, and to the subjective interpretation of outcomes. Most importantly, the user can amend the narrative – albeit subject to the coded limitations imposed by software – via the editing of existing information and the addition of new data layers. Far from passive, the visualization of these digital landscapes represents a dynamic recombination of individuals' interpretations with others' contributed understandings: a point that boosters of locative media emphasize frequently (Turner 2006).

Perhaps what marks the excitement of Google Earth, and by extension of locative media in general, is not the object of the gaze but the pleasure of "*the gaze itself*" (Žižek 1991: 91, original emphasis). Along just these lines, Kirsty Best (2010: para. 6) argues that "we need to see users as desiring subjects positioned at a cultural moment where the digital information screen has been enlisted as a central driver of both utility and pleasure." Best's argument is that the screen, working to satisfy a desire for monitoring, is a key site/sight in the gaze of the contemporary subject of locative media. But in her analysis, the screen is also duplicitous, working to construct consent to our own surveillance, to interpellate us into our own discipline as we "take up the part offered to us by the technology" (para. 28). In this view, the innocent transparency suggested by the screen belies the fact that its function is founded on the opacity of its coded innards.

This argument provides a useful foil to optimistic claims about the creative and liberating potential of locative media. Whether Kingsbury and Jones' (2009) vision of "intoxicated" adventuring – searching for the quirky, reveling in the excitement of *not* quite being able to see the blurry naked people of Google Earth (p. 507) – is representative of typical, utilitarian engagements with locative media is debatable. Kingsbury and Jones' (2009) article argues, and Gwilym Eades' response (2010) emphasizes, the importance of eschewing an oversimplified binary reading (from Nietzsche) of a rational, Apollonian cartographic discourse as a counterpoint to intoxicated/Dionysian adventuring in Google Earth. These readings suggest that digital mappings ought – as we would argue – be apprehended not as either/or, as inherently limiting and rational (qua Apollonian), or as inherently liberating and playful (qua Dionysian), but consistent with Nietzschean holism as ambivalent cultural products that work in subjective ways, for different people in different contexts but always within the constraints of code.

Like Walter Benjamin's wandering *flâneur* of the Parisian Arcades, emerging technologies create the conditions of possibility for a corresponding "anonymous wandering detective," the e-*flâneur*, as it were, of locative media (Kingsbury and Jones 2009: 504). But locative technologies entail not only the potential for new, panoptic ways of seeing on the part of the consumer/subject – who may display, manipulate, and author locationally referenced data which, a generation ago, were either unavailable or not readily available to the public – but also new ways to *be* coded and made visible. Increasingly, the public is seen and seeing through the digital artifacts of a geocoded life.

## Coding Bodies: Subjects of/to Locative Media

We should be careful not to make unsustainable, exaggerated, or ethnocentric claims about the ways in which locative media always, everywhere, and for everyone work in particular, limiting, or liberating ways (Laegran 2002; Valentine, Holloway, and Bingham 2002; Madge and O'Connor 2005). As Eades (2010) rather gravely warns us, "our children, our teachers, and our future selves," and not only "playful dilettantes, and the like" (p. 672), use and are subject to these technologies – a criticism of a perceived tendency in the literature toward "wanton" (p. 672) accounts of technologically savvy white males' playful experimentation in/with digital technologies. Thus, we invoke Doreen Massey's (1991) argument about the politics of writing time–space compression to argue that the story of a high-tech world of ubiquitous connectivity and interactive digital mapping is, to some extent, the story of middle-class academics and is not, by any means, a universal experience of space for myriad others positioned differentially in respect of processes of globalization, digitalization, and the cod(e)ification of society. The stories of intoxicated *flâneurs* and their dalliances with code-mediated landscapes are not the only stories to be told.

There is a scarcity within the locative media literature to date of explicit engagement with questions of gender (Elwood 2008). Although emerging work on locative media within cultural geography tends generally to be consistent with broadly poststructuralist epistemologies, it seems that much remains to be understood about the ways in which, for example, locatively mediated visualities entail particular gendered gazes and thus particular gendered subjects/ objects of knowledge (Nash 1996; Kwan 2002). To what extent and in what ways do specific technologies and changes in the embodied interfaces between humans and computers work toward or against a "utopian dream of the hope for a monstrous world without gender" (Haraway 1991: 116)? Addressing such questions will require taking seriously the potentiality for differentiation and experimentation inherent in emerging technologies. Doing so might also entail more empirically grounded, finer-grained, and "modest" work on/toward alternatives to complement more universalized utopian/dystopian synopses in the manner of Thrift's Lifeworld (2011).

Geographers have begun to examine the articulations of race with locative technologies. Developing the concept of cyberscapes – the cloud of user-generated spatial data about a location – Crutcher and Zook (2009) show how online representations of post-hurricane Katrina New Orleans reflected extant geographies of residential segregation. That user annotations were heavily concentrated in predominantly white areas of the city is significant in a variety of ways. Most basically, it points to the ever present question of digital divides: the race, gender, and class basis of access to and usage of emerging technologies. Perhaps more significantly, it points to the question of racialization of cyberscapes. Echoing recent work on racialized landscape (e.g., Schein 2009), we know that landscape is not innocent, however naturalized the exclusionary discourses materialized in the cultural landscape might appear (McDowell 1983; Bondi and Domosh 1998). In that sense it is a crucial project for critical cultural geographers to query just whose landscape visions are embedded into taken-for-granted base maps via ostensibly democratic practices of crowdsourcing (Leszczynski 2012) and with what effects.

These questions of positionality and ethnocentrism suggest a need more fully to engage with subjectivity and locative media as a crucial methodological issue for geographers studying these phenomena. By now, there are clear cases in the literature that show very directly how particular digital mapping technologies work through code to produce particular kinds of subjects (and objects) of knowledge (e.g., Wilson forthcoming). Maps that are navigated, manipulated, authored – *inhabited* – by lay audiences are, intuitively, qualitatively different creatures than static paper maps of old, although we should be careful about positing an epochal paper/digital divide and (thus) throwing out two decades or more of work on critical cartography which itself draws attention to the incomplete, processual, performative, becoming qualities of maps in general (Harley 1989; Crampton 2009a). Ubiquitous electronic maps thus have the potential to produce both a "knowing, empowered imperial audience and its subjects" (Thrift 2011) through the seeing/seen articulation of the new geospatial economy of visuality/visibility (Crampton 2009b). But the precise techniques and practices by which this subjectification proceeds, and the extent to which it can be contested or appropriated differentially by variously situated actors, can only be explicated with further work on specific empirical cases. And in the case of locative media, these cases must include code as one of the elements at play.

For example, in the context of a neighborhood-based exercise in Seattle involving the geotagging of assets/deficiencies, Wilson (forthcoming) argues that the particular practices of "training the eye," along with the embodied interaction of bodies and machines, produce particular kinds of geocoding subjects who, despite in some cases recognizing the silences, simplifications, and politics inherent in categorization/codification of their lay knowledges, nevertheless participate in such disciplined/disciplining practices. The knowledge recorded by neighborhood survey participants becomes objectified (Wilson forthcoming) – stripped of the subjective practices of its capture – in order to render it combinable (Latour 1990) with other participants' data for transmission in a format legible to state agencies and funding bodies. Wilson's work suggests that in the specific case of the neighborhood evaluation survey on which he reports, the act of codifying/cod(e)ifying knowledges works to discipline bodies toward particular practices of knowledge production: that is, to see the world in terms of categories. Specifically, for Wilson, this suggests the potential for the collapse of the social, of heterogeneity, of tacit knowledge, embodied experiences, and uncertainty into categorical certainty, into legible and actionable data. In a double move, then, the practice of cod(e)ification – rendering knowledge as (quantitative) data – objectifies knowledge, stripping the subjective content both from its production (the neighborhood residents' engagement with the handheld computer devices) and from its referents (for example, eliding the social processes underpinning homelessness and graffiti in favor of documenting their identifiable visual markers in the material landscape).

Beyond this rather specific case of neighborhood asset mapping, similar impulses can be observed in the arena of social networking. Consumer digital technologies including social networking platforms are key sites in which individuals negotiate, claim, and assert identity in a variety of ways. The management of "profiles" (albeit a degree of management delineated by the coded parameters of the social networking platform) entails a regime of visibility intrinsic to the social and professional lives of many young people and even adults in which subjects think, construct themselves, and are conditioned to present themselves as entities (the profile/username) with attributes (age, sex, pictures, hometown, music videos, favorite quotations, and so forth). The entity–attribute model of profile building suggests a broader categorization imperative on which indexability, comparison, and aggregation rely, and acts as a powerful limiting/structuring architecture for constructing identities and the conduct of social lives. The "structured generativity" of social networking platforms is coded specifically to guide customization and feedback, thus creating an economy of appropriate perpetual and permanent display. Indeed, much of the burgeoning volume of highly personal digital traces of individuals comes not from official databases but from the contributions of users themselves via social networking, blogging, and other electronic projections: a process named by Mann (2004) and others as "sousveillance."

The merciless memory of the online world immortalizes images, histories, data on which reputations, relationships, and careers are made and broken, raising significant ethical challenges. The vast databases and archives of information derived from online surveillance and sousveillance have no necessary expiration date. There is no clear binary division, then, between, say, the liberatory self-expression of sousveillance and the pernicious infringement of state or corporate surveillance. Hypothetically, we are headed toward "a society that never forgets" (Dodge and Kitchin 2007: 442), where a fine-grained data trail appends to individuals through time, space, and landscape, stored for all eternity and accessible to those who would put such a record to work in achieving more or less "good" outcomes. Such a prospect raises potential privacy concerns even above and beyond those related to real-time monitoring of bodies in space through CCTV, GPS, and the like, prompting technological as well as philosophical responses to the problematic of forgetting (Curry 1997; Bridwell 2007). In response, Dodge and Kitchin (2007) propose a framework for forgetting based on a normative ethics around the desirability of forgetting: "forgetting is not a weakness or a fallibility, but is an emancipatory process," they suggest (p. 441).

Part of this challenge and building on this work on the cod(e)ification of place is to take seriously the temporal dimensions of coded landscapes and subjects. Specifically, in the next section we turn to questions of memory, and code's role in the inscription of locatively mediated landscape as a more or less unwitting autobiography of social life. The digital traces of past interactions – placemarks, Tweets, photographs, and numerous other digital artifacts – represent a record, albeit highly exclusionary, of actions, behaviors, and representations potentially infinite and merciless in scope. In tandem with questions about the algorithmic smoothing (thus elision) of disparate narratives and dissenting voices in a new politics of remembering, we also reflect on the ethics of a politics of forgetting (Dodge and Kitchin 2007).

## Coding Memory and Memorialization

Consider these two cases: the first is the experience of a Google Street View user exploring a temporally flattened downtown block of Lexington, Kentucky. When you begin your walk you are confronted with an empty construction lot with bare earth and surrounded by a chain link fence. As you turn the corner, something strange happens: the rubble disappears, the sun comes out, pedestrians walk the previously torn-up sidewalk. As you look back down the blocked-off street, buildings have reappeared. The parking meters beside the jewelry store are occupied; business and life go on as normal. You turned away for less than a minute to circle to the far side of the block, and in that time the architecture has been reconstructed, businesses reinstated, and the weather transformed.

Second is the case of the Bronze Soldier memorial in Tallinn, Estonia: a controversial World War II memorial erected by Soviet authorities in the late 1940s. The monument represents a point of tension between, broadly, ethnic Russians and Estonians who read its claims about the oppressions or glories of the Soviet era rather differently. In 2007 the statue was relocated, amidst much protest and some violence, from its central city location to a military cemetery. But search for the "Bronze Soldier of Tallinn" in Google Maps and the apparent relocation is less straightforward. Indeed, the first and only search result identifies the former location; multiple photographs and annotations (uploaded to various online photo-sharing communities) highlight the original site (Graham, Zook, and Boulton 2011).

Rarely are the ambivalent temporalities of web information as stark as in the cases described here, and one might contend that such inconsistencies are inevitable and innocuous. But subjective experiences of place in the code-mediated world entail the recombination of

(a)

(b)

**Figure 36.1** Google Street View images of Downtown Lexington.

multiple discourses and multiple temporalities into indeterminate presents. Thus, not only does the locative mediation of landscape entail the melding of distinct spaces (of cyberspace, of memory, of the location itself), but also of distinct temporalities: the latent, temporally ambiguous digital cloud "out there" waiting to be accessed, used, and combined in place, even as the digital already shapes the materiality of place in important ways (Graham 2010).

The reviews, placemarks, and photographs that annotate everyday landscapes through Google Maps and similar applications are often of uncertain origin: perhaps scraped from web directories, fed from third-party sites, or actively contributed by users. Geolocated images of a downtown block of Lexington or the Bronze Soldier represent interventions in, or more or less witting authorship of, the meaning of this contested landscape. Posted for nostalgia, or simply as a ready means of storage, they remain accessible as a weight and resource for future searches. Divorced temporally from their time of creation and posting, and freed from the thick encumbrances of motive or indifference of their creators, these images stand as markers of place, memorials of motives now unknown. They represent histories of place but are simultaneously interventions in the ongoing layering of meanings that continuously reconstruct place anew.

**Figure 36.2** Google Maps search results for "Bronze Soldier of Tallinn."
Source: © 2011 Google Map data © 2011 Tele Atlas.

Michel de Certeau offers a potential vocabulary for thinking through the temporality of the locatively mediated landscape. In his terms, the trace can be thought of as synecdoche, where the fragment is made to "play the role of the whole" (1984: 101); the Yelp.com online review stands in for the totality of "worst food ever" and the social conditions and memories elided and evoked by such a codification. This raises the fundamental question of who is participating in this codification and which voices are missing. As noted earlier, there are clear gendered and racialized dimensions to the digital mediated landscapes under construction (Kwan 2002; Elwood 2008).

Amongst the layered cartographies of planners, maps, and the "strange toponymy [of place names] that is detached from actual places" (p. 104) floats another immanent field – of memory and affect. Increasingly, that which has been experienced is captured, however incompletely, as a digital marker – a Tweet, a review, a piece of georeferenced detritus which the innards of code collects and uses to populate the coded landscapes of locative media. In this way, memorialization via annotation becomes "anti-museum" in de Certeau's words; cyberspace has no specific time and no particular place, or existence (an echo, a ghost, a shadow) beyond its embodied articulation with the materiality of experience. Manuel Castells' conception of timeless time is also apt here: "time is compressed . . . de-sequenced, including past, present, and future occurring in a random sequence" (2000: 12–13). If we embody – and in our engagements with the materiality and digitality of landscape it embodies – traces of past encounters, past experiences, past fears, and past decisions, then the present, not to mention the future, becomes far less stable, less given and less natural (Edensor 2005) – but nonetheless geocoded, annotated, claimed in ways that again reflect the positionality of the voices that have and have not been heard.

By considering those intangible and material/codified traces of spatial practice, we can imagine an experience of place outside of the contrived spectacles of the Google Earth and the hyperreal (post)modern city – a code-supported, individual/subjective, emotional experience of digitally augmented ghosts, echoes, and relics that goes far beyond deliberately structured regimes of visuality. The echoes of past presences (as filtered through the coded and subjective authoring of locative media) are flattened into a temporally destitute present: the ever-present now. As such there is fertile ground for exploration, theoretical and empirical, of the implications for these digitally inscribed social hauntings of place (cf. Pile 2005). Such is the goal of the Walking Through Time smartphone application developed by the Edinburgh College of Art. Here, users explore present-day urban spaces using a historical map overlay. The authors explain:

> people will choose to navigate their city not in the technologically determined "present" in which the map is as up-to-date and "fresh" as possible, but may prefer to use an old landscape which is occupied by ghosts. Walking through streets that aren't "cleansed" of memories, or monitored by spooks that want to guide our interpretation of the past in order to sustain our fear of particular ghosts, may help us "see" the trauma that remains in a place and tread with understanding around its scars. (Fields 2010)

In such a project – explicitly evoking the past – as in digitally mediated experiences of place more generally, this formulation of presence = present(s) speaks to the uncertain afterlife of locative annotations, mappings that are never dead, but do work – perhaps even jarring, uncomfortable, irruptive work – in producing futures.

## Conclusion

If we are to develop theoretically and politically informed (and informing) accounts of the ways in which locative media technologies work in practice, the study of these technologies cannot be left "only to those who would unproblematically reproduce excitable futurist advocacy or reduce 'improving' [them] to a technical/technological challenge" (Boulton 2010) toward more perfect visibility and knowledge of populations. But neither ought crucial questions about the spaces and subjects of locative media and the work of information technologies more generally be left solely in the domain of Internet-, cyber-, and other hyphenated niche geographies/geographers of technology.

Although the exciting, cutting-edge locative media technologies that are mainstream or emerging today will, doubtless, appear archaic, comical even, a decade from now, "technological futurity" is, as Sam Kinsley (2010) argues, "a complex array of performative and proactive dispositions towards the future" (p. 6), located within problematic and differentially situated politics of anticipation. It is the goal of this chapter to provoke discussion about the ways in which existing theoretical and methodological frameworks within cultural geography and social theory are providing useful lenses for understanding the emerging practices associated with the geoweb. Moreover, we also emphasize the need for renewed, empirical examination of the texture and ambivalence of specific locative media products focusing on particular technologies, particular places, and particular individuals. Thus we ought to keep a critical distance in our writing (about) digitality and digital futures both from eulogies to liberatory e-*flâneurie* (with all the assumptions of privilege these entail) and from monolithically dystopian imaginaries of a Big Brother Lifeworld, Inc. of technologically determined servitude.

Work on locative media is moving toward developing critical accounts of the ways in which these technologies mediate embodied engagements with landscape and cultural geographies. In parallel, geographers are also beginning to engage more fully with questions of subjectivity, the changing nature of expertise, and the uneven and differentiated access to and usage of these technologies. Such questions establish the workings of the locatively mediated landscape as an important and central topic for cultural landscape scholarship and for critical geographical attention more generally.

## References

Amoore, L. and Hall, A. (2009) Taking people apart: Digitised dissection and the body at the border. *Environment and Planning D: Society and Space*, 27 (3), 444–464.

Best, K. (2010) Concealing screens: Consent, control and the desiring user. *Reconstructions*, 10 (2).

Bondi, L. and Domosh, M. (1998) On the contours of public space: A tale of three women. *Antipode*, 30 (3), 270–289.

Boulton, A. (2010) Guest editorial. Just maps: Google's democratic map-making community? *Cartographica*, 45 (1), 1–4.

Bridwell, S. (2007) The dimensions of locational privacy. In *Societies and Cities in the Age of Instant Access*, ed. H. Miller. New York: Springer.

Castells, M. (2000) Materials for an exploratory theory of the network society. *British Journal of Sociology*, 51 (1), 5–24.

Conzen, M. (1984) Landownership maps and county atlases. *Agricultural History*, 58 (2), 118–122.

Cosgrove, D. (1984) Prospect, perspective and the evolution of the landscape idea. *Transactions of the Institute of British Geographers*, 10 (1), 45–62.

Crampton, J. (2009a) Cartography: Maps 2.0. *Progress in Human Geography*, 33 (1), 91–100.

Crampton, J. (2009b) Cartography: Performative, participatory, political. *Progress in Human Geography*, 33, 840–848.

Crang, M. and Travlou, P. (2001). The city and topologies of memory. *Environment and Planning D*, 19, 161–177.

Crang, M. and Graham, S. (2007) Sentient cities: Ambient intelligence and the politics of urban space. *Information Communication and Society*, 10 (6), 789–817.

Crang, M., Crang, P. and May, J. (1999) *Virtual Geographies: Bodies, Space and Relations*. London: Routledge.

Crutcher, M. and Zook, M. (2009) Placemarks and waterlines: Racialized cyberscapes in post-Katrina Google Earth. *Geoforum*, 40 (4), 523–534.

Curry, M.R. (1997) The digital individual and the private realm. *Annals of the Association of American Geographers*, 87, 681–699.

Daniels, S. (1989) Marxism, culture, and the duplicity of landscape. In *New Models in Geography*, ed. R. Peet and N. Thrift. London: Unwin Hyman.

De Certeau, M. (1984) Walking in the city. In *The Practice of Everyday Life*. Berkeley: University of California Press.

Dodge, M. and Kitchin, R. (2005) Code and the transduction of space. *Annals of the Association of American Geographers*, 95 (1), 162–180.

Dodge, M. and Kitchin, R. (2007) Outlines of a world coming in existence: Pervasive computing and the ethics of forgetting. *Environment and Planning B: Planning and Design*, 34 (3), 431–445.

Eades, G. (2010) An Apollonian appreciation of Google Earth. *Geoforum*, 41, 671–673.

Edensor, T. (2005) The ghosts of industrial ruins: Ordering and disordering memory in excessive space. *Environment and Planning D: Society and Space*, 23, 829–849.

Elwood, S. (2008) Volunteered geographic information: Future research directions motivated by critical, participatory, and feminist GIS. *GeoJournal*, 72 (3/4), 173–183.

Fields (2010) Exhuming spectral cities. http://www.chrisspeed.net/?p=293 (accessed October 31, 2012).

Foster, H. (ed.) (1988) *Vision and Visuality*. Seattle: Bay Press.

Fuller, M. (ed.) (2008) *Software Studies: A Lexicon*. Cambridge, MA: MIT Press.

Goodchild, M. (2007) Citizens as sensors: The world of volunteered geography. *GeoJournal*, 69 (4), 211–221.

Gore, A. (1998) The digital earth: Understanding our planet in the 21st century. Speech given at the California Science Center, Los Angeles, California, January 31. http://www.isde5.org/al_gore_speech.htm (accessed October 31, 2012).

Graham, M. (2010) Neogeography and the palimpsests of place: Web 2.0 and the construction of a virtual earth. *Tijdschrift voor Economische en Sociale Geografie*, 101 (4), 422–436.

Graham, M., Zook, M. and Boulton, A. (2011) Augmented reality in urban places: Contested content and the duplicity of code. Manuscript under review.

Graham, S. (2005) Software-sorted geographies. *Progress in Human Geography*, 29 (5), 562–580.

Haraway, D. (1988) Situated knowledges: The science question in feminism and the privilege of partial perspective. *Feminist Studies*, 14 (3), 575–599.

Haraway, D. (1991) A cyborg manifesto: Science, technology, and socialist-feminism in the late twentieth century. In *Simians, Cyborgs and Women: The Reinvention of Nature*. New York: Routledge, pp. 149–181.

Harley, J.B. (1989) Deconstructing the map. *Cartographica*, 26 (2), 1–20.

Kingsbury, P. and Jones, J.P. (2009) Walter Benjamin's Dionysian adventures on Google Earth. *Geoforum*, 40 (4), 502–513.

Kinsley, S. (2010) Practising tomorrows? Ubiquitous computing and the politics of anticipation. Unpublished PhD thesis, University of Bristol.

Kitchin, R. and Dodge, M. (2011) *Code/Space: Software and Everyday Life*. Cambridge, MA: MIT Press.

Kwan, M.-P. (2002) Feminist visualization: Re-envisioning GIS as a method in feminist geography research. *Annals of the Association of American Geographers*, 92, 645–661.

Laegran, A.S. (2002) The petrol station and the Internet café: Rural technospaces for youth. *Journal of Rural Studies*, 18 (2), 157–168.

Latour, B. (1990) Drawing things together. In *Representation in Scientific Practice*, ed. M. Lynch and S. Woolgar. Cambridge, MA: MIT Press.

Leszczynski, A. (2012) Situating the geoweb in political economy. *Progress in Human Geography*, 36 (1), 72–89.

Mackenzie, A. (2002) *Transductions: Bodies and Machines at Speed*. London: Continuum.

Madge, C. and O'Connor, H. (2005) Mothers in the making? Exploring liminality in cyber/space. *Transactions of the Institute of British Geographers*, 30 (1), 83–97.

Mann, S. (2004) "Sousveillance": Inverse surveillance in multimedia imaging. *Proceedings of the 12th Annual ACM International Conference on Multimedia*. New York: ACM Press.

Massey, D. (1991) A global sense of place. *Marxism Today*.

McCormack, L. (1991) "Good fences make good neighbors": Geography as self-definition in early modern England. *Isis*, 82 (4), 639–661.

McDowell, L. (1983) Towards an understanding of the gender division of urban space. *Environment and Planning D: Society and Space*, 1 (1), 59–72.

Nash, C. (1996) Reclaiming vision: Looking at landscape and the body. *Gender, Place and Culture,* 3 (2), 149–170.

Pile, S. (2005) Spectral cities: Where the repressed returns and other short stories. In *Habitus: A Sense of Place,* ed. J. Hillier and E. Rooksby. Sydney: Ashgate.

Rose, G. (2006) *Visual Methodologies.* London: Sage.

Schein, R. (1993) Representing urban America: 19th-century views of landscape, space and power. *Environment and Planning D: Society and Space,* 11, 7–21.

Schein, R. (1997) The place of landscape: A conceptual framework for interpreting an American scene. *Annals of the Association of American Geographers,* 87 (4), 660–680.

Schein, R. (2009) A methodological framework for interpreting ordinary landscapes: Lexington, Kentucky's Courthouse Square. *Geographical Review,* 99 (3), 377–404.

Thrift, N. (2011) Lifeworld Inc – and what to do about it. *Environment and Planning D: Society and Space,* 29 (1): 5–26.

Thrift, N. and French, S. (2002) The automatic production of space. *Transactions of the Institute of British Geographers,* 27, 309–335.

Turner, A. (2006) *Introduction to Neogeography.* Sebastopol, CA: O'Reilly Media.

Valentine, G., Holloway, S. and Bingham, N. (2002) The digital generation? Children, ICT and the everyday nature of social exclusion. *Antipode,* 34 (2), 296–315.

Wilson, M. (forthcoming) "Training the eye": Formation of the geocoding subject. *Social and Cultural Geography.*

Žižek, S. (1991) Grimaces of the real, or when the phallus appears. *October,* 58, 44–68.

Zook, M. (2010) Digiplace and cyberscapes: Rethinking the digital divide in urban America. In *eChicago 2009,* ed. K. Williams. Champaign: University of Illinois at Urbana-Champaign Graduate School of Library and Information Science.

# Chapter 37

# Affect and Emotion

## Ben Anderson

## Hope

How are affects and emotions part of how life is lived and takes place? What difference might attending to affect and emotion make to cultural geography? In this chapter I explore these questions by considering the difference that recent work on affect and emotion makes to the concept of culture and by reflecting on different ways of thinking about the politics of affective or emotional life. First, though, I turn to three vignettes to open up the question of why affect and emotion matter.

### Events of Hope

For seventeen days families, friends, and then a global media audience waited. Trapped in the emergency shelter of a collapsed mine 2,300 feet into the earth in Chile, 33 miners waited to be rescued. During this period, hope was kept alive and lost, given and received. The first images of the men gave hope to the families who waited in the self-titled Camp Hope as the ordeal went on. Here is how Caraloa Narvaez, the wife of Raul Bustos, one of the trapped miners, expressed her hope in the context of a previous disaster they had survived together:

> In the earthquake we just had to keep on living, we had our lives . . . this is the same. It is producing much anguish, isolation, fear. But we're alive. My husband is alive down in that mine and we will have another happy ending.[1]

In his inaugural address to the University of Tübingen in 1961, the Marxist process philosopher Ernst Bloch, speaking in the shadow of Nazi Germany, asked a simple question about

*The Wiley Blackwell Companion to Cultural Geography*, First Edition.
Edited by Nuala C. Johnson, Richard H. Schein, and Jamie Winders.
© 2013 John Wiley & Sons, Ltd. Published 2016 by John Wiley & Sons, Ltd.

the event of hope: can hope be disappointed? His answer was yes, to be hope, it must be disappointable. Hopes and hoping open up a point of contingency in the here and now. Indeed:

> Hope must be unconditionally disappointable ... because it is open in a forward direction, in a future-orientated direction; it does not address itself to that which already exists. For this reason, hope – while actually in a state of suspension – is committed to change rather than repetition, and what is more, incorporates the element of chance, without which there can be nothing new. (Bloch 1998: 341)

## Atmospheres of Disappointed Hope

On January 19, 2009, a new US president speaks at his inauguration. Employing the prophetic voice of the African-American church and revitalizing the future-orientated promise of the American Dream, he regularly interrupts his speech with a refrain: "yes we can, yes we can." Obama evokes a moment of hope amid danger, a moment of promise. Three years on, what remains of the atmosphere of hope catalyzed by Obama's words? Amid the ravages of job losses and a continuing economic crisis, perhaps Obama's "audacious" hope has been lost; all that remains are memories of a future that never was. Perhaps, though, the atmospheres of hope live on, taking new form, becoming attached to new promises. For some, hope has been catalyzed and kept alive by the different promises of a future offered by the Tea Party movement or the Occupy protests. For others, perhaps, hope remains rooted in the daily struggles of what Lauren Berlant (2007) characterizes as an "aspirational normativity": a "reinvestment in the normative promises of capital" as a way of going on in a present disorganized by the forces we call capitalism and neoliberalism.

## Knowing Hope

Every month since 1967, the Conference Board, a business membership and research association, has released a monthly US "consumer confidence index." Designed to measure the degree of optimism about the economy, as expressed in patterns of spending and saving, the index establishes trends in consumers' affectively imbued relation to the future. Writing on November 22, 2010, a research advisor at the Federal Reserve Bank of San Francisco, Sylvain Leduc, notes that economists were worried about the US economy:

> Indicators of consumer confidence have been at depressed levels in recent months. Business sentiment is also low, reflecting uncertainty about US fiscal policy and the perception that economic weakness may be prolonged. This lack of confidence raises the risk that pessimism can become entrenched and self-reinforcing, further dampening the nascent recovery. (Leduc 2010: November 22)

Influenced by Keynes' now-famous comment about the role of "animal spirits" in driving economic activity, economists have long debated whether confidence is an independent economic variable and, thus, a "business cycle driver." Although there is no consensus as to whether confidence is cause or effect, changes in the "degree of optimism" of a population are measured and presented graphically so that trends can be identified and a range of economic actions undertaken.

These three examples exemplify different ways in which affects and emotions become part of how life is lived and organized and, as such, hint at the range of phenomena that a cultural geography of affect and emotion might learn to attend to. In the first example of the trapped miners, hope opens up a moment of difference in the context of a shared situation of misery and suffering. Hope is kept alive, if only just; and the suffering that marks the present is disrupted, if only momentarily. In the second example, disappointed hope becomes akin to an affective atmosphere coexisting with memories of the future Obama promised, simultaneously absent and present, material and immaterial. In the third example, hope is named, known, and rendered actionable. Techniques are deployed by economists to know optimism and macroeconomic policy responds to aggregate fluctuations in optimism.

Given the diversity of ways in which affect and emotion are part of life, a simple affirmation provides the starting point for work on affect and emotion, one that is at the heart of Eve Kosofsky Sedgwick's (2003) discussion of affect. Sedgwick uses the term "affect" in a particular way, one that I touch on below. Nevertheless, the point she makes cuts across theories of affect and emotion. In the conclusion to her essay on the novelist Henry James, Sedgwick describes one affect, shame, as a "kind of free radical," by which she means that shame "attaches to and permanently intensifies or alters the meaning of – of almost anything" (2003: 62). Always insisting on the plural – *affects* rather than the singular *affect* – Sedgwick's deceptively simple starting point is shared by the recent work on affect and emotion in geography: the freedom of the affects to combine with more or less any aspect of life. *This means that there can never be a carefully circumscribed affectual or emotional geography separate from other geographies, cultural or otherwise.* Returning to the three examples, affects or emotions such as hope may become part of global media events, the contemporary condition as embodied and expressed in responses to a politician, or macroeconomic policy in the midst of an ongoing financial crisis.

What the recent attention to affect and emotion promises is, then, a cultural geography attentive to the dynamics of how life is lived and how a life takes place. In the following section, I briefly summarize what work on affect and emotion holds in common: a break with a "regulative idea" of culture based on signification. Touching on the difference different theories of affect and emotion make, I argue that a key issue is how to understand the way affective/emotive relations are organized. The following section then considers the multiple ways of being political in relation to affect and emotion that are currently being experimented with in cultural geography. Here, I draw out how these ways of being political have different connections with the cultural politics that follow the cultural turn. To conclude, I speculate on a series of future issues for work on affect and emotion. Following Colls (2012), throughout the chapter, I try to keep open the multiple, partially connected trajectories that cross and connect recent work on affect and emotion.

## Affect/Emotion and the Concept of Culture

Naming real-world referents, concepts, and something close to an ethos, the terms "affect" and "emotion" have been used by geographers and others to describe a heterogeneous range of phenomena: background moods such as depression, moments of intense and focused involvement such as euphoria, immediate visceral responses of shame or hate, shared atmospheres of hope or panic, eruptions of passion, fleeting feelings of boredom, societal moods such as anxiety or fear, neurological bodily transitions such as a feeling of aliveness, amongst much else. In human geography alone, the terms have been used to understand a wonderfully diverse range of geographies; masculinities (Thien 2009), family photography (Rose 2010), mental health (Parr 2008), fathering (Aitken 2009), popular geopolitics (Carter and McCormack 2006), landscape (Wylie 2009), new forms of work (Woodward and Lea 2010), race and racism (Lim 2010; Swanton 2010), street performance (Simpson 2008), video games (Ash 2010), alcohol use (Jayne *et al.* 2010), obesity (Evans 2009), dance (McCormack 2003), war and violences (Anderson 2010; Adey 2010), therapeutic landscapes (Conradson 2005), animals and other non-humans (Greenhough and Roe 2011), and mobilities (Bissell 2008), to name but some.

Whilst clearly heterogeneous, this work shares a starting assumption that affects and emotions are not discrete properties of an individual mind or body. As Pile (2010) rightly identifies, a central claim of most recent work has been that emotions and/or affects are relational phenomena and/or emergent from relations. Although these two claims are not quite the same, the broad relational position, nevertheless, has the important initial effect of cutting the link between either category and an individual existing separately from a world that he/she only secondarily relates or refers to. On this understanding, affects and emotions are always-already collective in the sense that they emerge from and express ways in which life takes place and is organized. Consequently, the geographies of affect and emotion will be a function of the specific relational configurations that affects/emotions are a part of and emerge from.

To return to one of the examples I started with – Obama's inauguration – we could say that for some people, disappointed hope emerges from a complex field that includes the pain of ongoing adjustment to living in a financial crisis, the continuation of forms of military violence, and the reality of inequalities. However, affects and emotions are not reducible to the material collectives that they emerge from. They have an efficacy as elements within those collectives. Staying with the example of disappointed hope, we could speculate on how such an atmosphere might become part of the conditions for the emergence of new political movements or might confirm already-existing alignments to the promise of democracy (Berlant 2011). As this last point intimates, affects and emotions are never autonomous (cf. Massumi 2002a). They are always-already imbricated with other dimensions of life, without being reducible to them. To understand the composition of particular relational configurations, a range of "mid-level" concepts have been used in the analysis of particular substantive geographies of affect and emotion (such as apparatus, ecology, network, infrastructure, regime of feeling, feeling rules).

What is at stake, then, is how cultural geography relates to the world. Indeed, we can consider this shared orientation to affect and emotion to herald a break with one "regulative idea" of what culture is: culture as a "signifying system" (after Seigworth 2006; Grossberg 2010). By this I mean a style of analysis associated with some tendencies within the "new" cultural geography that focuses on how meaning is generated and structured through human signifying systems. This version of what culture is and does has four formal characteristics (after Grossberg 2010: 187; Massumi 2002b: xiv). First, human access to the world is mediated. Second, mediation occurs through structured systems of signification that exist prior to the subject and are given names such as discourses, ideologies, or narratives. Third, mediation occurs through the active formation and organization of meaning, albeit in various ways. Through this process, the world comes to take on significance and becomes meaningful to and for particular situated subjects. Fourth, the critical question becomes the degree to which the subject is made in conformity with the system of signification that she/he is reduced to an instantiation or expression of. Of course, this version of what culture is coexists with others in cultural geography. It has also resulted in many profound insights about the ways in which the workings of signifying systems link up with economic, political, and other forces. For this reason, any concern with affect or emotion owes a debt to a particular form of linguistic–discursive constructionism, not least for stressing the historicity of emotional/ affectual categories, recognizing the dangers of universalism, and showing how there is no such thing as a pure, unmediated experience.

Nevertheless, the attention to the dynamics of life and living that is at the heart of work on affect and emotion involves a reworking of this version of culture around two points, both of which make the relation between affect or emotion and signification into a question to be rethought. First, access to the world occurs through the active powers of *embodiment*, albeit an embodiment constituted in some form of relational configuration. It is in and through bodies – and their specific differences, limits, and potentials – that living takes place or life is expressed. Access to the world does not only occur through some form of discursive mediation, whether through signification or representation. This does not mean that affect/ emotion and signification or representation are separate. It means, instead, that we need to rethink how they are connected beyond the assumption that a system of signification precedes lived experience and pre-positions subjects. Perhaps this rethinking might involve focusing on how particular forms of verbal expression accompany and shape the experience of emotions. Maybe it could involve thinking of how images work performatively as devices that move bodies affectively (Latham and McCormack 2009).

Second, and consequently, attention shifts from system/structure (however framed) to the *processes, events, and practices* through which meaning temporarily emerges, coalesces, and becomes part of the organization of affectual/emotional life. Aware of the risk of equating emotion/affect with the immediate and the unformed, recent work has attempted to "multiply the modalities, practices, and agencies of mediation" (Grossberg 2010: 189) to include but extend beyond the categories, frameworks, and classifications through which experience is organized. Practically, this extension has involved carefully tracing how affective/emotive life is formed and organized through multiple processes and practices, including the discursive but extending to a variety of materialities and other non-discursive apparatuses. Examples include Swanton's (2010) inventive ethnography of how race emerges through the materialities of urban multiculture, Rose *et al.*'s (2010) careful account of the emotional life of buildings, and Greenhough and Roe's (2011) nuanced comparison between animals and humans in experimental environments.

What this work opens up are a number of questions about order: what are the different ways that bodies are formed through particular affects and emotions; how to understand the geo-historical conditions that shape how different bodies feel; and how do affects and emotions relate to the many ways in which such orders and orderings fall apart, disappear, or otherwise change, to name but a few questions. Stepping back from work that has tied the emphasis on relations to specific theories of affect and emotion, the more general claim of relationality is but a starting point. Understood as an analytic position, relationality is a claim that can be and has been made about any and all phenomena human geography examines (Anderson and Harrison 2010). Whilst I agree with the basic proposition, arguing that entities are "relationally constituted" has become automatic, a habit to be mastered and repeated. Little more than the most basic starting point, it tells us nothing specific about affect and emotion – what they do or what difference attending to them might make to cultural geography. Indeed, in the background to the three examples in the introduction is an assumption that hope is not just one thing: it is a way of relating to the world in the first example of waiting for news, a collective phenomenon in the case of disappointed hope, and an object-target in the example of consumer confidence. The question is, then, how are the terms used, with what effect, and to what purpose?

Here, matters get complicated because different uses of the terms affect and emotion do not neatly map onto discrete areas of work such as "affectual geographies" and "emotional geographies" (cf. Pile 2010). If affect and emotion were once downplayed and marginalized, as feminist work has rightly insisted, both terms are now subject to multiple definitions and uses. Within cultural theory alone, there are at least six definitions of the term affect, for example (Thrift 2004; Seigworth and Gregg 2011). Emotion is probably more various and contested as a category, given its intimacy with the birth of the psychological sciences (Dixon 2003). What this variability means is that the meaning or function of particular terms cannot be assumed. Given this variability, let's consider just a few ways in which "affect" and "emotion" might be used in cultural geography, briefly relating each back to the three examples of hope and showing how they involve different orientations to the world.

Take *affect* first. If we were to find inspiration in a combination of Deleuze and corporeal feminism, then we might pay attention to the asubjective or presubjective lines of force that subjects are formed through. We may, for example, understand how a set of shared affects given the name "hope" infused Obama's inauguration. At once both singular and diffuse, ephemeral and structural, hope becomes akin to an affective atmosphere that is "perpetually forming and deforming, appearing and disappearing, as bodies enter into relation with one another" (Anderson 2009: 78). By comparison, if we learn from the mixture of Silvan Tomkins and queer theory (Sedgwick 2003), then our focus might be on the relays between non-intentional bodily reactions and specific encounters. "Hope" might be a mixture of one or more "basic emotions" plus specific practices of cognition. By contrast, if affect is understood quantitatively as dischargeable energy and qualitatively on a pleasure/unpleasure dichotomy, as it is in some psychoanalytical traditions, then what we take hope to be changes again.

Now compare with *emotion*, a term that is similarly multiple. If we follow an analytic distinction between affect as "intensity" and emotion as "subjective content" (Massumi 2002a: 28), then a focus on emotion means attention is paid to all the ways in which the derivative, circumscribed realm of personal emotion becomes impersonal affect and vice versa. We might, with Stewart (2007), become sensitive to the incoherent or incommensurate in ordinary life, learning to experiment with circuits and flows of feeling. However, if one starts from a different position on what an emotion is and does, then we might learn to attend to different events or processes. One example would be if it was thought that emotions always have intentional objects (see Nussbaum 2007), then, the question would be, how is a singular reference for an emotion, the unique object necessary for an emotion, formed and how does it endure? We might ask how objects of hope or fear are channeled in particular ways to mediate a subject's relation to particular others, for example. By contrast, if emotions were thought to be the name given for a subject's phenomenal experience, then our focus might be on describing experience as it happens (Davidson 2003). Alternatively, we might follow someone like Rei Terada (2001: 13) in her combination of deconstruction and phenomenology and trace how "Emotions arise from others' subsidence, from reflection on emotions, and from the absence of any particular thing to feel." Finally, if we learned from Foucault's genealogies, our emphasis might be on all the ways in which emotions are named, known, and categorized through techniques such as a "consumer confidence index."

Differences in the use of "affect" and "emotion" in cultural geography, then, matter because they concern the kinds of entities that cultural geography should learn to attend to. For example, how should work on affect and emotion relate to the recent explosion of interest in brain science and neurological materials (compare McCormack (2007) and Papoulias and Callard (2010) on the neurological)? Should we center a subject in our analyses; and, if so, how do we understand the relation between specific subjects and the structures and processes they live and adjust to?

It is worth stressing that different uses of the terms cross between different "approaches" to the study of affect and emotion, often unsettling easy categorizations. For example, use of the term "affect" in geography has predominantly been associated with a broad range of what have been named as non-representational theories, particularly those associated with Giles Deleuze (McCormack 2003; Thrift 2007). However, as Colls (2012) argues in an important intervention, recent critiques of non-representational theory have themselves downplayed and marginalized feminist work in geography and elsewhere that uses the concept of affect (see Hayes-Conroy 2008; Clough 2007). Rather than offer a strict distinction between approaches, it is better to see the affect and emotion as sensitizing devices: means for attuning to dimensions of life and living in the wake of a break with an emphasis on "signifying systems." On the one hand, affect and emotion raise questions of Life, understood as the non-human, unhuman, or human forces that condition what comes to be experienced. For some, as Thacker puts it, Life is "a continuum or network of affects in which individuated subjects are more effects than causes" (2010: xiii; see Bennett 2010). On the other hand, there has been a concern with the situated dynamics of particular and historically and geographically varied ways of being alive in the world. Here, the emphasis is on the "experience of living" in and with a world (Thacker 2010: 5). These two orientations are not necessarily mutually exclusive; witness, for example, the emergence of post-phenomenological work (Simpson 2008; Ash 2010). They also do not simply map onto the terms "affect" and "emotion." Nevertheless, a key question has become whether the "phenomenal experience of emotions" (see Smith et al. 2009: 7) provides the empirical and theoretical starting point for an analysis of life or living or whether analysis starts with the powers or forces of a life that exceeds the human: "a pluriverse traversed by heterogeneities that are constantly doing things," as Jane Bennett (2010: 122) puts it (see Clough 2007). Despite this difference which follows from and enables particular orientations to subjects and the world, what is shared is a desire to sense and relate to the many ways of living and forms of life that make up the world.

## The Politics of Affect and Emotion

The reworking of the concept of culture, and the recent emphasis on the different ways in which life and living are organized, raise questions about the political implications of recent work on affect and emotion. For some, a concern with that which might appear to be most fleeting, or most ephemeral, about life and living is never going to matter politically. For others, extending questions of politics to affect and emotion might at best enable a focus on the surface effects of the real causal processes that we give names like neoliberalism or globalization. Either way of dismissing the politics of affect and emotion would be a serious mistake. As Smith et al. (2009) rightly note, the categories we use to understand the harmful or damaging effects of power carry assumptions about affective or emotional life. What the turn to affect and emotion requires, then, is that the assumptions carried in terms such as alienation, exclusion, or belonging are made explicit and reworked. More specifically, we can identify a number of partially connected ways of being political that follow from the renewed attention to life and living across cultural geography. These ways of being political are not necessarily new; and it would be a mistake to understand them as only a response to new forms of power in the early twenty-first century, although they are doubtless linked to a recognition of new forms of biopower (Clough 2007). All are also indebted to the disruptive effect of feminist work on the relations between the phenomenal experience of living and structures of oppression, inequality, and exclusion (see, in geography, Pain 1997; Valentine 1989; Bondi 2005). Partially connected, and far from internally homogeneous, each way of being political offers a means of understanding and intervening in the relation between power and life. As such, they offer different routes toward a politics of life and living.

The first way of being political is to reveal and critique how powerful actors intentionally manipulate subjects by appealing to specific affects and emotions. Closely linked to the ghostly presence of theories of ideology, here, the aim is to show how individuals and/or groups are taught or made to feel in particular ways. For example, we are repeatedly told we live in a "culture of fear" in which the channeling of fear is used to legitimize action (Furedi 2006). What may be presumed to be most natural, an individual's emotions, is revealed by the critic as an imposition intimately connected to extra-affective/emotive forces. The role of the analyst, then, is to deploy critique to reveal the hitherto hidden machinations of power, often by deploying a trope of manipulation (Barnett 2008).

Closely linked, a second way of being political is to diagnose the existence of new forms of control that address subjects as affective beings (Isin 2004). In an update to Foucault's (1978) original concern with two forms of biopower (biopolitics and discipline), critics have shown how neuroscience and other forms of knowledge are used by states, corporations, and other actors to govern subjects. Whitehead *et al.* (2011), for example, show how Behaviour Change policies in UK public policy have drawn on new sciences of behavior to intervene in "predictably irrational" decisions. In this context a concern with how affect is produced as an object-target of intervention is intertwined with a diagnosis of the contemporary condition, in ways that complement and extend now-longstanding work on governmentality and various Psy knowledges. Recently, this work has begun to turn to a diagnosis of the interconnections between capitalism and contemporary geopolitics, particularly around forms of security and war such as aerial bombing or counterinsurgency (Anderson 2010; Massumi 2009; Pain 2009; Adey 2010).

Third, and slightly differently, work has attempted to give voice to emotional or affective experience as a way of bearing witness to peoples who have been sidelined, downplayed, marginalized, or othered (Wright 2010; Puar 2007). Crossing a concern with the ordinary and the traumatic, and with the ways that the traumatic can be ordinary and the ordinary traumatic (Berlant 2011), this work has disclosed rich archives of experience associated with different structures and processes of oppression and inequality (Ahmed 2004). For the most part, this politics is influenced by queer and feminist work and based around notions of voice and witnessing that attempt to create resonances between events, subjects, and publics. Often, the style of work is self-consciously affective, experimenting with new modes of presentation (Stewart 2007).

Fourth, and following on, a range of work has shown how categories of social difference – race, gender, sexuality – are made in and through particular organizations of affect (Colls 2012; Swanton 2010; Lim 2010; Hayes-Conroy 2008; Saldanha 2007). Here, the emphasis is on the patterning of affective relations and capacities and how forms of inequality, damage, and harm are (re)produced through and via affects. By attending with care to the ongoing composition of social differences, this work comes charged with a certain type of optimism, even as it shows the operation of sedimented relations of power. It demonstrates the fragility of formations that may appear solid, self-evident, and settled. At its best, rethinking categories of social difference such as race or sexuality through affect orientates inquiry to how bodies "aggregate" (Saldanha 2010) into distinct social formations.

Fifth, inspired in particular by corporeal feminism and a range of "new vitalisms" (Bennett 2010), other work has experimented with the affective relations and capacities layered into our encounters with each other and other forces. Sharing a wager that more is needed than moralistic judgment to motivate ethical or political action, together with a diagnosis of the politically debilitating effects of certain forms of critique, a range of work has experimented with techniques, sensibilities, and concepts that aim to work on what Connolly (2002) calls the "relays" between thought and action. Moralistic judgment may be supplemented by a positive attachment to the existing world, for example. Hence, the recent interest in enchant-ment (Woodyer 2012), anger (Henderson 2008), or generosity (Darling 2011) as three affects or emotions imbued with political and ethical action, whether that be the concern for human/non-human others or acts of refusal and resistance.

Sixth, some recent work on affect has experimented with ways of attending to the difference, divergence, and differentiation opened up by events (after Anderson & Harrison 2010): the fleeting potential that follows the event of a sexually charged glance between two people (Lim 2007), the performative force and sense of mutability found in dance and the performing arts (Dewsbury 2000), the potential for better ways of being touched in protests (Dewsbury 2007; Woodward and Lea 2010). Critique becomes affirmative – no longer an exercise in debunking or fault finding in which the critic is separate from the process judged but a means of cultivat-ing "turning points" through which new possibilities or potentialities of living differently may be witnessed, invented, and acted on. There are strong connections here with a recent flourish-ing of interest in utopianism as a way of bringing futures into the here and now (Kraftl 2007).

What distinguishes these six ways of being political are different framings of the relation between affect/emotion (and their mediation) and forms of power, differences that take us back to the question of how affective and emotive life is organized. For some, affect is an object of forms of power that is named, known, categorized, measured, and exploited. For others, something about affective/emotional life exceeds forms of power and may, variously, hint to a life outside power's reach or herald something better. Of course, ways of being political in relation to affect and emotion are not exhausted by the above list. We might think, for example, of the role that the category of "passion" plays in work on radical democracy (Featherstone 2007). Nor do they necessarily follow directly from a set of theoretical com-mitments. For example, a concern with manipulation can occur whether affect is theorized as an asubjective intensity or the experience of a subject (Barnett 2008). By comparison, the effort to create new affectively charged events crosses non-representational performance work and feminist-inspired participatory research (see Gibson-Graham 2006). Instead of mapping onto discrete, internally coherent "affectual" and "emotional" approaches, what the different ways of being political struggle with is a promise that attending to spaces of affect and emotion offers a way for cultural geographers to engage with how life is organized and a life takes place.

## Concluding Comments

My presentation of various ways of being political has been purposively open. Ways of being political emerge from a complex mix of uses of the terms affect and emotion, specific political commitments and passions, and situated problems, concerns, and issues. For this reason, it is a mistake to read off politics from a theory or to assume that any particular approach has a particular politics. That said, we should note that what links the different ways of being political is the basic presumption that modalities of power work in relation to affective and emotional life but that life and living are not simply a secondary effect of forms of power. In the background to this assumption is a question which takes us back to the implications of work on affect and emotion for contemporary cultural geography: does the "turn" to affect/emotion herald a new "regulative idea" of what culture is and, thus, a significant change in what cultural geography is and does? If the turn to affect and emotion involves at the very least a renewed questioning of the equation between culture and "signifying systems," has an alternative "regulative idea" of culture developed in the midst of a concern for the dynamics of living and life?

Tentatively, we could follow Seigworth (2006) and say that the turn to affect and emotion complements and extends the tradition of thinking of culture as a "whole way of life," that is the tradition associated primarily with Williams' (1977) emphasis on culture as an interlocking set of "specific indissoluble real processes" and based on a practical concern for lived experience. It complements this variegated tradition by providing a richer, more nuanced sense of the "life" of ways of life and extends it by showing how that life, whether understood in human or more-than-human terms, is conditioned by a range of extra affective/emotive processes, including but not limited to forms of signification. However, amid the proliferation of empirical work on affect and emotion, it is still too early to determine whether a new version of culture has or will emerge. What can be said is that simply posing the question of whether recent interest in affect and emotion inaugurates a new "regulative idea" of culture suggests a number of issues for future research, including how to understand the relations between affect/emotion and practices of thinking (to include everything from deliberation to daydreaming); how to understand how discursive mediation through forms of signification and representation works alongside other forms of mediation to condition affectual and emotional life; and how to hold together the structural and ephemeral, the material and the immaterial, in empirical work on affectual/emotional life. Answering these questions, and the others posed in this chapter, might result in a cultural geography attuned to life and living and able to make a difference in a world where affects or emotions such as hope are part of everything from global media events to macroeconomic policy.

## Acknowledgments

My thanks to Jamie Winders for her really helpful editorial comments (and her patience). The chapter owes much to discussions over the last few years with Peter Adey, Rachel Colls, and Paul Harrison.

## Notes

1   http://www.telegraph.co.uk/news/worldnews/southamerica/chile/7969012/Wife-of-Chilean-miner-tells-how-she-survive-earthquake-six-months-ago.html (accessed October 30, 2012).

## References

Adey, P. (2010) *Aerial Life: Spaces, Mobilities, Affects*. Oxford: Blackwell.

Ahmed, S. (2004) *The Cultural Politics of Emotion*. Edinburgh: Edinburgh University Press.

Aitken, S. (2009) *The Awkward Spaces of Fathering*. Aldershot: Ashgate Press.

Anderson, B. (2009) Affective atmospheres. *Emotion, Society and Space*, 2, 77–81.

Anderson, B. (2010) Morale and the affective geographies of the "War on Terror." *Cultural Geographies*, 17, 219–236.

Anderson, B. and Harrison, P. (2010) The promise of non-representational theories. In *Taking-Place: Non-Representational Theories and Human Geography*, ed. B. Anderson and P. Harrison. Aldershot: Ashgate Press, pp. 1–36.

Ash, J. (2010) Architectures of affect: Anticipating and manipulating the event in practices of videogame design and testing. *Environment and Planning D: Society and Space*, 28 (4), 653–671.

Barnett, C. (2008) Political affects in public space: Normative blind-spots in non-representational ontologies. *Transactions of the Institute of British Geographers*, 33 (2), 186–200.

Bennett, J. (2010) *Vibrant Matter: A Political Ecology of Things*. Durham, NC: Duke University Press.

Berlant, L. (2007) Nearly utopian, nearly normal: Post-Fordist affect in *La Promesse* and *Rosetta*. *Public Culture*, 19 (2), 273–301.

Berlant, L. (2011) *Cruel Optimism*. Durham, NC: Duke University Press.

Bissell, D. (2008) Comfortable bodies: Sedentary affects. *Environment and Planning A*, 40 (7), 1697–1712.

Bloch, E. (1998) Can hope be disappointed? In E. Bloch, *Literary Essays*, trans. A. Joron. Stanford: Stanford University Press, pp. 339–345.

Bondi, L. (2005) Making connections and thinking through emotions: Between geography and psychotherapy. *Transactions of the Institute of British Geographers*, 30, 433–448.

Carter, S. and McCormack, D. (2006) Film, geopolitics and the affective logic of intervention. *Political Geography*, 25 (2), 228–245.

Clough, P. (2007) Introduction. In *The Affective Turn*, ed. P. Clough. Durham, NC: Duke University Press, pp. 1–33.

Colls, R. (2012) Feminism, bodily difference and non-representational geographies. *Transactions of the Institute of British Geographers*, 37, 430–445.

Connolly, W. (2002) *Neuropolitics: Thinking, Culture, Speed*. Minneapolis: University of Minnesota Press.

Conradson, D. (2005) Freedom, space and perspective: Moving encounters with other ecologies. In *Emotional Geographies*, ed. J. Davidson, L. Bondi, and M. Smith. Aldershot: Ashgate Press, pp. 103–116.

Darling, J. (2011) Giving space: Care, generosity and belonging in a UK asylum drop-in centre. *Geoforum*, 42, 408–417.

Davidson, J. (2003) "Putting on a face": Sartre, Goffman, and agoraphobic anxiety in social space. *Environment and Planning D: Society and Space*, 21, 107–122.

Dewsbury, J.-D. (2000) Performativity and the event: Enacting a philosophy of difference. *Environment and Planning D: Society and Space*, 18 (4), 473–497.

Dewsbury, J.-D. (2007) Unthinking subjects: Alain Badiou and the event of thought in thinking politics. *Transactions of the Institute of British Geographers*, 32 (4), 443–459.

Dixon, T. (2003) *From Passions to Emotions: The Creation of a Secular Psychological Category*. Cambridge: Cambridge University Press.

Evans, B. (2009) Anticipating fatness: Childhood, affect and the pre-emptive "war on obesity." *Transactions of the Institute of British Geographers*, 35, 21–38.

Featherstone, D.J. (2007) Skills for heterogeneous associations: The Whiteboys, collective experimentation and subaltern political ecologies. *Environment and Planning D: Society and Space*, 25 (2), 284–306.

Foucault, M. (1978) *The History of Sexuality: An Introduction*, vol. 1. London: Penguin.

Furedi, F. (2006) *Culture of Fear*. 2nd edition. London: Continuum.

Gibson-Graham, J.-K. (2006) *A Postcapitalist Politics*. Minneapolis: University of Minnesota Press.

Greenhough, B. and Roe, E. (2011) Ethics, space and somatic sensibilities: Comparing relationships between scientific researchers and their human and animal experimental subjects. *Environment and Planning D: Society and Space*, 29 (1), 47–66.

Grossberg, L. (2010) *Cultural Studies in the Future Tense*. Durham, NC: Duke University Press.

Hayes-Conroy, A. (2008) Taking back taste: Feminism, food, and visceral politics. *Gender, Place, and Culture*, 15 (5), 461–473.

Henderson, V. (2008) Is there hope for anger? The politics of spatializing and (re)producing an emotion. *Emotion, Space and Society*, 1 (1), 28–37.

Isin, E. (2004) The neurotic citizen. *Citizenship Studies*, 8 (3), 217–235.

Jayne, M., Valentine, G., and Holloway, S. (2010) Emotional, embodied and affective geographies of alcohol, drinking and drunkenness. *Transactions of the Institute of British Geographers*, 35 (4), 540–554.

Kraftl, P. (2007) Utopia, performativity and the unhomely. *Environment and Planning D: Society and Space*, 25 (1), 120–143.

Latham, A. and McCormack, D. (2009) Thinking with images in non-representational cities: Vignettes from Berlin. *Area*, 41 (3), 252–262.

Leduc, S. (2010) Confidence and the business cycle. FRBSF Economic Letters. November. http://www.frbsf.org/publications/economics/letter/2010/el2010-35.html (accessed October 30, 2011).

Lim, J. (2007) Queer critique and the politics of affect. In *Geographies of Sexualities*, ed. K. Browne, J. Lim, and G. Brown. London: Ashgate Press, pp. 53–67.

Lim, J. (2010) Immanent politics: Thinking race and ethnicity through affect and machinism. *Environment and Planning A*, 42, 2393–2409.

Massumi, B. (2002a) *Parables for the Virtual: Movement, Affect, Sensation*. Durham, NC: Duke University Press.

Massumi, B. (2002b) Introduction: Like a thought. In *A Shock to Thought: Expression after Deleuze and Guattari*, ed. B. Massumi. London: Routledge, pp. xiii–xxxix.

Massumi, B. (2009) National enterprise emergency: Steps toward an ecology of powers. *Theory, Culture and Society*, 26 (6), 153–185.

McCormack, D. (2003) An event of geographical ethics in spaces of affect. *Transactions of the Institute of British Geographers*, 4, 488–507.

McCormack, D. (2007) Molecular affects in human geographies. *Environment and Planning A*, 39 (2), 359–377.

Nussbaum, M. (2007) *Upheavals of Thought: The Intelligence of Emotions*. Cambridge: Cambridge University Press.

Pain, R. (1997) Social geographies of women's fear of crime. *Transactions of the Institute of British Geographers*, 22, 231–244.

Pain, R. (2009) Globalized fear? Towards an emotional geopolitics. *Progress in Human Geography*, 33, 466–486.

Papoulias, C. and Callard, F. (2010) Biology's gift: Interrogating the turn to affect. *Body and Society*, 16 (1), 29–56.

Parr, H. (2008) *Mental Health and Social Space: Towards Inclusionary Geographies?* Oxford: Wiley-Blackwell.

Pile, S. (2010) Emotions and affect in recent human geography. *Transactions of the Institute of British Geographers*, 35 (1), 5–20.

Puar, J. (2007) *Terrorist Assemblages: Homonationalism in Queer Times*. Durham, NC: Duke University Press.

Rose, G. (2010) *Doing Family Photography: The Domestic, the Public and the Politics of Sentiment*. Aldershot: Ashgate.

Rose, G., Degen, M., and Basdas, B. (2010) More on "big things": Building events and feelings. *Transactions of the Institute of British Geographers*, 35, 334–349.

Saldanha, A. (2007) *Psychedelic White: Goa Trance and the Viscosity of Race*. Minneapolis: University of Minnesota Press.

Saldanha, A. (2010) Skin, affect, aggregation: Guattarian variations on Fanon. *Environment and Planning A*, 42, 2410–2427.

Sedgwick, E. (2003) *Touching Feeling: Affect, Pedagogy, Performativity*. Durham, NC: Duke University Press.

Seigworth, G. (2006) Cultural studies and Gilles Deleuze. In *New Cultural Studies: Adventures in Theory*, ed. G. Hall and C. Burchall. Edinburgh: Edinburgh University Press, pp. 107–127.

Seigworth, G. and Gregg, M. (eds.) (2011) *The Affect and Cultural Theory Reader*. Durham, NC: Duke University Press.

Simpson, P. (2008) Chronic everyday life: Rhythmanalyzing street performance. *Social and Cultural Geography*, 9 (7), 807–829.

Smith, M., Davidson, J., Cameron, L., and Bondi, L. (2009) Geography and emotion: Emerging constellations. In *Emotion, Place and Culture*, ed. M. Smith, J. Davidson, L. Cameron, and L. Bondi. London: Ashgate, pp. 1–18.

Stewart, K. (2007) *Ordinary Affects*. Durham, NC: Duke University Press.

Swanton, D. (2010) Sorting bodies: Race, affect, and everyday multiculture in a mill town in northern England. *Environment and Planning A*, 42, 2332–2350.

Terada, R. (2001) *Feeling in Theory: Emotion After the "Death of the Subject."* Cambridge, MA: Harvard University Press.

Thacker, E. (2010) *After Life*. Chicago: University of Chicago Press.

Thien, D. (2009) Death and bingo? The Royal Canadian Legion's unexpected spaces of emotion. In *Emotion, Place and Culture*, ed. M. Smith, J. Davidson, L. Cameron, and L. Bondi. London: Ashgate, pp. 207–226.

Thrift, N. (2004) Intensities of feeling: Towards a spatial politics of affect. *Geografiska Annaler*, 86 (B1), 57–78.

Thrift, N. (2007) *Non-Representational Theory: Space, Politics, Affect*. London: Routledge.

Valentine, G. (1989) The geography of women's fear. *Area*, 21 (4), 385–390.

Whitehead, M., Jones, R., and Pykett, J. (2011) Governing irrationality, or a more than rational government? Reflections on the rescientization of decision making in British public policy. *Environment and Planning A*, 43 (12), 2819–2837.

Williams, R. (1977) *Marxism and Literature*. Oxford: Oxford University Press.

Woodward, K. and Lea, J. (2010) Geographies of affect. In *The Sage Handbook of Social Geographies*, ed. S. Smith, R. Pain, S.A. Marston, and J.P. Jones III. London: Sage, pp. 154–175.

Woodyer, T. (2012) Ludic geographies: Not merely child's play. *Geography Compass*, 6 (6), 313–326.

Wright, M. (2010) Geography and gender: Feminism and a feeling of justice. *Progress in Human Geography*, 34 (6), 818–827.

Wylie, J. (2009) Landscape, absence and the geographies of love. *Transactions of the Institute of British Geographers*, 34 (3), 275–289.

Chapter 38

# Tourism

*Chris Gibson*

## Introduction

This chapter takes a trip through cultural geographical work on tourism. Before we depart, I wish to clarify that, like Coles *et al.* (2006), I do not see disciplines as natural "homes" for particular questions or paradigms. The geographical does, however, mark a particular neighborhood of inquiry – a place that fosters certain kinds of research being done (Mee 2006). It is in this light that I consider tourism within cultural geography – as simply something about which cultural geographers embark on generating new knowledge. In this chapter I am interested in how geographies of tourism have been done, to what effect and how these have been situated and mediated.

Both the rapid rise of tourism in the twentieth century and its complexity have shaped the conduct and location of research. As a newly important industry in the 1970s and 1980s, emerging in the same era that academic specialisms and publication outlets proliferated, tourism growth was mirrored by a boom in research on its dimensions, management, marketing, and economics – and geographers contributed to this body of scholarship (e.g., Butler 1980). Tourism became more strongly supported by government, particularly in countries like Australia, Spain, and Aotearoa/New Zealand, where new schools in tourism and hospitality studies were established that became bases for applied research and industry training (Coles *et al.* 2006). Accordingly, in tourism studies the link between academic knowledge production and the interests of the state became particularly visible. Researchers were also drawn to tourism from other disciplines such as sociology, anthropology, and geography to ask questions of cultural representations, expectations and interactions, and issues of authenticity and identity connected with the tourist experience (MacCannell 1976; Cohen 1988; Urry 1990). Indeed, it is arguably still under-recognized that it was through engagements

*The Wiley Blackwell Companion to Cultural Geography*, First Edition.
Edited by Nuala C. Johnson, Richard H. Schein, and Jamie Winders.
© 2013 John Wiley & Sons, Ltd. Published 2016 by John Wiley & Sons, Ltd.

with tourism that significant advances in "new" cultural approaches in the social sciences were made in the 1980s.

Despite repeated calls to take tourism seriously (Britton 1991; Franklin and Crang 2001), tourism geography still somehow appears to occupy a liminal position in academia: no one disputes its inclusion in geographical, sociological, or anthropological research, but many view tourism as little more than a minor specialism or pursuit of the frivolous or fun (Hall 2005). Richard Butler (2004: 151) tells a particularly vivid story about the refusal by editors of the *Annals of the Association of American Geographers* to publish anything on leisure, recreation, or tourism, "regardless of quality, until a change of editors and policy well in the 1980s." Things are obviously much improved since then, yet many tourism researchers within geography still complain of marginalization.

This seems more than a little odd, given the tourism industry's economic clout, its multiple and complicated entanglements across rich and poor worlds, the links regularly forged between tourism research and policy, and the sheer ubiquity of travel in modern life. Researching tourism provides opportunities to connect and productively exploit tensions between social, cultural, economic, physical, and environmental geography – the sort of synthetic and boundary transgressing work that disciplinary commentators so consistently urge us to pursue (Matthews and Herbert 2004).

With this in mind, in this chapter I navigate a course through some prominent themes in tourism geographies. I am by no means comprehensive: I have consciously eschewed tourism research of a more management-focused bent, and instead draw attention to critical tourism geographies – critical in the sense of research that seeks to unsettle systems of domination, orthodoxies, injustices, and oppressions (Gibson 2009). Critical tourism research therefore usually stems from Marxist, feminist, postcolonial, queer, environmentalist, or poststructuralist theories. I organize my discussion below around hermeneutic "threads" – which are admittedly neither complete nor perfectly linear. The first such thread starts with neo-Marxist research critiquing tourism capitalism (very much the antecedent for later critical tourism geographies), and then discusses post-capitalist and relational approaches to understand the situatedness of tourism work, livelihoods, and performativities. The second thread considers the theme of spaces of encounter, embodiment, and ethics.

## Critiques of Tourism Capitalism

In a classic essay, Steve Britton (1991) sought to highlight the scale and import of tourism as a capitalist industry. Global tourism had grown exponentially since the 1950s, with the emergence of jet air travel and larger disposable incomes in the working and middle classes of the industrialized West. In Britain alone the number of holidays jumped from around 25 million in 1950 to more than 55 million by the early 1990s (Williams 1998) – yet geographers had not taken tourism particularly seriously. For Britton (1991: 451), tourism had become "a major internationalized component of Western capitalist economies; it is one of the quintessential features of mass consumer culture and modern life." By 2010, tourism was generating as much as $919 billion in export earnings, and more than 980 million trips were taken internationally (World Tourism Organization 2012).

Critical of descriptively "thin" studies, Britton sought to properly theorize tourism. Marxian frameworks had not been adequately applied to tourism. And yet tourism was also different; simple transference of old theoretical concepts onto tourism would not suffice (Agarwal *et al.* 2000; Debbage and Ioannides 2004). Tourism reconfigured trust (consumers being distant and therefore unable to sample before purchase); brought consumers to far-away places (mutating understandings of distance and markets); relied on commodifying culture (complicating use and exchange value); and created destinations as products that were spatially fixed. This altered the capacity for transnational capital mobility – a corporation could not easily move the Taj Mahal as they might a factory or call center.

Britton (1991: 455) originally theorized a "tourism production system" – less a single industry than an amalgam of sectors, each with their own geographies, divisions of labor, and competitive dynamics. Some still use the idea of a tourism production system (e.g., Yamamoto and Gill 2002; Mosedale 2006). Others are now less convinced that a "system" can be so neatly depicted, reflecting disciplinary suspicion with all-encompassing explanations, and further recognition that "production" and "consumption" are unnecessarily divisive analytical categories (d'Hauteserre 2006). Tourism has become a particularly slippery phenomenon to theorize.

In the 1980s, tourism had gone through phases of corporate concentration and expansion, with airlines privatized, the internationalization of hotel chains, and evermore sophisticated systems for travel and accommodation booking. Since then, further privatization, concentration, and sophistication in market competition and control has been subject to geographical analysis (Coles and Hall 2008; Weaver 2008). Mass tourism is increasingly controlled by large conglomerates with interests in real estate (e.g., US-based Cendant Corp.), finance (Thomas Cook), and telecommunications (Virgin). Airlines, hotel chains, and Internet companies consolidate powerful positions. Diversification, market risk, and the complexity of tourism's supply-side encourage further commodification, horizontal and vertical integration, and strategic alliances (Mosedale 2006; Coles and Hall 2008).

However, tourist capitalism has remained loose enough to enable others to enter markets and fuel further cycles of commodification (Lloyd 2006). Tourism's thirst for "the new," its reliance on local knowledge and low entry barriers have triggered further fragmentation, specialization, and diversification. Space continually emerges for small operators, itinerant stallholders, artisans, sex-workers, drug-dealers, and musicians to seek livelihoods (Gibson 2007; Turner 2007), resulting in slippages across capitalist and non-capitalist and formal and informal sectors.

Tourism consequently shapes material spaces: spatial fixity encourages market domination as strong players out-muscle small firms for space and control in iconic destinations. Simultaneously, new destinations characterized by small operators and the informal sector are "discovered" by intrepid travelers and guide book reviewers tired of mass tourism, and in turn these places experience inward-investment, property development, and corporate encroachment (McGregor 2000). The result is the production of tightly controlled, privatized, "enclavic" spaces aimed at complete revenue capture (like theme parks, resorts, and cruise ships), as well as the noisy, heterogeneous spaces of the informal sector (Edensor 2000; Lloyd 2006; Weaver 2005). Always contradictory, tourism capitalism tends toward corporate oligopoly but becomes more fragmented and complex, blending with other economic forms at its edges.

Accordingly, tourism has diversified into a multitude of niches. Although sometimes focusing solely on consumption, and at risk of becoming a mere list of "instances, case studies, and variations" (Franklin and Crang 2001: 1), the proliferation of niche tourism studies attests to the kaleidoscopic character of tourism capitalism. Vivid niches include "dark tourism" (focusing on sites of death, including war and genocide locations – Stone and Sharpley 2008), "wild" tourism (diversified from birdwatching to whale watching and even "carnivore tourism" – Ednarsson 2006); "alcotourism" (around drinking cultures – Bell 2008); slum tourism (Tourism Concern 2008); medical tourism (whether for essential or cosmetic surgery – Connell 2006), and sex tourism (Ryan and Hall 2001). Across each of these are variegated rationales for travel, diverse internal market structures, multiple divisions of labor, and complex politics of intersectionality and identity.

Debates also rotate around defining the boundaries of tourism, given that tourism is a "polyglot" amalgam of industries and activities (Ioannides and Debbage 1997: 229). Tourism relies on embodied consumption of "experiences" and "encounters," and the industry is reliant on gatekeepers such as travel writers and booking agents, as well as transport infrastructures, "natural" attractions such as national parks, and dedicated material production such as souvenirs, luggage, hiking boots, guide books, airplanes, and hotel beds. Some overlapping industries are wholly dedicated to serving tourists; others less so. Tourism has for instance fueled off-shore outsourcing and privatization in medical services as people increasingly travel to combine surgery and holidays. Such entanglements have spurred contestation over the very category of "the tourism industry." For Leiper (2008: 237), the singular "tourism industry" is now redundant: "the contention that tourism is supported by one giant industry has no robust theoretical foundation." Singular categories cannot capture tourism's fluidity or promiscuity.

Analytically, then, tourism is less a "production system" and more a hybrid economic formation blending people, different industries, the state, "nature," the informal sector, the capitalist and non-capitalist economies, and all manner of technologies, commodities, and infrastructures (d'Hauteserre 2006). The "trick" of tourism capitalism is its ability to commodify entire places and all they contain; to spill outwards from the edges of organized capital to saturate all other elements of place (Crouch 2000). You and everything in your town are part of its commodification potential as a tourist destination.

For other critics, "tourism" has become overly fetishized, "as a thing, a product, a behaviour" (Franklin and Crang 2001: 2), belying its inseparability from other forms of mobility (Hall 2005; Sheller and Urry 2006). Boundaries between mobilities have blurred with the rise of medium-term business travel, working holidays, overseas volunteering, "return home" trips within diasporic communities, seasonal work in ski resorts, "snowbirding," and "grey nomadism" (Allon et al. 2008; Coles and Timothy 2004; Duncan 2008). Tourism's very premise – travel – is much older than industrial capitalism; but travel is now more commonplace and complex as capitalism and society become more sophisticated and interconnected, and yet ever more fractured and contradictory.

## Working Lives and Livelihoods

Irrespective of the complexity required to theorize tourism, the reality is that for millions of people, working lives are spent serving, cleaning, performing, or producing goods and services for those who travel. Travel continues to structure people's lifeworlds and livelihoods (Connell and Rugendyke 2008). It is uncomplicated – and yet still vitally important – to stress as Britton (1991) did that much work created by travel is poorly paid, deskilled, and insecure – if not dangerous. Recent reports by UK-based NGO Tourism Concern document the worst cases, including belittling treatment of trekking porters undertaking dangerous work in Tanzania, Peru, and Nepal; forced labor camps on tourism projects in Myanmar; and the complete absence of minimum wage or hours of work laws in the Maldives (Tourism Concern 2008). Cruise ships often fly "flags of convenience" to circumvent national industrial relations laws (Lee-Ross 2006). Unsurprisingly, conditions are generally worse in the majority/poor world, where trade union activities are scarce or repressed (Riley 2004). In the Dominican Republic, for instance, tourism "deskills and devalues workers, marginalizing them from tourist development and sexualizing their labor. The majority of people are relegated, at best, to positions of servitude in low-paid jobs in the formal sector" (Cabezas 2008: 21). Awful cases of the trafficking of children for work in sex tourism have been documented in Thailand, Mexico, the Philippines, and Brazil (ECPAT International 2008).

Gender relations intersect with divisions of labor, rates of pay, and career opportunities, and can worsen in periods of crisis (Thrane 2007). After Indonesia's 2000 riots, casualized female staff from certain ethnic groups were laid off first in the tourism sector, a labor market which was already dominated by men because of religious and educational exclusion (Fallon 2008). Yet, some in the poor world may still prefer tourism to the drudgery and dirt of agricultural labor (Connell and Rugendyke 2008). Tourism's hybrid and contradictory economic formations are matched by intricate mosaics of employment and welfare circumstances. Because tourism brings customers directly and visibly in contact with workers, complex and sometimes uncomfortable collisions are generated, such as when corporate business travelers and low-paid cleaners pass by in corridors of downtown hotels (McNeill 2008); or when African-American tourists visit Brazil, ushering in a reconfiguration of power relationships within a diasporic community sharing supposedly "common" roots (Pinho 2008). Relational spaces of class, linguistic, and industrial tensions materialize.

Tourism both catalyzes labor mobility (attracting workers to destinations) and mobilizes workers to travel to other places on holiday, where local workers may in turn have limited capacity to be mobile (Riley 2004). In Thailand, for example, villagers excluded from traditional forest resources migrated to Bangkok to find incomes to survive (Wong 2008). In the Cook Islands workers were needed from Fiji because Cook Islanders had themselves migrated to New Zealand (Connell and Rugendyke 2008). In New Orleans, in-migrating tourism workers spurred gentrification in districts neighboring the French Quarter (Gladstone and Préau 2008). How tourism catalyzes entanglements of class, social relations, mobilities, and working and recreating lives – and in particular material, architectural spaces – is increasingly an agenda for geographical research.

## Performing Tourism Work/er

As an early researcher in the field, Britton explored how workers such as flight attendants and hotel cleaners both provided services and were commodified bodies – to be gazed upon, sexualized, or simply judged against yardsticks of "good" service: "the behaviour and qualities of the waiter, room service person, tour guide, or steward are as important as the physical labour service they undertake" (Britton 1991: 459). Recent scholarship has revealed how tourism workers negotiate expected codes of behavior and appearance. In Toronto, a hotel workers' union tried to transform images of lowly "service providers" into valued "cultural workers" (Tufts 2006). On cruise ships poor pay and conditions led to distinct organizational cultures amongst otherwise heterogeneous workers (Lee-Ross 2006). In Fiji, place marketing combined with colonial legacies created expectations that hotel workers appear and behave "as willing subordinates, eagerly smiling and anxious to please" (Kanemasu 2008: 116). Options for resistance were limited, yet diverse tactics emerged, including retaining some autonomy over bodily appearance, "switching off" performed behaviors, and lampooning employers away from the tourist gaze. Malam (2008: 135) emphasized the role of compromise: for young male workers in Thai beachside bungalows and bars, for instance, pay was poor (or non-existent); yet migrating to work in tourism remained attractive, because it "open[ed] up possibilities for the performance of masculine subjectivities which would otherwise be subject to surveillance and censure." Tourism facilitated sexual encounters with wealthy tourist women that "enable[d] the men to renegotiate their positioning in wider Thai society, and thereby challenge the marginalized identity labels that are ascribed to them." Amidst continued exploitation are stories of the negotiation of manifold identities.

## Encounter

Beyond its industrial and labor market structure, at the heart of tourism is *encounter* – perhaps its defining, distinguishing feature (Crouch *et al.* 2001). We travel to encounter other places, landscapes, people, sights, weather. Tourism encounters are immediate, embodied, and geographical; everyone with sufficient means to travel experiences them. Tourism both feeds off the "desire for distraction from the demands and drudgery of everyday routines" (Britton 1991: 452–453) and relies on bodily displacement and immersion in unfamiliar environments. Despite a propensity to *avoid* encounter on holiday (in favor of the poolside or the view from the bus), most tourism arises from the simple human need for social interaction, the "need to be with others" and to "regress into childhood in order to play" (Ryan 2002: 28, 33). Tourism is more than escapism, evidenced by continued growth in niche travel, educational tours, working holidays, and sex tourism – and it involves leaving the "safety bubble" of the tour bus or hotel, to be "*doing something* in the places they visit rather than being endlessly spectatorially passive" (Franklin and Crang 2001: 13). Tourists are consumers, translators, collectors, detectives – everyday cultural and political geographers (Crouch 2000) – seeking to make sense of the world and their place in it.

Tourism has a strong visual preoccupation – thus John Urry's book *The Tourist Gaze* (1990) has been particularly influential among geographers and others. It is a book "focused upon tourists' ways of seeing, the power inherent in their gaze upon attractions as well as the power inherent in the manipulation of tourism representations and experiences" (Hannam 2002: 229). Tourism brings consumers within visible proximity of workers in destinations, in contrast to other forms of commodity production which frequently distance or shield consumers from seeing how goods are made. Women's labor is frequently used for cleaning and serving in tourism; but unlike women in the textiles trade or electronics assembly industry, worker conditions are at best only partially hidden from tourists, and usually are quite visible (in hotels, bars, planes) (McNeill 2008). As Waitt *el al.* (2007) have demonstrated, the preponderance of guilt and shame amongst tourists, as common emotional responses to travel, attests to this. At one level then, travel encounters between producers and consumers render more transparent the embodied politics of tourism.

Having said this, much remains concealed, and tourism encounters are packaged, with worker decorum frequently stage-managed for tourist consumption. This is particularly so in cultural tourism, which commodifies ethnic difference and vernacular culture to bring order and predictability. As Robinson (2001: 54) reminds us, few tourists seek total immersion in a different culture. Instead, "the tourist seeks safe glimpses of cultural difference, and can often be satisfied with simulacra." Tourism commodifies place, guiding tourists' movements and controlling what they are drawn to gaze upon. Indeed, Britton (1991: 452) claimed that traveling was "not free time in any absolute sense, but subject to rules of permissible forms and sanctioned behaviour." Tourism's apparently "free" or spontaneous encounters are regulated and are a source of profit, even when, in the case of the backpacker in Southeast Asia, a sense of being "off the beaten track" prevails (Lloyd 2006). Given this, it is entirely understandable that in academia and activist circles the tourist gaze has often been conceived as another means of entrenching neocolonialism or imperialism (Robinson 2001). Indeed this is particularly seen to be the case when historical injustices against indigenous and minority groups are glossed over in attempts to maximize experiential appeal for tourists.

One response has been the emergence of an ethical tourism industry. In parallel to the fair trade movement, tourist enterprises can now badge themselves as "ethical" in terms of environmental standards, work practices, and cultural sensitivity. Where ethical tourism succeeds most is in promoting improvements to living and working conditions of workers, challenging the exploitative means of corporate tourism production, and raising awareness of unacceptable practices. Frequently community owned and supported through non-profit organizations, ethical tourism enterprises promise honesty and integrity, and provide hope of an alternative economy through which ethical/unethical practices are brought into sharper relief.

Yet a distinction is worthy of being made between attempts to insert more ethical practices into the superstructure of the tourism industry and envisioning what an ethics of tourism might encompass in the moments and spaces of encounter. That more ethical enterprises might now exist cannot guarantee ethical *conduct* (whatever that might be), nor counteract the variability of how tourism encounters actually transpire. Cultural exchanges take place in unfolding circumstances, relationships develop (or deteriorate), and reactions are negotiated (Johnston 2007). The "new moral tourist" (Butcher 2003) seeks non-intrusive encounters that reconnect sensitively with nature and culture – all good intentions. But ethical tourism risks becoming another opportunity for cosmopolitan travelers, who distance themselves from mass tourists, to accumulate cultural capital and consider themselves superior – adding to the "right" luggage and adventure wear as markers of distinction (Britton 1991: 454). Ethical tourism which hopes to overturn a binary opposition between oppressor (tourist) and oppressed (host community, tourism labor) may not always succeed unambiguously in reality.

Despite exploitation, tourism workers negotiate marginality and improve their life chances (Malam 2008), and while this does not preclude opposition to capitalistic relations of work, it acknowledges possibilities of resistance and the presence of ambiguous encounters in the moments and spaces of travel. In the context of sexual politics, Waitt *et al.* (2008: 785) argued that

> representations of the gay tourist as a passive consumer, whizzing around the commercial gay circuit, are rather simplistic . . . Indeed, the presence of international tourism amenities and associated travellers in non-Western nations might even *help* constitute alternative expressions of same-sex desire and identity . . . and do so on the political terms of local sexual dissidents rather than those of "Western imperialists."

Backpackers are a case in point: becoming part of the tourism workforce is for many part of the travel experience – a particular preference that complicates binary readings of tourism as poor Third World workers in servitude to rich Westerner consumers (Duncan 2008). Even mass tourism – so frequently depicted as tourism's dark heart, with its low-wage labor, environmental damage, and cheap cultural stereotypes – involves local populations establishing and defending front and back zones of encounter: places to entertain and to escape; places to perform formulaically for tourists, allowing everyday life to take place away from the tourist eye (Butcher 2003). By contrast, slum-dwellers meeting Western tourists in a pro-poor ethical tourism experience must revisit Western expectations of "slum life" every time they greet, serve, or accompany tourists through their neighborhoods. Limitations and contradictions are apparent even for the most well-meaning or best-designed ethical tourism enterprises.

## Sensory Encounters: Beyond Ethical Essentialism

Accordingly, recent work in tourism studies has focused on the complexity and materiality of tourism encounters. Beyond sight, researchers are now analyzing the other senses and how encounters are experienced in an affective, embodied fashion, through touch, sound, and taste. It is possible, for instance, for tourists to "internalize a place through its food" (Everett 2008: 337). Sensory encounters inform geographical analysis of material space, its surveillance, governance, and affective possibilities. Music, for instance, can mark out tourist space, define its borders, and makes its tourists feel invited (or unwelcome). An example of this is New Orleans, where both before and after Hurricane Katrina jazz marked sections of the French Quarter as tourist-friendly (Gibson and Connell 2005). At street parades and festivals, sound has been shown to be pivotal in tourists participating with a sense of joyous abandon rather than reserved observation of the local culture (Duffy et al. 2007).

The simple pleasure of feeling sun and sand on the skin is central to the beach's ubiquitous attraction in tourism, while cultural norms governing bodily exposure and decorum prevail and shape the sensory environment (Obrador-Pons 2007). Similarly, in Third World informal sector sites – markets, bazaars, streetscapes – bodily proximity, smell, heat, and noise have long invoked the exotic. For Robinson (2001: 40), "what tourists seem to feed from is the apprehension of conflict and the emotional responses brought out by the tangible recognition of difference."

The senses trigger specific bodily and emotional responses and encourage human interactions, from the festival parade to the nightclub – and geographers have begun to examine these dimensions of tourism in some detail over the last decade. Tourism is visceral, and frequently relies on what are considered hedonistic practices: sun-baking, dancing, drinking, taking drugs, pursuing sexual encounters, and becoming part of the "noise and din of the disco and the sweat of the massage parlour" (Ryan 2002: 27). Accordingly, tourism research has been refreshed by experts on space and sexuality, offering analysis of the complexities of sexual encounters, as correctives to a cerebral view of the world as an "asexual terrain, a world seemingly devoid of lust, passion and sex" (Waitt et al. 2008: 782). Within regulated spaces unpredictable encounters are still possible; while in the heat of the moment, "sensory and social overload" renders self-conscious tourist behavior impossible; "rehearsed tourist roles have little coherence in these settings" (Edensor 2001: 77).

Geographers have also sought to situate tourism encounters as moments of interaction between humans and non-humans. Waitt and Lane (2007) traced how "wilderness" comes to be understood through bodily encounters with nature among four-wheel drive tourists in the remote Kimberley region of outback Australia. In another study from the same part of the world, White and White (2008: 42) explored how isolation and transience combined to catalyze new social relationships, as encounters with strangers "offered comfort and companionship in what they perceived to be a hostile and alien environment." In neighboring New Zealand, a new "wedding tourism" industry relying on "pure" landscapes of snow-capped mountains, glaciers, and forests has tended to promote a naturalizing and romanticizing of heterosexuality where landscape and bodies are entwined (Johnston 2006). In contrast, in Borneo, humans simply "got in the way" of enjoyment of nature, and instead boundaries were reinforced between tourists and wild nature (Markwell 2001).

## Toward a Relational (and Spatial) Ethics of Tourism?

Analysis of tourism's encounters is now more attentive to how bodies and materials interact in fluid, complicated ways. For me, hope rests in how such work contributes to ongoing critical research agendas that seek to produce a better world through heightened ethical practices. The danger is that with a highly nuanced description of how bodies, materials, and "nature" are brought together in tourism encounters, the exercise of power is relegated to background status. And yet, there is much value in an ability to locate precisely the agents, moments, and techniques of the exercise of power. One avenue is to deploy concepts of embodiment and affect to trace an anatomy of power in the spaces of tourism encounter – whether planned or "serendipitous" – to highlight collisions of class, gender, race, and identity (Saldanha 2005), their spatial referents and dynamics, and to identify the intimate mechanics of discrimination, as in Tomsen and Markwell's (2007) analysis of hostility and violence at the Sydney Gay and Lesbian Mardi Gras. Encounters in tourism's material spaces elicit emotional responses of guilt, shame, concern – all potentially productive (if complex) responses (Waitt et al. 2007). How are ethical dilemmas confronted in encounters, and resolutions to them rehearsed?

Alongside the pervasive danger of exploitation and environmental damage are possibilities in the moments of encounter to learn, to address injustices, and to demonstrate commitment to equality – to extend relations of care. Given the possibility to interrupt dominance is everpresent, "moral gateways" can be opened (or closed) by tourism, via the "embodied knowledge derived from travelling, witnessing, climbing, walking, touching, and being touched" (Waitt et al. 2007: 248). Analysis of the moral gateways opened (or closed) by tourism encounters underpinned Waitt et al.'s (2007: 261) recommendations to national park managers: about whether cross-cultural signage worked, and whether restrictions on tourist movements intended to respect local indigenous communities in fact had the opposite effect, making tourists feel guilty to be there, and thus more estranged. There are other possible practical lessons from micro-analysis of encounters. Indeed, confrontation and tactile intensity can be harnessed to enable "symbolic excavation" of difficult or suppressed memories. In America's Deep South museums invite tourists to touch the material objects and landscapes of slavery – shackles and chains – heightening the drama of encounter, and forcing museum visitors to "participate in the memory work of not forgetting or trivializing the enslaved and their experiences" (Alderman and Campbell 2008: 338). There are indubitably other similar opportunities for museums and galleries to enlist tactility toward educational and curative goals.

## Conclusion

Tourism continues to occupy both a central and ambiguous space within academic geography. Geographers' engagements with tourism have not been limited to research foregrounding tourism as the subject of analysis. Much influential research in geography discussing tourism has done so only in the context of wider concerns such as poverty, postcolonialism, and the rights of indigenous peoples; identity and intersectionality, heteronormativity, racism, and sexism. A related point is that many cultural geographers would probably not consider themselves tourism geographers or may not even list tourism as a specialist research interest. Geography is thus a particular kind of disciplinary locale for the creation of knowledges on tourism where thematic boundaries are regularly transgressed in productive ways, by researchers who work on tourism, but sometimes only the context of a wider mix of concerns.

Finally – and mindful of the perennial depiction of tourism geography as "shallow" and "frivolous" – something needs to be said about the possibility of reclaiming tourism as fun. Holiday escapism may well tempt ignorance of unethical practices, but does that mean dismissing fun as a possible site of analysis? Surely there is something in the unexpected surprises and comforts of strangers (White and White 2008), in the transient and transgressive spaces of festivals, backpacker hostels and bars (Wilson and Richards 2008), that enables community and communality to be remade in unlikely ways. Even that most stereotypically mundane form of mass tourism, family holidays, provides meaningful encounters, because having fun together cements human relationships. Without tourism, the world would be dull – and more pointedly, tourism's only alternative, immobility, is an invitation to xenophobia. For this reason alone tourism warrants further analysis and reflection.

## References

Agarwal, S., Ball, R., Shaw, G., and Williams, A.M. (2000) The geography of tourism production: Uneven disciplinary development? *Tourism Geographies*, 2, 241–263.

Alderman, D. and Campbell, R. (2008) Symbolic excavation and the artefact politics of remembering slavery in the American South. *Southeastern Geographer*, 48, 338–355.

Allon, F., Anderson, K., and Bushell, R. (2008) Mutant mobilities: Backpacker tourism in "global" Sydney. *Mobilities*, 3, 73–94.

Bell, D. (2008) Destination drinking: Toward a research agenda on alcotourism. *Drugs: Education, Prevention and Policy*, 15, 291–304.

Britton, S. (1991) Tourism, capital, and place: Towards a critical geography of tourism. *Environment and Planning D: Society and Space*, 9, 451–478.

Butcher, J. (2003) *The Moralization of Tourism: Sun, Sand . . . and Saving the World?* London: Routledge.

Butler, R. (1980) The concept of a tourist area cycle of evolution: Implications for management of resources. *Canadian Geographer*, 24, 5–12.

Butler, R. (2004) Geographical research on tourism, recreation and leisure: Origins, eras and directions. *Tourism Geographies*, 6 (2), 143–162.

Cabezas, A.L. (2008) Tropical blues: Tourism and social exclusion in the Dominican Republic. *Latin American Perspectives*, 53, 21–36.

Cohen, E. (1988) Authenticity and commoditization in tourism. *Annals of Tourism Research*, 15, 371–386.

Coles, T. and Hall, C.M. (2008) *International Business and Tourism: Global Issues, Contemporary Interactions*. London: Routledge.

Coles, T., Hall, M., and Duval, D.T. (2006) Tourism and post-disciplinary enquiry. *Current Issues in Tourism*, 9, 293–318.

Coles, T. and Timothy, D.J. (2004) *Tourism, Diasporas and Space*. London: Routledge.

Connell, J. (2006) Medical tourism: Sea, sun, sand and . . . surgery. *Tourism Management*, 27, 1093–1100

Connell, J. and Rugendyke, B. (2008) *Tourism at the Grassroots: Villagers and Visitors in the Asia-Pacific*. London: Routledge.

Crouch, D. (2000) Places around us: Embodied lay geographies in leisure and tourism. *Leisure Studies*, 19, 63–76.

Crouch, D., Aronsson, L., and Wahlström, L. (2001) Tourist encounters. *Tourist Studies*, 1, 253–270.

Debbage, K. and Ioannides, D. (2004) The cultural turn? Toward a critical economic geography of tourism. In *A Companion to Tourism*, ed. A.A. Lew, C.M. Hall, and A.M. Williams. Oxford: Blackwell, pp. 99–109.

D'Hauteserre, A.-M. (2006) A response to "Tracing the commodity chain of global tourism" by Dennis Judd. *Tourism Geographies*, 8, 337–342

Duffy, M., Waitt, G., and Gibson, C. (2007) "Get into the groove": The role of sound in creating a sense of belonging in street parades. *Altitude*, 8, 1–22.

Duncan, T. (2008) The internationalization of tourism labour markets: Working and playing in a ski resort. In *International Business and Tourism*, ed. T. Coles and C.M. Hall. London: Routledge.

ECPAT International (2008) *Combating Child Sex Tourism*. Bangkok: ECPAT.

Edensor, T. (2000) Staging tourism: Tourists as performers. *Annals of Tourism Research*, 27, 322–344.

Edensor, T. (2001) Performing tourism, staging tourism: (Re)producing tourist space and practice. *Tourist Studies*, 1, 59–81.

Ednarsson, M. (2006) Attitudes towards large carnivores and carnivore tourism among tourism entrepreneurs in Sweden. *Revue de Geographie Alpine*, 94, 58–67.

Everett, S. (2008) Beyond the visual gaze? The pursuit of an embodied experience through food tourism. *Tourist Studies*, 8, 337–358.

Fallon, F. (2008) Sustainability and security: Lombok hotels' link with local communities. In *Tourism at the Grassroots*, ed. J. Connell and B. Rugendyke. London: Routledge, pp. 164–178.

Franklin, A. and Crang, M. (2001) The trouble with tourism and travel theory? *Tourist Studies*, 1, 5–22.

Gibson, C. (2007) Music festivals: Transformations in non-metropolitan places, and in creative work. *Media International Australia*, 123, 65–81.

Gibson, C. (2009) Geographies of tourism: Critical research on capitalism and local livelihoods. *Progress in Human Geography*, 33 (4), 527–534

Gibson, C. and Connell, J. (2005) *Music and Tourism*. Bristol: Channel View.

Gladstone, D. and Préau, J. (2008) Gentrification in tourist cities: Evidence from New Orleans before and after Hurricane Katrina. *Housing Policy Debate*, 19, 137–175.

Hall, C.M. (2005) Reconsidering the geography of tourism and contemporary mobility. *Geographical Research*, 43, 125–139.

Hannam, K. (2002) Tourism and development I: Globalization and power. *Progress in Development Studies*, 2, 227–234.

Ioannides, D. and Debbage, K. (1997) Post-Fordism and flexibility: The travel industry polyglot. *Tourism Management*, 18, 229–241.

Johnston, L. (2006) "I do Down Under": Naturalizing landscapes and love through wedding tourism in New Zealand. *ACME*, 5, 191–208.

Johnston, L. (2007) Mobilizing pride/shame: Lesbians, tourism and parades. *Social and Cultural Geography*, 8, 29–41.

Kanemasu, Y. (2008) Weapons of the workers: Employees in the Fiji hotel scene. In *Tourism at the Grassroots*, ed. J. Connell and B. Rugendyke. London: Routledge, pp. 114–130.

Lee-Ross, D. (2006) Cruise tourism and organizational culture. In *Cruise Ship Tourism*, ed. R.K. Dowling. Wallingford: CABI, pp. 41–50.

Leiper, N. (2008) Why "the tourism industry" is misleading as a generic expression: The case for the plural variation, "tourism industries." *Tourism Management*, 29, 237–251.

Lloyd, K. (2006) Catering to the backpacker: The development trajectory of backpacker enclaves in Vietnam. *Tourism Recreation Research*, 31, 65–73.

MacCannell, D. (1976) *The Tourist*. New York: Schocken.

Malam, L. (2008) Spatializing Thai masculinities: Negotiating dominance and subordination in Southern Thailand. *Social and Cultural Geography*, 9, 135–150.

Markwell, K. (2001) "An intimate rendezvous with nature?" Mediating the tourist–nature experience at three tourist sites in Borneo. *Tourist Studies*, 1, 39–57.

Matthews, J.A. and Herbert, D.T. (eds.) (2004) *Unifying Geography: Common Heritage, Shared Future*. London: Routledge.

McGregor, A. (2000) Dynamic texts and tourist gaze: Death, bones and buffalo. *Annals of Tourism Research*, 27, 27–50

McNeill, D. (2008) The hotel and the city. *Progress in Human Geography*, 32, 383–398.

Mee, K. (2006) The perils and possibilities of hanging out with geographers. *Geographical Research*, 44.4, 426–430.

Mosedale, J. (2006) Tourism commodity chains: Market entry and its effects on St. Lucia. *Current Issues in Tourism*, 9, 436–458.

Obrador-Pons, P. (2007) A haptic geography of the beach: Naked bodies, vision and touch. *Social and Cultural Geography*, 8, 123–141.

Pinho, P.D. (2008) African-American roots tourism in Brazil. *Latin American Perspectives*, 35, 70–86.

Riley, M. (2004) Labor mobility and market structure in tourism. In *A Companion to Tourism*, ed. A.A. Lew, C.M. Hall, and A.M. Williams. Oxford: Blackwell, pp. 135–145.

Robinson, M. (2001) Tourism encounters: Inter- and intra-cultural conflicts and the world's largest industry. In *Consuming Tradition, Manufacturing Heritage*, ed. N. Alsayyad. New York: Routledge, pp. 34–67.

Ryan, C. (2002) Motives, behaviours, body and mind. In *The Tourist Experience*, ed. C. Ryan. London: Continuum.

Ryan, C. and Hall, C.M. (2001) *Sex Tourism: Marginal People and Liminalities*. London: Routledge.

Saldanha, A. (2005) Trance and visibility at dawn: Racial dynamics in Goa's rave scene. *Social and Cultural Geography*, 6, 707–721.

Sheller, M. and Urry, J. (2006) The new mobilities paradigm. *Environment and Planning A*, 38, 207–226.

Stone, P. and Sharpley, R. (2008) Consuming dark tourism: A thanatological perspective. *Annals of Tourism Research*, 35, 574–595.

Thrane, C. (2007) Earnings differentiation in the tourism industry: Gender, human capital and socio-demographic effects. *Tourism Management*, 29, 514–524.

Tomsen, S. and Markwell, K. (2007) *When the Glitter Settles: Safety and Hostility At and Around Gay and Lesbian Public Events*. Newcastle, NSW: University of Newcastle Press.

Tourism Concern (2008) http://www.tourismconcern.org.uk (accessed October 30, 2012).

Tufts, S. (2006) "We make it work": The cultural transformation of hotel workers in the city. *Antipode*, 38, 350–373.

Turner, S. (2007) Small-scale enterprise livelihoods and social capital in Eastern Indonesia. *Professional Geographer*, 59, 407–420.

Urry, J. (1990) *The Tourist Gaze*. London: Sage.

Waitt, G., Figueroa, R., and McGee, L. (2007) Fissures in the rock: Rethinking pride and shame in the moral terrains of Uluru. *Transactions of the Institute of British Geographers*, 32, 248–263.

Waitt, G. and Lane, R. (2007) Four-wheel drivescapes: Embodied understandings of the Kimberley. *Journal of Rural Studies*, 23, 156–169.

Waitt, G., Markwell, K., and Gorman-Murray, A. (2008) Challenging heteronormativity in tourism studies: Locating progress. *Progress in Human Geography*, 32, 781–800.

Weaver, A. (2005) Spaces of containment and revenue capture: "Super-sized" cruise ships as mobile tourism enclaves. *Tourism Geographies*, 7, 165–184.

Weaver, A. (2008) When tourists become data: Consumption, surveillance and commerce. *Current Issues in Tourism*, 11, 1–23.

White, N. and White, P. (2008) Travel as interaction: Encountering place and others. *Journal of Hospitality and Tourism Management*, 15, 42–48.

Williams, S. (2008) *Tourism Geography*. London: Routledge.

Wilson, J. and Richards, G. (2008) Suspending reality: An exploration of enclaves and the backpacker experience. *Current Issues in Tourism*, 11, 187–202.

Wong, T. (2008) Communities on edge: Conflicts over community tourism in Thailand. In *Tourism at the Grassroots*, ed. J. Connell and B. Rugendyke. London: Routledge, pp. 198–213.

World Tourism Organization (UNWTO) (2012) http://media.unwto.org/en/press-release/2012-01-16/international-tourism-reach-one-billion-2012 (accessed October 30, 2012).

Yamamoto, D. and Gill, A.M. (2002) Issues of globalization and reflexivity in the Japanese tourism production system. *Professional Geographer*, 54, 83–93.

Chapter 39

# Borders and Border-Crossings

*Anssi Paasi*

## Borders: Neglected Elements in Cultural Geography?

"Border" has been a keyword for geographers since the end of the nineteenth century when Friedrich Ratzel published his book on political geography. Ratzel regarded borders as measures and expressions of the power of the organic state, as dynamic rather than static peripheral "organs." Such ideas were callously exploited in geopolitics before and during World War II, when the "wrong" location of borders was often used to justify violent expansion of territories (Paasi 1996). After the war, scholars typically regarded borders as physical lines separating states, or "artifacts on the ground" (Agnew 2008), and studied border landscapes, their functional roles in social and economic interaction and their perceptions, thus echoing the wider philosophical and methodological developments in geography (Prescott 1987; Newman and Paasi 1998). These abstract lines became crucial in understanding such notions as state, territory, and sovereignty. At the local and regional level, borders were lines between jurisdictions or voting districts.

Political–geographic views largely defined how borders have been understood in geographic research. While borders have been deeply embedded in both traditional and contemporary cultural–geographic thinking and research, their versatile roles have been curiously neglected in cultural geography. Nevertheless, many cultural–geographic themes and concepts are crucially related to borders, the practices of bordering, and border-crossings. Think, for example, of the role of borders in understanding mobility, transnational flows, citizenship, national/regional identity, diaspora, political and ethnonational conflicts or in examining the representations of "cultural regions" and ideologies of cultures as hermetically sealed and spatially fixed. Recognition of the complex and contested cultural–geographic meanings of borders requires recognition that traditional line-based views must be expanded radically in

*The Wiley Blackwell Companion to Cultural Geography*, First Edition.
Edited by Nuala C. Johnson, Richard H. Schein, and Jamie Winders.
© 2013 John Wiley & Sons, Ltd. Published 2016 by John Wiley & Sons, Ltd.

both a scalar sense (i.e., from the human body and local to the national and global) and in a locational sense (i.e., where borders are located and crossed).

This chapter will scrutinize the meaning of borders in human geography and try to illustrate that "border" is an important category not only for political but also for cultural geographers who have mapped and represented "bounded spaces" for various purposes at various spatial scales. It asks how critical cultural geography could contribute to border studies and raises new questions about bounded spaces. Current relational thinking, represented by scholars such as Doreen Massey (1995), provides some answers to this question, since it challenges all kinds of borders that are taken for granted. This critical perspective is crucial in the contemporary world where the flows of capital and information cross borders easily but where human border-crossings are highly selective. Immigrants, refugees, and displaced people often face borders and the processes of bordering in different ways than do transnational capitalists, highly educated elites, or even tourists. This situation forces the researchers to consider not only how they should conceptualize borders but also where contemporary borders and boundary producing practices are actually "located." It also forces scholars to reflect on how cultural practices and discourses are mobilized in bordering and what is the impact of borders themselves. This chapter addresses such questions and hereby opens border studies to recognize wider cultural perspectives.

To develop these ideas, this chapter first lays out the backgrounds for the rapid rise of interdisciplinary border studies. From there, it examines the rise of relational thinking and its challenge to both political–geographic and cultural–geographic understanding of borders. As has been well documented, borders and identities are often closely associated. The third section of this chapter, however, problematizes this idea in cultural–geographic terms. The penultimate section provides a theoretically informed, empirically illustrated discussion of where borders and boundary producing practices are located. Finally, the chapter concludes with suggestions for further research.

## The Expansion of Border Studies since the 1990s

Borders rapidly became highly important during the 1990s, in the wake of the end of the Cold War's dividing line between the capitalist and socialist blocs, the rise of many new states from the ruins of the former socialist states, the awakening of "old" nations and ethnic groups, and the acceleration of globalization. The enlargement of the European Union has also raised the importance of borders, as the EU has endeavored to foster cross-border activities inside the Union to decrease the importance of borders between member states. At the same time, however, it has striven to control more effectively its external limits and border-crossings. European borders have, thus, become a major "laboratory" in border studies. On the other side of the Atlantic, the traditional laboratory has been the US–Mexican border which has gained new importance through accelerating migration of Mexican immigrants into the United States and the post-9/11 political climate across North America. In both Europe and the United States, external borders have become sites where contradictions related to exclusionist nationalism and neoliberal globalizing capitalism come together in bordering practices (Nevins 2002).

A number of political geographers, international relations scholars, sociologists, literary theorists, and anthropologists have entered border studies in Europe and elsewhere (Anderson 1996; Paasi 1996; Shapiro and Alker 1996; Michaelsen and Johnson 1997; Donnan and Wilson 1999; Nevins 2002). This interdisciplinarity soon led to new theoretical developments. Cultural, feminist, postcolonial, postmodern, and poststructuralist approaches provided theoretical backgrounds for these studies that often challenged the "given" border-lines between social and cultural entities. Instead of looking at concrete border contexts, scholars increasingly critically reflected on such dichotomies as us/them, good/bad, inside/outside, or friends/enemies, which have been significant in both European thinking and other cultural traditions (Dalby 1990). Also, the power relations embedded in the making of borders and in their use as ideological tools in governance and security schemes emerged on the agenda. Some researchers mapped the historical, social, and cultural dimensions of "concrete borders" that have been exploited in the production and reproduction of territories.

Much of this initial work was done by anthropologists who studied the symbolic and cultural meanings of borders at various scales (Cohen 1986; Donnan and Wilson 1999). Over time, however, geographers started to study borders by bringing "political" and "cultural" together. Their work showed that local, national, and international processes and events fuse in ostensibly local borders. Following the anthropological tradition, geographers also showed the need for ethnographic methods to help reveal the meanings of cultural and symbolic borders in everyday life (Paasi 1996; Megoran 2004).

The representatives of critical geopolitics, often drawing their inspiration from poststructuralist thinking, proposed that attention had to be paid to boundary producing *practices* rather than to borders *per se* (Ó Tuathail and Dalby 1998). Dalby (1990) paved the way for such efforts by analyzing US foreign policy discourses and revealing how the borders between "us" and "them" were created in Cold War narratives. Many geographers and international relations scholars similarly analyzed how borders are constructed in foreign policy and security discourses (Campbell 1992; Walker 1993) or as part of the institutionalization of territories (Paasi 1996). Cultural–geographic approaches were expanded by other scholars who studied various forms of popular geopolitics and used novels, comics, and movies as their research materials (Dittmer 2010). Feminist geographers took new steps and defined security beyond the established binaries of inside/outside, or same/different, thus contesting the often-militarized bounded interpretations of security (Sharp 2007). Feminists also noted how borders, identity, and difference largely constructed and shaped the space of agency, the mode of participation in which people acted as citizens in the multi-layered polities to which they belonged (Yuval-Davis 1997).

Deepening globalization has given rise to contested narratives on borders. For some authors, borders are increasingly porous, de-territorializing, or even residual phenomena in the emerging "borderless world" (Ohmae 1995). For others, borders are highly important and require continuous theoretical and empirical reflection (Paasi 2003). The 9/11 terrorist attacks in the United States turned the attention of scholars to the relationship between borders and security issues. The simultaneous flows of immigrants and refugees has increased the complexity of these border relationships. Borders, border-crossings, and security became deeply intertwined and led scholars to consider such issues as transnationalism or cosmopolitanism, which force us to look beyond ostensibly "separate" spatial scales to connections across them. New approaches and theoretical debates have encouraged geographers interested in borders to go beyond subdisciplinary boundaries and to see that borders are not mere lines but processes, social institutions, and symbols. Borders stretch all over societies and even beyond formal state borders. Therefore, they reflect complex scalar issues related to territoriality, iconographies, identities, and resistance.

The previous discussion condenses and briefly contextualizes the changing role of borders as research objects in geography. Yet the development of border studies has not been linear.

New themes have not simply replaced old ones. Rather, old and new approaches have bolstered each other. Similarly, empirical and theoretical themes have varied, since border studies reflect wider social processes and relations, contextual features, and existing theoretical and methodological trends in academic research (Paasi 2011).

## Cultural Borders and the Challenge of Relational Thinking

Previous discussion raises the question of how borders "work" when they have once been established. Agnew (2008) suggests that borders work in two ways. First, borders have real effects when they are used to limit or allow movements of things, money, and people, a function that seems to have hardened borders since 9/11 in spite of globalization and all manner of flows. Second, borders entrap us into thinking about and acting in the world in territorial terms, that is, they "limit the exercise of intellect, imagination, and political will" (Agnew 2008: 176). In similar fashion, Balibar (1998) reminds us "that what can be demarcated, defined, and determined maintains a constitutive relation with what can be thought". The challenge for border scholars, then, is not only to map the increasingly complex functions of borders or their impacts on mobility but also, following Agnew's lead, "to think and then act beyond their present limitations" (2008: 176).

Previous sections showed that for political geographers, borders were for a long time largely given constituents of territories that separated "power containers" (i.e., states) from each other (Agnew 2008), although political geographers have gradually expanded their views on borders. Borders have also been important practical instruments for cultural geographers, who have used them to map and delimit the complexities of the Earth's surface. Such instrumental use to *distinguish* regional spaces from each other and to classify them on cultural and physical grounds has been significant since the institutionalization of academic geography. "Bounded spaces" were constructed at all scales, from subnational and national to international, to classify information or to help governance and education. Such bordering practices have characterized geography around the world but particularly in the North American tradition of cultural geography, where tracing and representing "cultural regions" or "cultural realms" has motivated cultural geographers until recent times (see Shortridge 1984; de Blij and Muller 2007). In spite of their ostensible neutrality, such cultural classifications of space are deeply political, or at least can be politically exploited.

The apparent objectivity of regional borders and their location has been continually called into question in the history of geography. Already in 1939, Hartshorne argued in *The Nature of Geography* that the problem of establishing the boundaries of a region presented a dilemma for which geographers had no reason to hope for an "objective" solution. Kimble (1951), for his part, later noted that regional geographers might be trying to put "boundaries that do not exist around areas that do not matter."

Current relational thinkers continue this critique, extending it from geographical regions to all "bounded spaces" that they want to challenge. Massey (1995: 67), for example, proposed that borders do not embody any "eternal truth of places" but, rather, are drawn by society to serve particular purposes. They are "socially constructed." Borders are as much the products of society as are other social relations which constitute social space. Massey also argues that borders inevitably cut across other social relations that constitute social space: the places that borders enclose are never culturally "pure" (cf. Sibley 1995). Borders at all scales are also "an exercise of power" and can be constructed as protection by the relatively weak, as a form of resistance identity (Castells 2007), or by the strong, as a way to protect the privileged position they have (Massey 1995).

Massey (2005) has also traced more generally how a specific hegemonic understanding of the nature of space and the relation between space and society developed within the history of modernity. One part of this understanding was an assumption of the isomorphism between space/place on the one hand and society/culture on the other. Respectively, local communities were thought to have their "localities," cultures their "regions," and nations their "nation-states." Space and society were, thus, assumed to map on to each other and were "divided up." Hence, Massey argues, cultures, societies, and nations were imagined to have an integral relation to "bounded" spaces that were internally coherent and differentiated from each other by separation. She suggests that this imagination that regards space as divided/regionalized came to be seen as progressive and natural and, indeed, continues to reverberate today.

Relational approaches have also called into question the state-centric views of the world that have dominated border thinking in political geography. Agnew (1994) labels the modernist understanding of state territory as the "territorial trap" and suggests that this trap rests on three assumptions that are typically taken for granted. First, the territorial trap assumes that the sovereignty, security, and political life of the modern state require a bounded territorial space. Second, it assumes that there is a fundamental opposition between the internal and external affairs of a state. Third, it assumes that the territorial state functions as a geographical container for modern society in which *state* borders are regarded as coincident with *political* or *social* borders. This assumption, in turn, has led to the idea, often supported by nationalists, that the world is composed of firmly delimited, mutually exclusive territories, each of which has its own collective identity.

Relational thinking, thus, accentuates the notion that borders are social constructs that always reflect power relations. Because all borderings of space are based on human choice and motivations and, thus, emphasize power relations, their cartographic representations (maps), so typical in cultural geography, similarly display power relations (Wood 1992). This point is particularly evident in the case of supra-state "meta-geographies." Lewis and Wigen (1997) define meta-geography as a set of spatial structures through which people order their knowledge of the world. It is well known that such meta-geographies, bounded spaces, and dividing lines have been crucial in the tradition of geopolitics where scholars, beginning with Halford Mackinder, have constructed nationalistically tuned representations of the world's major borderlines, regions, and their power relations (cf. ÓTuathail 1996).

Meta-geographic representations are powerful tools in geographic education. Textbooks in regional and cultural geography courses in schools and universities, for example, have long included maps, regional divisions, and border lines drawn on the basis of chosen "cultural traits" (e.g., the "cultural realms" in de Blij 1981 or the "realms of the world" in de Blij and Müller 2007). Such maps create an image of separate, bounded cultures or regions, thus omitting or at least simplifying the observations made by anthropologists almost a century ago that much of what we label as "culture" has always been based on cultural diffusion and loans. However, global cultural dividing lines were rarely seriously questioned in geography before relational thinkers brought the issue of borders to the agenda. Ó Tuathail (1996), for example, wrote a profound commentary on Samuel Huntington's (1996) well-known but much-criticized ideas on the "clash of civilizations" and the idea of separate cultures with "fault lines" between them. Yet Ó Tuathail did not pay attention to the fact that geographers have produced such maps and dividing lines for decades and used them to educate generations of geographers and other citizens.

Similarly to relational thinkers in geography, critical anthropologists have questioned the bounded cultural spaces and territorializing concepts of identity used in everyday language, in nationalist discourses, and even in scholarly studies of nationalism, nations, and refugees (Malkki 1992; Gupta and Ferguson 1992). In spite of this fact, cultural backgrounds are still important, even within a globalizing and hybridizing world, and often show the power of spatial imaginaries and cultural socialization. This fact became evident in the Danish cartoon incident of 2006, in which cartoons depicting the prophet Mohammed raised fury among groups of Muslims around the world, showing not only the sensitiveness of cultural and religious values but also their political role in mobilizing and creating "cultural" lines or negative stereotypes (Ridanpää 2009).

## Borders and Identities

New interest in borders and the rise of border studies were also related to another important social category: identity. This link harkens back to the fact that the "border phenomenon" is significant not only in the context of state borders but also in the case of many socially and culturally meaningful spaces, from the human body to local and regional administrative units, from the turfs of gangs to no-go areas and red-line zones. Borders are often related to the notion of "belonging" (Cohen 1986). While belonging is typically associated with identity, cohesiveness, and fixity, it is increasingly important in the context of mobilities and border-crossings (Kirby 2010; Adey 2010). The global transformations since 1989 have refocused attention not only on economic and informational flows but also on the displaced person, the migrant and the "stranger," people who are often separated and dispossessed from their history (Bromley 2000). While nationalist ideologies and histories generated by the state often narrate national identities as coherent, homogeneous, and territorialized phenomena, such identities (or belonging) are not "natural." Instead, imagined identity communities are constructed and bounded for particular purposes. Consider, for example, that while there exist less than 200 states in the world, there are probably 500–600 nations, groups of people understanding themselves as a unity based on culture, language, or ethnicity. Nationalist ideologies underlining "bounded identities" may be mobilized by states to create "cohesiveness"; but they are always contested by other borders that resonate with ethnicity, gender, generation, or class.

As relational thinkers have shown, borders between spaces (and cultures) need not be defined or understood as possessing either a singular meaning or location. Instead of fixed identities, what matter are dynamic and hybrid identifications and cultural possibilities (Massey 2005). Yet, some scholars have proposed that while collective identity is not generated naturally but is "socially constructed," it is still produced by the social construction of borders themselves (Mach 1993; Jenkins 2004). As Sarap (1994: 95) puts it, "identities are not free-floating, they are limited by borders and boundaries." Eisenstadt and Giesen (1995) have suggested that constructing borders and demarcating certain realms presupposes symbolic codes of distinction. They argue that the core of all codes of collective identity is formed by a distinction between "us" and "others" but also stress that these simple codes are connected by various discourses with other social and cultural distinctions such as sacred–profane, center–periphery, past–present–future, or inside–outside.

Bordering, ordering, and collective identity-building, then, are now understood as processes (Albert et al. 2001; Paasi 2003). To this argument we must add recognition of the fact that diverging forms of power are significant in bordering practices. This point is illustrated by Pratt (1999), who has suggested that democratic imaginary is not tied to producing a "good" identity for citizens but to maintaining an arena of conflict by keeping the process of boundary construction alive and open to contestation. Also, theorists of radical democracy suggest that (contingent and precarious) identities are defined through difference, that is, through the construction of a constitutive outside (Mouffe 1993).

Much current cultural–geographic thinking, thus, accentuates the openness and porousness of borders, the hybridity of cultures, and non-essentialist identities. These ideas are often related to mobility and the rise of transnational flows. Yet it is important not to essentialize such views or to isolate them from wider contexts and social practices. Pratt (1999) has discussed what she calls an overvaluing of mobility and hybridity and argues that even non-essential identities are also boundary projects: identities are constructed "through identifying who one is not." Such identities emerge from "historical geographies of conflict and difference," and these geographies themselves work to stabilize identities. Pratt reminds us that some identities are more mobile than others but that all involve exclusion and the construction of multiple and complex borders. Rethinking borders and contexts is, therefore, a perpetual challenge for cultural geographers.

## Parallel Modalities of Borders

In the last ten to fifteen years it has become more common to think of territorial borders as not located merely at the outer limits of territorial spaces. Thus, if state borders are understood as marking the spread of societal and political control into, and even outside, of the state, there must also be other ways to understand *how* borders exist "outside" of such lines. I suggest that an analysis of such modalities renders it possible to understand why an idea of the "fixity" of borders seems so persistent even in today's globalizing world and how such exclusive dividing lines can be so rapidly mobilized in wars, other conflicts, racism, or xenophobia.

How should we understand the location of borders? Despite speculation about a borderless world, state borders are – some visibly, some less visibly – still firmly located at the border areas as expressions of territoriality (O'Dowd 2010); and some of them, like the US–Mexico border, are increasingly effectively controlled (Nevins 2002) . Yet borders are more than policed lines. As social processes, borders are stratified in the wider institutionalization of territories and may, therefore, be "located" in a number of institutionalized practices, discourses, and symbols throughout state territory, and even outside of it (Paasi 1996). Balibar (1998) suggests that borders are so dispersed that they are "everywhere." This claim should not be understood literally, and this section will show that state borders come into being in and through a number of institutional and symbolic practices and discourses in specific sites that are mobilized by states but also by activists in civil society. Further, *how* current state borders exist is dramatically changing; and this change is related to supra-state geo-economic integration, forced and voluntary mobilities, rescaling of security threats, and the "technologization" of surveillance.

In what follows, I will discuss two modalities for such an understanding of contemporary borders. They can be labeled as *discursive landscapes of social power* and *technical landscapes of social control* (cf. Paasi 2009, 2011). Both modalities are historically and spatially contingent and are in operation simultaneously. However, the former resonates more clearly with such notions as nation, national identity, nationalism, and memory and the latter with state, sovereignty, citizenship, governance, security, and control. Technical landscapes of social control often "stretch" outside of state territories, but both modalities destabilize and relocate borders as mere lines on the ground.

## Discursive Landscapes of Social Power

Gottmann (1973) stressed the dynamism of territories and noted how political and economic interests combine in versatile ways in the trilogy of territory, population, and governmental organization. He also underscored the power of symbolism, values, beliefs, and ethics. Even in a globalizing world, states continue to play a crucial role in the politics of place-making and in the creation of the ostensibly "naturalized" links between places and people (cf. Gupta and Ferguson 1992). The legislation generated by the state, practices of territorial governance, and the instruments used in national socialization, for instance, aim at constructing the limits of nationality, citizenship, and identity by defining the borders of inclusion and exclusion (Isin and Wood 1999). Territory is a historically contingent process dependent on a "disorganized heterogeneity of situational projects" that make territory itself calculable (Hannah 2009). Such projects reflect not only authority, supremacy, and sovereignty but also the development of technologies such as cartography, land-surveying, statistics, accounting, and the military which ensured control over the land (Elden 2011). Elden suggests that a territory is a part of a specific rationality, a "political technology" that is dependent on calculation as much as on control and conflict. Borders, too, are simultaneously instruments and expressions of territoriality. Territoriality – the attempts of individuals and groups to control territories and population politically, culturally, and economically – persists in such social practices as classification by area, communication of borders, and control over access to territories and things within them (Sack 1986). In this context, borders are both symbols and institutions that are mobilized ideologically to produce inclusion and exclusion and the imagined "purification" of space (Sibley 1995). Borders can, therefore, be effectively used to produce and reproduce the limits of an imagined community of "us" and "them," friends and enemies.

Discursive landscapes of social power are crucial in such efforts. They become gradually institutionalized with the rise of the state territory and, due to this "processual" character, often lean on and mobilize memories. These landscapes are perhaps not "everywhere" but include key sites and elements such the border landscapes, border-guarding structures (e.g., watch-towers, customs buildings, technical equipment, even border guards themselves), and practices (e.g., passport checking, biometric testing). A fitting example of the fact that "borders" may exist far away from border areas is London's Heathrow Airport, where you can find, in the middle of the state, the sign "the UK border." Discursive landscapes of social power also include material, nationalized landscapes, memorials (place specific or general such as the tombs of the "Unknown Soldier"), and national commemorations, as well as nationalized events such as flag and independence days, which literally transform borders into part of the territory's heritage and iconography and contribute to the production and reproduction of collective identities (Paasi 2011). Particularly significant elements of such performances are military landscapes that perpetually reproduce memories and images of us and the Other (or enemy). All of these examples imply an emotional bordering that can take place at various sites throughout the national territory and become part of the political technologies used in the reproduction of territory itself.

Discursive landscapes of social power are also embedded in the media and in the national socialization through sites like schools. These landscapes contribute to maintaining the existing social order and tend to provide a specific hegemonic "reading" of societal norms and

values. A more omnipresent institution is the national legislation on borders, which is ubiquitous in the state but is particularly visible when implemented in certain sites like border
areas or airports. All these examples show not only the complex locations of contemporary
borders but also the simultaneity of "borders" at various spatial scales, which are sometimes
fused in various social and political processes.

The meanings attached to borders may also vary across localities. Borders often mean
different things for those living in the immediate, concrete border area than for those living
elsewhere in a state. Yet nationalized landscapes effectively "spread" borders elsewhere and
interpellate people as part of the imagined national community (Paasi 1996). The fact that
these landscapes project their meanings through various everyday forms of "banal nationalism" (Billig 1995) makes them persistent in daily life. Whether people cross them or
not, borders are present in daily life via the news and weather maps, for example. Similarly,
borders are reproduced in novels, poems, and various forms of popular culture, such as
movies, cartoons, and television (cf. Dittmer 2010).

Concrete border landscapes have been, and still are in most cases, effectively symbolized.
However, borders can also be performed and, thus, reproduced in various ways in bordering
*practices*. This bordering can occur on a daily basis through performances that make the
existing state power effectively visible. A powerful example is the India–Pakistan border,
where large audiences on both sides of the border witness theatrical flag-lowering ceremonies
which are loaded with masculine–military emanation and national symbolism (Figure 39.1).
Memories of borders and bounded spaces can also be enacted in other kinds of performances.
The "War Opera" performed at the Swedish–Finnish border city of Haparanda in summer
2009 is an example of a temporary artistic performance that mobilizes the memories of a
past border conflict (the 1809 war between Sweden–Finland and Russia) and transforms the
war and memories into the present in the context of the current border area (Figure 39.2).
Prokkola (2008) has shown, using the "Smuggling Opera" presented at this border, how
cultural and artistic work can be exploited in mediating the collective memory of a state
border. She also showed how such performances can be mobilized to contest the hegemonic
narrative of a national border by bringing back to life the memories of a local smuggling
culture that earlier challenged this border.

**Figure 39.1** Performing the border: flag-lowering ceremony at India-Pakistan border.
Source: photo by Anssi Paasi.

**Figure 39.2** Memorializing the past conflict: War Opera at the Swedish–Finnish border.
Source: photo by Anssi Paasi.

**Figure 39.3** The relicts of Berlin Wall on sale.
Source: photo by Anssi Paasi.

Borders can also be performed in the form of exhibitions. A primary example of this point is the relic border of the Berlin Wall that, since the beginning of the 1990s, has reminded locals and visitors of this key dividing line of the Cold War. This border is memorialized not only by the remains of the wall itself and the small concrete pieces of it that are sold to tourists, who spread this memory around the world, but also by the Berlin Wall Museum, which has a permanent exhibit and temporary displays of art related to the history of the Wall (Figure 39.3). This ostensibly local border, thus, effectively brings together national and international scales and memories.

One more example that radically widens the view of borders as lines is the fate of the communist iconography that was effectively used to "bound" and ideologically integrate the

**Figure 39.4** Art from the communist period in the Moscow metro.
Source: photo by Anssi Paasi.

meta-geography of the communist bloc and its member states. In contemporary Moscow, the layers of Soviet-era communist symbolism are so deeply embedded in the local cultural heritage, "topography," and landscape (architecture of buildings, monuments, and memorials) as well as in the "networked topology" of daily life (for instance, in the decor of underground stations), that this symbolism will doubtless remain alive within the current capitalist regime (Figure 39.4). Yet it will perpetually gain cultural meanings that bring former symbols, commercial aims, and even irony together. On the other hand, in several former socialist states like Poland, Hungary, and Lithuania, efforts have been made to forbid the use of communist symbols. Similarly, the Parliament of Georgia approved the so-called "Freedom Charter" in spring 2011, which envisages the removal of monuments bearing Soviet symbols and renaming of streets and towns whose names evoke memories of the country's socialist past. These acts have been made partly in the name of "national security." Thus, in these states, the symbolism of the former "meta-geography" of the socialist bloc is exploited to create a constitutive "outside" and a border that is used to constitute a new national "inside." Even so, counter-hegemonic or resistance identities have their competing iconographies in these sites (Paasi 2009), as is clear in the graffiti and murals that bring together local and distant events and struggles (Figure 39.5).

## Technical Landscapes of Social Control

It is thus evident that borders widely exist in a society as an expression of discursive landscapes of social power. This point also holds true in the case of the mechanisms used in surveillance and social control. Through such mechanisms, borders spread deep into societies and also outside of them. Borders have become increasingly complex elements of control in a contemporary world characterized by various flows of people, ideas, ideologies, and goods and by a fluctuating fear of terrorism. Researchers speak of a "gated globalism," which suggests that globalization and re-bordering are advancing hand-in-hand. This advancement raises a need to study what Andrijasevic and Walters (2010) call the international government of borders. In contemporary border studies, some of the most rapidly developing themes are the relations between mobility, identities, and borders – issues that are crucially related to citizenship, the selectiveness of state-based control and all manner of classification practices

**Figure 39.5** A mural in Beechmount Avenue, Belfast, calling for solidarity against oppression in Ireland and Catalonia.
Source: photo by Anssi Paasi.

that "borders" enact. This focus has motivated research on control mechanisms and biopolitical practices employed in monitoring borders, border-crossings, and profiling (the bodies of) borders-crossers, whether they are tourists, business people, immigrants, or displaced persons. It has also accentuated the links between border and security studies.

Complicated monitoring systems have been developed to inspect, screen, and classify mobile subjects (Sparke 2006; Winders 2007; Adey 2010; Johnson *et al.* 2011). Amoore (2006) has developed the concept of the biometric border to indicate the dual-faced phenomenon related to new technologies in border management and the exercise of biopower. In these ways, some suggest, people themselves "become borders" (cf. Balibar 1998). Biometric identity technologies, databanking, digital surveillance, and risk analysis "reveal not a blockaded boundary but a border that follows transboundary migrants as they move within and between national territories," suggests Martin (2011). Detention centers are material examples of bordering that occurs inside the technical landscapes of control. Similarly, airports have become significant locations in current border studies, since they are places where state power, mobility, geopolitics, and geo-economics coalesce as a problem of security which accentuates various combinations of surveillance and disciplinary practices (Martin 2010).

Emerging control mechanisms also stretch borders beyond state territories and transform borders into networks with state-centric nodes. Cowen and Smith (2009), for instance, have shown how the post-9/11 "layered-security" thinking has led the United States to develop new forms of border control that support the emerging contradictory spatialities of geopolitics and geo-economics. One aspect of these efforts has been the reconfiguration of the geographic location of the national border and the legal and social technologies for governing workers, migrants, citizens, and commodities. One of Cowen and Smith's examples is the Container Security Initiative (CSI), which installs US border patrols at ports around the world to identity potential terrorism risks. The mission statement of US Customs and Border Protection states that "We safeguard the American homeland at and beyond our borders." Similarly, the UK border agency tells in its homepage how it is "a global organization with 25,000 staff – including more than 9,000 warranted officers – operating in local communities, at our borders and across 135 countries worldwide" (http://ukba.homeoffice.gov.uk/aboutus/).

Another example of these emerging control mechanisms, this time related to crossing of "real" state borders, is the utilization of citizens as voluntary observers of illegal mobilities. This kind of "vigilantism" has a long tradition in the United States. The Texas Virtual Border Watch Program is a fitting example of such observing. This "innovative real-time surveillance program designed to empower the public to proactively participate in fighting border crime" has been established by the Texas Border Sheriff's Coalition (TBSC) in a public–private partnership to deploy a virtual community watch (http://www.texasborderwatch.com/about.php). This site has attracted a number of voluntary participants to monitor illegal border-crossings via thirty cameras available on the Internet. Koskela (2011) has studied the complex politics of watching/being watched within this "patriotic voyeuristic" scheme, as well as the ethics of such action. The program's homepage suggests that "it is a well-established fact that citizen involvement in community watch programs such as this one reduces crime." Koskela points out how such activity contributes to the social production of "the criminal" and "suspicious activity" that overlooks the various background reasons for border-crossing mobility (poverty, lack of opportunity, political oppression).

## Future Challenges

This chapter has suggested that instead of looking at borders as given "political" lines on the ground or viewing borders as neutral *objects* of political geography, a wider perspective is needed. The key aim has been, first, to problematize how "bounded spaces" and power relations embedded in boundary producing practices have manifested themselves in geographical thinking and research and, second, to show how a more versatile, culturally sensitive view on borders and border-crossings is possible. The chapter argues that bounded spaces have long been almost given instruments in political and cultural–geographic thinking, indicating the close connections between geography and the national(ist) project in many countries.

Building on this critique, the chapter, then, laid out some alternative ways of looking at borders that could help to understand their contradictory political and cultural roles. As it showed, the key *location* of a national(ist) symbolic border does not lie merely at the concrete border landscape but rather occurs in different sites and reflects the perpetual nation-building process and diverging nationalist practices. Border scholars must trace the roots and geographies of such complex manifestations of borders. The analysis of discursive landscapes of social power brings in a strong cultural–geographic view. At the same time, the rise and spread of the "technical borders of social control" show that a remarkable rescaling and reorganization is occurring in border-producing practices and in the "stretching" of state borders around the globe. This stretching occurs at the same time that the discursive landscapes of social power are being maintained, or even strengthened around the world, often in the name of national security. Both modalities of borders are, thus, in operation simultaneously, weaving cultural–symbolic and material practices together and strengthening a national community as a bounded, calculable unit in a way that harks back to the basic functions of "state territoriality" (Paasi 2011). It is clear, then, that both modalities of borders argue for considerably expanding the idea of the border as a "dividing line." To do so, however, border scholars must not only theorize borders but also study them *contextually* in relation to such cultural and political categories as state, nation, citizenship, memory, and everyday life, thus contributing to a wider conceptual and empirical understanding of these categories.

## References

Adey, P. (2010) *Mobility*. London: Routledge.

Agnew, J. (1994) The territorial trap: The geographical assumptions in international relations theory. *Review of International Political Economy*, 1, 53–80.

Agnew, J. (2008) Borders on the mind: Re-framing border thinking. *Ethics and Global Politics*, 1, 175–191.

Albert, M., Jacobson, D., and Lapid, Y. (eds.) (2001) *Identities, Borders, Orders*. Minneapolis: University of Minnesota Press.

Amoore, L. (2006) Biometric borders: Governing mobilities in the war on terror. *Political Geography*, 25, 336–351.

Anderson, M. (1996) *Frontiers: Territory and State Formation in the Modern World*. Cambridge: Polity.

Andrijasevic, R. and Walters, W. (2010) The international organization for migration and the international government of borders. *Environment and Planning D: Society and Space*, 28, 977–999.

Balibar, E. (1998) The borders of Europe. In *Cosmopolitics*, ed. P. Cheah and B. Robbins. Minneapolis: University of Minnesota Press, pp. 216–229.

Billig, M. (1995) *Banal Nationalism*. London: Sage.

Bromley, R. (2000) *Narratives for a New Belonging*. Edinburgh: Edinburgh University Press.

Campbell, D. (1992) *Writing Security*. Minneapolis: University of Minnesota Press.

Castells, M. (2007) *The Power of Identity*. Oxford: Blackwell.

Cohen, A.P. (1986) *Symbolizing Boundaries*. Manchester: Manchester University Press.

Cowen, D. and Smith, N. (2009) After geopolitics: From the geopolitical social to geoeconomics. *Antipode*, 41, 22–48.

Dalby, S. (1990) *Creating the Second Cold War*. London: Pinter.

De Blij, H. (1981) *Geography: Regions and Concepts*. Chichester: Wiley.

De Blij, H. and Muller, P. (2007) *The World Today: Concepts and Regions in Geography*. Chichester: Wiley.

Dittmer, J. (2010) *Popular Culture, Geopolitics, and Identity*. Lanham: Rowman and Littlefield.

Donnan, H. and Wilson, T.M. (1999) *Borders: Frontiers of Identity, Nation and State*. Oxford: Berg.

Eisenstadt, S.N. and Giesen, B. (1995) The construction of collective identity. *European Journal of Sociology*, 36, 72–102.

Elden, S. (2011) Territory. In *The Wiley-Blackwell Companion to Human Geography*, ed. J. Agnew and J. Duncan. Oxford: Wiley-Blackwell, pp. 260–270.

Gottmann, J. (1973) *The Significance of Territory*. Charlottesville: University of Virginia Press.

Gupta, A. and Ferguson, J. (1992) Beyond "culture": Space, identity, and the politics of difference. *Cultural Anthropology*, 7, 6–23.

Hannah, M. (2009) Calculable territory and the West German census boycott movements of the 1980s. *Political Geography*, 28, 66–75.

Hartshorne, R. (1939) *The Nature of Geography*. Lancaster, PA: Association of American Geographers.

Huntington, S. (1996) *The Clash of Civilizations*. New York: Simon and Schuster.

Isin, E.F. and Wood, P.K. (1999) *Citizenship and Identity*. London: Sage.

Jenkins, R. (2004) *Social Identity*. London: Routledge.

Johnson, C., Jones, R., Paasi, A., Amoore, L., Mountz, A., Salter, M., and Rumford, C. (2011) Interventions on rethinking "the border" in border studies. *Political Geography*, 30, 61–69.

Kimble, G. (1951) The inadequacy of the regional concept. In *London Essays in Geography*, ed. L. Dudley Stamp and S.W. Wooldridge. London: Green, Longmans, pp. 151–174.

Kirby, P.W. (2010) *Boundless Worlds: An Anthropological Approach to Movement*. Oxford: Berghahn.

Koskela, H. (2011) "Don't mess with Texas!" Texas Virtual Border Watch Program and the (botched) politics of responsibilization. *Crime Media Culture*, 7, 49–65.

Lewis, M.W. and Wigen, K.E. (1997) *The Myth of Continents: A Critique of Metageography*. Berkeley: University of California Press.

Mach, Z. (1993) *Symbols, Conflicts and Identity*. Albany: State University of New York Press.

Malkki, L. (1992) National geographic: The rooting of peoples and the territorialization of national identity among scholars and refugees. *Cultural Anthropology*, 7, 24–44.

Martin, L. (2010) Bombs, bodies, and biopolitics: Securitizing the subject at the airport security checkpoint. *Social and Cultural Geography*, 11, 17–33.

Martin, L. (2011) "Catch and remove": Detention, deterrence, and discipline in US noncitizen family detention practice. *Geopolitics*, 17, 312–334.

Massey, D. (1995) The conceptualization of place. In *A Place in the World*, ed. D. Massey and P. Jess. Oxford: Oxford University Press, pp. 45–85.

Massey, D. (2005) *For Space*. London: Sage.

Megoran, N. (2004) The critical geopolitics of the Uzbekistan–Kyrgyzstan Ferghana Valley boundary dispute, 1999–2000. *Political Geography*, 23, 731–764.

Michaelsen, S. and Johnson, D.E. (eds.) (1997) *Border Theory*. Minneapolis: University of Minnesota Press.

Mouffe, C. (1993) *The Return of the Political*. London: Verso.

Nevins, J. (2002) *Operation Gatekeeper*. New York: Routledge.

Newman, D. and Paasi, A. (1998) Fences and neighbours in the postmodern world: Boundary narratives in political geography. *Progress in Human Geography*, 22, 186–207.

O'Dowd, L. (2010) Sociology, states and borders: Some critical reflections. *Environment and Planning D: Society and Space*, 28, 1031–1050.

Ohmae, K. (1995) *The End of the Nation-State*. New York: Free Press.

Ó Tuathail, G. (1996) *Critical Geopolitics*. London: Routledge.

Ó Tuathail, G. and Dalby. S. (1998) Introduction: Rethinking geopolitics. In *Rethinking Geopolitics*, ed. G. Ó Tuathail and S. Dalby. London: Routledge, pp. 1–15.

Paasi, A. (1996) *Territories, Boundaries and Consciousness*. Chichester: Wiley.

Paasi, A. (2003) Boundaries in a globalizing world. In *Handbook of Cultural Geography*, ed. K. Anderson, M. Domosh, S. Pile, and N. Thrift. London: Sage, pp. 462–472.

Paasi, A. (2009) Bounded spaces in a "borderless world": Border studies, power and the anatomy of territory. *Journal of Power*, 2, 213–234.

Paasi, A. (2011) A "border theory": An unattainable dream or a realistic aim for border scholars? In *A Research Companion to Border Studies*, ed. D. Wastl-Walter. Aldershot: Ashgate Press, pp. 11–31.

Pratt, G. (1999) Geographies of identity: Marking boundaries. In *Human Geography Today*, ed. D. Massey, J. Allen, and P. Sarre. Cambridge: Polity, pp. 151–167.

Prescott, J.V.R. (1987) *Political Boundaries and Frontiers*. London: Unwin Hyman.

Prokkola, E.-K. (2008) Border narratives at work: Theatrical smuggling and the politics of commemoration. *Geopolitics*, 13, 657–675.

Ridanpää, J. (2009) Geopolitics of humour: The Muhammed Cartoon Crisis and the *Kaltio* comic strip episode in Finland. *Geopolitics*, 14, 729–749.

Sack, R.D. (1986) *Human Territoriality*. Cambridge: Cambridge University Press.

Sarap, M. (1994) Home and identity. In *Travellers' Tales: Narratives of Home and Displacement*, ed. G. Robertson *et al*. New York: Routledge, pp. 93–104.

Shapiro, M.J. and Alker, H.R. (eds.) (1996) *Challenging Boundaries*. Minneapolis: University of Minnesota Press.

Sharp, J. (2007) Geography and gender: Finding feminist political geographies. *Progress in Human Geography*, 31, 381–387.

Shortridge, J. (1984) The emergence of "Middle West" as an American regional label. *Annals of the Association of American Geographers*, 74, 209–220.

Sibley, D. (1995) *Geographies of Exclusion*. London: Routledge.

Sparke, M. (2006) A neoliberal nexus: Economy, security and the biopolitics of citizenship on the border. *Political Geography*, 25, 151–180.

Walker, R. (1993) *Inside/Outside: International Relations as Political Theory*. Cambridge: Cambridge University Press.

Winders, J. (2007) Bringing back the (b)order: Post-9/11 politics of immigration, borders, and belonging in the contemporary US South. *Antipode*, 39, 920–942.

Wood, D. (1992) *The Power of Maps*. London: Routledge.

Yuval-Davis, N. (1997) National spaces and collective identities: Borders, boundaries, citizenship and gender relations (inaugural lecture). London: University of Greenwich.

Chapter 40

# The Imperial Present: Geography, Imperialism, and its Continued Effects

*John Morrissey*

In our time, direct colonialism has largely ended; imperialism, as we shall see, lingers where it has always been, in a kind of general cultural sphere as well as in specific political, ideological, economic, and social practices.

Edward Said (1993: 9)

## Introduction

The era of formal imperialism and colonial expansion may be over but its political economies, its hegemonic knowledges, and its composite array of prevailing and hybrid cultures remain. Indeed, in so many ways, the imperial/colonial moment is not past. As Derek Gregory (2004: xv) reminds us, many in the "West" in particular "continue to think and act in ways that are dyed in the colors of colonial power," and if the long/global war on terrorism has divulged anything, it is that imperialism's power-knowledge assemblages and abstracted Manichean registers are as potent as ever. Even those interventionary practices that have been recast in the more benevolent language of "democratization," "reconstruction," "securitization," and "development" still betray a (neo)liberal imperial urge, and frequently serve to reinforce long-established imperial modalities of power.

This chapter reflects on this imperial present by exploring some of the focal themes and theoretical concerns of geographers working on imperialism today. I begin by sketching the development of "postcolonialism," arguably the most important theoretical and political influence in geography in recent years that has both extended and renewed critical engagements with imperialism, past and present. I outline a number of these key engagements, including the focus on the various functions and legacies of imperial discourse, the import of decentering hegemonic imperial geographical knowledges, and the problem of positionality

*The Wiley Blackwell Companion to Cultural Geography*, First Edition.
Edited by Nuala C. Johnson, Richard H. Schein, and Jamie Winders.
© 2013 John Wiley & Sons, Ltd. Published 2016 by John Wiley & Sons, Ltd.

and representation in geo-graphing the complexities and contradictions of imperialism's myriad overlapping worlds. The chapter then addresses the critical challenge of theorizing resistance, before concluding with an outlining of the enduring imperial modalities of power operative in our contemporary moment.

## Imperialism, Postcolonialism, and Geography

Imperialism has been viewed as "symptomatic of an epistemological malaise at the heart of Western modernity – a propensity to monopolize and dictate understanding of what counts as right, normal and true, and denigrate and quash other ways of knowing and living" (Clayton 2009a: 94). And certainly the operation of imperial power on every continent rested, and of course continues to rest, on a range of monopolized cultural and geopolitical discourses concerned with race, difference, political–economic correction, and so on. However, it is important to remember too that imperialism on the ground has always involved social, economic, and cultural interactions that were, and are, far more varied, complex, and contradictory than many assume (Thomas 1994; Loomba 1998; Duncan 1999; Blunt and McEwan 2002; Legg 2007).

Imperialism "on the ground" is also typically referred to of course as "colonialism," and one of the initial challenges in studying imperialism and colonialism is that of thinking through their always intertwined connections and frequently interchangeable meanings (Lester 2000; Blunt 2005; Morrissey 2013). Differentiating between the two is far from straightforward. To begin with, their political and cultural meanings and manifestations have overlapped and varied greatly, both geographically and over time (Loomba 1998). In the contemporary moment, some opt to speak of "the colonial" rather than "the imperial" to insist on the "active" implication of the verb "to colonize"; Derek Gregory, for example, argues that "constellations of power, knowledge, and geography" continue to "colonize lives all over the world" (Gregory 2004: xv). Other distinctions drawn underline differences of scale, and for sure questions of scale are important. Robert Young, for instance, conceives of imperialism as "driven by ideology from the metropolitan centre and concerned with the assertion and expansion of state power," whereas he sees colonialism as operating "on the periphery" and being largely "economically driven" (Young 2001: 16–17). Young's work is both brilliant and incisive, but perhaps this distinction is a little too neat. Though we can certainly think of colonialism as typically imperialism's endgame at the "local," it would be a mistake to either consider the local as always "on the periphery" or overlook imperialism's perennial concerns with localized technologies of occupation and economic production. In other words, we can never be too neat in differentiating between imperialism and colonialism, and in opting in this chapter to speak of "the imperial" more prominently, I want to particularly attend to questions of relationality, and I want to insist too on imperialism as not just an "ideology" reified by hegemonic discourse, but also very much as an active "practice," replete with an array of functioning technologies of power.

Since the 1980s, the key theoretical influence in geographical approaches to the study of imperialism has been "postcolonialism." Drawing on the work of Edward Said, Homi Bhabha, and Gayatri Spivak, amongst others, postcolonial critiques in geography have coalesced around a number of overarching aims (Said 1978, 1993; Bhabha 1983, 1994; Spivak 1987, 1988). These include: decolonizing and decentering Eurocentric/Western constellations of geographical knowledge; acknowledging the difficulties of "positionality" and dangers of locating postcolonial critique outside historical and contemporary imperial relations of power; challenging falsely conceived bounded geographies of "core" and "periphery"; and demonstrating the "overlapping" and "intertwined" geographies and social productions of imperial and anti-imperial worlds, past and present (Blunt and McEwan 2002; Clayton 2008). One could say that postcolonial geographers share a common goal of theorizing critical conceptions of how imperial and colonial relations of space and governmentality were constructed, represented, normalized, and enacted. For Jonathan Crush (1994: 336–337), postcolonial geography is about

> the unveiling of geographical complicity in colonial dominion over space; the character of geographical representation in colonial discourse; the de-linking of local geographical enterprise from metropolitan theory and its totalizing systems of representation; and the recovery of those hidden spaces occupied, and invested with their own meaning, by the colonial underclass.

For Edward Said, perhaps the most influential postcolonial theorist, historical "imperialism" equated to "the practice, the theory, and the attitudes of a dominating metropolitan centre ruling a distant territory," while "colonialism" was "almost always a consequence of imperialism" and involved "the implanting of settlements on distant territory" (1993: 8). Conceding that "direct colonialism" has now ended, Said has shown how imperialism "lingers where it has always been, in a general cultural sphere as well as in specific political, ideological, economic, and social practices" (1993: 8). For Said, neither imperialism nor colonialism are "a simple act of accumulation and acquisition"; rather, both are "supported and perhaps even impelled by impressive ideological formations that include notions that certain territories and people *require* and beseech domination, as well as forms of knowledge affiliated with domination" (1993: 8). And certainly imperial interventions, past and present, have always been predicated on the production of any given geography that "requires" reduction, reconstruction, regulation, and reform.

Imperialism in practice relied, and continues to rely, upon key technologies of power on the ground. These include cartography, military capability, and legal registers to underwrite colonial violence and (bio)political governmentality. If military capacity was enabled via the law, so too of course was the economic endgame of imperialism: "accumulation by dispossession" (on this last point, see Harvey 2003; cf. Harris 2004). Before either took place, however, it was geography and cartography that prepared the imperial "fields of intervention" across the globe, and in recent years a number of revealing histories of geography have highlighted the role of geographical methods, practitioners, institutions, and societies in imperial practices of exploration and colonization (e.g., Godlewska and Smith 1994; Ploszajska 2000; Driver 2001; Heffernan 2003). Cartography in particular was central in the "disciplining" and "disseminating" of imperial knowledges, with maps playing a pivotal role of visual control and serving to both mirror and reinforce political, economic, and cultural hegemony. Consider, for example, how sixteenth-century Ireland was systematically geographed as a Western frontier of England in need of renewed imperial intervention. Abraham Ortelius' map of "Hibernia" in 1573, for instance (Figure 40.1), is just one example of a much broader assemblage of contemporary geographical representations (ranging from patronized maps, woodcuts, and travel writings to state papers) that were used to script Ireland as requiring both geopolitical securitization (from the threat of then-prominent naval rival, Spain) and civilizing settlement of New Englishmen in what was depicted as a degenerated Old English colony with a seemingly expansive and largely uninhabited Gaelic western frontier.

**Figure 40.1** *Hibernia, 1573.*
Source: A. Ortelius, *Additamentum Theatrum Orbis Terrarum.* Dublin: Neptune Gallery.

In contemporary geography, an important starting point in understanding cartography's functioning at the heart of imperialism is the work of Brian Harley (1988, 1989). Harley's sustained critique of the Cartesian and positivist foundations of mapmaking revealed both the power of maps and the fundamental falsity that they can "mirror accurately some aspect of 'reality' which is simple and knowable and can be expressed as a system of facts" (Harley 1989: 82). Methodologically based on semiotics and deconstruction, his work has been especially influential in highlighting the inherent power relations that are reified cartographically in scriptings of human geography (Wood 1993; Dorling and Fairbairn 1997; Cosgrove 2005). For Harley, maps always possessed the potent capacity of "reifying power, reinforcing the status quo, and freezing social interaction within chartered lines"; and his vital contribution to historical geography has been instrumental too in "the broader problematization of all forms of geographical representation," past and present (Harley 1988: 302–303). In this sense, his work is still a significant influence in critiques of contemporary imperialism and its enduring reliance on the persuasive, abstracted power of cartographic representation, whether that be via GIS or otherwise, in the name of security, surveillance, or reconnaissance (Pickles 1995; Farish 2009).

The broader critical tradition that has emerged in geography of situated, contextualized, and historicized analyses of imperialism gives it a particular strength and relevancy, but it is important to underline that theoretical influences have not solely come from postcolonialism, but rather more eclectically from a range of other critical and often complementary positions/ politics too, such as feminism, Marxism, and political ecology. Collectively, however, the rich array of geographical work on imperial discourses and technologies of power has served to complicate, differentiate, and bring into view the multiple conflicting pasts and continued complex effects of imperialism (Blunt and Rose 1994; Lester 2000; Blunt and McEwan 2002). It has problematized, too, monolithic accounts of imperialism and ostensibly static and bounded notions such as the "frontier" as appropriate conceptual tools in theorizing colonial relations and resistance; with many opting for the concept of the "contact zone" to signal

the overlapping nature of imperialism's intricate human geographies on the ground (Routledge 1997; Morrissey 2005; Nally 2009). Much recent work in historical and cultural
geography has also exhibited an interest in the experiences of "dislocation" for both colonizer
and colonized, and this concern has opened an important trajectory of work focused on
questions of "hybridity" and, more specifically, on the hybrid nature of "colonial subjectivities," as a number of edited volumes attest (Blunt and Rose 1994; Blunt and McEwan 2002;
Raju *et al.* 2006). As a final point here, a range of methodological questions respecting issues
such as scale and locationality, what constitutes the "field" or the "archive," and how different
theoretical perspectives and techniques of analysis can facilitate critical accounts of imperialism, have also been fruitfully engaged with in recent years (Wishart 1997; Duncan 1999;
Nash and Graham 2000; Withers 2002; Black 2003; Ogborn 2003).

## Imperialism and Discourse

In one of his earliest works, the literary critic Homi Bhabha (1983: 199) notes how imperialism "produces the colonized as a fixed reality which is at once an 'other' and yet entirely
knowable and visible". Bhabha's point here is that the "colonized" must always be first
produced through "discourse," and it is this "imperial" or "colonial" discourse that legitimizes
and sustains imperialism in practice (though both "imperial discourse" and "colonial discourse" are commonly used interchangeably, it is sometimes confusing to do so; for the
purposes of this chapter, I use the term "imperial discourse" hereafter). The careful deconstruction of imperial discourse is pivotal to our understanding of how imperialism works. I
have outlined elsewhere how imperial discourse can be defined as "the prevailing representations of imperial power" that seek to "normalize imperial mindsets and the rights of colonial
intervention" and simultaneously to lay claim to the power to "represent" the colonized
(Morrissey 2013). The anthropologists John and Jean Comaroff are particularly instructive
on this latter point, the question of claiming representational power over the subaltern or
"Other":

> the essence of colonization inheres less in political overrule than in seizing and transforming
> "others" by the very act of conceptualizing, inscribing, and interacting with them on terms not
> of their own choosing; in making them into the pliant objects and silenced subjects of our scripts
> and scenarios; in assuming the capacity to "represent" them. (Comaroff and Comaroff 1991: 15)

For the Comaroffs, the power of representation or discourse was key to the European colonization of Africa, for example, which they argue was ultimately "less a directly coercive
conquest than a persuasive attempt to colonize consciousness, to remake people by redefining
the taken for granted surfaces of their everyday world" (1991: 313).

In recent years, a particular focus on discourse in approaches to the study of imperialism
and colonialism, in geography and a range of other disciplines including especially anthropology and English, has proven to be intellectually emancipatory in a number of ways. In the
context of the broader postcolonial critique since the 1980s, a more politicized academy has
engendered a research trajectory that, for Ania Loomba, has sought to both divulge and
dismantle the pervasive power of imperial discourse, its "ideas and institutions, knowledge
and power" (1998: 54). Loomba is joined by many in underlining the role that imperial
discourse played, and continues to play, in imperial practice. Nicholas Thomas, for instance,
asserts that imperial practice has always been crucially underpinned discursively, "through

signs, metaphors, and narratives," and observes how even "its purest moments of profit and violence have been mediated and enframed by structures of meaning" (1994: 2). Thomas' point here is that in any imperial intervention we find that imperial violence is carefully scripted as "necessary." Furthermore, the typical imperial endgame of economic expropriation is commonly discursively marginalized by prioritized political and cultural discourses such as the notion of "bringing civilization." Thomas also reminds us of the constitutive, rather than external, nature of imperial discourse. In other words, functioning imperial discourses do not work to simply "mask, mystify, or rationalize forms of oppression that are external to them"; rather they are "also expressive and constitutive of colonial relationships in themselves" (1994: 2).

This focal question of the constitutive, material context through which imperial discourse and imperial practice work in tandem is taken up by Dan Clayton when he warns against "reducing imperialism to discourse," and insists upon "the need to materially ground understanding of imperialism's operations" (2009b: 374). History is replete, of course, with multiple forms of imperial discourse serving to constitutively frame, regulate, and enact colonial order and regimes of truth (Mitchell 1991). In historical and cultural geography in recent years, more sustained engagement with the particularity and relationality of the discourses and practices of colonialism in the colonized worlds themselves has emerged (Lester 2001; Morrissey 2003; Raju *et al.* 2006; Legg 2007; Stanley 2008). And this work has taken up, in effect, Jim Duncan and Denis Cosgrove's earlier call for the complexities of imperialism and colonialism to be "unravelled through localized and historically specific accounts" (1995: 127).

Before concluding on imperial discourse, it is important to acknowledge in particular the key influence of Edward Said in much work on imperialism in historical and cultural geography over the last twenty-five years. Certainly, a fundamental starting point in understanding the pivotal role of discourse at the heart of imperialism everywhere is his foundational text *Orientalism*, which was first published in 1978 and has since inspired the rise of what is now referred to as "postcolonial studies." Said's brilliant prose and incisive and courageous politics (especially in the context of his native Palestine) has been particularly inspiring for many. *Orientalism* explored the historical emergence of a powerful European imperial imaginary of the Orient in which the West is continually positioned discursively via a powerful and indeed therapeutic set of binaries, such as us/them, superior/inferior, rational/irrational, and civilized/barbaric. The endgame for Said was that all-pervasive and dominant imperial discourses of what he called the "Other" or "Otherness" served to habitually underpin the operation of imperial power in practice by literally ascribing "reality and reference," and that ascendant imperial power in turn rendered imperial discourses hegemonic (Said 1978: 321; in this sense, Said was drawing in particular on Michel Foucault's notion of the "power–knowledge couplet"). In introducing the concept of "imaginative geographies" in his later work, *Culture and Imperialism*, in 1993, Said further theorized how the "Other" is typically imagined, vilified, and scripted in abstracted, essentialist, and deeply consequential ways.

Many geographers have drawn on Said's writings to deconstruct the operation of imperial power in a wide range of historical and geographical contexts (Gregory 2001; Lester 2001; Blunt 2005; Clayton 2008). Said's work has come in for some critique (such as for his proclivity toward the written texts of high culture when theorizing imperial discourse, and his rather limited theorizing of the agency of anti-imperial resistance); however, on the whole, his "critical deconstruction of the historical language, power relations, and subject positions of the western 'Self' and the external 'Other' continues to have an enduring and fruitful legacy" (Morrissey 2013). As Nicholas Thomas (1994) reminds us, imperialism is an ongoing cultural process in which the "Other" is persistently represented in ways that legitimize racial and cultural differences. And imperial discourse also continues to legitimize interventionary practices across the planet – from "geopolitics" to "development." As Edward Said argued so lucidly in one of his last works before his death, abstracted and Manichean imperial geographical knowledges centrally underpinned and ultimately served to guarantee the launch of what is now the long war on terror:

> Without a well-organized sense that these people over there were not like "us" and didn't appreci-
> ate "our" values – the very core of traditional Orientalist dogma – there would have been no war.
> (Said 2003: xv)

## Imperialism and Resistance

In theorizing resistance to imperialism, a key influence and important point of departure for many contemporary postcolonial thinkers is the work of French writer and revolutionary, Frantz Fanon – and especially his *The Wretched of the Earth*, first translated into English in 1963. Homi Bhabha, for instance, in seeking to reject historicist or linear conceptions of causality and inheritance in terms of "anti-colonial struggle," underlines the usefulness of a Fanonian conception of "continuance," in which "the practice of action" has an everyday temporality and an agency constituted in "the singularity of the "local" (Bhabha 2001: 39, 40). For Fanon, the anti-colonial struggle must always be about a "fight which explodes the old colonial truths"; it must have a politics that are "national, revolutionary, and social"; and it must have a violence "committed by the people" and "organized and educated by its leaders" (Fanon 1963: 147). This, for Fanon, was how to live "inside history," to generate new "social truths," "new facts," and "new meanings," because without the knowledge forged in "the practice of action," resistance was "nothing but a fancy-dress parade and the blare of the trumpets" (1963: 147).

Perhaps Fanon's greatest intellectual contribution is his engagement with the question of "revolutionary violence," the narration of which has been so discursively subjugated over time by the hegemonic power of imperial discourse. In recent years, postcolonial geographers have shown how on every continent there are long and complex narratives of anti-imperial revolutionary violence and resistance that are under-theorized and often no more than foot-notes to history – from Ireland to India, from Ceylon to Vietnam (Morrissey 2003; Raju *et al.* 2006; Duncan 2007; Clayton 2008). Their limited narration is perhaps for various reasons, ranging from methodological concerns of archives, access, and language to arguably a lingering Western and Anglophone worldview that serves to reinforce a metropolitan-centered historiography of imperialism (Lester 2000; Blunt 2005). Mostly, however, resistance to imperialism is not the prioritized story because it is commonly not "our" story, and, in the contemporary world, let us not forgot the enduring representational power of monopolized imperial discourses that can delegitimize resistance as irrational, barbaric "insurgency," for example, and thereby negate meaningful political and intellectual engagement with the peren-nially scripted "Other."

Inspired by the broader postcolonial critique of imperialism by writers such as Fanon, Bhabha, and others, a range of important recent work in historical, political, and cultural geography has addressed the fundamental need for decolonizing and decentering hegemonic imperial geographical knowledges (Blunt and McEwan 2002; Clayton 2009b). A key over-arching challenge in much of this work has involved recovering and accounting for the counter-imperial discourses of the subaltern, and geo-graphing the complex spaces and prac-tices of anti-imperial resistance – from autoethnography to legal and constitutional opposi-tion, from economic sabotage to political violence (Crush 1994; Pratt 1994; Pile and Keith 1997; Blunt and McEwan 2002; Featherstone 2005a; Watts 2009).

Theorizing anti-imperial resistance and the violence of the "anti-colonial struggle" is not just important historiographically, of course. Engaging, narrating, and learning from the geographies of past anti-imperial struggles matter a great deal for understanding resistance to contemporary imperial interventions (Butz 2002; Smith 2003; Jhaveri 2004; Featherstone 2005b; Kearns 2009). Consider, for example, the repeated and myopic shortcomings of Western geopolitical and cultural explanations for the so-called "insurgency" during the recent Iraq war (Gregory 2008). It is, of course, vital too that we do not overly romanticize or suspend critique when it comes to resistance. As Homi Bhabha writes, we must "eschew the springing wolf's instinct of total annihilation and the messianic blast of the revolutionary gust of wind" (2001: 40). David Nally (2009: 622) observes, for instance, that inflecting ideo-logical visions of resistance with Spivak's notion of "strategic essentialism" or using "ethnic categories in order to further certain perceived emancipatory goals" are neither straightfor-ward nor unproblematic endeavors in practice. For Nally, "where ethnic identities are culti-vated, and human differences underscored, there is often a vast gap between emancipatory and egalitarian politics" (2009: 622).

Over time, the complex networking of both imperial practice and anti-imperial resistance ensured the manifestation of mutually constitutive political, economic, and cultural produc-tions in both the "metropole" and "periphery" (Lester 2001; Featherstone 2008). Foucault called this the "boomerang effect" (Foucault 2003: 103). Just as imperial endeavors were frequently *ad hoc* and certainly not monolithic or static in character, indigenous responses were typically fluid too and indeed often contradictory, reflecting the entangled co-constitution of the worlds of the colonizer and colonized. In other words, there is always a relational nature to resistance. As Foucault (1978: 95) put it, "where there is power, there is resistance, and yet, or rather consequently, this resistance is never in a position of exteriority in relation to power." And this key conceptual challenge has variously been engaged in recent postcolo-nial critiques in geography, as David Butz (2002: 15–16) observes:

> An important dimension of these recent examinations has been the effort to describe how the material and discursive aspects of domination and resistance relate; that is, to use the notion of resistance to understand subjectivity as well as agency among subordinate populations. Much of the conceptual context for this effort comes from postcolonial analyses of subaltern subjectivities.

It is vital, ultimately, to avoid either bounding or essentializing the worlds of the imperial or anti-imperial past or present. This is part of Gregory Castle's call to adapt a "regional approach" to challenge and complicate what he refers to as "the tendency toward a col-lectivist postcolonialism" (2001: xi). He draws on Homi Bhabha's (2001) notion of "ver-nacular cosmopolitanism" to insist on the situated, geographical diversity of imperial practice on the ground. For Castle (2001: xii), vernacular cosmopolitanism serves to rein-force "the fundamental importance of *location*, the felt experience of the local, which is not collectivized or sublated in a universal historical narrative." And geographers, in particular, have been especially mindful of this broader postcolonial critique in endeavoring to offer carefully contextualized, historically and geographically situated research of the intricate spaces of the imperial past and present on every continent (Lester 2000; Blunt 2005; Clayton 2009a).

## Conclusion: Imperialism's Continued Effects

What are the ways in which imperialism "lingers" today, as Edward Said once observed? Certainly, imperialism lingers in the discursive, in the persistence of functioning imperial knowledges, and all of their abstracted and essentialist equations of geography, difference, and threat. As Derek Gregory (2004) has shown, the so-called "war on terror," the interventionary war of our time, has served to reify a Manichean sense of "good" and "evil," of "friend" and "enemy," of "us" and "them" – all built on well-established imperial registers of Orientalism. And this is not just important in the "cultural sphere." As Bradley Klein (1994: 5) explains in his brilliant book, *Strategic Studies and World Order*, Western geopolitics and its interventionary "strategic violence" continues to draw upon "a variety of discursive resources" that are "widely construed as rational, plausible, and acceptable." Chief amongst these discursive resources are an array of reductive cultural binaries predicated upon simplified dichotomous geographies such as us/them, civilized/barbarous, and inside/outside. As Klein underlines, what geopolitics does, together with explicit academic support from strategic studies in particular, is to "provide a map for the negotiating of these dichotomies in such a way that Western society always winds up on the 'good' . . . side of the equation" (1994: 5). The consequences in terms of legitimated geopolitical violence then become clear:

> Our putative enemy, whatever the form assumed by its postulated Otherness – variously the Soviet Union, or Communism, guerilla insurgents, terrorism, Orientals, Fidel Castro, Nicaragua, Qaddafi, Noriega, or Saddam Hussein – simultaneously is endowed with all of these dialectically opposed qualities. Strategic violence is then called in to mediate the relationship, patrol the border, surveil the opponent, and punish its aggression. (Klein 1994: 5–6)

Contemporary geopolitics extends historical imperialism in various ways, and not just in terms of its perpetuation of imperial registers of difference and Otherness. It relies upon an array of biopolitical modalities of power, for instance, that were first initiated in the era of high colonialism, as Jim Duncan and David Nally have shown respectively for nineteenth-century Ceylon and Ireland – both drawing in particular on Michel Foucault's recently translated lectures on biopolitics and governmentality (Duncan 2007; Nally 2008; Foucault 2007, 2008). And as others have outlined, the legal and biopolitical operations of geopolitical interventions today are sustained by an array of well-established liberal imperial discourses that legitimize the necessity of emergency powers in the name of national security (Gregory 2006; Dillon 2007; Kearns 2008; Barder 2009). Contemporary imperial geopolitics also works to script the necessity of continued military–economic securitization of the global political economy – and that political economy was built, of course, during the imperial era. As J.A. Hobson (1938: 106) noted over a century ago, the "economic root of imperialism is the desire of strong organized industrial and financial interests to secure and develop at the public expense and by the public force private markets for their surplus goods and their surplus capital." For Hobson, the "necessary means to this end" centrally involved "war, militarism, and a 'spirited foreign policy'" (1938: 106). Today, as Thomas Pogge dolefully observes, "affluent Western states" may no longer practice "slavery, colonialism, or genocide," but they "still enjoy crushing economic, political, and military dominance over a world in which effective enslavement and genocides continue unabated" (2008: 6). And certainly there has been no shortage of recent calls to extend Western military and political economic ascendancy via aggressive imperial geopolitics (Kaplan 2009; cf. Dalby *et al.* 2009).

Contemporary imperialism has been critiqued by geographers in at least four principal ways: first, focus has been given to the persistence of hegemonic cultural registers of difference via imperial discourses of ethnicity, race, religion, gender, and sexuality (Gregory 2004; Blunt 2005; Clayton 2009b; Kearns 2009); secondly, attention has been directed to the political economy of continued Western global hegemony and accelerated capitalist accumulation (Harvey 2003; Jhaveri 2004; Smith 2005; Nally 2011); thirdly, critical geopolitical accounts have underlined the abstracted discursive production of military interventionary spaces (and particularly so in the context of the so-called "war on terror") (Ó Tuathail 2003; Graham 2005; Dalby 2007; Hyndman 2007); and, fourthly, geographers have sought to interrogate the multiple practices of interventionism in our contemporary world and their consequent contested forms of securitization and governmentality (Desbiens 2007; Stanley 2008; Fluri 2009; Morrissey 2011). There has, of course, been much overlap of perspective too, and arguably one of the most important overarching characteristics of contemporary geographical critiques of imperialism is a particular proficiency in contextualizing and theorizing discursive and material productions of space, especially in the complex contexts of postcolonialism, neoliberalism, environmental justice, and political violence (Sullivan 2006; Featherstone 2008; Cowen 2009; Watts 2009).

In conclusion, the recent invasions of Afghanistan and Iraq and the rapacious exercise of crude Western power in the Middle East and elsewhere have brought into sharp relief a series of questions concerning the continued geopolitical and cultural maneuverings of imperialism. Geographers have sought to shed light on multiple aspects of imperial practice today, along with an array of pervasive, prioritized interventionary rationales. In critiquing abstract geopolitical, geo-economic, and developmental forms of imperialism, a key concern has been to theorize and insist upon more humane, nuanced, and critical human geographies. Nicholas Thomas perhaps put it best when he reminded us that "relations of cultural colonialism are no more easily shrugged off than the economic entanglements that continue to structure a deeply asymmetrical world economy" (1994: 10). This is precisely why critical human geography today is marked by explicit concerns about imperialism's lasting cultures, its persistent interventionism, and its continued effects.

## Acknowledgments

My thanks to Nuala Johnson, David Nally, and Anna Stanley for their comments, and to Andrew Bonar Law at the Neptune Gallery in Dublin for his kind permission to use Figure 40.1.

# References

Barder, A.D. (2009) Power, violence and torture: Making sense of insurgency and legitimacy crises in past and present wars of attrition. In *The Geopolitics of American Insecurity: Terror, Power and Foreign Policy*, ed. F. Debrix and M. Lacy. New York: Routledge, pp. 54–70.

Bhabha, H. (1983) Difference, discrimination and the discourse of colonialism. In *The Politics of Theory*, ed. F. Barker, P. Hulme, M. Iverson, and D. Loxley. Colchester: University of Essex Press, pp. 194–211.

Bhabha, H. (1994) *The Location of Culture*. London: Routledge.

Bhabha, H. (2001) Unsatisfied: Notes on vernacular cosmopolitanism. In *Postcolonial Discourses: An Anthology*, ed. G. Castle. Oxford: Blackwell, pp. 39–52.

Black, I.S. (2003) Analysing historical and archive sources. In *Key Methods in Geography*, ed. N.J. Clifford and G. Valentine. London: Sage, pp. 475–500.

Blunt, A. (2005) Colonialism/postcolonialism. In *Cultural Geography: A Critical Dictionary of Key Concepts*, ed. D.Atkinson, P.Jackson, D.Sibley, and N.Washbourne. London: I.B. Tauris, pp. 175–181.

Blunt, A. and McEwan, C. (eds.) (2002) *Postcolonial Geographies*. London: Continuum.

Blunt, A. and Rose, G. (eds.) (1994) *Writing Women and Space: Colonial and Postcolonial Geographies*. New York: Guilford Press.

Butz, D. (2002) Resistance, representation and third space in Shimshal Village, Northern Pakistan. *ACME: An International Journal of Critical Geographies*, 1, 15–34.

Castle, G. (ed.) (2001) *Postcolonial Discourses: An Anthology*. Oxford: Blackwell.

Clayton, D. (2008) Le passé colonial/impérial et l'approche postcoloniale de la géographie Anglophone. In *L'Empire des Géographes: Géographie, Exploration et Colonisation, XIXe–XXe Siècle*, ed. P. Singaravélou. Paris: Belin, pp. 219–234.

Clayton, D. (2009a) Colonialism. In *The Dictionary of Human Geography*, 5th edition, ed. D. Gregory, R. Johnston, G. Pratt, M. Watts, and S. Whatmore. Oxford: Wiley-Blackwell, pp. 94–98.

Clayton, D. (2009b) Imperialism. In *The Dictionary of Human Geography*, 5th edition, ed. D. Gregory, R. Johnston, G. Pratt, M. Watts, and S. Whatmore. Oxford: Wiley-Blackwell, pp. 373–374.

Comaroff, J. and Comaroff, J. (1991) *Of Revelation and Revolution, Volume 1: Christianity, Colonialism and Consciousness in South Africa*. Chicago: University of Chicago Press.

Cosgrove, D. (2005) Mapping/cartography. In *Cultural Geography: A Critical Dictionary of Concepts*, ed. D. Atkinson, P. Jackson, D. Sibley, and N. Washbourne. London: I.B. Tauris, pp. 27–33.

Cowen, D. (2009) Containing insecurity: US port cities and the "war on terror." In *Disrupted Cities: When Infrastructure Fails*, ed. S. Graham. New York: Routledge, pp. 69–84.

Crush, J. (1994) Post-colonialism, decolonization and geography. In *Geography and Empire*, ed. A. Godlewska and N. Smith. Oxford: Blackwell, pp. 333–350.

Dalby, S. (2007) Regions, strategies and empire in the global war on terror. *Geopolitics*, 12 (4), 586–606.

Dalby, S., Kearns, G., Morrissey, J., and Toal, G. (2009) Geography writes back: Responses to Kaplan's "The Revenge of Geography." *Human Geography*, 2 (2), 33–51.

Desbiens, C. (2007) "Water all around, you cannot even drink": The scaling of water in James Bay/Eeyou Istchee. *Area*, 39 (3), 259–267.

Dillon, M. (2007) Governing through contingency: The security of biopolitical governance. *Political Geography*, 26 (1), 41–47.

Dorling, D. and Fairbairn, D. (1997) *Mapping: Ways of Representing the World*. London: Longman.

Driver, F. (2001) *Geography Militant: Cultures of Exploration and Empire*. Oxford: Blackwell.

Duncan, J. (1999) Complicity and resistance in the colonial archive: Some issues of method and theory in historical geography. *Historical Geography*, 27, 119–128.

Duncan, J. (2007) *In the Shadows of the Tropics: Climate, Race and Biopower in 19th Century Ceylon*. Aldershot: Ashgate.

Duncan, J. and Cosgrove, D. (1995) Editorial: Colonialism and postcolonialism in the former British Empire. *Ecumene*, 2 (2), 127–128.

Fanon, F. (1963) *The Wretched of The Earth*, trans. C. Farrington. New York: Grove Press.

Farish, M. (2009) Maps and the state. In *International Encyclopedia of Human Geography*, vol. 6, ed. R. Kitchin and N. Thrift. Oxford: Elsevier, pp. 442–454.

Featherstone, D.J. (2005a) Atlantic networks, antagonisms and the formation of subaltern political identities. *Social and Cultural Geography*, 6 (3), 387–404.

Featherstone, D.J. (2005b) Towards the relational construction of militant particularisms: Or why the geographies of past struggles matter for resistance to neoliberal globalization. *Antipode*, 37 (2), 250–271.

Featherstone, D.J. (2008) *Resistance, Space and Political Identities: The Making of Counter-Global Networks*. Oxford: Wiley-Blackwell.

Fluri, J. (2009) "Foreign passports only": Geographies of (post)conflict work in Kabul, Afghanistan. *Annals of the Association of American Geographers*, 99 (5), 986–994.

Foucault, M. (1978) *The History of Sexuality: Volume 1, An Introduction*. New York: Vintage.

Foucault, M. (2003) *Society Must Be Defended: Lectures at the Collège de France, 1975–1976*, trans. D. Macey. London: Penguin.

Foucault, M. (2007) *Security, Territory, Population: Lectures at the Collège de France, 1977–1978*, trans. G. Burchell. Basingstoke: Palgrave Macmillan.

Foucault, M. (2008) *The Birth of Biopolitics: Lectures at the Collège de France, 1978–1979*, trans. G. Burchell. Basingstoke: Palgrave Macmillan.

Godlewska, A. and Smith, N. (eds.) (1994) *Geography and Empire*. Oxford: Blackwell.

Graham, S. (2005) Remember Fallujah: Demonizing place, constructing atrocity. *Environment and Planning D: Society and Space*, 23 (1), 1–10.

Gregory, D. (2001) (Post)colonialism and the production of nature. In *Social Nature*, ed. N. Castree and B. Braun. Oxford: Blackwell, pp. 84–111.

Gregory, D. (2004) *The Colonial Present: Afghanistan, Palestine, Iraq*. Oxford: Blackwell.

Gregory, D. (2006) The black flag: Guantánamo Bay and the space of exception. *Geografiska Annaler B*, 88 (4), 405–427.

Gregory, D. (2008) The biopolitics of Baghdad: Counterinsurgency and the counter-city. *Human Geography*, 1 (1), 6–27.

Harley, J.B. (1988) Maps, knowledge and power. In *The Iconography of Landscape: Essays on the Symbolic Representation, Design and Use of Past Environments*, ed. D. Cosgrove and S. Daniels. Cambridge: Cambridge University Press, pp. 277–312.

Harley, J.B. (1989) Historical geography and the cartographic illusion. *Journal of Historical Geography*, 15 (1), 80–91.

Harris, C. (2004) How did colonialism dispossess? Comments from an edge of empire. *Annals of the Association of American Geographers*, 94 (1), 165–182.

Harvey, D. (2003) *The New Imperialism*. Oxford: Oxford University Press.

Heffernan, M. (2003) Histories of geography. In *Key Concepts in Geography*, ed. S.L. Holloway, S.P. Price, and G. Valentine. London: Sage, pp. 3–22.

Hobson, J.A. (1938/1902) *Imperialism: A Study*, 3rd edition. London: George Allen and Unwin.

Hyndman, J. (2007) Feminist geopolitics revisited: Body counts in Iraq. *Professional Geographer*, 59 (1), 35–46.

Jhaveri, N. (2004) Petroimperialism: US oil interests and the Iraq War. *Antipode*, 36 (1), 2–11.

Kaplan, R. (2009) The revenge of geography. *Foreign Policy*, 172, 96–105.

Kearns, G. (2008) The geography of terror. *Political Geography*, 27 (3), 360–364.

Kearns, G. (2009) *Geopolitics and Empire: The Legacy of Halford Mackinder*. Oxford: Oxford University Press.

Klein, B.S. (1994) *Strategic Studies and World Order: The Global Politics of Deterrence*. Cambridge: Cambridge University Press.

Legg, S. (2007) *Spaces of Colonialism: Delhi's Urban Governmentalities*. Oxford: Blackwell.

Lester, A. (2000) Historical geographies of imperialism. In *Modern Historical Geographies*, ed. B. Graham and C. Nash. London: Prentice Hall, pp. 100–120.

Lester, A. (2001) *Imperial Networks: Creating Identities in Nineteenth Century South Africa and Britain*. London: Routledge.

Loomba, A. (1998) *Colonialism/Postcolonialism*. London: Routledge.

Mitchell, T. (1991) *Colonizing Egypt*. Berkeley: University of California Press.

Morrissey, J. (2003) *Negotiating Colonialism*. London: HGRG, Royal Geographical Society.

Morrissey, J. (2005) Cultural geographies of the contact zone: Gaels, Galls and overlapping territories in late medieval Ireland. *Social and Cultural Geography*, 6 (4), 551–566.

Morrissey, J. (2011) Closing the neoliberal gap: Risk and regulation in the long war of securitization. *Antipode*, 43 (3), 874–900.

Morrissey, J. (2013) Imperialism and empire. In *Key Concepts in Historical Geography*, ed. J. Morrissey, D. Nally, U. Strohmayer, and Y. Whelan. London: Sage.

Nally, D. (2008) "That coming storm": The Irish Poor Law, colonial biopolitics and the Great Irish Famine. *Annals of the Association of American Geographers*, 98 (3), 714–741.

Nally, D. (2009) Ethnicity and resistance, historical geographies of. In *International Encyclopedia of Human Geography*, vol. 3, ed. R. Kitchin and N. Thrift. Oxford: Elsevier, pp. 620–625.

Nally, D. (2011) The biopolitics of food provisioning. *Transactions of the Institute of British Geographers* NS, 36 (1), 37–53.

Nash, C. and Graham, B. (2000) The making of modern historical geographies. In *Modern Historical Geographies*, ed. B. Graham and C. Nash. London: Prentice Hall, pp. 1–9.

Ogborn, M. (2003) Finding historical data. In *Key Methods in Geography*, ed. N.J. Clifford and G. Valentine. London: Sage, pp. 101–115.

Ó Tuathail, G. (2003) "Just out looking for a fight": American affect and the invasion of Iraq. *Antipode*, 35 (5), 856–870.

Pickles, J. (ed.) (1995) *Ground Truth: The Social Implications of Geographic Information Systems*. New York: Guilford Press.

Pile, S. and Keith, M. (eds.) (1997) *Geographies of Resistance*. London: Routledge.

Ploszajska, T. (2000) Historiographies of geography and empire. In *Modern Historical Geographies*, ed. B. Graham and C. Nash. London: Prentice Hall, pp. 121–145.

Pogge, T. (2008) *World Poverty and Human Rights*, 2nd edition. Cambridge: Polity.

Pratt, M.L. (1994) Transculturation and autoethnography: Peru, 1615–1980. In *Colonial Discourse/ Postcolonial Theory*, ed. F. Barker, P. Hulme, and M. Iversen. Manchester: Manchester University Press, pp. 24–46.

Raju, S., Kumar, M.S., and Corbridge, S. (eds.) (2006) *Colonial and Post-Colonial Geographies of India*. New Delhi: Sage.

Routledge, P. (1997) A spatiality of resistances: Theory and practice in Nepal's revolution of 1990. In *Geographies of Resistance*, ed. S. Pile and M. Keith. London: Routledge, pp. 68–86.

Said, E. (1978) *Orientalism: Western Conceptions of the Orient*. New York: Pantheon.

Said, E. (1993) *Culture and Imperialism*. New York: Knopf.

Said, E. (2003) *Orientalism*. London: Penguin.

Smith, N. (2003) *American Empire: Roosevelt's Geographer and the Prelude to Globalization*. Berkeley: University of California Press.

Smith, N. (2005) *The Endgame of Globalization*. New York: Routledge.

Spivak, G.C. (1987) *In Other Worlds: Essays in Cultural Politics*. London: Methuen.

Spivak, G.C. (1988) Can the subaltern speak? In *Marxism and the Interpretation of Culture*, ed. C. Nelson and L. Grossberg. Urbana: University of Illinois Press, pp. 271–313.

Stanley, A. (2008) Citizenship and the production of landscape and knowledge in contemporary Canadian nuclear fuel waste management. *Canadian Geographer*, 52 (1), 65–83.

Sullivan, S. (2006) The elephant in the room? Problematizing "new" (neoliberal) biodiversity conservation. *Forum for Development Studies*, 33 (1), 105–135.

Thomas, N. (1994) *Colonialism's Culture: Anthropology, Travel and Government*. Cambridge: Polity.

Watts, M. (2009) Neo-colonialism and developmentalism. In *International Encyclopedia of Human Geography*, vol. 3, ed. R. Kitchin and N. Thrift. Oxford: Elsevier, pp. 123–130.

Wishart, D. (1997) The selectivity of historical representation. *Journal of Historical Geography*, 23 (2), 111–118.

Withers, C.W.J. (2002) Constructing "the geographical archive." *Area*, 34 (3), 303–311.

Wood, D. (1993) *The Power of Maps*. London: Routledge.

Young, R.J.C. (2001) *Postcolonialism: An Historical Introduction*. Oxford: Blackwell.

Chapter 41

# Postcolonialism

*Declan Cullen, James Ryan, and Jamie Winders*

## Introduction

. . . He sees that more children have raised their hands to ask questions.

"Yes, Joseph."

"You have told us about black history. You have been telling us about our heroes and our glorious victories. But most seem to end in defeat. Now I want to ask my question . . . If what you say is true, why then was it possible for a handful of Europeans to conquer a continent and to lord it over us for four hundred years? How was it possible, unless it is because they have bigger brains, and that we are the children of Ham, as they say in the Christian Bible?"

He suddenly starts fuming with anger. He knows that a teacher should not erupt into anger but he feels his defeat in that question. Maybe the journey has been long and they have wandered over too many continents and over too large a canvas of time.

"Look, Joseph. You have been reading eeh, American children's encyclopedia and the Bible. They used the Bible to steal the souls and minds of ever-grinning Africans, caps folded at the back, saying prayers of gratitude for small crumbs labelled aid, loans, famine relief while big companies are busy collecting gold and silver and diamonds, and while we fight among ourselves saying I am a Kuke, I am a Luo, I am a Luhyia, I am a Somali . . . and . . . and . . . There are times, Joseph, when victory is defeat and defeat is victory."

Thiong'o (1977: 238)

This passage is taken from Ngugi wa Thiong'o's 1977 novel, *Petals of Blood*. The story is set in Ilmorog, a new town on the edge of the Trans-Africa Highway in Kenya. In this scene, Mr. Karega, a teacher and trade unionist, dreams about an incident in his classroom. Mr. Karega is one of four town inhabitants who become prime suspects following the murder of the local directors of the foreign-owned Theng'eta Brewery. The novel tells the story of these four characters, setting their uneasy relationships and personal histories against the backdrop

*The Wiley Blackwell Companion to Cultural Geography*, First Edition.
Edited by Nuala C. Johnson, Richard H. Schein, and Jamie Winders.
© 2013 John Wiley & Sons, Ltd. Published 2016 by John Wiley & Sons, Ltd.

of post-independence Kenya. In this postcolonial territory, as in the classroom scene dreamt by Karega, Kenya's history of colonial domination has evolved into new post-independence struggles against the combined forces of foreign capitalism and the interests of a new, propertied African elite. In *Petals of Blood*, as in many of his other novels, Thiong'o paints a vivid sense of Kenya's social and political landscape following independence from British rule in 1963 and the persistence of material and ideological colonial processes in a postcolonial era. His novels offer powerful critiques of both British colonial mentalities and the ways in which colonial attitudes linger in the economic, cultural, and social processes of postcolonial nationhood. Thiong'o's fifth novel, *Devil on the Cross* (1982), written while he was detained without trial by Kenyan authorities, was dedicated "To all Kenyans struggling against the neo-colonial stage of imperialism." The combination of literary imagination and resolutely anti-colonial struggle that Thiong'o's work displays has ensured his reputation well beyond Kenya. His work is widely read in the West, where it is often categorized under the headings of "commonwealth" or "postcolonial" literature.

We refer to Thiong'o here since he is one of a number of writers whose work deals with the territory of postcolonialism not as an abstract theoretical concept but as the very landscape upon which the lives of individuals and societies are shaped. His work, thus, provides a useful starting point for an engagement with the theme of "postcolonial geographies," since it prompts the question: what does it mean to describe something as "postcolonial?" Does postcolonial refer to a time period, a place, a condition, a theoretical stance, or a political practice? Is such an all-encompassing descriptive term as the postcolonial even useful? Before we address these questions, it is worth noting that the relationship between postcolonialism and cultural geography is a highly significant one. This point may seem obvious in a chapter included in a companion to cultural geography. Nonetheless, interest in postcolonialism marks one of the more striking ways in which cultural geographers (and indeed, human geographers more generally) have responded to major intellectual and theoretical currents within the social sciences and humanities in the last two or three decades. Cultural geographies and postcolonialism share a concern with understanding the complex circuits, networks, and flows through which geographies of identity, difference, and inequality are produced in and through landscapes (e.g., Braun 2002; Nash 1999; Sarmento 2009; Sioh 2010; Kipfer 2007; Nagar 1997; Goonewardena and Kipfer 2006). More broadly, a parallel exists between cultural geography and postcolonialism in the nature of criticisms leveled at both for promoting studies of the immaterial, textual, and symbolic at the expense of the substantive, material processes of history and geography (Nash 2002). Notwithstanding such charges, the terms postcolonial and postcolonialism, as well as related concepts like hybridity, remain central elements of human geography.

Cultural geographers in particular have taken a profound interest in postcolonialism as both a substantive research agenda focused on particular processes and geographical sites and a set of theoretical approaches grounded in specific ways of engaging global and local processes (e.g., Shurmer-Smith 2002; Anderson and Domosh *et al.* 2002; Blunt and McEwan 2002). In cultural geography, postcolonialism has prompted a variety of work, from explorations of different imaginative geographies to accounts of the cultural dimensions of European colonialism, from the spatial strategies of colonial rule to the cultural spaces of anti-colonial and postcolonial resistance, past and present (e.g., Blunt and Wills 2000; Sidaway 2000; Yeoh 2001; Noxolo 2006). The proliferation of a *postcolonial* cultural geography, however, has not always led to clarification over the term postcolonialism itself. Indeed, the vast array of "postcolonialisms" deployed in geographical texts often results in little overall sense of what

postcolonial geographies might actually be. It is high time to reassess the kinds of contributions that cultural geographers can make to postcolonialism as a field.

What, however, are postcolonial geographies? Attempts to answer this question immediately face a range of complex questions concerning the scope and definition of the term
postcolonial. Google "postcolonial" or "postcolonialism" and you will find a bewildering
amount of material from literature, anthropology, history, international relations, cultural
studies, and geography, as well as pieces from artists, writers, and filmmakers. Given this
range of users, it is unsurprising that what is meant by postcolonialism has been the subject
of intense debate for at least three decades. Is postcolonialism a movement, era, or condition?
Should there be a hyphen between "post" and "colonialism?" Is the term too frequently, and
too vaguely, used to hold effective meaning (Ashcroft et al. 1995; see also Rattansi 1997)?
Robert Young (2001), for example, favors the term "tricontinentalism" as a more precise
geographical and cultural encapsulation that developed after the first conference of the
Organization of Solidarity of the Peoples of Africa, Asia, and Latin America at Havana in
1966. Walter Mignolo, by contrast, argues for attention to the *damnés*, a term he draws from
Frantz Fanon's writings to describe "all those whose dignity has been and continues to be
stripped away by the logic of coloniality" (Mignolo 2005: 388–389). Thinking through the
lens of the *damnés*, Mignolo argues, creates an opportunity for de-coloniality, for both
"moving toward a world in which many worlds could coexist" (2005: 392) *and* decentering
the production of knowledge itself by beginning from the margins.

Along similar lines, many commentators have warned against the use of postcolonial to
describe a single or universal condition (McClintock 1995; Loomba 2005), a warning that
also applies to the related terms colonialism and imperialism. While colonialism refers generally to the establishment and formal colonization of territory by an alien occupying force,
imperialism describes the broader exercise of political, economic, military, and/or cultural
domination that can occur without direct settlement. For both terms, however, the forms
that domination took were geographically and temporally specific. Argentina in the nineteenth century, for example, was clearly a recipient of British economic and cultural
imperialism but not British colonialism, since it was never formally colonized. For these
reasons, it is necessary to distinguish among the different kinds of colonialism, depending
upon the type and degree of settlement in the colonial territory, and, thus, the kinds of postcolonialisms emerging from different colonial practices (see Mishra and Hodge 1994).
Postcolonial geographies are as varied as the forms of colonialism and imperialism that
produced them, and any discussion must start from this framing of postcolonialism as geographically contingent.

Charting a course through these debates about what the postcolonial entails and how
it should be approached is not always easy. At this juncture it is, thus, helpful to identify
two main applications of the term postcolonialism, both of which circulate around the
meanings of the prefix "post." In the first, and earlier, application, postcolonialism describes
the historical condition of people, states, and societies *after* colonialism. In this context,
postcolonial is applied to states that experienced European decolonization, particularly in
Africa and Asia, in the second half of the twentieth century. A second way of thinking about
postcolonialism is as a movement or set of theories, ideas, and practices committed to anti-
colonial struggle, to moving *beyond* colonialism not so much in a temporal sense but in a
political sense. From this second definition, postcolonialism becomes a form of political
practice that offers new perspectives on relations and inequalities across scales and seeks
to recast colonial relationships and their legacies. The foundations for this second

understanding can be found in the writings of novelists and critics engaged in anti-colonial struggles, a group including Frantz Fanon, Aimé Cesaire, Albert Memmi, and Ngugi Wa Thiong'o, as well as the varied articulations of tricontinentalism described above (Young 2001). The currency of this second notion of postcolonialism was firmly established through the development of postcolonial criticism and theory. The foundational work of Edward Said (1978, 1993), Homi Bhabha (1990, 1994), and Gayatri Spivak (1987, 1988), the holy trinity of postcolonial theory, helped produce a body of knowledge that takes as its object the language and practice of colonialism and the formation of colonial subjectivities. It is not our intention to review this literature here, since there are several guides to postcolonial studies that accomplish this task (e.g., Williams and Chrisman 1993; Ashcroft *et al.* 1995; Pieterse and Parekh 1995; Young 2001; Goldberg and Quayson 2002). We merely note that this second sense of postcolonialism is most widely recognized within contemporary Anglo-American geography and forms the theoretical basis of the scholarship discussed in the remainder of this chapter.

## Postcolonialism in Geography

Vis-à-vis geography's engagement with postcolonialism, Derek Gregory argues that a post-colonial approach includes the following elements:

1 a "close and critical reading of colonial discourse";
2 an understanding of "the complicated and fractured histories through which colonialism passes from the past into the present";
3 a mapping of "the ways in which metropolitan and colonial societies are drawn together in webs of affinity, influence and dependence";
4 a sensitivity to the "political implications" of the way history is constructed. (Gregory 2009: 561)

Such a notion of postcolonialism, common in contemporary cultural geography, does not assume that colonialism has ended but, instead, frames postcolonialism as an attitude of critical contestation of colonialism and its discursive and material legacies. In doing so, it positions postcolonialism not only as a lens for understanding postcolonial places and land-scapes but also as a political and theoretical approach to relations and dynamics in a world overdetermined by colonial practices themselves (see also Blunt and Wills 2000; Robinson 2003). As Gregory's definition suggests, a solely temporal definition of postcolonialism is insufficient, since forms of neocolonial or neo-imperial domination persist long after the flags of Western colonial powers were lowered in their colonial territories. Indeed, the world today arguably consists of *multiple* colonialisms: quasi-colonialism, internal colonialism, and neo-colonialism, as well as new ideologies of imperialism (Furedi 1994, cited in Sidaway 2000: 603). Within geography, Gregory has examined this new imperialism of the United States and Britain in the Middle East and the roles played by imaginative and material colonial geographies in shaping "the colonial present" (Gregory 2004; Kearns 2006). Given the current geopolitical situation, one might ask if an end of colonialism and imperialism is even possible in a world where economic, political, and cultural ties grounded in a colonial past continue to sustain and structure global inequalities in a colonial present. For this reason, it is essential that we constantly reassess and maintain a critical perspective on the political meanings of postcolonialism as it applies to the condition of different political entities

(Sidaway 2000; Lionnet 2000), *even as* we remain focused on the imperial realities in the world around us.

At their most basic, then, postcolonial geographies encompass studies that draw on post-colonial perspectives to understand various forms of and resistances to colonial and imperial domination in the past and present and across a diverse set of spatial locations. Postcolonial geographies also take seriously the spatial practices and individual and collective subjectivities that are bound up with these pairings of colonial domination and resistance. As a distinct dimension of contemporary human geography, postcolonial geographies have been credited with an ambitious range of aims (Blunt and Wills 2000; Crush 1994), from revealing geo-graphical complicity in colonial practices to problematizing the sites from which geographic knowledge is produced, from recovering the perspectives of subaltern voices to interrogating how erasures were produced through landscapes and spatial arrangements across scales.

Building on and consolidating these aims, we identify here three broad themes within postcolonial geographies that coalesce around the dynamics between power and difference at the heart of postcolonialism. First, the study of postcolonial geographies helps us under-stand the different ways in which geographical knowledge has shaped, and been shaped by, colonial power relations in different locations and the ways that geographic practices them-selves can be "postcolonialized." Second, examining postcolonial geographies sheds light on the complex spatialities, effects, and expressions of colonial power and identities, both past and present, particularly vis-à-vis the interplay between colonial metropole and periphery. Third, careful consideration of postcolonial geographies demonstrates the ways that colonial practices have been encountered and resisted by colonized peoples within their everyday worlds and the forms of subjectivity produced through and productive of these encounters. The remainder of this chapter looks at each of these themes in turn to show the diverse contributions cultural geographers can make to the field of postcolonialism.

## Colonialism, Geographic Knowledge, and Postcolonial Practices

A major strand of postcolonial work in geography has focused on the relationship between geographic knowledge and colonial power (Driver 1992). In the 1990s, work on geographic knowledge's link to colonialism was strongly influenced by critical explorations of colonial discourse that threw into sharp relief the ways that knowledge and power were implicated in the operation of colonialism *and* in the production of geographic knowledge (Driver 1992; Blaut 1993). Edward Said's 1978 book *Orientalism* marked a major initiative in this direction through its analysis of how the "Orient" was constructed in the Western imagination as the other of the West. Said's work and the debates around it have had a lasting impact within cultural geography (e.g., Jansson 2003; Gregory 1994; Winders 2005). Many geographers, for example, were taken with his concept of imaginative geography and his argument that categories such as "the East" and "the West," supposedly fixed blocks of geographical reality, were constructed through language and cultural imagery in travel writing and other texts, yet also shaped by wider grids of power (Gregory 1995; Driver 1992).

Such insights from postcolonial work on the relationship between forms of knowledge and the operations of colonial power fostered scholarship that exposed the ways in which the discipline of geography developed hand in hand in the nineteenth and twentieth centuries with Western colonialism and imperialism (Bell *et al.* 1995; Driver 1992, 2001; Godlewska and Smith 1994; Livingstone 1992), with the fashioning of imperial space (Edney 1997; Clayton 2000), and with the promotion of imperial citizenship (Ploszajska 2000; Maddrell

1996). Works in this vein also considered the relationship between empire and geographical knowledge more broadly, through cultural representations from travel writing to photography (Blunt 1994; Gregory 1995; Duncan and Gregory 1999; Godlewska 2000; Ryan 1997). Of course, the boundaries between the academic discipline of geography and wider geographical discourses are neither fixed nor impermeable; and a great deal of work has examined the construction and movements of different kinds of knowledge across this divide in the context of colonial power. In particular, geographers have analyzed how specific spaces and sites from the intimate and spectacular colonial encounters on the margins of empire to the arenas of knowledge production in metropolitan centers of colonial calculation themselves enabled, and sometimes undermined, colonial authority (e.g., Miller and Reill 1996; Lambert and Lester 2006).

These questions of knowledge and power, however, are not exclusively historical issues. Indeed, they are an essential part of the project of decolonizing the discipline of geography itself, a project that became prominent in the 2000s (Shaw *et al.* 2006; Radcliffe 2005; Johnson *et al.* 2007). Such a task is not simply the writing of critical histories of the discipline that expose its relationship to empire, although such works help form the basis of subsequent efforts to postcolonialize geography. Instead, this newer body of work also involves rethinking the epistemological and institutional boundaries of the discipline itself. Work in this vein includes efforts to rethink the discipline's institutional structures and practices, from teaching (Ashutosh and Winders, 2009) to hiring decisions (Morin and Rothenberg 2011) to research (Dikec 2010). This writing also pays close attention to institutional hierarchies of place that determine excellence and stature in scholarship and publishing (Robinson 2003; Berg 2004) and that frame *where* geographic knowledge comes from and how it acquires authority (Gilmartin and Berg 2007; Jazeel 2007). Thus, a central aspect of postcolonial geography has become the task of decentering the usual starting points and norms in both the production of geographic knowledge *and* the practice of geographic scholarship (Jazeel and McFarlane 2010). Indeed, postcolonial perspectives in geography increasingly challenge us not only to look beyond the West in our research and teaching but also to consider the ways in which geographical categories such the West are themselves formulated and constructed as invisible standards, models, and categories in the production of geographic knowledge (Sidaway 2000; Robinson 2003, 2005).

Those engaged with postcolonial geographies, then, must be sensitive to these critiques of the Eurocentric and totalizing tendencies of Western knowledge, especially as they apply to cultural geography. As Sidaway (2000) puts it, "at their best and most radical, postcolonial geographies will not only be alert to the continued fact of imperialism, but also thoroughly uncontainable in terms of disturbing established assumptions, frames and methods" (606–7). While much work has shown the fallacy of believing that it is possible to step outside inherited categories of knowledge and language, an important task for those engaged in postcolonial geographies is to question taken-for-granted narratives and frameworks of geographical knowledge and to envision and enact postcolonial geographic practice.

## Charting (Post)colonial Spaces and Identities

A second major theme of postcolonial geographies, one that is closely allied to explorations of the relationship between geographical knowledge and colonial power described above, is a concern with both the spatial operations of colonial power and the expression of colonial and postcolonial identities in different kinds of sites. Research in this vein began with careful considerations of landscapes of colonialism and imperialism, especially from historical geographers, who were some of the first to take up postcolonial studies in their work in geography (Harris 1996; Nash 1994; Sluyter 2002). Through the study of practices of urban planning, architecture, and related cultural forms, cultural geographers soon joined this work, examining the expressions of colonial and postcolonial identities in various kinds of landscapes (Anderson and Jacobs 1997; Duncan 2002; McGuinness 2004).

In the last two decades, such research has focused on the varied geographic effects of multiple colonialisms and imperialisms. A number of scholars, for example, have considered how racial discourses and discrimination were central to colonialism itself and had distinctive spatial dimensions and effects across colonial contexts from colonial Swaziland and the Eastern Cape Colony (Crush 1996; Lester 2000) to eighteenth- and nineteenth-century Ireland (Gibbons 2000). Racial discourses associated with colonialism, these works have shown, were produced through a range of practices and texts, including those of medicine, science, and acclimatization (Livingstone 1999). In colonial Sierra Leone, for example, contemporary theories of race and tropical disease were used to legitimate evolving policies of racial segregation (Frenkel and Western 1988). Along similar lines, nineteenth-century colonial practices in the tropics were filtered through a range of discourses, including those of geography, medicine, and race (Duncan 2000; Arnold 2000; Howell 2000). Colonial knowledge and practices also established a pseudo-scientific relationship between race, nature, and landscape to rationalize and reinforce colonial authority, domination, and spatial hierarchies.

Many studies of postcolonial geographies have also emphasized the complex ways in which categories of race, gender, sexuality, and class were interwoven and forged across colonial spaces not only to bolster colonial power but also to create spaces for its destabilization (Blunt and Rose 1994; McClintock 1995; McClintock et al. 1997). Ideas of domesticity in British India in the late-nineteenth and early-twentieth centuries, for example, were shaped by gendered and spatially articulated meanings of "home" produced in both India and England that brought the metropole and the colony together in the intimate space of the domestic (Blunt 2005; Thomas 2007). Critical analyses of travel writing have been another avenue for exploring the flows of colonial power and influence and the complicated networks linking the imperial metropolis and colonies (Pratt 1992; Blunt and Rose 1994; McEwan 1996). More recently, cultural geographers have begun to explore postcolonial geographies in places not normally considered part of colonialism's spatial reach. Through work on postcolonial spaces and practices in Canada, the American South, and elsewhere (Braun 2002; Winders 2005; Butz 2011; Kincaid 2006; Morin 2002; Harris 2004), such scholarship brings postcolonial studies to new places and, in the process, pushes the geographic and theoretical limits of its scope.

Interest in the spatial networks of colonial power is also evident in the rich body of geographic work on imperial and postcolonial cities (Driver and Gilbert 1999; Jacobs 1996; Legg 2007; Yeoh 2001) and, more recently, on what Goonewardena and Kipfer (2006) call "postcolonial urbicide" and the new forms of imperialism worked on postcolonial subjects around the world. Urban and imperial historians have long been interested in the ways colonial cities were shaped by forces of European colonialism (King 1990). Building on this work, a range of cultural geographers have examined how the form, representation, and use of European cities, notably capital cities such as London and Paris, have also been shaped by (post)colonial practices, politics, and performance. In doing so, cultural geographers have brought questions of colonialism's reach back to the metropoles, highlighting the (post)colonial networks that made cities in the colonies, Europe, and the United States equally, if differently, imperial (Domosh 2004). Just as we must understand the cultural geography of a city like Cairo by reference to the imperial networks that linked it to London and Paris, these works show that we must understand the changing geography of cities like London with reference to their position within the wider British Empire (Driver and Gilbert 1999).

Recent accounts of the formation of imperial cities have also examined their heterogeneity and possibilities for alternative articulations of empire. Jonathan Schneer (1999), for example, has shown how London provided the setting for the evolution of *anti*-imperial politics, particularly through the 1900 Pan-African conference and the Indian and Irish nationalist movements. Moreover, in London, urban spaces such as Trafalgar Square, constructed to symbolize imperial power, were subsequently appropriated as sites of protest and resistance to imperialism (Mace 1976). These works clearly demonstrate the need to consider not only manifestations of colonial and imperial power in urban landscapes but also resistances to and redefinitions of such displays of power.

One significant model for such an approach is Brenda Yeoh's work on the colonial city of Singapore. Yeoh (1996) explores the overlapping domains of the colonial project and the colonized world, within the physical setting of Singapore. To do so, she draws upon a range of historical sources to trace various kinds of resistance to colonial authority in late-nineteenth and early-twentieth-century Singapore, from attempts by indigenous people to evade official strategies of disease control to the 1888 Verandah Riots by Chinese residents reacting to restrictions on their use of urban space. Yeoh, thus, envisions the colonial city as a space of multiple conflicts and negotiations in which practices of resistance are entangled in complex patterns with discourses and practices of colonial domination.

Collectively, these works on colonial cities pay close attention to the ways identities are imagined and performed in (post)colonial urban contexts (Nagar 1997). As Jacobs observed,

> In contemporary [postcolonial] cities people connected by imperial histories are thrust together in assemblages barely predicted, and often guarded against, during the inaugural phases of colonialism. Often enough this is a meeting not simply augmented by imperialism but still regulated by its constructs of difference and privilege. (Jacobs 1996: 4)

Jacobs' accounts of postcolonial cultural geographies in Britain and Australia show that postcolonial perspectives are essential in understanding both the intertwined geographies of center and periphery apparent in (post)colonial cities and the complex interactions between power, difference, and resistance wrapped up in such encounters. Robinson (2005) has pushed this perspective even further, asking what it means to rethink the urban itself from a postcolonial perspective and to make spaces beyond Europe and North America the starting point of theorizing and understanding urban geographies. As she argues, in urban studies, modernity has been considered the preserve of only a few privileged world cities while poorer, marginal cities have been "profoundly excluded from the theoretical imaginary of urban modernity" (Robinson 2006, x; see also Ragharum and Madge 2006). In response, she suggests, we should theorize the urban from the margins, so to speak, to emphasize diversity and cosmopolitanism rather than reinforce a hierarchical ranking of cities and urban spaces in the production of geographic knowledge.

## Postcolonial Geographies of Encounters and Resistance

A third, if less developed, strand of work within postcolonial geographies takes the spaces of colonial encounter and resistance, mentioned in the last section, as its starting point. As a movement, postcolonialism has long been concerned with the struggles of ordinary people against forces of imperial and colonial power. Indeed, postcolonial theory itself emerged from various anti-colonial movements that mobilized political practice and radical ideas against colonial domination (Young 2001). Despite postcolonial theory's roots in such political struggles, those most exploited in society – invariably, the poor, women, and children – have often been left out of studies of colonial history, anti-colonial struggles, or political independence, which focus instead on elite postcolonial actors and large-scale struggles. One group of scholars, the Subaltern Studies collective, has pioneered work designed to address this oversight and to recover the hidden voices and actions of subaltern groups through alternative readings of official or elite records and the use of alternative historical sources such as oral history and songs (e.g., Guha and Spivak 1988). Such work rejects the elitist models of both imperial and nationalist history, focusing instead upon the experiences of people whose lives and agency have, to date, been ignored. Some commentators – most famously, Gayatri Spivak – have questioned attempts to represent the lives of the marginalized, arguing that it is not possible to recover fully the silenced subaltern voices because any act of dissent is always already entangled within dominant discourses it might be resisting. Instead, Spivak points to the necessity of decolonizing dominant discourses themselves, notably of gender (Spivak 1987, 1988), and of identifying the mechanisms that created subaltern silences, rather than "recovering" silenced voices.

It has long been recognized in geography and beyond that colonialism involves contact, conflict, and compromise between different groups within what Mary Louise Pratt calls the "contact zone," that space where "disparate cultures meet, clash, and grapple with each other, often in highly asymmetrical relations of domination and subordination" (1992: 4). Many geographic accounts of colonialism and imperialism, however, in concentrating on the processes and practices of domination, have paid less attention to perspectives of the colonized and their processes of negotiation and resistance. In response, Yeoh argues for "geographical accounts of the colonized world which move away from depicting it as a passive, flattened out world, stamped upon by more powerful others and fashioned solely in the image of colonialism" (2000: 162). Instead, she urges, geographers must pay close attention to the everyday worlds of colonized people, to "re-filter colonial discourse through 'other' lenses" and to "reconceptualize the 'contact zone' in terms of contest and complicity, conflict and collusion, and to tackle the unwritten history of resistance" (2000: 149).

In this way, the notion of contact zones offers new ways of thinking about and approaching colonial encounters and the negotiation of colonial authority. Within cultural geography, however, postcolonial theory is also gradually shaping research methods themselves. Spivak's (1988) much-cited aphorism, "the subaltern cannot speak," has been especially influential, forcing scholars to think critically about what they actually do when they read archives against the grain and "give voice" to research participants. In similar fashion, Chakrabarty's (2000) call to "provincialize" European intellectual hegemony has forced geographers to think about where they start, literally and figuratively, in their efforts to understand the world around them. In all these ways, postcolonial theory is changing how cultural geography is conducted. Raghuram and Madge (2006), for example, argue that operationalizing a postcolonial method, particularly a commitment to emancipatory politics, helps us move beyond Eurocentric "world picturing." To do so, they suggest, we first must think about the politics behind our research questions and "how these might ideally arise out of dialogue with the research subjects" (2006: 271). Equally important, Raghuram and Madge (2006) address academic positionality, arguing that we must acknowledge the identities we bring to the field and their connections to our investments in the broader geopolitical context of the academy. This postcolonial focus on why we do research, how we theorize it, and what effects our locations have on the knowledge we produce has been taken up most directly outside cultural geography in development geographies (Noxolo 2006; Raghuram and Madge 2006), feminist geography (e.g., Nagar 2002), and, to a lesser extent, economic geography (Pollard and Samers 2007; Pollard et al. 2009). Cultural geographers, however, can learn much from these works *and* contribute to them, as some already are (e.g., Anderson and Domosh 2002; Blunt and McEwan 2002).

Another potentially fruitful avenue for cultural geographers is engagement with postcolonial countercultural praxis, notably in the work of community programs, artists, and filmmakers (McCarthy and Dimitriadis 2000). Catherine Nash (1994), for example, explored the emergence of new cartographies of postcolonial and gender identities in the landscape art of contemporary Irish women artists. Along similar lines, Jane Jacobs has explored alternative postcolonial maps in her account of an Aboriginal art trail near Brisbane, Australia. Together, these studies show how specific projects of individual or community art can promote new renditions of space that creatively reappropriate colonial maps and subvert their conventional contours of power.

To date, this innovative work of artists and filmmakers on postcolonial geographies has been under-appreciated by cultural geographers but offers much potential. Anthropologist Paul Stoller (1994), for example, has studied films made by the ethnographic filmmaker Jean Rouch from the 1940s to the 1960s, showing how Rouch's work offered an incisive, sophisticated critique of the ethnographic encounter and French colonialism in Africa. One of Rouch's late films, *Petit à Petit* (1969), portrays the experience of two West African entrepreneurs, Damoré and Lam, visiting Paris to observe the habits of the French "tribe," with a view to opening a luxury hotel in Niamey, Niger. With humor and dexterity, the characters turn the tables on Europeans. Here, Parisians, not Africans, are scrutinized and visualized. In one scene, Damoré poses as a doctoral student and, wielding anthropometric calipers, sets about making bodily measurements of willing Parisians in the Place Trocadero. In this and other work, Rouch skillfully transforms the observer into the observed and exposes academic complicity with colonial power and racism. By exploring such countercultural productions, cultural geographers can further their critique of colonial knowledge and amplify the contested nature of colonial and postcolonial culture.

## Conclusion: Locating Postcolonial Geographies

As we noted at the start of this chapter, some commentators on postcolonialism have been concerned that the term has been used so frequently, and with so little focus, that it might have lost any effective meaning (Ashcroft et al. 1995). Might postcolonial geographies be simply another variant on an already over-extended theme, something destined to produce more heat than light? Could postcolonial geographies be just an attempt by geographers to colonize academic territories of postcolonial studies and theory (Barnett 1997)? These scenarios might materialize if geographers simply appropriate and rehearse existing or outdated ideas, if we apply postcolonialism in an uncritical way and fail to scrutinize our own procedures and practices in producing knowledge. As this chapter has shown, cultural geographers have a great deal to learn, and unlearn, from postcolonial studies in our efforts to decolonize the geographical imagination and geographic practice itself (Pieterse and Parekh 1995; Thiong'o 1986; Spivak 1988).

As we have also tried to indicate in this chapter, however, cultural geography itself has much to contribute to the study of colonial, imperial, and postcolonial power, practices, and spaces. In particular, studies of the landscapes of postcolonialism involve significant questions of space, place, and territory. As a number of commentators have observed, the work of postcolonial critics, from Said's imaginative geography to Bhabha's third space, is often profoundly geographical in its *theoretical* emphasis (Blunt and Wills 2000). At the same time, many critics point out that such theoretical analyses of colonial discourse have a limited relevance *because* they are over-generalized and decoupled from the "real" geographies of the world around us (e.g., Mitchell 1997). What is needed instead are more studies that take account of the specific geographic and historical conditions and circumstances in which colonial power operated. It is here where cultural geography comes in. If discussions of postcolonialism are not located in time and space, they fail to grasp how colonial power, and struggles against it, worked, and continue to work, through both spectacular and mundane material geographies of daily life. The conventional preoccupations of geographers with space and place position them well to ground often-abstract debates within postcolonial studies and, in so doing, to engage with the material as well as the discursive, the physical as well as the symbolic, dimensions of colonialism and its legacies (Driver 1992; Barnett 1997; Yeoh 2001).

We began this chapter by discussing how varied notions of postcolonialism have found an increasingly influential place within cultural geography. It is now clear that this flow of ideas goes in both directions and that cultural geographers have distinct contributions to make to the field of postcolonial studies. As Shurmer-Smith argues, cultural geographers are well placed to employ postcolonial theory in the deconstruction of a range of postcolonial cultural artifacts, including films, novels, poems, music, and theater, to reveal and confront continuing forms of imperial and colonial prejudice and discrimination. As she also notes, however, cultural geographers must think more critically about the process by which cultural products are legitimated through what Mitchell terms "post-imperial criticism" emerging from metropolitan centers of authority (Mitchell 1992, cited in Shurmer-Smith 2002: 76). In this way, cultural geographers must interrogate the processes by which unequal power dynamics between center and periphery are produced and maintained in the academy and beyond vis-à-vis not only cultural artifacts but also broader geopolitical relations in which some groups and places live out the fantasies of a new imperialism and some groups and places live out the realities of a colonial present whose forms of structural, discursive, and very material violences look hauntingly familiar (Gregory 2004). The production, legitimation, and reception of (postcolonial) cultural products, and practices, therefore, are intensely geographical, and intensely political, processes.

The making of postcolonial cultural geographies, then, is not only a matter of deconstructing cultural representations for the marks of imperial and colonial power. It is also, as we have noted, also an exploration of the everyday cultural worlds of colonial and postcolonial subjects and their efforts to reshape the contact zones of colonial encounters and postcolonial landscapes, from London to Lagos. The fact that postcolonial geographies, like postcolonial studies more generally, stem from Western and metropolitan institutions, notably universities, does not prohibit us from developing radical new perspectives or fostering links with worldwide political movements to highlight inequalities and promote social justice (see, for example, Blunt and Wills 2000). To do so, however, cultural geography must not only pay critical attention to postcolonial spaces, practices, and identities but also further the project of postcolonializing geography itself. The fact that some postcolonial critiques have shown how the language and techniques of geography placed it squarely as an imperial science should not stop us from attempting to explore the shape of *post*colonial geographies.

As part of an evolving body of work, postcolonial geographies occupy an increasingly important position within human geography. Across the discipline, postcolonial perspectives continue to challenge geographers to think more deeply about the process of colonialism and their lingering presence. Within cultural geography, thinking more carefully about postcolonial geographies encourages us to employ new understandings of "culture" to better understand the operations of colonial power and challenge Eurocentric knowledges. The culture of colonialism, as this chapter has shown, is not located simply in the world of texts and representations but also in the material and performed realities of the everyday. Nor is culture a separate domain that can be isolated from or explained by colonialism's economic or political dimensions. Instead, cultures of empire must be considered in their full and complex articulations with other forms of colonial rule (Dirks 1992). Finally, postcolonial geographies must be sensitive to the precise cultural and historical differences in the operation of and resistance to forms of colonial power. By undertaking work that locates colonial and postcolonial geographies more precisely in time and space, geographers can continue to shape the development of this field and to probe the lingering effects of colonialism on the cultural landscapes of the present and future.

## References

Anderson, K. and Domosh, M. (2002) North American spaces/postcolonial stories. *Cultural Geographies*, 9, 125–128.

Anderson, K. and Jacobs, J. (1997) From urban Aborigines to aboriginality and the city: One path through the history of Australian cultural geography. *Australian Geographical Studies*, 35, 12–22.

Arnold, D. (2000) "Illusory riches": Representations of the tropical world, 1840–1950. *Singapore Journal of Tropical Geography*, 21, 6–18.

Ashcroft, B., Griffiths, G., and Tiffin, H. (eds.) (1995) *The Post-Colonial Studies Reader*. London: Routledge.

Ashutosh, I. and Winders, J. (2009) Teaching *Orientalism* in introductory human geography. *Professional Geographer*, 61.4, 547–560.

Barnett, C. 1997. "Sing along with the common people": Politics, postcolonialism, and other figures. *Environment and Planning D: Society and Space*, 15.2, 137–154.

Bell, M., Butlin, R., and Heffernan, M. (eds.) (1995) *Geography and Imperialism, 1820–1940*. Manchester: Manchester University Press.

Berg, L. 2004. Scaling knowledge: Towards a *critical geography* of critical geographies. *Geoforum*, 5, 555–558.

Bhabha, H. (1990) *Nation and Narration*. London: Routledge.

Bhabha, H. (1994) *The Location of Culture*. London: Routledge.

Blaut, J. (1993) *The Colonizer's Model of the World: Geographical Diffusionism and Eurocentric History*. New York: Guilford Press.

Blunt, A. (1994) *Travel, Gender, and Imperialism: Mary Kingsley and West Africa*. New York: Guilford Press.

Blunt, A. (2005) *Domicile and Diaspora: Anglo-Indian Women and the Spatial Politics of Home*. Oxford: Blackwell.

Blunt, A. and McEwan, C. (eds.) (2002) *Postcolonial Geographies*. New York: Continuum.

Blunt, A. and Rose, G. (eds.) (1994) *Writing Women and Space: Colonial and Postcolonial Geographies*. New York: Guilford Press.

Blunt, A. and Wills, J. (2000) *Dissident Geographies: An Introduction to Radical Ideas and Practice*. New York: Prentice Hall.

Braun, B. (2002) Colonialism's afterlife: Vision and visuality on the Northwest Coast. *Cultural Geographies*, 9, 202–247.

Butz, D. (2011) Introduction: Places postcolonialism forgot (and how to find them) *ACME*, 10, 42–47.

Chakrabarty, D. (2000) *Provincializing Europe: Postcolonial Thought and Historical Difference*. Princeton: Princeton University Press.

Clayton, D. (2000) *Islands of Truth*. Vancouver: University of British Columbia Press.

Crush, J. (1994) Post-colonialism, de-colonization, and geography. In *Geography and Empire*, ed. N. Smith and A. Godlewska. Oxford: Blackwell, pp. 333–350.

Crush, J. (1996) The culture of failure: Racism, violence and white farming in colonial Swaziland. *Journal of Historical Geography*, 22.2, 177–197.

Dikec, M. (2010) Colonial minds, postcolonial places. *Antipode*, 42.4, 801–805.

Dirks, N. (ed.) (1992) *Colonialism and Culture*. Ann Arbor: University of Michigan Press.

Domosh, M. (2004) Postcolonialism and the American city. *Urban Geography*, 25.8, 742–754.

Driver, F. (1992) Geography's empire: Histories of geographical knowledge. *Environment and Planning D: Society and Space*, 10, 23–40.

Driver, F. (2001) *Geography Militant: Cultures of Exploration and Empire*. Oxford: Blackwell.

Driver, F. and Gilbert, D. (eds.) (1999) *Imperial Cities: Landscape, Display and Identity*. Manchester: Manchester University Press.

Duncan, J. (2000) The struggle to be temperate: Climate and "moral masculinity" in mid-nineteenth century Ceylon. *Singapore Journal of Tropical Geography*, 21, 34–47.

Duncan, J. (2002) Embodying colonialism? Domination and resistance in nineteenth-century Ceylonese coffee plantations. *Journal of Historical Geography*, 28, 317–338.

Duncan, J. and Gregory, D. (eds.) (1999) *Writes of Passage: Reading Travel Writing*. London: Routledge.

Edney, M. (1997) *Mapping an Empire: The Geographical Construction of British India, 1765–1843*. Chicago: University of Chicago Press.

Frenkel, S. and Western, J. (1988) Pretext or prophylaxis? Racial segregation and malarial mosquitoes in a British tropical colony: Sierra Leone. *Annals of the Association of American Geographers*, 78, 211–228.

Gibbons, L. (2000) Race against time: Racial discourse and Irish history. In *Cultures of Empire: A Reader*, ed. C.Hall. Manchester: Manchester University Press, pp. 207–223.

Gilmartin, M. and Berg, L. (2007) Locating postcolonialism. *Area*, 39, 120–124.

Godlewska, A. (2000) *Geography Unbound: French Geographic Science from Cassini to Humboldt*. Chicago: University of Chicago Press.

Godlewska, A. and Smith, N. (eds.) (1994) *Geography and Empire*. Oxford: Blackwell.

Goldberg, D. and Quayson, A. (2002) *Relocating Postcolonialism*. Oxford: Blackwell.

Goonewardena, K. and Kipfer, S. (2006) Postcolonial urbicide: New imperialism, global cities and the damned of the earth. *New Formations*, 7.3, 23–33.

Gregory, D. (1994) *Geographical Imaginations*. Oxford: Blackwell.

Gregory, D. (1995) Between the book and the lamp: Imaginative geographies of Egypt, 1849–1850. *Transactions of the Institute of British Geographers* , NS 20, 29–57.

Gregory, D. (2004) *The Colonial Present*. Oxford: Blackwell.

Gregory, D. (2009) Postcolonialism. In *The Dictionary of Human Geography*, ed. R. Johnston *et al.* Oxford: Blackwell, pp. 561–562.

Guha, R. and Spivak, G. (eds.) (1988) *Selected Subaltern Studies*. Oxford: Oxford University Press.

Harris, C. (1996) *The Resettlement of British Columbia: Essays on Colonialism and Geographical Change*. Vancouver: University of British Columbia Press.

Harris, C. (2004) How did colonialism dispossess? Comments from an edge of empire. *Annals of the Association of American Geographers*, 94.1, 165–182.

Howell, P. (2000) Prostitution and racialized sexuality: The regulation of prostitution in Britain and the British Empire before the Contagious Diseases Acts. *Environment and Planning D: Society and Space*, 18, 321–339.

Jacobs, J. (1996) *Edge of Empire: Postcolonialism and the City*. London: Routledge.

Jansson, D. (2003) Internal Orientalism in America: W.J. Cash's *The Mind of the South* and the spatial construction of American national identity. *Political Geography*, 22, 293–316.

Jazeel, T. (2007) Awkward geographies: Spatializing academic responsibility, encountering Sri Lanka. *Singapore Journal of Tropical Geography*, 28, 287–299.

Jazeel, T. and McFarlane, C. (2010) The limits of responsibility: A postcolonial politics of academic knowledge production. *Transactions of the Institute of British Geographers*, 35, 109–124.

Johnson, J., Cant, G., Howitt, R., and Peters, E. (2007) Creating anti-colonial geographies: Embracing indigenous people's knowledges and rights. *Geographical Research*, 45, 117–120.

Kearns, G. (2006) Naturalizing empire: Echoes of Mackinder for the next American century? *Geopolitics*, 11, 74–98.

King, A. (1990) *Urbanism, Colonialism and the World Economy: Cultural and Spatial Foundations of the World Urban System*. London: Routledge.

Kinkaid, A. (2006) *Postcolonial Dublin: Imperial Legacies and the Built Environment*. Minneapolis: University of Minnesota Press.

Kipfer, S. (2007) Fanon and space: Colonization, urbanization, and liberation from the colonial city to the global city. *Environment and Planning D: Society and Space*, 25, 701–726.

Lambert, A. and Lester, A. (eds.) (2006) *Colonial Lives Across the British Empire*. Cambridge: Cambridge University Press.

Legg, S. (2007) *Spaces of Colonialism: Delhi's Urban Governmentalities*. Oxford: Blackwell.

Lester, A. (2000) Historical geographies of imperialism. In *Modern Historical Geographies*, ed. B. Graham and C. Nash. London: Pearson Education, pp. 100–120.

Lionnet, F. (2000) Transnationalism, postcolonialism or transcolonialism? Reflections on Los Angeles, geography, and the uses of theory. *Emergences: Journal for the Study of Media and Composite Cultures*, 10.1, 25–35.

Livingstone, D. (1992) *The Geographical Tradition*. Oxford: Blackwell.

Livingstone, D. (1999) Tropical climate and moral hygiene: The anatomy of a Victorian debate. *British Journal for the History of Science*, 32, 93–110.

Loomba, A. (2005) *Colonialism/Postcolonialism*, 2nd edition. London: Routledge.

Mace, R. (1976) *Trafalgar Square: Emblem of Empire*. London: Lawrence and Wishart.

Maddrell, A. (1996) Empire, emigration and school geography: Changing discourses of imperial citizenship. *Journal of Historical Geography*, 22, 373–387.

McCarthy, C. and Dimitriadis, G. (2000) Art and the postcolonial imagination: Rethinking the institutionalization of Third World aesthetics and theory. *Ariel*, 31.1/2, 231–254.

McClintock, A. (1995) *Imperial Leather: Race, Gender, and Sexuality in the Colonial Contest*. New York: Routledge.

McClintock, A., Mufti, A., and Shohat, E. (1997) *Dangerous Liaisons: Gender, Nation, and Postcolonial Perspectives*. Minneapolis: University of Minnesota Press.

McEwan, C. (1996) Paradise or pandemonium? West African landscapes in the travel accounts of Victorian women. *Journal of Historical Geography*, 22.1, 68–83.

McGuinness, M. (2002) Geographies with a difference? Citizenship and difference in postcolonial urban spaces. In *Postcolonial Geographies*, ed. A. Blunt and C. McEwan. New York: Continuum, pp. 99–114.

Mignolo, W. (2005) On subalterns and other agencies. *Postcolonial Studies*, 8.4, 381–407.

Miller, D. and Reill, P. (eds.) (1996) *Visions of Empire: Voyages, Botany and Representations of Nature.* Cambridge: Cambridge University Press.

Mishra, V. and Hodge, B. (1994) What is post-colonialism? In *Colonial Discourse and Post-Colonial Theory,* ed. P. Williams and L. Chrisman. New York: Columbia University Press, pp. 285–288.

Mitchell, K. (1997) Different diasporas and the hype of hybridity. *Environment and Planning D: Society and Space,* 15.5, 533–553.

Morin, K. (2002) Postcolonialism and Native American geographies: The letters of Rosalie La Flesche Farley, 1896–1899. *Cultural Geographies,* 9, 150–180.

Morin, K. and Rothenberg, T. (2011) Our theories, our selves: Hierarchies of place and status in the US academy. *ACME,* 10, 158–168.

Nagar, R. (1997) The making of Hindu communal organizations, places, and identities in postcolonial Dar es Salaam. *Environment and Planning D: Society and Space,* 15, 707–730.

Nagar, R. (2002) Footloose researchers, "traveling" theories, and the politics of transnational feminist praxis. *Gender, Place and Culture,* 9 (2), 179–186.

Nash, C. (1994) Remapping the body/land: New cartographies of identity, gender and landscape in Ireland. In *Writing Women and Space: Colonial and Postcolonial Geographies,* ed. A. Blunt and G. Rose. New York: Guilford Press, pp. 227–250.

Nash, C. (1999) Irish placenames: Post-colonial locations. *Transactions of the Institute of British Geographers,* ns 24, 457–480.

Nash, C. (2002) Cultural geography: Postcolonial cultural geographies. *Progress in Human Geography,* 26.2, 219–230.

Noxolo, P. (2006) A postcolonial critique of "partnership" in Britain's development discourse. *Singapore Journal of Tropical Geography,* 27, 254–269.

Pieterse, J. and Parekh, B. (eds.) (1995) *The Decolonization of Imagination: Culture, Knowledge and Power.* London: Zed Books.

Ploszajska, T. (2000) Historiographies of geography and empire. In *Modern Historical Geographies,* ed. B. Graham and C. Nash. London: Pearson Education, pp. 121–145.

Pollard, J. and Samers, M. (2007) Islamic banking and finance: Postcolonial political economy and the decentring of economic geography. *Transactions of the Institute of British Geographers,* ns 32, 313–330.

Pollard, J., McEwan, C., Laurie, N. and Stenning, A. (2009) Economic geography under postcolonial scrutiny. *Transactions of the Institute of British Geographers,* 34, 137–142.

Pratt, M. (1992) *Imperial Eyes: Travel Writing and Transculturation.* New York: Routledge.

Radcliffe, S. (2005) Development and geography: Towards a postcolonial development geography. *Progress in Human Geography,* 29, 291–298.

Raghuram, P. and Madge, C. (2006) Towards a method for postcolonial development geography? Possibilities and challenges. *Singapore Journal of Tropical Geography,* 27, 270–288.

Rattansi, A. (1997) Postcolonialism and its discontents. *Economy and Society,* 26, 480–500.

Robinson, J. (2003) Postcolonalizing geography: Tactics and pitfalls. *Singapore Journal of Tropical Geography,* 24.3, 273–289.

Robinson, J. (2005) Urban geography: World cities, or a world of cities. *Progress in Human Geography,* 29.6, 757–765.

Ryan, J. (1997) *Picturing Empire: Photography and the Visualization of the British Empire.* London: Reaktion Books.

Said, E. (1978) *Orientalism.* New York: Pantheon.

Said, E. (1993) *Culture and Imperialism.* New York: Knopf.

Sarmento, J. (2009) A sweet and amnesic present: The postcolonial landscape and memory making in Cape Verde. *Social and Cultural Geography,* 10.5, 523–544.

Schneer, J. (1999) *London 1900: The Imperial Metropolis.* New Haven: Yale University Press.

Shaw, W., Herman, R. and Rebecca-Dobbs, G. (2006) Encountering indigeneity: Re-imagining and decolonizing geography. *Geografiska Annaler B,* 88, 267–276.

Shurmer-Smith, P. (2002) Postcolonial geographies. In *Doing Cultural Geography*, ed. P. Shurmer-Smith. London: Sage, pp. 67–77.

Sidaway, J. (2000) Postcolonial geographies: An exploratory essay. *Progress in Human Geography*, 24.4, 591–612.

Sioh, M. (2010) Anxious enactments: Postcolonial anxieties and the performance of territorialization. *Environment and Planning D: Society and Space*, 28.3, 467–483.

Sluyter, A. (2002) *Colonialism and Landscape: Postcolonial Theory and Applications*. Lanham: Rowman and Littlefield.

Spivak, G. (1987) *In Other Worlds: Essays in Cultural Politics*. New York: Methuen.

Spivak, G. (1988) Can the subaltern speak? In *Marxism and the Interpretation of Culture*, ed. C. Nelson and L. Grossberg. London: Macmillan, pp. 271–313.

Stoller, P. (1994) Artaud, Rouch and the cinema of cruelty. In *Visualizing Theory: Selected Essays from V.A.R. 1990–1994*, ed. L. Taylor. New York: Routledge, pp. 84–98.

Thiong'o, N. (1977) *Petals of Blood*. London: Heinemann.

Thiong'o, N. (1982) *Devil on the Cross*. London: Heinemann.

Thiong'o, N. (1986) *Decolonizing the Mind: The Politics of Language in African Literature*. London: Heinemann.

Thomas, N. (2007) Embodying imperial spectacle: Dressing Lady Curzon, Vicereine of India 1899–1905. *Cultural Geographies*, 14, 369–400.

Williams P. and Chrisman, L. (eds.) (1993) *Colonial Discourse and Post-Colonial Theory*. New York: Columbia University Press.

Winders, J. (2005) Imperfectly imperial: Northern travel writers in the postbellum US South, 1865–1880. *Annals of the Association of American Geographers*, 95.2, 391–410.

Yeoh, B. (1996) *Contesting Space: Power Relations and the Urban Built Environment in Colonial Singapore*. Kuala Lumpur: Oxford University Press.

Yeoh, B. (2000) Historical geographies of the colonized world. In *Modern Historical Geographies*, ed. B. Graham and C. Nash. London: Pearson Education, pp. 146–166.

Yeoh, B. (2001) Postcolonial cities. *Progress in Human Geography*, 25.3, 456–468.

Young, R. (2001) *Postcolonialism: An Historical Introduction*. Oxford: Blackwell.

# Index

Note: page numbers in italics denote illustrations

AAG (Association of American
  Geographers)  63, 343
Abel, E.  243
Aberystwyth University  176, 177
abnormality, mapping of  426
Aboriginal peoples  64, 299, 333,
  419, 517
Access and Benefit Sharing regimes  325
accommodation  294, 298
accumulation
  by dispossession  388–9, 496
  primitive  211, 214, 216, 217
Acker, J.  96
actor network theory  233, 234, 315, 334,
  336
Adams, P.C.  122, 124
adaptation  309, 312–13, 371–2, 374,
  377–8
Adbusters  392–3
Adey, P.  414
adventure tourism  231
aesthetic nuisance litigation  245–8
affect  36–8, 40n4, 457
  body  36–7, 230–1
  culture  454–8
  embodiment  473
  and emotion  11, 452, 454

  environment  36
  Klein  400
  materiality  26, 149
  non-representational theory  36, 230,
    458
  social difference  459–60
  space of  400–1
Afghanistan  503
African Americans
  feminists  76
  health regulations  111
  lived experience  63–4
  parallel politics  108
  politics of remembering  187
  street names  189
  see also black women
*Ageing and Place* (Andrews & Phillips)
  251–2
aging  9
  class  252–3
  identity  251, 252, 253
  loneliness  255
  public space  269
  relational approach  253, 254
  spatiality  254–8
  studies of  250, 251–2
Agnew, J.A.  7, 141, 176, 481, 482

*The Wiley Blackwell Companion to Cultural Geography*, First Edition.
Edited by Nuala C. Johnson, Richard H. Schein, and Jamie Winders.
© 2013 John Wiley & Sons, Ltd. Published 2016 by John Wiley & Sons, Ltd.